Nong Khai
Loei
Udon Thani
Mukdahan
Khon Kaen
NORTHEAST
THAILAND
Ubon
Ratchathani
Khorat
Chanthaburi
F THAILAND
attani
Yala Narathiwat

P9-BIT-997

KHORAT PLATEAU
Pages 258–271

MEKHONG RIVER VALLEY
Pages 272–293

WESTERN SEABOARD
Pages 314–331

EASTERN SEABOARD
Pages 302–313

BANGKOK
Pages 66–145

0 kilometres 100

0 miles   100

EYEWITNESS *TRAVEL GUIDES*

THAILAND

DORLING KINDERSLEY
LONDON • NEW YORK • SYDNEY • MOSCOW

A DORLING KINDERSLEY BOOK

PROJECT EDITOR Rosalyn Thiro
ART EDITORS Ian Midson, David Rowley
EDITORS Jonathan Cox, Marcus Hardy, Tim Hollis,
Lesley McCave, Sean O'Connor
DESIGNERS Susan Blackburn, Des Hemsley,
Tim Mann, Malcolm Parchment, Adrian Waite
MAP CO-ORDINATORS Emily Green, David Pugh
RESEARCHER Warangkana Nibhatsukit

MANAGING EDITOR Vivien Crump
MANAGING ART EDITOR Jane Ewart
DEPUTY EDITORIAL DIRECTOR Douglas Amrine
DEPUTY ART DIRECTOR Gillian Allan

PRODUCTION David Proffit
PICTURE RESEARCH Victoria Peel
DTP DESIGNER Ingrid Vienings

CONTRIBUTORS
Philip Cornwel-Smith, Andrew Forbes, Tim Forsyth,
Rachel Harrison, David Henley, John Hoskin, Gavin Pattison,
Jonathan Rigg, Sarah Rooney, Ken Scott

MAPS
Clare Brown, Sophie Dawson, Samantha James, Phil Rose,
Jennifer Skelley (Lovell Johns Ltd)

PHOTOGRAPHERS
Philip Blenkinsop, Stuart Isett, Kim Sayer, Michael Spencer

ILLUSTRATORS
Stephen Conlin, Gary Cross, Richard Draper,
Roger Hutchins, Chris Orr & Assocs, John Woodcock

Film output by Graphical Innovations, London
Reproduced by Colourscan, Singapore
Printed and bound in Italy by A. Mondadori, Verona

First published in Great Britain in 1997
by Dorling Kindersley Limited
9 Henrietta Street, London WC2E 8PS

Copyright 1997 © Dorling Kindersley Limited, London

Visit us on the World Wide Web at http://www.dk.com

A CIP CATALOGUE RECORD IS AVAILABLE FROM THE BRITISH LIBRARY.

ISBN 0 7513 0407 7

Transliteration of Thai words in this book mostly follows the
General System recommended by the Thai Royal Institute, but
visitors will encounter many variant spellings in Thailand. Details
such as telephone numbers, opening hours, prices and travel
information are correct at the time of going to press, but are liable
to change. The publishers cannot accept responsibility for any
consequences arising from the use of this book.

We would be delighted to receive any corrections and
suggestions for incorporation in the next edition. Please write to:
Deputy Editorial Director, Eyewitness Travel Guides,
Dorling Kindersley, 9 Henrietta Street, London WC2E 8PS.

CONTENTS

HOW TO USE THIS GUIDE 6

Lakshman and Sita, characters
from the Ramakien

INTRODUCING THAILAND

Cho fas, Wat Pan Tao in Chiang Mai

◁ The *chedis* of Wat Chong Klang reflected in the tranquil waters of Chong Kham Lake, Mae Hong Son

EYEWITNESS *TRAVEL GUIDES*

THAILAND

Hat Maenam, a beach on Ko Samui in the Gulf of Thailand

Carved pumpkin

The Khmer shrine at Phimai

HOW TO USE THIS GUIDE

THIS GUIDE helps you to get the most from your holidays in Thailand. It provides both detailed practical information and expert recommendations. *Introducing Thailand* maps the country and sets it in its historical and cultural context. The five regional chapters, plus *Bangkok*, describe important sights, using maps, pictures and illustrations. Features cover topics from architecture and crafts to wildlife and sport. Hotel and restaurant recommendations can be found in *Travellers' Needs*. The *Survival Guide* has practical information on everything from transport to personal safety.

BANGKOK

The centre of Bangkok has been divided into five sight-seeing areas. Each has its own chapter, which opens with a list of the sights described. The *Further Afield* section covers the best sights outside the centre. All sights are numbered and plotted on an area map. The information for each sight follows the map's numerical order, making sights easy to locate within the chapter.

A locator map shows where you are in relation to other areas of the city centre.

All pages relating to Bangkok have red thumb tabs.

Sights at a Glance lists the chapter's sights by category: *Wats and Palaces; Museums and Monuments; Parks and Districts; Markets and Notable Roads.*

1 Area Map
For easy reference, the sights are numbered and located on a map. Sights in the city centre are also marked on the Street Finder on pages 138–45.

2 Street-by-Street Map
This gives a bird's-eye view of the key areas in each chapter.

Stars indicate the sights that no visitor should miss.

A suggested route for a walk is shown in red.

3 Detailed Information
The sights in Bangkok are described individually. Addresses, telephone numbers, opening hours and other practical information are also provided. The key to the symbols used is on the back flap of the book.

1 Introduction
The landscape and character of each region is outlined here, showing how the area has developed and what it has to offer the visitor today.

THAILAND AREA BY AREA

Apart from Bangkok, Thailand has been divided into ten regions, each of which has a separate chapter. The most interesting towns and places to visit have been numbered on a *Pictorial Map*.

Each area of Thailand can be identified quickly by its colour coding, shown on the inside front cover.

2 Pictorial Map
This shows the main road network and gives an illustrated overview of the whole region. All entries are numbered and there are also useful tips on getting around the region by car, train and other forms of transport.

3 Detailed Information
All the important towns and other places to visit are described individually. They are listed in order, following the numbering on the Pictorial Map. Within each entry, there is detailed information on important buildings and other sights.

Story boxes explore related topics.

For all the top sights, a Visitors' Checklist provides the practical information you need to plan your visit.

4 Thailand's Top Sights
These are given one or more full pages. Three-dimensional illustrations reveal the layouts and interiors of historic monuments. Interesting town and city centres are given street-by-street maps, featuring individual sights.

INTRODUCING
THAILAND

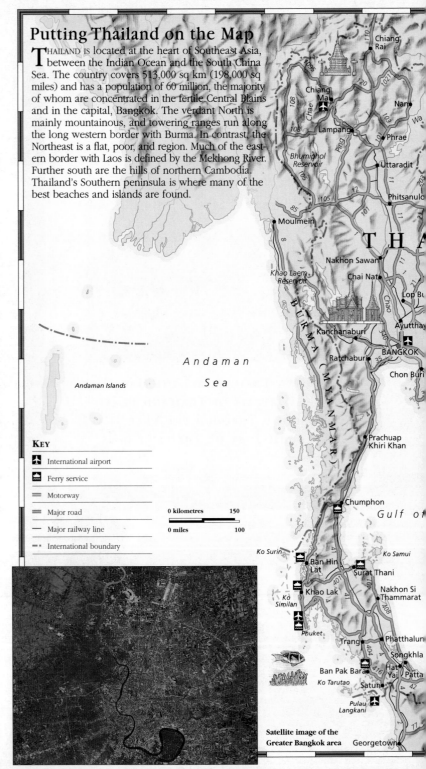

Putting Thailand on the Map

THAILAND IS located at the heart of Southeast Asia, between the Indian Ocean and the South China Sea. The country covers 513,000 sq km (198,000 sq miles) and has a population of 60 million, the majority of whom are concentrated in the fertile Central Plains and in the capital, Bangkok. The verdant North is mainly mountainous, and towering ranges run along the long western border with Burma. In contrast, the Northeast is a flat, poor, arid region. Much of the eastern border with Laos is defined by the Mekong River. Further south are the hills of northern Cambodia. Thailand's Southern peninsula is where many of the best beaches and islands are found.

KEY

✈ International airport

⛴ Ferry service

▬ Motorway

▬ Major road

— Major railway line

-·- International boundary

0 kilometres   150

0 miles   100

Andaman Islands

Andaman Sea

Chiang Rai

Chiang Mai

Nan

Lampang

Phrae

Wa

Bhumiphol Reservoir

Uttaradit

Phitsanulo

Moulmein

T H A

Khao Laem Reservoir

Nakhon Sawan

Chai Nat

Lop Bu

Kanchanaburi

Ayuttha

BANGKOK

Ratchaburi

Chon Buri

B U R M A   (M Y A N M A R)

Prachuap Khiri Khan

Chumphon

Gulf of

Ko Surin

Ban Hin Lat

Ko Samui

Surat Thani

Khao Lak

Nakhon Si Thammarat

Ko Similan

Phuket

Trang

Phatthalun

Songkhla

Ban Pak Bara

Hat Yai

Patta

Ko Tarutao

Satun

42

Pulau Langkani

Satellite image of the Greater Bangkok area   Georgetown

◁ **Spectacular limestone cliffs and turquoise waters characteristic of the Phi Phi islands in the Andaman Sea**

Satellite image of Southeast Asia

Northern Thailand

AN EXTENSIVE ROAD NETWORK covers most of the North, North-east and Central Plains of Thailand. Air-conditioned buses run between many of the major towns, and local buses are plentiful. Only in isolated border areas are road links unreliable. The railway system connects Bangkok to the Central Plains and Chiang Mai, and most main towns in the North-east. Bangkok and Chiang Mai have inter-national airports and many major towns are served by domestic flights.

KEY TO AREAS

- Northwest Heartland
- Far North
- North Central Plains
- South Central Plains
- Khorat Plateau
- Mekhong River Valley
- Bangkok

BURMA (MYANMAR)

Mae Sai
Sop Ruak
Chiang Saen
Chiar Khor
Tha Ton
Fang
Chiang Rai
Pai
Chiang Dao
Phrao
Wiang Pa Pao
Mae Hong Son
Phayao
CHIANG MAI
Ngao
Lamphun
Lampang
Mae Sariang
Phra
Si Satchanalai
Uttarao
Sawankhalok
Sukhothai
Tak
PHITSANULOK
Mae Sot
Kamphaeng Phet
Umphang
NAKHON SAWAN
Uthai Thani
Cha Nat
Sangkhla Buri
Sing Buri
A Tho
Suphan Buri
Kanchanaburi
Non t
Nakho Pathor
RATCHABURI
Samut Songkhram
Phetchaburi
Cha-am
Hua Hin

Bangkok

Bangkok is afflicted by some of the world's worst traffic congestion. If you have no alternative but to travel to or around the city by road, then at least try to avoid the rush hours, holiday week-ends and the rainy season (June to October) when the streets can be flooded.

Ayutthaya
Don Muang
Nonthaburi
Min Buri
Nakhon Pathom
Chanthaburi
Samut Prakan

BANGKOK AND ENVIRONS

0 kilometres 20

0 miles 10

Chiang Mai

Chiang Mai has excellent road and rail connections with Bangkok and the rest of the Thailand. The "Super Highway" loops around most of the city and provides links to the airport and main routes into the city.

CHIANG MAI AND ENVIRONS

Doi Saket

Chiang Rai

San Sai

118

DOI SUTHEP

Nam Mae Tueng

1001

107

1004

1014

106

1006

Chiang Mai

11

San Kamphaeng

1147

0 kilometres   10

0 miles   5

Mae Sariang

Saraphi

108

1030

Lamphun, Lampang

LAOS

Nong Bua

Nan

Chiang Khan

211

VIENTIANE

212

Nong Khai

222

201

212

103

Loei

210

Udon Thani

Ban Chiang

22

Nakhon Phanom

201

22

Renu Nakhon

Sakhon Nakhon

That Phanom

12

2

213

Mukdahan

Phetchabun

KHON KAEN

12

209

Kalasin

212

21

113

201

Maha Sarakham

214

Roi Et

Khemmarat

Chaiyaphum

225

Selaphum

202

Bua Yai

202

Yasothon

23

212

Suwannaphum

214

UBON RATCHATHANI

Khong Chiam

217

21

205

201

Phimai

Buri Ram

219

226

Sirindhorn Dam

KHORAT (Nakhon Ratchasima)

226

218

219

Surin

221

24

op uri

Phra Phutthabat

2

24

214

Saraburi

304

YUTTHAYA

ang Pa-in

Prachin Buri

CAMBODIA

319

ANGKOK

304

33

Chachoengsao

Aranyaprathet

CHON BURI

317

Ko chang

Si Racha

344

36

attaya

Rayong

3

Ban Phe

Chanthaburi

attahip

Ko Samet

318

Laem Ngop

Trat

Ko Chang

0 kilometres   100

0 miles   50

KEY

✈ International airport

⛴ Ferry service

━━ Motorway

━━ Major road

══ Minor road

── Railway line

▪▪▪ International boundary

Southern Thailand

Thailand's long coastline, fine beaches and idyllic offshore islands are a major attraction for visitors to the Gulf of Thailand and the South. Good-quality roads stretch from the Cambodian border in the east to the Malaysian border in the south, and along the western Andaman Sea coast. Air-conditioned buses operate regularly between the main towns. There is one north-south railway line from Bangkok which passes through, or has connections with, most of the towns on the Gulf of Thailand. The Eastern Seaboard has good road connections with Bangkok but the railway line terminates at Sattahip. Ferry services from ports to the main islands are frequent, and it is possible to buy tickets in Bangkok which combine train, bus and ferry journeys. Ko Samui and many towns have regional airports and Phuket is served by international flights.

Key to Areas

- Eastern Seaboard
- Bangkok
- Western Seaboard
- Upper Andaman Coast
- Deep South

YUTTHAYA

Bang Pa-in
onthaburi

ANGKOK

Prachin Buri

Chachoengsao

Aranyaprathet

CHON BURI

Ko
ichang

Si Racha

attaya

attahip

Rayong

Ban Phe

Chanthaburi

Ko Samet

Laem Ngop

Trat

Ko
Chang

Ko
Kut

Khlong Yai

C A M B O D I A

Gulf of
Thailand

V I E T N A M

SONGKHLA

HAT YAI

Pattani

Yala

Narathiwat

Tak Bai

Sungai
Ko-Lok

Betong

M A L A Y S I A

KEY

✈ International airport

⛴ Ferry service

▬ Motorway

▬ Major road

═ Minor road

── Railway line

─ ∙ ─ International boundary

| 0 kilometres | 100 |
| 0 miles | 50 |

MILEAGE CHART

BANGKOK										
432 **695**	*CHIANG MAI*			10 = Distance in miles						
487 **785**	**112** **180**	*CHIANG RAI*		**10** = Distance in kilometres						
161 **260**	**481** **775**	**540** **870**	*KHORAT*							
484 **780**	**916** **1475**	**972** **1565**	**646** **1040**	*NAKHON SI THAMMARAT*						
233 **375**	**208** **335**	**258** **415**	**283** **455**	**717** **1155**	*PHITSANULOK*					
534 **860**	**969** **1560**	**1022** **1645**	**696** **1120**	**209** **336**	**770** **1240**	*PHUKET*				
590 **950**	**1022** **1645**	**1077** **1735**	**751** **1210**	**100** **161**	**823** **1325**	**307** **495**	*SONGKHLA*			
196 **315**	**627** **1010**	**683** **1100**	**248** **400**	**680** **1095**	**428** **690**	**730** **1175**	**786** **1265**	*TRAT*		
391 **630**	**581** **935**	**630** **1015**	**230** **370**	**876** **1410**	**373** **600**	**696** **1120**	**981** **1580**	**556** **895**	*UBON RATCHATHANI*	
351 **565**	**248** **400**	**360** **580**	**189** **305**	**835** **1345**	**270** **435**	**885** **1425**	**941** **1515**	**546** **880**	**248** **400**	*UDON THANI*

A PORTRAIT OF THAILAND

SET WITHIN A LUSH, TROPICAL LANDSCAPE, *Thailand is a theatre of cultural and sensual contrasts for the visitor. The long, rich heritage and abundant natural resources of this proud Buddhist nation jostle for space within the dynamism of a country undergoing rapid industrialization. In turns zestful and tranquil, resplendent and subtle, Thailand is always compelling.*

Thailand is located in a fertile monsoon belt midway between India and China, the two civilizations that have moulded Southeast Asia. But the Thais have long delighted in their distinctive culture. For instance, though the Tai (rather than Thai) ethnic group probably originated in Southern China sometime in the first millennium AD, their tonal language is quite unlike any form of Chinese. Moreover, the elegant Thai script, though derived from that of ancient Southern India, is distinct.

Tuk-tuk

Today, Thailand is a member of the Association of Southeast Asian Nations (ASEAN), though Thais still take pride in a long tradition of independence. Unlike all her immediate neighbours, Burma (Myanmar), Laos, Cambodia and Malaysia, the country never fell to a European colonial power. More fundamentally, though, the Thai sense of identity is allied with Theravada Buddhism and the monarchy. Both have been dignified institutions since the Sukhothai period (13th–14th century), an era when the first real Thai kingdom flourished. Indeed, the colours of the modern Thai flag *(thong trai rong)* symbolize the three forces of Buddhism (white), the monarchy (blue) and the nation (red).

Colourful *korlae* fishing boats in the clear waters of Southern Thailand

◁ Young men parading in Old Sukhothai for the annual Loy Krathong Festival

Today, the great majority of Thailand's 60 million inhabitants regard themselves as Thai. Hill tribes are the most obvious ethnic minority groups, but it is the Chinese who form the largest (and most integrated) group. The various peoples live relatively peaceably nowadays, though in 1939, in a wave of nationalism encouraged by Prime Minister Phibun Song-

Downtown Bangkok, a rapidly modernizing, expanding area of the city

kram, the country's name was changed from Siam to Prathet Thai (Thailand), or "land of the Thai people".

The country is divided into four main regions, and there are many subtle differences between the peoples and dialects of the Central Plains, North, Northeast and South. Each region also has its own topographical identity. The North is an area of forested mountains, where hill-tribe minorities coexist with mainstream society. In the South, the narrow Kra Peninsula presents a 2,500-km (1,500-mile) coastline with a hilly interior of rainforests and rubber plantations. Malay-Muslim culture is a major influence here.

Between these two extremes are the Central Plains, the cradle of Thai civilization and a fertile, rice-growing region. Near the mouth of the Chao Phraya River, the capital, Bangkok, sprawls ever further each year. Though its 200-year-old palatial splendour can still be discerned, the city is among the world's most congested and polluted. Different again is Northeast Thailand (also widely known as Isan), the poorest part of the country occupying the Khorat Plateau, its eastern border with Laos defined by the Mekong River. In this semi-arid region traditional farming communities, many of them Thai-Lao, eke out a subsistence living.

ECONOMIC DEVELOPMENT

Rice and other agricultural crops were long the mainstays of the Thai economy, and farming is still regarded with great respect by Thais. From the mid-1980s, however, a concerted export drive, backed by an attractive climate for foreign investment, triggered an unprecedented economic boom. For several years Thailand enjoyed double-digit growth, and, while the pace slowed in the 1990s, the economy continues to grow at around eight per cent annually as Thailand consolidates its position as one of Asia's new "tiger" economies. Raw materials top the country's list of

Fisherman on the Mekong, the river defining Northeast Thailand's border

Noodle vendor at Damnoen Saduak Floating Market, a colourful and popular sight near Bangkok

imports, while the leading exports include garments, electrical goods, mechanical equipment, seafood products, gems and jewellery.

Tourism is now the single largest foreign exchange earner in Thailand. The country annually hosts more than six million visitors, but the tourist infrastructure has developed unevenly. Bangkok, Chiang Mai and the beach resorts attract the vast majority of visitors, and have deluxe hotels ranking among the world's best. Other regions, such as the Khorat Plateau, see relatively few visitors and have limited tourist facilities.

Economic success has, unfortunately, been achieved at a price. Transport infrastructure in particular has lagged behind economic growth, resulting in Bangkok's notorious traffic chaos. Commerce and communications are concentrated in Bangkok, putting increasing strain on a capital with a population of some seven million and rising, while the rest of the country largely remains rural. The new wealth remains concentrated in the hands of a few, and if the rampant poverty associated with some Asian countries is generally absent, there is nevertheless a widening gulf between the haves and have-nots. Education is also failing to keep pace with development. Though Thailand boasts one of the highest literacy rates in Asia, schools and colleges now face the challenge of producing a generation with the skills needed to maintain economic growth in the 21st century.

The environment has taken many blows in the last 50 years, during which forest cover has declined from 70 per cent of the land area to less than 20 per cent. Many animal species have lost their habitats and been hunted almost to extinction. On the positive side, conservation awareness is increasing, and measures are being taken to preserve what remains of the nation's rich natural bounty.

Muslim Thai in Southern Thailand

SOCIETY AND POLITICS

In spite of the pressures of change, Thai society is relatively stable. The concept of the extended family is important in Thailand, as in other parts of Asia. Children live with their parents, often sleeping in the same room, until marriage. Living alone is rare. Elders are always accorded respect within families and in society.

Elephant in Bangkok, surprisingly not a rare sight

There is no caste system, but the social hierarchy, topped by the monarchy, is quite rigid. Social standing is mainly dictated by wealth and family connections. Women have less standing than men, despite playing a major role in the economy, mainly as labourers and white-collar workers.

Seated Buddha image, one of thousands in Thailand

Hierarchy permeates daily life in many ways. The traditional greeting, the *wai*, in which the hands are brought together near the chin, is always initiated by the inferior, and the height of the *wai* reflects the social gap between the parties. If the gap is extreme, inferiors may approach their superiors on their knees. Other rules of etiquette, such as never raising the voice, transcend class. Despite such rules that they apply to themselves, Thais are renowned for their tolerance of other cultures and friendliness to visitors. Offence is taken only if there is any perceived disrespect to the king or Buddhism.

There is no criticism of the king in Thailand's press. Constitutional since 1932, the monarchy is revered almost as much as when kings were *chakravatin,* or "lords of life". Kingship and

religion are inextricably linked in Thailand. The present monarch, King Bhumibol Adulyadej (Rama IX), served as a monk in his youth and presides over some major religious ceremonies. He is the longest-reigning living monarch in the world, having ascended to the throne in 1946, and has won widespread respect for his devotion to welfare and environmental projects throughout Thailand. The monkhood *(sangha),* some 250,000 strong, plays a crucial social role. Most teenage boys become monks for a few months, which is seen as

Garland of jasmine, a ubiquitous sight

fortuitous for their families, especially their mothers, as well as a rite of passage. Some enter the monkhood properly later in life and may choose its austere precepts for life. Monks conduct numerous Buddhist rites, ranging from festivals to everyday blessings and other social events. In rural areas, they traditionally play an important role as school teachers, a profession that in Thailand is perhaps held higher in regard than anywhere else in the world.

In contrast, politicians are held in far less respect, and the Thai press makes no hesitation in criticizing the running of the country. Parliamentary politics are plagued by old-style patronage and privilege and are still threatened by military coups: there have been 19, mostly peaceful,

Lisu women and children during the Thai New Year, in April

Monks chanting in Pali, the language of Theravada Buddhism

coups or attempted coups since 1932. A mass pro-democracy demonstration in 1992 ended in bloodshed when the army opened fire. A great tragedy, the event did at least succeed in raising public awareness and securing a broader base for democratic reform.

THAI CULTURE AND ARTS

Thailand's classical arts have developed almost exclusively (and anonymously) in the service of Theravada Buddhism. Accordingly, the best showcase is the *wat*, where traditional architecture, typified by sweeping, multi-tiered roofs, countless Buddha

images and murals, and decorative arts, such as woodcarving, stucco relief, gilt, lacquer, coloured glass mosaic and mother-of-pearl inlay, are all used to striking effect.

The literary tradition of Thailand is confined mostly to classic tales, the most important of which is the Ramakien, an ancient moral epic with its origins in the Indian Ramayana. Such sagas provided the narrative content for the once-thriving performing arts, best preserved today in highly stylized classical dance-drama called *khon* and *lakhon*. Thailand's most notable literary figure is the 19th-century poet Sunthorn Phu.

Lakhon dancers at a Buddhist shrine

Avant-garde and neo-traditionalist painting is booming, while the film industry thrives on a diet of comedies, thrillers and period dramas. One very popular novel, *The Four Reigns* (1953), was written by former Prime Minister Kukrit Pramoj. A few films, such as *Luk Isan* (1978), set in the Northeast, and a number of books tackle social issues.

On the sporting front, Thailand's world-renowned, unique style of kick boxing draws big crowds, while other traditional pastimes range from *takraw*, a game not unlike volleyball, but using the feet, to kite-flying. Numerous colourful festivals, many linked to both Buddhism and the changing seasons, are celebrated with exuberance. Whatever the activity, Thais believe that life should be *sanuk* – "fun". *Sanuk* can be found in all things, from eating – something for which Thais have a passion – to simply going for a stroll with friends.

Cho fas, or roof finials, at the Grand Palace, Bangkok

Monsoon Country

Thailand's pre-eminent crop

THE RICE CYCLE, upon which the Thais have long believed their health, wealth and happiness depends, is governed by the advance and retreat of the monsoon rains. As most people in the kingdom define themselves as *chao na,* rice farmers, the monsoon could be said to govern the cycle of life. This analogy is seen clearly in many Thai beliefs and practices. The rice goddess must be honoured before cultivation if the crop is to be bountiful. The rice grain contains a spirit *(kwan)* and is planted in the rainy season to become "pregnant". The Thai word for irrigation *(chon prathan)* translates as "gift of water".

The Central Plains *of Thailand enjoy good conditions for wet rice cultivation. The flat paddy fields become flooded in the rainy season.*

Bundles of rice seedlings ready for transplanting

Transplanting takes place in the rainy season, when the heavy clay soil is saturated.

A "calling for rains" *Buddha image – a standing posture with both arms pointing to the earth – is found in some Northern wats. The rice crop depends on rain.*

Songkran, *or Thai New Year, in April, is a water festival marking the imminent end of the cool, dry season. People celebrate by pouring or throwing water over each other.*

MONSOON SEASONS

"Monsoon" comes from the Arabic *mawsim* (season). It refers to South Asia's seasonal winds (not heavy rain). In Thailand, the southwest monsoon is the rainy season; the northeast monsoon is dry, called the cool season; and between these periods is the hot season.

The southwest monsoon *comes from the Indian Ocean with rain-laden clouds, from about June to October. Most days there are downpours, though Thailand's east coast is fairly dry.*

Flooding in Bangkok at the end of the rainy season

Seedlings transplanted in rows

RAINY SEASON

Flooded paddy fields

Machinery *has replaced animals on many farms, reflecting the increasing mechanization of the Thai farming industry. However, ploughing and cultivating the land is still hard work.*

The main harvest *for lowland wet rice cultivation takes place in the middle of the cool season. Entire families and villages labour in the fields at this busy time, cutting off the golden stalks with sickles.*

Water channel between fields

Seedlings need to be semi-submerged

Threshing *is usually undertaken in the rice fields by the same labourers who have harvested the crop. The stalks are beaten to separate the grain from the chaff. The grain is then dried in the sun.*

TRANSPLANTING

Since most varieties of rice can only propagate in flood conditions, rice seedlings may initially be nurtured in nursery fields, where irrigation can be carefully managed and monitored. Later these seedlings will be transplanted into flooded paddy fields.

The northeast monsoon *from central Asia usually blows from November to March, bringing relatively cool, dry conditions to Thailand, though rains often affect the east coast.*

Between the two monsoons *the land heats up, creating an area of low pressure above it. Eventually the high pressure over the Indian Ocean moves inland, and the monsoon cycle begins again.*

Golden stalks ready for harvesting

Floodwaters recede

COOL SEASON

Stubble burnt at end of rice cycle

Hot, dry earth

HOT SEASON

The Landscape and Wildlife of Thailand

THAILAND STRETCHES from south of the Tropic of Cancer to about 1,000 km (620 miles) north of the Equator; its tropical climate is affected by two monsoons *(see pp22–3)*. Varied topography and a gentle climate have led to a rich diversity of flora and fauna. Limestone hills in the North are clad in dense tropical forest. Open forest is more usual in the Northeast and Central Plains, while the South and Gulf have superb coastlines and pockets of rainforest. Many habitats are threatened by industry and tourism; deforestation is rife and some animal species face extinction *(see p209)*. As a result, many national parks have been established. The first, Khao Yai *(see pp174–5)*, opened in 1962.

Green parakeet

Coconut palms on the island of Ko Samui in the Gulf of Thailand

MONTANE TROPICAL FOREST

This type of forest is made up mostly of broadleaf evergreens and some deciduous trees such as laurel, oak and chestnut. Mosses, ferns and epiphytic orchids, growing on other plants, are common.

OPEN FOREST

The most common trees in the open forest, also called savanna forest, are dipterocarps, a family of trees native to Southeast Asia. The ground around them is often carpeted by coarse scrub.

Atlas moths are the world's largest species. The female is larger than the male.

Sambar, Thailand's largest deer, can be seen on the Central Plains and in the Northeast.

Serow, a type of antelope, are becoming increasingly rare in the hills of Northern Thailand.

Capped gibbons are found mainly on the southern edge of Northeast Thailand. They are extremely agile.

Palm civets are nocturnal. They are found in tropical forests but may also live near humans and eat cultivated fruit.

Wild boars have been heavily hunted in the past. They feed mainly on grass.

THAI FLOWERS

The diversity of Thailand's flowers reflects its range of natural habitats. Most famous of all are its orchids; there are some 1,300 different varieties. Unfortunately, illegal collection has led to them becoming quite rare in the wild. Other flowers are used as spices and for medicinal purposes.

The mallow flower, a relative of the hibiscus, is common throughout Southeast Asia.

Mountain pitcher plants are insectivorous. Their prey falls into the "pitcher" where the plant's juices slowly dissolve it.

Lotus lilies' seed pods and stems are edible. Other lilies are grown for ornament only.

Orchids (see p210) come mainly from Northern Thailand; they are prized for their beauty.

WETLANDS

Freshwater swamp forests have been decimated by farming, though some survive in the South. River basins and man-made lakes and ponds can be found all over Thailand.

Dusky leaf-monkeys are found in the Thai-Malay peninsula. Three other species of leaf-monkey also live in Thailand.

Painted storks migrate to Thailand's swamps to breed. During this time the pigment in their faces turns pink.

Purple swamp hens are common. Long-toed feet allow them to walk on floating vegetation.

COASTAL FOREST

The seeds of coastal trees such as pines and Indian almond are transported on sea currents, thus ribbons of coastal forest are found all over Southeast Asia. Thailand's coastal forests are now threatened by farming and tourism.

Green turtles are the only herbivorous sea turtles; they feed on sea grass and algae and are nocturnal.

Lizards are common in island forests. Most eat insects, though some species eat mice and small birds.

Crested wood partridges are found in the South, in areas of coastal, lowland forest.

Thai Buddhism

AT LEAST 90 per cent of Thais practise Theravada Buddhism. This was first brought to the region from India around the 3rd century BC, and is based on the ancient Pali canon of the Buddha's teachings (Tripitaka). However, Thai practice incorporates many Hindu, Tantric and Mahayana Buddhist influences. The worship of Buddha images, for instance, is a Mahayana Buddhist practice. Animist beliefs in spirits and the magical, and in astrology, are also widespread. Thais believe that Buddhism is one of three forces that give their kingdom its strength, the other two being the monarchy and nationhood. Religious rituals colour daily life, especially in the form of merit-making *(see p125)*.

King Bhumibol, *like many kings before him, spent time as a monk. For Thais, this act reinforces the notion that Buddhism and the monarchy are unified powers.*

Monk with Thai flags

Siddhartha sets out to attain Enlightenment.

Most Thai males *are ordained as monks at adolescence – a major rite of passage. They usually spend at least a few months as monks, earning merit for themselves and their families. Few Thai women become nuns.*

Applying gold leaf to Buddha images is a popular act of merit-making. Books of gold leaf can be readily purchased at temples, and the thin leaves are applied in profusion on Buddha images, wat *deco-ration and murals.*

STORY OF THE BUDDHA

The Buddha was born Prince Siddhartha Gautama in India in the 6th century BC. He gave up his riches to seek Enlightenment, and later taught the way to *nirvana.* Statues of the Buddha *(see p163)* and murals depicting his previous ten lives *(jatakas)* abound in Thailand.

The family *is held in high regard in Thailand. A senior monk will be asked by the family for his blessing at child-naming ceremonies, weddings, to bless a new house or car, or simply after a donation to the* wat *has been made. Children are taught the simple moral codes of Buddhism from an early age.*

Walking meditation is practised by most monks. Here, the most senior monk leads the line in circumambulating the temple clockwise. Meditation on the nature of existence is a major way in which Buddhists progress towards Enlightenment – "Buddha" literally means "One who is Enlightened".

Vishnu, with four arms, is one of the three principal Hindu gods.

Thai folding book painting, c.1900

Heavenly beings *(devas)* bear the Prince through the air.

Incantations in the ancient Pali script

A ring of jasmine symbolizes the beauty of the Buddha's teachings and, as it perishes, the impermanence of all life. Vendors offer wreaths of jasmine to be hung in cars and at shrines.

Cremation ceremonies *are sober but not morbid; they are a rite of passage from this life to the next. The scale of the pyre reflects the status of the deceased. Chulalongkorn's funeral* (see pp62–3) *was one of the grandest.*

Ritualistic tattooing *is an ancient Hindu-Buddhist custom. Such tattoos are believed to act as powerful talismans against bad forces.*

THE BASIC TENETS OF BUDDHISM

Buddhist cosmology encompasses many states of being and heavenly realms. Buddhists believe in perpetual reincarnation, whereby each life is influenced by the actions and deeds of the previous one. This underlying philosophy of cause and effect, known as *karma,* is symbolized by the "wheel of law". Enlightenment *(nirvana)* is the only state that will end the cycle of rebirth. To reach this, Buddhists try to develop morality, meditation and then wisdom (the "three pillars"). Following certain codes of behaviour in each life, including the basic principles of tolerance and non-violence, assists in this aim.

The "wheel of law" on the Thai flag of Buddhism

The Wat Complex

A WAT IS A COLLECTION OF BUILDINGS within an enclosure serving various purposes: Buddhist monastery, temple and community centre. There are about 30,000 *wats* in Thailand. Their construction is often funded by wealthy patrons – contributing to a *wat* is a good way to make merit *(see p125)*. Each period of Thai history has seen modifications to *wat* architecture, and the exact layout and style of buildings vary considerably. However, the basic layout of most *wats* follows set principles, as do the functions of different buildings.

A mondop is a square-based structure topped with either a spire, as pictured here with the mondop at Wat Phra Kaeo (see pp76–9), or a cruciform roof. The edifice contains an object of worship or sacred texts.

A Bodhi tree is found in many *wats*. According to Buddhist lore, the Buddha sat beneath one as he attempted to attain Enlightenment *(see pp26–7)*.

A wall or cloister may enclose the main part of the temple (known as the phutthawat*). A cloister sometimes houses a row of Buddha images, and murals may be painted on its walls.*

Monks' living quarters and dormitories are in a separate compound known as the *sanghawat*.

The *sala kanparien* is a small meeting hall, sometimes the venue for lectures on the holy scriptures.

Minor *salas* (halls) act as meeting places for pilgrims.

The **ho trai**, *or library, is used to house holy scriptures. A comparatively rare feature of* wat *complexes, they come in an assortment of shapes and sizes; this one at Wat Paknam in Bangkok is typical of a* ho trai *in a city* wat. *A* ho trai *in the countryside may have a high base, or be surrounded by water to minimize damage from insects.*

Ornamental pond

IMPORTANT WATS

Wats whose names begin with Rat-, Racha- or Maha- have been founded by royalty or contain highly revered objects (with names often prefaced by "Phra"). There are about 180 important *wats* in Thailand, and this imagined *wat* is typical. The *bot* and *wihan* are grand affairs and there are a number of minor *salas*, as well as extensive monks' quarters. Lesser *wats* have fewer buildings and sometimes no *wihan*.

A chedi *is a solid structure encasing a relic of the Buddha, such as a hair or fragment of bone, or the ashes of a king.* Wat *complexes are often built expressly to surround a sacred* chedi.

The wihan, *an assembly hall, is very similar to, but usually larger than, a* bot *and not demarcated by* bai semas. *There may be several* wihans. *This one at Wat Rachabophit (see p87) is, like several in Bangkok, an eclectic mix of architectural styles.*

Buddha images in the cloister help mark the divide between the profane, outer world and the inner, sacred *wat.*

Bai semas, sacred boundary stones, are used to demarcate the consecrated ground of the *bot.*

The cho fa, *which means "tassle of air" is the most recognizably Thai architectural detail. Its shape is thought to derive from a highly stylized* garuda, *a fierce bird featured in Hindu mythology.*

Entrance to *wat*

The bot *(sometimes called an* ubosot*), or ordination hall, is reserved mainly for monks. Stylistically, it is similar to a* wihan. *It faces east and often houses the* wat's *main Buddha image, as seen here at Wat Suthat (see pp86–7), Bangkok.*

Ho rakangs *or bell towers are used to toll the hour and summon monks to prayer. This one at Wat Rakhang (see p121) is a comparatively large, ornate structure.*

Religious Architecture

THAILAND'S RELIGIOUS SITES span more than 11 centuries. The materials used to build them invariably determine how much of each site can be seen today. Hindu-Buddhist Khmer temples were built of stone and, where restored, are fairly complete. Generally, all that is left of the *wihans* and *bots* (*see pp28–9*) of the Buddhist temples at Sukhothai and Ayutthaya are foundations and stone pillars, though some stone structures such as *chedis* and *mondops* are still standing. There are many fine examples of later Lanna and Rattanakosin Buddhist temples.

Gilded pediment of *wihan*, **Wat Saket** (*see p83*)

KHMER (9TH TO 13TH CENTURIES)

Stone temple complexes, or *prasats*, in Northeast Thailand were built by the Khmers (*see pp254–5*). Most have staircases or bridges lined with stone *nagas* (serpents) leading to a central sanctuary; this is usually decorated with carved stone reliefs depicting Hindu myths, and topped by a *prang* (tower). The two most important Khmer sites in Thailand are Prasat Hin Khao Phnom Rung (*pp270–71*) and Prasat Hin Phimai (*see pp266–7*).

Khmer *prangs* symbolized Mount Meru, the mythical abode of the gods.

Lintels and pediments over the entrances depict Hindu and Buddhist deities.

The inner chamber of the *prang* housed either a *lingam* (*see p255*) or a Buddha image.

Naga antefix on the *prang* of
Prasat Hin Khao Phnom Rung

Central sanctuary of Prasat Hin Khao Phnom Rung

SUKHOTHAI (MID-13TH TO 15TH CENTURIES)

The cities of Sukhothai (*see pp184–7*) and Si Satchanalai (*see pp188–90*), witnessed the most radical architectural leap in Thai history. Amid sacred Khmer ruins, King Si Intharathit (*see p54*) and his successors built *wihans* and *bots* to house Buddha images. *Chedis*, modelled on Sri Lankan bell-shaped reliquary towers (*see p188*), were added. Vast new temple complexes, such as Wat Mahathat (*see pp186–7*), sometimes incorporated a unique development, the lotus-bud *chedi*.

Central lotus-bud *chedi*

Small *chedis* surround the main one.

Niches (foreground) once housed stucco Buddhas.

Some *chedis* (background) show Khmer influence.

A frieze of walking monks is carved around the base.

Mondop **housing a Buddha**
image at Wat Si Chum (*see p185*)

Six (illustrated) of the nine *chedis* **at the heart of Wat Mahathat**

AYUTTHAYA (MID-14TH TO LATE 18TH CENTURIES)

The architects of Ayutthaya *(see pp166–71)* looked to the past, subtly modifying such features as Khmer *prangs* and Sri Lankan-style *chedis*. Temple buildings were ornate structures, with elaborate *cho fas* and door and window pediments. Few *bots* or *wihans* survived the Burmese sack of 1767 *(see p56)*; one exception is Wat Na Phra Men *(see p170)*.

Carved Buddhas sit in the niches of the *prang*.

The ringed spire of the *chedi* tapers to a fine point.

This chedi has an entrance to the relic chamber.

Surviving Ayutthayan *wihan* of Wat Na Phra Men

Sri Lankan-style *chedi* of Wat Phra Si Sanphet *(see pp168–9)*

Corncob-shaped *prang* of Wat Ratchaburana *(see p166)*

LANNA (MID-13TH TO 19TH CENTURIES)

Religious buildings during the Lanna period in the North *(see pp58–9)* were inspired first by Dvaravati architecture *(see pp52–3)*, then later by Sukhothai, Indian and Sri Lankan styles. Lanna's golden age was in the 14th–15th centuries. Unfortunately, few buildings remain from this period. Later 18th–19th-century *wats*, seen in such towns as Chiang Mai *(see pp214–17)*, often feature intricate woodcarving, gilded *cho fas* and murals.

Square-based *chedi* of Wat Chiang Man, Chiang Mai

Intricately carved and gilded gables

Low, sweeping roofline

Cho fas, Wat Pan Tao, Chiang Mai   Lanna *wihan* of Wat Phra Sing, Chiang Mai

RATTANAKOSIN (LATE 18TH CENTURY TO PRESENT)

After the devastation of Ayutthaya the Thais attempted to recreate their lost past. The first *bots* and *wihans* built in the new capital, Bangkok, were similar to Ayutthayan structures; the most notable examples can be seen at Wat Phra Kaeo *(see pp78–9)*. Later temple buildings were grander and more elaborate. In the 19th century buildings such as Wat Benchamabophit *(see pp102–3)* and Wat Rachabophit *(see p87)* were built, incorporating Western elements. The Rattanakosin style is also known as the Bangkok style.

Gilded *cho fas* and detailing set off the green, red and orange of the roof tiles.

Western-style, stained-glass window, Wat Benchamabophit

Eight *bai semas* (boundary stones) encircle the *bot*.

Early Rattanakosin *bot*, Wat Suthat *(pp86–7)*

Traditional Thai Houses

TRADITIONAL THAI HOUSES are well adapted to the tropical climate. Many are raised on stilts to protect from flooding. A steeply slanting roof helps to channel rainwater off the house, and natural materials such as hardwoods, bamboo and dried leaves help keep the building cool. The design also reflects spiritual beliefs. The innermost room is believed to be the abode of the spirits of family ancestors, and this is usually used as the sleeping quarters. Traditional Thai houses are most often seen in rural areas, though grand versions may be found in cities.

Plantation house, Northern Thailand

NORTHERN HOUSES

Northern Thailand can be relatively cool. As a result, the windows of Northern houses are smaller than those in the rest of the country. The kitchen and living areas are often joined together, which makes good use of the available heat. Outer walls are commonly built to slope outwards, towards the roof, for strength. In more rural areas of Northern Thailand some houses have thatched roofs.

Decorative *kalae*, a traditional feature of Northern houses

Traditional Northern houses, constructed from teak

Plain *kalae*

Slanted walls

Typically *the whole structure of a Northern house is raised on pillars. An open balcony running along the front of the house is common, as are plain or decorative* kalae.

Front veranda

CENTRAL PLAINS HOUSES

In the hot Central Plains, a large, centrally situated veranda is the dominant feature of many traditional houses, and acts for much of the year as an outside living area. Some houses in the Central Plains have covered verandas running along the sides of the main structure. Sometimes, a communal veranda will have several houses clustered around it. A relatively recent addition to houses found in the Central Plains is wood-panelled walls.

Panelled walls

Ngao

Central veranda

Gate

Wood-panelled gable

The gables *often have decorative features called* ngaos, *the origins of which can be traced to Khmer architecture.*

HOUSES ON WATER

River houses can be found in the Central Plains. The *khlongs* of early
Bangkok *(see p123)* had many floating shop-houses. Such houses are
very practical in areas prone to seasonal flooding. Houses can either be
anchored to posts above the water line, or built on bamboo rafts so that
during flood conditions they are able
to float on the rising waters.

Thatched roof

Loosely fitted floorboards

Anchor post

Floating houses, Sangkhla Buri *(see p158)*

Houses *close to the river's
edge are often anchored on
posts. Floorboards are loosely
fitted so that they move with
the water beneath them.*

ROYAL HOUSES

Royal houses and mansions are typically a mixture of Thai
temple and house styles, and Western architecture. The main
structural material of such buildings is usually teak, which gives
them their distinctive rich, red colour. Windows and doors
usually have ornate frames and pediments, which are
themselves sometimes decorated in gilt bronze.

**Window pediment, Prince of
Lampang's Palace *(see p133)***

Cho fa   **Teakwood roof tiles**

The Red House *at the National
Museum (see pp84–5) is a
typical royal house. As its name
reflects, it is built entirely of teak,
and, like a temple, has cho fas.*

SPIRIT HOUSES

Spirit houses can be found in the
grounds of many Thai homes. They
are small structures, usually elevated
on poles, and house the spiritual guardian of the prop-
erty. Resembling both dolls'
houses and bird-tables,
they come in an astonish-
ing collection of styles:
sometimes simple replicas of the
houses to which they belong, at
other times elaborate models of
religious buildings. Spirit houses are

**Decorated
spirit house**

erected to placate the spirits of the
land, traditionally before the construction of the main house (or
shop) begins. They are then
adorned, preferably daily,
with incense, flowers and
food to further mollify
the spirits. Spirit worship
predates Theravada Bud-
dhism *(see pp26–7)* but
the flexibility of Thai religion means
that worship of the Buddha and
spirits is a normal part of daily life.

The Art of Thai Food

Elaborately carved melon

THAI FOOD IS JUSTIFIABLY renowned for its quality and diversity – and for being as much a feast for the eyes as for the stomach. The simplest of dishes is often served with a carved carrot flower or a spring onion tassel; a full-blown Royal Thai meal in a high-class restaurant may be accompanied by spectacular virtuoso fruit and vegetable sculptures. The cooking and presentation techniques of Thai cuisine are so respected that Bangkok's celebrated cookery schools attract pupils from all over the world. For the majority of Thais, eating is an informal, social activity. Whether it is an important family occasion, such as a wedding, an impromptu outdoor garden party or a colourful festival, food will play a central role. Many restaurants serving Northern *khantoke* dinners may be aimed at tourists, but the principal of communal sharing of food is genuinely Thai.

The pre-rice planting festival *in Northern Thailand, like many Thai festivals, involves the preparation and consumption of a wide variety of food.*

White radish petals around a papaya heart

Royal Thai cuisine *is based on the dishes that at one time were served only at the Thai court. It is characterized by complex cooking methods and elaborate decoration. Royal Thai cooking also often uses ingredients that are (or were) expensive, such as ice for chilled dishes.*

Papaya has a firm texture and is a popular fruit to carve.

Cucumber carved into leaves

Radish

Khantoke *is a traditional way of eating in Northern Thailand. Guests sit on raised platforms around a circular table and share a selection of typical Northern dishes served with sticky rice.*

FRUIT AND VEGETABLE CARVING

Few visitors to Thailand fail to be impressed by the exquisitely carved fruit and vegetables that accompany many dishes in restaurants. Spring onions are transformed into tassels and chrysanthemums; carrots and chillies become flowers; and tomatoes are magically turned into roses. The practice was once the preserve of the women of the royal court. Today, most Thais know the basic carving skills, but few have the dexterity and application needed to master the more advanced techniques. Skilled practitioners, capable of producing astonishingly elaborate creations, are highly esteemed.

Demonstrating the art of vegetable carving

Cookery schools provide trainee chefs and interested amateurs with a grounding in Thai cooking techniques, although most chefs learn their trade over a period of years in a restaurant kitchen. The most famous schools are in Bangkok (see p446).

Miang kham, *a snack dish of ginger, coconut, lemons, red onions, dried shrimps, peanuts and a syrup sauce, is presented here with a typical Thai attention to detail. The idea that food should look as good as it tastes applies to simple as well as elaborate dishes.*

Thai pumpkin

Carrot

Pumpkin

Beetroot, expensive in Thailand, is sometimes replaced by dyed carrot.

***Rice** is endowed with spiritual significance in Thailand (see pp22–3) as well as being the central pillar of the country's cuisine. Here, Brahmins present offerings of rice in a Bangkok temple.*

Luk chub *are exquisite sweetmeats made to resemble tiny vegetables. Because few people possess the skills to make them, they are very expensive and eaten only on special occasions.*

Cucumber petals

***A communal meal** is the subject of this 19th-century temple mural. Although the Thais are inveterate snackers, sitting down for a full meal is still an important social event. Weddings and funerals often seem like excuses to eat and drink as much as is possible in a limited period of time. Eating out of doors, in a pavilion or a garden, is a popular way of dining in Thailand and is known as* suan ahan. *On Sundays many* wats *host a large communal meal.*

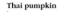

The Ramakien

THE RAMAKIEN, the Thai version of the Indian Rama-yana, is an allegory of the triumph of good over evil. The hero, Rama, is a paragon of virtue; the ideal king. The villain, the demon king Tosakan, is a tragic character of great dignity. This epic tale is thought to have become established after the Thais occupied Angkor in the 15th century. It has been an inspiration for painting and classical drama. All the Chakri kings have taken Rama as one of their names, and the old capital of Ayutthaya *(see pp166–71)* was named after Ayodhya, a fictional kingdom in the story.

Hun krabok (rod puppets), in a scene from the Ramakien

Monkey armies accompany Rama to Longka.

Buildings and chariots are painted in Thai style though the story is set in India and Sri Lanka.

Rama is a skilled archer, as this bas-relief marble panel at Wat Pho (see pp88–9) shows. Rama wins Sita's hand by stringing a bow that no other suitor is able even to lift.

THE STORY

Rama, the heir to the throne of Ayodhya, is sent into exile for 14 years, through the intrigues of his step-mother. His wife, Sita, and brother Lakshman go with him deep into the forest. Tosakan, the demon king of Longka (Sri Lanka), abducts Sita and carries her off to his island kingdom in the hope of marrying her. The brothers pursue him. Hanuman, the white monkey god, volunteers his services. Together they win the alliance of two monkey kings, Sukrip and Chompupan, each with a powerful army. They march south to the coast opposite Longka. The monkey armies build a road of stone through the sea and lay siege to Longka. Many victorious battles are waged against Tosakan's demon armies. Finally, when all his champions have been defeated, Tosakan fights Rama and is killed. Rama then crowns his ally, Piphek (Tosakan's banished brother), as King of Longka, and returns with Sita to resume his reign in Ayodhya.

Mural at Wat Phra Kaeo: Hanuman using his tail as a bridge

Many demons were overcome by Rama during his forest exile. Some recognized his divine nature. As they died, his blessings released them from the punishment of being reincarnated as a demon in the next life.

Nang yai shadow plays (see p373), based on the Ramakien, were first documented in the 15th century. Today this art form is rarely performed in Thailand but can still be seen in Cambodia.

Ignoring Western perspective, the sea is narrowed to allow both countries in the tale to be seen.

Rama in the chariot rides high above his followers, as befits a king.

RAMAKIEN MURALS AT WAT PHRA KAEO
The Ramakien is beautifully depicted through a series of 178 colourful murals, dating from the late 18th century, at Wat Phra Kaeo *(see pp76–9)*. In this scene Hanuman displays his supernatural powers to assist Rama in rescuing Sita by building a stone causeway across the sea.

Hanuman finds Sita imprisoned by the wicked king of Longka, Tosakan. He gives her Rama's ring and tells her she will soon be rescued.

THE MAIN CHARACTERS
Hundreds of characters are featured in the many episodes of the epic Ramakien. However, the central thread of the drama is carried by the five most important figures, who are described below.

Rama, often depicted with a deep green face, is an incarnation of the god Vishnu. Rama's purpose is to defeat the demon race whose power threatens the gods.

Sita, the daughter of Tosakan's consort and incarnation of the goddess Lakshmi, remains loyal to Rama while held captive by the evil Tosakan.

Lakshman, Rama's loyal younger brother, is often shown in gold. He accompanies Rama into exile in the forest.

Hanuman, the white monkey, son of the wind god, is totally devoted to Rama, but still finds time to seduce beautiful women.

Tosakan (meaning "ten necks"), the demon king of Longka, has multiple heads and arms. In the Indian version of the Ramayana he is called Ravanna.

Thai Theatre and Music

T HE TWO PRINCIPAL FORMS of classical Thai drama are *khon* and *lakhon*. *Khon* was first performed in the royal court in the 15th century, with story lines taken from the Ramakien *(see pp36–7)*. The more graceful *lakhon*, which also features elements from the *jataka* tales *(see p26)*, was originally performed inside the palace, but moved outside at a later date. Both *khon* and *lakhon* involve slow, highly stylized, angular dance movements set to the music of a *phipat* ensemble.

Classical Thai dancer

Students learn *gestures by imitating their teacher. Training begins at an early age (when limbs are still supple) and includes a sequence of moves known as the Alphabet of Dancing (mae bot).*

Graceful gestures typify classical Thai drama. Here, weapons are raised to attack the enemy.

White mask of Hanuman *(see p37)*

Ganesh, the elephant god

Khon **masks**, *decorated with gold and jewellery, are treated as sacred objects with supernatural powers.*

Lavish costumes, made of heavy brocade and adorned with jewellery, are modelled on traditional court garments.

Khon **and** lakhon **performances** *are often staged at outdoor shrines. Dancers are hired to perform to the resident god by supplicants whose wishes have been granted.*

A KHON PERFORMANCE

In *khon* drama, demons and monkeys wear masks, while human heroes and celestial beings sport crowns. As the story is told mainly through gestures, *khon* can be enjoyed by non-Thais. Visitors today are most likely to see performances at restaurants catering for tourists.

INSTRUMENTS OF CLASSICAL THAI MUSIC

A *mahori* ensemble shown in a mural

Thailand's classical music originated in the Sukhothai era. The basic melody is set by the composer, but, as no notation is used, each musician varies the tune. He or she adopts the character of their instrument, like actors in a play. A tuned percussion ensemble, or *phiphat*, accompanies theatre performances and boxing matches *(see p40)*. A *mahori* ensemble includes stringed instruments.

Ranat **(xylophones)**

The keys of a flat xylophone produce a different tone from those of a curved xylophone.

Likay, *by far the most popular type of dance-drama, is a satirical form of* khon *and* lakhon. *The actors wear gaudy costumes and the plot derives from ancient tales, laced with improvised jokes and puns.*

Khon *and* lakhon *troupes, employed by the royal palace until the early 20th century, are now based at Bangkok's Fine Arts Department.*

Finger extensions, *emphasizing the graceful curves of a dancer's hands, are seen in* lakhon *performances and in "nail dances" of the North.*

This mural *at Wat Benchamabophit, Bangkok, depicts a scene from a* khon *performance. In it, Erawan, the elephant mount of Indra, descends from heaven.*

Natural-looking make-up enhances the features of characters who do not wear masks. This replaces a heavy white paint that was traditionally worn.

Hun krabok *puppets*, *rodded marionettes, are operated by hidden threads pulled from under the costume.* Hun krabok *performances are very rare today.*

Khong wong lek (small gong circle)

Chake ("crocodile")

The hollowed hardwood body is inlaid with ivory.

Small gongs are struck by the player to give the tune's basic melody.

The strings of a *chake* are plucked. It accompanies fiddles and flutes in a string ensemble.

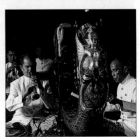

A phiphat mon *ensemble*, *including a vertical gong circle, plays at funerals.*

Thai Boxing

THAI BOXING *(muay thai)*, Thailand's unique national sport, is gaining popularity worldwide. It was first documented in 1411, but probably evolved from an earlier form of armed combat, *krabi-krabong*. *Muay thai* is highly ritualistic – many techniques are inspired by battle stories from the Ramakien *(see pp36–7)*. The country's first famous boxer was Nai Khanom Dtom, who in 1774 defeated ten Burmese fighters. Due to a high injury rate, the sport was banned in the 1920s. In 1937 it was revived with rules for protecting fighters.

Nai Khanom Dtom

In the stadium, *the audience becomes excited, shouting encouragement to the boxers. Thais bet furiously, often staking large sums on their favourite fighter. Bouts between famous boxers can be sold out well in advance.*

This manuscript, *which dates from the early 20th century, depicts a fight between two Thai boxers.*

Phone Kingphet *was the first world champion Thai boxer. He trained in the cool climate of Phu Kradung National Park (see pp276–7) in preparation for his numerous bouts abroad.*

Training gear
varies in style from camp to camp.

Feet are kept bare in training sessions, though ankle covers may be worn for protection during a match.

TYPES OF MOVES

Points are awarded for each blow to the opponent. The groin is not a valid target, and biting and head-butting are not allowed. A match may end with a spectacular knockout.

The jumping downward strike elbow *is a physically demanding move. It gives the boxer an excellent vantage point over his opponent.*

A ringside **phipat** ***band*** *is an essential element of a Thai boxing match. During the opening ceremony, the music is soft in tone; when the fighting begins it switches to a more upbeat "fight melody". As the action becomes more frenzied, the music increases in tempo, adding tension to the match.*

Amulets (see p74), *worn around one or both biceps during the match, are believed to offer protection to the boxer while fighting. They consist of a piece of cord which usually contains a Buddha image or a herb that is thought to be lucky.*

WHERE TO SEE THAI BOXING

Matches are held at Ratchadamnoen Stadium (p443) every Mon, Wed, Thu & Sun. Thursday's contests are shown on Thai TV Channel 9. Lumphini Stadium (p443) has matches on Tue, Fri & Sat. For other towns, check venues.

Fists are bound with cloth for protection during training. Before 1937, glass-impregnated hemp was often used, to injure the opponent.

The **wai kru**, *a ritual bow, is the first part of the* ram muay, *a gesture of respect to the trainer (kru) and the spirit of boxing. In honour of their training camp, boxers often take its name as their surname.*

Before the match, the boxer performs a slow, solemn dance (ram muay). The exact movements differ according to the boxer's camp, but usually involve sweeping arm motions, which are said to draw the power of earth, air, fire and water into the body.

THAI BOXING VERSUS WESTERN BOXING

Thai boxing, or "kick boxing", exerts parts of the body not used in Western boxing, such as the feet and elbows. Thai boxing matches are also faster paced, and are thus limited to five rounds of three minutes, each separated by a short break. Professional boxers, who may start the rigorous training as young as six, often retire by 25. Several Thai boxers have won Western boxing titles.

Kicks are common in Thai boxing. A high kick to the neck, as shown here, may knock out a rival. A push kick, in which one boxer pushes the sole of his foot into the face of the other, is regarded as a great insult to the opponent.

***Knee books** can be devastating. To perform a "rising knee", aimed at either the head or body, the boxer pushes down his rival's head, bringing his knee up to hit it.*

***Elbows deliver** fierce blows to the face, and, like knee strikes, are often decisive in matches. An elbow strike is more powerful than a punch, the weakest blow.*

Festivals in Thailand

THAI FESTIVALS are rarely solemn occasions, and few countries celebrate them with so much fun and colour. Annual rites and festivities, marking religious devotion or the passage of seasons, have long been an integral part of Thai life. A 13th-century inscription reads: "Whoever wants to make merry, does so; whoever wants to laugh, does so." This still applies today, with scores of festivities taking place each month.

Phi Ta Khon, held in Dan Sai and Loei

The main festivals, such as Songkran, are celebrated nationwide, with the most exuberant activities taking place in Bangkok and other major cities. Each region has its own unique festivals, too. Many festival dates change each year, as they follow the lunar calendar.

Decorated oxen, paraded for Bangkok's Royal Ploughing Ceremony

BANGKOK

SONGKRAN, the Thai New Year, is celebrated nationally from 12th–14th April *(see p44)*. In Bangkok, festivities take place at Sanam Luang, where a revered Buddha image is bathed as part of the merit-making rituals. Over the years, the festival has become a boisterous affair involving water throwing in which few people escape getting soaked.

Visakha Bucha *(see p45)*, in May, marks the birth, death and Enlightenment of the Buddha, all said to have occurred on the same day of the year. It is celebrated with candlelight processions around important temples.

The Royal Ploughing Ceremony is held at Sanam Luang at the start of the rice-planting season in May *(see p44)*. The display features oxen ploughing and Brahmin priests sowing rice seeds. The oxen predict the coming year's harvest by selecting one of several types of food offered to them.

The Golden Mount Fair *(see p46)* is in November. With its fun fair, performers and candlelight processions, this is Thailand's best temple fair.

December's Trooping of the Colours in the Royal Plaza is the best of many nationwide celebrations marking King Bhumibol's birthday *(see p47)*.

CENTRAL PLAINS

EVERY MARCH, pilgrims flock to the Temple of the Holy Footprint near Saraburi for the elaborate Phra Phutthabat Fair *(see p44)*, which has theatre and folk music performances.

Full-moon night in November is the occasion for Loy Krathong. It is celebrated throughout the country, but most magically amid the ruins of Old Sukhothai *(see p185)*, where it is said to have originated. The festival is held in honour of Mae Kongkha, the goddess of rivers and waterways, and takes place by rivers, lakes and ponds. Small lotus-shaped vessels carrying offerings for Mae Kongkha are floated to take away the sins of the past year and to bring good luck for the future.

Khwae River Bridge Week (late November/early December), held at Kanchanaburi, marks the building of the infamous bridge with historical displays and a dramatic sound and light show.

NORTHERN THAILAND

BO SANG, which is famous for its hand-painted umbrellas, holds an Umbrella Fair every January. Umbrella painting competitions, umbrella exhibitions, parades and a "Miss Bo Sang" beauty contest are part of the festival.

Northern Thailand shows off its beautiful blooms to full effect during Chiang Mai's Festival of Flowers in February, when parades of lavish floral floats fill the town with colour. Events include floral exhibitions, handicraft sales and a beauty pageant.

Mae Hong Son comes alive during its Poi Sang Long Festival, held in late March

Painting umbrellas for the Umbrella Festival in Bo Sang

Young Buddhist novices at the Poi Sang Long Festival in Mae Hong Son

or early April. The highlight of this Buddhist festival is a mass ordination ceremony for Shan boys. Wearing sumptuous costumes, the novices parade through the town before exchanging their finery for simple monks' robes in a symbolic gesture of renouncing worldly goods.

NORTHEAST THAILAND

NORTHEAST THAILAND is renowned for its unique festivals. In May, the town of Yasothon hosts the Bun Bang Fai (Rocket Festival), perhaps the most thrilling of Thailand's regional celebrations. This two-day event, accompanied by much high-spirited revelry, is staged to ensure plentiful rains during the coming rice-planting season. On the first day there is a parade of carnival floats, as well as fun fairs, music and folk dancing. The next day, huge, home-made rockets are let off.

Dan Sai and Loei, both in Loei province, are known for their Phi Ta Khon Festival *(see p279)*, held in June. Celebrations begin with a

parade, where locals dressed as ghosts follow a Buddha image through the streets of town to make Buddhist merit and call for rain.

Ubon Ratchathani has a Candle Festival in July, its own version of the nationally celebrated "beginning of the rains retreat", or Khao Phansa *(see p45)*. As part of the celebrations, huge, intricately carved beeswax candles are exhibited on floats in the town before being presented to temples, where they burn throughout the rainy season.

The national holiday of "end of the rains retreat", or Ok Phansa, is celebrated in particular style at Nakhon Phanom in October with the Illuminated Boat Procession. Intricately fashioned model boats carrying single candles are set adrift on the Mekhong River at nightfall.

GULF OF THAILAND

MODERN-STYLE merrymaking is found at Pattaya, which hosts the week-long Pattaya Festival in April. Floral float parades, beauty contests and firework displays feature amid a non-stop carnival atmosphere. One of Thailand's most colourful water festivals is the Receiving of the Lotus Festival, which is celebrated in

late October at Bang Phli, just south of Bangkok. Here, Ok Phansa is marked by a ceremony in which a locally revered Buddha image is showered with thousands of lotus buds while it is paraded by barge along Khlong Samrong, the local canal. Lively crowds, thronging the canal banks, throw flowers until only the image's head remains visible above the mounting floral offerings. Other events include boat races, boxing matches fought on poles placed across the canal and *likay* theatre shows.

Displays of self-mortification, part of the Vegetarian Festival, Phuket

SOUTHERN THAILAND

TRADITIONAL Southern culture gets an airing at the week-long Narathiwat Fair (last week of September). This features races between brightly painted traditional *korlae* fishing boats *(see p378)*, as well as dove-cooing contests and performances of Southern music and dance.

For sheer spectacle, it is hard to beat Phuket's Vegetarian Festival (late September/ early October, *see p350*). This nine-day festival, marking the start of Taoist Lent, is celebrated by people of Chinese ancestry. During the festival followers eat only vegetarian food and take part in acts of self-mortification, such as piercing the body with skewers, with no apparent harm.

Mud-covered revelers at Dan Sai, Northeast Thailand

THAILAND THROUGH THE YEAR

THE THAI YEAR revolves around the monsoon seasons – which dictate the year's farming activities – and the religious calendar. Most religious festivals are Buddhist, and often observed on significant days of the lunar cycle, such as full moon. Festivals may also mark a seasonal change, such as the end of the rains, or a related agricultural event, such as the beginning of the planting season. The three seasons – wet, cool and hot – are

Celebration of Loy Krathong, Sukhothai

produced by the southwest and northeast monsoons (see pp22–3). At the start of the wet season farmers plant rice seedlings. The rice-growing period is the traditional time for boys to enter the monkhood for a few weeks. In the cool season the drier weather ripens the crop, which is gathered before the hot season. Village life then slows down. During most weeks a festival is held somewhere in the country, especially in the cool season.

HOT SEASON

HIGH TEMPERATURES combined with high humidity make this an uncomfortable time, April being especially hot. With the fields empty and rivers running low, the landscape appears faded and spent in the bright sunshine. Considering the heat, it is not surprising that Thailand's traditional New Year, Songkran, is celebrated with water.

Water throwing during Songkran celebrations in Chiang Mai

MARCH

ASEAN Barred Ground Dove Fair (first week), Yala. Dove-singing contest that attracts bird lovers from as far away as Cambodia, Malaysia, Singapore and Indonesia.
Phra Phutthabat Fair (first or second week), Saraburi. Celebration of the annual pilgrimage to the Temple of the Holy Footprint (see p162).

Temple of the Holy Footprint during the Phra Phutthabat Fair

Bangkok International Jewellery Fair (third week). Thailand's largest, most important gem and jewellery trade show. Held in large hotels around Bangkok.
Poi Sang Long Festival (late Mar/early Apr), Mae Hong Son. Mass ordination of 15- and 16-year-old-boys, who dress up as princes in memory of the Buddha's origins.

APRIL

Chakri Day (6 Apr). Commemorates Rama I founding the Chakri Dynasty. The Royal Pantheon – which displays statues of former kings – in Wat Phra Kaeo's grounds, Bangkok, is open to the public on this day only.
Songkran (12–14/15 Apr). Traditional Thai New Year. Celebrated nationwide, but Chiang Mai has the reputation for the most fun (see p226).

Pattaya Festival (mid-Apr). Features a week of food and floral floats, beauty contests and a huge firework display.
Phnom Rung Fair (Apr full moon). Daytime procession and a night-time sound and light show at Prasat Hin Khao Phnom Rung (see pp270–1).

MAY

Coronation Day (5 May). Ceremony to mark the crowning of King Bhumibol.
Royal Ploughing Ceremony (early May), Bangkok. Observes the official start of the rice-planting season with an elaborate royal rite at Bangkok's Sanam Luang.
Bun Bang Fai (Rocket) Festival (second week), Northeast Thailand. Home-made rockets are fired to ensure plentiful rains amid a carnival atmosphere. Celebrated exuberantly at Yasothon (see p264).

AVERAGE DAILY HOURS OF SUNSHINE

equate precautions against sunburn and sunstroke should be taken. Sun cream, a sun hat and sunglasses are highly recommended. Drinking plenty of water reduces the risk of dehydration.

Visakha Bucha celebrations at Wat Benchamabophit, Bangkok

Visakha Bucha *(May full moon)*. Most important date on the Buddhist calendar. Celebrates the birth, Enlightenment and death of the Buddha. Sermons and candle-lit processions at temples.

RAINY SEASON

T HE RURAL SCENE comes alive with the advent of the annual rains, which soften the soil ready for ploughing. Once the rice has been planted, there is a lull in farming activity. This coincides with the annual three-month Buddhist Rains Retreat, the period when young men traditionally enter the monkhood for a brief period. This is something that young Thai men should do at least once in their lives. The rainy season is a good time to observe the ordination ceremonies held throughout Thailand, which blend high-spirited festivities with deep religious feelings.

JUNE

Phi Ta Khon Festival

(mid/late Jun), Loei. An event unique to the Dan Sai district of Loei province, comprising masked players re-enacting the legend of Prince Vessandon, the Buddha's penultimate incarnation *(see p279)*.

JULY

Asanha Bucha *(Jul full moon)*. Second of the year's three major Buddhist festivals. Commemorates the anniversary of the Lord Buddha's first sermon to his first five disciples.

Khao Phansa *(Jul full moon)*. Marks the start of the three-month Buddhist Rains Retreat (which is also referred to as Buddhist Lent), when monks remain in their temples to devote themselves to study and meditation. Young men are ordained for short periods.

Young man in ordination robes

Candle Festival *(Jul full moon)*, Ubon Ratchathani. Unique festival held in the Northeast to mark the beginning of Khao Phansa. Features parades of carved candles (made by villagers from all over the province) displayed on floats and later presented to temples throughout the city. Some candles are several metres tall *(see pp292–3)*.

AUGUST

Her Majesty the Queen's Birthday *(12 Aug)*. Buildings and streets are lavishly decorated in honour of Queen Sirikit's birthday. The most elaborate decorations can be seen in Bangkok, especially along Ratchadamnoen Avenue and around the Grand Palace, where the streets and government offices are exuberantly adorned with coloured lights.

Parade of candles at the Ubon Ratchathani Candle Festival

ERAGE MONTHLY RAINFALL (BANGKOK)

Rainfall Chart
Thailand's rainfall is not evenly distributed. The southern peninsula has the highest, some 2,400 mm (95 inches) annually; the north and central regions receive 1,300 mm (51 inches). In many places, torrential rain falls almost daily during the rainy season, usually from June to October.

SEPTEMBER

Food and Fruits Fair *(first week)*, Nakhon Pathom. Held at Thailand's largest Buddhist temple, Phra Pathom Chedi. Cooking, folk theatre and floral floats.
Thailand International Swan-Boat Races *(mid-Sep)*, Bangkok. Races held on the Chao Phraya River. Attracts top Thai and foreign rowing teams.
Narathiwat Fair *(last week)*. A good opportunity to experience Southern culture.
Vegetarian Festival *(late Sep/early Oct)*. Trang and Phuket provinces *(see p350)*. Self-mortification rituals following abstinence from meat.

Mangoes on display at Nakhon Pathom

OCTOBER

Chulalongkorn Day *(23 Oct)*, Bangkok. Commemorates the death of Rama V (King Chulalongkorn). Floral tributes are placed by the King's equestrian statue by the Royal Plaza in Bangkok.
Receiving of the Lotus Festival *(late Oct)*, Bang Phli *(see p43)*. The end of the rains celebrated by pouring lotus buds over a locally revered Budda image.
Ok Phansa *(Oct full moon)*. Nationwide celebration of the Lord Buddha's reappearance on Earth after a season spent preaching in heaven. Marks the end of the Buddhist Rains Retreat.
Krathin *(begins Oct full moon)*. One-month period during which monks are presented with new robes.
Nan Boat Races *(late Oct)*. Festive regatta *(see p245)*.
Illuminated Boat Procession *(Oct full moon)*, Nakhon Phanom. Boats with candles and offerings set afloat down the Mekhong River. Entertainments provided in the town *(see p286)*.

Colourful spectacle of the boat races at Nan in Northern Thailand

COOL SEASON

AFTER THE RAINS the skies clear and the air cools to a comfortable warmth. The countryside looks its best, lush and green from the rains, with full rivers and waterfalls. In general this is the best time to visit Thailand, especially during the coolest months of December and January. Numerous festivals, to celebrate of the end of the rains, afford a period of relaxation before rural activity climaxes with the rice harvest in December and January.

NOVEMBER

Golden Mount Fair *(first week)*, Bangkok. Thailand's largest temple fair, held at the foot of the Golden Mount.
Elephant Roundup *(third week)*, Surin. Annual spectacle honouring the many and varied roles played by the elephant in Thailand's development *(see p268)*. More than 150 elephants take part in displays of forestry skills and a mock battle.
Khwae River Bridge Week *(late Nov/early Dec)*, Kanchanaburi. Commemorates the construction of the bridge by POWs and slave labour.
Loy Krathong *(Nov full moon)*. One of Thailand's best-loved national festivals. Pays homage to the goddess of rivers and waterways, Mae Khongkha. In the evening, people gather at rivers, lakes and ponds to float *krathongs*. Sukhothai is the best place to watch this festival *(see p185)*.

AVERAGE MONTHLY TEMPERATURE (BANGKOK)

Temperature Chart
For visitors from temperate climes, Thailand is hot and humid throughout the year, especially in the South. It is uncomfortably so during April and May, pleasantly so in November and December. Though it is less humid in Northern Thailand, it can be chilly at night during the coolest months.

DECEMBER

Trooping of the Colours *(3 Dec)*, Royal Plaza, Bangkok. A very impressive ceremony that offers a vivid picture of regal pageantry. It is presided over by the king and queen, and features members of the elite Royal Guards, arrayed in bright dress uniform. The guardsmen swear allegiance to the king and march past members of the royal family.

His Majesty the King's Birthday *(5 Dec)*. Government and private buildings throughout the country are elaborately decorated, and the area around the Grand Palace is illuminated. In the evening, crowds gather around Sanam Luang for celebrations. This occasion shows the deep respect Thais have for their king.

Soldiers in dress uniform for the Trooping of the Colours in Bangkok

JANUARY

Chinese New Year *(Jan/Feb)*. Not an official holiday, but this three-day festival is widely observed by the large number of Thais of Chinese origin.

Umbrella Fair *(mid-Jan)*, Bo Sang, Chiang Mai province. Celebrates traditional paper and wood umbrella making *(see p218)*.

Don Chedi Memorial Fair *(late Jan)*, Suphan Buri province. Marks the victory of King Naresuan of Ayutthaya over the Burmese. The highlight of the events is an elephant-back duel.

FEBRUARY

Festival of Flowers *(first week)*, Chiang Mai. Beautiful blooms of the North displayed on floral float parades.

Kite Flying Season *(Feb–Apr)*, Sanam Luang, Bangkok. Colourful displays and kite-flying contests.

Wat Phra Kaeo on the King's Birthday

Makha Bucha *(Feb full moon)*. Third of the year's major Buddhist festivals. Merit-making and candlelit processions at temples.

PUBLIC HOLIDAYS

Western New Year's Day (1 Jan)

Makha Bucha (Feb full moon)

Chakri Day (6 Apr)

Thai New Year – Songkran (12–14/15 Apr)

Labour Day (1 May)

Coronation Day (5 May)

Royal Ploughing Ceremony (early May)

Visakha Bucha Day (May full moon)

Asanha Bucha and Khao Phansa (Jul full moon)

Queen's Birthday (12 Aug)

Chulalongkorn Day (23 Oct)

King's Birthday (5 Dec)

Constitution Day (10 Dec)

Western New Year's Eve (31 Dec)

THE HISTORY OF THAILAND

THE HISTORY OF THAILAND is that of an area of Southeast Asia, rather than of a single nation, and over the centuries numerous peoples have made their home in this region. The most recent were the Tai of Southern China, who migrated south in the first millennium AD, and from whom most Thais today are descended.

Prehistoric Thailand was once regarded as a cultural backwater. In the Northeast of the country, however, archaeologists recently uncovered the earliest evidence of agriculture and metallurgy in Southeast Asia. Also among the finds were ceramic pots, some dating as far back as 3000 BC, which display a high level of artistic skill.

Votive tablet from Ayutthaya

The earliest known powers in the region were the Dvaravati Kingdom (6th–11th centuries AD), the Sumatran-based Srivijaya Empire (7th–13th centuries) and the Khmer Empire (9th–13th centuries) based at Angkor (*see p254*), all of which were heavily influenced by Indian culture and religion.

The Lanna Kingdom in the North and the Sukhothai Kingdom, which imported Theravada Buddhism to Thailand, in the Central Plains grew in power from around the 12th century. Today, Thai schoolchildren are taught that Sukhothai marks the beginning of their history. Of all its kings, Ramkamhaeng (1279–98) stands out; part heroic myth, part historical figure.

Sukhothai was conquered by the Kingdom of Ayutthaya – also Tai – in the 14th century. At its height Ayutthaya controlled most of what is now Thailand, and the city of Ayutthaya saw the arrival of the first Europeans. The city was destroyed by the Burmese in 1767. Subsequently, a new city, Krung Thep (Bangkok), was built further south, on the Chao Phraya River, and the Chakri dynasty founded. In the 19th century Kings Mongkut and Chulalongkorn modernized Thailand. During this period, Thailand resisted colonization by France and Britain.

A revolution in 1932 ended absolute monarchy, and in 1939 Phibun Songkram, formerly a soldier in the Thai army, changed the country's name from Siam to Thailand. More recently, in the 1980s and '90s, Thailand has become one of Asia's "tiger economies". Because of recent political instability, though, real democracy has been slower to arrive than economic success.

Dutch map of the city of Ayutthaya, probably drawn in the 17th century

◁ Chakri period painted screen, dating from the late 18th century

Prehistoric Thailand

Jewellery from Ban Chiang

HUNTER-GATHERERS were already established in the area of modern-day Thailand by around 40,000 BC. They lived in semi-permanent settlements and made tools from wood and stone. Ancient seed husks found in caves in Northern Thailand have led to speculation that agriculture began to develop around 9000 BC. Rice was being cultivated around 3000 BC. Subsequently, in the area of Ban Chiang, elaborate pottery and bronze work began to be produced. This Bronze Age culture is believed by some historians to be the earliest in the world.

PREHISTORIC SITES

- Spirit Cave and Banyan Valley Cave
- Phu Phrabat
- Ban Chiang and Ban Na Di
- Pha Taem
- Don Tha Phet and Ban Kao

Ban Kao Tripod
This three-legged, terra-cotta pot was made by Neolithic artisans around 2000 BC. It was found at Ban Kao (see p160) in the Central Plains.

The flared rim and slightly more complex geometric pattern on this black and white, cord-incised pot were new stylistic features.

Moulded shoulders

Bronze Axe Head
The earliest bronze artifacts found at Ban Chiang are thought to date from about 3000 BC. This axe head is from around 2000 BC.

A black and white pattern was created by incising the clay with cord.

Clay feet

3000–2000 BC

c.1600 B

Clay Moulds
Clay moulds confirm that bronze objects were cast at Ban Chiang and not imported from elsewhere.

BAN CHIANG POTTERY

Pots found at Ban Chiang *(see p262)* date from 3000 BC to AD 200. Until their discovery in 1966, this area of Southeast Asia was thought to have produced little of cultural merit in prehistoric times. These, and other finds, show that the indigenous peoples were capable of producing sophisticated, beautiful works of art.

TIMELINE

Bronze spearhead

50,000 BC	5000 BC	4000 BC	3000 BC	2000 BC	10
40,000 BC Hunter-gatherers in area of modern-day Thailand			**2000–1500 BC** Bronze artifacts created at Ban Chiang	**1000 BC** Cave and cliff paintings at Pha Taem *(p288)*	
6000 BC First pottery created by inhabitants of Spirit Cave	**3000 BC** Domestication of animals (pigs, dogs, chickens and cattle)				
	3500 BC Rice chaff left in Banyan Valley Cave – beginning of rice cultivation		**2000 BC** Clay and bronze pots created at Ban Kao	**1000 BC** Bronze animals cast at Don Tha Phet	
	9000–7000 BC Seed and plant husks left in caves in Northern Thailand may indicate the beginnings of agriculture		**3000 BC** Elaborate cord-marked pottery manufactured at Ban Chiang		

Iron Age Rooster

A find of bronze and iron artifacts at Don Tha Phet, near Kanchanaburi (see p160), includes this iron rooster from about 1000 BC.

Cave Painting

These paintings at Pha Taem date from around 1000 BC. The artists were probably descended from the early inhabitants of Ban Chiang.

WHERE TO SEE PRE-HISTORIC THAILAND

At Ban Chiang *(see p262)* visitors can see burial sites and artifacts housed in the Ban Chiang National Museum. More Ban Chiang artifacts can be seen in the Bangkok National Museum *(pp84–5)*. At Ban Kao *(p160)* there are burial sites and a museum, while cave paintings can be seen at Pha Taem *(p288)* and Phu Phrabat Historical Park *(p285)*.

***Burial sites** at Ban Chiang were filled with pots, which were placed around the dead.*

Paint rather than cord is used to create a complex geometric pattern.

Narrow stand

300 BC–AD 1

Rust-coloured geometric designs were painted onto a beige ground.

300 BC–AD 200

Bronze Bracelets

As well as practical objects, the craftsmen of Ban Chiang were skilled at making elaborate jewellery. These bracelets probably date from the height of Ban Chiang's Bronze Age, around 300–200 BC.

---

500 BC Bronzeware created at Ban Na Di

Limestone sculpture of Vishnu (4th century AD)

1st–6th centuries AD Indianized Kingdom of Funan exerts strong cultural influence on the area around the Central Plains

AD 1	100	AD 200	300	AD 400

1st century AD Indian merchants begin to arrive in the Thai peninsula *(see pp336–7)*

Ban Chiang pot (300 BC–AD 200)

3rd–5th centuries Kingdom of Dan Sun in South flourishes and trades with Indian merchants

The First States

FROM THE FIRST FEW CENTURIES BC Hindu and Buddhist missionaries from India and Sri Lanka came to Southeast Asia. Over the next millennium distinctly Indianized kingdoms emerged. The Dvaravati Kingdom (6th–11th centuries) flourished in what is now the heart

Srivijayan votive tablet

of Thailand; the Srivijaya Empire of Sumatra (7th–13th centuries) was strong in the peninsula *(see pp336–7)*; while the Khmer Empire (9th–13th centuries) expanded from Cambodia *(see pp254–5)*. The Tai, from southern China, migrated to the area from the 11th century onwards.

KHMER EMPIRE IN AD 960

☐ *Extent of Khmer Empire*

Flying Buddha *(8th–9th centuries) This Dvaravati sculpture shows the Buddha on the back of Panaspati, a strange beast that comprises Nandin the bull, Shiva's mount, and a garuda (a mythical bird).*

Vishnu, asleep on the back of the *naga*, dreams of a new universe.

Stone Relief
Dvaravati craftsmen were renowned for their stonework. They excelled at bas-reliefs such as this one, at Wat Suthat (see p86), which depicts Buddhist and Hindu figures.

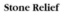

Dvaravati Deities
Dvaravati bas-reliefs, found in a cave near Saraburi, central Thailand, depict Brahma, Vishnu, the Buddha and flying figures.

The *naga* (serpent) bearing Vishnu represents the Milky Sea of Eternity.

TIMELINE

Early 6th century Mon people establish Dvaravati culture. They have already inherited Buddhism from Indian missionaries	**7th century** Srivijaya civilization expands from Sumatra	**8th century** Tai people inhabit the upland valleys of Laos, northern Vietnam and southern China

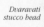

Dvaravati coin

500	600	700	800

Dvaravati stucco head

AD 661 Haripunchai said to be founded at Lamphun, Northern Thailand *(see p219)*, by Buddhist holymen

7th century Chamadevi of Lop Buri becomes Queen of the Dvaravati Kingdom

9th century Khmer Empire founded at Angkor

Devaraja
This Khmer bas-relief, one of many found at Angkor Wat (see pp254–5), shows the god-king, or devaraja, *King Suryavarman II (1113–50).*

Terracotta Lion *(8th-century)*
Dvaravati figures, such as this lion from Phetchaburi (see pp318–19), were influenced by earlier Gupta art from India.

The Creator,
Brahma, sitting on a lotus blossom springing from Vishnu's stomach, has the task of realizing Vishnu's dream of creating a new universe.

WHERE TO SEE THE FIRST STATES

Dvaravati, Srivijayan and Khmer artifacts can be seen at the Bangkok National Museum *(see pp84–5)* as well as at other regional national museums. Two Dvaravati-style *chedis* can be seen at Wat Chama Thewi in Lamphun *(p219)*. Phra Boro-mathat Chaiya *(p323)* is the best-surviving example of a Srivijayan temple. Khmer sites in Thailand include Prasat Hin Phimai *(pp266–7)* and Prasat Hin Khao Phnom Rung *(pp270–71)*.

***Prasat Hin Phimai** was built mostly during the reign of Sur-yavarman I in the 11th century.*

Srivijayan Buddha
This Buddha image, one of the most notable of the Srivijaya period, was found in Chaiya (see p323), an ancient city in peninsular Thailand.

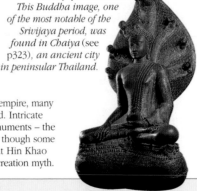

KHMER LINTEL

The Khmers built temples throughout their vast empire, many of which are in present-day Northeast Thailand. Intricate stone carvings are a striking feature of the monuments – the characters depicted *(see p37)* are mainly Hindu, though some are Mahayana Buddhist. This lintel, from Prasat Hin Khao Phnom Rung *(see pp270–71)*, depicts a Hindu creation myth.

11th–13th centuries Lop Buri incorporated into Khmer Empire as a significant provincial capital	**1001–1002** Reign of Udayadit-yavarman, who invades Haripunchai (Lamphun) following an assault on Lop Buri	**1229–43** Reign of Indravarman II	
		1115–55 Lop Buri tries to assert its independence from Khmer control	
900	**1000**	**1100**	**1200**
10th–12th centuries Srivijaya becomes involved in ruinous wars with Chola state in India	**11th–12th centuries** Population of Tai people increases in areas of present-day Thailand, then under Khmer control	**1113–50** Reign of Suryavarman II *Lop Buri Buddha*	**1181–1220** Reign of Jayavarman VII, the most powerful and innovative of the Khmer kings

The Sukhothai Kingdom

Sukhothai coin

SUKHOTHAI was the first notable kingdom of the Tai people, centred around the city of Sukhothai *(see pp184–7)* in the Central Plains. The Khmers referred to the Tai as *Siam*, a name that came to be used for this and subsequent Tai kingdoms. Theravada Buddhism achieved new expression during the Sukhothai period, in innovative architecture and images of the Buddha finely cast in bronze. Sukhothai was made powerful by its most illustrious ruler, Ramkamhaeng, but by 1320 was only a local power again.

SUKHOTHAI IN 1300

☐ *Sukhothai Kingdom*

Ramkamhaeng (c.1279–98)
This modern relief depicts Ramkamhaeng, Sukhothai's most illustrious ruler. He extended the kingdom and negotiated treaties with neighbouring states.

Inscription No. 1 (1292)
Ramkamhaeng is credited with inventing the Thai alphabet, and using it to record the history of Sukhothai on this stone.

Potteries and other industries were located north of the city.

Minor *wats* on low hills

Wat Chang Lom, the symbolic power centre

Rice fields and houses

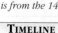

Roof Decoration
Ceramics were used to adorn buildings. This one is from the 14th century.

RECONSTRUCTION OF SI SATCHANALAI

Sukhothai's twin city, Si Satchanalai *(see pp188–90)* was the classic Thai *muang* or city-state. Within the walls was the symbolic power centre of the crown prince. Beyond were the life-giving waters of the Yom River, rice fields, homes and potteries, all within a ring of forested mountains, the outer limits of the *muang*.

TIMELINE

King Ramkamhaeng

1240	1260	1280

c.1240s Si Intharathit is first known king of Sukhothai

c.1279 Ramkamhaeng is made king; during his reign Sukhothai becomes a large kingdom

1287 Ramkamhaeng forges alliance with states of Lanna *(see pp58–9)* and Phayao

c.1270–79 Reign of Ban Muang; Sukhothai remains merely a local power

1283 According to legend, Ramkamhaeng modifies Sri Lankan script to create Thai alphabet

1294 Ramkamhaeng campaigns in the south, near Phetchaburi

Slate Engraving
This 14th-century engraving shows the Buddha being reincarnated as a horse. It is one of a series discovered at Wat Si Chum (see p185) at Sukhothai.

WHERE TO SEE THE SUKHOTHAI KINGDOM

The main sites are Sukhothai itself *(see pp184–7)*, Si Satchanalai *(pp188–90)* and Kamphaeng Phet *(pp182–3)*. Artifacts are housed in the Bangkok National Museum *(pp84–5)*, the Ramkamhaeng National Museum *(pp184–5)*, the Sawankha Woranayok National Museum *(p190)* and the Kamphaeng Phet National Museum *(see p182)*.

Minor *wat*

Sangkhalok Pottery
Sawankhalok was the old name for Si Satchanalai, where many kilns *(see pp150–1) were sited. From this derives the name Sangkhalok, given to 13th–15th-century pottery from the Sukhothai Kingdom.*

Rapids

Wat Sa Si (see p185) is just one of dozens of wats *at Sukhothai Historical Park.*

Royal Palaces

A Lak Muang
(city pillar) was built to appease the spirits of the land.

Walking Buddha
New, sophisticated techniques for casting bronze produced this classic 14th-century Walking Buddha image.

Four main *wats*
run parallel to the Yom River.

The perimeter was triple walled and moated; spikes around the moat deterred war elephants.

1298 Ramkamhaeng dies

End of 13th century Sukhothai first called Siam by Chinese

14th–15th-century Sangkhalok bowl

1346–7 Reign of Ngua Nam Thom

1300	1320	1340

1298–1346 Reign of Lo Thai, who succeeds Ramkamhaeng. Empire begins to unravel

1321 Tak, formerly part of Sukhothai, falls under Lanna control; Sukhothai is now a small kingdom, one of many competing states

14th–15th-century Sukhothai stoneware

1347–1368 Reign of Maha Thammaracha I

The Kingdom of Ayutthaya

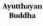
Ayutthayan Buddha

AYUTTHAYA SUPPLANTED SUKHOTHAI as the most powerful kingdom in Siam in the mid-14th century, and by 1438 had incorporated it into its empire. By the mid-16th century Ayutthaya controlled the entire Central Plains area and at its height held sway over much of what is now Thailand. The Ayutthaya period saw military, legal and administrative reforms and a flowering of the arts, as well as diplomatic and trade links with the West *(see pp152–3)*. Its end came after years of conflict with Burma, when in 1767 the capital was sacked.

AYUTTHAYA IN 1540

☐ *Kingdom of Ayutthaya*

Ayutthayan Frescoes
Few frescoes have survived. These, from the 15th century, are from Wat Ratchaburana in Ayutthaya (see pp166–71).

Votive Tablets
Clay and terracotta tablets from the Ayutthaya period often show the Buddha resplendent beneath a naga (serpent).

Gold Elephant
The Ayutthayans were masters at working gold. This elephant, studded with gems and crafted to look as though it is paying homage, was discovered in Wat Ratchaburana.

Ornate, stylized carvings

A huge oar at the stern helped steer the boat.

Gold lacquer was used to decorate the barges.

RECONSTRUCTION OF A ROYAL BARGE

When foreigners *(farangs)* first came to Ayutthaya, they often met the sight of grand royal barges. This illustration is based on French engravings in some of the first accounts of the opulent city of Ayutthaya to reach the West.

TIMELINE OF THE AYUTTHAYA KINGDOM

1351 Ayutthaya is established and Ramathibodi becomes king

1409–24 Reign of Intharacha

1448–88 Reign of Borommatrailokanat, who introduces far reaching administrative and legal reforms

1350	1400	1450	1500

1390 Ramesuan captures Chiang Mai in Lanna *(pp58–9)*

1431–2 Borommaracha II conquers Angkor

1491–1529 Reign of Ramathibodi II

1507–15 Ayutthaya at war with Lanna

Ayutthayan coin

Gilded Lacquer Cabinet
The craftsmen of Ayutthaya were adept at working wood. The doors of this cabinet are inlaid with gold; the pattern is of trees. Other such cabinets depict scenes from the jataka *or Westerners.*

WHERE TO SEE AYUTTHAYA

The city of Ayutthaya in the South Central Plains has some of the most spectacular ruins in Thailand *(see pp166–71)*. Ayutthayan artifacts are housed in the Chao Sam Phraya National Museum *(p168)* and in the Bangkok National Museum *(pp84–5)*.

***Wat Chai Watthanaram**, built by King Prasat Thong in 1630.*

Door Panel from Ayutthaya
This 17th–18th-century wood panel once formed part of the door of a temple. It was discovered in Wat Huntra in Ayutthaya.

Carving of the king

Royal insignia

The oarsmen would chant barge songs to keep paddling in time.

Deva Figure
Carved "angels", such as this 18th-century figure, were used in religious ceremonies.

1585–7 Naresuan defeats Burmese twice	*Ayutthayan soldier*	**1660** Narai tries to take Chiang Mai and Lampang in Lanna from Burmese rule, but is repelled by a Burmese army	**1766** Burmese forces, after taking Chiang Mai, besiege Ayutthaya
1555 Naresuan is born	**1593** Naresuan defeats Burmese at Battle of Nong Sarai *(pp58–9)*	**1685** First French mission in Ayutthaya	

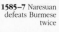

1550	1600	1650	1700	1750

1564 Burmese invade the kingdom of Ayutthaya	**1608** Siam sends its first diplomatic mission to Europe	**1662** Narai invades Burma	*King Narai*	**1767** Ayutthaya sacked, capital moves to Thon Buri
	1569–93 Ayutthaya under Burmese rule	**1688** Narai's death leads to "revolution" in Ayutthaya		

Lanna and Burmese Kingdoms

Lanna urn

THE NORTHERN KINGDOM of Lanna was established at the same time as Sukhothai and endured for 600 years. Its first ruler, Mengrai, extended Lanna rule into Burma, and the reigns of Ku Na and Tilok saw a golden age. Wars with Burma and Ayutthaya in the 16th and 17th centuries, however, led to decline. Ayutthaya had driven the Burmese out of Lanna once before, but in 1615 the Burmese took back the Lanna capital, Chiang Mai, for almost a century. In the late 18th century, newly allied Siamese and Lanna forces drove the Burmese out. Lanna remained autonomous into the 19th century.

LANNA IN 1540

☐ *Lanna Kingdom*

Golden Door
Decorated with gold leaf, this temple door is at Wat Phra That Lampang Luang (see pp224–5), one of the oldest Lanna structures in Thailand.

Naresuan, on his elephant, engages the Burmese crown prince.

Ayutthayan soldiers, in traditional helmets, rally round Naresuan.

Lanna Elephant
This bronze elephant, from the 16th century, was used as a pedestal upon which Buddhist merit offerings were presented.

Bronze Buddha
Buddha images, such as this one, from the 14th–15th century, are regarded as the pinnacle of classical Lanna art. After the Burmese took the north, this style of Lanna art declined.

BATTLE OF NONG SARAI (1593)
The Burmese attempted to control all of Siam, and, in 1564, invaded Ayutthaya. This 19th-century painting shows the Battle of Nong Sarai, when Naresuan (1590–1605) defeated the Burmese crown prince and Ayutthaya gained independence. In 1598 Ayutthaya drove Burma from the north, but in the 17th century the Burmese retook it.

TIMELINE OF LANNA AND BURMESE KINGDOMS

1259–1317 Reign of Mengrai; northern principalities unified

1289 Mengrai extends Lanna control into Burma

1292 Chiang Mai founded

1355–85 Reign of Ku Na leads to period of stability

1441-82 Reign of Tilok

1442–3 Ayutthaya sends an army against Lanna

1250	1300	1350	1400	1450	1500

1281 Mengrai conquers Haripunchai *(p219)*

1262 Chiang Rai *(pp240–1)* founded

1369 Ku Na invites a Sukhothai monk, a follower of Sri Lankan Buddhism *(p188)*, to establish a monastery in Chiang Mai

1456–7 Lanna and Ayutthaya are engaged in a protracted war for control of the upper Central Plains

King Mengrai

Model Wihan

Models of wihans are common throughout Thailand. This Lanna one, from the 18th–19th century, cast in bronze, has a high base, an exaggerated version of the bases found on many Lanna temple buidings.

WHERE TO SEE LANNA AND BURMESE THAILAND

Lanna artifacts can be seen in national museums at Chiang Mai, Lamphun *(see p219)* and Bangkok. Chiang Mai *(pp214–17)*, Chiang Khong *(p239)*, Lamphun and Lampang *(p226)* all have buildings that date from the Lanna period. Mae Hong Son *(pp206–7)* and Phrae *(pp248–9)* have buildings showing Burmese influence.

Burmese Dancer
This temple mural of a Burmese dancing girl is from Chiang Mai (see pp214–17). *A number of* wats *in the North bear similar indications of Burmese occupation.*

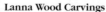

***The* ho trai** *(scripture library) of Wat Phra Sing, Chiang Mai, is one of the most notable late Lanna structures in Thailand.*

Burmese soldiers
wear simple bandanas around their heads.

Lanna Coin
During the 18th and 19th centuries, bronze rings were used as coinage in the Lanna Kingdom.

Lanna Wood Carvings
The pediment of the 19th-century wihan *at Wat Pan Tao (see p215) is typical of the elaborate work produced by Lanna wood carvers.*

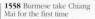

1550	1600	1650	1700	1750	1800

1558 Burmese take Chiang Mai for the first time

1593 Ayutthaya establishes independence from Burma at Battle of Nong Sarai

1660 Narai of Ayutthaya attempts to wrest control of North from Burmese but is repulsed

19th-century Lanna box

1615 Burma regains control over Lanna

1598 Naresuan of Ayutthaya expels Burma from the North, though this is short-lived

15th–17th-century Lanna Buddha

1727 General Thip proclaims himself king of Lampang after defeating Burmese

1776 Taksin of Thon Buri and Kawila of Lampang reconquer Chiang Mai

The Early Chakri Dynasty

Court dress, c.1850

AFTER THE SACK OF AYUTTHAYA, Taksin, an army general, established a new capital at Thon Buri, on the west bank of the Chao Phraya opposite what would later become Bangkok. He became king in 1768 and in ten years Siam was a regional power again. However, he became increasingly despotic and, in 1782, was ousted by the military commander Chao Phraya Chakri, who was later pronounced King Rama I. Chakri's descendant, King Mongkut (Rama IV), modernized Siam, opening it up to foreign trade and influence.

SIAM IN 1809

☐ *Siamese territories*

Chakri Kings
The reigns of Ramas I, II and III signalled an era of stable monarchical rule. Rama II was a literary man, while Rama III was a staunch traditionalist.

Khlongs are an important means of transportation

Chakri Throne
The Busok Mala Throne was built in the reign of Rama I and was used for important state occasions. It stands in the Grand Palace (see pp76–81).

The Grand Palace
(see pp76–81) was founded in the late 18th century; by the mid-19th century it is already vast.

Sir John Bowring
The Bowring Treaty (1855) allowed the British free trade. Later, Siam forged similar treaties with other colonial powers, thus avoiding annexation.

TIMELINE

Ramakien mural

1768 Taksin begins to re-establish Siamese Empire

1782 Rama I overthrows an increasingly despotic Taksin; relocates capital

1783 Wat Phra Kaeo begun

1785 Massive Burmese invasion repulsed

1797 Rama I "writes" Ramakien *(see pp36–7)*

1800 Burmese finally expelled from Siam

1805 Rama I appoints a committee of judges to reform Siamese law

1808–24 Reign of Rama II

1813 Siam withdraws from Cambodia leaving Vietnam as dominant power

| 1770 | 1780 | 1790 | 1800 | 1810 |

Thai Etiquette *(1855)*
In mid-19th century Siam, prostrating oneself before a superior was common. It was officially abolished by Rama V (see pp62–3).

(see pp62–3)

WHERE TO SEE EARLY CHAKRI THAILAND

Almost all the best examples of architecture from the early Chakri – or Rattanakosin *(see p31)* – period can be seen in Bangkok. The earliest Chakri building is the *bot* of Wat Phra Kaeo *(p76)*. Other examples include the *bot* of Wat Suthat *(pp86–7)*, the *wihan* of Wat Suthat, Wat Pho *(pp88–9)* and Phra Nakhon Khiri in Phetchaburi *(see p320)*.

Wat Suthat, *built in the early 19th century by Rama I, is the site of Bangkok's tallest* wihan.

Mongkut *(1851–68)*
Before coming to the throne Mongkut, pictured here with his favourite wife, travelled widely, meeting many Westerners.

Thon Buri, on the western bank of the Chao Phraya, is still just a small town.

EARLY BANGKOK (KRUNG THEP)

The Siamese capital was moved from Thon Buri to the east of the river in 1782 as a defence from the Burmese. Its official 43-syllable name matches the majesterial plans that Rama I had for his new city: the first two words, "Krung Thep", mean "city of angels". This mural from 1864 shows the temples and river houses of early Bangkok.

King Mongkut Mural
In this mural King Mongkut is in his palace observing an eclipse through a telescope, his subjects below him.

1824–1851 Reign of Rama III		**1840s** Siam dominant in Cambodia	**1855** Signing of the Bowring Treaty
Chakri coin			
1820	**1830**	**1840**	**1850**	**1860**
1826 Limited trade agreement, Burney Treaty, signed	**1830s** Siam goes to war in Cambodia, to defend Buddhism against the Vietnamese	*Rama IV (1855)*	**1868** Mongkut, Rama IV, dies. 15-year-old King Chulalongkorn accedes to the throne, his powers constrained by the appointment of a regent
	1827 Vientiane is sacked by Siamese army		

Reign of King Chulalongkorn

PERHAPS THE GREATEST KING of the Chakri dynasty, Chulalongkorn (1868–1910) carried on the modernization of Siam that his father, Mongkut, had started. Financial reforms were made, the government restructured and slavery abolished. Reform angered older ministers, the "conservatives" *(hua boran)*, and led to the Front Palace Crisis of 1875. This was also a time when Britain and France were consolidating their positions in Southeast Asia.

Rama V in Western garb

Chulalongkorn's policies and diplomacy kept the colonial powers at bay, though parts of Burma, Laos, Cambodia and the Malay states were ceded to them.

SIAM IN 1909

☐ *Siamese territories*

☐ *Ceded territories*

Rama V

Chulalongkorn (Rama V) came to the throne, under the guidance of a regent, at the age of 15. He had received an excellent Thai and Western education and was amply qualified for the task of reforming Siam.

Soldiers attending the cremation wore colonial uniforms.

Drummers wore traditional Thai headdresses.

Life on the Khlongs

At the end of the 19th century, and into the 20th, Bangkok was known as the "Venice of the East" (see p123).

Classical Dancers at Court

Many Siamese traditions, among them classical dance, remained unchanged. Scenes such as this were often recorded with the aid of new technology – photography.

TIMELINE

1874 Chulalongkorn (Rama V) introduces a series of reforms which anger the "conservatives" or *hua boran*

1887 Prince Devawongse attends the celebrations, in London, of Queen Victoria's 50th year; the prince studies European government with a view to reform in Siam

1870	1875	1880	1885

1874 Thai High Commissioner sent to govern Lanna

1875 Front Palace Crisis – the "conservatives" demonstrate their anger. Chulalongkorn has to tone down some of his reforms

1885 Enlightened Prince Devawongse made Foreign Minister

Tile detail, Wat Rachabophit

1888 New administrative system, centralizing power, is introduced

Franco-Siamese Crisis
In an attempt to consolidate her hold over Indochina, in 1893 France asserted sovereignty over Siamese-controlled Laos. This cartoon shows a French "wolf" hungrily assessing a Siamese "lamb".

Chulalongkorn's body was cremated in this funeral tower.

WHERE TO SEE LATE CHAKRI THAILAND

During the latter part of the 19th century there was little change in the basic style of religious buildings. Chulalongkorn, however, left his mark on some buildings in Bangkok. Wat Benchamabophit *(see pp102–3)* employs an eclectic mixture of Chinese, Italian and Khmer styles, while Wat Rachabophit *(p85)* displays traditional Thai and Western motifs.

At Wat Rachabopit, Rama V had the interior decorated in Italianate-Thai style.

CREMATION OF CHULALONGKORN

Chulalongkorn's cremation, held in Bangkok in 1910, was a grand state affair. As a great reformer, he was idealized by his subjects, and, even today, the people of Thailand commemorate his death on Chulalongkorn Day *(see p46).*

Modern Developments
Chulalongkorn promoted many new ideas; cars appeared in Bangkok at the beginning of the 20th century.

French gunboat

1893 French take control of Laos; leads to Franco-Siamese Crisis

1910 Chulalongkorn dies. His son Vajiravudh (Rama VI) comes to throne

1907 Cambodia ceded to the French

890   **1895**   **1900**   **1905**   **1910**

1892 New ministries are created to govern Siam

1893 Paknam Incident – French gunboats sail up the Chao Phraya River

1905 After years of gradual reform, slavery is finally abolished

1909 Siamese sovereignty over the Malayan states of Kelantan, Perlis, Terengganu and Kedah ceded to the British

Modern Thailand

Modern Thai flag

IN 1932 SIAM became a constitutional monarchy. Under Prime Minister Phibun Songkram, the 1930s saw rising nationalism: the country was renamed Prathet Thai (Thailand) and sided with Japan against the Allies in World War II. By contrast, during the Vietnam War in the 1970s, fear of Communism led Thailand to help the USA. Economic growth accelerated during the 1980s and '90s, pushing Thailand towards being one of Asia's "tiger economies". Military coups, however, have hindered democratization.

ASEAN IN 1997

☐ *Association of SE Asian Nations*

King Vajiravudh

Chulalongkorn's son Vajiravudh (1910–25) clashed with his father's senior advisors. To build a following of his own he created the elite corps, the Wild Tigers, in 1911.

Democracy Monument

A meeting place during pro-democracy rallies, this monument was built in 1939 to mark the revolution of 1932. The last major demonstration held here was in 1992.

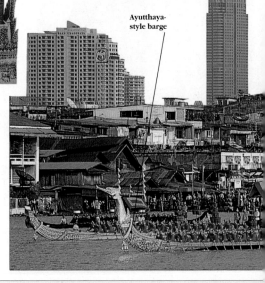

Ayutthaya-style barge

MODERN BANGKOK

With an official population of seven million in the 1990s (unofficially closer to ten million), Bangkok is growing in line with Thailand's economy. Unregulated development has left the city with a poor infrastructure. However, old traditions are still important. The 1982 Bangkok Bicentennial and celebrations of Bhumibol's 50th year as King in 1996 (shown here), featured traditional royal barges.

TIMELINE

Phibun Songkram

	1920	1930	1940	1950

1911 Wild Tigers, an elite paramilitary corps, formed

1917 Siam sends a small force of men to fight on the side of the Allies in WW I

1925 Prajadhipok becomes king

1932 Revolution; Siam made a constitutional monarchy

1934–8 Increasing power struggle between Phibun Songkram and Pridi Phanomyong

1935 Prajadhipok abdicates, Ananda Mahidol becomes king

1938 Phibun Songkram becomes PM

1939 Phibun renames Siam

1940 Thais invade Laos and Cambodia after fall of France to Germany

1941 Phibun capitulates to Japan; Pridi Phanomyong organizes underground resistance

1946 Phibun resigns; Pridi Phanomyong forms government

1946 Mahidol killed; Bhumibol made king

Traffic Congestion

As modern Bangkok has grown, so too has the problem of traffic congestion. Lack of proper road planning means that the city's streets are constantly gridlocked.

King Bhumibol

Against a backdrop of unstable politics, the revered King Bhumibol (Rama IX) has represented virtue and stability. Through his authority, the military coup and bloody demonstrations of 1992 were ended.

WHERE TO SEE MODERN THAILAND

Apart from palaces and *wats*, most 20th-century architecture in Thailand, particularly in Bangkok, tends to be very dull and functional. However, some of the many new buildings of the 1980s and '90s are worth a look if only for their sheer outrageousness (*see p117*). Modern resort hotels sometimes incorporate traditional touches.

The Robot Building, *in downtown Bangkok, was designed by Sumet Jumsai in the mid-1980s.*

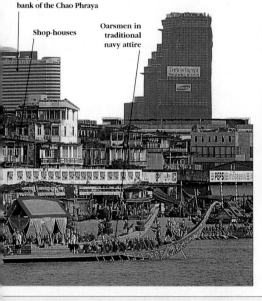

Luxury hotel on the west bank of the Chao Phraya

Shop-houses

Oarsmen in traditional navy attire

Tourism

Tourism is now one of the country's major industries – over six million people visit each year. It has both positive and negative effects on local culture.

1957 Sarit Thanarat becomes PM in coup; he ushers in the era of modern development, known as *samai pattana*

US fighter plane

1973–6 Turbulent democratic government; student demonstrations

1980s CPT a spent force; Thailand enters a period of rapid economic growth

1988 Fully democratic elections

1991 Military coup

1960	1970	1980	1990

1964 US military aircraft operate from Thai soil as Vietnam War escalates

1976 Massacre of students at Thammasat University brings huge support for the CPT (*see p278*)

1967 Thailand becomes founder member of the Association of Southeast Asian Nations (ASEAN)

1992 Massacre of pro-democracy demonstrators in Bangkok followed by democratic elections

King Bhumibol

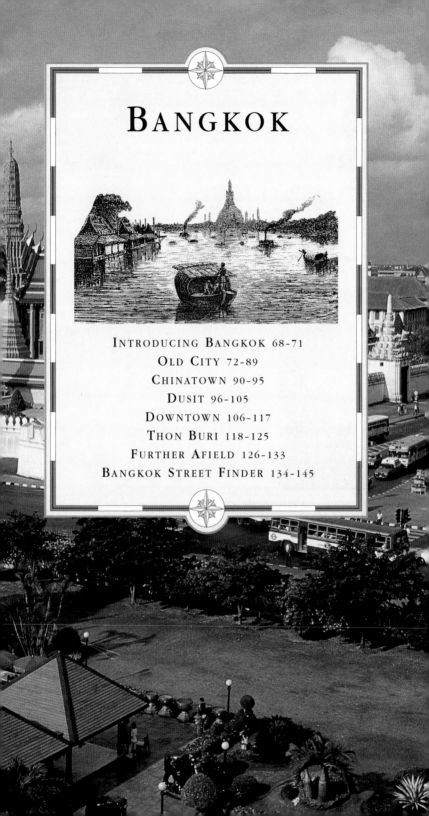

BANGKOK

Introducing Bangkok

THAILAND'S CAPITAL CITY, straddling the great Chao Phraya River, 20 km (12 miles) upstream from the Gulf of Thailand, is an exuberant, exhilarating, infuriating metropolis of seven million people. Founded by Rama I in 1782, this relatively young city is known to Thais as Krung Thep ("city of angels"), a shortened form of a full name in excess of 150 letters. Bangkok may be a lesson in the dangers of uncontrolled urban expansion, but it is also one of the world's most exciting cities. Its lively nightlife and markets, shops and restaurants, and magnificent *wats*, museums, palaces and parks, have something for everyone.

Guard statue at Wat Arun

The National Museum (see pp84–5) *contains a wealth of treasures, such as this 7th–8th-century head of the Buddha.*

OLD CITY
(see pp72–89)

THON BURI
(see pp118–125)

CHAO PHRAYA

The Grand Palace and Wat Phra Kaeo complex (see pp76–81) *is Bangkok's premier tourist attraction. The sacred Emerald Buddha, or Phra Kaeo, is housed in one of many splendid buildings.*

Wat Pho (see pp88–9) *is one of the oldest temples in the capital, dating originally from the 16th century. It is also a renowned centre for traditional medicine and contains the much respected Institute of Massage.*

Wat Arun (see pp120–21), *otherwise known as the Temple of Dawn, is one of Bangkok's best known landmarks. Its Khmer-influenced prangs are encrusted with thousands of pieces of broken porcelain.*

◁ Intricately decorated *prangs* of the Grand Palace and Wat Phra Kaeo embellishing Bangkok's skyline

Dusit Park (see pp98–9), with its leafy walkways, fascinating museums, Vimanmek Palace and neighbouring zoo, has enough attractions to provide a full day's sightseeing.

0 metres 1,000
0 yards 1,000

DUSIT
(see pp96–105)

Jim Thompson's House (see pp114–15), a beautifully decorated series of teak buildings, was once home to the famed American silk merchant.

CHINATOWN
(see pp90–95)

DOWNTOWN
(see pp106–117)

Chinatown (see pp90–95) is one of Bangkok's most hectic, colourful and intoxicating districts. Narrow streets overflow with markets and shops, such as this religious goods emporium.

GREATER BANGKOK AREA

Pathum Thani
Bang Yai
Nonthaburi
Min Buri
Phra Pradaeng
Samut Sakhon
Samut Prakan

0 kilometres 50
0 miles 25

The Old Farang Quarter (see pp108–9) was the commercial hub for foreigners in the 19th century. Some colonial buildings, such as the Portuguese Embassy, survive.

A River View of Bangkok

THE TWO GREAT RIVERS of the North, the Ping and the Nan, join at Nakhon Sawan in the Central Plains to form the Chao Phraya ("river of kings"), Thailand's most important waterway. This vital transport axis drains some of the country's most fertile rice-growing land. The stretch shown here is actually a canal, built in the 16th century as a short cut at a point where the Chao Phraya took a huge meander along what is now Khlong Bangkok Noi and Khlong Bangkok Yai. Along this busy "royal mile" you can catch glimpses of the Grand Palace, temples and colonial buildings, and experience a flavour of old Bangkok's colourful riverfront.

A typical Chao Phraya barge, transporting goods along the river

To Phra Pin Klao Bridge

The Buddhaisawan Chapel in the National Museum (see pp84–5) *is home to the Phra Buddha Sing, one of the most venerated Buddha images in Thailand after the Emerald Buddha. Elsewhere in the museum is a fabulous collection of arts and crafts from every period of Thai history. Exhibits include Buddha images, weapons and pottery.*

RIVERBOATS ON THE CHAO PHRAYA

The Chao Phraya is a major transport artery, both for goods and for people. Hefty rice barges, tiny boats laden with fruit and vegetables and a variety of ferry services continually ply the river. No visitor to Bangkok should miss seeing the city from the water, and jumping on the Chao Phraya Express is one of the easiest and cheapest ways to do so. The stops are indicated on the Street Finder (maps 1–2, 5–6). There are also cross-river ferries from almost every river pier, as well as countless long-tail boats which operate as buses or can be specially chartered to explore the city's *khlongs*.

Long-tail boat on the Chao Phraya

Wat Rakhang (see p121) *is a little visited but rewarding temple containing fine murals painted in the 1920s.*

0 metres	200
0 yards	200

Wat Phra Kaeo (see pp76–9) contains Thailand's most sacred Buddha image, the Emerald Buddha. The temple and palace complex is a superb collection of buildings with lavish decorative details.

Sanam Luang, ("field of kings"), the venue for national ceremonies, is one of Bangkok's few open spaces.

LOCATOR MAP

See Street Finder maps 1, 5

Wat Pho (see pp88–9), the city's oldest temple, dates from the 17th century. It is famed for its school of massage, as well as for fine details such as this painting of a Chinese soldier.

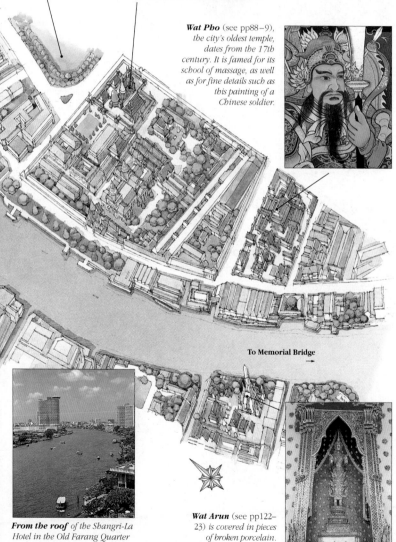

To Memorial Bridge

From the roof of the Shangri-La Hotel in the Old Farang Quarter (see pp108–9), there is an excellent view of the Chao Phraya River.

Wat Arun (see pp122–23) is covered in pieces of broken porcelain. This Buddha image is outside the main bot.

OLD CITY

Buddha images, ready for transit

As THE SPIRITUAL and historical heart of Bangkok, the Old City is dense with temples and shrines. Known as Rattanakosin, this was the centre of the new capital Rama I founded in 1782 *(see pp60–61)*. Remnants of a defensive wall can be seen between the Golden Mount and Wat Rachanat. Some of Thailand's finest Rattanakosin period architecture is within the Old City. The foremost example is the Grand Palace, within which is Wat Phra Kaeo, home of the country's most venerated image, the Emerald Buddha. South of here is Wat Pho, one of the city's oldest temples, while to the north lies Sanam Luang ("field of kings"), the site of royal ceremonies. Alongside Sanam Luang, the National Museum contains Southeast Asia's most impressive collection of artifacts. Two Buddhist universities are located in temples nearby: Wat Mahathat and Wat Bowonniwet. The latter is famed for its murals combining Western and traditional Thai styles.

SIGHTS AT A GLANCE

Wats

Grand Palace and Wat Phra Kaeo pp76–81 ❶

Wat Bowonniwet ❺

Wat Mahathat ❷

Wat Pho pp88–9 ⓯

Wat Rachabophit ⓬

Wat Rachanat ❼

Wat Rachapradit ⓭

Wat Saket and the Golden Mount ❽

Wat Suthat and the Giant Swing ⓫

Museums and Galleries

National Gallery ❹

National Museum pp84–5 ❸

Notable Roads and Districts

Bamrung Muang Road ❿

Monk's Bowl Village ❾

Monuments

Democracy Monument ❻

0 metres   500

0 yards   500

GETTING THERE

If you are staying near the river, the easiest way to get to the Old City is by ferry. The Chao Phraya Express piers of Chang and Maharaj are best for the Grand Palace while Tien and Rachinee are close to Wat Pho. Many buses go to the Old City.

KEY

- ▨ Street-by-Street map pp74–5
- ⚓ Riverboat pier
- ⚓ Chao Phraya Express pier
- 🚔 Police station
- ✉ Post office
- ⛩ *Wat*

◁ **The elaborately decorated roof of the Aphonphimok Pavilion, Grand Palace**

Street-by-Street: Around Sanam Luang

สนามหลวง

Portraits of the King, Sanam Luang

SANAM LUANG ("field of kings" or "royal ground") is one of the few sizeable open spaces in Bangkok. It is the traditional site for royal cremations, the annual kite-flying festival and the Royal Ploughing Ceremony *(see p44)*. Spiritually speaking, this area is one of the luckiest in the city, with the Grand Palace, the Lak Muang (City Pillar) shrine and the Amulet Market bordering Sanam Luang. Neighbouring streets overflow with salesmen hawking lotions, potions and amulets for luck, love, or protection from evil spirits. Astrologers gather to chart your stars or read your palm. Notable sights include Wat Mahathat, Thailand's most revered centre of Buddhist studies, and the National Museum.

LOCATOR MAP
See Street Finder map 1

Phra Chan Pier

Wat Mahathat
Meditation classes are held at the Buddhist university within this temple's compound. Dating from the 18th century, the wat is more notable for its bustling atmosphere than its buildings ❷

0 metres	500
0 yards	500

Tha Chang Chao Phraya Express Pier

MAHATHAT

TROK SILLAPAKORN

NA PHRA LAN

Silpakorn University of Fine Arts
This façade, facing Sanam Luang, fronts Thailand's most famous art school. The university regularly puts on excellent art shows in its exhibition hall. See the boards outside the entrance for details and opening times.

Entrance to Grand Palace and Wat Phra Kaeo

Western edge of Sanam Luang

To Lak Muang (City Pillar)

KEY

– – – Suggested route

AMULETS

The Thais are a highly superstitious people – those who do not wear some form of protective or lucky amulet are firmly in a minority. Amulets come in myriad forms and are sold in specialist markets, often near spiritually auspicious sites. Although many are religious in nature – such as tiny Buddha images and copies of sacred statues – others are designed for more practical purposes, such as model phalluses to ensure sexual potency. Amulets are such a big business that there are even magazines dedicated to them.

A selection of charms sold at stalls around Sanam Luang

Thammasat University, notable for its law and political science faculties, was the scene of student riots in the 1970s *(see p65).*

To Phra Pin Klao Bridge

★ **National Museum**
A magnificent range of arts and crafts from every period of Thai history are displayed in this huge museum ❸

The Gallery of Thai History at the National Museum provides a good introduction to the country.

PRA CHAN

NA PHRA THAT

Fortune Teller at Sanam Luang
Many Thais set great store by the predictions of fortune tellers and often visit those who gather on Sanam Luang near Wat Phra Kaeo.

★ **Kite Flying at Sanam Luang**
King Chulalongkorn (1868–1910) was a keen kite flyer and permitted Sanam Luang to be used for the sport. Fiercely contested kite fights can often be witnessed here between February and April.

STAR SIGHTS

★ **National Museum**

★ **Kite Flying at Sanam Luang**

Grand Palace and Wat Phra Kaeo ●

พระบรมมหาราชวังและวัดพระแก้ว

Detail on Phra Mondop Library

Construction of this remarkable site began in 1782, to mark the founding of the new capital and provide a resting place for the sacred Emerald Buddha (Phra Kaeo) and a residence for the king. Surrounded by walls stretching for 1,900 m (2,080 yards), the complex was once a self-sufficient city within a city. The Royal Family now lives in Dusit, but Wat Phra Kaeo is still Thailand's holiest temple. Many of the eclectic, colourful buildings are open to the public.

Wat Phra Kaeo's skyline, as seen from Sanam Luang

★ Bot of the Emerald Buddha
Devotees make offerings to the Emerald Buddha at the entrance to the bot, *the most important building in the* wat.

Emerald Buddha

Chapel of the Gandharara Buddha

Eight *prangs* border the east side of the *wat*.

★ Ramakien Gallery
Extending clockwise all the way around the cloisters are 178 panels depicting the complete story of the Ramakien.

TIMELINE

1750	1800	1850	1900	1950
1782 Official founding of new capital	**1809** Rama II introduces Chinese details	**1840s** Women's quarter laid out as a city within a city	**1880** Chulalongkorn, the last king to make major additions, involves 26 half-brothers in renovation of Wat Phra Kaeo	**1932** Chakri Dynasty's 150th year celebrated at palace

1783 Work begins on Wat Phra Kaeo, Dusit Throne Hall and Phra Maha Monthien

1855 New buildings epitomize fusion of Eastern and Western styles

1925 Rama VII chooses to live in the less formal Chitrlada Palace at Dusit. Grand Palace reserved for special occasions

1982 Renovation of the complex

Decorative Gilt Figures
Encircling the exterior of the bot are 112 garudas (mythical beasts that are half-man, half-bird). They are shown holding nagas *(serpents) and are typical of the* wat's *dazzling decorative details.*

VISITORS' CHECKLIST

Na Phra Lan Rd. **Map** 1 C5.
AC: 3, 6, 8, 12, 39, 44.
Chang, Tien. ☐ 8:30am–3:30pm daily. ● special ceremonies. 🎟 includes admission to Vimanmek Palace. ✗ in bot. 📷

Apsonsi
A mythical creature (half-woman, half-lion), Apsonsi is one of the beautiful gilded figures on the upper terrace of Wat Phra Kaeo.

Phra Mondop (library)

The Phra Si Rattana Chedi contains a piece of the Buddha's breastbone.

Upper Terrace

Ho Phra Nak (royal mausoleum)

Wihan Yot

WAT PHRA KAEO

Wat Phra Kaeo (shown here) is a sub-complex within the greater Grand Palace complex. The temple is Thailand's holiest shrine, but unlike other Thai *wats*, has no resident monks.

The Ho Phra Monthien Tham is the auxiliary library.

The Royal Pantheon

GRAND PALACE AND WAT PHRA KAEO

1 Entrance
2 Wat Phra Kaeo complex
3 Dusit Throne Hall
4 Aphonphimok Pavilion
5 Chakri Throne Hall
6 Inner Palace
7 Phra Maha Monthien Buildings
8 Siwalai Gardens
9 Rama IV Chapel
10 Boromphiman Mansion
11 Audience Chamber

KEY

☐ Wat Phra Kaeo complex
☐ Buildings
☐ Lawns

STAR FEATURES

★ Bot of the Emerald Buddha

★ Ramakien Gallery

Exploring Wat Phra Kaeo

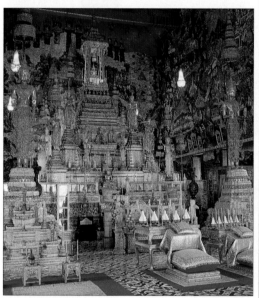

W HEN RAMA I ESTABLISHED the new capital of Bangkok in 1782 his ambition was to construct a royal temple along the lines of the grand chapels of previous capital cities. Symbolizing the simultaneous founding of the Chakri dynasty, this temple was to surpass its larger Sukhothai and Ayutthaya predecessors in the splendour of its design and decoration. The result of his vision was Wat Phra Kaeo, or Temple of the Emerald Buddha (officially known as Wat Phra Si Rattana Sasadaram), so called because the *bot* houses the Emerald Buddha image, brought here from Wat Arun *(see pp120–1)* in 1785.

Guard outside *chedi*

The Emerald Buddha crowning the ornate gilded altar inside the *bot*

THE BOT AND PERIPHERAL BUILDINGS

T HE MOST SACRED building within the palace complex, the *bot* of Wat Phra Kaeo was erected to house what is still the most revered image of the Buddha in Thailand: the Emerald Buddha.

The exterior doors and windows of the *bot* are inlaid with delicate mother-of-pearl designs. Along the marble base supporting the structure runs a series of gilt bronze *garudas* (half bird, half human). The staircase of the main entrance is guarded by Cambodian-style stone lions, or *singhas*.

Inside, the surprisingly small image of the Emerald Buddha sits in a glass case high above a golden altar. Carved from a single piece of jade (not emerald), it is 66 cm (26 in) tall and has a lap span of 48 cm (19 in). The Buddha has been attributed to the late Lanna School of the 15th century. It is dressed in one of three costumes: a crown and jewellery for the summer season; a golden shawl in winter; and a gilded monastic robe and head-dress in the rainy season. The reigning monarch or a prince appointed by him presides over each changing of the Buddha's attire in a deeply symbolic ceremony.

Inside the *bot* are murals from the reign of Rama III (1824–51). They depict the classic subjects of Thai mural painting, namely the Traiphum (Buddhist cosmology), the Buddha's victory over Mara (the god of death), and scenes from the previous lives of the Buddha – the *jatakas*. Around the temple are 12 open-sided *salas* (small pavilions) built as contemplative shelters.

Southeast of the *bot* is the 19th-century **Chapel of the Gandharara Buddha**. The bronze image of the Buddha calling the rains housed here is used in the Royal Ploughing Ceremony in May *(see p42)*. The bell in the nearby belfry is rung only on special occasions, such as New Year's Day.

THE UPPER TERRACE

O F THE FOUR structures on this elevated terrace, the **Phra Si Rattana Chedi**, at the western end, is the most striking. It was built by King Mongkut (Rama IV) to enshrine a piece of the Buddha's breastbone. The golden tiles decorating the exterior were later added by King Chulalongkorn (Rama V).

The adjacent **Phra Mondop**, used as a library, was built by Rama I as a hall to house Buddhist scriptures. Although the Library is closed to the public, the exterior is splendid in itself. The Javanese Buddha images on the four outer corners are copies of early 9th-century originals, which are now in the museum near the entrance

Gold Buddha images decorating the wall of the Phra Mondop

Mural depicting a scene from the Ramakien in the Ramakien Gallery

THE PRANGS, YAKSHAS AND RAMAKIEN GALLERY

SURROUNDING the temple complex is the cloister-like Ramakien Gallery, decorated with lavishly painted and meticulously restored murals. This is Thailand's most extensive depiction of the ancient legend of the Ramakien *(see pp36–7)*. The 178 panels were originally painted in the late 18th century, but damage from humidity means that frequent renovation is necessary. The murals are divided by marble pillars inscribed with verses relating the story, which begins opposite Wihan Yot and proceeds in a clockwise direction.

Guarding each gateway to the gallery is a pair of *yakshas* (demons). Placed here during the reign of Rama II, they are said to protect the Emerald Buddha from evil spirits. Each one represents a different character from the Ramakien myth: the green one, for example, symbolizes Tosakan, or the demon king.

The eight different-coloured *prangs* on the edge of the temple complex are intricately decorated with Chinese porcelain. They represent the eight elements of the Buddhist religion, including the Buddha, the Dharma (law), the *sangha* (monkhood) and the *bhiksunis* (female Buddhists).

to the palace complex. Outside the building are memorials to all the kings of the present Chakri dynasty, and bronze elephant statues representing the royal white elephants *(see p102)* from the first five reigns of the dynasty *(see pp60–1)*.

To the north of the *mondop* is a model of Angkor Wat in northwest Cambodia *(see pp254–5)*. The model was commissioned by Rama IV to show his people the scale and gracious splendour of 12th-century Khmer architecture – Cambodia during his reign being under Thai rule.

The **Royal Pantheon** houses life-size statues of the Chakri kings. Rama IV had intended the hall to hold the Emerald Buddha but decided that it was too small. The pantheon is open to the public only on Chakri Day *(see p44)*.

Ramakien figure outside *chedi*

minor members of the royal family. The Nak Buddha was moved into the neighbouring **Wihan Yot**, which is shaped like a Greek cross and decorated with Chinese porcelain.

Also on the Northern Terrace is the **Ho Phra Monthien Tham**, or Auxiliary Library, built by the brother of Rama I. The door panels, inlaid with mother-of-pearl, were salvaged from Ayutthaya's Wat Borom Buddharam. Inside, Buddhist scriptures are stored in fine cabinets.

THE NORTHERN TERRACE

HO PHRA NAK was originally constructed by Rama I in the late 18th century to enshrine the Nak (literally, alloy of gold, silver and copper) Buddha image that had been rescued from Ayutthaya. Rama III, however, demolished the original hall, preferring to build the present brick and mortar structure to house the ashes of

THE LEGEND OF THE EMERALD BUDDHA

In 1434 lightning struck the *chedi* of Wat Phra Kaeo in Chiang Rai in Northern Thailand *(see pp240–1)*, revealing a simple stucco image. The abbot of the temple kept it in his residence until the flaking plaster exposed a jadeite image beneath. Upon learning of the discovery, the king of Chiang Mai sent an army of elephants to bring the image to him. The animal bearing the Emerald Buddha, however, refused to take the road to Chiang Mai, and, treating this as an auspicious sign, the entourage re-routed to Lampang. The image was moved several more times over the next century, then was taken to Wat Pha Kaew in Laos *(see pp284–5)* in 1552. It was not until General Chakri (later Rama I) captured Vientiane in 1778 that the Emerald Buddha was returned to Thailand. It was kept in Wat Arun *(see pp120–1)* for 15 years, before a grand river procession brought it to its current resting place on 5 March 1785.

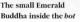

The small Emerald Buddha inside the *bot*

Exploring the Grand Palace

BUILT AT THE SAME TIME as Wat Phra Kaeo, the Grand Palace was the king's official residence from 1782 to 1946 although King Chulalongkorn (Rama V) was the last monarch to live here. Today, the royal family resides at Chitrlada Palace *(see p102)*. Throughout the palace's history, many structures have been altered or enlarged. Within the complex there are a few functioning government buildings, such as the Ministry of Finance, although most others are unused. Important ceremonies are still held in the Dusit Throne Hall and the Amarin Winichai Hall.

Decorative demon guardian

DUSIT THRONE HALL

THIS CROSS-SHAPED throne hall was originally built in 1784 as a reproduction of one of Ayutthaya's grandest buildings, Sanphet Maha Prasat *(see pp168–9)*. Five years later the hall was struck by lightning and rebuilt on a smaller scale. Crowned with a sumptuously decorated tiered spire, it is one of the finest examples of early Rattanakosin architecture *(see p31)*. Inside is a masterpiece of Thai art: the original Rama I teak throne, inlaid with mother-of-pearl. In the south wing is a window in the form of a throne. The hall is used for the annual Coronation Day celebrations *(see p44)*.

APHONPHIMOK PAVILION

KING MONGKUT (Rama IV) built this small wooden structure as a royal changing room for when he was

giving audiences at the Dusit Throne Hall. The king would be carried on a palanquin to the pavilion's shoulder-high first step. Inside the building he would change into the appropriate apparel for the occasion. The pavilion's simple structure, complemented by its elaborate decoration, makes it a building of perfect proportions: indeed, it is considered a glory of **Elephant statue by** Thai architecture. It **Chakri Throne Hall** inspired Rama V so much so that he had a replica built at Bang Pa-in *(see p171)*.

CHAKRI THRONE HALL

ALSO KNOWN AS the Grand Palace Throne Hall, Chakri Maha Prasat was built in Neo-Classical style by the British architect John Chinitz. Rama V commissioned the building in 1882 to mark the centenary of the Chakri dynasty, a fact reflected in the theme

of the sumptuous decoration. The structure was originally intended to have a domed roof, but the royal court decided that, in the interest of maintaining aesthetic harmony with the surrounding buildings, a Thai-style roof would be more appropriate.

Housed on the top floor of the Central Hall are the ashes of royal monarchs, while the first floor functions as the main audience hall where the King receives ambassadors and entertains foreign monarchs.

Behind the Niello Throne in the Chakri Throne Room is the emblem of the Chakri dynasty: a discus and trident. The paintings in the room depict diplomatic missions, including Queen Victoria welcoming Rama IV's ambassador in London. The East Wing is used as a reception room for royal guests. The long hall connecting the Central Hall with this wing is lined with portraits of the Chakri dynasty. In the West Wing is the queen's personal reception room. Portraits of the principal queens of Rama IV, Rama V and Rama VII decorate the hall between the Central Hall and this wing.

PHRA MAHA MONTHIEN BUILDINGS

THIS CLUSTER of connected buildings, located to the east of the Chakri Throne Hall, is the "Grand Residence" of the palace complex.

The focal point of the 18th-century **Amarin Winichai Hall**, the northernmost building of the group, is Rama I's boat-shaped Busok Mala Throne. When an audience was present, two curtains hid the throne as the king ascended, and, with an elaborate fanfare, the curtains were drawn back to reveal the king wearing a loose, golden gown and seemingly floating on the prow-like part of the throne. In the 19th century two British ambassadors were received in such manner here;

Exterior of the Dusit Throne Hall, with its elegant multi-tiered spire

Lavish decor of the connecting hall of the Chakri Throne Hall's West Wing

John Crawfurd by Rama II and Sir John Bowring by Rama IV. The hall is now used for state ceremonies such as the King's birthday speech.

Connected to the hall by a gateway through which only the king, queen and royal children may walk is the **Phaisan Thaksin Hall**. This was used by Rama I as a private hall when dining with family, friends and members of the royal court. In 1809 a Horom Rachaphisek Ceremony was performed in this hall to mark the coronation of the new king, Rama II. On the high altar is the Phra Siam Thewathirat, a highly venerated guardian figure, placed here by Rama IV.

The third building is the **Chakraphat Phiman Hall**. It served as a residence for the first three Chakri kings. It is still the custom for newly crowned kings to spend a night here as part of their coronation.

INNER PALACE

BEHIND A GATEWAY to the left of the Chakri Throne Hall is the entrance to the Inner Palace, which is closed to the public. Until the time of Rama VII, the palace was inhabited solely by women of the royal family: principal wives, minor wives and daughters. Apart from sons, who had to leave the palace on reaching puberty, the king was the only male allowed to live within its walls.

The palace functioned as a mini-city, with its own government and laws, complete with prison cells. Under the strict guidance of a formidable "Directress of the Inside", a small army of uniformed officers policed the area.

Rama III renovated the overcrowded and precarious wooden structures and, in the late 19th century, Rama V built small, fantastical Victorian-style palaces here for his favourite consorts. Because his successor, Rama VI, had only one wife, the complex was left virtually empty, and it eventually fell into disrepair.

One of the palace buildings that continues to function is the finishing school for the daughters of high-society Thai families. The girls are taught flower weaving, royal cuisine and social etiquette.

SIWALAI GARDENS

THESE BEAUTIFUL gardens, which are often closed for state functions, lie east of the Inner Palace and contain the **Phra Buddha Ratana Sathan**, a personal chapel built by Rama IV. The pavilion is covered in grey marble and decorated with white and blue glass mosaics. The marble *bai sema* (boundary stones) are inlaid with the insignia of Rama V, who placed the stones here, Rama II, who had the gardens laid out, and Rama IV.

The Neo-Classical **Boromphiman Mansion** in the gardens was built by Rama V as a residence for the Crown Prince (later King Rama VI). The building served as a temporary residence for several kings: Rama VII, Rama VIII and Rama IX (King Bhumibol). Today it is used as a guesthouse for visiting dignitaries.

AUDIENCE CHAMBER

VISIBLE FROM OUTSIDE the palace walls, this chamber – Phra Thinang Sutthaisawan Prasat – is located between Thewaphithak and Sakchaisit gates. It was built by Rama I as a place to grant an audience during royal ceremonies and to watch the training of his elephants. Rama III strengthened the wooden structure with brick, and decorative features were added later. These include the crowning spire and ornamental cast-iron motifs.

Mosaic-decorated Phra Buddha Ratana Sathan in the Siwalai Gardens

Entrance to the Buddhist University at Wat Mahathat

Wat Mahathat ❷

วัดมหาธาตุ

3 Maharaj Rd. **Map** 1 C5.
📞 *(02) 221 5999.* 🚌 *AC: 6, 8, 39.*
🚤 *Maharaj.* ⭘ *daily.*

THIS IS A LARGE, busy temple complex, interesting more for its atmosphere than for its architecture. Dating from the 1700s, the *wihan* and *bot* were both rebuilt between 1844 and 1851. The *mondop*, which gives the temple its name – "temple of the great relic" – has a cruciform roof, a feature rarely found in Bangkok.

The *wat* is the national centre for the Mahanikai monastic sect, and its compound contains one of Bangkok's two Buddhist universities (meditation classes are offered here at 7am, 1pm and 6pm in Section Five, near to the monks' quarters). There is also a traditional herbal medicine market; and, at weekends, numerous stalls selling a wide range of goods.

National Museum ❸

พิพิธภัณฑ์สถานแห่งชาติ

See pp84–5.

National Gallery ❹

หอศิลป์แห่งชาติ

4 Chao Fa Rd. **Map** 2 D4. 📞 *(02) 281 2224.* 🚌 *AC: 6, 11.* 🚤 *Phra Athit.* ⭘ *9am–4pm Wed–Sun.* ⬤ *public hols.* 📷 🚫

THAILAND'S MAIN art gallery, housed in the old mint building, was established in 1977. It concentrates on modern Thai and international art. Initially the gallery suffered from lack of funds, but in 1989 new wings were added. The high-ceilinged, spacious halls now attract exhibitions from all over Asia. Temporary shows of prominent Asian artists are often better than many of the permanent exhibits. Modern art can also be found at the Visual Dhamma Gallery *(see p132).* Check the *Bangkok Post* for details.

Modern sculpture at the National Gallery

Wat Bowonniwet ❺

วัดบวรนิเวศน์

240 Phra Sumen Rd. **Map** 2 E4.
📞 *(02) 280 0869.* 🚌 *AC: 11.*
⭘ *daily.*

HIDDEN IN QUIET, tree-filled grounds, this mid-19th-century temple was constructed by Rama III. The style bears his trademark Chinese influence. A central gilded *chedi* is flanked by two symmetrical chapels, the most interesting of which is next to Phra Sumen Road. The interior murals are attributed to monkpainter Khrua In Khong, who is famous for the introduction of Western perspective into Thai temple murals. As court painter to King Mongkut (Rama IV) he was exposed to Western ideas and adapted these to a Thai setting. The result was a series of murals that on first glance look wholly Western but which portray the same Buddhist allegories found in traditional Thai murals. For instance, a physician healing a blind man can be interpreted as the illuminating power of Buddhism. The images are all the more remarkable for the fact that Khrua In Khong never travelled to the West. The main Buddha image, Phra Buddha Chinasara, is one of the best examples from the Sukhothai period.

King Mongkut served as abbot here during his 27 years in the monkhood and founded the strict Tammayut sect of Buddhism, for which the temple is now the headquarters. Since Mongkut, many Thai kings have served their monkhoods at the *wat*, including the current monarch, King Bhumibol (Rama IX). The temple also houses Thailand's second Buddhist university. Across the road from the temple is a Buddhist bookshop that sells Englishlanguage publications.

Mid-19th-century, Western-style mural at Wat Bowonniwet

Democracy Monument 6

อนุสาวรีย์ประชาธิปไตย

Ratchadamnoen Klang. **Map** 2 E4.
M: 8. daily.

A FOCAL POINT during pro-democracy demonstrations, this monument (built 1939) commemorates the revolution of 1932 *(see p64)*. Each feature symbolizes the date of the establishment of Thailand's constitutional monarchy, on 24 June 1932.

The four wing towers are each 24 m (79 ft) high. The 75 cannons indicate the year 2475 of the Buddhist Era (1932), and the pedestal, containing a copy of the constitution, is 3 m (10 ft) high, referring to the third month of the Thai calendar (June).

The structure was designed by Silpa Bhirasi, an Italian sculptor who took a Thai name and citizenship.

Central edifice of Democracy Monument (1939)

Wat Rachanat 7

วัดราชนัดดา

Maha Chai Rd. **Map** 2 E4. M: 8.
9am–4pm daily.

THE MOST interesting feature at Wat Rachanat (also often spelt Ratchanaddaram) is the metal monastery. Originally conceived as a *chedi* to complement the temple proper, it evolved into an elaborate meditation chamber modelled on a 3rd-century BC Sri Lankan

One of hundreds of meditation cells at Wat Rachanat

temple (the original is now ruined). Passages dissect each level, running from north to south and east to west. The meditation cells are located at each intersection.

In the temple's courtyard is Bangkok's best amulet market. Tourists may face disapproval if they attempt to take one of the wide range of talismans home as a souvenir. Across the road, behind the old city walls, is the Doves' Village, where singing doves are sold for competitions.

Wat Saket and the Golden Mount 8

วัดสระเกศและภูเขาทอง

Chakkaphatdi Phong Rd. **Map** 2 F5.
AC: 8; M: 8. 8am–6pm daily.
Golden Mount Fair (Nov).

BUILT BY Rama I in the late 18th century, Wat Saket is one of the oldest temples in Bangkok. Visitors come mainly to climb the artificial hill topped with a golden tower within the grounds. Rama III attempted to build the first Golden Mount but the soft soil led to its collapse. King Chulalongkorn (Rama V) provided the necessary technology to create the 76-m (250-ft) high representation of the mythical Mount Meru seen today. It is believed to house relics of the Buddha presented to Rama V by the Viceroy of India. A circular staircase lined with curious

monuments and tombs leads to the top where there is a small sanctuary. The wonderful panoramic view from the gallery takes in the Grand Palace, Wat Pho and Wat Arun. The octagonal building opposite, Mahakan Fort, is one of 14 original watchtowers of the city walls.

Until the 1960s the Golden Mount was one of the highest points in Bangkok. Today, it still forms a prominent landmark although it is dwarfed by skyscrapers *(see p117)*.

During the 19th century the grounds of Wat Saket served a macabre function as a crematorium. The bodies of the poor were sometimes left for vultures and dogs. By contrast, a fair with dancing and a candle procession is now held in the grounds in November.

The Golden Mount, a distinctive Bangkok landmark

National Museum ❸

พิพิธภัณฑ์สถานแห่งชาติ

Colourful Bencharong drums

THE NATIONAL MUSEUM has one of the largest and most comprehensive collections in Southeast Asia and provides a splendid introduction to the arts, crafts and history of Thailand. Two of the museum buildings, the 18th-century Wang Na Palace and Buddhaisawan Chapel, are works of art in themselves. The chapel contains the venerated Phra Buddha Sing image and the palace an eclectic selection of artifacts from ancient weaponry to shadow puppets. The two wings of the museum are devoted mainly to art and sculpture. Other attractions include galleries of history and prehistory and the Royal Funeral Chariots Gallery. The labelling of the collection is not always helpful, so taking one of the frequent, free guided tours is highly recommended.

Doors of Throne Hall
These beautifully decorated black and gold lacquered doors to the Wang Na Palace date from the 19th century and show a strong Chinese influence.

Phra Buddha Sing
The history of this image, one of Thailand's holiest after the Emerald Buddha, is shrouded in legend. It probably dates from the 13th century and was brought here from Chiang Mai by Rama I in 1795.

King Rama IV Pavilion

Red Pavilion

The Gallery of Thai History houses the 13th-century Ramkamhaeng Stone. This is thought to be inscribed with the earliest extant example of the Thai script.

Ticket office

King Vajiravudh Pavilion

Pavilion of the Heir to the Throne

★ Buddhaisawan Chapel
Built in 1787, this beautiful building is decorated with some of the best Rattanakosin period murals in Thailand.

★ Royal Funeral Chariots Gallery
Several lavishly decorated, gilded teak chariots used in royal funeral processions can be seen in this gallery, including Racharot Noi, built in 1795.

★ Dvaravati Wheel of Law
This 8th-century stone wheel and deer symbolize the Buddha's first sermon in a deer park in Sarnath, India.

VISITORS' CHECKLIST

1 Na Phra That Rd. **Map** 1 C4.
((02) 224 1370. 🚌 AC: 39; M: 43, 53, 70, 80, 91. 🛥 Phra Athit. ◯ 9am–4pm Wed–Sun. ⬤ public hols. 🖼 🚫 🎥 🚻 🛗 🍴

Lop Buri Stone Lion
Lions were believed to be the protectors of Buddhist teachings. This 12th–13th-century sculpture once stood guard at a temple doorway.

First Floor

★ Sukhothai Buddha Image
This graceful 14th-century bronze image is finished in red lacquer and gold.

First Floor

Ayutthayan Head of the Buddha
The skill of Ayutthaya-period bronze casting is evident in this immense but delicate 15th–16th-century image, which stands 150 cm (60 inches) high.

Wang Na Palace

GALLERY GUIDE
The collection is displayed in several buildings set around the central Wang Na Palace. Art exhibits are arranged chronologically in the two wings (both of which have upper and lower levels), starting from the left (south) wing. The ticket office, near the entrance on Na Phra That Road, sells guide books.

KEY TO FLOORPLAN

- ☐ Gallery of Thai history
- ☐ Buddhaisawan Chapel
- ☐ Royal Funeral Chariots Gallery
- ☐ Throne Hall
- ☐ Miscellaneous arts and crafts
- ☐ Khmer, Lop Buri and Hindu art
- ☐ Mansion of King Pin Klao
- ☐ Dvaravati and Srivijayan art
- ☐ Lanna, Sukhothai, Ayutthayan and Rattanakosin art

STAR EXHIBITS

- ★ **Buddhaisawan Chapel**
- ★ **Royal Funeral Chariots Gallery**
- ★ **Dvaravati Wheel of Law**
- ★ **Sukhothai Buddha Image**

Monk's bowl being heated to blacken and finish the surface

Monk's Bowl Village (Ban Bat) ⑨

บ้านบาตร

Bamrung Muang Rd, Soi Ban Bat.
Map 2 F5. 🚌 *AC: 8; M: 8.*

MONKS' BOWLS were first used 2,500 years ago and are still widely used today in Buddhist countries for early morning alms-gathering *(see p125)*. Such bowls have been made at Monk's Bowl Village in Bangkok since the late 18th century. The village once stretched as far as Wat Saket *(see p83)*, but modern developments have reduced the village to just four homes and a cluster of small workshops. This area may be hard to find amid the maze of *sois*, but the bowls are sold at Wat Suthat.

The process of bowl making is time consuming and requires eight pieces of metal, representing the eight spokes of the wheel of Dharma. The first strip is beaten into a circular form to make the rim. Three pieces are then beaten to create a cross-shaped skeleton. Four triangular pieces complete the sides. After being welded in a kiln, the bowl is shaped, filed smooth and fired again to give an enamel-like surface. About 20 bowls are produced daily in the village.

At the centre of the maze of alleyways next to the small village hall is an unusual and intriguing shrine, constructed from old Chinese cylinder bellows, which is dedicated to the "Holy Teacher and Ancestor".

Bamrung Muang Road ⑩

ถนนบำรุงเมือง

Map 2 F5. 🚌 *AC: 8; M:8.*

BAMRUNG MUANG, like Charoen Krung *(see p110)*, was an elephant trail until the 20th century when it became one of Thailand's first paved roads. The stretch between Maha Chai Road and the Giant Swing provides an enlightening peek into the thriving business behind the Buddhist practice of merit-making. Along here the road is lined with shops selling religious paraphernalia: monks' robes, votive candles and Buddha images of all shapes and sizes, many rather incongruously packaged in cellophane. Monks shop here for temple essentials; other people buy offerings and shrines for the home. Although the religious objects look enticing

Plastic-wrapped Buddha image

to tourists, they are not intended as souvenirs: images of the Buddha cannot be taken out of the country without an export licence *(see p451)*.

Wat Suthat and the Giant Swing ⑪

วัดสุทัศน์และเสาชิงช้า

Bamrung Muang Rd. **Map** 2 E5.
🚌 *AC: 8; M: 8.* ⬜ *8:30am–6:30pm daily (wihan Sat & Sun only).*

THERE ARE SEVERAL superlatives for Wat Suthat, a temple that was begun by Rama I in 1807 and completed by Rama III. Its *wihan* is the largest in Bangkok. The art and architecture beautifully exemplify Rattanakosin style *(see p31)*. Its central Buddha, at 8 m (26 ft) high, is one of the largest surviving Sukhothai bronzes. This image was moved from Wat Mahathat in Sukhothai *(see pp54–5)* to Bangkok by Rama I. The

View through the immense portal of the *wihan* at Wat Suthat

murals in the immense *wihan* are some of the most celebrated in Thailand. Amazingly intricate, they depict the Trai-phum (Buddhist cosmology) and were restored in the 1980s. The teak doors to the *wihan* are also noteworthy, carved in five delicate layers and standing 5.5 m (18 ft) high. (One made by Rama II is now in the National Museum.) The cloister around the outside of the *wihan* is lined with 156 golden Buddha images.

In the square in front of Wat Suthat is a red-painted, lofty frame. The structure, known as the Giant Swing, is the remains of a swing used for a Brahmin ceremony, dedicated to the god Shiva, which used to be performed in the presence of royalty.

Wat Rachabophit ⑫

วัดราชบพิธ

Fuang Nakhon Rd. **Map** 2 D5.
🚌 60; AC: 8. 🚤 Thien. ⬤ 8am–8pm daily.

THE CIRCULAR FORM of Wat Rachabophit is a successful architectural blend of East and West. Construction of the temple began under King Chulalongkorn (Rama V) in 1869 and continued for over 20 years. The whole complex is splendidly decorated with porcelain tiles, which were made-to-order in China. The focal point is the central, Sri Lankan-style, gilded *chedi*, whose full height from the terrace is 43 m (140 ft).

Inside the *wat* are four Buddha images, each facing one of the cardinal points.

Rows of tiny carved figures on eaves of the *bot* at Wat Rachapradit

Leading off from the circular gallery are the *bot* to the north, the *wihan* to the south and two lesser *wihans* to the east and west; an unusual layout for a Thai *wat*.

East-West flourishes permeate the entire complex. The 10 door panels and 28 window panels of the *bot* are decorated with typically Thai mother-of-pearl inlay, which illustrates the insignia of five royal orders. The mouldings over the door depict King Chulalongkorn's seal. The carved, painted guards on the doors are distinctively *farang* (European), and the interior is decorated in an incongruous Italian Renaissance style.

Accessible through the temple grounds (parallel to Khlong Lot) is a fascinating royal cemetery rarely explored by visitors. The monuments to members of King Chulalongkorn's family are an eccentric mix of Khmer, Thai and European styles.

"Farang", Wat Rachabophit

Wat Rachapradit ⑬

วัดราชประดิษฐ์

Saran Rom Rd. **Map** 2 D5.
🚌 1, 3, 6, 9, 43, 60. 🚤 Thien.
⬤ daily.

LOCATED IN THE northeast corner of the former Saranrom Palace gardens (now the Ministry of Foreign Affairs), this charming, peaceful temple is rarely visited by tourists. It was built in the mid-19th century by King Mongkut (Rama IV) and his East-meets-West taste in architecture is apparent in the choice of building materials. The main *wihan*, for instance, is covered in forbidding grey marble. The interior murals were painted in the late-19th century and depict the festivals of the Thai lunar calendar. Among other scenes are some extravagant preparations for the Giant Swing ceremony, people celebrating the annual Loy Krathong water festival and an image of King Mongkut observing an eclipse of the moon *(see p61).*

Striking carvings adorn the doors, eaves and gables of the temple. Other notable edifices in the grounds of the *wat* include graceful pavilions, Khmer-style *prangs* and a grey marble *chedi*. Near to Wat Rachapradit, next to Khlong Lot, is a small gilded boar, a shrine to Queen Saowapha Phongsi (King Chulalongkorn's consort), who was born in the year of the pig.

THE SWING IN ACTION

Sao Ching Cha, the "Giant Swing" at Wat Suthat, was built in 1784 by Rama I. During ceremonies – Brahmin in origin – teams of four would swing in 180 degree arcs up to 25 m (82 ft) high. One participant would try to bite off a sack of gold hung from tall poles. The event, linked to the god Shiva swinging in the heavens, caused many deaths and was abolished in 1935.

Young Brahmins performing on Sao Ching Cha

Wat Pho ⑭

วัดโพธิ์

Farang guard

O FFICIALLY KNOWN AS Wat Chetuphon, Wat Pho is not only Bangkok's oldest and largest temple but also Thailand's foremost centre for public education. Unlike the Grand Palace *(see pp 76–81)*, it has a lively and lived-in dilapidated grandeur. In the 1780s Rama I rebuilt the original 16th-century temple on this site and enlarged the complex. In 1832 Rama III built the Chapel of the Reclining Buddha, housing the stunning image, and turned the temple into a place of learning. Today Wat Pho is a traditional medicine centre, of which the famous Institute of Massage is a part. Across Chetuphon Road is the temple monastery, home to some 300 monks.

Wihan
The western wihan *is one of four around the* main bot.

★ **Medicine Pavilion**
Embedded in the inner walls of this pavilion are stone plaques showing massage points. The pavilion is now a souvenir shop.

★ **Reclining Buddha**
The 46-m (150-ft) long gilded plaster and brick image fills the whole wihan

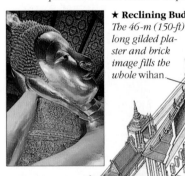

Small buildings
at this end of the *wat* are reserved for children.

Feet of the Reclining Buddha
The striking, intricate mother-of-pearl images on the soles of the feet of the Reclining Buddha represent the 108 lakshanas, *which are the auspicious signs of the true Buddha.*

The Phra Si Sanphet Chedi
encases the remains of a sacred Buddha image

Bodhi Tree
It is said that this grew from a cutting of the tr under which the Buddh meditated in India.

Ceramic Decoration
This porcelain design is on the Phra Si Sanphet Chedi.

Institute of Massage

VISITORS' CHECKLIST

Chetuphon Rd. **Map** 5 C1.
(02) 225 9595. AC: 6, 44.
Thien. 9am–5pm
daily.
Institute of Massage (02)
221 2974. 8am–5pm daily.

Main Bot
Wat Pho's bot houses a bronze meditating Buddha image salvaged from Ayutthaya by Rama I's brother. Scenes from the Ramakien (see pp36–7) are carved into the outer base and inner doors.

Miniature Mountains
This tiny stone mountain by the southern wihan is one of several within the complex. The statues of naked hermits are posed in the different positions of healing massage.

Visitors' entrance

***Farang* guards**
stand at the compound's inner gates. These huge stone statues with big noses, beards and top hats, are caricatures of Westerners.

STAR FEATURES

★ **Reclining Buddha**

★ **Medicine Pavilion**

TRADITIONAL MASSAGE

Since the 1960s Wat Pho has run the most respected massage school in the city. Traditional Thai massage *(nuat paen boran)* supposedly dates from the time of the Buddha and is related to Chinese acupuncture and Indian yoga. The highly trained masseurs at the *wat* specialize in pulling and stretching the limbs and torso to relieve various ailments ranging from general tension to viruses. Visitors can experience a massage or learn the art through a 10- or 15-day course in Thai or English.

Braving a traditional Thai massage at Wat Pho

CHINATOWN

Modern painting of a Chinatown street vendor

B ANGKOK'S CHINESE residents originally lived in the area where the Old City is today. When Rama I decided to move his capital across the river in 1782, the entire community was relocated. Since then the district around Yaowarat and Sampeng roads has been the focus of Chinese life in the city, although now it is also home to a small Indian community. Once the financial centre of Bangkok, Chinatown remains a thriving, bustling, noisy area. Between the two great traffic-choked thoroughfares of Yaowarat Road and Charoen Krung Road lies a maze of narrow alleyways packed with market stalls. The most accessible are the wholesale fabric market of Sampeng Lane and the diverse offerings of the vendors along Soi Isara Nuphap. Other major markets in Chinatown include Pak Khlong, Nakorn Kasem and Phahurat. Near to Hua Lamphong Station is Wat Traimit with its splendid interior and huge gold Buddha image. The area is peppered with Chinese shrines, many of which combine elements of Confucianism, Taoism, Mahayana Buddhism and animism. Old Chinese noodle shops patronized by mahjong-playing, singlet-clad men make interesting pit-stops.

SIGHTS AT A GLANCE

Wats
Wat Traimit ④

Markets
Pak Khlong Market ①
Nakorn Kasem ③
Phahurat Market ②

Historic Buildings
Hua Lamphong Station ⑤

GETTING THERE
Chinatown is easily accessible from the Chao Phraya Express Ratchawong pier, by bus along Charoen Krung Road or train to Hua Lamphong station.

0 metres 500
0 yards 500

KEY

	Street-by-Street map pp92–3
🚉	Railway station
	Riverboat pier
	Chao Phraya Express pier
🚓	Police station
🚓	Tourist police station
✚	Hospital with casualty unit
🛕	Wat

◁ **Bags of dried shrimps in one of Chinatown's numerous, pungent markets**

Street-by-Street: Central Chinatown

เยาวราช

Khanom dao – a soya sweet

THIS AREA IS CHINATOWN at its most atmospheric, with its vibrant colours, pungent smells, overwhelming cacophony and frenetic bustle. A cross-section of the district can be experienced by walking up Soi Isara Nuphap from Ratchawong pier. After Songwat Road, with its old wooden buildings, the street is lined with wholesale spice shops. Past the fabric market of Sampeng Lane, the pavement is crowded with fresh and preserved foods. Once over Yaowarat Road, with its countless gold shops and Chinese herbal medicine stores, snack stalls predominate before giving way, after crossing traffic-choked Charoen Krung Road, to sellers of Chinese religious paraphernalia.

Kao Market
Fresh produce, such as mushrooms, is sold at Kao ("old") Market, which has been here since the late 18th century.

Tang To Kang Gold Shop
This antique water filter is displayed at Tang To Kang, a seven-storey structure built as Chinatown's central Gold Exchange in the late 19th century.

To Sampeng Market

Sanchao Kun Oo
People who hope for luck in gambling leave offerings of vegetables in front of a gilded horse's head in this temple.

To Pak Khlong Market

0 metres	100
0 yards	100

Ratchawong

KEY

 Chao Phraya Express pier

To River City Department Store

Songwat Road
Despite the trucks transporting goods to the busy pier at Ratchawong, the old houses and commercial buildings along Songwat Road give a flavour of Chinatown as it was in the 19th century. This old wooden warehouse stands opposite Soi Thanam San Chao.

★ Neng Noi Yee

This Buddhist shrine combines elements of Confucianism and Taoism, attracting a wide range of devotees. The main chamber contains several gilded Buddha images.

LOCATOR MAP
See Street Finder map 6

Sanchao Dtai Hong Kong

At this popular temple, relatives of the dead burn "hell's banknotes" to provide for their loved ones in the afterlife (see p95). Devotees make merit by buying and freeing caged birds.

CHAROEN KRUNG

SOI CHAROEN KRUNG 10

PHLAB PHLA CHAI

SOI ISARA NUPHAP

YAOWAPHANIT

CHAROEN KRUNG

YAOWARAT

Li Thi Miew

This atmospheric temple within a courtyard is topped by fearsome dragons. Inside, incense smoke swirls around statues of Taoist deities.

To Hua
Lamphong
Station

This picturesque sausage shop is said to date from the 19th century.

To Wat
Traimit

Mai Market

Mai ("new") Market can't boast the pedigree of Kao Market, but it is still a good source of everyday and unusual items like snake parts for Chinese medicine.

★ Yaowarat Road

One of Chinatown's main traffic arteries, this bustling road is packed with gold shops, herbal sellers, cafés and restaurants.

STAR SIGHTS
★ Neng Noi Yee
★ Yaowarat Road

Vendor selling a wide range of chillies, Pak Khlong Market

Pak Khlong Market ❶

ตลาดปากคลอง

Maharaj Rd. **Map** 5 C2. 🚌 AC: 6. 🚢 Rachinee, Pak Khlong. 🔘 daily.

O PEN 24 HOURS A DAY, Pak Khlong Market provides the city with wholesale fresh flowers and vegetables. Known for offering the widest array of flowers in Thailand, it is a one-stop florist's dream. Deliveries begin to arrive from 1am and by dawn the display features roses, orchids, lotus, jasmine and even tulips from Holland. The widest variety of blooms can be seen at around 9am. Visitors can buy bouquets or floral basket arrangements.

Phahurat Market ❷

ตลาดพาหุรัด

Phahurat Rd. **Map** 6 D1. 🚌 1, 3, 53, 56.

T HIS PREDOMINANTLY Indian market offers all the tastes, sights and smells of Bombay. The main bazaar, which spills out around Phahurat and Chak Phet roads, specializes in fabrics. Downstairs, cloth merchants sell anything from tablecloths to wedding saris. The dimly lit upstairs section is devoted to traditional Indian accessories such as sandals and ornate jewellery.

In the surrounding streets are many delicious "hole-in-the-wall" Indian restaurants and samosa stalls. Off Chak Phet Road is Siri Guru Singh Sabha, a traditional Sikh temple.

Nakorn Kasem ❸

นครเกษม

Charoen Krung Rd. **Map** 6 E1. 🚌 AC: 1, 7.

P OPULARLY KNOWN AS Thieves' Market because stolen goods were allegedly once sold here, Nakorn Kasem has discarded its illicit past and now has a miscellaneous collection of shops selling metal wares, musical instruments and a wide range of ornaments.

Nearby is Saphan Han Market, a covered market along both sides of Khlong Ong Ang. Its speciality is electrical goods. The area is filled with smells wafting from nearby noodle stalls.

Wat Traimit ❹

วัดไตรมิตร

Tri Mit Rd. **Map** 6 F2. 🚌 AC: 1, 7; M: 5. 🔘 9am–5pm daily.

A LSO CALLED the Temple of the Golden Buddha, Wat Traimit is known principally for housing the world's largest solid gold Buddha. The gleaming 4-m (13-ft) high 13th-century Sukhothai image is made of 18-carat gold and weighs five tonnes.

The Buddha was discovered by accident in 1955. While extending the port of Bangkok, workers for the East Asiatic Company unearthed what appeared to be a plain stucco Buddha. The image was kept at Wat Traimit under a makeshift shelter for 20 years until a crane dropped it while moving it to a more permanent shelter. The plaster cracked, revealing the gold Buddha beneath. The statue had probably been encased in stucco to hide it from Burmese ransackers – a common practice during the Ayutthaya period *(see p56–7)*.

Local Chinese residents come here to worship the Golden Buddha and to make merit by rubbing gold leaf on the temple's smaller Buddha images.

Wat Traimit, which houses the revered Golden Buddha image

Hua Lamphong Station ❺

สถานีหัวลำโพง

Rama IV Rd. **Map** 7 A2. 📞 (02) 223 7010. 🚌 AC: 1, 7, 29; M: 5. 🔘 8:30am–6pm daily.

K ING CHULALONGKORN (Rama V), a great champion of modernization, was the instigator of rail travel in Thailand. The first railway line, begun in 1891, was a private line from Paknam to Hua Lamphong. Today, the historic station is Bangkok's main rail junction. From here, trains leave for the North, Northeast, the Central Plains and the South. The city's other station, Bangkok Noi, serves only the South.

The Chinese in Thailand

Warrior on the roof of a temple in Chinatown

THE FIRST CHINESE IMMIGRANTS arrived in Thailand as merchants in the 14th century. During the late 18th and early 19th centuries, following years of war in Thailand *(see p60)*, Chinese immigration was encouraged in order to help rebuild the economy. The subsequent integration of the Chinese into Thai society was so successful that by the mid-19th century half of Bangkok's population was of pure or mixed Chinese blood. There have been periods of anti-Chinese feeling and immigration restrictions, but the Chinese still dominate Thailand's commercial sector. Chinese traditions and beliefs remain strong in their communities.

Neng Noi Yee Temple in Bangkok is an important Mahayana Buddhist shrine which also incorporates elements of Taoism and Confucianism. The temple, with its glazed ceramic gables topped by Chinese dragons, is the focal point of the annual Vegetarian Festival (see p43).

"Hell's banknotes" are a form of klong fek – paper replicas of real objects, burned to provide for the dead during their next life.

Intricate Chinese designs feature on many cooking utensils, such as these kettles.

Fresh vegetables are essential to many Chinese dishes.

CHINESE SHOP-HOUSES

Shop-houses are a common feature of Chinatown. The family lives on the first floor while the ground floor is devoted to the family business, whether it is a small workshop or a store selling, for example, food or household goods.

Chinese opera, performed by travelling troupes, features a dramatic mixture of martial arts, acrobatics, singing and dance.

Dim sum, literally "touch the heart", can be sampled in many of the area's Chinese restaurants. The bite-sized snacks include prawn toast and pork dumplings.

Sign painting is not just a decorative art form. These good luck messages, written in gold, are said to ward off evil and sickness. They are displayed in great numbers during the Chinese New Year.

DUSIT

Detail from gates in Dusit Park

DUSIT IS THE CENTRE of Thai officialdom and an oasis of relative calm in a chaotic city. Tree-lined avenues, *khlongs*, old buildings and the low skyline have all been preserved here. King Chulalongkorn laid out the district along European lines, with grand vistas, broad boulevards and a geometric road grid surrounding his palaces. A century later, this remains Bangkok's royal quarter. Ratchadamnoen Avenue ("royal way") leads up to Vimanmek Palace and the royal museums in Dusit Park. Nearby is the royal "marble" temple of Wat Benchamabophit and Chitrlada Palace, the King and Queen's residence. Political power is also concentrated in Dusit. The National Assembly, Government House, several ministries and the Prime Minister's house are located here. By contrast, horse racing at the Royal Turf Club, *muay thai* boxing at Ratchadamnoen Stadium and animal encounters at the landscaped Dusit Zoo provide popular public entertainment.

SIGHTS AT A GLANCE

Wats and Churches
Dusit's Christian Churches ❷
Wat Benchamabophit ❿
Wat Indrawihan ❹

Museums
SUPPORT Museum ❻
Vimanmek Palace ❺

Notable Roads
Phitsanulok Road ❾
Ratchadamnoen Avenue ⓫

Landmark Buildings
Chitrlada Palace ❽

Markets
Thewet Flower
  Market ❸

Parks and Zoos
Dusit Park
  pp98–9 ❶
Dusit Zoo ❼

GETTING THERE
The Chao Phraya Express calls at Wat Sam Phraya, Wisut Kasat and Thewet piers. The latter is the most convenient stop for the majority of Dusit's sights. The area is well served by buses, particularly along Ratchadamnoen Avenue and Dusit's other main arteries.

0 metres   500
0 yards   500

KEY

▨ Dusit Park
    See pp98–9

▤ Riverboat pier

▥ Chao Phraya Express pier

ⓘ Tourist information

✚ Hospital with casualty unit

☒ Post office

🛕 *Wat*

✝ Church

◁ **Nuns relaxing on the steps of the main entrance to the SUPPORT Museum in Dusit Park**

Dusit Park ●

แผนผังสวนดุสิต

THIS SPLENDID PARK is the major attraction of the Dusit area. King Chulalongkorn (1868–1910), the first Thai sovereign to visit Europe, was determined to Westernize Bangkok, and the carefully manicured gardens, genteel architecture and teak mansions in Dusit Park bear testimony to his efforts. Highlights include Vimanmek Palace – the world's largest golden teak building – and the graceful Abhisek Dusit Throne Hall, which houses the SUPPORT Museum of traditional arts and crafts. A visit to the park, and to the neighbouring zoo (see p101), can easily occupy a whole day.

Topiary at Vimanmek Palace

LOCATOR MAP
See Street Finder maps 2, 3

King Bhumibol's Photographic Museums

Most of the photographs in these museums were taken by King Bhumibol, a keen photographer. The royal family features in many.

Royal Family Museum

Photographs and paintings of regal figures from the Chakri dynasty, such as this portrait of Maha Uparaja Bovornvijaya Jarn, the deputy king to King Rama V, can be seen in this museum.

Rank and Portrait Museum

Perimeter wall

Old Clock Museum

A small collection of ancient timepieces, gathered from various countries, is kept in this building. Many clocks are beautifully ornate, if quaintly eccentric in their time-keeping.

STAR FEATURES

★ **Vimanmek Palace**

★ **Abhisek Dusit Throne Hall**

Entrance and ticket office

★ Abhisek Dusit Throne Hall
This hall (see p101) is a fancifully ornamented white edifice. The major attraction inside is the SUPPORT Museum, with its collection of traditional, crafted artifacts, such as works using the exquisitely coloured wings of jewel beetles.

Lake

VISITORS' CHECKLIST

Map 2 F1. ☎ (02) 281 8166/
281 8824. 🚌 AC: 10.
Vimanmek Palace ⏱ 9am–
4pm daily. 📷 compulsory.
SUPPORT Museum ⏱ 9am–
4pm daily. **All other buildings**
⏱ 9am–4pm daily. ⬤ for
occasional royal ceremonies.
🎟 Grand Palace ticket (valid for
30 days) includes admission to
Dusit Park and to all buildings.
🚫 inside all buildings.

Bridge

Lakeside Pavilion
An elegant pavilion behind Vimanmek Palace affords a pleasant view over the lake to some particularly fine traditional Thai teak houses. The further bank is, however, closed to visitors.

Information office

★ Vimanmek Palace
More like a Victorian mansion than a Thai palace, this three-storeyed, golden teak structure (see pp100–1) was built using wooden pegs instead of nails. The palace is full of intriguing artifacts.

Royal Ceremonial Photographic Museum

Royal Carriage Museum
This museum contains the royal family's collection of unusual and interesting vehicles. Inside, there are two long mews lined with antique cars and ceremonial carriages.

0 metres	50
0 yards	50

Dusit's Christian Churches ❷
โบสถ์ดุสิตคริสเตียน

Map 2 E1. 🚌 *AC: 5.*

B Y THE BANK of the Chao Phraya River, just south of Ratchawithi Road, is a small group of Christian churches.

The first of these, **St Francis Xavier Church**, is near Krung Thon Bridge. Built in the early 1850s, it is notable for the statue of the saint atop its triple-arched portico frontage. Among its congregation are members of the local Vietnamese Catholic community, who settled here in 1934.

Just south is the smaller **Church of the Immaculate Conception**. It was built in 1837 by French missionaries on a site previously occupied by a Portuguese church.

Behind it is an even earlier church constructed in 1674, during King Narai's reign *(see pp56–7)*, by Father Louis Laneau for the early Portuguese community. Their descendants, and those of some Cambodian refugees who settled here in the late 17th century, still live in the parish. They take part in religious festivals here, hence the church's nickname, the Cambodian Church. It now houses the **Wat Mae Phrae Museum** (no set opening times) which contains holy relics and antiques, including a statue of the Virgin Mary, venerated in an annual ceremony held in October.

Porticoed entrance of St Francis Xavier Church

Modern mural of a reclining Buddha, Wat Indrawihan

Thewet Flower Market ❸
ตลาดดอกไม้เทเวศน์

Krung Kasem Rd. **Map** 2 E2. 🚌 *M:1,8.* **National Library** Samsen Rd. 📞 *(02) 281 5212.* ○ *9:30am–7:30pm daily.*

O NE OF BANGKOK'S premier plant and garden markets flanks both sides of Khlong Phadung Krung Kasem, west of Samsen Road. It stocks an enormous range of goods, including ornamental garden pots, orchids, trees and pond bases. Although Thewet Market is not as extensive as Chatuchak Market *(see p131)*, its prices are generally lower. It is a pleasant place to browse, even if you buy nothing.

Ornamental garden pots at Thewet Flower Market

Around the corner is the **National Library**, which contains a large collection of books in Thai and English. A number of Thai paintings hang in the lobby. The exterior incorporates several traditional Thai architectural touches *(see pp30–31)*, as do many government offices in the area.

Wat Indrawihan ❹
วัดอินทรวิหาร

Wisut Kasat Rd. **Map** 2 E3. 🚌 *M: 1, 8.* ○ *daily.*

Y OU CANNOT MISS the reason for Wat Indrawihan's fame: an impressive 32-m (105-ft) standing Buddha. The statue was commissioned in the mid-19th century by King Mongkut (Rama IV) to enshrine a relic of the Buddha from Sri Lanka. (Relics such as fragments of bone and hair are housed in countless Buddhist monuments worldwide.)

While admittedly not the most beautiful of Buddha images because of its rather flattened features, it stands out attractively against the sky. Its enormous toes make a bizarre altar for the many offerings presented, including garlands of flowers.

Inside the *bot* of Wat In (a popular abbreviation for the temple) are hundreds of Bencharong (five-colour) funerary urns. Traditional-style, modern murals can also be seen inside the *bot*. In another, smaller building, "lucky" water is sold in plastic bags.

Vimanmek Palace ❺
พระที่นั่งวิมานเมฆ

Ratchawithi Rd. **Map** 2 F1. 📞 *(02) 281 8166.* 🚌 *AC: 10.* ○ *9am–4pm daily.* 🎫 *(free for Grand Palace ticket holders).* 📷 *inside.* 📹 *compulsory.*

C ONSTRUCTED ENTIRELY without nails, the world's largest golden teak building was reassembled on this site in 1901, after being moved from its original location on Ko Sichang *(see pp306–7)*. It soon became a favoured retreat of King Chulalongkorn (Rama V) and his family and concubines while they were waiting for nearby Chitrlada Palace *(see p102)* to be completed. Apart from the king, the mansion was for women only. After closing in 1935 and falling into disrepair, this "celestial residence" was magnificently restored in 1982 at the request of Queen Sirikit for Bangkok's Bicentennial celebrations *(see pp64–5).*

The guided tour takes in 30 of the 81 rooms via circuitous corridors. Highlights include the audience chambers, the music room, sweeping staircases and the king's apartments, which are contained within an octagonal tower. The palace was the first building in Thailand to have electricity and an indoor bathroom: an early light bulb and a showerhead are two of the items on display.

Treasures from the Rattanakosin era include porcelain, furniture, betel-nut sets, the first Thai alphabet typewriter, state gifts from many foreign countries, hunting trophies and royal photographs. King Chulalongkorn was known for his taste in Western-style design, and the palace, with its verandas and high ceilings, has the appearance of a Victorian mansion.

Although the tour allows little time inside, visitors can walk around outside or sit in a lakeside porch, where Thai dancing *(see pp38–9)* and disquieting monkey acrobatics are staged twice daily.

Vimanmek Palace, the favourite summer residence of Rama V

Domed ceiling of the Ananta Samakorn Throne Hall

SUPPORT Museum ➏

พิพิธภัณฑ์ศูนย์ศิลปาชีพพิเศษ

Ratchawithi Rd. **Map** 2 F1.
📞 *(02) 281 8824.* 🚌 *AC: 10.*
🕐 *9am–4pm daily.* 📷

HOUSED IN the Abhisek Dusit Throne Hall beside Vimanmek Palace (and included on the same ticket), the SUPPORT Museum is a showcase for traditional crafts that have been saved from decline by Queen Sirikit, founder of the Promotion of Supplementary Occupations and Related Techniques (SUPPORT). One such craft is *yan lipao* weaving, which originated in Nakhon Si Thammarat *(see pp368–9).* The fine reed used in *yan lipao* lends itself to intricate patterns, its sheen giving the end product a lustre.

Crafts on display include nielloware, rattan, bamboo, celadon, lacquerware and an art form that uses the iridescent green-blue wings of jewel beetles. Some of the designs were created by members of the royal family. The training centre for SUPPORT is at the Bang Sai Folk Arts and Crafts Centre near Bang Pa-in *(see p171).* South of the Abhisek Dusit building is another throne hall, **Ananta Samakorn**. Dating from 1912, this ornate, Italianate building once housed the parliament. Today it is used for royal receptions and private functions. Its spectacular interior is open to the public only on Children's Day, the second Saturday in January.

Dusit Zoo ➐

สวนสัตว์ดุสิต (เขาดิน)

Rama V & Ratchawithi rds. **Map** 3 A2.
📞 *(02) 281 2000.* 🚌 *AC: 3, 10.*
🕐 *8am–6pm daily.* 📷

FORMING A GREEN wedge between Dusit Park and Chitrlada Palace are the lush gardens of Dusit Zoo. One of Asia's better zoos, it has reasonable space for birds and large mammals such as tigers, bears, elephants and hippos, although some of the other enclosures are much more confining. There are also elephant rides and several animal-feeding shows. The grounds were originally the private botanical gardens of Rama V, and some varieties of tropical flora are still cultivated here. The lawns, lakes and wooded glades are ideal for relaxing strolls. Other pursuits include eating at a café or simply watching Thai families enjoying a day out.

Black bear in Dusit Zoo

Chitrlada Palace ⑧

พระตำหนักจิตรลดา

Ratchawithi & Rama V rds. **Map** 3 B2.
🚌 AC: 3, 10; M: 4. ⬤ to public.

THE PERMANENT RESIDENCE of the king and queen is an early 20th-century palace set in extensive grounds (closed to the public), east of Dusit Zoo. Although the palace is hidden from view, the buildings used by King Bhumibol (Rama IX) for agricultural and industrial experiments are visible. In 1993 he became the first monarch in the world to earn a patent – for a waste water aerator.

The royal white elephants (there are currently 11) are trained and housed in the palace grounds.

Board celebrating King Bhumibol's 50 years' reign

The perimeter is illuminated from the King's Birthday (5 Dec) to New Year.

Phitsanulok Road ⑨

ถนนพิษณุโลก

Map 2 E2. 🚌 AC: 5, 9, 10; M: 8.

A NUMBER OF important state institutions are located along this major avenue, which cuts through the heart of Dusit. Travelling northwest past the Mission Hospital at the Sawankhalok Road end, the first of interest is **Ban Phitsanulok**. This mansion has been the official residence of the prime minister since it was restored in 1982. It was originally built in 1925 by Rama VI for Major General Phraya Aniruttheva. Designed by the same Italian architects who built the Ananta Sama-korn Throne Hall *(see p101)*, it is a riot of Venetian Gothic, with floral-shaped mullioned windows, spindly crenella-tions and a sweeping curved wing. It is not open to the public, and guests rarely stay overnight because it is widely believed to be haunted.

On the opposite side of the road is the grassy oval of the **Royal Turf Club**, one of Thai-land's two major horse-racing tracks *(see p113)*. Races alternate between the two tracks, and are held here from 12:30–6:30pm every other Sunday. The stands fill with punters from all levels of Thai society. Experiencing the banter and furious betting can often be as much fun as watching the race itself. The most prominent annual event that takes place here is the King's Cup, also known as the Derby Cup, on the first or second weekend of January.

Filling in the results at the end of a race at the Royal Turf Club

Government House, to the west, just past the Nakhon Pathom Road turning, is a fanciful, cream-coloured Neo-Venetian style building, which is used as the prime minister's office. It is closed to the public.

Wat Benchama-bophit ⑩

วัดเบญจมบพิตร

Nakhon Pathom Rd. **Map** 3 A3. 🚌
AC: 2, 3; M: 8. ⬤ 9am–5pm daily. 🗝

EUROPEAN INFLUENCE on Thai architecture *(see p31)* is exemplified by Wat Benchama-bophit, the last major temple to be built in central Bangkok. In 1899 King Chulalongkorn (Rama V) commissioned his architect brother Prince Naris and the Italian architect Hercules Manfredi to design a new *bot* and cloister for the

---

ROYAL WHITE ELEPHANTS

The importance of the white elephant *(chang samkhan)* in Thailand derives from a 2,500-year-old tale. The hitherto barren Queen Maya became pregnant with the future Buddha after dreaming of a white elephant entering her womb. Ever since the 13th century, when King Ramkamhaeng gave the animal great prestige, the reigning monarch's importance has been judged in part according to the number of white el-ephants he owns. Indeed, the white elephant's status as a national icon was symbolized by

Old manuscript depicting a white elephant

its presence on the Siamese flag until 1917. The origin of the phrase "white el-ephant", meaning a large, useless invest-ment, lies in the Thai tradition according to which all white el-ephants must belong to the king. They cannot be used for work and, therefore, have to be cared for at huge expense. Though referred to as white, the elephants are not fully albino. But tradition states that seven parts of their body – the eyes, palate, nails, tail hair, skin, hairs and testicles – must be close to white.

Singhas **guarding the entrance to Wat Benchamabophit**

Ratchadamnoen Avenue ⑪

ถนนราชดำเนิน

Map 1 D4. 🚌 *AC: 3, 6, 9, 39, 44; M: 8.*

PLANNED BY King Mongkut (Rama IV) in the style of a European boulevard, this thoroughfare has three parts.

The first section, Ratchadamnoen Nai ("inner"), starts at Lak Muang and skirts **Sanam Luang** *(see pp74–5)*, before veering east at the Royal Hotel as Ratchadamnoen Klang ("middle"). From here it passes the **Democracy Monument** *(see p83)* and 1930s mansion blocks – a vista featured in the film *Good Morning Vietnam.*

Just across Khlong Banglamphu, Ratchadamnoen Nok ("outer") turns north into the Dusit area. This stretch, shaded by trees, is flanked by ministries, the main TAT headquarters and **Ratchadamnoen Boxing Stadium** *(see p41).* Just before the ornate double bridge over Khlong Phadung Krung Kasem is the Thai-influenced modern building of the United Nations Economic and Social Commission for Asia and the Pacific (ESCAP).

The avenue culminates at the domed **Ananta Samakorn Throne Hall** *(see p101),* which looms up beyond the Chulalongkorn Equestrian Statue in the parade ground, the site of December's Trooping of the Colours ceremony *(see p47).*

Ratchadamnoen Avenue is decorated and illuminated in December, as part of King Bhumibol's birthday festivities.

original Ayutthaya-period temple which stood on the site. The nickname for the new *wat* ("Marble Temple") is derived from the grey Carrara marble used to clad the walls.

Laid out in cruciform style with cascading roof levels, the *bot* is elegantly proportioned. It contains another successful fusion of traditions: intricate Victorian-style stained-glass windows depicting scenes from Thai mythology. In the room housing the ashes of Rama V is the most revered copy of Phitsanulok's Phra Buddha Chinarat *(see pp150–51),* distinguished by a pointed halo. On display in the cloister are 53 different Buddha images, both originals and copies of images from around Thailand and other Buddhist countries, assembled by Rama V.

Within the *wat* is one of the three sets of doors inlaid with mother-of-pearl that were salvaged from Wat Borom Buddharam in Ayutthaya. The building in which Rama V lived as a monk features murals depicting events that occurred during his reign.

Wat Benchamabophit is a popular location for witnessing monastic rituals, from Buddhist holiday processions to the daily alms round *(see p125),* in which merit-makers donate food to the monks lined up outside the *wat* along Nakhon Pathom Road. This is a reversal of the usual practice whereby the monks go out in search of alms.

Annual Trooping of the Colours ceremony, Ratchadamnoen Avenue

Buddhist monks in the forecourt of the European-inspired Wat Benchamabophit ▷

DOWNTOWN

THE CENTRE OF Bangkok's vast and continually expanding downtown is the area spanning Silom and Ploen Chit roads. The business district originated in the 19th century in the Old Farang Quarter of Charoen Krung Road, where charming colonial buildings have been conserved around the Oriental Hotel. The concrete canyon of Silom is the preserve of business peo-

ple by day, but after dark its northern end is the heart of city nightlife. Further north, showcase stores line Ploen Chit and Rama I roads while the stalls of Silom Road and Siam Square provide cheaper shopping. Amid the tower blocks, Lumphini Park provides green relief, and a few traditional Thai buildings remain, such as Jim Thompson's House and Suan Pakkad Palace.

SIGHTS AT A GLANCE

Wats, Shrines and Churches
Assumption Cathedral ❷
Erawan Shrine ⓬
Maha Uma Devi Temple ❺
Wat Pathum Wanaram ⓭

Museums and Libraries
Jim Thompson's House
  pp116–17 ⓯
Neilson-Hays Library ❻
Suan Pakkad Palace ⓱

Notable Roads and Districts
Charoen Krung (New) Road ❸
Patpong ❼
Pratunam ⓰
Siam Square ⓮
Silom Road ❹

Parks and Sports Grounds
Lumphini Park ❾
Royal Bangkok Sports
  Club ⓫

Historic Buildings
Chulalongkorn University ❿
Oriental Hotel ❶

Zoos
Snake Farm ❽

GETTING THERE
Many buses run along the main roads. The Chao Phraya Express calls at Si Phraya, Wat Muang Khae and Oriental piers. The Skytrain is not yet open.

KEY

- ▨ Street-by-Street map pp108–9
- Skytrain station (not yet open)
- Riverboat pier
- Chao Phraya Express pier
- Police station
- Tourist police station
- Hospital with casualty unit
- ⊠ Post office
- Wat
- Church

◁ Office blocks and shopping centres on Rama IV and Silom roads, as seen from Lumphini Park

0 kilometres 1
0 miles 0.5

Street-by-Street: Old Farang Quarter

ย่านที่อยู่ของฝรั่งสมัยก่อน (ย่านเจริญกรุง)

Emblem on gate of French Embassy

THIS AREA was Bangkok's original port and foreign commercial district in the 19th century. In 1820 Portugal was granted land in Bangkok, which resulted in the Portuguese Embassy being constructed. Embassies for other countries, such as France, soon followed. These outside influences created an amalgam of Western and Eastern architectural styles. Charoen Krung (New) Road, the first road in Thailand to be paved, cuts through the Old Farang Quarter, and is home to gem traders, tailors and antique dealers. The elegant Assumption Cathedral faces Bangkok's only European-style square. The Quarter's back streets are surprisingly quiet and contain some attractive wooden houses.

Harmonique restaurant is one of a row of Chinese shophouses built around 1900

To Portuguese Embassy and GPO

SOI 34

SOI 36

The House of Gems is a tiny shop-cum-museum selling rocks and fossils. Geological oddities – such as dinosaur droppings and tektites (glassy meteorites) from Northeast Thailand – can be seen here.

The Old Customs House was built in the 1880s. Its exterior is now crumbling.

The French Embassy features pitched roofs and carved verandas.

The Haroon Mosque is a quaint stucco building with a Muslim graveyard. The mosque, which faces Mecca, is off a street lined with wooden houses, many displaying extravagantly carved grilles.

STAR SIGHTS

★ **Oriental Hotel**

★ **Assumption Cathedral**

★ **Oriental Hotel**
The world-renowned Oriental Hotel was established in 1876 by two Danish sea captains. In 1958 a new structure (the Tower Wing) was added, and in 1976 the River Wing, a ten-storey annexe, opened **1**

The China House, one of Bangkok's most expensive restaurants, is in a building dating from the reign of King Vajiravudh *(see p63)*. The structure next door, the Commercial Co. of Siam, was erected in the same era. It is built of wood and masonry and has been converted into offices.

LOCATOR MAP
See Street Finder map 6

★ Assumption Cathedral
This elegantly decorated cathedral was built in 1910. The cathedral's Rococo interior features a high, vaulted ceiling, and a striking marble altar from France ❷

CHAROEN KRUNG

SOI 38

ORIENTAL AVENUE (SOI 40)

ORIENTAL LANE

SILOM

SOI 42

SOI 42/1

SOI 44

SOI 46

0 metres 50
0 yards 50

↓ To Taksin Bridge

Shangri-La Hotel

The East Asiatic Company building is a Venetian-style edifice constructed in 1901.

Wat Suan Phu, situated near the Shangri-La Hotel, is distinguished by its carved wooden buildings and the Phra Bodhisattvakuan-In, a Chinese shrine positioned over a carp pond.

KEY

– – – Suggested route

Neo-Classical façade of the Authors' Wing of the Oriental Hotel

Oriental Hotel ❶

โรงแรมโอเรียนเต็ล

Oriental Ave, off Charoen Krung Rd.
Map 6 F4. ☎ *(02) 236 0400.*
🚌 75; M: 6. ⛴ *Oriental.*

REPEATEDLY VOTED the world's best hotel for its service and attention to detail, the Oriental was Thailand's first large hotel. It was established in 1876 and completely re-built in 1887. New wings have since been added. The hotel owes much of its charm to the Armenian Sarkies brothers, creators of the luxurious Raffles Hotel in Singapore. The Oriental's status, lavish decor and spectacular setting on the banks of the Chao Phraya River, account for its elevated prices.

The hotel's original, white-shuttered wing contains the renowned Authors' Suites. Somerset Maugham was one such author who stayed here in the 1920s. Recovering from a bout of malaria, he wrote of the "dust and heat and noise and whiteness and more dust" of Bangkok, though his perception of the city was to change once he was able to explore the *wats* and *khlongs.*

Classic, English-style high tea is served in the Authors' Lounge of the hotel, a riot of potted plants and fan-backed wicker chairs. A teak barge shuttles back and forth to the Sala Rim Naam on the opposite bank, one of the Oriental's eight highly acclaimed restaurants *(see p414).* Khon performances *(see pp38–9)* are staged here as guests dine. The hotel runs a respected school of Thai cookery.

Assumption Cathedral ❷

วัดอัสสัมชัญ

Oriental Lane, off Charoen Krung Rd.
Map 6 F4. 🚌 M: 5. ⭘ *daily.*

THIS ROMANESQUE-STYLE brick edifice was built in 1910 on the site of an earlier ca-thedral. Its rose window is flanked by twin squat towers. The richly ornamented, Rococo interior is dominated by a lof-ty, barrel-arched blue ceiling patterned with gold starbursts.

The cathedral faces a traffic-free, tree-shaded piazza, the site of several other Western-style buildings. These include the modern Assumption Col-lege, the Neo-Classical Catho-lic Mission and the Renaiss-ance-style Catholic Centre, which backs onto the river.

Charoen Krung (New) Road ❸

ถนนเจริญกรุง

Map 6 F2. 🚌 *AC: 4; M: 6.*

SKIRTING THE Chao Phraya River – from Wat Pho through Chinatown and on to Yannawa – Charoen Krung, or New Road (as it is often also called) is one of Bangkok's oldest thoroughfares.

Linking the Customs House and many trading companies, the road was once the centre of Bangkok's European com-munity. At their insistence it became Thailand's first paved highway. Still home to the gem and antique trades, today the road is choked with traffic pollution and noise, but side streets, lined with trees and old wooden buildings, can be bliss-fully serene. Along the road is the imposing **General Post Office**, whose brown stone façade is adorned with reliefs of *garudas* (mythical beasts, half bird, half human). In

Decorative wooden bells inside the spacious lobby of the Oriental Hotel

front is a statue of King Chula-longkorn. The coin and stamp stalls (open Sundays) outside the GPO and the **Bangrak Market** (open daily), selling clothing and fruit, give the area some human vibrancy.

Silom Road ❹

ถนนสีลม

Map 7 A4. 🚌 AC: 2, 4, 5, 15; M: 1, 2, 5.

THE COMMERCIAL HEART of Bangkok, Silom Road is becoming a polluted canyon of skyscrapers, shopping malls and elevated railway lines. Just a few decades ago the area consisted of orchards flanking a canal. One feature that remains unchanged is the many thousands of barn swallows who nest here from October to March, undaunted by the congestion.

Towards the river end of the road, and also on parallel Surawong Road, are several gem and silk shops. Near Patpong *(see p112)* is the Dusit Thani Hotel which overlooks Lumphini Park and the bustle of the local nightlife. Close by is Convent Road, taking its name from the **Carmelite Convent**, and also home to the Gothic-style **Anglican Christ Church**, built in 1904.

Street vendor pushing his cart

Maha Uma Devi Temple ❺

วัดศรีมหาอุมาเทวี

Corner of Silom and Pan rds. **Map** 7 B4. 🚌 AC: 2, 4; M: 2, 5. 🕐 7am – 6pm. 🎉 Deepavali (Nov).

TAMILS FOUNDED this colourful Hindu temple during the 1860s. They were part of an influx of Indians who decided to move to Bangkok when India was handed over to the British Crown in 1858.

The main temple building is topped by a gold-plated copper dome above a 6-m (20-ft) high façade depicting various Hindu gods. Always buzzing with activity, and often with

Multi-coloured deities on the roof of Maha Uma Devi Temple

live Indian music, the temple is also the focus for Deepavali (Festival of Lights) celebrations in November. An oil-lamp ritual is held most days at noon, and on Fridays at 11:30am there is a *prasada* (vegetarian ceremony), in which blessed food is distributed to devotees.

Although some Thais might call the temple Wat Khaek ("guests' temple"), a common cultural heritage means that many local Thais and Chinese also regularly worship here. The Hindu deities Shiva and Ganesh feature in Thai Buddhism, and Hindus regard the Buddha as one of the incarnations of Vishnu.

Neilson-Hays Library ❻

ห้องสมุดเนลสันเฮยส์

195 Surawong Rd. **Map** 7 B4. 📞 (02) 233 1731. 🚌 16, 93; M: 6. 🕐 9:30am – 4pm Mon – Sat; 9:30am – 12.30pm Sun.

HOUSED WITHIN an elegant building beside the British Club is the Neilson-Hays Library. Its 20,000 volumes form one of Southeast Asia's finest English-language collections. The library was built in 1921 in honour of Jennie Neilson-Hays, who was the mainstay of the Bangkok Library Association between 1895 and 1920. The internal domed rotunda is a modern art gallery.

WESTERN WRITERS IN BANGKOK

Western impressions of Thailand were for a long time heavily influenced by just one author – Anna Leonowens. An English teacher at the court of King Mongkut (Rama IV), Leonowens wrote the book that inspired the musical *The King and I*. However, the portrayal of the king as a comic figure stirred up anger in the country, and the book is now regarded as an unreliable historical source. Less controversially, Joseph Conrad wrote about his journey up the Chao Phraya in *The Shadow Line*, and Somerset Maugham described his impressions of Thailand in *The Gentleman in the Parlour*. These are just two of the Western authors commemorated by suites at the Oriental Hotel. Others include Noël Coward, Gore Vidal, Graham Greene and Barbara Cartland. The Oriental has also ventured into other literary projects: it is the venue for the annual prize-giving ceremony of the SEAWrite Award, established in 1969 to promote contact between writers in Southeast Asian countries.

Joseph Conrad in 1904

Entrance to Patpong, as seen in daytime from Silom Road

Patpong ❼

พัฒน์พงษ์

Silom Rd, Patpong 1 and 2. **Map** 7 C3.
🚍 AC: 2, 4, 5, 15; M: 1, 2.

THE PRIVATE STREETS of Patpong 1 and 2, named after
the one-time owner, Chinese
millionaire Khun Patpongpanit,
comprise what is probably
the world's most notorious
red light district. In the 1960s
the area was the home of
Bangkok's entertainment scene
– the go-go bars sprang up to
satisfy airline crews and US
GIs on leave during the Vietnam War. Since the 1970s,
the sex shows have been sustained mainly through tourist

patronage. A less visible homo-
sexual scene exists in adjacent
Silom Soi 6, while Soi Taniya's
hostess bars are frequented
mainly by Japanese clients.

The tourist police department monitors Patpong, and
the area is surprisingly safe. A
night market, filled with stalls
selling souvenirs and original
and fake fashions, gives the
area an incongruous, thin ve-
neer of respectability. A bookshop in the centre of Patpong
is one of Southeast Asia's major outlets for books on femi-
nism and exploitation. Many
visitors come to Patpong out
of mild curiosity rather than to
indulge in the flesh trade: most
leave feeling disturbed.

Snake Farm ❽

สวนงู

Rama IV Rd. **Map** 7 C3. 📞 *(02) 252
0161.* 🚍 *M: 2.* ⏰ *8:30am–4:30pm
Mon–Fri, 8:30–noon Sat, Sun & public
hols.* 🏷️ 🔲

FORMERLY CALLED the Pasteur
Institute, the Queen Sao-
wapha Snake Farm is run by
the Thai Red Cross. It makes
anti-snakebite serums and
informs the public about local
snakes. Unlike the more tourist-oriented farms, the empha-
sis here is on education.

Demonstrations of venom
milking take place twice daily
(once daily at weekends), pre-
ceded by an explanatory slide
show. Handlers open a snake's
mouth and pierce the cellophane lid of a glass jar with its
fangs. The milky venom then
squirts harmlessly into the jar.

Cobra before milking, Snake Farm

SEX WORKERS AND THEIR CLIENTS IN THAILAND

Historically, prostitution in Thailand was
reinforced by the institution of polygamy. Both
are now illegal, but the use of prostitutes by
Thai men is still widespread. Every-town has
at least one massage parlour. The glitzy broth-
els of Patpong and such towns as Pattaya
and Hat Yai may form the foreign perception
of the Thai sex industry but they are a relatively recent development, dating from the
presence of US servicemen in Thailand during
the Vietnam War. Some estimates put the number of sex workers as high as two million, but

Gaudy nightclub sign in central Bangkok

a more realistic figure is 250,000, one fifth
of whom are male. The majority of prostitutes
work for Thai clients, but a few service the
many tourists who come for so-called "sex
holidays". Increasingly, concern about exploitation, paedophilia, AIDS and sex tourism are
being voiced around the world, and countries
such as Sweden now prosecute their nationals
caught paying for sex with children abroad.

Many prostitutes come from the poorest
regions of Thailand or neighbouring countries
such as Burma. The income, and a somewhat
fatalistic attitude, can outweigh any social disapproval they may face. But some do not
become involved in the industry willingly,
and cases of beatings and imprisonment are
not uncommon. Health problems, stigma,
lack of skills and death from AIDS *(see p458)*
spell grim prospects for all sex workers.
Despite a government campaign and the work
of schemes by charities such as Empower,
AIDS statistics for the mid-1990s estimate the
number of prostitutes infected at 14 per cent
for the whole country, and up to 70 per cent
for provinces such as Chiang Rai.

Perfecting the art of t'ai chi chu'an early one morning in Lumphini Park

Lumphini Park 9

สวนลุมพินี

Map 8 D3. 🚌 *AC: 7; M: 6.*
⭕ *6am–9pm daily.*

NAMED AFTER the Buddha's birthplace in Nepal, Bangkok's principal green lung sprawls around two boating lakes. Dominating the Silom Road corner of the park is a statue of Rama VI.

The best time to visit is early morning, when it is used by Thais for jogging and Chinese for practising the rhythmic movements of t'ai chi chu'an. The superstitious can be seen consuming fresh snake blood and bile to keep ill health at bay, purchased from stalls along the park's northern edge. The park is a relaxing place to stroll and observe Thai families in their best attire, elderly Chinese playing chess and impromptu games of *takraw* (a type of volleyball in which the hands may not be used).

Chulalongkorn University 10

มหาวิทยาลัยจุฬาลงกรณ์

Phya Thai Rd. **Map** 7 C3. 🚌 *AC: 6, 10, 12, 29; M: 2, 5.* **Imaging Technology Museum** 📞 *(02) 218 5580.* ⭕ *Thu.* 🖼 **Art Gallery** 📞 *(02) 218 2961.* ⭕ *daily during exhibitions.* ⬤ *public hols.*

DEDICATED TO THE modern-minded king who founded it, Thailand's oldest, richest and most prestigious university covers two entire city blocks.

Chulalongkorn's central gardens, between the busy Phya Thai and Henri Dunant roads, are the site of several attractive buildings and a lake that is often used during the festival of Loy Krathong *(see p46).*

The **Imaging Technology Museum**, to the south of the lake, features hands-on photographic displays, including a room where you can process and develop your own film. Exhibitions of high-quality photography from Thailand and other countries are sometimes held in the museum gallery. Also within the university complex are an auditorium, which is used mainly for classical concerts, and an important contemporary **Art Gallery**, which stages various temporary exhibitions.

Royal Bangkok Sports Club 11

สโมสรราชกรีฑา

Henry Dunant Rd. **Map** 8 D2.
🚌 *M: 1, 4.* 📞 *(02) 255 1420.*
⭕ *noon–6pm alternate Sundays for races only.* 🖼

CONSIDERED TO BE Thailand's most exclusive social institution, the RBSC has a waiting list to prove it. It offers a wide range of sports to its members – including rugby, soccer and hockey – who form some of the top Thai teams in these sports. Non-members may enter to watch horse races at the club, one of Thailand's two principal race courses; the other is the Royal Turf Club on Phitsanulok Road *(see p102).*

Gambling is virtually a national institution in Thailand, and the RBSC gives Bangkokians the perfect opportunity to indulge in one of their favourite pastimes. On race days, thousands of punters from all social classes flock to the track. As the start of the race draws near, betting becomes increasingly furious, and huge electronic screens keep track of the odds on each horse and the total money wagered. Visitors are welcome to join in, and should watch the screens for clues as to which horse to bet on, although they may have to ask for help to fill out one of the Thai-language betting slips.

Horses on the home straight, Royal Bangkok Sports Club

The Siam Center, Rama I Road, one of Thailand's first shopping malls

Erawan Shrine ⑫

พระพรหมเอราวัณ

Ratchadamri Rd. **Map** 8 D1.
AC: 4, 5, 8, 11, 13, 15.

DRIVERS CAN BE SEEN taking their hands off the steering wheel to *wai* (a gesture of respect) as they pass the Erawan Shrine, such is the widespread faith in the luck that this landmark brings. The construction of the original Erawan Hotel in the 1950s, on the site now occupied by the Grand Hyatt Erawan Hotel, was plagued by a series of mishaps. In order to counteract the bad spirits believed to be causing the problems, this shrine dedicated to Brahma and his elephant mount, Erawan, was erected in front of the hotel. Ever since, the somewhat gaudy monument has been decked with garlands, carved wooden

Dancers in traditional Thai costume performing at the Erawan Shrine

elephants and other offerings in the hope of, or thanks for, good fortune. By the shrine are women in traditional costume. Anyone wishing to express gratitude at the shrine for recent good fortune can pay the dancers a substantial fee, and they will perform a thank you dance around it. Near the shrine, and along the nearby Phloen Chit and Sukhumvit roads, are several of Bangkok's most up-market shopping complexes *(see p431)*. Among them are Sogo, the Siam Center, the World Trade Center, the Gay Sorn Plaza, the Amarin Plaza and Le Meridien.

Wat Pathum Wanaram ⑬

วัดปทุมวนาราม

Rama I Rd. **Map** 8 D1. AC: 1, 6, 8;
M: 6. ◯ 7am–6pm daily.

THE MAIN REASON for visiting this temple is to see Phra Meru Mas, a reconstruction of the crematorium of the late Princess Mother. Following her cremation at Sanam Luang *(see pp74–5)* in March 1996, her remains were transferred to these grounds in an elaborate procession. The crematorium is a rare example of ancient craftmanship, featuring ornate stencils and lacquered sculptures. It represents Mount Meru, the heavenly abode of the gods in the Tripitaka *(see p26)*.

Siam Square ⑭

สยามสแควร์

Rama I Rd. **Map** 7 C1. AC: 1, 8;
M: 1, 6, 8.

STREET SHOPPING is fast disappearing in Bangkok as shopping malls proliferate. The principal exception to this phenomenon is the network of *sois* (alleys) collectively known as Siam Square, between Chulalongkorn University *(see p113)* and the Siam Center.

The square is packed with independent shops and stalls selling, in particular, music, books, accessories and clothing – much of it by enterprising young Thai designers.

Rama I Road, on one side of the square, is the showcase for Thailand's film industry. Three grand cinemas – the Scala, the Lido and the Siam – are located here. On the western edge of the square, on Phaya Thai Road, is the **Mah Boon Krong Centre**, which houses a department store and various shops and stalls. Beyond it is the **National Stadium**, Thailand's main arena for major soccer and other sports events. However, the future of the entire district looks uncertain: it is feared that the land may be redeveloped when its lease expires in 2001.

Movie poster on Rama I Road

Jim Thompson's House ⑮

บ้านจิมทอมป์สัน

See pp116–17.

Pratunam ⑯

ประตูน้ำ

Map 4 E5. AC: 12.

ALTHOUGH IT IS off the beaten tourist track, Pratunam district is worth a brief visit. The lively and characterful **Pratunam Market** is a vast warren of stalls, shops and workshops, trading mostly in everyday goods such as fresh produce and clothing. Just west of the market is the

Bargain-price clothing for sale at Pratunam Market

Modernist **Baiyoke Tower**, which reigned briefly as the tallest building in Bangkok from 1987 until 1995. Despite evidence of subsidence in the surrounding ground, permission was granted for construction of the adjacent **Baiyoke Tower II**, which will have twice as many storeys (90).

Suan Pakkad Palace ⑰

วังสวนผักกาด

352 Si Ayutthaya Rd. **Map** 4 D4.
C (02) 245 4934. **▤** 3, 39, 72; M: 38. **◻** 9am–4pm Sun–Thu. **☑**

T HIS PALACE, actually a group of five traditional teak houses, was originally the home of Prince and Princess Chumbhot. The houses were assembled in the 1950s within a lush garden landscaped out of a cabbage patch – *suan pakkad* in Thai – which gives the palace its name. Each building has been converted into a museum and together they house an impressive private collection of art and artifacts which once belonged to the royal couple.

The eclectic assortment ranges from Khmer sculpture, betel-nut sets and pieces of antique lacquered furniture, to Thai musical instruments and exquisite shells and crystals. More important, perhaps, is the first-class collection of whorl-patterned red and white Bronze Age pottery, excavated from tombs at Ban Chiang *(see p262)* in Northeast Thailand.

The highlight for most visitors, though, is the Lacquer Pavilion, which was built from two exquisite temple buildings retrieved by Prince Chumbhot from Ayutthaya province.

Immaculately crafted, charmingly detailed black and gold lacquered murals inside each edifice depict scenes from the Buddha's life and the Ramakien *(see pp36–7)*. They also portray ordinary Thai life from just before the fall of Ayutthaya in 1767 *(see pp56–7)*. These murals are some of the only ones to survive from the Ayutthaya period. Scenes include foreign traders exchanging goods, graphic battle scenes, everyday market scenes, as well as gruesome depictions of hell.

Elegant façade of the Lacquer Pavilion at Suan Pakkad Palace

BANGKOK'S MODERN ARCHITECTURE

Away from Bangkok's many *wats* and palaces, an apparently endless mass of dull concrete towers, monotonous rows of shop-houses and gaudy mock-classical edifices give this vast city the overall impression of a sprawling urban jungle rather than the Oriental splendour visitors might expect.

Nonetheless, there are a small number of modern buildings within the city that were designed by visionary architects. Postmodern architecture of an international standard is particularly noticeable along Sathorn Tai and Silom roads. Other interesting buildings include the Thai Airways headquarters and the triple-towered "Elephant Building".

One of Bangkok's most progressive design companies is Plan Architecture, responsible for a number of striking buildings in the city,

Baiyoke Towers I and II in Downtown Bangkok

including the Baiyoke Towers I and II, the bullet-shaped Vanit Building II on Soi Chidlom and the amazingly narrow Thai Wah II Tower on Sathorn Tai Road. Thailand's most famous, and perhaps most witty, modern landmark is probably the Bank of Asia's head office on Sathorn Tai Road. Dr Sumet Jumsai's innovative, bizarre design has earned it the nickname, the "Robot Building" *(see p65)*.

Perhaps the two most sophisticated examples of "Thai Modernism", both of which are hotels, were designed by Westerners. The roof of the Siam Inter-Continental was designed to resemble a traditional "Mongkut" crown, while the gardens of the elegant Sukhothai evoke the serene waterscape of the old capital of the same name *(see pp184–7)*.

Jim Thompson's House ⑮

บ้านจิมทอมป์สัน

**Khmer
singha in
the garden**

O NE OF THE BEST-PRESERVED traditional Thai
houses in Bangkok and finest museums
in the country is the former home of Jim
Thompson. The entrepreneurial American
revived the art of Thai silk weaving *(see
pp256–7)* following its demise during World
War II. His house stands in a flower-filled
garden across from the ancient silk weavers'
quarter of Ban Khrua. In 1959 Thompson
dismantled six teak houses in Ban Khrua
and Ayutthaya province and reassembled them
here in an unconventional layout. Thompson
was an avid collector of antiquities and artworks from all
over Southeast Asia. His distinguished array, which spans 14
centuries, is attractively displayed, and left much as it was
when he mysteriously disappeared in 1967. Unlike many
other domestic museums, this feels like a lived-in home.

Master Bedroom
*Fine 19th-century paintings of
the* jataka *tales line the walls of
this room.*

**Guest
bedroom**

★ Jataka Paintings
*This panel, in the entrance hall,
is one of eight early 19th-century
paintings in the house showing
scenes from the Vessantara*
jataka *(see p26). These depict
Prince Vessantara as an incarnation of the Buddha.*

**★ Burmese
Carvings**
*This wooden figure
of an animist Nat
spirit is among
Thompson's exten-
sive collection of
Burmese images. When
Buddhism developed
in Burma it incorp-
orated the pre-existing
worship of Nat spirits.*

**One of six tradi-
tional teak houses**

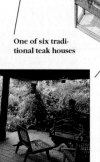

View of the Garden
*The terrace looks out onto
the garden, Khlong San Sap,
and across to Ban Khrua.*

STAR EXHIBITS

★ **Jataka Paintings**

★ **Burmese Carvings**

★ **Dvaravati Torso of
the Buddha**

KEY TO FLOORPLAN

- ☐ Bedrooms
- ☐ Study
- ☐ Entrance hall
- ☐ Drawing room
- ☐ Dining room
- ☐ Secure room
- ☐ Other exhibition space

Drawing Room
Situated on the right is a 13th-century U Thong sandstone head of the Buddha, while the 18th-century carved wooden figures in the alcoves are of Burmese spirits.

VISITORS' CHECKLIST

6 Soi Kasemsan 2, Rama I Rd. **Map** 3 C5. ☎ (02) 215 0122. 🚌 15, 47, 73; AC: 8; M: 6, 8. 🕐 9am–5pm daily. 🚫 📷 in house. 🎥 compulsory. 🚻 🍴

The *khlong* (canal) was once used by silk weavers, who dried threads of silk on poles along the banks.

Porcelain Chamberpot
This cat, made of Chinese porcelain, is in the guest bedroom.

First floor

Dining Room
Beautiful blue and white Ming porcelain adorns the walls of this room.

★ **Dvaravati Torso of the Buddha**
This torso, made of limestone, is in the garden. Dating from the early Dvaravati period (6th century), it is said to be one of the oldest surviving Buddha images in Southeast Asia.

Spirit house with offerings

Ground floor

entrance

The teak houses, the oldest dating from 1800, were erected with some walls reversed so that exterior carvings now face the interior.

WHO WAS JIM THOMPSON?

An architect by profession, Thailand's most famous American came here in 1945 as the Bangkok head of the Office of Strategic Services (OSS), a forerunner of the CIA. In 1948 he founded the Thai Silk Company Ltd, turning the ailing industry into a thriving business once again. Thompson became a social celebrity in Bangkok and finally achieved mythical status following his disappearance on Easter Sunday 1967 while walking in the Cameron Highlands in Malaysia. Explanations for his vanishing include his falling from a path or having a heart attack to more sinister suggestions of CIA involvement.

Jim Thompson inspecting Thai silk in 1964

THON BURI

KNOWN ORIGINALLY AS Ban Kok ("village of the wild plum"), Thon Buri was the capital of Thailand for 15 years between 1767 and 1782. When Rama I moved his capital across the river its original name followed and, though Thais refer to the capital as Krung Thep, it remains known as Bangkok to foreigners. Thon Buri wasn't linked by bridge to Bangkok until 1932 and was officially incorporated into the city only in 1971. Today this area preserves a distinct identity, offering a sleepier version of Bangkok proper. The best way to explore Thon Buri is by boat. Meandering down the intricate network of canals, the visitor sees scenes of river life – stilt houses, small temples, mansions and floating shops. On Khlong Bangkok Noi is the Royal Barge Museum with its lavishly decorated boats. Further south there are some interesting riverside *wats* along the Chao Phraya River, the most prominent and famous of which is Wat Arun.

Chinese statue at Wat Arun

SIGHTS AT A GLANCE

Wats and Churches
Church of Santa Cruz ❼
Wat Arun pp122–3 ❺
Wat Kalayanimit ❻
Wat Prayun ❽
Wat Rakhang ❹
Wat Suwannaram ❶

Museums
Museums at the Siriraj Hospital ❸
Royal Barge Museum ❷

Monuments
Taksin Monument ❾

GETTING THERE
Cross-river ferries operate from all the Chao Phraya piers. The Chao Phraya Express has two stops on the Thon Buri side: Thon Buri Railway Station and Phrannok. Buses and taxis reach Thon Buri via Taksin, Memorial and Phra Pin Klao bridges.

KEY
🛳	Riverboat pier
🛥	Chao Phraya Express pier
🚓	Police station
⊠	Post office
✚	Hospital with casualty unit
🛕	*Wat*
☾	Mosque

◁ **Detail of the elaborate ceramic decoration, made up of thousands of pieces of broken porcelain, on Wat Arun**

Buddha in classic *bhumisparsa mudra* posture, Wat Suwannaram

Wat Suwannaram ❶

วัดสุวรรณาราม

Charan Sanit Wong Rd, Khlong Bangkok Noi. **Map** 1 A3. 🚤 *hire a long-tail from any pier.* ⭘ *daily.*

W AT SUWANNARAM was constructed by Rama I on the foundations of a temple dating from the Ayutthaya era. It was renovated by Rama III and finally completed in 1831. The temple complex provides a graceful example of early Rattanakosin archi-

tecture *(see p31)*, in which a few traces of the Ayutthaya style still linger. The well-restored murals of the main *wihan,* some of the best of the early 19th century, are attributed to two renowned painters of the third reign, Luang Vichit Chetsada and Krua Khonpae.

Western perspective had not permeated Thai mural painting at the time: scenes are depicted as aerial views with figures shown at the same size whether they are in the foreground or background. On the side panels are depictions of the last ten tales of the *jataka* (the Buddha's previous lives). On the south wall are the Buddhist cosmological kingdoms, while the entrance wall is dominated by a lively scene of the Buddha's victory over Mara. Notice the hairstyles of the third reign (1824–51): the heads of both sexes are shaven to leave a small patch of hair at the top. Also, look out for a Christian cross on a hermit's hut, evidence that missionaries were active in Thailand at the time.

Hamsa, on prow of the king's barge

Royal Barge Museum ❷

พิพิธภัณฑ์เรือพระที่นั่ง

Khlong Bangkok Noi. **Map** 1 B3. 📞 *(02) 424 0004.* 🚌 *7, 9,19.* 🚤 *hire a long-tail from Chang pier.* ⭘ *8:30am–4:30pm daily.* 🚫 📷

H OUSED WITHIN a huge warehouse-like structure is a collection of Thailand's most ostentatious boats, the royal boats. Paintings of fabulous Ayutthayan barges *(see pp56–7)* engaged in battles and stately processions, together with archive photographs of royal barge ceremonies in Bangkok over the last 150 years, have provided some of the most splendid visions of Thailand presented to the world via postcards and tourist brochures. Nowadays, though, the vessels are rarely seen cruising the Chao Phraya River as they have been housed at the museum since 1967. The barges are reproductions of some built 200 years ago by Rama I, who had copied Ayutthayan originals.

In 1981 most of the royal barges underwent an expensive face-lift. They came out in all their gilded glory during the 1982 Bangkok Bicentennial celebrations *(see p64)*, for the King's 60th birthday in 1987 and for the Golden Jubilee of his reign on 7 November 1996. For such auspicious occasions more than 50 barges sail in a lengthy procession down the Chao Phraya. Most of the 2,000 oarsmen – dressed in traditional uniforms – are sea cadets, a fitting crew for boats that were once the naval fleet.

The vessel in the centre of the museum, Supphanahongsa ("golden swan"), is the most important royal barge. Made from a single piece of teak, it is over 50 m (165 ft) long and weighs 15 tonnes. In action it requires a highly-trained crew of 64. The mythical, swan-like bird Hamsa rears up from its prow. Anantanagaraj, a barge bearing a multi-headed *naga* and a Buddha image, is reserved for conveying monks'

Superbly detailed 19th-century mural at Wat Suwannaram

Fearsome figurehead on a gun barge built in the reign of Rama I

robes. Narai Song Suban Rama IX is the first new barge to be built during the present king's reign. It is 44 m (145 ft) long and can carry 50 people.

Museums at the Siriraj Hospital ❸
พิพิธภัณฑ์โรงพยาบาลศิริราช

Arun Amarin Rd. **Map** 1 B4.
📞 (02) 411 0211. 🚌 81, 91.
🚢 Phrannok. 🕐 8:30am–4pm Mon–Fri. 🌑 public hols. 🚫

TEN MEDICAL MUSEUMS are located at this hospital, of which the **Museum of Forensic Medicine** is the best known. It houses grue-some objects, such as the preserved figure of Si-oui, a man who suffocated and ate

seven children. Thai parents often threaten naughty chil-dren with his ghost. In the only other museum of note, the **Congdon Museum of Anatomy**, are still-born Siamese twins. Such twins are so-named because the famous Chang and Eng, who toured the world in the mid-19th century, were from Siam, as Thailand was then known.

Wat Rakhang ❹
วัดระฆัง

Soi Wat Rakhang. **Map** 1 B5.
🚌 57, 83. 🚢 Phrannok. 🕐 daily.

WAT RAKHANG was the last major temple to be constructed by Rama I in the early 19th century. The fine murals in the main *wihan*, which were painted between

1922 and 1923 by a monk, Phra Wanawatwichit, include recognizable scenes of Bang-kok. Although the capital has changed much since then, the Grand Palace, which stands just across the river from Wat Rakhang, is easy to identify. In the murals, the palace is shown in the middle of an imaginary attack. There is also an elaborate depiction of a royal barge procession.

The raised wooden library (*ho trai*) of Wat Rakhang, in the west of the compound, was used as a residence by Rama I before he became king. The building's eave supports, delicately carved bookcases and gold and black doors are all considered to be period masterpieces. Inside the library are murals depicting scenes from the Ramakien and a portrait of Rama I.

Wooden façade of the raised library at Wat Rakhang

LIVING ON WATER: THE ERA OF THE THAI KHLONGS

Ayutthaya and Bangkok, both on the flood plain of the Chao Phraya River, were cities that grew along countless little canals and streams known as *khlongs*. Bangkok was once a floating city. In the 1840s all but about ten per cent of its popu-lation of 400,000 lived on the *khlongs*. Houses built on rafts could be moored wherever there was space (*see p33*).

Stilt houses lining the banks of the *khlongs* provided a somewhat more stable habitat. Although roads now cover most of Bangkok's eastern waterways, many still exist in Thon Buri,

where life still largely revolves around the *khlongs*. Children splashing in the water are a common sight, and early each morning water-borne vendors cruise up and down, selling everything from Chinese pastries and coffee to fruit, vege-tables and cooking utensils. The favoured *khlong* vessel today is the long-tailed power-boat – one was memo-rably commandeered by Roger Moore as James Bond in the movie *The Man with the Golden Gun*. Visitors can easily charter their own from Chang pier to explore the Thon Buri *khlongs*.

Bangkok in the 1890s, before the age of roads and land-based dwellings

Wat Arun ❺

วัดอรุณ

Ceramic flower on main *prang*

W̶AT ARUN, named after Aruna, the Indian god of dawn, is a striking Bangkok landmark. It owes its name to the legend that, in October 1767, King Taksin arrived here at sunrise from the sacked capital, Ayutthaya. He soon enlarged the tiny temple which stood on the site into a Royal Chapel to house the Emerald Buddha *(see pp78–9)*. Rama I and Rama II were responsible for the size of the current temple: the main *prang* is 67 m (220 ft) high and the circumference of its base is 234 m (768 ft). In the 19th century King Mongkut (Rama IV) added the ornamentation created with broken pieces of porcelain. The monument's style, deriving mainly from Khmer architecture *(see pp254–5)*, is unique in Thailand.

Multi-Coloured Tiers
Rows of demons, decorated with pieces of porcelain, line the exterior of the main prang.

CENTRAL MONUMENT OF WAT ARUN

The monument's design symbolizes Hindu-Buddhist cosmology. The central *prang* (tower) is the mythical Mount Meru, and its ornamental tiers are worlds within worlds. The layout of four minor *prangs* around a central one is a symbolic mandala shape.

★ **River View of Temple**
This popular image of Wat Arun, as seen from the Chao Phraya, appears on the ten-baht coin and in the Tourism Authority of Thailand (TAT) logo.

Top terrace

One of the eight entrances

Minor *prangs* at each corner of the *wat*

Chinese Guards
These figures, at the entrances to the terrace, complement the Chinese-style porcelain decorating the prangs.

Gallery of the Bot
Elsewhere in the temple complex are the usual buildings found in a wat. *This image of the Buddha in the main* bot *sits above the ashes of devotees.*

STAR FEATURES

★ **Ceramic Details**

★ **River View of Temple**

Indra's weapon, the *vajra* or thunderbolt, at the crest

SYMBOLIC LEVELS

The Devaphum (top) is the peak of Mount Meru, rising above four subsidiary peaks. It denotes six heavens within seven realms of happiness.

The Tavatimsa Heaven (central section), where all desires are fulfilled, is guarded at the four cardinal points by the Hindu god Indra.

The Traiphum (base) represents 31 realms of existence across the three worlds (Desire, Form and Formless) of the Buddhist universe.

Stairs on the Central Prang
The steep steps represent the difficulties of reaching higher levels of existence. Visitors can climb halfway up when restoration work allows.

Small Cove
On the second level of the central prang *are many small coves, inside which are* kinnari, *mythological creatures, half-bird, half-human.*

Decoration of the Four Minor Prangs
Inside the niches of each minor prang *are statues of Nayu, the god of wind, on horseback.*

Mondops at the cardinal points

★ **Ceramic Details**
Much of the colourful porcelain used to decorate the prangs *was donated by local people. The flowers depicted are said to evoke the vegetation of Mount Meru, home of the gods.*

Wat Kalayanimit 6

วัดกัลยาณิมิตร

Soi Wat Kanlaya. **Map** 5 B2. 🚌 AC: 6.
⬤ 8:30am–4:30pm daily.

THIS DILAPIDATED TEMPLE complex is one of the five temples built in Bangkok by Rama III (1824–51). The monarch was known for his taste for Chinese design, as can be seen from the Chinese statuary dotted around the courtyard (brought to Thailand as ballast on empty rice barges returning from China) and the Chinese-style polygonal *chedi*.

The complex's *wihan* is immense yet gracefully proportioned and contains a large sitting Buddha image. In the temple grounds is the biggest bronze bell in Thailand.

Near the *wat*, on the other side of Khlong Bangkok Yai, is **Wichai Prasit Fortress**, built to guard the river approach to Thon Buri when Ayutthaya was the dominant city in Thailand (*see pp56 – 7*).

Thailand's biggest bronze bell, in the bell tower of Wat Kalayanimit

Church of Santa Cruz 7

วัดซางตาครู้ส

Soi Kudi Chain. **Map** 5 C2. 🚌 AC: 6, 12. ⬤ 6am and 7pm Sun (for Mass). 🚫 inside the church.

THIS PASTEL YELLOW church is one of the most prominent reminders of the community of Portuguese merchants and missionaries who lived here in the

Newly released turtles feeding on fruit in the pond at Wat Prayun

mid-19th century. The church was originally built in the late 18th century, during the brief period when Thon Buri was the capital of Thailand (*see pp60–61*). It was rebuilt by Bishop Pallegoix in 1834, and again in 1913. The church is known in Thai as Wat Kuti Chin ("Chinese monastic residence"), a term derived from the subtle Chinese influences apparent in its architecture.

Although only a few houses of Portuguese origin remain in the muddle of alleyways surrounding the temple, the Portuguese legacy can still be seen in the private Catholic shrines that are tucked away among Thai shop-houses.

Wat Prayun 8

วัดประยูร

Pratchatipok Rd. **Map** 5 C2. 🚌 AC: 6; M: 5. ⬤ 7am–4:30pm daily.

THE CURIOUS artificial hill at the entrance to this temple was created on a whim of Rama III. While reading by candlelight, the king observed the interesting wax formation of the melting candle. He then asked one of his courtiers, Prayun Bunnag, to create a hill in the same shape. The hill is dotted with bizarre shrines, miniature *chedis*, *prangs*, grottoes and tiny temples, but is perhaps most memorable for its ornamental pond, filled with hundreds of

turtles. Devotees buy the turtles nearby and then release them into the pond. This act of setting free confined creatures (which more commonly takes the form of releasing caged birds) is a way of gaining merit for future lives.

The temple *bot*, although in a state of disrepair, has doors and window shutters decorated with mother-of-pearl. The large *chedi* has a circular cloister surmounted by smaller *chedis*.

Taksin Monument 9

อนุสาวรีย์พระเจ้าตากสิน

Pratchathipok Rd. **Map** 5 C4.
🚌 AC: 6, 10; M: 4, 5.

LOCATED ON THE busy Wong-wian Yai roundabout, this 20th-century equestrian statue commemorates King Taksin (ruled 1767–82), who moved the capital to Thon Buri after the destruction of Ayutthaya by the Burmese in 1767.

In 1950 the commission to design the monument was given to Professor Silpa Bhirasri, the Italian "father" of Thai

Detail of King Taksin monument

modern art who took a Thai name and citizenship. The striking statue took three years to complete, and was finally unveiled in 1954. Each year, on 28 December – the anniversary of

King Taksin's Coronation – many Thais come to pay homage at the statue.

Popular Buddhist Rituals

The act of merit-making is an essential part of religious life in Thailand *(see pp26–7)*. Practised both by monks and lay people, it reflects an awareness that good deeds lead to good outcomes, such as happiness, either in this life or the next (as a more fortunate rebirth). To accumulate merit is a way of taking responsibility for one's own *karma* (destiny). Becoming a monk, even for a short period, or sponsoring the ordina-

Child offering a lotus bud

tion of a monk, is the ultimate way of making merit, and a devout Buddhist monk adheres to strict rules in his daily life. In some rituals – such as the alms round – the lives of monks and lay people interact. Other everyday habits of ordinary people focus on the local temple: the shared act of decorating a Buddhist shrine strengthens community ties. Devout lay people, meanwhile, may meditate and worship at a private shrine in their own home.

The daily alms round (pindabat) *takes place shortly after dawn, when monks leave their temples to search for their daily meal. Giving food to monks is a popular way for lay people to earn merit and practise generosity (the act of* dana). *Monks are only permitted to eat food that has been offered to them and they must consume it before noon.*

Meditation *purifies the mind and clears it of distractions. It is practised regularly by all monks and some lay people.*

Shaving the head *is a ritual for monks on the day of the full moon. This mural shows a novice being shaved for ordination.*

Pavilion at Wat Phra Kaeo

Gold leaf put on the Buddha image honours his teachings.

Offerings for the Buddha are usually symbolic. Lotus buds represent the purity of the Buddha's thoughts.

Incense sticks, in groups of three, symbolize the Buddha, the *dharma* (teachings) and the *sangha* (monkhood). Candles stand for the light of understanding.

VISITS TO THE WAT

Many lay people in Thailand go to their local *wat* at least once a week. Typically they make offerings to an image of the Buddha, listen to the monks chanting and to a *dharma* talk, and receive blessings. Food is prepared to offer to the monks and as a communal meal. The local community often funds building or restoration works.

FURTHER AFIELD

MANY INTERESTING SIGHTS lie outside central Bangkok. Extending eastwards is Sukhumvit Road, with a plethora of shops, restaurants, small galleries and museums. Shopaholics will also not want to miss the superb Chatuchak Market or the spectacle of Damnoen Saduak Floating Market, west of the city. To the south and east are a clutch of theme and amusement parks, including the Ancient City, a tranquil park containing replicas of important Thai monuments. Nearby is the Croco-

Thai classical dancer

dile Farm, where reptile wrestling is the major draw, while Safari World offers further wildlife encounters. Culture lovers will enjoy the art and antiques in the Prasart Museum. Pleasant day trips include the green suburb of Nonthaburi and, to the west, the relaxed provincial towns of Ratchaburi and Nakhon Pathom. The latter is the site of the world's tallest Buddhist monument, Phra Pathom Chedi. Another popular excursion is west to the Thai culture shows and elephant rides at the Rose Garden.

SIGHTS AT A GLANCE

Towns
Nakhon Pathom ❹
Nonthaburi ❺
Ratchaburi ❶

Museums and Cultural Theme Parks
Ancient City ⓫
Prasart Museum ❿
Rose Garden ❸

Notable Roads
Sukhumvit Road ❼

Swimming Pools
Siam Park ❾

Markets
Chatuchak Market ❻
Damnoen Saduak Floating Market ❷

Zoos
Crocodile Farm ⓬
Safari World ❽

GETTING THERE
Many tour companies offer day-trips to popular sights such as the Rose Garden, Safari World and Ancient City. Local bus routes also serve most sights.

KEY

☐	Main sightseeing area
☐	Built-up area
✈	Airport
═	Motorway
═	Major road
▪▪	Road under construction
═	Minor road

20 km = 12 miles

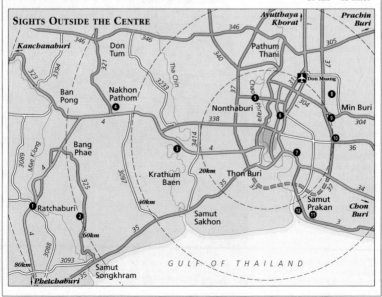

◁ **Lychee seller at Damnoen Saduak Floating Market in Ratchaburi province**

Palm-shaded Wat Mahathat, the main sight at Ratchaburi

Ratchaburi ❶

ราชบุรี

Ratchaburi province. 🏛 *85,000.*
🚉 🚌 🛈 *TAT, Phetchaburi (032) 471005.*

O RIGINALLY AN estuarine
port at the mouth of the
Klong River, Ratchaburi is now
30 km (19 miles) from the sea.
During the Ayutthaya period
(see pp56–7) the town was
sacked twice, in 1765 and
1767, by invading Burmese
armies en route to besiege
the capital city of Ayutthaya.

Nowadays, Ratchaburi makes
a pleasant place to stop on
the way to Kanchanaburi and
the Western Seaboard. Some
visitors stay overnight if visiting Damnoen Saduak Float-
ing Market the next morning.

The town has few sights but
Wat Mahathat is worth a visit.
Its *prang*, allegedly modelled
on the main *prang* at Angkor
Wat *(see pp254–5)*, dates from
the 15th century, although
the temple complex may
have been founded as early
as the 8th or 9th century.
Inside the *prang* are faint
traces of murals from the 15th
century, as well as partially
restored stucco work.

Artifacts in the **Ratchaburi
National Museum** include
archaeological finds such as
fine Khmer sculptures and
stucco decorations excavated
from Muang Khu Bua, a Dvaravati site south of Ratchaburi.

🏛 Ratchaburi National Museum

Woradej Rd. [*(032) 321513.*
◻ *Wed–Sun.* ◼ *public hols.* 🚫

ENVIRONS: The caves of Khao
Ngu, 6 km (4 miles) northwest of Ratchaburi on Highway 3087, contain some early
Dvaravati art. The splendid
reliefs of Buddha images
found in Tham Rusi and
Tham Fa Tho are probably of
greatest interest. Aggressive
macaques congregate in the
area surrounding the caves.

Damnoen Saduak Floating Market ❷

ตลาดน้ำดำเนินสะดวก

2 km (1 mile) W of Damnoen Saduak,
Ratchaburi province. 🚉 🚌 🛥 *or
join tour from Bangkok.* ◻ *dawn–
10am daily.* 🛈 *TAT, Phetchaburi
(032) 471005.*

I N CONTRAST to the numerous
floating markets in Bangkok
that are now organized solely
for the benefit of tourists, this
is a fairly unspoilt example.

Located near Damnoen
Saduak – 100 km (62 miles)
southwest of Bangkok – the
market is a labyrinth of narrow
khlongs (canals). The small
wooden boats are paddled
mainly by female traders, most
of whom are dressed in traditional blue farmers' shirts – *mo
hom* – and conical straw hats.
The fresh produce, including
fruit, vegetables and spices,
comes straight from the farm.
For the benefit of the tourists,
some boats sell souvenir straw
hats and refreshments.

The floating market actually
consists of three markets. The
largest, **Ton Khem**, is on
Khlong Damnoen Saduak. On
the parallel *khlong* is **Hia Kui**,
where structures anchored to
the banks function as ware-
houses selling souvenirs to
large tour groups. To the
south, on a smaller *khlong*, is
Khun Phitak, which is the
least crowded market.

The best way of getting
around the three markets is by
boat: trips can be taken along
the *khlongs* or to see nearby
coconut plantations. The best
time to arrive is between 7am
and 9am, when the Floating
Market is in full swing.

Trading Thai-style at the bustling Damnoen Saduak Floating Market

Thai Fruits and Vegetables

THAILAND'S CLIMATE and soil conditions are conducive to the cultivation of a huge variety of fruits and vegetables throughout the year. Well known tropical fruits, including papaya, watermelon, mango and pineapple, are unmistakable, but the orchards and farms of Thailand also offer a wealth of produce that may be less familiar to many visitors. Among the not-to-be-missed treats are the mangosteen, the grapefruit-like pomelo, the much-prized durian and the sweet-fleshed, hairy rambutan. Thai fruits are sold sliced as snacks by street vendors everywhere, and the full range of fresh produce can be seen at most markets.

Bright red, fresh rambutans

Longans have a transparent, succulent flesh around a smooth pip.

Mangoes can be eaten unripe and sour (green) or ripe and sweet (yellow).

Mangosteens are the king of Thai fruit. Their tasty flesh has a melt-in-the-mouth texture.

Durians are a favourite with Thais. The pungent smell and flavour are an acquired taste.

Guavas, crisp and sour fruits, are best enjoyed with a sweet chilli dip or as a refreshing juice.

Jackfruits, similar in appearance to durians, only larger, have a sticky flesh with a tangy flavour.

Gourds

Pea aubergines

Baby tomatoes

Aubergines

Thai vegetables include several types of makhua *(the tomato and aubergine family). Gourds and aubergines are frequently used in curries.*

Spring onions

Coriander

Chillies

Thai cuisine makes liberal use of chillies, galingale, tamarind and lemon grass to flavour dishes, balancing spiciness with coconut milk and sugar. Coriander and spring onions are popular garnishes.

The peaceful, immaculately maintained Rose Garden

Rose Garden ❸

สวนสามพราน

Off Hwy 4, 32 km (20 miles) W of Bangkok. **[** (034) 322 7724. **🚌** AC: 6, 15, 9, 10, or join tour from Bangkok. **◯** 6am–6pm daily (show at 2:45pm). **🦽**

THIS WELL MANICURED garden, west of Bangkok, is part of the Rose Garden Country Resort. Although there are tennis courts, a swimming pool and a golf course on the site, the chief attraction for the majority of visitors is the daily show of traditional Thai culture. Packed into the one-hour show are demonstrations of traditional Thai dancing *(see pp38–9)*, ancient sword fighting, a Thai wedding, the ordination of a monk *(see p26)*, and Thai boxing *(see pp40–1)*. The model Thai village within the grounds is a showcase for fruit-carving, basket-weaving and other crafts.

ENVIRONS: Just north of the Rose Garden is the **Samphran Elephant Ground and Zoo**, featuring crocodile wrestling and elephant rides. Further west, on the way to Nakhon Pathom, the **Human Imagery Museum** has fibreglass statues of notable figures in Thai history, including the Chakri kings *(see pp60–1)* and a number of renowned monks.

🎪 Samphran Elephant Ground and Zoo
[(02) 284 1873. **◯** daily. **🦽**
🏛 Human Imagery Museum
Pinklao-Nakhon Hwy. **[** (034) 332 109. **◯** daily. **🦽**

Nakhon Pathom ❹

นครปฐม

Nakhon Pathom province. **👥** 92,000. **🚌 🚆 ℹ** TAT, Bangkok (02) 226 0060. **🍴** daily. **🎉** Phra Pathom Chedi Fair (Nov); Food and Fruit Fair (Dec).

SOME 67 KM (42 MILES) to the west of Bangkok, Nakhon Pathom was a major centre of the Dvaravati Kingdom, which thrived from the 6th to the 11th centuries AD *(see pp52–3)*.

The highlight of the town is the **Phra Pathom Chedi**, on Phetkasem Highway. This huge monument, housing a standing Buddha image of large proportions, is one of the most important places of pilgrimage in Thailand. The original *stupa* (a non-Thai *chedi*) on this site is thought to have been built sometime between the 2nd century BC and the 5th century AD. It commemorated the arrival of the first Buddhist missionaries in Thailand, allegedly sent here from India in the 3rd century BC. The building fell into decay in the 11th century and was not restored until the early 19th century when King Mongkut had the old shrine encased in a *chedi*. The spire was completed by King Chulalongkorn. The *chedi*, beautifully adorned with golden tiles, dominates the town, and at 120 m (395 ft) in height is the tallest Buddhist monument in the world.

Southeast of the *chedi* is the **Phra Pathom Chedi National Museum**, with a magnificent collection of locally excavated pieces from the Dvaravati period, including stone Wheels of the Law *(see p27)*, as well as stuccoed panels from Chedi Chula Prathon, a 7th–8th century monument east of town.

West of the *chedi* is the early 20th-century **Sanam Chan Palace**. Although the palace itself is closed to the public, the peaceful grounds are open, and the palace's unusual mix of architectural styles can be viewed.

🏛 Phra Pathom Chedi National Museum
Khwa Phra Rd. **[** (034) 242 500. **◯** Wed–Sun. **●** public hols. **🦽**
🏛 Sanam Chan Palace
Off Phetkasem Hwy.
Grounds ◯ daily.

Nakhon Pathom's *chedi*, the world's tallest Buddhist monument

Nonthaburi pier, as seen from the Chao Phraya River

Nonthaburi 5

นนทบุรี

Nonthaburi province. 60,000.
🚉 🚌 🚤 ℹ *TAT, Bangkok
(02) 226 0060.* 🎪 *Wed, Sat.*

APPROXIMATELY 10 km (6 miles) north of Bangkok, Nonthaburi offers a relaxing slice of provincial life. The town is best reached by riverboat from one of Bangkok's express piers. The journey takes 50 minutes and offers several interesting sights, the first of which is the Royal Boat House near Wat Sam Phraya pier, where some of the royal barges are kept. Others are housed at the Royal Barge Museum in Thon Buri (*see pp120–1*). Past the Krung Thon Bridge is a small community of rice barges on the east bank, and shortly before Nonthaburi pier is **Wat Khian**, a temple that is half-submerged in the river.

Nonthaburi has a pleasant, provincial atmosphere that contrasts with the chaos and pollution of the capital just down the river. The town is particularly well known for the quality of its durian fruit (*see p129*) – reflected in the unusual decoration of the lampposts on the promenade. You may find the famously smelly fruit for sale in Nonthaburi's colourful, lively market by the side of the river. A round-trip boat ride from Nonthaburi along Khlong Om will take you on a slow-paced journey

Door of *bot*, Wat Chalerm Phrakiet

through durian plantations and past riverside houses. Another worthwhile excursion from Nonthaburi is the river journey to **Wat Chalerm Phrakiet**, situated on the west bank of the Chao Phraya. The *wat*, which occupies the site of a 17th-century fortress was built by Rama III in the 19th century in honour of his mother, who is believed to have lived in the vicinity.

One of the most striking features of the temple is the intricate detailing, including porcelain tilework, on the doors, gables and window frames of the *bot*. Behind the *bot* is a *chedi* that was added by Rama IV. Enclosed by castellated walls, the attractive temple grounds are dotted with rockery, sculpted trees and Chinese-style wooden statues, including one, perhaps surprisingly, of Santa Claus.

Chatuchak Market 6

ตลาดจตุจักร

Chatuchak district. 🚌 *AC: 2, 3, 9, 10 12, 13, 29, 39, 44;* M: 8.
ℹ *TAT, Bangkok (02) 226 0060.*
🕐 *7am – 8pm Sat & Sun.*

THAILAND'S BIGGEST MARKET is staged each weekend in a northern suburb of Bangkok, between the Northern Bus Terminal and Bangsu Railway Station. The market moved to this location in 1982 because it had outgrown its original site on Sanam Luang (*see pp74–5*). Now it is a chaotic collection of over 6,000 stalls, which together occupy the space of five football fields. It is always full of throngs of eager shoppers, many of whom spend a whole day browsing among the merchandise displays.

The huge variety of goods on offer ranges from fresh seafood to antiques, and from Siamese fighting fish to second-hand jeans. The plant section offers a good introduction to Thai flora, while the food stalls display every conceivable ingredient of Thai food, fresh from the farm or the sea. The antique and hill-tribe sections sell a good selection of artifacts and textiles, both fake and genuine, from all over Thailand and neighbouring countries.

The market has been referred as the "wildlife supermarket of the world", due to some endangered species, such as leaf monkeys, being illegally sold here. Thankfully, such trade is now declining.

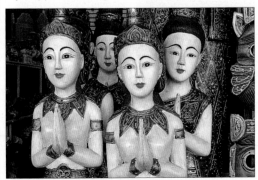

Traditional Thai wooden figures for sale at Chatuchak Market

Sukhumvit Road ●
ถนนสุขุมวิท

Phra Khanong district. 🚌 *AC: 1, 8, 11, 13.*

THIS ROAD BEGINS at the eastern end of Bangkok's downtown and continues all the way to the Cambodian border in Trat province (*see p313*). In Bangkok it is the main thoroughfare of an expanding business quarter popular with foreigners.

Though it is a long way from Bangkok's best-known sights, the area has numerous good quality, moderately priced hotels and restaurants, and a few attractions of its own.

Foremost of these is the **Siam Society**, which was founded in the early 1900s (by a group of Thais and foreign residents under the patronage of Rama VI) to research, rediscover and preserve Thai culture. Within the grounds are two traditional teakwood Northern Thai houses that comprise the country's only genuine ethnological museum. The Kamthieng House, a farm dwelling, was transported piece by piece in the 1960s to Bangkok from the bank of the Ping River, near Chiang Mai. The Sangaroon House is a later addition donated by the architect Sangaroon Ratagasikorn who – inspired by the utilitarian beauty of rural

A mock up of a traditional sleeping area in the Kamthieng House

Hotels, restaurants and offices lining Sukhumvit Road

utensils – amassed a sizeable collection. It is a good example of Central Plains style (*see p32*). Also in the grounds is a reference library on Thai culture, open to visitors. The *Journal of the Siam Society* is one of Asia's most respected publications on art history, culture and society.

Near to the Siam Society, the **Visual Dhamma Art Gallery** is dedicated to the best in contemporary Thai art and is preferred by some to Thailand's National Gallery, situated in the heart of the Old City (*see p82*). It houses a permanent display of Thailand's leading modern artists: Vasan Sitthiket, Montien Boonma, Mit Jai La and Kamin Lertchaiprasert.

Next to the Eastern Bus Terminal, the **Bangkok Planetarium**, with its hands-on exhibitions, may be of interest to those who have time to spare while waiting for a bus.

The **Queen's Park** is easily found between sois 22 and 24, while the larger **King's Royal Park** is further out towards Samut Prakan. With its botanical gardens and area for water sports, this park is one of Bangkok's most pleasant oases. The park also has an exhibition on the king's life.

🏛 **Siam Society**
131 Soi Asoke, Sukhumvit Rd, Soi 21. 🕻 *(02) 259 4999.* ☐ *Mon–Sat.*

🏛 **Visual Dhamma Art Gallery**
44/28 Soi Asoke, Sukhumvit Rd, Soi 21. 🕻 *(02) 258 5879.* ☐ *Mon–Sat.*

🏛 **Bangkok Planetarium**
928 Sukhumvit Rd. 🕻 *(02) 392 5951.* ☐ *Wed–Sun.* ● *public hols.* 🎫

🌿 **Queen's Park**
By Soi 22, Sukhumvit Rd. ☐ *daily.*

🌿 **King's Royal Park**
Soi Udonsuk, Sukhumvit Rd, Soi 103. 🕻 *(02) 328 1385.* ☐ *daily.* 🎫

Safari World ●
ซาฟารีเวิลด์

99 Ramindra Road, Minburi district. 🕻 *(02) 518 1000.* ☐ *9am–5pm daily.* 🎫

THIS CAR-SAFARI PARK offers eight different natural habitats over a 5-km (3-mile) drive. Among the animals on view are tigers, elephants, giraffes, lions and zebras, and rare species such as white pandas. A marine park features dolphin shows. Other entertainment includes elephant and orang-utan shows, and a bird park with a walk-in aviary.

Siam Park ●
สวนสยาม

101 Mu 4 Sukha Phiban 2 Rd, Minburi district. 🕻 *(02) 517 0075.* 🚌 *AC: 12.* ☐ *10am–6pm Mon–Fri, 10am–7pm Sat, Sun & public hols.* 🎫

SIAM PARK, a water and amusement centre, is a great place to cool off from the heat of the Thai sun. Its attractions include huge waterslides, a

Sculpture at the Queen's Park

gentle whirlpool and an artificial lake. Water permeates Thai culture in many ways, not least at Songkran (New Year), when everyone gets soaked on the streets (see p44 and p226). However, Thais have never been particularly keen swimmers. This may change if more complexes like Siam Park are built.

The facilities are well maintained and there are restaurants and lifeguards. There is also an amusement park with rickety fairground rides and a mini-zoo. As Bangkok families descend upon the park in numbers at the weekend, it's best to visit during the week.

Ornate interior of Lanna Pavilion at the Prasart Museum

Prasart Museum ⑩
พิพิธภัณฑ์ปราสาท

9 Soi Krungthepkretha 4a, Bang Kapi district. 【 (02) 379 3607.
▥ M: 10. ◯ 10am–3pm Fri–Sun; Mon–Thu by appointment. ▨ ⊘ ⓖ compulsory.

T HE PRIVATELY OWNED Prasart Museum is known to few tourists and Bangkokians, but the journey out to this elegant museum, set in landscaped tropical gardens, will be worthwhile for anyone who loves Thai art. The collector, Prasart Vongsakul, started to acquire Thai antiques in 1965 when he was only 12 years old. The buildings in which they are housed are also of interest, designed by the collector himself either as direct replicas or playful combinations of his favourite palaces and pavilions from around the country.

Ancient City ⑪
เมืองโบราณ

Sukhumvit Rd, Bangpu, Samut Prakan province. 【 (02) 323 9253. ▥ 25 to Bangpu, then 3, or join tour from Bangkok. ◯ 8am–5pm daily. ▨

M UANG BORAN, which roughly translates as "Ancient City", is an outdoor cultural theme park financed and created in the early 1970s by the art-loving philanthropic owner of Thailand's largest Mercedes-Benz dealership.

The park makes a surprisingly worthwhile visit. The peaceful grounds, shaped roughly like Thailand itself, display numerous replicas of important monuments in Thailand as well as actual buildings and sculptures that have been restored to their former grandeur. Replicas are one third real size.

All the Thai art periods are represented, including a few mythical and literary ones such as at the Garden of Phra Aphaimani, inspired by a 19th-century verse play (see p308). Some of the buildings, for example the Sanphet Prasat Palace, which once stood near Wat Phra Si Sanphet in Ayutthaya (see pp168–9), are reconstructions of monuments destroyed centuries ago in battle and so provide the only testaments to past glories.

The selection and construction of monuments was overseen by Thailand's top art historians. The resident army of craftsmen can often be seen maintaining the park.

Wrestling, the most spectacular show at the Crocodile Farm

Crocodile Farm ⑫
ฟาร์มจระเข้

Old Sukhumvit Highway, Samut Prakan province. 【 (02) 387 1168. ▥ AC: 11 to Samut Prakan, then songthaew, or join tour from Bangkok. ◯ 8am–5pm daily. ▨

T HE LARGEST of Thailand's crocodile farms and supposedly the largest in the world, this breeding park-cum-zoo is home to some 30,000 reptiles. Fresh- and saltwater species are included, ranging from South American caimans to crocodiles from the Nile.

In the breeding section you can see crocodiles hatching and in various stages of growth. You can also see them transformed into hand-bags and key-rings in the souvenir shop. Wrestling shows are held regularly, and feeding time happens at 4:30–5:30pm. A visit to the crocodile farm is popularly combined with a day trip to the Ancient City.

Reconstruction of the Prince of Lampang's Palace, Ancient City

BANGKOK STREET FINDER

FINDING YOUR WAY around Bangkok can be a challenge. The lack of standard transliterations for Thai words means that the street names listed here will not always match those seen on street signs. Additionally, some streets are known by more than one name – for example, Charoen Krung Road is New Road and Wireless Road is Witthayu Road. Most major roads *(thanons)* have numerous numbered (and sometimes named) *sois* and *troks* (minor roads and lanes) leading from them. Odd numbered *sois* usually lead off one side of a road, even numbers off the other. Be warned that there can be considerable distances between *sois* – for instance, *sois* 6 and 36 off Phetchaburi Road are more than 3 km (2 miles) apart. Major sights, markets and ferry piers are also listed in this gazetteer.

The quickest way to get around Bangkok for humans and canines

KEY

▢ Major sight	🚓 Police station	≡ Expressway
▢ Place of interest	🚓 Tourist police station	⫶ Road under construction
▢ Other building	🜊 *Wat*	— One-way street
🚉 Railway station	🛕 Hindu temple	▬ Street market
🚉 Skytrain station (not yet open)	✝ Church	
⚓ Riverboat pier	🅲 Mosque	
⚓ Chao Phraya Express pier	⊠ Post office	0 metres 400
ℹ Tourist information	— Railway line	0 yards 400
✚ Hospital with casualty unit	═ Skytrain route (not yet open)	**Scale for Street Finder pages**

0 kilometres   2

0 miles   1

THE CENTRAL PLAINS

Introducing the Central Plains

T HE FERTILE PLAINS stretching northwards from Bangkok
are the nation's rice basket and the historic heartland of the Tai people. Here lie the impressive ruined
cities of the old Sukhothai *(see pp54–5)* and Ayutthaya
kingdoms *(see pp58–9)*. Today this is the country's
most wealthy and densely populated region, with fast-
expanding towns surrounded by fields of sugar cane
and rice. In the forested hills that border the
Central Plains are national parks with spectacular waterfalls and a wide range of wildlife, providing a pleasant scenic contrast.

Si Satchanal
Chalieng
Historical Pa

Kamphaeng Phet

Si Satchanalai-Chalieng Historical Park
(see pp188–90) *encompasses the ruins of one
of the most important Sukhothai cities, as well
as the remains of an earlier Khmer settlement.*

SOUTH
CENTRAL
PLAINS
(see pp154–175)

Kamphaeng Phet *(see*
pp182–3) contains a
wealth of Sukhothai-
era monuments and
ruins and, within
the old city walls, a
fine museum display-
ing ceramics such as
this 15th-century pot.

Kanchanaburi

Kanchanaburi *(see pp160–61)*
is near the site of the infamous
bridge built over the Khwae Yai
River during World War II. A
museum and cemetery in the
town provide a moving testa-
ment to the Asian labourers and
Allied troops who died.

◁ **The remains of a *bot*, featuring a huge, seated Buddha image, Wat Mahathat, Sukhothai**

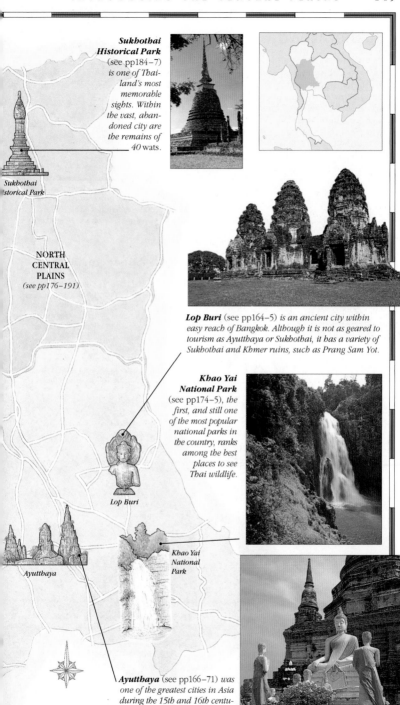

Sukhothai Historical Park (see pp184–7) is one of Thailand's most memorable sights. Within the vast, abandoned city are the remains of 40 wats.

Sukhothai Historical Park

NORTH CENTRAL PLAINS (see pp176–191)

Lop Buri (see pp164–5) *is an ancient city within easy reach of Bangkok. Although it is not as geared to tourism as Ayutthaya or Sukhothai, it has a variety of Sukhothai and Khmer ruins, such as Prang Sam Yot.*

Khao Yai National Park (see pp174–5), *the first, and still one of the most popular national parks in the country, ranks among the best places to see Thai wildlife.*

Lop Buri

Ayutthaya

Khao Yai National Park

0 kilometres   50

0 miles   25

Ayutthaya (see pp166–71) *was one of the greatest cities in Asia during the 15th and 16th centuries. Extensive ruins scattered through the modern town evoke the splendour of the city's past.*

Sukhothai Art

THE PROLIFIC ARTISANS of the Sukhothai School (late 13th–15th centuries) adapted stylistic elements from Sri Lanka, Burma and other neighbouring countries to produce some of Thailand's finest works of art. Numerous Buddha images of immense beauty and fluidity were cast in bronze. The "Walking" Buddha – a posture which is otherwise rare in Buddhist art – is perhaps the best-known artistic achievement of the period. The Sangkhalok *(see p190)* ceramics industry also flourished, and its fine wares, including pale blue-green celadons, were exported all over Asia until the middle of the 16th century.

The Walking Buddha *posture possibly represents the Buddha's descent from Tavatimsa Heaven after he had visited his mother.*

Bronze *replaced stone as the preferred material for Buddha images during the Sukhothai period. It allowed a far more delicate detailing of the Buddha's hair and facial features.*

PHITSANULOK BUDDHA

Located in Wat Phra Si Rattana Mahathat in Phitsanulok, this 14th-century Buddha image, known properly as Phra Phuttha Chinarat, is one of the most revered in all of Thailand, second only to the Emerald Buddha in Bangkok. Cast in bronze and later gilded, the serene figure is a supreme example of late Sukhothai art.

This bronze Vishnu, *a Hindu god, is in the classic Sukhothai style. Brahmin priests, who presided over some court ceremonies, probably ordered figures like this to be made.*

Wedge-shaped joints

The flame-like "halo" around Phra Phuttha Chinarat, ending in *naga* heads, is unique.

Fingers all of the same length

***Sukhothai* bai semas** *(boundary stones, see p29) were fashioned from slate into leaf shapes. This one, at Wat Sorasak in Sukhothai, is inscribed with details of a land grant.*

Monochrome ceramic gable decorations, *such as this one from Wat Phra Phai Luang, Sukhothai, are a typical architectural flourish from the period.*

Ceramic finials, *found on many roofs, were sometimes fashioned as dragons. Such decorations show a fusion of Khmer and Chinese styles.*

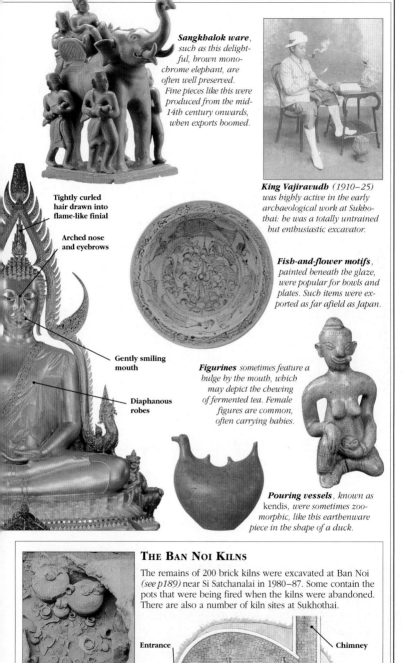

Sangkhalok ware, such as this delightful, brown monochrome elephant, are often well preserved. Fine pieces like this were produced from the mid-14th century onwards, when exports boomed.

King Vajiravudh (1910–25) was highly active in the early archaeological work at Sukhothai: he was a totally untrained but enthusiastic excavator.

Tightly curled hair drawn into flame-like finial

Arched nose and eyebrows

Fish-and-flower motifs, painted beneath the glaze, were popular for bowls and plates. Such items were exported as far afield as Japan.

Gently smiling mouth

Figurines sometimes feature a bulge by the mouth, which may depict the chewing of fermented tea. Female figures are common, often carrying babies.

Diaphanous robes

Pouring vessels, known as kendis, *were sometimes zoo-morphic, like this earthenware piece in the shape of a duck.*

THE BAN NOI KILNS

The remains of 200 brick kilns were excavated at Ban Noi *(see p189)* near Si Satchanalai in 1980–87. Some contain the pots that were being fired when the kilns were abandoned. There are also a number of kiln sites at Sukhothai.

Entrance

Chimney

Foreigners in Ayutthaya

THROUGHOUT THE 16TH AND 17TH centuries Ayutthaya was one of the most important trading centres in Asia, attracting not only merchants but also missionaries, adventurers and mercenaries from around the world. Portuguese visitors arriving in the 16th century found a riverine city of canals, and magnificent flotillas of barges. They brought firearms to trade, and military advisers to help Ayutthaya against the Burmese. The Dutch and English followed in the 17th century and established trading ware-houses. The Japanese came to buy animal hides, while French Jesuits and Persians competed for

European illustration of a Siamese official

religious converts. Some foreigners, including Constantine Phaulkon, sought political influence.

St Joseph's Church (see p170) *stands south of Ayutthaya's main island. Originally built during the reign of King Narai (1656–88) by French missionaries, it has been restored many times since.*

Royal Palace

Lacquerware *was a speciality of Ayutthaya. Like other as-pects of life in the city, the decorative arts reflected the influence of foreigners or* farangs. *These doors depict farang traders.*

MAP OF AYUTTHAYA
The involvement of Europeans in Siamese affairs led to the publication of several maps of Ayutthaya. This French map, probably an 18th-century copy of one drawn in the 17th century, shows the location of the French, Portuguese and Siamese quarters. The European spelling of Ayutthaya at that time was Iudia.

Siamese quarter **Chao Phraya River**

The first French to arrive in Ayutthaya, in 1662, were Jesuit mission-aries. In 1681 the French asked permission for a full diplomatic mission to visit the city. It arrived in 1685, headed by the envoy from Louis XIV, Chevalier de Chaumont. A Siamese envoy later returned with him to France. This painting shows him being received at court by the Sun King, Louis XIV.

French Jesuit missionaries *came to Ayutthaya to convert King Narai to Catholicism. They failed in this but encouraged him to cultivate an interest in astronomy. This illustration shows him watching a lunar eclipse in 1685. Following the Jesuits' tutelage he watched a partial solar eclipse in 1688. Narai favoured the Jesuits and gave them land to build churches and schools.*

Chillies *were first imported from South America by the Portuguese, who established a trading treaty with the Siamese in 1516. They quickly grew in popularity and today chillies are an essential ingredient in numerous Thai dishes.*

Siamese quarter

Chinese quarter

French quarter   **Portuguese quarter**

Royal barges *and other boats crowded the waterways of Ayutthaya. Often the first sight that greeted visitors to the city was a convoy of royal barges. As a result, Ayutthaya became known as the "Venice of the East".*

The VOC *(Dutch East India Company) first visited Ayutthaya in 1604. A trading warehouse was set up in 1634, but by the 1670s trade had declined. The warehouse in Ayutthaya was later destroyed by the Burmese.*

CONSTANTINE PHAULKON

The influence of foreigners in Ayutthaya was greatest under King Narai (1656–88). Most notorious of those who came to Ayutthaya was the Greek adventurer Constantine Phaulkon, who arrived in 1678 in the employ of the English East India Company. Attracting the attention of Narai, he quickly moved on to become the king's personal confidant and chief minister. He later advised Narai against Dutch and English interests in Ayutthaya. The French, meanwhile, were allowed to station 600 soldiers in the kingdom. Amid much political wrangling in court, Narai was viewed as cultivating strong ties with Louis XIV, whose ambition was to convert him and Siam to Catholicism, and some people feared a French takeover. When Narai died in 1688 all ties with foreigners were cut, and Phaulkon was executed.

Constantine Phaulkon, prostrate before the Siamese king, Narai

SOUTH CENTRAL PLAINS

F OR CENTURIES, *the broad flood plain of the Chao Phraya, which bisects the South Central Plains north to south, has been Thailand's rice basket as well as its most densely populated region. The river remains a vital link between the country's cultural heartland and its present-day capital, Bangkok. The old capital of Ayutthaya, upstream from Bangkok, is the region's most popular sight.*

Ayutthaya was one of the greatest mercantile centres in Asia during the 14th–18th centuries. Its fabulous temples and palaces, built around the confluence of the Chao Phraya, Lop Buri and Pasak rivers, were regarded with wonder by foreigners. In 1767 it was sacked by the Burmese, and the capital was forced to move downstream to Bangkok. The remains of monuments from the earlier period stand among more modern buidings and each day attract hundreds of visitors on round trips from Bangkok.

Kanchanaburi, to the west of Bangkok, is another popular day trip from the capital. During World War II the Japanese built a railway from here to the Three Pagodas Pass near Burma, along an old Burmese invasion route. Little of the railway was ever used, but at Kanchanaburi visitors can see poignant reminders of this gruelling episode, when thousands of Asian labourers and Allied POWs died.

Despite these and other noteworthy sights, the region still has relatively few tourist facilities. Towns such as Lop Buri – an old Khmer outpost with several Khmer *prangs* – and the pilgrimage site of Phra Phutthabat are unknown to the majority of tourists.

There is some accommodation in the Khwae Noi River Valley, along the route to the Three Pagodas Pass. This region is surrounded by a vast expanse of forest and grassland, including two wildlife sanctuaries and the Erawan, Sai Yok and Chaloem Rattanakosin national parks. At the eastern edge of the South Central Plains, Khao Yai, the oldest national park, is the best place in Thailand to see wild elephants and many other animals.

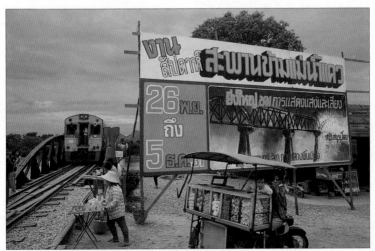

The bridge over the Khwae Yai River at Kanchanaburi, a poignant reminder of World War II

◁ **Wat Mahathat, built in 1384, one of the largest temples at the ancient site of Ayutthaya**

Exploring the South Central Plains

THE CHAO PHRAYA RIVER BASIN is fertile terrain, perfect for rice production. It is no coincidence that the kingdoms of Lop Buri and, later, Ayutthaya, the capital of which is the premier sight of the region, were founded here. East of the wide plain, Khao Yai is the country's oldest and most accessible national park. Kanchanaburi, in the west, is the site of the notorious Death Railway of World War II. From there, a road winds up to the Three Pagodas Pass on the Burmese border, passing near numerous national parks and wildlife sanctuaries.

Chiang Mai

Burma

THREE PAGODAS PASS

1 SANKHLA BURI

Khwae Yai

3438

2

THUNG YAI NARESUAN AND HUAI KHA KHAENG

UTHAI TH

CHALOEM RATTANAKOSIN NATIONAL PARK

7

3086

333

3306

DON C

0 kilometres 25

0 miles 25

SAI YOK NATIONAL PARK

3

4 ERAWAN NATIONAL PARK

U THONG

324

3199

3086

5

PRASAT MUANG SING

6 KANCHANABUR

3209

3274

3087

Ratcha

Phetch

Memorial stones at POW cemetery, Kanchanaburi

KEY

▬▬	Motorway
▬▬	Major road
▬▬	Minor road
▬▬	Scenic route
═══	River
☀	Viewpoint

GETTING AROUND

Many hotels in Bangkok arrange day tours of Ayutthaya and Kanchanaburi. Boat tours up the Chao Phraya River, from Bangkok to Ayutthaya via Bang Pa-in, are also popular. Roads from Bangkok fan out across the region, providing fast and easy access by bus or car, though leaving Bangkok itself is time consuming. Kanchanaburi, Ayutthaya and Lop Buri can be reached by rail. A small airport serves Lop Buri.

Buddhas at Wat Yai Chai Mongkhon, Ayutthaya

SEE ALSO

- *Where to Stay* pp391–2

- *Where to Eat* pp415–16

Chanthara Phisan Hall, in grounds of King Narai's Palace, Lop Buri

On the way to market, Three Pagodas Pass

Sangkhla Buri ❶
สังขละบุรี

Kanchanaburi province. 👥 *21,000.*
🚌 *from Kanchanaburi.* ℹ️ *TAT,
Kanchanaburi (034) 511200.* 🛍️ *daily.*

IN THE CENTRE of Sangkhla
Buri is a market, where,
among other things, you can
buy Burmese curries and
samosas, as well as books
written in the Mon language.

However, the main attrac-
tion of this isolated trading
town, which is populated by
Mon and Karen tribespeople
(see p196) as well as Thais,
is its serene lake-side location.
The lake is effectively a large
reservoir, formed by the dam-
ming of the Khwae Noi River
further downstream. Some-
times, late in the dry season,

the drowned remains of
old villages and forests
can be seen sticking up
out of the calm surface
of the lake's waters.

The north shore of the
lake is overlooked by the
unusual *chedi* of
Wat Wangwiwekaram.
In the covered gallery
beside it a daily market
sells goods from Burma,
Indonesia and else-
where, including *lungis*
(sarongs) and simple
woodcarvings. Visitors
can reach the *wat* on foot
by crossing a wooden
bridge, which spans the
wide shallow inlet of the
lake. A large settlement,
consisting predominantly
of Mon tribespeople, has
grown up in close proximity
to the *wat*. An interesting
daily market is held here in
the early morning.

ENVIRONS: At the **Three
Pagodas Pass**, 23 km (14
miles) northwest of Sangkhla
Buri, right on the Burmese border, are situated three small,
physically unimpressive, whitewashed *chedis*. For centuries
this pass, which is less than
300 m (985 ft) above sea
level, was used as an invasion
route. During World War II,
the Burma-Siam Railway *(see
pp160–61)* passed through
here, and the route the track
took can still be seen beside
the Burmese border. Nowa-
days, the pass is a quiet trading
(and smuggling) route between
the Indian Ocean to the west

and mainland Southeast Asia.
Visitors to this region are
usually permitted to cross the
border on a one-day visa *(see
p451)* to the Burmese town of
Pyathonzu. However, visitors
should note that the relations
between Thailand and Burma
are often uneasy, at times
verging on the hostile, and
mean that this situation is
prone to change at any time.

Thung Yai
Naresuan and Huai
Kha Khaeng ❷
เขตรักษาพันธุ์สัตว์ป่าห้วยขาแข้ง

Kanchanaburi, Tak and Uthai Thani
provinces. ℹ️ *TAT, Tak (055) 514341;
Kanchanaburi (034) 511200; Forestry
Dept (02) 579 0529.* 🚌 *from
Kanchanaburi.* 📷

THESE TWO HUGE, adjacent
wildlife sanctuaries, covering 6,220 sq km (2,400 sq
miles) and surrounded by a
further 6,000 sq km (2,320 sq
miles) of protected forest,
form one of the most important conservation areas in
Southeast Asia. They are
listed jointly as a UNESCO
World Heritage Site, and are
home to some of Thailand's
largest remaining wild elephant
herds as well as several endangered carnivores, such as
tigers, clouded leopards and
Malaysian sun bears. The
enormous gaur, a species of
wild cattle, and the country's
last wild buffalo herds also
live within the sanctuary. Rare

Herd of wild buffalo, native to Thung Yai Naresuan and Huai Kha Khaeng wildlife sanctuaries

Tourist accommodation in the tranquil Sai Yok National Park

species of gibbon can also be seen. At Huai Kha Khaeng there is a nature trail for visitors, but neither wildlife sanctuary is really geared up for large numbers of visitors – permission for large parties to enter the parks can be obtained from the Bangkok Forestry Department.

Sai Yok National Park ❸
อุทยานแห่งชาติไทรโยค

Kanchanaburi province. Park HQ off Hwy 323, 100 km (62 miles) NW of Kanchanaburi. *TAT, Kanachanaburi (034) 511200; Forestry Dept (02) 579 0529 (inc bungalow bookings).* from Kanchanaburi.

SAI YOK was the site of a large Japanese army barracks and POW labour camp during World War II. The 500-sq km (190-sq mile) national park was established in 1980 and today is renowned for its tranquil river scenery and the impressive Sai Yok Yai waterfall, which tumbles into the Khwae Noi River near to the park headquarters.

Accommodation is available in simple park bungalows or on pleasant houseboats, and boats can be chartered – unfortunately at quite considerable expense – to some nearby caves. The caves are home to the 3-cm (1-inch) long Kitti's hog-nosed bat, considered by some to be the world's smallest mammal, and which was discovered in 1973 by Thai naturalist Kitti Thonglongya.

ENVIRONS: The Burma-Thailand Railway Memorial Trail, south of Sai Yok, pays tribute to prisoners who died during the excavation of the Konyu railway cutting. Near to the cutting, which was given the name "Hellfire Pass" by the many prisoners of war who laboured through the night by torchlight, was the "Pack of Cards Bridge". This rickety 300-m (985-ft) long, 25-m (82-ft) high structure was built at perilous speed with green timber and, as a result, heavy loss of life – the structure collapsed three times during its construction.

The trail, set up with funding from the Australian government, winds up to Konyu cutting through a bamboo grove. The railway track has long since been removed.

Plaque in memory of POWs, Hellfire Pass

Erawan National Park ❹
อุทยานแห่งชาติเอราวัณ

Kanchanaburi province. Park HQ off Hwy 3199, 65 km (40 miles) NW of Kanchanaburi. *TAT, Kanchanaburi (034) 511200; Forestry Dept (02) 579 0529 (inc bungalow bookings).* from Kanchanaburi.

IN THE LUSH FOREST of the 550-sq km (210-sq mile) Erawan National Park, the nearest park to Kanchanaburi, are the stunningly beautiful **Erawan falls**, which drop through a series of cascades and shady rock pools. While park rangers still find occasional tiger prints, visitors are more likely to see pig-tailed and rhesus macaques, and some 80 bird species. The Visitors' Centre offers a slide show about the park and there is a pleasant, but strenuous, 2-km (1-mile) hiking trail which climbs up beside the falls. This is one of Thailand's most popular national parks, and at weekends and holidays it gets very crowded. The large limestone cavern of Tham Wang Badan, situated on the west side of the park, contains many colourful stalactites and stalagmites.

ENVIRONS: The Huai Khamin falls, which are located in the nearby **Si Nakharin National Park**, do not receive as many visitors as the Erawan falls but are, nevertheless, quite impressive and worth making the trip. Visitors to the park can also make excursions by boat out onto the Si Nakharin reservoir, either from the Kradan pier or from Si Sawat, a small market town situated on the eastern shore of the reservoir.

🏞 Si Nakharin National Park
108 km (67 miles) N of Kanchanaburi. *daily.*

The Erawan falls, named after the Hindu god Indra's elephant mount

Central sanctuary of Prasat Muang Sing near Kanchanaburi

Prasat Muang Sing ❺
ปราสาทเมืองสิงห์

Off Hwy 323, 43 km (27 miles) W of Kanchanaburi, Kanchanaburi province. ■ TAT, Kanchanaburi (034) 511200. ■ from Kanchanaburi to Tha Kilen, then songthaew. ○ daily. ◪

THE RUINS of Muang Sing beside the Khwae Noi River date from around the 13th century and mark the westernmost point of expansion of the Khmer Empire (see pp254–5). Earthen ramparts surround an inner wall of laterite which forms a rough rectangle about 1 sq km (245 acres). Near the centre of this are the ruins of the Buddhist sanctuary, Prasat Muang Sing. It stands on a raised laterite platform, and, like most Khmer temples, faces east, in alignment with the city of Angkor. To the northwest of the *prasat* lie the ruins of a similar, but smaller, edifice.

Although the Muang Sing temple complex looks Khmer, some art historians believe it was actually built by local artisans in imitation of the occupying Khmers – the sanctuary, for example, lacks the stylistic details that are normally associated with Khmer sites. It was probably built after the reign of Jayavarman VII (1181–1220) as the Khmer Empire began to decline, and its power in this region was fading. A museum at the site displays artifacts excavated here.

ENVIRONS: Southeast of Muang Sing is Ban Kao, a prehistoric settlement discovered in the 1940s by Dutch archaeologist van Heekeren, a prisoner on the Burma-Siam Railway. The **Ban Kao Museum** houses stone tools and ornaments.

▲ **Ban Kao Museum**
35 km (22 miles) W of Kanchanaburi.
○ Wed–Sat. ◪

Kanchanaburi ❻
กาญจนบุรี

Kanchanaburi province. ▨ 54,000. ▨ ▨ ▨ TAT, Saeng Chuto Rd, Kanchanaburi (034) 511200. ● daily. ◪ Khwae River Bridge Week (Nov/Dec).

THOUGH SURROUNDED by strikingly beautiful limestone hills and vast expanses of sugar cane, Kanchanaburi is best known for its associations with the infamous Burma-Siam Railway. Constructed in 1942–3 it crosses over the Khwae Yai River just to the north of Kanchanaburi town centre. At the small station beside the bridge are a number of steam locomotives dating from the period. There is also a memorial to those who died during the war, which was erected by the Japanese administration in 1944. Today, 77 km (47 miles) of the railway remain, and the trip along it from Kanchanaburi to Nam Tok is one of the most interesting in Thailand.

Sign, Kanchanaburi station

The building of the railway cost the lives of more than 100,000 Asian labourers and 12,000 Allied prisoners of war. The **Kanchanaburi War Cemetery**, containing the graves of almost 7,000, mostly British and Australian prisoners, is one of two war cemeteries in the town. This poignant place is immaculately maintained by the Commonwealth War Graves Commission.

The smaller of the two cemeteries, **Chung Kai Cemetery**, contains 1,740 graves, and lies on the north bank of the Khwae Noi River, a short ferry ride from the centre of town. Nearby is **Wat Tham Khao Pun**, overlooking the river and the Burma-Siam Railway, which at this point heads south towards Ban Kao and Prasat Muang Sing. In the grounds of the *wat* complex a network of narrow passages leads through a gaudily lit cave system filled with Buddha images.

In the **JEATH War Museum**, housed in Wat Chai Chumphon, visitors can see three replicas of the bamboo huts used to house prisoners of war in the camps that sprang up along the Burma-Siam Railway during the war. The huts display paintings, sketches and photographs of life in the camps and along the railway line. JEATH is an acronym for Japan, England, Australia and America, Thailand and Holland, some of

Steel bridge over the Khwae Yai River, Kanchanaburi

the countries whose nationals worked on the railway. Many survivors and victims' relatives visit Kanchanaburi each year.

Accommodation at Kanchanaburi includes a number of unusual river-side raft houses.

🏛 **Kanchanaburi War Cemetery**
Saeng Chuto Rd. ◯ daily.

🏛 **Chung Kai Cemetery**
Ban Kao Rd. ◯ daily.

🏛 **JEATH War Museum**
Wisuttharangsi Rd. ◯ daily. 📷

Farmers cultivating crops in the hills around Kanchanaburi

Chaloem Rattanakosin National Park ❼
อุทยานแห่งชาติเฉลิมรัตนโกสินทร์

Kanchanaburi province. Park HQ off Hwy 3086, 97 km (60 miles) NW of Kanchanaburi. 🛈 TAT (034) 511200; Forestry Dept (02) 579 0529 (inc bungalow bookings). 🚌 from Kanchanaburi to Nong Pru, then songthaew. ◯ daily. 📷

THIS BEAUTIFUL and isolated national park is one of Thailand's smallest, at just 59 sq km (23 sq miles). The main trail runs beside a stream which passes through a cavern, Tham Than Lot Noi, to emerge in a thickly forested, steep-sided ravine. The path continues for 2,500 m (8,200 ft), climbing steeply beside the Trai Trung falls to Tham Than Lot Yai, a limestone sink-hole, and a small Buddhist shrine. On weekday mornings, you may find that you are the only visitor in this delightful spot.

THE BRIDGE OVER THE KHWAE YAI RIVER AND THE BURMA-SIAM RAILWAY

The first railway bridge over the Khwae Yai River, near Kanchanaburi, was built of wood, using Allied and Asian slave labour. In 1943 it was abandoned for an iron bridge, which was repeatedly bombed and damaged by the US Air Force from late 1944. In 1945, after only a short period in service, the bridge was put out of commission. After the war this infamous river crossing was immortalized in David Lean's film, *The Bridge on the River Kwai* (1957).

The bridge was part of an immense project, the 414-km (255-mile) Burma-Siam Railway, conceived by the Japanese after the Allies blockaded sea routes in 1942. It ran from Nong Pladuk, 50 km (30 miles) southeast of Kanchanaburi, to Thanbyuzayat near the coast in Burma. Built under appalling conditions, it operated for only two years. Around 60,000 Allied prisoners of war and 300,000 Asian labourers were forced to work 18-hour shifts on its construction, with many losing their lives to cholera, malaria, malnutrition and, most tragically, to maltreatment. It is said that one man died for each sleeper laid. One reason for such a brutal regime was that the Japanese followed a samurai code. They despised the disgrace of surrender and treated the Allied prisoners of war as if they had forfeited all human rights. The present-day bridge at Kanchanaburi was rebuilt, as part of Japanese war reparations, with two girders from the Japan Bridge Com-

Painting by prisoner of war in the JEATH War Museum, Kanchanaburi

pany of Osaka. It has now become a place of pilgrimage for veterans and relatives of those who died. Kanchanaburi has two cemeteries and a museum; the exhibits in the latter present a particularly moving evocation of this extremely harrowing episode of World War II history.

Prisoners of war on the wooden bridge over the Khwae Yai River (c.1942–3)

The beautifully tended Chung Kai Cemetery, Kanchanaburi

The Chinese shrine of San Chao Pho, Suphan Buri

Suphan Buri **❽**
สุพรรณบุรี

Suphan Buri province. 👥 42,000.
🚌 🚆 **ℹ** TAT, Ayutthaya (035)
246077. 🎎 Don Chedi Fair (Jan).

LIKE MANY large towns in
this region, Suphan Buri
came to prominence with the
rise of Ayutthaya in the 14th
century. The attractive art and
architecture of the town are
known to few tourists.

Near the centre of town is
the beautiful *prang* of Wat
Phra Si Rattana Mahathat, restored in the Ayutthaya period
and again in the 20th century.
At Wat Pa Lelai, on the edge
of Suphan Buri, is a huge
Buddha image from the Dvaravati period *(see pp52–3)*. To
the east is San Chao Pho, a
colourful Chinese shrine. Wat
Phra Rup, on the other side of
the Suphan Buri River, houses
a reclining Buddha image and
a carved wooden Footprint of
the Buddha. The *bot* of nearby Wat Pratu San contains
striking 19th-century murals
of the Buddha's life.

ENVIRONS: The large white
monument of **Don Chedi**, 31
km (20 miles) from Suphan
Buri, marks the site of the battle of Nong Sarai, between the
Burmese and Thai forces led
by King Naresuan *(see p58)*.
The **U Thong National Museum** houses 6th–11th-century
Dvaravati artifacts, excavated
nearby, and Khmer art.

**🏛 U Thong National
Museum**
7 km (4 miles) SW of Suphan Buri.
⬜ daily. ⬛ public hols. 🎫

Ang Thong **❾**
อ่างทอง

Ang Thong province. 👥 23,000. 🚌
ℹ TAT, Ayutthaya (035) 246077.
🛵 daily.

THIS SMALL TOWN is a useful
base from which travellers
who are interested in Thai
images of the Buddha can
visit three little known but
rewarding sites nearby. To
the south of Ang Thong,
Wat Pa Mok houses a
reclining Buddha image
from the 15th century.
Wat Khun In Pramun
is to the northwest. In
its grounds is a huge
reclining Buddha im-
age, about 50 m (165
ft) long, dating from
the Ayutthaya period.

At **Wat Chaiyo Wora
Wihan**, to the north of
Ang Thong, a *wihan* houses a
third enormous, seated image
of the Buddha from the Rattanakosin period, called the
Phra Maha Phuttha Phim.

**Wat Pha Mok, which houses a 15th-
century Buddha, near Ang Thong**

Lop Buri **❿**
ลพบุรี

See pp164–5.

Phra Phutthabat **⓫**
พระพุทธบาท

Saraburi province. **ℹ** TAT, Lop Buri
(036) 422768. 🚌 from Saraburi,
then samlor. ⬜ 7am–6pm daily.
🎎 Phra Phutthabat Fair (Mar).

IN THE EARLY 17th century,
King Song Tham of Ayut-
thaya sent a group of monks
to Sri Lanka to pay homage to
a revered Footprint of the
Buddha. (According to legend,
these Footprints actually show
where the Lord Buddha
walked upon the Earth.) The
monks were surprised to be
told by the Sri Lankans that,
according to scriptures, there
was a Footprint in Thailand.
Song Tham, on hearing this,
ordered a search for the
Footprint. It was found
by a hunter pursuing a
wounded deer – the
animal vanished into the
undergrowth only to re-
emerge healed. On
closer inspection, the
hunter found a water-
filled pool shaped like
a footprint. He drank
from it and was mirac-
ulously cured of a skin
disease. The king, on
learning of this, had a
temple built on the site,
which subsequently became
one of the most sacred places
of worship in Thailand.

Today, the 1.5-m (5-ft) long
Footprint, Phra Phutthabat, lies
in an ornate *mondop*, restored
in the late 18th century after
the earlier buildings were destroyed by the Burmese in
1765. A museum here displays
offerings by pilgrims, who
flock to the sight each year.
Phra Phutthabat is also the
name of the small town here.

ENVIRONS: At **Phra Phuttha-
chai** ("Buddha's shadow"),
about 40 km (25 miles) southeast of Phra Phutthabat, a
faint Buddha image, probably
painted by a hermit, can be
seen on a cliff face. Pilgrims
often visit this site on the
journey to Phra Phutthabat.

**Bell, Phra
Phutthabat**

Gestures of the Buddha

Buddha images throughout Thailand for the most part follow strict rules laid down in the 3rd century AD. There are four basic postures: standing, sitting, walking and reclining; the first three are associated with daily activities of the Buddha, the last with the Buddha's final moments on earth as he achieved *nirvana*. These postures can be combined with hand and feet positions, to create a variety of attitudes *(mudras)* which represent key Buddhist themes. King Rama III (1824–51) drew up a list of 40 attitudes to be used by sculptors, but many of these are rare. Most images in Thailand represent a dozen or so attitudes, the seated image in *bhumisparsa mudra* occurring most frequently.

Exposition (vitarkha mudra) *symbolizes the first public discourse given by the Buddha, to five ascetics in a deer park in India. On this Sukhothai-era image, the thumb and forefinger form a circle – the "turning of the wheel of law" (see p27).*

TOUCHING THE EARTH

Bhumisparsa is the most common *mudra*. It symbolizes an important episode in the Buddha's life when he sat in meditation under a Bodhi tree in Bodh Gaya, India, refusing to move until he attained Enlightenment. While his enemy, Mara, offered temptations such as nubile maidens and feasts, the Buddha touched the ground to attract the attention of the Earth goddess, so that she could see his resistance. Just after this he achieved Enlightenment.

Right hand pointing to the Earth

Left hand resting in lap

Legs in lotus position

Meditation (dhyana mudra) *is signified with a sitting posture, shown by this modern Buddha image from Southern Thailand. Both hands are positioned palms up, the right over the left, as still practised by meditating Buddhists.*

Reassurance (abhaya mudra) *symbolizes the Buddha's offer of protection to his followers. The raised right hand is also representative of an episode in which the Buddha settled a heated dispute over water.*

Restraining the waters *is a variation of abhaya mudra. The two hands of this Ayutthayan Buddha image are held palms forwards, fingers pointing upwards. It refers to an episode when the Buddha calmed the floodwaters of the Nairanjana, a tributary of the Ganges in Northern India.*

Reclining Buddhas, such as this one at Ayutthaya, usually represent the point of parinirvana or ultimate nirvana.

Street-by-Street: Lop Buri ⓾

ลพบุรี

ONE OF THAILAND'S oldest cities, Lop Buri was known as Lavo in the Dvaravati period *(see pp52–3)* and subsequently became an important outpost of the Khmer Empire *(see pp254–5)*. The Khmer *prang* in the grounds of Wat Phra Si Rattana Mahathat, and those of Prang Sam Yot, date from this time. With the decline of the Khmer Empire and the rise of the Sukhothai Kingdom *(see pp54–5)*, Lop Buri struggled to retain its independence, until, in the 14th century, it was linked by marriage to the emerging state of Ayutthaya *(see pp58–9)*. It reached its political peak in the 17th century when the Ayutthayan King Narai (1656–88) briefly moved his capital here to avoid a threatened Dutch blockade. Today, the thriving modern town of Lop Buri lies to the east of the old city.

Wat Sao Thong Thong
The wihan at this wat was modified by King Narai so the buildng could be used as a Christian chapel – he replaced Thai windows with Western-style Gothic designs.

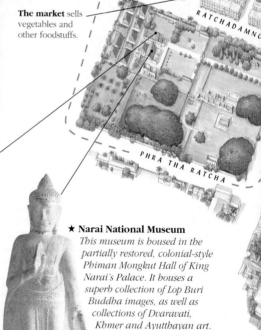

The market sells vegetables and other foodstuffs.

★ **King Narai's Palace**
Abandoned after Narai's death, parts of the palace, including the Chanthara Phisan Hall, were later restored by King Mongkut (see p61).

★ **Narai National Museum**
This museum is housed in the partially restored, colonial-style Phiman Mongkut Hall of King Narai's Palace. It houses a superb collection of Lop Buri Buddha images, as well as collections of Dvaravati, Khmer and Ayutthayan art.

STAR SIGHTS

★ **King Narai's Palace**

★ **Narai National Museum**

★ **Wat Phra Si Rattana Mahathat**

★ **Prang Sam Yot**

KEY

‒ ‒ ‒ Suggested route

Phaulkon Residence

This palace was built by King Narai for his favoured minister, the Greek Constantine Phaulkon. Phaulkon encouraged Narai to forge close ties with the French, often excluding other foreigners, though his hidden motive was to aid Louis XIV's attempt to convert Narai to Christianity. When this came to light it alarmed the Ayutthayan court; when Narai died in 1688 Phaulkon was executed (see p153).

Prang Khaek

This Hindu shrine has three brick towers. It is believed by some to date as far back as the 8th century.

WICHAYEN

RATCHADAMNOEN

PHRA YAM CHAMKAT

NA WAT

To railway station

★ Prang Sam Yot

The Lop Buri style was a variation, by local artisans, of already established Khmer art and architecture; this shrine is archetypal. The three prangs were originally consecrated as a Hindu shrine; Buddha images were added later to two of them.

★ Wat Phra Si Rattana Mahathat

This wat complex encloses ruins from two distinct eras. At its centre is a 12th-century, Khmer prang, decorated with finely detailed stucco work. The site also includes Ayutthayan chedis and a wihan added by King Narai.

0 metres 75
0 yards 75

Ayutthaya

พระนครศรีอยุธยา

Ayutthayan bracelet

T HE CITY OF AYUTTHAYA was founded around 1350 by Ramathibodi I (1351–69), who came here to escape an outbreak of smallpox at Lop Buri. By the early 15th century Ayutthaya had become a major power. Sukhothai *(see pp54–5)* fell to Ayutthaya in 1438. Foreign traders arrived in the early 16th century *(see pp152–3)* and much evidence of Ayutthaya's splendour comes from their accounts. In the early 18th century, after years of war, decline set in, and in 1767 the Burmese sacked the city. Today, the ruins stand among the modern buildings of the provincial town.

Stucco and brick *singhas* around the main *chedi* of Wat Thammikarat

🔲 Wat Mahathat

วัดมหาธาตุ

Naresuan Rd. 🔲 *daily.* 🖋
Wat Mahathat is one of the largest and most important *wat* complexes in Ayutthaya. It was probably founded in the late 14th century by King Borommaracha I (1370–88). Other buildings were added by his successor, Ramesuan (1388–95). The central *prang*, which has now collapsed, once stood 50 m (165 ft) high.

European-style Pisai Sayalak Tower, behind the Chan Kasem Palace

🔲 Wat Ratchaburana

วัดราชบูรณะ

Naresuan Rd. 🔲 *daily.* 🖋
Across the road from Wat Mahathat is Wat Ratchaburana, its *prang* now restored. It was built in the early 15th century by King Borommaracha II (1424–48) on the cremation site of his two brothers, who died in a power struggle. Both of them had wanted to succeed their father, Intharacha I (1409–24), to the throne. Rob-

bers looted the crypt in 1957 and escaped with a huge cache of gold artifacts, only a few of which were recovered. A steep, narrow staircase now descends to the crypt where visitors can see the faded remains of Ayutthayan frescoes *(see p56)*.

🔲 Chan Kasem Palace

วังจันทรเกษม

Uthong Rd, opposite the night market. 🔲 *daily.*
In the northeast corner of the main island stands the Chan Kasem Palace or Wang Na. It was built in 1577 by the illustrious Naresuan, the son of King Maha Thammaracha (1569–90), before he became king. When Naresuan came to the throne in 1590, the palace became his permanent residence. The buildings seen today, however, date from the reign of King Mongkut (1851–68), as the palace was razed by the Burmese in 1767. It houses a large collection of Buddha images and historical artifacts. Behind the Chan Kasem Palace is the **Pisai Sayalak Tower**, once used as an astronomical observatory by King Mongkut.

🔲 Wat Thammikarat

วัดธรรมิกราช

Off Uthong Rd. 🔲 *daily.* 🖋
At this picturesque site are the dilapidated remains of a large, early Ayutthayan, octagonal *chedi* surrounded by stucco and brick lions or *singhas*. Beside the *chedi* is the ruin of a *wihan*, slowly succumbing to weeds and trees. A beautiful U Thong Buddha head recovered from here is now in the Chao Sam Phraya National Museum *(see p168)*.

🔲 Wang Luang

วัดหลวง

Off Uthong Rd. 🔲 *daily.* 🖋
To the west of Wat Thammikarat is Wang Luang, the northern extension of the royal palace built by King Borommatrailokanat (1448–88) in the mid-15th century. Successive monarchs added a number of pavilions and halls. Wang Luang was razed by the Burmese in 1767. The best preserved of the buildings of the former royal palace is the **Trimuk Pavilion**. It was built during the reign of King Chulalongkorn (1868–1910) on the site of earlier foundations.

19th-century Trimuk Pavilion, in the grounds of Wang Luang

Wat Phra Si Sanphet

See pp168–9.

Wihan Phra Mongkhon Bophit

วิหารพระมงคลบพิตร

Off Klong Tho Rd. 🕒 *daily.* 📷

This *wat* contains one of Thailand's largest bronze Buddha images. Now gilded, it probably dates from the late 15th century, though it has undergone numerous restorations. In 1767 Burmese invaders destoyed much of the *wihan*, and damaged the image's head and right hand. The image was left open to the sky until the 1950s when the *wihan* was rebuilt.

Wat Phra Ram

วัดพระราม

Off Patone Rd. 🕒 *daily.* 📷

A chronicle relates that Wat Phra Ram was built in 1369 on the cremation site of King Ramathibodi (1351–69) by his son, Ramesuan. The elegant *prang* visible today, however, is the result of later renovation by King Borommatrailokanat (1448–88). The *prang* is decorated with *garudas*, *nagas* and walking Buddha images. Surrounding it are *wihans* and a *bot*. The *wat* casts beautiful reflections in nearby lily ponds.

15th-century, corncob-shaped *prang* at Wat Phra Ram

VISITORS' CHECKLIST

Phra Nakhon Si Ayutthaya province. 🏠 *71,000.* 🚉 Off Bang Ain Rd. 🚌 Off Naresuan Rd. 🚤 🛈 *TAT, Si Sanphet Rd, Ayutthaya (035) 246076.* 🕒 *daily.*

Wat Lokaya Sutharam

วัดโลกยสุธาราม

Off Klong Tho Rd. 🕒 *daily.* 📷

This *wat* is the site of a 42-m (140-ft) long, whitewashed reclining Buddha image. Large Buddha images such as this do not always depict the Buddha's death, but sometimes, as in this instance, an occasion when the Buddha grew 100 times in size to confront the demon Rahu. The image now lies in the open air, the original *wihan* having been destroyed by the Burmese; 24 octagonal pillars are all that remain of this *wihan*. The *wat* also houses the ruins of a *bot* and *chedis*.

AYUTTHAYA TOWN CENTRE

Ayutthaya Historical Study Centre ⑧
Chan Kasem Palace ⑫
Chao Sam Phraya National Museum ⑦
St Joseph's Church ⑮
Wang Luang ②
Wat Chai Watthanaram ⑭
Wat Lokaya Sutharam ①
Wat Mahathat ⑨

Wat Na Phra Men ⑬
Wat Phanan Choeng ⑰
Wat Phra Ram ⑥
Wat Phra Si Sanphet ④
Wat Phutthaisawan ⑯
Wat Ratchaburana ⑩
Wat Suwan Dararam ⑪
Wat Thammikarat ③
Wihan Phra Mongkhon Bophit ⑤

KEY

🚉 Railway station

🚌 Coach station

🚤 Riverboat pier

🛈 Tourist information

🏛 Wat

| 0 metres | 250 |
| 0 yards | 250 |

🏠 Chao Sam Phraya National Museum

พิพิธภัณฑ์เจ้าสามพระยา

Intersection of Rotchana Rd and Si Sanphet Rd. ⬚ *daily.* 🎫

Among the exhibits at this museum is a small collection of magnificent gold artifacts, including a jewel-encrusted sword, gold slippers and jewellery. Discovered in the crypt of Wat Ratchaburana's central *prang* when it was looted in 1957, they are among

Deity on wooden door-panel

the few items from the *wat* to have survived the sack of Ayutthaya by the Burmese *(see pp58–9)*. Other artifacts exhibited in the museum include bronze Buddha images and wooden door panels from *wats* around Ayutthaya.

🏠 Ayutthaya Historical Study Centre

ศูนย์ศึกษาประวัติศาสตร์อยุธยา

Rotchana Rd. ⬚ *daily.* 🎫

This study centre houses interesting audio-visual displays depicting Ayutthaya's history and trading relations. There is also a reconstructed model of Wat Phra Si Sanphet. Funded by the Japanese government, the centre stands in what was the Japanese quarter at the time when Ayutthaya was at the height of its power.

🏯 Wat Suwan Dararam

วัดสุวรรณดาราราม

Uthong Rd. ⬚ *daily.*

This temple was completely destroyed by the Burmese but later rebuilt by Rama I (1782–1809). The *ubosot* is usually locked, but it is worth requesting the key to see the murals commissioned by Rama VII (1925–35), depicting scenes from the time of King Naresuan. Among them is a mural of the Battle of Nong Sarai, which was fought against the Burmese in 1593 *(see p58)*.

Nearby is a section of the old city defences, Phom Phet, which were a strategically important look-out post over the Chao Phraya River.

Wat Phra Si Sanphet

วัดพระศรีสรรเพชญ์

FOUNDED BY KING BOROMMATRAILOKANAT during the 15th century as a state temple, Wat Phra Si Sanphet was later added to by his son, Ramathibodi II, who built two *chedis* to house the relics of his father and brother. The third *chedi* was built by Borommaracha IV to house the remains of Ramathibodi II. The site was extended by subsequent rulers until the Burmese sack of 1767 *(see pp58–9)*. Partially renovated in the 20th century, many of its treasures are now kept in museums.

The Prasat Phra Narai was cruciform in shape. All that remains of it today are the foundations.

The ashes of Ramathibodi II (1491–1529) are enshrined in this *chedi*, built in the mid-16th century by Borommaracha IV.

RECONSTRUCTION

Overgrown with weeds and trees until the beginning of the 20th century, Wat Phra Si Sanphet is still a ruin, albeit partially restored. This artist's impression gives an idea of its glory before it was sacked.

Drawing of Chedis
Lying empty after it was sacked by the Burmese, Ayutthaya became the focus of scholarly interest. Henri Mouhot, who drew this image, was one of many late 19th-century visitors. Wat Phra Si Sanphet has been under the protection of the Thai Fine Arts Department since 1927.

VISITORS' CHECKLIST

Off Si Sanphet Rd, Ayutthaya.
⬚ 9am–5pm daily. 📷

Wooden Door
This door was probably once situated in the entrance to Wihan Phra Si Sanphet. It dates from the reign of Rama-thibodi II. A collection of such doors is displayed in the Chao Sam Phraya Museum.

Three Chedis
Apart from the ashes of kings, caskets of precious Buddha images and royal regalia were buried in the chedis' *central chambers.*

The ashes of Borommaracha III
(1463–88), the brother of Ramathi-bodi II, are buried in this *chedi.*

Entrance to Chedi
The entrance chamber to the chedi *is a scaled down version of a Khmer mandapa (entrance chamber to a Khmer sanctuary). Ayutthayan builders modified many older architectural features, such as Khmer prangs and Sri Lankan bell-shaped chedis.*

The ashes of Boromma-trailokanat (1448–88) are buried in this *chedi,* the only one to survive the Burmese sack. The other two had to be restored.

Stairway leading to entrance of hollow *chedi*

A Footprint of the Lord Buddha was housed in this elegant, spired *mondop.*

Wihan Phra Si Sanphet
The main wihan – *the entrance to the* wat – *once housed the principal Buddha image of Phra Si Sanphet.*

Exploring Ayutthaya: the Outer Sites

Buddha, Wat Na Phra Men

THE CENTRAL ISLAND of Ayutthaya stands at the confluence of the Chao Phraya, Lop Buri and Pasak rivers. The town's most imposing sites are to be found on the central island. However, a short *samlor* ride, by bridge, over any of the rivers, which more or less encircle it, will bring you to many more sites of interest. Wat Na Phra Men is one of Ayutthaya's most beautiful *wats*, while St Joseph's Church offers a glimpse of Ayutthaya's connections with Western trading powers *(see pp152–3)* during the city's heyday. The main part of modern Ayutthaya sprawls to the east of the island, over the Pasak River and beyond.

A roundup of wild elephants at the elephant kraal (1890)

Wat Na Phra Men
วัดหน้าพระเมรุ
Opp Royal Palace, nr Sa Bua Canal. (035) 252163. ☐ *daily.*
Across a bridge to the north of the main island is Wat Na Phra Men, one of the most beautiful of Ayutthaya's monasteries, and one of the few to survive the Burmese sacking of the city in 1767 *(see p56)*. Thought to date from the reign of Intharacha II (1488–91), it was restored during the reign of King Borommakot (1733–58), and again in the mid-19th century. In the *wihan* is a Dvaravati, seated Buddha image, Phra Kanthararat, which was moved here from Nakhon Pathom in the mid-16th century. The murals covering the *wihan* walls have now almost completely disappeared. Its doors are from the early 19th century. In the adjacent *bot* is a gilded Buddha image, probably from the reign of King Prasat Thong (1629–56).

Elephant Kraal
พระที่นั่งเพนียด
N of main island. ☐ *daily.*
Further to the north is the elephant kraal. It is thought that the original structure, built by King Yot Fa (1547–8), stood within the confines of the old city wall. The present kraal, built later, was in use well into the 19th century – wild elephants would be driven here for training as pack animals or war mounts for senior officers. In the middle of the stockade is a shrine where the elephant guardian is thought to live.

Wat Phu Khao Thong
วัดภูเขาทอง
2 km (1 mile) W on Hwy 309. ☐ *daily.*
To the west, the original *chedi* of Phu Khao Thong was constructed by King Bayinnaung of Burma to celebrate his capture of Ayutthaya in 1569. Additions were made in 1744–5 by the Thai King Borommakot.

Wat Chai Watthanaram
วัดไชยวัฒนาราม
W bank of Chao Phraya river, SW of main island. ☐ *daily.*
This *wat* was built by King Prasat Thong in 1630. The central *prang* is surrounded by eight smaller ones, decorated with stucco reliefs depicting images such as the Buddha preaching to his mother in the Tavatimsa Heaven. All the *prangs* have been restored.

St Joseph's Church
โบสถ์เซนต์ยอเซฟ
SW of main island on the Chao Phraya River. ☐ *daily.*
St Joseph's, overlooking the Chao Phraya River, has been the site of Catholic worship for over 300 years. The original 17th-century structure was destroyed by the Burmese in 1767. The present church was built during the 19th century.

Wat Phutthaisawan
วัดพุทไธศวรรย์
S of main island. ☐ *daily.*
East from St Joseph's is Wat Phutthaisawan, also located on the river bank. It has a restored 14th-century *prang* surrounded by a cloister filled with Buddha images.

Wat Kuti Dao
วัดกุฎีดาว
E of main island. ☐ *daily.*
This *wat* originally dated from the early Ayutthaya period, but the ruins here today are of an 18th-century renovation by King Phumintharacha. The *chedi* is flanked by a *wihan* and a *bot* with distinctive arched windows and doors.

Bell-shaped *chedi*, part of the ruined Wat Kuti Dao

Reclining Buddha in a ruined *wihan* at Wat Yai Chai Mongkhon

🕍 Wat Pradu Songtham
วัดประดู่ทรงธรรม
N of railway station, E of main island.
⭘ *daily.*
Inside the *wihan* of Wat Pradu Songtham are the remains of murals dating from the early Rattanakosin period *(see p31).* These recount the life of the Buddha, and also show images of daily life, including one of a performance of the Ramakien at a fair. Outside is a bell tower topped by a small *chedi* from the late Ayutthaya period.

🕍 Wat Maheyong
วัดมเหยงค์
E of main island. ⭘ *daily.*
The partially reconstructed ruins of Wat Maheyong date from the reign of King Borommaracha II (1424–48). The principal, bell-shaped *chedi* shows a clear stylistic link with earlier Sukhothai *chedis*, while all around the rectangular base are the remnants of stucco elephants. Other *chedis* at this site also show Sukhothai influence.

🕍 Wat Yai Chai Mongkhon
วัดใหญ่ไชยมงคล
SE of main island. ⭘ *daily.* 🎫
The *chedi* here, one of the largest in Ayutthaya, was built by King Naresuan (1590–1605) to celebrate his victory over the Burmese at Nong Sarai in 1593 *(see pp58–9).* Flanking steps up to the *chedi* are two *mondops* housing seated Buddha images. On the northeast side of the *wat* is a ruined *wihan* containing a reclining Buddha.

🕍 Wat Phanan Choeng
วัดพนัญเชิง
SE of main island. ⭘ *daily.*
This *wat* has been renovated over the years and houses the large, 14th-century, seated image of Phra Chao Phanan Choeng. The *wihan* was built in the mid-19th century.

🏛 Ban Yipun
บ้านญี่ปุ่น
SE of main island on Hwy 3059.
⭘ *daily.* 🎫
Once the site of a 17th-century Japanese settlement, today a museum here displays exhibits that explain Ayutthaya's foreign relations at the time.

Bang Pa-in ⑬
บางปะอิน

Nakhon Si Ayutthaya province.
🚶 *5,000.* 🚌 🚐 🚆 ℹ *TAT, Ayutthaya (035) 246076.* ⭘ *daily.*

Visitors to Bang Pa-in stop off, for the most part, just to visit **Bang Pa-in Palace**, whose exuberant, 19th-century buildings stand in stark contrast to nearby Ayutthaya. It is thought that a royal palace was first built at Bang Pa-in by King Prasat Thong (1629–56), to mark the birth of his son and successor, King Narai. With the defeat of Ayutthaya by the Burmese in 1767 the site fell into ruin; the present buildings date from the reigns of Mongkut (1851–68) and Chulalongkorn (1868–1910).

The beautiful pavilion, Phra Thinang Aisawan Thipha-at ("divine seat of personal freedom"), at the centre of an ornamental lake, was built for Chulalongkorn in 1876 together with the Phra Thinang Warophat Phiman ("excellent and shining abode"), to the left. Behind are the terracotta- and white-striped lookout tower, Ho Withun Thasana built by Chulalongkorn in 1881, and the Chinese-style mansion, Phra Thinang Wehat Chamrun, built as a gift for him by an association of Chinese merchants in 1889. Visitors can cross a canal by cable car to Wat Niwet Tham Prawat, which was built by Chulalongkorn in 1877–8.

🏛 Bang Pa-in Palace
พระราชวังบางปะอิน
Bang Pa-in district. ⭘ *daily.* 🎫

The Phra Thinang Aisawan Thipha-at pavilion, Bang Pa-in Palace

Khao Yai National Park

อุทยานแห่งชาติเขาใหญ่

Begonia flower

WHEN IT WAS ESTABLISHED in 1962, Khao Yai was Thailand's sole national park. Today there are well over 100 parks but this one still remains popular. Sprawling over 2,000 sq km (770 sq miles), the park encompasses a wide variety of habitats, including sub-montane evergreen forests and grasslands. There are also several mountains of around 1,000 m (3,300 ft), including Khao Khieo, south of the park headquarters. Wildlife is abundant and includes many endangered mammals such as elephants, gibbons, tigers, leopards and Malaysian sun bears, as well as more than 300 bird species. Visitors to the park are advised to hire a guide for trips to more remote areas.

White-Handed Gibbon
These tailless apes use their long arms to move swiftly and agilely through the trees.

SARABURI

Elephant salt lick

Watchtower

Watchtower

Radar station

Khao Khieo 1,287 m (4,223 ft)

NAKHON NAYOK

BANGKOK

Endangered Species
Khao Yai is home to a few of the 500 or so tigers left in Thailand. These noble animals can be found surprisingly close to the park's headquarters; visitors should treat them with respect.

Siamese Fireback Pheasant
Thailand's national bird, this pheasant spends its days on the ground where it feeds on small insects, seeds and fruit. It roosts at night in the trees.

Deciduous forest
grows in the park's low-lying areas.

Haeo Suwat Waterfall
Located along the upper reaches of the Lam Takhong River, this waterfall is one of many dotted around Khao Yai. From March to May each year many varieties of orchids can be seen flowering around the waterfall. Elephants have been known to drown while crossing near waterfalls when the rains are very heavy.

Sub-Montane Evergreen Forest

This type of forest often contains deciduous trees such as chestnuts. It grows at Khao Yai's highest altitudes, 1,000 m (3,300 ft) to 1,351 m (4,450 ft) above sea level.

VISITORS' CHECKLIST

Khorat, Nakhon Nayok, Saraburi and Prachin Buri provinces. Park HQ off Hwy 1, NE of Bangkok. ■ TAT, Khorat (044) 213666; Forestry Dept (02) 579 0529 (inc bungalow bookings). ▤ Pak Chong, then bus or songthaew. ● sometimes during heavy rainfall. ◪ ◪ ▯

KHORAT

● **PAK CHONG**

Sambar Stag

Sambar are the largest species of deer in Thailand and are primarily forest dwellers. Though hunted by tigers and leopards, humans are its main predator. It is now common only in well protected conservation areas.

Semi-evergreen rainforest can be seen above 600 m (1,950 ft).

▲ Khao Kamphaeng 974 m (3,196 ft)

▲ Khao Wong 146 m (479 ft)

Earthball Fungus

This parasitic fungus is found in humid evergreen forests all over Southeast Asia. Like many parasitic plants, its presence encourages the growth of its host.

PRACHIN BURI

0 kilometres   10

0 miles   10

KEY

═══	Motorway
═══	Major road
═══	Minor road
▬ ▬	Park border
■	Park headquarters
Ⓐ	Camping and bungalows
☆	Viewpoint

Lam Takhong River

Rainfall in Khao Yai National Park is usually in excess of 3,000 mm (120 inches) per year. Streams swollen by the rains flow off forested slopes forming rivers, among them the Lam Takhong River. Wildlife living around this river includes kingfishers, cormorants, elephants and macaques.

NORTH CENTRAL PLAINS

THE FURTHER NORTH *the visitor travels through the Central Plains the more sparsely populated the countryside becomes – the landscape here is typified by gentle, rolling hills and rice farms. There are few interesting modern cities in this region. Its major attractions are ancient city ruins, relics of an illustrious past when competing princedoms and city-states fought each other for land and power.*

Visitors to Thailand travelling north from Bangkok tend not to stop off in the North Central Plains, but instead press on to the major destination of Thailand's second city, Chiang Mai. However, some of the most fascinating ruins in Southeast Asia are found here.

In the 13th century, during the reign of King Ramkamhaeng *(see p54)*, one city, Sukhothai, came to dominate the region to such an extent that its influence was felt far beyond Thailand's present boundaries. But its power was shortlived and by the mid-14th century the region was once more a collection of fiefdoms. The ruins the kingdom left behind at Sukhothai, and at its satellite cities of Kamphaeng Phet and Si Satchanalai, still inspire wonder. Recently they have been extensively restored and turned into well managed historical parks.

Other places of interest in the region include the prosperous trading centre Phitsanulok, which is at the heart of a transport network connecting the region to Bangkok and the North. This, and other towns, support a mainly rural, local rice-farming economy. The hillier areas, in the west and northeast of the region, are the setting for a number of national parks and wildlife sanctuaries. These provide a much needed refuge for endangered plant and animal species *(see pp24–5)* whose habitats are threatened by the impact of illegal logging and the widespread loss of land to agriculture.

Around Mae Sot the influence of Burma is felt; the town is characterized by Burmese architecture, and a common sight is Karen and Shan tribespeople and Burmese who cross the border at this point to trade.

Farmer raking unhusked rice; a typical rural scene in the North Central Plains

◁ Reclining and sitting Buddha images at Wat Phra Kaeo, Kamphaeng Phet

Exploring the North Central Plains

THIS PART OF THE COUNTRY acts as a bridge between the crowded heartland of modern Thailand to the immediate south, and the rolling hills of the North. The region has no big cities, and the majority of tourists do no more than overnight in small, provincial towns near the magnificent ruins of ancient Sukhothai, the first Thai capital. Predominantly, this is rice-farming country, flanked to the east, north and west by hills. National parks in some of the hilly areas help protect endangered flora and fauna. Magnificent forest scenery and spectacular waterfalls can be found along the western border with Burma, around Mae Sot and remote Umphang. Here, a hint of Burma spills across the border in the shape of Karen and Shan tribespeople and Burmese architecture, goods and food.

Buddha under *naga* at Wat Chumphon Khiri, Mae Sot

SEE ALSO

- ***Where to Stay*** pp392–3
- ***Where to Eat*** pp416–17

KEY

▬▬▬	Major road
▬▬▬	Minor road
▬▬▬	Scenic route
▬▬▬	River
☀	Viewpoint

*Map labels:*
Lampang
Chiang Mai
SI SATCHANAL
SI SATCHANALAI
CHALIEN
HISTORICAL PAR
Bhumibol
Reservoir
SUKHOTHA
HISTORICA
PAR
TAKSIN
MAHARAT
NATIONAL
PARK
TAK
LAN SANG
NATIONAL
PARK
MAE SOT
Ping
KAMPHAENG PHET
Moi
KHLONG LAN NATIONAL PARK
UMPHANG
MAE WONG
NATIONAL
PARK
UMPHANG
WILDLIFE
SANCTUARY

Wat Traphang Thong, a monastery surrounded by a lotus-filled pond at Sukhothai Historical Park

Prang of Wat Phra Si Rattana Mahathat, a 14th-century temple at Phitsanulok

0 kilometres 25

0 miles 25

GETTING AROUND

Sukhothai Historical Park is on the itineraries of some tour companies. However, most visitors use public transport for sights in the region. Phitsanulok, an important transport hub, is the only major town in the region that is served by the regular train service connecting Bangkok to the North. It also has a small airport, as do Mae Sot and Sukhothai. Highway 1 passes through Kamphaeng Phet and Tak. Local buses run to all towns, and a network of main roads connect nearly all the sights. Only Umphang remains isolated, at the end of a spectacular, winding road from Mae Sot.

SIGHTS AT A GLANCE

Kamphaeng Phet **5**
Khlong Lan National Park **4**
Mae Sot **1**
Phitsanulok **8**
Si Satchanalai-Chalieng Historical Park pp188–90 **7**
Sukhothai Historical Park pp184–7 **6**
Tak **2**
Thung Salaeng Luang National Park **9**
Umphang **3**

Wat Chumphon Khiri, Mae Sot, Tak province

Mae Sot ❶
แม่สอด

Tak province. 👤 70,000. ✈ 🚌
ℹ TAT, Tak (055) 514341. 🏪 daily.

I N THE mid-19th century
Burmese and Shan mer-
chants, crossing the Moei
River from Burma in the west,
helped to establish Mae Sot
as a prosperous market town.
In more recent years, trade in
Burmese hard woods and
gemstones, both legal and
smuggled, has brought considerable wealth to this small
town. Today Mae Sot retains
the feel of a frontier town and
makes a relaxing stopover for
travellers. Gem traders, usually
ethnic Chinese, can often be
seen huddled on Mae Sot's
pavements, negoti-
ating with buyers
from Bangkok and
other parts of Thai-
land. Because of its
location and trading
history, Mae Sot has
a distinct Burmese
flavour, evident in
architecture and
market goods.

Trilingual shop
signs can be seen on
the main streets,
Burmese-language
publications are sold
in the shops, and
Burmese people
wearing traditional
sarongs (lungis) can
be seen walking
along the streets.
During the morning
food market – one of
Thailand's most picturesque
and characterful – Karen and
Burmese traders haggle with
Thais and Indians.

North of the market is **Wat
Chumphon Khiri**, which
has a magnificent Burmese
chedi decorated with golden
mosaic tiles. On the southeast
side of town is the Muslim
quarter; at its centre is the
small **Nurul Islam Mosque**.

Dotted around the town are
a number of other temples that
have both Karen and Shan
characteristics.

ENVIRONS: Some 5 km (3
miles) west of Mae Sot is **Wat
Thai Watthanaram**. In the
rear courtyard is a huge,
Burmese-style, reclining
Buddha image built in 1993
and a gallery of 28 seated
Buddha images. A further 1
km (1,100 yards) beyond Wat
Thai Watthanaram, a bridge
over the Moei River (built in
the mid-1990s) links Mae Sot
to the Burmese border town of
Myawadi. Clustered around the
foot of the bridge is a large
market selling an odd mix of
Thai, Burmese, Indonesian and
Chinese goods.

South of Mae Sot are the **Pha
Charoen falls**, a popular spot
for picnicking and bathing.

**Monks in the grounds of Wat Bot
Mani Sibunruang, Tak**

Tak ❷
ตาก

Tak province. 👤 48,000. ✈ 🚌
ℹ TAT, Mahatthaibamrung Rd, Tak
(055) 514341. 🏪 daily.

D URING MUCH of the 13th
century, Tak was a western
outpost of the Sukhothai
Kingdom. After the death of
King Ramkamhaeng and the

Reclining, Burmese-style Buddha in the courtyard of Wat Thai Watthanaram, near Mae Sot

Umphang ❸
อุ้มผาง

Tak province. ⛰ *20,000.* 🚌 *to Mae Sot, then songthaew.* ℹ *TAT, Tak (055) 514341.* 📅 *daily.*

P ART OF UMPHANG'S charm lies in the journey, as the road from Mae Sot is one of Thailand's most scenic. The village – its population consisting largely of Karen tribespeople – is surrounded by the lush forests of **Umphang Wildlife Sanctuary**, rich in bird life and small mammals. In recent years Umphang has become popular for rafting, hiking and elephant treks, but its isolation has kept most of the tourist hordes away. Here too are many cascades and rapids (including one of the country's highest waterfalls, **Thi Lo Su**), caves and Karen settlements. Several agencies in Umphang or Mae Sot can arrange treks. Visitors should avoid school holidays, when this region is crowded and accommodation scarce.

🏕 Umphang Wildlife Sanctuary
150 km (93 miles) S of Mae Sot on Hwy 1090. ℹ *Forestry Dept (02) 579 0529.* 🏕

One of many waterfalls in the **Umphang Wildlife Sanctuary**

subsequent collapse of the Sukhothai Empire *(see pp54–5)*, the town came under the influence of the Lanna Kingdom *(see pp58–9)* to the north. Today Tak sprawls along the left bank of the Ping River and much of the Lanna influence can still be seen in the teak houses hidden away in quiet lanes at the southern end of town. The houses here date from the late 19th and early 20th centuries.

Wat Bot Mani Sibunruang also shows Northern influences with its finely decorated, Lanna-style *bot* and a small *sala* containing a much revered Buddha image called Luang Pho Phutthanom.

Nearby is a statue of King Taksin, a former governor of Tak, who, after the sacking of Ayutthaya by the Burmese in 1767, established a new capital at Thon Buri, now part of Bangkok *(see pp60–1)*.

ENVIRONS: The 105-sq km (40-sq mile) **Lan Sang National Park** has tracks leading to several beautiful waterfalls. These are best visited during or soon after the rainy season *(see pp22–3)*; at other times of year there is little water. To the north of Lan Sang National Park is the **Taksin Maharat National Park**, the highlight of which is a steeply descending trail to the huge *ton krabak yai* or big krabak tree, which is some 50 m (165 ft) tall, and

has a girth of 16 m (50 ft). The park offers bird-watching opportunities, boasting a variety of species including the tiger shrike and forest wagtail. Also in the park are the nine-tiered Mae Ya falls.

🏕 Lan Sang National Park
20 km (12 miles) W of Tak, off Hwy 105. 🏕

🏕 Taksin Maharat National Park
15 km (9 miles) W of Tak, off Hwy 105. ℹ *Forestry Dept (02) 579 0529.* 🏕

THAILAND-BURMA BORDER REFUGEES

Scattered along Thailand's western border are more than 30 refugee camps, where about 100,000 Karen and other ethnic groups shelter from the totalitarian regime in Burma (Myanmar). The Karen tribespeople, who have long occupied an area straddling Burma and Thailand, are Burma's largest ethnic minority. The British were supposed to grant the Karen an autonomous homeland within Burma after World War II, but this did not happen. Following pro-democracy demonstrations in Burma in 1988, and the subsequent crack down, opposition MPs and ethnic minorities fled east to refugee villages. It is in such villages that the Karen organize their struggle for an independent state. The Burmese army sporadically ventures into Thailand, attacking and shelling Karen settlements. The Thai government does not openly condemn Burma, and the Thai army does not usually intervene on behalf of the Karen.

Boy soldiers in the rebel army of the Karen tribespeople

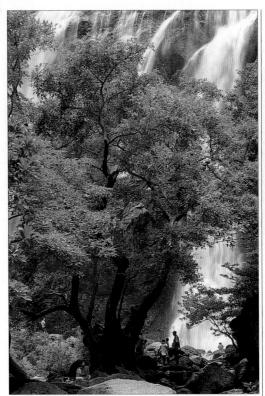
Waterfall in Khlong Lan National Park, Kamphaeng Phet province

Khlong Lan National Park ④

อุทยานแห่งชาติคลองลาน

Kamphaeng Phet province. Park HQ 6 km (4 miles) off Hwy 1117, S of Kamphaeng Phet. *TAT, Tak (055) 514341; Forestry Dept (02) 579 0529 (inc bungalow bookings).* from Kamphaeng Phet.

THIS 300-SQ KM (116-sq mile) national park was gazetted in 1982. Formerly, the area was controlled by Communist insurgents, and inhabited by a number of hill tribes. Initially the tribes lived within the park but were later relocated because they were regarded as a threat to the wildlife, which includes gaur, tiger and the Asiatic black bear.

The highlight of the park is the Khlong Lan waterfall, which is easily accessible from the park headquarters. It falls 95 m (310 ft) into a pool ideal for a refreshing swim. At the foot of the road leading up to the waterfall is a small market selling Hmong handicrafts – a government rehabilitation scheme for the hill tribes relocated from the park.

The adjacent **Mae Wong National Park** is good for hiking and bird-watching, and there are some facilities for visitors. Until the late 1980s it was populated by Hmong, who have also been relocated as part of ongoing conservation measures. Park staff confirm that the number of birds and mammals is steadily increasing. An old road running through the centre of the park is now overgrown, but it does make a good walking trail. Simple accommodation in bungalows is available near the park headquarters.

✗ Mae Wong National Park
Park HQ SW of Kamphaeng Phet, off Hwy 1, 60 km (37 miles) along Hwy 1242. *Forestry Dept (02) 579 0529 (inc bungalow bookings).*

Kamphaeng Phet ⑤

กำแพงเพชร

Kamphaeng Phet province. *29,000. TAT, Tak (055) 514341. daily. Nop Phra-Len Plang (Feb), Kluay Khai Muang Kamphaeng (Sep).*

THERE HAS BEEN a settlement at this site on the banks of the Ping River since the 11th century, when a northern prince, fleeing a Burmese attack in the area of present-day Fang *(see p232)*, brought his followers here. The community initially survived as an outpost of the Khmer Empire *(see p52)* and, during the 13th century, as part of the Sukhothai Kingdom.

On the east bank lie the impressive remains of the **Old City**, dating from the early 15th century, and which once formed part of a satellite city to the mighty Sukhothai *(see pp184–7)*. Located within its walls is the **Kamphaeng Phet National Museum**. In this collection are several fine 16th-century bronzes of Hindu deities, including a standing image of Shiva and torsos of Vishnu and Lakshmi. There are also stucco and terracotta fragments from Kamphaeng Phet's many ruins.

The Old City walls also enclose two important ruins from the late Sukhothai period. Close to the National Museum, **Wat Phra Kaeo** is the Old City's largest site, containing the ruins of several *wihans*, a

Renovated stone elephant at Wat Phra Kaeo, Kamphaeng Phet

Kamphaeng Phet National Museum and surrounding gardens

bot at the eastern end, a *chedi* from the late Sukhothai period and the laterite cores of a number of Buddha images. At the western end of the site are three more partly restored Buddha images. Neighbouring **Wat Phra That** has a fine late Sukhothai, octagonal-based *chedi*. One admission charge covers all ruins in the Old City.

The modern town of Kamphaeng Phet, for the most part, sprawls to the south of the Old City. It mostly comprises commercial buildings, though it also has a riverside park and a few traditional wooden houses, as well as some tourist-oriented facilities.

A *samlor* ride northwest of the Old City are the **Aranyik Ruins**, the area of many forest *wats* once used by a meditational order called the Forest Dwelling Sect. Built during the 14th–16th centuries, the sheer number of ruins at Aranyik attest to the popularity of the sect, which achieved prominence in Thailand during the Sukhothai era. With the assistance of UNESCO, parts of the site have now been restored and landscaped.

The *wihan* at Wat Phra Non, near the entrance, once contained a large reclining Buddha, but this is so badly damaged as to be almost indiscernible. Nevertheless, a number of laterite columns from the *wihan* are still standing. On each side of the *mondop* at Wat Phra Si Iriyabot are images of the Buddha in different postures, though all are damaged. The standing

Buddha on the west side has been partially restored. In the ruined *bot* of Wat Sing (found in the northern part of the Aranyik site) is the laterite core of a Buddha image.

Most impressive of the Aranyik *wats* is **Wat Chang Rop**, consisting mostly of the remains of a very large, square-based *chedi*, flanked by the forequarters of some elephants in laterite. On a few of these, the original stucco decoration has been restored. However, little of the Sri Lankan-style bell-shaped *chedi* is still standing. Among two dozen or so other sites dotted around Aranyik, many of them

scarcely visible in thick undergrowth, Wat Awat Yai is one of the few now cleared of vegetation.

Back in the modern part of town, other half-forgotten monuments, such as the Sukhothai brick *chedi* of **Wat Kalothai**, can be seen tucked away in quiet lanes. Many such sites have now fallen into considerable disrepair but their sheer quantity is an indication of the importance of Kamphaeng Phet during the Sukhothai and Ayutthaya periods.

West of the city, the large, white Burmese-style *chedi* of **Wat Phra Boromathat** was built in the late 19th century on the site of three 13th–14th century *chedis*, the earliest of which was constructed by King Si Intharathit of Sukhothai (c.1240–70) to house some relics of the Lord Buddha. Also to the west are the laterite walls of **Thung Setthi Fort**, which once protected this side of the city.

🛕 **Kamphaeng Phet National Museum**
Old City. ☐ *Wed–Sun.*
● *public hols.* 🎫
🏛 **Aranyik Ruins**
NW of Old City. ☐ *daily.* 🎫
🏰 **Thung Setthi Fort**
Off Hwy 1, W of town. ☐ *daily.*

KAMPHAENG PHET'S HISTORICAL SITES

SUKHOTHAI

KEY

● Wat Chang Rop

Wat Awat Yai ●

▓▓ City walls

↖ TAK   ARANYIK

● Wat Sing

Wat Phra Si Iriyabot ●

● Wat Phra Non

OLD CITY

Thung Setthi Fort ●

● Wat Phra Kaeo

Wat Phra Boromathat ●   ● Wat Phra That

Kamphaeng Phet National Museum

0 metres   500

0 yards   500

Wat Kalothai ●

↓ NAKHON SAWAN

Sukhothai Historical Park ❻

อุทยานประวัติศาสตร์สุโขทัย

Buddha, Wat Traphang Ngoen

T HE UNESCO WORLD HERITAGE site of Old Sukhothai lies to the west of the modern town. It is a potent reminder of the ancient Sukhothai Kingdom, which arose in the early 13th century from what had been a distant outpost of the Khmer Empire. Under the leadership of the Tai warrior King Ramkamhaeng, the city came to dominate the Central Plains *(see pp54–5)*. The abandoned city that can be seen today is the best preserved and most popular sight in Central Thailand. On-going restoration has revealed the amazing symmetry of its layout and offers the visitor a remarkable insight into a time when Thai art and culture reached its apex.

Exploring Sukhothai Historical Park

The site of Old Sukhothai has around 40 temple complexes spread over an area of about 70 sq km (28 sq miles). At its centre is the walled Royal City, protected by moats and ramparts. Many of the most important ruins are within this inner compound. The layout of Old Sukhothai, as with many major Thai cities *(muangs)*, follows fixed principles: a large, central

wat complex surrounded concentrically by walls, river, rice fields and, beyond, forested mountains. Another example of this, on a smaller scale, is Si Satchanalai *(see pp54–5)*.

One way to see the ruins of the Royal City is by bicycle: shops beside the old east gate hire them by the day for a small fee. A quick test ride is advised as some are in poor condition, and an early start is recommended so as to avoid the mid-day heat.

The Royal City

Entering from the east, the first *wat* within the city walls is Wat Traphang Thong, which is situated on an islet in a small lotus-filled lake. The Sri Lankan-style *chedi* dates from the mid-14th century, and a small *mondop* beside it enshrines a stone Footprint of the Buddha, still worshipped by resident monks.

The **Ramkamhaeng National Museum** houses photographs, taken around

Khmer-style, laterite *prangs*, part of Wat Si Sawai

PLAN OF OLD SUKHOTHAI

- Wat Phra Phai Luang
- Wat Si Chum
- TAK
- Wat Saphan Hin
- Wat Sorasak
- San Ta Pha Daeng
- Wat Sa Si
- King Ramkamhaeng Monument
- Wat Chang Lom
- Wat Chana Songkhram
- East Gate
- Wat Traphang Thong
- Wat Pa Mamuang
- Ramkamhaeng National Museum
- NEW SUKHOTHAI PHITSANULOK
- Wat Phra Yun
- Wat Traphang Ngoen
- Wat Si Sawai
- Wat Chedi Sung

KEY

- Wat Mahathat *(see pp186–7)*
- City walls
- Information office

0 metres 500
0 yards 500

- Wat Chetuphon
- Wat Chedi Si Hong

Façade of the Ramkamhaeng National Museum

VISITORS' CHECKLIST

13 km (8 miles) W of New Sukhothai, Sukhothai province. ■ TAT, Phitsanulok (055) 252742. ⊠ ⊟ New Sukhothai, then songthaew. ☐ 8:30am–4:30pm daily. ⊠ ⊟ ⊠ Loy Krathong and Candle Festival (Nov). **Ramkamhaeng National Museum** ☐ 8:30am–4pm daily. ⊠

1900–20, of Sukhothai's ruins prior to renovation and a large collection of artifacts. At the heart of the moated city is **Wat Mahathat** *(see pp186–7)*, the most important *wat* complex in Sukhothai.

Nearby, Wat Takuan has a restored, Sri Lankan bell-shaped *chedi*. Several Buddha images found in the vault of the *chedi* are thought to date from the early Sukhothai period, though they remain something of a mystery.

To the southwest, at Wat Si Sawai, are three 12th–14th-century Khmer-style *prangs*, thought to pre-date the Tai takeover of the city.

The *bot* of Wat Traphang Ngoen, mentioned in Ramkamhaeng's famous Inscription No. 1 *(see p54)*, lies in an artificial rectangular lake.

Copper Buddha images and Chinese pottery were recovered from Wat Sa Si, also at the centre of an artificial lake. These are now in the Ramkamhaeng National Museum.

Nearby, Wat Chana Songkhram has a restored, squat Sri Lankan-style *chedi*. A smaller *chedi* here dates from the Ayutthaya period.

To the north of Wat Mahathat is the modern **King Ramkamhaeng Monument**. Beyond lies San Ta Pha Daeng, a 12th-century Khmer shrine which once housed sandstone Hindu icons, now in the Ramkamhaeng National Museum.

Wat Sorasak, a small, brick, bell-shaped *chedi*, dates from the early 15th century. The square base is supported by 24 stucco elephants.

East of the Royal City

Wat Chang Lom, a bell-shaped *chedi* similar to one at Si Satchanalai *(see p190)*, has 36 brick and stucco elephants around its base. It represents mythical Mount Meru, supported by elephants. Beyond is Wat Chedi Sung, a beautiful *chedi* with a high, square base typical of the late Sukhothai era.

North of the Royal City

Wat Phra Phai Luang, a Khmer-style complex, is thought to be part of the original mid-13th century settlement, built when this region was part of the Khmer Empire. Only one of the three laterite *prangs*, decorated with stucco fragments, is extant. Nearby, the *mondop* of Wat Si Chum houses an immense seated Buddha image, which peers out through a narrow opening.

Reconstructed stucco elephant heads at Wat Sorasak

LOY KRATHONG AT SUKHOTHAI

Loy Krathong *(see p46)* occurs at the November full moon to mark the end of the rainy season and the main rice harvest. The festival has its origins in the Hindu tradition of thanking the water god for the rains. *Krathongs,* bowls fashioned out of banana leaves holding lighted candles, are floated on water after dark. Though celebrated all over Thailand, the most exuberant festivities take place at Old Sukhothai. Nowadays, the festival includes folk dancing and *son et lumière* shows.

Loy Krathong festivities at the Sukhothai Historical Park

Wat Mahathat

วัดมหาธาตุ

Arch on central *chedi*

W̲AT MAHATHAT was the spiritual centre of the Sukhothai Kingdom. The central *chedi* was founded by Si Intharathit (c.1240–70), first king of Sukhothai, and rebuilt in the 1340s by Lo Thai (1298–1346) to house relics of the Buddha. Buildings were added to the complex by successive kings: by the time it was abandoned in the 16th century it had some 200 *chedis* as well as numerous *wihans* and *mondops*.

Ornamental pond

Bell-shaped *chedi*

★ **Lotus-Bud Chedi**
At the epicentre of the wat *complex is this classic Sukhothai lotus-bud* chedi. *The remains of beautiful stucco decoration can be seen in patches.*

Multi-Layered Chedi
At the western end of a minor wihan *are the crumbling remnants of a large, square-based, multi-layered* chedi. *It is built out of brick.*

Octagonal *chedi*

STAR FEATURES

★ **Frieze of Walking Monks**

★ **Lotus-Bud Chedi**

★ **Phra Attharot Buddha Images**

★ **Frieze of Walking Monks**
A stone frieze runs around the square base of the central group of chedis. *It depicts monks processing around the shrine – a ritual called* pradaksina.

Remains of Bot
To the north of the central chedi are the remains of a bot, with a large, seated Buddha. Like all major Buddha images in Thailand, it faces the east.

Perimeter wall

0 metres   25

0 yards   25

★ Phra Attharot Buddha Images
Flanking the central chedis are two Buddhas, both known as Phra Attharot – a literal reference to their size – housed in mondops.

Remains of Wihan
Aligned on an east-west axis with the central group of chedis *is the main* wihan. *The only remains today are columns that once supported a roof and a seated Buddha image.*

Exploring the Outer Sights
Along a low ridge of hills, around 3.5 km (2 miles) west of the ramparted royal city is another string of ruins that form part of the Sukhothai Historical Park. Most important of these is **Wat Saphan Hin**, where a 12.5-m (41-ft) high Buddha image, Phra Attharot, similar to the Buddha images of the same name at Wat Mahathat, stands on a low summit. There is another large image, similar to Phra Attharot, at Wat Phra Yun, though the head and hands are missing.

Closer to the west city wall is Wat Pa Mamuang, of archaeological importance for the inscriptions discovered here relating to King Lo Thai.

To the south are the ruins of Wat Chetuphon where a *mondop* contains the remains of four Buddha images in varying postures *(see p163)*; two are in good condition, but of the other two, one is missing below the waist and the other has virtually disappeared. At Wat Chedi Si Hong, the base of the laterite brick *chedi* is lined with stucco elephants, interspersed with divinities.

Beyond the southern edge of the Historical Park loom the hills of **Ramkamhaeng National Park**. Covering 342 sq km (133 sq mile), this is home to serow, gaur and wild pig.

🗙 Ramkamhaeng National Park
S of Sukhothai off Hwy 101.
ℹ️ *Forestry Dept (02) 579 0529 (inc bungalow bookings).*

Farmer cultivating rice in the fields surrounding Sukhothai

Si Satchanalai-Chalieng Historical Park ❼

อุทยานประวัติศาสตร์ศรีสัชนาลัย-ชะเลียง

DURING THE 13TH CENTURY, the Sukhothai Kingdom con-
solidated its power in the Central Plains by building a
number of satellite cities. The most important of these was
Si Satchanalai. Today, its ruins lie on the right bank of the
Yom River, 7 km (4 miles) south of modern Si Satchanalai.
One of the best examples of a Thai *muang (see pp54–5)*,
it was laid out along fixed cosmological lines – temple
complexes lay at its heart, surrounded by city walls, rivers
and forest. It is considered by many historians to be
the apogee of Thai city planning. The nearby ruins of
Chalieng are thought to be an earlier Khmer settlement,
an outpost of that empire dating from the time of Jayavarman VII (1181–1220). At the height of the Sukhothai
Kingdom, Si Satchanalai was twinned with the city of
Sukhothai. A royal road, the Phra Ruang, linked the two.

Laterite columns and central
chedi at Wat Nang Phaya

The Main Wats
At the heart of the moated city
a huge Sri Lankan-style, bell-
shaped *chedi* forms the centrepiece of **Wat Chang Lom** *(see
p190)*. To the south is **Wat
Chedi Chet Thaeo**, around
whose central lotus-bud *chedi*
are many smaller ones in
different styles, some containing stucco Buddha images.
One of these *chedis* is a smaller
version of the famous lotus-
bud *chedi* at Wat Mahathat at
Sukhothai *(see pp186–7)*.

At **Wat Nang Phaya**, the
wihan is decorated with fine
stucco reliefs from the
Ayutthaya period, especially
on the exterior. There is also
a Sri Lankan-style, 15th–16th-
century *chedi*. The *wihan*'s
grille-like windows here are

The central, lotus-bud *chedi* of Wat Chedi Chet Thaeo

Exploring the Park
The ruins of Si Satchanalai
are not as grandiose as those
of Sukhothai but are in some
ways more interesting. They
have not been as extensively
restored, and fewer tourists
visit the site. The ruins evoke
a once powerful city which,
although not a seat of government of the Sukhothai
Kingdom, was the city of the
deputy king and an important
commercial centre in the 14th
and 15th centuries. Its most
important trade was in ceramics *(see pp150–1)*, for which
it was renowned all over
Southeast Asia and China.

Today, the ruins at Si
Satchanalai cover an area of
roughly 7 sq km (3 sq miles)
and are surrounded by a
moat 12 m (40 ft) wide. A
good way to tour the site is
by bicycle; there is a bicycle
hire-shop located half-way
between Si Satchanalai and
Chalieng. Visitors can also
ride around the ruined city

on the back of an elephant.
An information centre located
in front of the Ram Narong
Gate houses a small exhibition
of artifacts found at the site
and photographs of Si Satchanalai's many monuments.

SRI LANKAN INFLUENCE

During the Sukhothai period,
Theravada Buddhism, which
had developed independently
in Sri Lanka, arrived in Thailand. With it came Sri Lankan,
bell-shaped *chedis*, reliquary
towers symbolizing the ringing out of the teachings of
the Buddha. The three-tiered
base symbolizes hell, earth
and heaven; rings on the
spire represent the 33 levels
of heaven. A second layer
of symbolism designates the
base as the Buddha's folded
robes, the *stupa* as his alms
bowl and the spire as his
staff. The entire *chedi* also
symbolizes Mount Meru.

Ringed
spire

Box-shaped
harmika

Three-
tiered
base

Bell-shaped
stupa

Sri Lankan-style *chedi* of Wat Suwan
Khiri, overlooking Si Satchanalai

also characteristic of Ayutthaya, and less complete examples of this style can be seen elsewhere around the park. Nearby stands Wat Lak Muang, a small, Khmer-style shrine built as the city foundation shrine.

Minor Wats

On a low, wooded hill north of Wat Chang Lom stands Wat Khao Phnom Phloeng, once the site of ritual cremations. Also among the ruins are a seated Buddha, a *chedi* and a number of columns that once supported a *wihan* roof.

On a hill top, further west, all that remains of Wat Suwan Khiri is a single *chedi*, though there are great views from here over the rest of the city.

Beyond the City Walls

Further west, on a mountain outside the city walls, is a row of ruined monasteries reached by a shady path. At the top of the path is the large, ruined *chedi* of Wat Khao Yai Bon.

There are many other minor ruins scattered within and outside the moated site, and while some have been restored, others comprise little more than the base of a *wihan* or *chedi*. The *mondop* of Wat Hua Khon, for example, once contained seven stuccoed standing Buddha images; today only three are still plainly identifiable. North of the old Tao Mo Gate is Wat Kuti Rai.

There are two rectangular *mondops* here, both built entirely from laterite. Their pediments retain holes for beams, suggesting that they were once linked to other buildings. Inside one *mondop* is a seated Buddha image.

To the north are the kiln sites of Ban Pa Yuang and Ban Noi, where some of the finest Sangkhalok ceramics were produced. A sign of the times is that villagers nearby sell modern replicas to supplement their farming incomes.

Chalieng

Situated 1 km (1,090 yds) to the southeast is the settlement of Chalieng, pre-dating the city of Si Satchanalai and in all likelihood built by the Khmers *(see pp254–5)* as a staging post for travellers. Some of the ruins that can be seen today date from later.

The laterite shrine of **Wat Chao Chan** was built in the Bayon style as a Mahayana Buddhist structure. The *wihan* and *mondop*, now ruins, were added later and reflect a move towards Theravada Buddhism.

Surrounded on three sides by a tight bend of the Yom River, the most important of the Chalieng sites is **Wat Phra Si Rattana Mahathat**, the buildings of which reflect a range of architectural styles from Sukhothai to Ayutthayan. The original Sukhothai lotus-

VISITORS' CHECKLIST

57 km (35 miles) N of New Sukhothai, Sukhothai province.
i *Information Centre (055) 611179 or TAT, Tak (055) 514341.*
from New Sukhothai to Si Satchanalai, then samlor.
○ *8:30am–4:30pm daily.*

Ancient kiln site, north of the walled city at Ban Pa Yuang

bud *chedi* was built over with a huge Khmer-influenced, Ayutthayan *prang*, one of the finest structures of its type in Thailand. Nearby, a seated Buddha, sheltered under the head of a *naga*, sits inside a half *chedi*. Also close by are remains of stucco reliefs of walking Buddhas, said to be some of the very finest examples of Sukhothai sculpture.

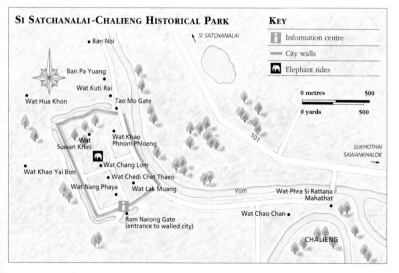

SI SATCHANALAI-CHALIENG HISTORICAL PARK

KEY

i Information centre

City walls

Elephant rides

SI SATCHANALAI

- Ban Noi
- Ban Pa Yuang
- Wat Kuti Rai
- Wat Hua Khon
- Tao Mo Gate
- Wat Suwan Khiri
- Wat Khao Phnom Phloeng
- Wat Chang Lom
- Wat Khao Yai Bon
- Wat Chedi Chet Thaeo
- Wat Nang Phaya
- Wat Lak Muang
- Ram Narong Gate (entrance to walled city)

0 metres 500
0 yards 500

101

SUKHOTHAI
SAWANKHALOK

Yom

Wat Phra Si Rattana Mahathat

Wat Chao Chan

CHALIENG

Wat Chang Lom
วัดช้างล้อม

BUILT IN THE REIGN of Ramkamhaeng, this monument is thought to be the first Sri Lankan-style *chedi* of the Sukhothai Kingdom. The style was later copied throughout Si Satchanalai and Sukhothai.

Tapered, ringed spire

Sri Lankan, bell-shaped *chedi*

Stucco elephants around the base of the *chedi*

A frieze of figures, believed to be walking Buddha images, is carved into the shaft just below the ringed spire.

The trunks were probably broken off by invading Burmese.

The staircase was used by pilgrims wishing to make the symbolic journey between earth and heaven.

RECONSTRUCTION OF WAT CHANG LOM
This shows the *wat* as it might have looked in the Sukhothai era. It stood in the centre of Si Satchanalai.

Exploring Sawankhalok

With the introduction, by Chinese potters, of new firing techniques, the kilns around Si Satchanalai and Sukhothai became some of the most important producers of ceramics in Southeast Asia. At their most prolific, during the 14th–16th centuries, as the Sukhothai Kingdom came under the control of the Kingdom of Ayutthaya, it is thought that over 200 potteries lined the banks of the Yom River. They produced a variety of pottery termed Sangkhalok – a derivation of Sawankhalok, the name that was given to Si Satchanalai during the period of Ayutthaya's rule in the region. Today the name applies only to the small town

Sangkhalok pottery

of Sawankhalok, where the **Sawankha Woranayok National Museum** is located. This houses an expansive selection of Sangkhalok ceramics *(see pp150–1)*, which includes plates, storage jars, bowls, temple roof tiles, figures used in religious ceremonies and everyday statues that may have been toys. A large number of the ceramics on display were salvaged from ships wrecked in the Gulf of Thailand on their way to trade with India, China, the Philippines and Indonesia. The museum also contains a collection of religious sculptures taken from Sawankhalok's nearby Wat Sawankharam – many were donated to the *wat* by the villagers who unearthed them.

Exploring Si Satchanalai National Park

Founded in 1981, this park covers an area of 213 sq km (82 sq miles) and consists mainly of low hills. Dotted around the park are the Tad Dao, Tao Don, Huai Sai and Huai Pa Cho waterfalls. The Tara Wasan and Kang Khao caves are also worth visiting. The park is good for birdwatching with more than 70 species having been recorded. Few large mammals inhabit the park, though it is believed that there is a small number of wild elephants living here.

🏠 **Sawankha Woranayok National Museum**
Sawankhalok, 17 km (11 miles) S of Si Satchanalai. ⬜ *Wed–Sun.* 🏷
🗲 **Si Satchanalai National Park**
N of Si Satchanalai-Chalieng Historical Park, off Hwy 101. ⬜ *daily.* 🏷

Green and ochre roof tiles at Wat Phra Si Rattana Mahathat, Phitsanulok

Phitsanulok **8**

พิษณุโลก

Phitsanulok province. 88,000. TAT, 209/7–8 Borommatrailokanat Rd, Phitsanulok (055) 252742. Wed, Sat. Phra Buddha Chinarat (Jan/Feb), Phitsanulok Boat Races (Oct).

MANY VISITORS pass through this town as it is an important transport hub, connecting Bangkok and the Central Plains to Northern Thailand.

There has been a settlement here from as early as the mid-14th century, when **Wat Phra Si Rattana Mahathat** was built on the bank of the Nan River. Initially, this *wat* complex, also called Wat Yai, probably housed a Sukhothai lotus-bud *chedi*, which was later replaced by the tall Ayutthayan *prang* that can be seen today. It was built by the Ayutthayan king Borommatrailokanat (1448–88), who ruled from Phitsanulok after 1463 in order to wage a military campaign against the Kingdom of Lanna (*see pp58–9*). The golden tiles on the antefixes of the *wat* were added during a later renovation by King Chulalongkorn (1868–1910).

Inside the west *wihan* is the revered Buddha image Phra Buddha Chinarat (*see pp150–1*), made of gilded bronze and dating from the 14th century. It attracts pilgrims from all over Thailand and, consequently, a small industry of religious paraphernalia

The Phra Buddha Chinarat image

has grown up around it. In the gallery outside the *prang* are scores of Buddha images. Across the road, in the *bot* of **Wat Ratchaburana**, are some faded 19th-century murals, depicting scenes from the Ramakien (*see pp36–7*).

Sergeant Major Thawee's Folk Museum houses a collection of rural folk crafts – wood and bamboo animal traps, farm tools and basketry. Across the street is the affiliated **Buddha Foundry**, where visitors can watch bronze Buddha images being forged.

ENVIRONS: 5 km (3 miles) south of Phitsanulok is the Ayutthayan, laterite *prang* of **Wat Chulamani**. It was built in Khmer style by King Borommatrailokanat in 1464, a year after he moved his capital from Ayutthaya to Phitsanulok. He was ordained as a monk here in 1465 after abdicating

in favour of his son. Eight months later he returned to the throne and, until his death in 1488, continued to rule Ayutthaya from Phitsanulok.

🏛 Sergeant Major Thawee's Folk Museum
26/43 Wisuth Kasat Rd. (055) 258715. Tue–Sun. **Buddha Foundry** Mon–Sat.

Thung Salaeng Luang National Park **9**

อุทยานแห่งชาติทุ่งแสลงหลวง

Phitsanulok province, Park HQ 80 km (50 miles) E of Phitsanulok. TAT, Phitsanulok (055) 252742; Forestry Dept (02) 579 0529 (inc bungalow bookings). from Phitsanulok to Nakhon Thai, then songthaew.

WITH ITS EXPANSES of open meadow interspersed with forest, this 1,262 sq km (487 sq mile) park offers good hiking and bird-watching. Barking deer can also be seen and, occasionally, elephants are found at the salt licks. The beautiful cascades of Kaeng Sopha lie 9 km (6 miles) from the park headquarters. Further west, along the main highway, are the Poi falls and the smaller Kaeng Song rapids.

ENVIRONS: At **Khao Kho**, to the east, is a rehabilitation scheme for the Hmong, displaced through involvement in anti-Communist fighting in the 1970s–80s. The King takes great interest in the scheme and has a palace nearby.

The thinly forested Thung Salaeng Luang National Park

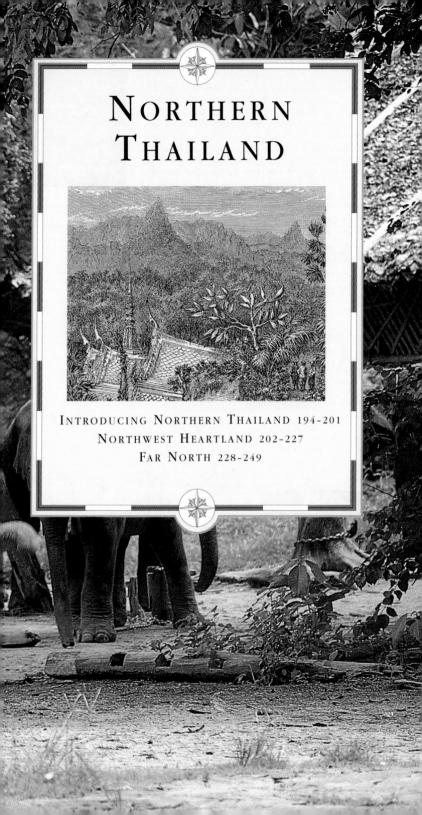

NORTHERN THAILAND

Introducing Northern Thailand

NORTHERN THAILAND, home of the ancient Lanna king-dom (see pp58–9), offers a great diversity of activities. The old Lanna capitals of Chiang Mai and Chiang Rai are filled with ancient monuments and museums, and markets selling the distinctive local textiles and handicrafts. Smaller towns, such as Nan and Lamphun, offer a more low-key charm. Away from the main settlements, the scenery of Northern Thailand is stupendous: mountains, forests (some of them teak), rice fields set in verdant valleys and several spectacular national parks. The more adventurous visitor can join a trek to remote villages inhabited by hill tribes where elements of lifestyle have changed little in hundreds of years.

Mae Hong Son (see pp206–7), *a rapidly developing tourist centre, is particularly popular with budget travellers. The town's main attraction is its beautiful mountain setting.*

Chiang Mai (see pp214–17) *is justly famed for its 300 temples, fine shopping, distinctive Northern cuisine and (despite its size) relaxed pace of life.*

Mae Hong Son

Chiang Mai

NORTHWEST HEARTLAND (see pp202–227)

Doi Inthanon National Park

Lampang

Doi Inthanon National Park (see pp220–21) *incorporates the highest mountain in Thailand. Visitors come for the stunning scenery, including several waterfalls, and rich wildlife.*

Lampang (see pp224–7) *is a thriving town which hosts colourful festivals. It contains a number of important* wats *and a museum of Lanna artifacts.*

◁ **The Elephant Training Centre, southeast of the town of Chiang Dao**

Doi Tung (see p233), *a mountain set in beautiful forested country, is crowned by an important pilgrimage site.*

Doi Tung

Chiang Rai

FAR NORTH
(see pp228–249)

Chiang Rai (see pp240–41) *has long dwelt in the shadow of nearby Chiang Mai, but is now rapidly developing into a significant tourist centre in its own right. Its monuments may not be as numerous as those of Chiang Mai, but the city is an excellent source of hill-tribe handicrafts and a major starting point for trekkers.*

Nan

0 kilometres   50

0 miles   25

Nan (see pp244–5) *is a wealthy, sleepy town with several quirky wats, a good museum and a spectacular mountain setting. Every October the Nan River is filled with colourful canoes taking part in the Lanna boat races.*

The Hill Tribes of Thailand

Ceremonial mask

THERE ARE SIX MAIN GROUPS of hill dwellers living in Northern Thailand: the Akha, Hmong, Lisu, Karen, Lahu and Mien. These semi-nomadic peoples, some 500,000 in total, began to arrive here at the end of the 19th century, pushed out of their native Tibet, Burma and China by civil war and political pressures. Though widely referred to as hill tribes, this label is rather general as each group has its own heritage, clothing, language, religion and culture. However, the future of the hill tribes is uncertain. Traditionally, most use the slash-and-burn method (swiddening) to grow crops, abandoning land once it is exhausted. But competing pressures on land are drawing them into the Thai market economy. Some are also becoming dependent on tourist hand-outs.

This 1890s portrait is of Lahu women. Most hill tribes still wear traditional dress, though Western clothing is widely available.

Bamboo sections are pounded rhythmically to honour leaders during the Swing Ceremony.

Young Lisu women and girls wear black turbans adorned with multicoloured threads, mainly for important celebrations, such as New Year. Silver jewellery, sewn on to their clothes, is a display of the family's wealth.

This Hmong house has been accidentally destroyed by fire. To improve living conditions and economic opportunities, and to stop swiddening, the government aims to integrate hill tribes into the Thai way of life.

FESTIVALS AND GATHERINGS
Colourful ceremonies mark rites of passage such as birth, death and marriage. Here, the Akha gather for a festival.

New Year is the most important date in the Lisu calendar. A tree is planted in front of each house in the village. A shaman and a priest then perform a ritual to cleanse the village of the past year's bad elements, while young people dance around the trees.

In the past, some hill tribes earned extra income from opium production. They are now encouraged to grow "new" crops, such as cabbages.

Akha houses *are characterized by a large porch connected to a square living area with a stove. They are usually constructed on high ground near the tribe's rice fields.*

Akha people *strive to maintain a traditional way of life, the "Akha Way". This is proving more difficult as fertile land disappears and animal numbers are depleted. Here, a villager carries out the vital chore of collecting wood.*

An ornate headdress, decorated with silver or, increasingly, aluminium, is worn by Akha women.

A sash, weighed down with coins and beads, distinguishes women from girls.

While many Lahu women *no longer wear traditional dress on a daily basis, they still weave distinctive shoulder bags (yam) from brightly coloured fabrics.*

Mien clothing *is particularly distinctive. Women embroider colourful patterns onto black or indigo cloth and stitch red pompons onto caps worn by children.*

Karen typically *build houses in lowland valleys, cultivating by crop rotation rather than slash-and-burn. They are the largest and least nomadic tribe.*

SPIRITUAL BELIEFS

Many hill-tribe beliefs and practices are based on animism. Villages often have two religious leaders: a priest, who performs rituals and communes with the local guardian spirit, and a shaman, who has the power to consult directly with the spirit world. Rituals influence most decisions in a village, including where it is sited. But as tribes are drawn into modern life, traditional practices and medicine are coming under threat.

Mien tools used during shamanistic ceremonies

Northern Arts and Crafts

Pale green celadon bowl

NORTHERN THAILAND IS RENOWNED for its handicrafts. The high quality of crafts produced today, such as wooden carvings, silverware, fabrics, ceramics, silk and lacquerware, reflects centuries of Northern Thai, or Lanna, expertise. The region's ethnic minorities and hill tribes *(see pp196–7)* also produce distinctive embroidery, paintings and silverware. Chiang Mai *(see pp214–17)* is the main crafts centre, while villages such as Bo Sang and San Kamphaeng *(see pp218–19)* specialize in particular crafts. In factory-shops, visitors can watch crafts being made. Antiques and excellent copies, especially wood carvings, are sold in outlets in Chiang Mai. Though teak logging has been strictly controlled in Thailand since 1989, wooden crafts produced from imported teak are still widely sold.

Ornate Akha *headdresses feature silver coins and hollow baubles that are expertly crafted by the men of the hill tribe.*

***Animal figures**, intricately carved from wood (in many cases teak), often feature in Northern wats. Such wooden crafts are still produced throughout the North, despite the ban on unregulated teak logging.*

Northern lacquerwork *typically consists of a red lacquer-coated wood or bamboo base decorated with a yellow pattern. This is a 19th- or 20th-century box.*

Curved legs were designed to fit over the back of the elephant, near its head.

ROYAL HOWDAH
Before the advent of the car, elephants were used for transport in Thailand. People sat in howdahs, or elephant chairs, on the elephants' backs. Howdahs stood some 1.5 m (5 ft) high, and their decoration revealed their passengers' status. The most basic form, used by the lower classes, consisted of a seat with raised sides. Howdahs used for transporting royalty and aristocrats, such as this one from Northern Thailand, featured ornate woodcarving and usually had a roof.

Umbrellas are the main craft items *produced in Bo Sang. They are made of lacquered paper, stretched over a bamboo frame, then painted with traditional motifs, such as elephants.*

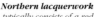

Betel sets *consist of several containers used to hold the ingredients for betel-chewing (a popular activity in Southeast Asia) – betel leaf, limestone ash and the narcotic areca palm fruit. A gold set was a sign of status.*

Wooden roof brackets, *seen on religious buildings, are for decoration rather than support. They often depict* nagas *(serpents) and other animals.*

A roof, made from lacquered woven bamboo, offered shelter from the heat.

Silver ceremonial *jewellery is worn for village festivals and other important occasions. While hill tribes still use old silver, melted down from Indian and Burmese coins, many Thai silversmiths in Chiang Mai nowadays rely on imported silver of a lower quality.*

Handles were used for support during bumpy rides. Royal elephant seats were more comfortable than ordinary ones.

In Thailand, *even everyday items are decorated, such as this wooden clapper, which is painted with a flower motif. A clapper is traditionally worn by water buffaloes so they can be located if they stray.*

Delicately fashioned woodcarving featured only on elephant chairs used by affluent members of society.

TEXTILES OF NORTHERN THAILAND

Embroidering a striped Lahu bag

Textile production in Northern Thailand dates from the early Lanna period, and the region is renowned for its silk and cotton. Chiang Mai and San Kamphaeng are centres for silk clothing – also made in the Northeast *(see pp256–7)* – including the traditional *pha sin* (woman's sarong). Outlets also sell furnishings and cottonware produced in Pasang *(see p219)* such as the *pha koma* (man's sarong). Chiang Khong factory-shops produce Thai Lue cotton fabrics in stunning colours *(see p239)*, while hill tribes make and sell brightly patterned fabrics. Most textiles can be bought as lengths or as ready-made items.

A traditional cotton design

A 19th-century *pha sin*

Birds of Northern Thailand

NORTHERN THAILAND lies on the Eastern Asia Flyway, a major flight path for migrating birds. Thailand boasts some ten per cent of the world's bird species, 380 of which have been recorded in the hills around Chiang Mai. Most of these are migratory birds that have flown south in winter to the warmer climes of Thailand's forested hills. In recent years, steps have been introduced to protect bird habitats, under threat from deforestation. But many sites in the North, especially Doi Suthep *(see pp212–13)* and Doi Inthanon *(see pp220–21)* national parks, still provide a habitat for numerous bird species.

SELECTED MIGRATION ROUTES

— Arctic warblers

— Siberian rubythroats

— Herons

Black-crowned night-herons *are nocturnal birds. They have a black crest, nape and back, whitish underparts and grey wings. Resident in various countries, they migrate to low altitudes in Northern Thailand.*

Changeable hawk-eagle

The red-breasted parakeet, of deciduous woodlands, is threatened by the illegal trade in birds.

Red-wattled lapwings, *named for the red patch of skin in front of the eye, reside near streams and in open forest. When alarmed they emit a loud, shrill call.*

Teak tree

Silver pheasants *live at various altitudes, typically over 700 m (2,300 ft). Their red feet and long tail distinguish them from other types of pheasants. They are also bred in captivity to be sold for food – because of their depleted numbers, pheasants are protected.*

Pheasant-tailed jacanas *have long legs, toes and claws that enable them to walk on leaves in lowland rivers, foraging for food.*

Purple herons are wetland birds that can be seen near forest streams. They have a slender, rufous (red-brown) neck.

**0–500 M
(0–1,640 FT)**
ABOVE SEA LEVEL

Coral-billed ground-cuckoos are difficult to observe because they are rare, shy birds.

Long-tailed broadbills, *so called for their short heavy bill and long tail (unique in broadbills), live at high altitudes in Northern Thailand. They feed on insects, probing for them in trees or catching them while in flight.*

Gould's sunbirds live at high altitudes. The male is far more colourful than the female, with a metallic blue, crimson and yellow body.

Asian paradise flycatchers *can be resident or migratory, nesting on upper slopes. The females and immature males have a brown body and a black head. Fully developed males are more stunning in colour, with a white tail and a blue beak.*

Great Indian hornbill

Siberian rubythroats *migrate to the upper slopes of Northern Thailand's evergreen forests. The characteristic red patch on the throat is present only in the male.*

Epiphyte-covered trees

1,500–2,500 M (4,900–8,200 FT)

Bay owls are distinguished from other owls by a loud, musical whistle.

Silver pheasant

Strangler fig

500–1,500 M (1,640–4,900 FT)

Greater racket-tailed drongos *are resident at medium-range elevations in Northern Thailand. They feed almost entirely on insects, flying out repeatedly from the same branch, often in small groups. Their long tails are tipped with a vane or "racket" that ripples as the bird flies.*

BIRD HABITATS AT DIFFERENT ALTITUDES

Deciduous dipterocarp trees clothe the foothills of Northern Thailand. Here, teak forests provide a habitat for kalij pheasants, wagtails and parakeets, and migratory wetland birds such as herons. Higher up the slopes, bazas, hornbills, hill mynas and shikes are drawn to mixed evergreen and deciduous forests. Oaks and epiphytic plants, such as ferns, thrive on the hill tops, where arctic warblers, owls and other small birds live.

TIPS FOR BIRD-WATCHING

• The best time to see birds is during the "winter" months, from January to April, when resident birds are mating and most migratory species arrive. Avoid the wet season (June–October), when heavy rain and leeches can be a problem.
• National park headquarters provide leaflets detailing bird-watching trails. Guided trips can often be arranged.
• Take binoculars, plenty of water, insect repellent and a compass. Try to wear dark green or inconspicuous clothing.
• Many birds are shy, so be patient. Walk quietly to avoid rustling leaves, and do not walk straight towards the bird.

NORTHWEST HEARTLAND

NORTHWEST THAILAND *is the heartland of Lanna Thai. The ancient city of Chiang Mai, famed for its many fine temples and handicrafts, is the focal point for visitors. This and smaller towns are set in verdant valleys among thickly forested mountains. The Northwest is also home to a number of ethnic minorities, and the rich mix of diverse cultures and scenery is most enticing.*

Chiang Mai, superbly sited in the Ping River Valley, was once the capital of the Lanna Kingdom. In the 12th–18th centuries this kingdom, strongly influenced by Burma, ruled over what is now Northern Thailand, and local Thais remain proud of their Lanna heritage. Indeed, the silverwork, woodcarving, pottery and other crafts of the North are regarded by many as the most exquisite in Thailand. Nowhere in the country are crafts more readily available than in Chiang Mai and its environs.

Chiang Mai is also a useful base from which to explore the mountains and villages. Trekking to hill-tribe villages is a popular, though controversial, activity. Although most trekkers are genuinely interested in hill-tribe culture, there is a danger that villages will become dependent on tourism and that traditional ways of life will be lost forever.

In the west, close to the Burmese border, the remote towns of Mae Hong Son and Mae Sariang are in some ways more Burmese than Thai. The *wats*, for instance, have multi-roofed *chedis* reminiscent of Burmese temples. North of Chiang Mai, the streets of Chiang Dao are lined with two-storey teak buildings, a reminder that the surrounding countryside was once rich in teak forests. To the south of Chiang Mai, Lanna influence can again be seen in temples and museum artifacts within the cities of Lampang and Lamphun. The latter also has surviving traces of the older Kingdom of Haripunchai.

Thailand's highest mountain, Doi Inthanon, lies west of Chiang Mai, within a national park with good facilities. Here can be seen dramatic waterfalls and a wide range of wildlife, including hundreds of migratory birds.

Boy lighting a candle at Wat Phra That Lampang Luang, one of several major *wats* in the Northwest

◁ Woman cleaning umbrellas in the handicraft village of Bo Sang, near Chiang Mai

Exploring the Northwest Heartland

THE NORTHWEST HEARTLAND is a geographically spectacular region. Towering mountains, many with densely forested slopes, stretch to the Burmese border, and contrast with the gentler scenery of the Ping and Taeng river valleys. Trekking in this beautiful landscape, with its wealth of wildlife and fascinating hill-tribe villages, is a major activity in the Northwest Heartland. Cultural attractions are also plentiful, including the ancient temples of Chiang Mai, Lamphun and Lampang, and the unmissable Wat Phra That Lampang Luang.

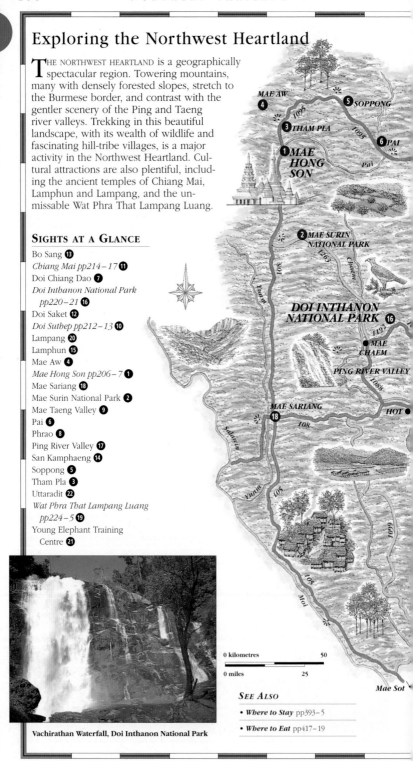

SIGHTS AT A GLANCE

Vachirathan Waterfall, Doi Inthanon National Park

SEE ALSO

• *Where to Stay* pp393–5

• *Where to Eat* pp417–19

Elaborately decorated pillars inside the *bot* of Chiang Mai's Wat Chiang Man

GETTING AROUND

Apart from the highways around Chiang Mai, most roads in this area are poor. Lampang and Mae Hong Son have domestic airports, and there is an international airport at Chiang Mai, the main transport hub. Many trains and buses run each day between Chiang Mai and Bangkok (11–13 hours by train, via Uttaradit and Lampang; about ten hours by coach). Frequent local bus services link most towns and villages in the region. Isolated sights are best reached by *songthaew*, while guided treks and organized coach tours are a good way of seeing larger areas.

KEY

〰️	Motorway
▬	Major road
▭	Minor road
▭	Scenic route
〰	River
☀	Viewpoint

Elephants at the Young Elephant Training Centre

Street-by-Street: Mae Hong Son ❶

แม่ฮ่องสอน

BEAUTIFULLY SITED in a valley ringed by forested mountains, Mae Hong Son sprang up in 1831 from a small camp where elephants were tethered. The town remained largely isolated until it was linked by a paved highway to Chiang Mai in 1965. The province has traditionally been dominated by nearby Burma, as shown by its architecture. Shan and Karen people, who make up most of the population, continue to move across the border to live in Mae Hong Son and its environs. Today, the tranquil town is growing as a resort and trekking centre. In the cool season, you may need to wear a jumper or jacket here.

To Airport

★ **Wat Hua Wiang**
This teak temple has a Burmese-style, multi-roofed design. The bot – *in an advanced state of decay – houses an important brass Buddha image, Phra Chao Phla La Khaeng, which was transported here from Burma.*

UDOM CHAONITHET

The Night Bazaar sells crafts and Thai Lue fabrics.

Daily Market
This lively, pungent market, which almost spills onto the airport runway, sells a range of fresh produce, Burmese textiles and trekking supplies. Local hill tribes are often seen here.

PRADIT CHONG KHAM

SINGHANAT BAMRUNG

THE PADAUNG WOMEN

Many tours from Mae Hong Son visit the "long-neck women" of the area. These women, of the Padaung, or Kayan, tribe, are distinguished by their long necks, lengthened from childhood by brass rings. Among the explanations for this old practice are that it protects the women from tiger attacks or that it is a way of enhancing their looks. This practice had begun to die out until recently when the Padaung realized tourists would pay to die out until recently when the Padaung realized tourists would pay to photograph the women.

"Long-neck women" of the Padaung tribe

Traditional Shan teak houses can be seen along this street.

Chong Kham Lake
This lake, which was originally a bathing pool for elephants, can be especially stunning in the early-morning mists that enshroud the town.

VISITORS' CHECKLIST

Mae Hong Son province.
🏠 6,000. ✈ 1 km (1,100 yds) NE of Chong Kham Lake.
🚌 Khunlum Phraphat Rd.
ℹ TAT, Chiang Mai (053) 248604.
🏛 Singhanat Bamrung Rd (053) 611812. 🕐 daily. 🎊 Poi Sang Long Festival (late Mar/early Apr); Chong Para Festival (Oct).

★ Wat Chong Kham
Wat Chong Kham (c.1827), which was built by the Shans, features a multi-roofed chedi. The wat houses a revered 5-m (16-ft) seated Buddha image.

★ Wat Chong Klang
Built in the late 19th century, this temple has distinctive white and gold chedis. Painted glass panels depicting the jataka tales (see p26) can be seen on request.

Post office

Fitness park

Wat Doi Kong Mu, on a hill top to the west of town, has superb views of the town and area.

To Wat Doi Kong Mu

0 metres   25

0 yards   25

KEY

– – – Suggested route

STAR SIGHTS

★ **Wat Hua Wiang**

★ **Wat Chong Kham**

★ **Wat Chong Klang**

Khunlum Phraphat Road
Craft shops, restaurants and tour companies line Mae Hong Son's main street. Hill-tribe textiles and antiques are among the items that can be bought.

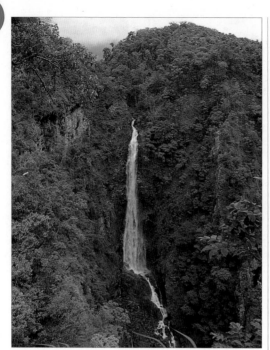

The spectacular Mae Surin waterfall in Mae Surin National Park

Mae Surin
National Park ❷
อุทยานแห่งชาติน้ำตกแม่สุริน

Mae Hong Son province. Park HQ
2.5 km (1.5 miles) off Hwy 108, 8 km
(5 miles) N of Mae Hong Son *TAT,
Chiang Mai (053) 248604; Forestry
Dept (02) 579 0529 (inc bungalow
bookings).* 🚌 *from Khun Yuam,
then songthaew.* ⭘ *daily.* 🖼

THIS SMALL PARK is the highlight of the area south of
Mae Hong Son. Much of it is
covered with lowland forest,
providing a habitat for mammals such as the Malaysian sun
bear, Asiatic black bear and
barking deer. Bird species include drongos and hornbills.
Mae Surin waterfall, which at
100 m (330 ft) is one of the
highest in Thailand, is reached
on a dirt road east of Pang Mu.
Also accessible from this dirt
road is Thung Bua Thong
("wild sunflower meadow"),
which blooms spectacularly
in November and December.
Raft trips along the Pai River,
which flows through the park,
can be arranged at guesthouses
in Mae Hong Son and Pai.

Tham Pla ❸
ถ้ำปลา

Mae Hong Son province. Off Hwy
1095, 17 km (11 miles) N of Mae
Hong Son. *TAT, Chiang Mai (053)
248604.* 🚌 *Mae Hong Son, then
songthaew, or join tour.* 🖼

LOCATED NORTH OF Mae Hong
Son, this scenic spot can
be visited on a day trip from
the town. Tham Pla ("fish
cave") is actually a pool and
stream at the base of a limestone outcrop, so named because of the huge carp that live
in it. Visitors make merit by
buying papaya to feed to the
fish. The peaceful surrounding
gardens are perhaps the site's
most attractive feature.

Mae Aw ❹
แม่ออ

Mae Hong Son province. 🚶 800.
🚐 Mae Hong Son, then songthaew,
or join tour. *TAT, Chiang Mai
(053) 248604.* 🗓 *daily.*

SITUATED in the mountains
near the Burmese border,
Mae Aw is a remote settlement
built by members of the Kuomintang, or KMT (see p232).
Apart from superb views, the
village offers an intriguing
insight into life in an isolated
border village. But fighting still
sometimes breaks out between
rival factions over control of
the local opium trade, following the overthrow of Khun Sa
(see p223) in 1996.
The best way to get to Mae
Aw is with a tour from Mae
Hong Son or by jeep. Before
you come, check with the local
tourist information office that
there is no fighting in the area.

Soppong ❺
สบปง

Mae Hong Son province. 🚶 700.
🚐 from Mae Hong Son. *TAT,
Chiang Mai (053) 248604.* 🗓 *daily.*

THE SMALL VILLAGE OF Soppong
(sometimes called Pang
Mapha on local maps) is
perched some 700 m (2,200 ft)
up in the mountains. With its
fine views, beautiful surround-

Highway 1095 as it passes through Soppong

Muslim children in Pai, part of the town's mixed community

ing teak forests and air of tranquility, Soppong is becoming an increasingly popular resort. Many trekkers pass through here on the way to visit local hill-tribe villages populated by Lisu and Shan (a minority originally from Burma). The village itself has a thriving market where local tribespeople congregate daily.

ENVIRONS: Tham Lot, north of Soppong, is one of the largest cave systems in Southeast Asia. The three adjoining caverns form a vast subterranean canyon, which is cut through by a large stream. The distinctive stalactites and stalagmites are especially impressive. The discovery of artifacts and huge, roughly carved teak coffins indicates that the caves were inhabited thousands of years ago. Visitors may cross the stream by raft or by elephant. Guided visits can be arranged at local guesthouses.

🏠 Tham Lot
8 km (5 miles) N of Soppong, Mae Hong Son province. ⏰ *daily.*
📷 *(for guide and lantern).*

Pai ❻
ปาย

Mae Hong Son province. 🚶 *8,000.*
🚌 *from Mae Hong Son.* ℹ️ *TAT,*
Chiang Mai (053) 248604. 📅 *daily.*

PAI HAS A FAST-GROWING reputation as one of Northern Thailand's top beauty spots, and is popular with trekkers and lovers of mountain scenery. Originally an old Shan settlement, the town and surrounding area have, in recent decades, become populated by Lisu and Lahu hill tribes, Muslims from Burma, and Yunnanese from China.

The yellow and white tiles and multi-layered roofs of **Wat Klang**, between the coach station and the Pai River, are typical of Shan temples. The hilltop **Wat Phra That Mae Yen**, just east of Pai, was also built by the Shan. The carved wooden doors of the main *wihan* depict scenes from nature and human life. The temple gives sweeping views of the valley.

Guided treks of the area *(see p211)* can be arranged at many guesthouses in town.

THAILAND'S ENDANGERED WILDLIFE

With its diversity of landscapes, Thailand is an ideal habitat for a vast range of flora and fauna. In the 20th century, however, poaching and deforestation have led to the extinction of many species, including the kouprey (a type of wild cattle) and Schomburgk's deer. Some animals are caught for food; some, including gibbons, are sold as pets, while others, like snakes, are killed through fear. Of Thailand's 282 mammal species, about 40 are endangered and while laws exist to protect these animals, they are not always enforced. Almost all of Thailand's large mammals are in danger of extinction, and many others, including the white-handed gibbon, are, at best, rare. This alarming state of affairs is not confined to mammals: ten per cent of the country's 405 reptiles and amphibians are also endangered.

Rock python – its favoured forest habitat is rapidly disappearing

A rare white-handed gibbon

TIGERS IN THAILAND
The increasing demand for dried tiger parts in traditional Chinese medicines has led to the worldwide demise of this great creature. Of the few thousand tigers that remain in Asia, about 500 are estimated to be living in Thailand, particularly in the Khao Yai National Park *(see pp174–5)*. In 1995 the Royal Forest Department established a conservation project to try to prevent the tiger from dying out altogether in Thailand.

Pavilions and carp-filled pool in front of Tham Chiang Dao

Doi Chiang Dao ❼

ดอยเชียงดาว

12 km (7.5 miles) W of Chiang Dao, Chiang Mai province. 🄸 *TAT, Chiang Mai (053) 248604.* 🚍 *from Chiang Mai to Chiang Dao, then songthaew.*

A T 2,285 M (7,500 FT), Doi Chiang Dao is the third-largest mountain in Thailand. Home to several Lisu and Karen villages, it features a mixture of tropical and pine forests. Today, this peak and the surrounding area, characterized by rugged limestone scenery and dense teak forest, are more of an attraction than the nearby town, Chiang Dao.

Running for some 14 km (8.5 miles) underneath the mountain is a network of caves, **Tham Chiang Dao**, best reached from Chiang Dao town. Most of the caves house statues of the Buddha, which, over the years, have been left

by Shan pilgrims from Burma. The highlight of the bat-inhabited caves, however, are their huge stalactites and stalagmites. Lanterns and guides can be hired in order to make the most of these impressive features. The tours take visitors along an illuminated walkway through the caves.

Near the caves is a temple, **Wat Tham Chiang Dao**, with a Buddhist meditation centre and a small room displaying gongs and other instruments. Beyond a huge tamarind tree, by a pond, is an old Burmese-style *chedi*. Nearby, a small market offers a wide selection of locally gathered forest roots, herbs and spices.

East of Doi Chiang Dao, and dominated by the peak, is **Chiang Dao town**, with its traditional teak buildings along the main street. It was founded in the 18th century as a place

Façade of Wat Tham Chiang Dao, near Doi Chiang Dao

of exile for *phi pop*, ("spirit people"), who were suspected of being possessed by evil spirits. In fact, the symptoms of their true illnesses, such as malaria, had been mistaken as signs of madness.

The **Elephant Training Centre Chiang Dao**, southeast of Chiang Dao, is located in a wooded area beside a stream. The daily displays feature elephants bathing, and lifting and dragging logs. Elephant rides may also be taken.

Tham Tup Tao, 48 km (30 miles) north of Chiang Dao, are two large caverns. Tham Pha Kha ("light cave") houses two large Buddha images and a stalagmite carved in the shape of a group of elephants. Inside Tham Pha Chak ("dark cave"), which can be explored only by lantern, is a bat colony.

🄼 **Tham Chiang Dao**
Off Hwy 107, 5 km (3 miles) NW of Chiang Dao. ◯ *daily.* 🄵 🄲
🄼 **Elephant Training Centre Chiang Dao**
E of Hwy 107, 15 km (9.5 miles) SE of Chiang Dao, Chiang Mai province.
🄲 *(053) 298 553.* ◯ *daily (displays 9–10am and 10–11am).* 🄵
🄼 **Tham Tup Tao**
W of Hwy 107, Chiang Mai province.
◯ *daily.* 🄵 🄲

Phrao ❽

พร้าว

Chiang Mai province. 🄼 *55,000.* 🚍 *from Chiang Mai.* 🄸 *TAT, Chiang Mai (053) 248604.* 🄰 *daily.*

A SMALL MARKET TOWN, Phrao is a meeting place for Thai traders and hill-tribe people. Until quite recently, Phrao was relatively isolated from other towns. Today, Highway 1150 connects it with Wiang Pa Pao *(see p242)*, making it more accessible. Phrao is still off the main tourist track. The town's main sight is its covered market which sells traditional textiles and a wide range of locally grown fruit and vegetables.

ENVIRONS: Heading east towards Wiang Pa Pao, Highway 1150 passes through spectacular forest scenery. Here, several Lisu and Hmong hill-tribe villages can be seen.

ORCHIDS IN THAILAND

Seen on logos throughout Thailand, the orchid is the country's most famous flower. There are over 1,300 varieties of wild orchid in Thailand, most of which are dependent on forests. But while their natural habitat is threatened by deforestation, millions are being cultivated for export to overseas markets.

A pink orchid, one of the most popular colours for the overseas markets

Export began in the 1950s, and burgeoned in the 1980s when the first orchid farms were established. In 1991 the value of exports peaked at about US$ 80 million. Since then, as consumer trends have changed in important markets such as Japan, this figure has started to decline.

A leisurely rafting trip along the Taeng River

Mae Taeng Valley ➒

แม่แตง

Chiang Mai province. 🚉 🚌 *Chiang Mai, then songthaew.* ℹ️ *TAT, Chiang Mai (053) 248604.*

THE AREA AROUND Mae Taeng, especially the vicinity of the Taeng River to the northwest of the town, is very popular with trekkers. In recent years, the land has been terraced and irrigated to improve agricultural production. The variety of crops grown has created an attractive contrast of landscapes. However, most trekkers come here not only for the peaceful surroundings but also to witness everyday scenes in the region's many Lisu, Karen and Hmong villages. Other activities, including river rafting and elephant rides, can be combined with treks in the area. The **Mae Taman Rafting and Elephant Camp** is located amid peaceful scenery on a dirt road to the west of Highway 107, and arranges rafting trips on the Taeng River. Elephant rides and bullock cart rides can also be taken. A nearby guesthouse, set on the banks of the river, offers accommodation.

🏠 **Mae Taman Rafting and Elephant Camp**
15 km (9.5 miles) W of Hwy 107.
⭕ *daily.* 🎫

Hmong women, wearing their distinctive woven textiles

TREKKING AROUND CHIANG DAO

Northern Thailand is renowned for its trekking *(see p446)*. Treks in the area around Chiang Dao and Mae Taeng often combine visits to hill-tribe villages with an elephant ride or raft trip through the stunning scenery. Most three-day treks from Chiang Mai, which can be arranged by guesthouses or trekking companies in the city, incorporate this area. Among the region's interesting towns are Mae Taeng, Phrao and Chiang Dao, all of which have long been at the interface between the Thai-dominated lowlands and the uplands, where the hill tribes live. It is vital to trek with a guide who is familiar with the area and hill-tribe etiquette. Typical routes, lasting two to three days, are marked below.

Tourists enjoying an elephant ride, Chiang Dao

SIGHTS NEAR CHIANG DAO

Fang

Doi That
1,802 m
(5,912 ft)

Soppong

1095

Doi Chiang Dao
2,285 m
(7,500 ft)

Wiang
Pa Pao

Chiang
Mai

KEY

▬▬	Major road
—	Minor road
- - -	Trek route

0 kilometres 25

0 miles 20

Doi Suthep ⑩

ดอยสุเทพ

DOI SUTHEP is a much-visited, thickly forested mountain within the twin-peaked Doi Suthep-Doi Pui National Park. Near its 1,601-m (5,250-ft) summit is Wat Phra That Doi Suthep, one of the most revered Buddhist shrines in Northern Thailand. The mountain is also popular with birdwatchers and trekkers. From Chiang Mai, a paved road snakes up the hillside to a village with restaurants and souvenir shops. From here there is a choice of a steep climb or funicular railway to the *wat*. Minor attractions on Doi Suthep include waterfalls, a Hmong village and, further along the road, the English-style gardens of Phuping Palace.

Buddha image by *chedi*

Murals in Cloister
The murals depict scenes from the Buddha's life.

★ **Central Chedi**
This striking gold-plated Lanna structure is a 16th-century extension of the original. The four multitiered gold umbrellas around it, onto which pilgrims apply gold leaf (see p26), are adorned with intricate filigree.

White Elephant Monument
According to legend, in the 1390s King Ku Na's elephant selected the site of the chedi by marching up the mountain, trumpeting and turning three times.

WAT DOI SUTHEP
Enshrining sacred relics, the *wat* at the top of Doi Suthep, founded in the 14th century, is regarded by many as the symbol of Lanna Thailand *(see pp58–9)*.

Naga Staircase
Flanked by impressive nagas, this sweeping staircase has almost 300 steps. The less energetic can take the funicular railway up to the temple.

STAR FEATURES
★ **Central Chedi**
★ **Panoramic Views**

Buddha Images in the Main Wihan
The gold Buddha images in the 16th-century wihan are the most important within the temple complex. The huge image at the back is surrounded by several smaller ones.

VISITORS' CHECKLIST

12 km (7.5 miles) NW of Chiang Mai, Chiang Mai province. ℹ️ TAT, Chiang Mai (053) 248604; Forestry Dept (02) 579 0529 (inc bungalow bookings). 🚆 🚌 Chiang Mai then songthaew. **Wat Doi Suthep** ⬜ 6am–6pm daily. **Palace Gardens** ⬜ 8:30am– 5pm Sat & Sun when royal family not in residence (phone to check). **Phuping Palace** ⬤ to public.

Library

Temple Bells
The original use of these miniature bells was to call the monks and the laity to worship. Today, there is a constant tinkling from visitors ringing them for good luck.

This is one of several buildings in the complex used as accommodation by monks.

Campanile
This decorative bell tower, near the steps up to the main wihan, is distinctive for its multi-coloured, layered roof.

Funicular railway

WILDLIFE AROUND WAT DOI SUTHEP

With its rich and varied wildlife, Doi Suthep-Doi Pui National Park is a great attraction for nature lovers. Despite the deforestation of the western side of the park due to agriculture and the building of tourist accommodation, the park is rich in plants, butterflies and birds, such as the green cochoa. Though people have killed or driven out many indigenous mammals, 60 species still live here, including the Burmese ferret badger.

Black-collared starling, a resident of the park

★ Panoramic Views
From the edge of the temple complex there are breathtaking views over the forests of Doi Suthep-Doi Pui National Park, and of Chiang Mai city, situated to the southeast.

Street-by-Street: Chiang Mai ⓫

เชียงใหม่

Typical Chiang Mai lantern

THAILAND'S SECOND most important city, Chiang Mai (literally, "new city"), was chosen in 1292 by King Mengrai to replace Chiang Rai *(see pp240–41)* as the capital of his Lanna Kingdom *(see pp58–9)*. Under Mengrai, Chiang Mai became a major base for Theravada Buddhism. It was during this period and the subsequent reign of King Tilok that many fine *wats* were built within the walled city, which is still the most atmospheric area. Today, visitors are increasingly drawn to Chiang Mai not only for its beautiful temples, but also for its excellent shopping and trekking facilities and up-market hotels and restaurants.

To Suan Dok Gate

Tourist police

Old Chiang Mai
The first bridge across the Ping River was built in 1950. Others were later added to cope with the city's growth.

Mengrai Kilns *(see p433)* sells a wide range of ceramics.

Mengrai Kilns

SAMLAN

SOI 7

Wat Muen Ngon Kong
This wat has exquisite lattice work and a Lanna chedi topped by a Burmese finial.

Wat Phra Chao Mengrai has a decorated ceremonial gate.

KEY

– – – Suggested route

STAR SIGHTS

★ **Wat Phra Sing**

★ **Wat Chedi Luang**

Wat Phan Waen
A typical Northern Thai temple, Wat Pan Waen is set within peaceful compounds, which provide relief from the city heat. The doors of the wihan are decorated with religious images.

★ Wat Phra Sing
This wat *was built in 1345 to house King Kham Fu's ashes. The Wihan Lai Kham is a superb Lanna structure with carved and gilded pediments. Murals inside depict everyday life in 19th-century Chiang Mai.*

VISITORS' CHECKLIST

Chiang Mai province. 168,000. 3 km (2 miles) SW of Chiang Mai. Charoen Muang Rd. Chiang Mai Arcade. TAT, 105/1 Chiang Mai–Lamphun Rd (053) 248604. main office: same address as TAT (053) 248130. daily. Festival of Flowers (Feb), Intakin Festival (May), Mango Fair (May), Food Festival (Dec), Winter Fair (late Dec/early Jan).

Wat Phan Tao
The well-preserved Lanna wihan *is notable at this* wat. *Its roof, supported by columns, is decorated with Lanna* cho fas *(see p31).*

★ Wat Chedi Luang
The spacious, triple-roofed wihan *houses panels depicting scenes from the* jataka *tales (see p26).*

Wat Chang Taem

0 metres	100
0 yards	100

CITY OF SPLENDID WATS

Though 45 times smaller than Bangkok, Chiang Mai boasts almost as many *wats* as the capital. Most were built during the city's most prosperous period – from the 13th to the mid-16th centuries – when it was a major religious centre. Many *wats* in Chiang Mai survive from this period, but most were altered by the Burmese, who subsequently ruled the city. Nevertheless, Chiang Mai's architecture is still thought to epitomize Lanna style *(see pp58–9)*, with features such as elaborate woodcarvings on temple pillars and doors.

The 19th-century Wihan Lai Kham, Wat Phra Sing

RATCHADAMNOEN

CHABAN

RATCHAMANKHA

SOI 7

Exploring Chiang Mai

Burmese carving

OFTEN CALLED the "rose of the North", Chiang Mai deserves its reputation. Its most important *wats*, notably Wat Chedi Luang and Wat Phra Sing, are situated within the old walled area of the city. The moat bounding the historic centre is still intact, but the walls were largely destroyed during World War II. There is also much to see outside the old city, including Wat U Mong – one of the area's oldest forest *wats* – and the excellent National Museum. Northeast of the river is the old colonial sector, with its characteristic mansions. Chiang Mai thrives on its crafts trade *(see pp198–9)*, as shown by the wide range sold at Warorot Market and the Night Bazaar, and along Tha Phae Road.

One of the murals inside Wat Phra Sing's Wihan Lai Kham

⛩ Wat Phra Sing
วัดพระสิงห์

W end of Ratchadamnoen Rd, near Suan Dok Gate. ⬭ daily.
Construction of this temple, the largest in Chiang Mai, began in 1345, though the *bot* dates from 1600. The Wihan Lai Kham ("gilded hall"), decorated with murals of everyday life, houses the revered golden Phra Buddha Sing. Like its namesakes in Bangkok *(see p84)* and Nakhon Si Thammarat *(see p369)*, the image is said to have originated in Sri Lanka.

⛩ Wat Chedi Luang
วัดเจดีย์หลวง

Phra Pok Klao Rd. ⬭ daily.
Within the compound of this temple is the spot where King Mengrai was killed by lightning in 1317. The revered Emerald Buddha image was briefly housed in the *wat* in the 15th century – a previous attempt to bring it to Chiang Mai failed *(see p79)*. The *chedi*, once 90 m (295 ft) high, was damaged by an earthquake in 1545.

⛩ Wat Chiang Man
วัดเชียงมั่น

Off Ratcha Phakhinai Rd. ⬭ daily.
King Mengrai allegedly resided in this temple, the city's oldest, while his new capital was being built. Its features include Lanna teak pillars and a *chedi* surrounded by stone elephant heads. The *wihan* houses the Buddha Sila image, thought to have been carved in Northern India in the 6th century BC.

⛩ Tha Phae Gate
ประตูท่าแพ

Tha Phae Gate marks the beginning of Tha Phae Road, the commercial hub of Chiang Mai. Located here are bookshops, department stores and handicraft shops. Further east, the road becomes Highway 1006, along which are shops and factories selling silk, celadon, lacquerware and other crafts.

⛩ Suan Dok Gate
ประตูสวนดอก

This is the city's western gate, marking the start of Suthep Road, along which three important temples are situated.

◪ Night Bazaar
ไนท์บาซาร์

Chang Khlan Rd. ⬭ 6–11pm daily.
With its wide range of goods at competitive prices, this easily rivals Bangkok's Chatuchak Market *(see p131)*. Inside are endless stalls selling hill-tribe crafts, leather goods and clothing. The top floor specializes in antiques. Beware of fakes *(see p431)*, especially at the stalls outside the market. This is also a good place to try Chiang Mai's Burmese-influenced cuisine. Shops on Wualai Road, south of Chiang Mai Gate, sell the best silverware and textiles.

◪ Warorot Market
ตลาดวโรรส

N of Tha Phae Rd. ⬭ daily.
During the day, this covered market sells clothing and hill-tribe crafts, often at lower prices than the Night Bazaar. Local fruits, spices and tasty dishes are also available. By night, it is the venue of a colourful flower market.

Shoppers browsing around Chiang Mai's lively Warorot Market

ENVIRONS: There are many sights outside the city centre that warrant a visit. Most can be reached by bicycle, motor-bike, *songthaew* or *tuk-tuk*. For longer excursions, most hotels and guesthouses offer trekking tours to hill-tribe villages *(see pp196–7)*. There are also many organized tour operators located on Tha Phae Road.

To the north of the city is the **Chiang Mai National Museum**. Its varied collection ranges from Haripunchai terracottas to Lanna heads of the Buddha, the largest of which is some 3 m (10 ft) tall.

Sited in the grounds of Chiang Mai University is the **Tribal Research Institute**. Its small museum and library detail the history of the area's ethnic minorities. Treks to hill-tribe villages can also be arranged here.

On Kaew Narawat Road, to the northeast of the city, is **McCormick Hospital**. This working hospital is typical of Chiang Mai's 19th- and 20th-

Buddha image, National Museum

century architecture, much of which was built by missionaries and officials of the British teak logging companies who came here from Burma.

Just west of Suan Dok Gate, on Suthep Road, is **Wat Suan Dok**. The temple was built in 1383 to house relics of the Buddha, while the open-sided *wihan* was restored in the 1930s. The small *chedis* contain ashes of members of Chiang Mai's former royal family. Near the entrance is a school of Thai massage.

Further along Suthep Road, set in picturesque forest scenery, is the 14th-century **Wat U Mong**. Some of the original underground tunnels leading to the monks' cells can still be explored. Also of note is a disturbing image of a fasting Buddha. Nearby **Wat Ram Poeng** offers meditation courses. The library keeps versions of the Theravada Buddhist canon in English, Chinese and other languages.

Façade of the 14th-century Wat Suan Dok

Wat Chet Yot, distinctive for its seven-spired *chedi*, is set in spacious grounds. Its stuccoed design is based on the Mahabodhi Temple of Buddh Gaya in India, where the Buddha achieved Enlightenment.

🛕 **Chiang Mai National Museum**
Off Superhighway. ☐ Wed–Sun.
● *public hols.* 🖾
🛕 **Tribal Research Institute**
Chiang Mai University, off Huai Kaew Rd. ☐ Mon–Fri. ● *public hols.*

CHIANG MAI CITY CENTRE

Night Bazaar ⑦
Suan Dok Gate ①
Tha Phae Gate ⑤
Warorot Market ⑥

Wat Chedi Luang ③
Wat Chiang Man ④
Wat Phra Sing ②

KEY

	See pp214–15
🏠	Tourist police
ℹ	Tourist information
🛕	Wat

0 metres 500
0 yards 500

Doi Saket **⑫**
ดอยสะเก็ด

Off Hwy 1019, 16 km (10 miles) NE
of Chiang Mai, Chiang Mai province.
ℹ *TAT, Chiang Mai (053) 248604.*
🚍 🚗 *Chiang Mai, then* songthaew.
◯ *daily.* 🎫

F ORMING A TRIANGLE with Bo
Sang and San Kamphaeng,
the mountain of Doi Saket is
an ideal sight to combine with
these two towns on a day trip
from Chiang Mai.

The main reason for visiting
Doi Saket is its hilltop temple,
Wat Doi Saket, which offers
stunning views of the Chiang
Mai valley. The *wat* is reached
by a steep staircase of 300
steps, flanked on either side by
a *naga*. The temple complex
includes a modern *wihan*,
painted in red and gold, and a
white *chedi*. There is a huge,
seated Buddha on the hill top
and seven smaller Buddhas,
one for each day of the week.

**Red and gold modern *wihan* of
the hill top Wat Doi Saket**

Women constructing ornamental umbrellas in the village of Bo Sang

Bo Sang **⑬**
บ่อสร้าง

Chiang Mai province. **🏠** *5,000.*
🚌 *from Chiang Mai.* **ℹ** *TAT,
Chiang Mai (053) 248604.* **🛍** *daily.*
🎪 *Umbrella Fair (Jan).*

L OCATED 9 KM (6 MILES) east of
Chiang Mai, Bo Sang is
known throughout Thailand
as the "umbrella village" on
account of the decorative umbrellas produced here. The
village is made up almost entirely of shops and factories
involved in this craft.

Each umbrella has a wooden
handle, bamboo ribs and a
covering of oiled rice paper,
silk or cotton. Craftsmen will
usually add names or a personalized design in bold colours
if requested. The annual fair
includes competitions, exhibitions and a beauty contest.

Other handicrafts, including silverware, celadon
(a greyish-green porce-
lain) and lacquerware,
are also sold here.

Aside from its umbrella making, Bo Sang is also the heart
of a farming community. In the
wet season (June–October),
the rice fields are a deep
green colour. From November
to January, the fields dry out
and turn golden. Farmers
then thresh the rice by hand.

Many houses in and around
Bo Sang are traditional, wood-
en Northern Thai structures
(see p32) with spacious rooms.
They are typically built on
stilts and set in small gardens.

San Kamphaeng **⑭**
สันกำแพง

Chiang Mai province. **🏠** *5,000.*
🚌 *from Chiang Mai.* **ℹ** *TAT, Chiang
Mai (053) 248604.* **🛍** *daily.*

T HIS SMALL VILLAGE, with its
old, wooden buildings and
narrow streets, is renowned for
its silk and handicraft products.
There are many factories here
selling good quality silk,

NAGAS: MYTHICAL SERPENTS

Naga figures, seen throughout Thailand, are protective
serpents. Acting as guardians against bad spirits, they often
flank the walls of temples or the staircases up to them, and
may also be carved on roofs, doors, gables and windows.
The significance of *nagas* is deep-rooted throughout Buddhist Asia, though their meaning may vary slightly according
to the country, with overlaps between Buddhism and Hinduism.
In Buddhism, their origins can be traced back to an episode in
the *jataka* tales *(see p27)* in which a *garuda*, or mythical bird,
attacks and subdues a *naga* that is trying to harm the Buddha.
The *naga* subsequently becomes the Buddha's guardian. Its
protective powers are shown when Mucilinda, a king of the
nagas, grows several heads to shelter the Buddha from a thun-
derstorm. *Nagas* are also believed to control rainfall and are
worshipped as givers of water during Songkran *(see p226)*.

**Two-headed *naga* of
Wat Chedi Luang,
Chiang Saen
*(see p238)***

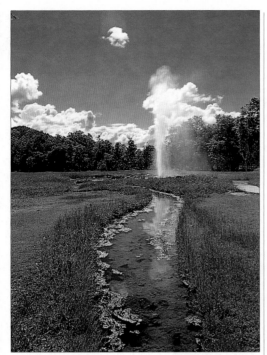

Geyser bursting through the ground at the San Kamphaeng Hot Springs

teak furniture, silverware, lacquerware, jade or celadon. Prices can be high, though bargaining *(see p455)* often reduces the cost significantly. An interesting feature of most of the silk factories are their exhibits of the silk-making process. The whole procedure is shown *(see pp256–7)*, from silk moths, through the unravelling of the cocoons, to the weaving of dyed silk thread on traditional wooden looms.

ENVIRONS: To the east of San Kamphaeng, just past the village of Mu Song, are the caves of **Tan Muang On**, with impressive stalactites and stalagmites. Further east are the **San Kamphaeng Hot Springs**, offering therapeutic baths in rich, hot mineral water. Here, geysers spurt out of the ground to an incredible height.

Tan Muang On
14 km (8.5 miles) E of San Kamphaeng.
○ daily.

San Kamphaeng Hot Springs
20 km (12.5 miles) E of San Kamphaeng. ○ daily.

Lamphun ⓯
ลำพูน

Lamphun province. 🏠 14,000. 🚉
🚌 ℹ TAT, Chiang Mai (053) 248604.
🚍 daily. 🎉 Lamyai Festival (Aug).

THIS ANCIENT TOWN was the capital of the Haripunchai Kingdom from AD 750–1281. Today, Lamphun is made up of large wooden houses beside the Kuang River, and is characterized by its peaceful atmosphere, ancient temples and surrounding countryside of rice fields.

Lamphun's most important temple is **Wat Phra That Haripunchai**. The present compound was probably founded in AD 1044 by King Athitayarai of Haripunchai, though the 46-m (150-ft) high central *chedi*, topped by a nine-tier umbrella of pure gold, is thought to date from 897. In the 1930s, the temple was renovated by Khrubaa Siwichai, one of the most revered monks

in Northern Thailand. One unusual structure is the rare, pyramid-shaped *chedi* in the northwest of the compound. The large *bot* houses a reclining Buddha image, while a 15th-century Lanna Buddha is kept in the main *wihan*. Adjoining it is a 19th-century library, with a staircase flanked by *nagas*. To the right of the library is an open pavilion displaying a huge gong cast in 1860, alleged to be the largest in the world. Outside the main compound is a smaller *bot*, inside of which is a so-called "happy Buddha", a fat, smiling Chinese-style image.

The nearby **Lamphun National Museum** is small but excellent. It has carvings and artifacts from many periods, especially the Dvaravati, Haripunchai and Lanna kingdoms. Modern artifacts include an ornate black and gold howdah *(see pp198–9)* and *naga* decorations. The collection of Buddha images covers many schools of sculpture.

Wat Chama Thewi (or Wat Kukut), just west of Lamphun on Highway 1015, is noted for its two *chedis*, thought to be among the oldest in Thailand. Both built in 1218, they are the last surviving examples of Dvaravati architecture. The larger, tiered structure is adorned with Buddha images, and the smaller one is decorated with Hindu gods.

🏛 Lamphun National Museum
Inthayongyot Rd, opposite Wat Phra That Haripunchai. ○ Wed–Sun. 🈲

ENVIRONS: **Pasang**, a small town 30 km (19 miles) south of Lamphun, produces excellent cottonwear of unique designs, especially sarongs and shirts. They are sold through many outlets in the town. Lamphun province, in particular the town of Nong Chang Kheun, to the north, is renowned for its *lamyai*, or longan *(see p129)* fruit. It is celebrated in a festival which features competitions and a Miss Lamyai beauty contest.

Buddha head, Lamphun National Museum

Doi Inthanon National Park ⑯

อุทยานแห่งชาติดอยอินทนนท์

The rare *hyper-icum garrettii*

DOI INTHANON, at 2,565 m (8,400 ft), is the highest mountain in Thailand. It is located in the 272-sq km (105-sq mile) Doi Inthanon National Park, and, being only 58 km (36 miles) from Chiang Mai, is a popular destination for one-day excursions. The park has many types of habitat and a wide range of mammals, such as leopard cats, pangolins and flying squirrels. The area is also popular for bird-watching, being home to nearly 400 bird species, many from North Asia (including mountain hawk eagles and Eurasian woodcocks). Karen and Hmong peoples *(see pp196–7)* also live here. In contrast with the rest of Thailand, the climate on Doi Inthanon can be chilly, so visitors to the park are advised to take warm clothing.

Twin Chedis
This shrine is inside one of th twin chedis of Phra That Nap arethanidon, built in honour King Bhumibol's 60th birthda

Spectacular View
Walkers on Doi Inthanon are treated to impressive views. On a clear day it is possible to see for many kilometres over the forested landscape.

Doi Inthanon 2,565 m (8,400 ft)

Mae Pan waterfall

Siriph water

MAE CHAEM

Sphagnum Moss
Doi Inthanon's cool climate allows plants such as mosses, ferns and lichens to thrive. At the mountain's summit, sphagnum mosses form a kind of "bog", the only habitat of this kind in Thailand.

Montane evergreen forests are found on the upper levels of Doi Inthanon.

Timber Beetle
For protection, this beetle's markings ape the warning coloration of wasps. Its larvae are hatched in the trunks or branches of trees.

0 kilometres 2

0 miles 2

Orchids

Wild orchids are in abundance on Doi Inthanon. On the higher slopes of the mountain, 2,500 m (8,200 ft) above sea level, pink and white orchids (see p210) can be seen draped over the branches of evergreen trees.

White-Crested Laughing Thrush

This bird takes its name from its distinctive white crest. Its common habitat is the forest crowning the upper slopes of Doi Inthanon.

Deciduous and sub-montane forests are found in low-lying areas of the national park.

Vachiratarn waterfall

Borichinda cave

Mae Klang waterfall

CHIANG MAI ↑

Chom Thong

HOT ↙

Hmong Tribespeople

The Hmong (see p196) have been here since the 1890s. Their slash-and-burn agriculture has led to deforestation, but government schemes to reduce this are now underway.

KEY

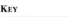

═══ Road

– – Trail

—•— Park border

ⓘ Park headquarters

🔺 Camping and bungalows

❊ Viewpoint

Mae Ya Waterfall

This is estimated to be the highest waterfall in the whole of Thailand. Falling over 250 m (820 ft), Mae Ya waterfall is also one of the most beautiful sights at Doi Inthanon.

Rural landscape around Hot, a town in the Ping River Valley

Ping River Valley ⑰

หุบเขาแม่น้ำปิง

Chiang Mai province. **ℹ** *TAT, Chiang Mai (053) 248607.* **🚌** *Chiang Mai, then songthaew.*

NEARLY 600 KM (370 miles) long, the Ping River is one of the major watercourses in Northern Thailand. It rises on the Burmese border, and flows on to the Bhumibol Reservoir before merging with the Chao Phraya River at Nakhon Sawan, in the Central Plains. The valley is a rural area, where traditional life can still be observed. There are also many tourist attractions along the way.

Wooden carving on the *bot* of Wat Phra That Si Chom Thong

Chom Thong, just south of Chiang Mai, at the junction of Highway 108 and the road to Doi Inthanon National Park *(see pp220–21)*, is a small but busy town. It boasts one major sight, **Wat Phra That Si Chom Thong**. The *wat* was built to enshrine a relic of the Buddha, and is still an important pilgrimage site for Buddhists. Many will try to make the journey at least once a year. This *wat* is also widely considered to be one of the most beautiful in Northern Thailand. The gilded *chedi*, built in 1451, is Burmese in design, as is the mid-16th-century *bot*, which features intricate woodcarvings

depicting flowers, birds and *nagas (see p218)*. A meditation centre and a room displaying thrones, religious antiques and weapons, are also located within the temple complex.

The deep Chaem River Valley, west of Chom Thong, is known locally for its many varieties of butterfly and moth. Several villages, spread along the twisting road within the valley, are known collectively as the town of **Mae Chaem**. The town, once famous for weaving, is now modernizing rapidly. Its main temple, **Wat Pa Daet**, is worth visiting for its well-preserved Lanna buildings and extensive murals.

At the southern end of the valley is the small town of **Hot**. Originally located 15 km (10 miles) further downstream, the town was relocated to its present site in 1964, when the land was flooded to form the Bhumibol Reservoir. Today, this reservoir is a major source of Thailand's electricity. Ruins of the original town can still be seen beside the reservoir, though they are limited to only a few *chedis*. Excavation of the site has turned up amulets, stucco carvings and gold jewellery. These artifacts are now on display in Chiang Mai's National Museum *(see p217)*. Modern-day Hot, meanwhile, is an important market town, and a useful staging post for journeys westwards to the town of Mae Sariang.

Mae Sariang ⑱

แม่สะเรียง

Mae Hong Son province. **🚶** *49,000.* **🚌 ℹ** *TAT, Chiang Mai (053) 248607.* **🛍** *daily.*

MAE SARIANG is a small, pleasant town on the Yuam River. The area has long historical links with nearby Burma, a fact which is reflected in Mae Sariang's architecture and by its large community of Burmese Muslims. People of the Karen hill tribe – the area's main ethnic group – can be seen in the central market.

Two temples near the bus station have Burmese features: multi-layered roofs and vivid orange and yellow exterior ornamentation. **Wat Chong Sung** (also called Wat Uthayarom) was built in 1896, while **Wat Si Bunruang** dates from 1939.

ENVIRONS: The area around Mae Sariang is mountainous and forested, with many winding roads. Organized trips by boat or *songthaew* (which can be arranged in town) make the 45-km (30-mile) journey from Mae Sariang to **Mae Sam Laep**, a Karen settlement on the Burmese border next to the Salawin River. This river was once infamous for drug running and gem smuggling. Today, Mae Sam Laep is a staging post for the (mostly illegal) teak log trade. Political troubles in Burma have made this area a zone for refugees, though some minorities from Burma, such as the Lawa, have lived here longer than Thais.

Chedi of the 19th-century Wat Chong Sung in Mae Sariang

The History of Opium in Thailand

OPIUM WAS FIRST grown in Northern Thailand in the late 19th century when hill tribes *(see pp196–7)* arrived from Southern China, where the drug was a major commodity. Grown on poor soil at high altitudes and easily transported, it was in fact their most profitable cash crop. Opium production was outlawed in Thailand in 1959, but flourished nonetheless during the Vietnam War. It was during this lucrative period that power struggles erupted

Opium poppies

for control of the Golden Triangle's *(see pp236–7)* poppy fields. The KMT *(see p232)*, allowed by the Thai government to control the illicit drugs trade, and the Shan United Army, based in Burma, were the largest of the many contenders, who also included the Thai, Burmese and Lao armies. Opium production has been cut by more than 80 per cent since the 1960s and most hill tribes now grow other crops. However, Thailand is still used as a channel for opium produced in nearby countries.

Smoking opium *in purpose-built dens became popular in parts of Asia – especially China – in the 19th century.*

Britain and China *fought the Opium Wars of 1839–42 and 1856–60 over British rights to import opium from India. After the wars the drug was legalized in China and freely traded.*

Short sickles, used to score poppy heads, are just some of a number of poppy-cultivating implements exhibited in the House of Opium.

The thin hillside soil easily supports poppies which favour the low-nutrient, high-alkaline conditions at altitudes of over 1,000 m (3,300 ft).

OPIUM PRODUCTION

This mural in the House of Opium Museum, Sop Ruak *(see p238)*, is one of a series showing traditional poppy harvesting for opium production, a process normally carried out in December and January. The museum also houses artifacts depicting the war between the KMT and the Shan United Army.

Since the 1980s, *new cash crops, including cabbages, tea and coffee, have begun to replace poppies grown for opium production. Today, fields of these new crops are a common sight in Northern Thailand.*

King Bhumibol, *concerned about opiate addiction in his country, and the illegal drugs trade, has been particularly active in encouraging replacement crops.*

Wat Phra That Lampang Luang ⑲
วัดพระธาตุลำปางหลวง

China cow by the main *chedi*, where devotees make merit

Ⓞ NE OF THE MOST renowned temples in Northern Thailand, Wat Phra That Lampang Luang is also one of the most attractive. The main buildings were constructed in the late 15th century on the site of an 8th-century fortress. This had been built on a mound to protect it from attack, and was further fortified by three parallel earthen ramparts separated by moats. The ramparts are still visible in the village around the present *wat*. In 1736 a local hero, Tip Chang, successfully defended the temple from the Burmese. The buildings are distinctive for their graceful architecture and richly coloured interiors, while the revered Phra Kaeo Don Tao image, allegedly carved from the same jadeite block as the Emerald Buddha (*see p79*), is kept in the museum behind the main complex.

Buddha in Wihan Phra Phut
A huge Buddha image sits inside the 13th-century wihan, *the oldest building on the site.*

Wihan Phra Phut
With its beautifully carved façade and two-tiered roof, this wihan, *from 1802, is a masterpiece of Lanna architecture.*

Bodhi tree

Main entrance

Five Buddhas in Wihan Luang
The huge, open-sided main wihan, *which dates from 1496, has an elegant, three-tiered roof. Inside are five seated Buddha images.*

STAR FEATURES

★ **Main Chedi**

★ **Murals in Wihan Nam Tam**

Main Staircase
Flanked by nagas, *this stairway leads up to a 15th-century ceremonial gatehouse.*

Ho Phra Phuttabat
*This small, elevated
mondop houses a
sculpture of the
Buddha's Footprint,
which is worshipped
by pilgrims during
important festivals.
Women may not
enter the building.*

Bot

Wihan Phra Sao Sila

VISITORS' CHECKLIST

Off Hwy 1, 25 km (16 miles) SW
of Lampang, Lampang province.
🗣 TAT, Chiang Mai (053) 248604.
🚌 Lampang, then songthaew or
taxi, or join tour from Lampang,
Chiang Mai or Lamphun.
🕙 9am–4pm daily. 🎫
🎉 Luang Wiang Lakhon (Feb).

★ Main Chedi
*The subtle green and blue
hues of the 15th-century
chedi are due to centuries of
rainfall, which have oxidized
the copper. Inside is a hair,
said to be from the Buddha.*

★ Murals in Wihan Nam Tam
*These faded murals, which depict
16th-century life and scenes from
the jataka tales (see p26), adorn the
walls of what may be Thailand's
oldest surviving wooden structure.*

**Ku in Wihan
Luang**
*The Buddha
image, Phra
Chao Lang
Thong, which
dates from
1563, sits in
this gilded
brick ku (Lao-
style prang).*

Wihan Ton Kaew

Pillar Detail
*This black lac-
quered pillar,
inlaid with
gold, is typical
of the intricate
decoration of
the whole tem-
ple complex.*

Horse-drawn carriages, the main form of transport in Lampang

Lampang ⑳

ลำปาง

Lampang province. 👥 70,000.
✈ 🚌 🚐 ℹ TAT, Chiang Mai
(053) 248604. 🏛 daily. 🎎 Luang
Wiang Lakon (Feb).

THE SECOND LARGEST TOWN in Northern Thailand, Lampang is still growing rapidly as a trading centre. It offers much of the historic interest of Chiang Mai, but without the overt commercialization. Lampang is also a good base for excursions and travel within Northern Thailand.

The town was originally inhabited in the 7th century. The following century, when it was still called Kelang Nakorn, it became part of the Haripunchai Empire, which centred on Lamphun *(see p219)*. In the 19th century, British traders came here from Burma and turned the town into a centre for teak production, bringing Burmese loggers and craftsmen with them. The result was the many teak houses and Burmese-style temples seen throughout the town today. Teak furniture is just one of the traditional crafts still produced in Lampang; others are cottonware and ceramics.

Modern-day Lampang is distinctive for its brightly coloured horse-drawn carriages, another tradition to survive the years. This mode of transport was introduced to Lampang in the 19th century, and it is the only town in Thailand that uses it.

One of the most important temples in Northern Thailand is **Wat Phra That Lampang Luang** *(see pp224–5)*, to the southwest of the town, which is renowned for its impressive 19th-century murals.

Lampang town focuses on the south side of the Wang River, although the main sights are found to the north of it. Of its temples, the most interesting is **Wat Phra Kaeo Don Tao**. The *wat* is thought to have been built about the same time the town was founded, but only the 50-m (165-ft) *chedi* survives from the original buildings. The distinctive *mondop* is notable for its nine-tier teak roof with intricate carvings and a bronze Buddha in the Mandalay style.

Between 1436 and 1468 the temple housed the revered Emerald Buddha, or Phra Kaeo *(see p77)*, which was later moved to Bangkok's Wat Phra Kaeo. During the same period, a similar jasper Buddha image, now in Wat Phra That Lampang Luang, was kept there. Within the compound is the **Lanna Museum**, displaying religious Lanna artifacts.

Ban Sao Nak ("many pillars house"), southeast of Wat Phra Kaeo Don Tao, is a Lanna structure built in 1896. It takes its name from the 116 square teak pillars supporting the building. Now a museum, it is furnished with Burmese and Thai antiques. The sumptuous decoration includes lacquerware, ceramics and silverware. **Wat Pongsanuk Tai**, to the west of Ban Sao Nak, is a distinctive late 18th-century

Interior of Ban Sao Nak, Lampang, decorated with antique crafts

---

SONGKRAN FESTIVITIES IN THE NORTH

Celebrated nationwide, but most exuberantly in and around Chiang Mai, Songkran *(see p42)* is one of Thailand's major festivals. Held over three days from 12th–14th April (though celebrations carry on until the 15th in towns such as Chiang Mai), Songkran marks the start of the Buddhist New Year. This public holiday has, over the centuries, evolved from a purely religious event, in which Buddha images are bathed with water to purify them, into a much greater celebration of water in the hot season. Nowadays, buckets of water are thrown over everyone in the streets (unsuspecting tourists make the best targets). Some of Songkran's original customs, such as younger Thais paying respect to their elders and monks by sprinkling their hands with perfumed water, are also maintained.

River procession in Lampang, part of the Songkran festivities

Performance at the Young Elephant Training Centre near Lampang

Lanna temple with a copper *chedi*. An enclosure in the *mondop* contains a Bodhi tree which is surrounded by four Buddha images.

The 19th-century Burmese-style **Wat Si Chum**, located in the south of the city, is constructed mostly from beautifully carved teak. The exquisite lacquerwork inside the main chamber shows life in Lampang during the 19th century.

🏛 **Lanna Museum**
Phra Kaeo Rd. 📞 *(053) 211364.*
⬚ *daily.* 🈺
🏛 **Ban Sao Nak**
Ratwana Rd. ⬚ *daily.* 🈺

Young Elephant Training Centre ㉑
ศูนย์ฝึกลูกช้าง

Off Hwy 11, 37 km (23 miles) NW of Lampang, Lampang province. 🛈 *TAT, Chiang Mai (053) 248604.* 🚉 🚌 *Lampang, then songthaew.* ⬚ *daily.* 🈺

ONE OF THE BEST elephant training camps in Northern Thailand, this one is less tourist-oriented than many others. About 12 animals, aged three to five years, arrive here each year to be trained, and there are about 100 in total. Although their ability peaks between the ages of 40 and 50, the elephants may remain at the camp until the official retirement age of 60.

During the five-year training period the elephants learn a variety of tasks in the nearby forest, including stacking, carrying and pushing logs. Nowadays, such daily chores are part of the regular performances put on principally for tourists. Visitors can get close to the elephants by feeding them fruit. Also on the site is a small museum, which focuses on the culture and the history of elephants in Thailand *(see p243).*

ENVIRONS: On the opposite side of the highway is the **Thung Kwian Forest Market**. It sells a wide range of wild plants and medicinal and culinary herbs, as well as lizards, beetles and snakes. Recent government campaigns have attempted to end the sale of endangered species *(see p209)* at the market, though some, such as pangolins (scaly anteaters), are still sold here.

Poster for Young Elephant Training Centre

🏪 **Thung Kwian Forest Market**
Off Hwy 11, 35 km (22 miles) NW of Lampang. ⬚ *daily.*

Uttaradit ㉒
อุตรดิตถ์

Uttaradit province. 👥 *43,000.* 🚉
🚌 🛈 *TAT, Chiang Rai (053) 717433.*
🛒 *daily.* 🎪 *Langsat Fair (Oct).*

THIS PROVINCIAL CAPITAL, relatively free of modern development and tourist paraphernalia, features on few visitors' itineraries. Nevertheless, the town's location makes it a convenient staging post between the North Central Plains and Northern Thailand.

Uttaradit rose to prominence during the Sukhothai era, and just prior to the collapse of the kingdom at the end of the 13th century, the town marked its northern border. Uttaradit's most famous citizen was King Taksin, who was born here in the mid-18th century. He reunited Thailand after the Burmese sacked Ayutthaya in 1767. The town is made up of old teak buildings and narrow streets. The main temple of interest is **Wat That Thanon**, behind the train station. Inside is the Luang Pho Phet, a revered bronze Lanna Buddha.

To the west of Uttaradit is **Wat Phra Boromathat**, which is also known as Wat That Thung Yang. Its *wihan* is an example of the Lao Luang Prabang architectural style.

Uttaradit province is renowned for the quality of its agricultural produce, particularly the *langsat* fruit.

Busy main street of Uttaradit, the birthplace of King Taksin

FAR NORTH

THE FAR NORTH *of Thailand is known as the Golden Triangle – the meeting point of Thailand, Burma and Laos and an area historically associated with opium production. Nowadays, this picturesque region with numerous hill-tribe villages attracts large numbers of trekkers. Less well known delights in the Far North include, southeast of the Golden Triangle, quiet towns such as Phrae and Nan.*

The fertile flood plains of the Mekhong, which touch the tip of the Far North before running east into Laos, contrast with the breathtaking beauty of the mountains in the west and east of the area. Here can be found remote villages inhabited by hill tribes such as the Mien and Akha, who still preserve their traditional way of life. There are also settlements populated by ex-Chinese Nationalist soldiers and their descendants, who migrated here after Mao Tse-tung's Communist army won the Chinese civil war in 1949.

Chiang Rai is the main town in the Far North. Though not picturesque, it has a few sights and is used as a trekking base. Of greater interest are the towns strung out by the Mekhong along the Burmese and Lao borders, including the ancient city of Chiang Saen and Chiang Khong, a Thai Lue settlement.

Most visitors to Northern Thailand travel from Chiang Mai to Chiang Rai, and then north to the Golden Triangle, thus some sights to the east are relatively unknown. The old, walled settlement of Phrae, for instance, with some of Thailand's largest teak buildings, is visited by few tourists, despite being easily accessible from the Central Plains and Chiang Mai. The town of Nan is more remote, set in a valley far from the main highway to the Golden Triangle. The diversion is worthwhile, if only to see the murals at Wat Phumin. Northeast of here, Doi Phu Kha National Park offers superb birdwatching. To the south of Nan, and far from the beaten track, is extraordinarily diverse scenery ranging from the earth pillars of Sao Din and Phrae Muang Phi to the vast Sirikit Reservoir.

Thai Lue farmer ploughing the fields in the time honoured way

◁ **Young Lisu women sporting their elaborate and colourful traditional costumes**

Exploring the Far North

THE NORTHERNMOST region of Thailand is, for many people, synonymous with the Golden Triangle. This semi-mythical region around the meeting point of three national borders still conjures up images of untamed wilderness, remote hill-tribe villages and fugitive opium barons. There remains more than a grain of truth in this reputation, but the Far North is also developing rapidly as a tourist destination, centred around the one-time capital of the Lanna Kingdom, Chiang Rai. The major attraction for visitors is the spectacular and varied geography of the region, best explored by foot or motorbike. Touring through the mighty forested mountains along the Burmese and Lao borders, and beside the winding Mekhong, as it skirts the tip of the region, is a richly rewarding experience.

SIGHTS AT A GLANCE

TACHILEK ●
MAE SAI ⑤
④ DOI TU
⑥
GOLDEN
TRIANGLE
TOUR
MAE SALONG ③
1089
②
THA TON
① FANG
Chiang Mai
CHIANG
RAI
⑩
MAE SARUAI ⑪
118
Phrao
⑫ WIANG
PA PAO
Chiang Mai
⑬
PHAYAO
120
NG
1035
Lampang
Sukboth

KEY

▬▬	Major road
▭▭	Minor road
▭▭	Scenic route
⌐	River
☆	Viewpoint

A gathering of Lisu tribeswomen in traditional costume

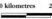

0 kilometres	25
0 miles	15

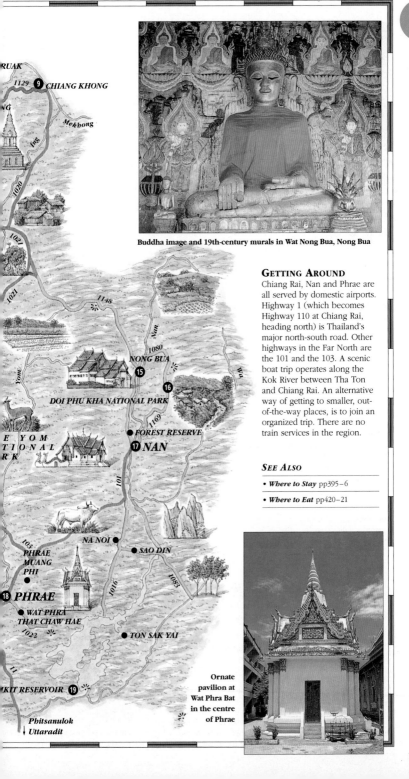

Buddha image and 19th-century murals in Wat Nong Bua, Nong Bua

GETTING AROUND

Chiang Rai, Nan and Phrae are all served by domestic airports. Highway 1 (which becomes Highway 110 at Chiang Rai, heading north) is Thailand's major north-south road. Other highways in the Far North are the 101 and the 103. A scenic boat trip operates along the Kok River between Tha Ton and Chiang Rai. An alternative way of getting to smaller, out-of-the-way places, is to join an organized trip. There are no train services in the region.

SEE ALSO

- *Where to Stay* pp395–6
- *Where to Eat* pp420–21

Map labels:

RUAK
1129 **9 CHIANG KHONG**
NG
Mekhong
Ing
1020
1021
1021
1148
Nam
1080 **NONG BUA 15**
Yom
16
Wa
DOI PHU KHA NATIONAL PARK
1169
E YOM **FOREST RESERVE**
TIONAL **17 NAN**
R K
101
103
NA NOI
SAO DIN
PHRAE MUANG PHI
1016
1083
18 PHRAE
WAT PHRA THAT CHAW HAE
1022
TON SAK YAI
11
KIT RESERVOIR **19**
Phitsanulok ↓ *Uttaradit*

Ornate pavilion at Wat Phra Bat in the centre of Phrae

Karen tribespeople trading their wares at Fang's daily market

Fang ➊

ฝาง

Chiang Mai province. 🏚 *10,000*.
🚌 *from Chiang Mai.* ℹ *TAT, Chiang Mai (053) 248604.* 📅 *daily.*

THIS SMALL TOWN was founded as a trading centre in 1268 by King Mengrai, who took advantage of the site's strategic location at the head of a valley. At the beginning of the 19th century the town was destroyed by Burmese raiders, and lay deserted until 1880. Today Fang is effectively a frontier town between the areas inhabited by Thais and hill tribes (*see pp196–7*). The local Mien, Karen and Lahu tribes sell their goods at Fang's market, and this has once again made it an important trading centre.

Fang is characterized by two-storey teak houses. The influence of nearby Burma is evident in many structures, such as **Wat Jong Paen**, located in the far north of town. The most impressive temple in Fang, it features a Burmese-style, multi-roofed *wihan*.

ENVIRONS: Drug trading in the Fang area has been significant in the past, and fighting between rival drug factions in Burma still occasionally spills across the border. It is therefore wise to check the situation with the local tourist office before venturing on a guided trek. Sights in the region include, some 10 km (6 miles) west of Fang, sulphur springs, whose natural energy is used to power a nearby geothermal plant. To the southwest of Fang, Highway 1249 leads to the peak of **Doi Ang Khang**, via several Lisu, Lahu and Hmong hill-tribe villages.

Tha Ton ➋

ท่าตอน

Chiang Mai province. 🏚 *4,000*.
🚌 *from Chiang Mai to Fang, then songthaew.* ℹ *TAT, Chiang Mai (053) 248604.*

LOCATED ON A BEND in the Kok River, picturesque Tha Ton is essentially a staging post for riverboats which make regular trips from here to Chiang Rai. Excursions can be arranged at guesthouses in town, and may often be combined with visits to nearby hill-tribe villages or hot springs. Tha Ton's chief tourist attraction is **Wat Tha Ton**, which is notable for a huge white Buddha with a striking golden topknot. The temple dominates the town from its hillside location to the west, offering panoramic views of the surrounding countryside.

Imposing white Buddha overlooking Tha Ton

ENVIRONS: The road leading from Tha Ton to Doi Mae Salong, 43 km (26 miles) to the northeast, takes in impressive mountain scenery and villages along the Burmese border.

Mae Salong (Santikhiree) ➌

ดอยแม่สะลอง (ดอยสันติคีรี)

Chiang Rai province. 🏚 *950.* 🚌 *Chiang Rai, then songthaew.* ℹ *TAT, Chiang Rai (053) 717433.* 📅 *daily.*

ONE OF THE most important settlements in the recent history of Northern Thailand, the hillside town of Mae Salong is also one of the most scenic. Mae Salong was founded in 1962 by the Kuomintang (KMT), or Chinese Nationalist Army, following their defeat in China by Mao Tse-tung in 1949. It became a centre for exiled Chinese soldiers, who used it as a base for incursions into China. The Thai military agreed to let the KMT stay if they helped to suppress Communism, which they believed would become rife among the hill tribes at the time of the Vietnam War. In return for their help, the KMT were allowed to control and tax the local opium trade. As a result, the area around Mae Salong was relatively lawless and dangerous until the 1980s.

When Khun Sa, the opium warlord (*see p223*), retreated to Burma in the early 1980s, the Thai government began to have some success in pacifying the area. This was helped when, soon after the end of this turbulent period, Mae Salong was officially renamed Santikhiree ("hill of peace"), in an attempt to rid the town of its former image. The new term is used for both the town and the 1,200-m (3,950-ft) peak

Chinese medicinal herbs and spices for sale at Mae Salong market

Modern temple on the hill top of Doi Mae Salong

that rises above it, Doi Mae Salong. A temple was recently built at the summit, giving spectacular views of the surrounding rolling hills, which are dotted with hill-tribe villages. Akha and Mien villagers can be seen at the market in Mae Salong, though the town's main population is made up of old KMT soldiers and their descendants. The sight of low, Chinese-style houses made of bamboo, and the sound of Yunnanese (a Chinese dialect) give the overall impression that Mae Salong is more of a Chinese than Thai town.

A road built to Mae Salong in the early 1980s made the settlement less isolated. Opium production is now suppressed, having been replaced by new cash crops such as cabbages, tea and Chinese herbs and medicines. This produce is sold in the town's market.

Doi Tung ❹

ดอยตุง

Chiang Rai province. ℹ TAT, Chiang Rai (053) 717433. 🚌 from Mae Chan or Mae Sai to turn-off for Doi Tung, then songthaew to summit.

THE MOUNTAIN of Doi Tung is an impressive limestone outcrop dominating the Mekhong flood plain near Mae Sai. The narrow road snakes through beautiful monsoon forest, winding its way up to the 1,800-m (5,900-ft) peak. On a clear day the views of Burma and lowland Thailand from the summit are especially stunning.

The name of the mountain means "flag peak", so called because in AD 911 King Achutarat of Chiang Saen ordered a giant flag to be flown from the summit to mark the site where two *chedis* were to be built, allegedly to house a piece of the Buddha's collarbone. Still a major pilgrimage site, the *chedis* are at the heart of **Wat Phra That Doi Tung**, which was renovated in the early 1900s. Also here is a large, rotund Chinese-style Buddha image. Pilgrims throw coins into its navel to make merit.

The area around Doi Tung has historically been the site of opium production, the poppy fields guarded by hill tribespeople and the KMT. In recent years the area has become the focus for a rural development project aimed at increasing central government control over the area. In 1988 **Doi Tung Royal Villa** was built on the mountain as part of a plan to increase tourism in the area and to discourage nearby hill tribes from producing opium. Originally a summer residence for the late mother of King Bhumibol, the villa has an attractive flower garden and a restaurant. While the scheme has largely succeeded, local hill-tribe villagers have become dependent on hand-outs from the development project and from tourists.

Doi Tung is now connected to the other main settlements of the area by good roads. These make fascinating driving into regions that were once the preserve of drug barons. Mae Salong and Mae Sai may be reached by these routes, via Lahu and Akha hill-tribe villages. Although a strong Thai army presence has reduced drug trading in the area substantially, visitors are advised not to leave main roads.

🏛 **Doi Tung Royal Villa**
Hwy 1149. ⬤ to public. **Palace Gardens** ☐ daily. 📷

The hillside of Doi Tung, cultivated with new crops aimed at replacing opium as the main source of income

Terraced plantation adjoining a formal garden, on a hillside in the beautiful Golden Triangle region ▷

Mae Sai ❺

แม่สาย

Chiang Rai province. 🏯 10,000.
🚌 🛈 TAT, Chiang Rai (053) 717433.
🗓 daily.

THE NORTHERNMOST town in
Thailand, Mae Sai is separated from Burma only by a
bridge. Every day, the town
bustles with traders from the
neighbouring country who
come here to trade their wares.
Among the handicrafts for sale
are lacquerware, gems and
jade items, mostly made in
Burma. Though the town itself is nondescript, there are
good views over the Sai River
to Burma. **Wat Phra That Doi
Wao** also has a good outlook.

ENVIRONS: For a small fee in
US dollars, visitors may usually
cross the bridge to the Burmese town of **Tachilek**. Check
the current political situation
with the Burmese Embassy *(see
p451)* or with a tour operator,
as this determines whether visitors can travel further into Burma. Tachilek looks much like
Mae Sai and thrives on its market selling a variety of goods.
  South of Mae Sai is **Tham
Luang**, a large cave complex
with crystals that change colour
in the light. Further south are
more caves, **Tham Pum** and
Tham Pla, with lakes inside.

🦇 **Tham Luang**
Off Hwy 110, 6 km (3.5 miles) S of Mae
Sai. ◯ daily. 🈸 🎫
🦇 **Tham Pum and Tham Pla**
Off Hwy 110, 13 km (8 miles) S of
Mae Sai. ◯ daily. 🈸 🎫

**Brick warehouses near the Burmese
border, just outside Mae Sai**

Golden Triangle Driving Tour ❻

THE GOLDEN TRIANGLE is a 195,000 sq-km
(75,000 sq-mile) area spanning parts of
Thailand, Laos and Burma, the three countries of the "triangle". The area is historically connected to the opium and heroin
trades (thus "golden"), but has much more
to interest visitors. This tour takes in its best
features: superb views of the "apex" of the
Golden Triangle, where the three countries
meet; hill-tribe villages nestling amid stunning mountain scenery; and the historical
towns of Chiang Saen and Chiang Khong.
  Illicit opium trading is thought to continue in
the region, however, and visitors should take extra care
near the Burmese border, which can be dangerous.

**Lanna
carving,
Chiang Saen**

Saam Yekh Akha ③
As in every Akha vil-
lage, small sculptures
of people, represent-
ing human life, deco-
rate the village gates.
These are meant to
warn spirits that only
humans may enter.

Doi Mae Salong ②
This mountain, the site of the mainly
Chinese settlement of Mae Salong *(see
pp232–3)*, is set amid beautiful
rolling scenery.

1089

Pha Dua ④
This Mien village
sells textiles and handi-
crafts. Visitors may also see
elaborate rituals and ceremonies based on the local hill
tribe's religion, a mixture of
animism and Chinese Taoism.

Tha Ton ①
Located near the Burmese
border, Tha Thon *(see p232)*
is a staging post between the
lowlands and the mountains.
A huge white Buddha image,
visible from miles around,
faces eastwards over the town
and surrounding countryside.

TIPS FOR DRIVERS

Tour length: 200 km (125 miles).
Stopping-off points: Mae Sai,
Chiang Saen, and Chiang Khong
all have restaurants, guesthouses
and petrol stations. Smaller roads
may be difficult for passing, especially in the wet season, so it is best
to use the numbered roads above.

0 kilometres   15

0 miles   10

Mae Sai ⑥
Wat Phra That Doi Wao, on a hill top outside Mae Sai, is the town's best temple. The *bot* features carvings of the Buddha.

Doi Tung ⑤
This impressive mountain is the site of the Doi Tung Royal Villa *(see p233)*, which has a colourful, English-style flower garden.

Sop Ruak ⑦
This village *(see p238)*, with its restaurants and shops, thrives on its location at the meeting point of Thailand, Burma and Laos.

BURMA (MYANMAR) • *Tachilek*

LAOS

THAILAND

e Chan •

Rai •

KEY

Major road
Minor road
Country boundary
Viewpoint

Chiang Khong ⑩
Though most people pass non-stop through Chiang Khong *(see p239)* en route to Laos, the town's Wat Luang is well worth seeing.

Wat Phra That Pha Ngao ⑨
This 10th-century temple *(see p239)* is superbly sited on a hill top south of Chiang Saen, and offers exhilarating views of the surrounding countryside. It is distinctive for its bas relief work on the *wihan* and its *chedi* of shiny white marble.

Chiang Saen ⑧
Visitors should not miss this town *(see pp238–9)* of ruined temples and teak trees, once the capital of a small kingdom. Today it boasts an excellent branch of the National Museum and a daily market specializing in Thai Lue fabrics and souvenirs.

Farmers using traditional methods to cultivate rice in paddy fields near Chiang Saen

The Golden Triangle Apex (Sop Ruak) ❼

สามเหลี่ยมทองคำ (สปรวก)

50 km (31 miles) NE of Chiang Rai, Chiang Rai province. 🚌 *from Chiang Saen.* 🚤 *from Chiang Saen.* ℹ️ *TAT, Chiang Rai (053) 717433.*

THE APEX OF THE Golden Tri- angle is the point at which the borders of Thailand, Burma and Laos meet. The junction, at a bend in the Mekhong Riv- er, is near the village of **Sop Ruak**. Historically, the "Golden Triangle" referred to a much wider region – the area of Northern Thailand, Burma and Laos in which opium was pro- duced *(see p223)*. Nowadays, though, the term refers to a much smaller area and is as- sociated with Sop Ruak village.

Sop Ruak, eager to take advantage of its location, is growing rapidly as a tourist destination, as evidenced by its many shops, restaurants and hotels. A museum, the **House of Opium**, displays artifacts relating to opium production. It details a battle between the KMT army *(see p232)* and the now-deposed opium lord, Khun Sa *(see p223)*, over con- trol of the local opium trade. The battle, which established the notoriety of the Gold- en Triangle, took place nearby in 1967.

But the area's main attraction is undoubt- edly the Mekhong. Boat trips give su- perb views of for- ested Laos and of the Golden Triangle Paradise Resort in Burma. The resort, with a casino, was built in Burma as gambling is illegal in Thailand.

Lanna carving, National Museum

🏛 House of Opium
212 House of Opium, SE of Sop Ruak village centre. ⬜ *daily.* 📷

Chiang Saen ❽

เชียงแสน

Chiang Rai province. 👥 *11,000.* 🚌 🚤 ℹ️ *TAT, Chiang Rai (053) 717433.* ⬜ *daily.*

ONE OF THE oldest towns in Thailand, Chiang Saen is set beautifully on the bank of the Mekhong River. The town was founded in 1328 by Saenphu, the grandson of King Mengrai, as a powerful fortification with many temples. There is evidence, however, from some of Chiang Saen's monu- ments, that suggests the town may be much older. In 1558 Chiang Saen was captured by the Burmese. It was liberated by King Rama I in 1804, who burned it to the ground to prevent its recapture. The present town was established in the early 1880s. Today, Chiang Saen is a quiet and peaceful settle- ment boasting an impressive number of monuments that survived the razing. The Fine Arts Department in Bangkok lists 66 ruins inside the walled town and 75 beyond.

The largest temple in Chiang Saen is **Wat Chedi Luang**. Its 58-m (190-ft) octagonal *chedi*, built between the 12th and the 14th centuries, is a classic Chiang Saen (more commonly known as Lanna) structure. Beside the temple is a small market selling textiles and souvenirs made by the Thai Lue, an ethnic minority from

Mural in the House of Opium showing tools used to harvest poppies

China who came to the area in the 18th century. Also nearby is the **Chiang Saen National Museum**, with a collection of stone carvings from the Lanna period, Buddha images and artifacts relating to hill-tribe culture (*see pp196–7*).

The town's most attractive temple is **Wat Pa Sak**, ("teak forest temple"), located outside the old walls to the west. The monument consists of seven separate ruined structures set among teak trees, which give the *wat* its name. The *chedi*, built in 1295, is the oldest in town. It is carved with flowers and mythological beasts.

On a hill to the northwest of Chiang Saen is **Wat Phra That Cham Kitti**, which is thought to date back to the 10th century. Although the temple has little of architectural interest, it gives impressive views of the town and the Mekhong.

Just south of Chiang Saen is the hilltop **Wat Phra That Pha Ngao**. This temple, with a white pagoda, offers stunning views of the river and the Golden Triangle region.

🏠 **Chiang Saen National Museum**
Phahon Yothin Rd. ⬜ *Wed–Sun.* ⬤ *public hols.* 📷
🏛 **Wat Pa Sak**
Near Chiang Saen Gate. ⬜ *daily.* 📷

Typical Thai Lue fabrics for sale in Chiang Khong

Chiang Khong ❾
เชียงของ

Chiang Rai province. 👥 *12,000.* 🚌 🚐 ℹ *TAT, Chiang Rai (053) 717433.* 🏨 *daily.*

SITUATED ON THE bank of the Mekhong River, Chiang Khong town is all that remains of the much larger territory of Chiang Khong, most of which was lost to the French in 1893 when they claimed it as part of French Indochina (the rest of this land now forms part of Laos). A growing border town, Chiang Khong is largely dominated by events in Laos. The town was one of the key points of arrival for refugees after the Communist victory in Laos in 1975 (*see p285*).

There is a large Thai Lue community here too, and shops sell their distinctive, multi-coloured textiles. Chiang Khong's main temple is the 13th-century **Wat Luang**, in the town centre. On a hillside just northwest of town is a cemetery where some 200 Chinese KMT soldiers, killed in battles against Communists in the area since the 1960s, are buried.

ENVIRONS: Visitors can take a ferry to **Huay Xai**, just inside the Lao border. To do so, you must obtain a visa for Laos from a travel agency in Chiang Khong or from the Lao Embassy in Bangkok (*see p451*). An important trade centre, Huay Xai boasts the 19th-century **Wat Chan Khao Manirat**.

THAILAND'S TEAK INDUSTRY

The use of teak (*Tectona grandis*) in Thailand dates back many centuries. Its favourable properties, including strength and resistance to pests and disease, made it a natural choice for use in buildings and furniture, while its fine grain traditionally lent itself to intricate carving. However, reckless over-logging has led to disastrous deforestation, and, as a result, most commercial teak logging and export was banned in 1989. Pockets

Transporting teak logs on the Chao Phraya River

of teak may still be seen in its natural habitat – low-lying deciduous forests of up to 600 m (1,950 ft) in elevation, with rich, moist soil (such forest is characteristic of Northern Thailand) – or in large new plantations. The trees are easily recognizable by their huge size – they can grow up to 100 m (330 ft) when mature – and by their large, floppy leaves, which fall off during the dry period of November to May. Thailand's historic use of teak is evident in rural parts of the country, such as in the old wooden houses of provincial towns, including Phrae (*see pp248–9*) and Ngao (*see p242*), both located in the North.

Lowland teak forest in Northern Thailand

Chiang Rai ⑩

เชียงราย

THIS ANCIENT TOWN was founded in 1262 by King Mengrai. He decided that the site, in a basin between mountains, would be ideal for the new capital of the Lanna Kingdom *(see pp56–7)*. However, the capital was transferred to Chiang Mai only 34 years later and Chiang Rai declined in importance. Today it is known as the "gateway to the Golden Triangle". While the modern town may lack the charm and architectural interest of Chiang Mai, it has a number of sights worthy of attention.

Detail of carved peacock, Wat Phra Sing

Exploring Chiang Rai

With its varied ethnic groups and beautiful surrounding scenery, Chiang Rai, the capital of Thailand's northernmost province, feels far removed from Bangkok or even Chiang Mai. Evidence of the town's historic importance can be seen in monuments such as Wat Phra Kaeo, even though modern development is becoming increasingly prominent.

The construction of new hotels for tourists, who use Chiang Rai as a trekking base, and of second homes for the wealthy people of Bangkok, have made the town one of the fastest growing in Thailand. Economic activity in the area is expected to grow even further as trade increases with China, just 200 km (120 miles) to the north. New development focuses mainly on the area between the old market off Suk Sathit Road and Phahon Yothin Road, with the newest hotels on the outskirts of town and by the airport. Resorts have been built on many of the islands in the Kok River.

▲ Wat Phra Kaeo

วัดพระแก้ว

Trirat Rd. ⬤ *daily.*
This is the city's most revered temple. According to legend, lightning struck and cracked the *chedi* in 1436, revealing a plaster cast statue encasing the Emerald Buddha (actually made of jadeite). Today Thailand's most holy Buddha image is housed in Bangkok *(see p79)*. A replica, presented in 1991, is now kept here. The *wat* dates from the 13th century and is also notable for its fine *bot*, decorated with elaborate woodcarving, and the Phra Chao Lang Thong, one of the largest surviving bronze statues from the early Lanna period *(see pp58–9)*.

▲ Wat Chet Yot

วัดเจ็ดยอด

Chet Yot Rd. ⬤ *daily.*
This small temple, named for its unusual, seven-spired *chedi*, is similar in appearance to its namesake in Chiang Mai *(see pp216–17)*. The front veranda of the main *wihan* has a mural depicting astrological scenes.

▲ Wat Phra Sing

วัดพระสิงห์

Singhakhrai Rd. ⬤ *daily.*
Built in the late 14th century, Wat Phra Sing is a typical Northern wooden structure, with low, curved roofs. The main *wihan* houses a replica of the Phra Sing Buddha in Chiang Mai's Wat Phra Sing *(see pp214–17)*. Also of interest are the carved medallions below the windows of the *bot*, which depict birds and animals. Around the Bodhi tree are images of the Buddha.

Staircase leading up to a seated Buddha image at Wat Mungmuang

▲ Wat Mungmuang

วัดมุ่งเมือง

Uttarakit Rd. ⬤ *daily.*
A rotund Buddha image with one hand raised in the *vitarkha mudra* position *(see p163)* dominates this *wat*. The murals in the main *wihan*, depicting local mountain scenery and scenes of flooding and pollution, reflect the concern of Thais at the rapid growth of their cities, an issue of particular relevance in Chiang Rai.

▲ Wat Doi Chom Thong

วัดพระธาตุดอยจอมทอง

Doi Chom Thong Hill. ⬤ *daily.*
This temple, built in the 1940s, is located on a hill top outside the town. It is on this spot that King Mengrai is said to have decided upon the location of his new capital. In the *wihan* is Chiang Rai's original *lak muang*, or "city pillar", traditionally erected in Thailand to mark the founding of a new city. The temple has good views of the river.

***Wihan* of Wat Phra Sing, housing a replica of Chiang Mai's Phra Sing Buddha**

Overbrook Hospital, an example of Chiang Rai's colonial architecture

Overbrook Hospital

โรงพยาบาลโอเวอร์บรุ๊ค

Trirat Rd. (053) 711336.

This working hospital is typical of the colonial architecture created by Westerners in the 19th and 20th centuries, when the city was a base for missionaries and traders. Such buildings are slowly being swamped in Chiang Rai as modern development proceeds apace. This trend is likely to continue as ever more trekkers and package tourists, demanding ever more comprehensive facilities, are attracted to the wild beauty of the mountainous Golden Triangle region (*see pp236–8*).

Hill Tribe Museum

ศูนย์พัฒนาและสงเคราะห์ชาวเขา

Phahon Yothin Rd. (053) 719167. Mon–Sat.

This small museum and crafts centre was established in 1990 by the non-profit-making Population and Community Development Association (PDA), also known for raising awareness of Thailand's AIDS problem (*see p112*). As well as informing tourists of the plight of hill tribes (*see pp196–7*), volunteers at the centre work with the tribespeople themselves, educating them on how to cope with threats to their traditional lifestyle from a rapidly modernizing society. The centre displays and sells hill-tribe crafts (*see pp198–9*). These can also be bought at the market and in shops around the centre of town.

ENVIRONS: Chiang Rai is growing as a base for visiting the rest of the Far North. Vehicle hire, guided treks on foot and organized excursions can all be arranged

Tourists riding an elephant at Ruamit

VISITORS' CHECKLIST

Chiang Rai province. 45,000. 8 km (5 miles) N of Chiang Rai. off Prasopsuk Rd. Kok River pier. TAT, 448/16 Singhakhrai Rd, Chiang Rai (053) 717433. on the floor below TAT office, (053) 717779. daily. Pho Khun Mengrai Festival (Jan); Lychee and Nang Lae Pineapple Fair (May).

through tour companies and many of the guesthouses in town. Also on offer are boat trips along the Kok River, including excursions westwards to the village of **Tha Ton** (*see p232*). **Ruamit**, some 20 km (12 miles) west of Chiang Rai, can be reached by an hourlong boat ride. This village was originally inhabited solely by the Karen tribe, although many different hill tribes now live here. Elephants can then be taken to travel overland to further Akha and Mien villages.

CHIANG RAI TOWN CENTRE

Hill Tribe Museum ⑦
Overbrook Hospital ③
Wat Chet Yot ⑥
Wat Doi Chom Thong ①
Wat Mungmuang ⑤
Wat Phra Kaeo ②
Wat Phra Sing ④

MAE SAI
GOLDEN TRIANGLE
Airport

Kok

KRAISORN SIT
AT-AM NUAI
RAT DET DAMRONG
THA NAM
KO LOI
SINGHAKHRAI
UTTARAKIT
ASIAN
UTTARAKIT
RATTANAKHET
WISET
NONG SI CHAENG
WIANG
UTTARAKIT
THANALAI
BANPHA
RATCHAYOTHA
PRAKAN
PHAHON YOTHIN
CHET YOT
PHAHON YOTHIN
CHAO CHAI
ASIAN
PRASOPSUK
SAN KHONG NOI
SATHAN PHAYABAN
CHIANG MAI, PHAYAO, LAMPANG

KEY

Coach station
Local bus station
Tourist information
Wat
Mosque

0 metres   250
0 yards   250

Mae Saruai
แม่สรวย

Chiang Rai province. 🏘 *5,000.* 🚌
Chiang Rai, then songthaew. ℹ *TAT,
Chiang Rai (053) 717433.* 🏪 *daily.*

Situated on a plain between mountains and jagged limestone outcrops, this small market town is a popular meeting place for hill tribes, particularly Akha *(see pp196–7).* Mae Saruai is modernizing rapidly, and new agriculture, including flower production, is replacing traditional crops such as rice.

Environs: Cars can be hired in Chiang Rai to visit the Akha hill-tribe villages. The remote ones are accessible on motorbikes or by trekking. Ban Saen Chareon, 10 km (6 miles) west of Mae Saruai, was the subject of a major study of the Akha.

Wiang Pa Pao
เวียงป่าเป้า

Chiang Rai province. 🏘 *10,000.*
🚌 🚌 *Chiang Mai, then songthaew; or*
🚌 *Chiang Rai, then songthaew.* ℹ
TAT, Chiang Rai (053) 717433. 🏪 *daily.*

An important market town, Wiang Pa Pao is picturesquely located in a long, thin, green valley surrounded by mountains. The town is composed mainly of two-storey teak buildings, characteristic of Northern Thailand, and has quiet back streets shaded by teak trees. Many hill-tribe villagers who live in the area, especially Lisu and Akha, come

Chedi and wiban of Wat Si Sutha-wat, Wiang Pa Pao's main temple

The main street in Mae Saruai, with its two-storey buildings

to trade at its market. Wiang Pa Pao's main tourist attraction is **Wat Si Suthawat**, to the east of the main road through town. This spacious old temple, with distinctive, curled *nagas* flanking the sweeping staircase that leads up to the main *wiban*, is surrounded by teak trees.

Phayao
พะเยา

Phayao province. 🏘 *22,000.* 🚌 ℹ
TAT, Chiang Rai (053) 717433. 🏪 *daily.*

This quiet provincial capital, spectacularly sited beside a large lake, was possibly first settled in the Bronze Age. Later abandoned, it was resettled in the 12th century, when it became an independent city state. Today, Phayao is divided into two parts. The older district is confined to the promontory jutting into the lake. With its narrow streets and teak houses, it is more pleasant than the newer part.

Wat Si Komkan, situated just north of town by the lake, dates from the 12th century. Its modern *wiban* houses a 16th-century, 16-m (52-ft) Buddha image, which is thought to be the largest in the whole of Northern Thailand. The *wiban* is surrounded by 38 heads of the Buddha in the Phayao style – distinguished by their rounded heads and pointed noses – dating from the 14th century.

Ngao
งาว

Lampang province. 🏘 *12,000.* 🚌
from Lampang or Chiang Rai. ℹ *TAT,
Chiang Mai (053) 248604.* 🏪 *daily.*

Like many towns in Northern Thailand, Ngao's historical association with the teak trade is evident in its buildings. The suspension bridge over the Yom River offers wonderful views of the town, with its teak houses on stilts backing onto the fertile river valley.

Ngao's principal temple is **Wat Dok Ban**, on the east side of town. It is distinctive for its wall surrounded by about 100 kneeling angel figures of different colours.

Environs: Mae Yom National Park, northeast of Ngao, is centred on the Yom River, one of Northern Thailand's main watercourses. More than 50 species of birds have been observed in the park, as well as many mammals, including the serow (a type of antelope), pangolin (scaly anteater), wild pigs and barking deer.

Angel at Wat Dok Ban, Ngao

Within the park is the **Dong Sak Ngan Forest**, notable for its tall teak trees. The forest can be reached only on foot.

✈ **Mae Yom National Park**
18 km (11 miles) NE of Ngao.
ℹ *Forestry Dept (02) 579 0529.*
🅾 *daily.* 🚫

Elephants in Thailand

As well as playing a very important practical role in Thai history, elephants have traditionally been of great spiritual significance. They were first mentioned centuries ago in Hindu and Buddhist texts and since then have enjoyed a higher status in Thailand than any other animal. However, although wild elephants have been protected by law since 1921, deforestation and, to a lesser extent, poaching have reduced their numbers to just a few thousand. The introduction of machines for logging, followed by a ban on most commercial logging in 1989, has led to a sharp fall in the number of captive elephants, too. While tourists may still come across these being ridden by *mahouts*, a surer way to see them is at shows at elephant camps.

White elephant on a former Siamese flag

Elephants were used in war, as depicted in this old manuscript

WORKING ELEPHANTS

Although most logging is officially banned in Thailand, elephants are still used for transporting logs in some areas. They are often looked after by one handler for all their life, and cause less damage than modern machinery.

Able to run up to 20 km (12 miles) an hour, elephants were frequently used by hunters.

This 19th-century training manual shows how to tame wild elephants.

SACRED ELEPHANTS

The spiritual significance of elephants derives from Ganesh, the Hindu god of knowledge and the remover of obstacles, who is a young boy with an elephant's head. The significance of white elephants *(see p102)*, the most revered of all, has its roots in Buddhism. Only the king may own them.

Mural of elephants in one of the Buddhist heavens, Wat Suthat, Bangkok (see pp86–7).

Royal white elephants, said to represent the monarch's power, are the most sacred elephants.

Nong Bua ⑮
หนองบัว

Nan province. 🏠 5,000. 🚌 Nan,
then songthaew. 🛈 TAT, Chiang Rai
(053) 717433. 🏛 daily.

THIS PICTURESQUE VILLAGE,
situated on a flat, fertile
plain beside the Nan River, is
characterized by traditional
teak houses on stilts and neat
vegetable gardens. It is one of
a number of villages in Nan
province inhabited by the Thai
Lue, an ethnic minority related
to the Tai people of Southern
China, who began to settle in
the region in 1836.

Wat Nong Bua, which was
built in 1862, has features
typical of a Thai Lue temple,
including a two-tiered roof and
a carved wooden portico. Its
murals are thought to be the
work of the same artists who
painted those at Wat Phumin
(see pp246–7). Though the
murals at Wat Nong Bua are
more faded than Wat Phumin's,
their depictions of 19th-century
life are just as fascinating. As
at Wat Phumin, scenes from
the *jataka* tales *(see pp26–7)*
are also featured here.

To the west of town is a
textile factory, where traditional Thai Lue fabrics are
made using hand-oper-
ated looms. The distinc-
tive, multi-coloured
fabrics can be bought in
the adjacent shop.

Nong Bua is the site
of a two-day festival
held every three years
in December (1999,
2002, and so on), dur-
ing which the villagers pay
homage to their ancestors.

A 19th-century mural depicting a hunting party, Wat Nong Bua

Doi Phu Kha National Park ⑯
อุทยานแห่งชาติดอยภูคา

Visitors' Centre off Hwy 1256, 75 km
(47 miles) NE of Nan. 🛈 TAT, Chiang
Rai (053) 717433; Forestry Dept (02)
579 0529. 🚌 Nan, then songthaew.

RANGED AROUND the 2,000-m
(6,550-ft) peak of Doi Phu
Kha, this is one of the
most recently created
national parks in
Thailand. For years,
the area was widely
considered to be a
hotbed of Com-
munist infiltra-
tion. Some of the
hill-tribe villagers here were
suspected of sympathizing
with the Communists, and
were kept isolated from visitors. Tourism in the
park is therefore still
in its infancy.

Doi Phu Kha has
two main attractions,
the most obvious being its
beautiful scenery, such as

**Short-tailed
magpie, Doi Phu
Kha National Park**

caves and waterfalls. The visitors' centre provides information on forest walks and
opportunities for bird-watching.

The other main point of
interest in the park and the
surrounding area is the hill-
tribe villages, particularly Mien
and Hmong *(see pp196–7)*,
and lowland ethnic minorities
such as the Htin and Thai Lue.

Currently, there are few good
roads or tourist facilities within
the park. However, the more
adventurous will be rewarded
by an area which is still relatively free of development.

Nan ⑰
น่าน

Nan province. 🏠 23,000. ✈ 🚌
🛈 TAT, Chiang Rai (053) 717433. 🏛
daily. 🎉 Nan Provincial Fair (Oct/Nov),
Golden Orange Festival (Dec/Jan).

NAN DEVELOPED as an
isolated kingdom in the
13th and 14th centuries. It fell
under the influence of the
Sukothai and Lanna kingdoms
(see pp 54–7), then surrendered
to Burmese control in 1558. In
1788 the town became a vassal
state of Bangkok, though it
kept its autonomy and independent rulers until it officially
became part of Thailand in
1931. Today, Nan is a prosperous town on the Nan River.

Wat Phumin *(see pp246–7)*,
in the south of town, is without doubt the most important
sight in Nan. Just north of it is
the **Nan National Museum**,
which is housed in an impressive former royal palace dating
from 1903. The ground floor
is dedicated to the ethnic

Thai Lue farmers working in the rice fields around Nong Bua

groups of Nan province, including the Hmong and Mien hill tribes. The second floor has a comprehensive selection of artifacts relating to the history of the region, including archaeological finds and weapons. Notable items include a "black" elephant tusk weighing 18 kg (40 lb), supported by a sculpted *khut* (mythological eagle). Thought to date from the 17th century, the tusk is actually dark brown.

The collection of Buddhas includes some rare Lanna and Lao images. Also exhibited are sky rockets made by local farmers for the Bun Bang Fai (Rocket Festival) *(see pp42–3)* held each May in Northeast and parts of Northern Thailand. Unusually for Thai museums, many of the exhibits are labelled in English.

Façade of the *bot* of the 14th-century Wat Suan Tan in Nan

Nearby is **Wat Phra That Chang Kham**, with a magnificent 14th-century *chedi* resting on sculpted elephant heads. The *bot* and the *wihan*, both featuring attractive woodcarving on their façades, are guarded by *singhas* (mythological lions). Among Nan's other temples is **Wat Suan Tan**, in the northwest of town, with a 40-m (130-ft) *chedi*, crowned by a white *prang* – a rounded, Khmer-style tower which is very rarely seen in Northern Thailand. Housed in the *wihan* is a bronze Buddha image, Phra Chao Thong Thip. The image was made to the order of the king of Chiang Mai in 1449 after he conquered Nan. According to legend, the monarch gave the city's craftsmen just one week to make it.

Just southeast of Nan is the revered **Wat Phra That Chae Haeng**. Dating from 1355, the temple is set in a square compound on a hill top overlooking the Nan valley. Its gilded Lanna *chedi* is just over 55 m (180 ft) high. This, and the huge *nagas* (serpents) flanking the staircase, can be seen from several miles around. The multi-layered roof of the *wihan* is Lao in style.

"Black" elephant tusk in Nan National Museum

↑ Nan National Museum
Hwy 101. ☐ *Wed–Sun.* 📷

ENVIRONS: Despite its many attractions, the far-flung and mountainous province of Nan was, until fairly recently, one of the most remote and inaccessible areas in Thailand. In the past few years, better roads have greatly improved connections to the province, and it is now among the country's fastest growing tourist destinations.

To the north of Nan is **Tham Pha Tup Forest Reserve**, a limestone cave complex set in a forested area. There are some 17 caves here, which are impressive for their stalactites and stalagmites. About half of them can be reached by marked trails.

Another natural feature of the region is **Sao Din**, literally "earth pillars", which are located off Highway 1026, about 30 km (19 miles) to the south of Nan. These sculpted clay columns, created by erosion, stick out of depressions in the ground. The pillars have the same eerie appearance as those at Phrae Muang Phi in Phrae province *(see p249)* and have been used as a backdrop for many Thai films.

✗ Tham Pha Tup Forest Reserve
Off Hwy 1080, 12 km (7 miles) N of Nan. 🛈 *Forestry Dept (02) 579 0529.* ☐ *daily.* 📷

TRADITIONAL BOAT RACES IN NAN

Each year, at the end of October, boat races take place on the river at Nan. The races are the highlight of the two-week Nan Provincial Fair, which attracts visitors from all over Thailand. The tradition of the boat races is thought to have begun towards the end of the 19th century, and marks the start of the Krathin season *(see p46)*, when the city's menfolk present new robes to the local monks. The boats, some 30 m (98 ft) in length, can hold up to 50 rowers. Each one is carved from a single log and decorated to look like a dragon-serpent or *naga (see p218)*. The sides are brightly painted with traditional motifs.

Boats competing during annual races on the Nan River

Wat Phumin
วัดภูมินทร์

O NE OF THE MOST BEAUTIFUL TEMPLES in Northern Thailand, Wat Phumin was founded in 1596 by the ruler of Nan. The *wat* was renovated in the mid-19th century and again in 1991, and is notable for its cross-shaped design, elaborate coffered ceiling, carved doors and pillars. The highlight, however, is undoubtedly its murals. These were originally thought to have been painted by Thai Lue *(see p244)* artists during the 19th-century renovation. But the apparent depiction of French troops, unknown in the area before the French annexation of part of Nan province in 1893, suggests a date in the mid-1890s. Three main themes can be picked out from the murals: the life of the Buddha, the *jataka (see p26)* tale of his incarnation as Khatta Kumara, and scenes depicting everyday life in Nan.

Rich Official
This lavishly dressed man, smoking a pipe, may depict the ruler of Nan who commissioned the murals.

★ Central Buddha Images
Four identical gilded Sukhothai images (see pp150–51), *sit back-to-back facing the cardinal points.*

Decorative Pillars
These red, black and gold pillars are all carved with the same floral pattern. The bases of some pillars feature elephant motifs while others depict devas *(Hindu gods).*

Descending Serpents
This mural shows poisonous snakes sent by angry gods to punish an unruly king in the story of Khatta Kumara.

STAR FEATURES

★ **Central Buddha Images**

★ **Story of the Buddha Mural**

Courting Couple
This mural gives an insight into clothing worn in 19th-century Nan. The tattooed man, with a Thai Lue hair-style, may be one of the artists.

VISITORS' CHECKLIST

On south bank of Nan River, Phak-wang Rd, centre of Nan town.
◻ 8:30am – 4:30pm daily.

★ Story of the Buddha Mural
The mural on the northern wall above the main door is particularly outstanding. Located at the very top of the image is the Buddha and on a lower plane are his disciples. In the bottom half, Khatta Kumara and his friends are depicted on their way to a city with a palace, which Khatta later rebuilds after its destruction by snakes and birds.

Nagas (serpents) flank the steps at the front and back of the building.

Main entrance

The Arrival of Europeans in Nan
This scene shows characters wearing European clothes. The figures in berets may be French, and the mural could be a direct reference to the takeover of part of Nan province by the French in 1893.

Boy, Mother and Elephant's Footprint
In this scene, Khatta Kumara is with his mother. She bore him after drinking the god Indra's urine from an elephant's footprint. Indra had descended to earth in the form of an elephant.

Street-by-Street: Phrae ⑱

แพร่

Buddhist shrine inside the museum at Wat Luang

Wᴵᵀᴴ ɪᴛꜱ ᴅɪꜱᴛɪɴᴄᴛɪᴠᴇ ᴄʜᴀʀᴍ and identity, Phrae is appealing yet surprisingly little-visited. The town was built beside the Yom River in the 12th century and remained an independent city state until it came under Ayutthayan control. In the 18th century, the town was taken by the Burmese and later became a base for Burmese and Lao teak loggers. Burmese influence is obvious in Phrae's temples, which also have Lanna features. The town prospers on agricultural produce from the surrounding fertile valley, as shown by the growing commercial district outside the walled town. Remains of the old city walls and moat can be seen in the northeast of town.

★ Wat Luang
Phrae's oldest temple (12th century) is entered through a section of old city wall. The octagonal Lanna chedi is notable for its elephant caryatids. Swords, jewellery and photographs are displayed in the museum.

Wat Phra Non, a 17th-century Lao temple, houses a reclining Buddha image.

To Wat Phra Non

To Ban Prathup Chai

Wat Phra Ruang
Several architectural styles are blended at this temple. The cruciform bot is more characteristic of temples in nearby Nan. The Lao wihan has delicately carved doors, shown here. The chedi is Lanna.

Wat Phra Bat
The Lao bot of Wat Phra Bat dates from the 18th century, while the wihan – housing a revered Buddha image, is modern. Part of a Buddhist university, the temple is often bustling with monks.

KHAMLUE I

KHAMLUE

KHUMDERM

LUKMUANG

PHRA RUANG

NARIRUT

Wat Si Chum

The plain interiors of the
bot *and* wihan *contrast with
the ornate Buddha images
inside. Unfortunately, the
chedi is in a state of ruin.*

★ Teak Houses

*These teak houses
are typical of Phrae.
Their roofs are deco-
rated with* kalae, *a
feature of Northern
Thai houses (see p32).*

Public Park

*This park is ideal for relaxing after
visiting Phrae's sights. Unusually for
Thai towns, it is located in the centre.*

To Wat Chom
Sawan and
old city walls

0 metres   100

0 yards   100

KEY

= = = Suggested route

STAR SIGHTS

★ Wat Luang

★ Teak Houses

ENVIRONS: Wat Chom Sawan,
in the northeast of Phrae, is an
early 20th-century Shan temple with a distinctive, copper-
crowned Burmese *chedi*.

To the west of Phrae is **Ban
Prathup Chai**, one of Thailand's largest teak houses. The
structure, with its lavish, ornate
pillars and furniture, was assembled in the mid-1980s.
Even though teak logging was
not then banned *(see p239)*,
spare teak logs from nine other
houses were used to build it.

To the southeast is **Wat
Phra That Chaw Hae**, thought
to date from the 12th–13th
centuries. Staircases, flanked
by *nagas* and stone lions,
lead through a teak forest up
to the hilltop *wat*. The temple
is named after the satin-like
cloth *(chaw hae)* that worshippers wrap around the 33-m
(110-ft) gilded *chedi*. Inside is
the revered Phra Chao Than
Chai, believed to grant wishes.

Phrae Muang Phi is a popular excursion from Phrae.
This surreal landscape *(muang
phi* means "ghost city") comprises pillars of soil and rock
that rise from the ground like
mushrooms. Like Sao Din in
Nan province *(see p245)*, they
are the result of the erosion
of clay beneath a hard crust.

🏠 **Ban Prathup Chai**
1 km (1,100 yards) W of Phrae.
🗓 *daily.* 🖼

🛕 **Wat Phra That Chaw Hae**
8 km (5 miles) SE of Phrae, Phrae
province. 🚌 *Phrae, then* songthaew.
🗓 *daily.* 🖼

⛰ **Phrae Muang Phi**
Off Hwy 101, 18 km (11 miles) NE
of Phrae, Phrae province. 🚌 *Phrae,
then* songthaew.

Sirikit Reservoir ⑲
เขื่อนสิริกิติ์

45 km (28 miles) SE of Phrae, Uttaradit
province. 🚌 *Nan or Uttaradit, then*
songthaew.

NAMED AFTER Queen Sirikit,
and set amid splendid
scenery, this reservoir and dam
were created in the mid-1970s
on the Nan River, a tributary
of the Chao Phraya. Built to
control flooding, the dam also
provides electricity and water
for farmers in the area.

NORTHEAST
THAILAND

Introducing Northeast Thailand

THE KHORAT PLATEAU, which takes up most of the Northeast, is mostly barren scrubland; its main focus is the city of Khorat. To the north and east of this region and separating it from neighbouring Laos is the Mekhong River Valley. Along the Thai side of the river lie small towns and villages, some with small quays and beaches. Known locally as Isan, the Northeast has an extremely rich history. One of the first areas in the world where rice was cultivated, silk woven and bronze produced, it fell under Khmer rule in the 9th–13th centuries. Isan's proximity to Laos and Cambodia and its largely infertile land mean that it is seen by many Thais as a poor relation. Most of its people are ethnically Lao and are known for their friendly openness.

Nong Khai

Phu Kradung National Park

Phu Kradung National Park
(see pp276–7), with a steep-sided plateau at its centre, is home to fabulous animal and plant life.

KHORAT PLATEAU
(see pp258–271)

Prasat Hin Phimai

Prasat Hin Phimai (see pp266–7), dating from the 11th–12th centuries, is one of the most extensively restored Khmer temple complexes in Thailand.

Prasat Hin Khao Phnom Rung

Prasat Hin Khao Phnom Rung
(see pp270–71), covering a huge area, is one of Thailand's finest examples of Khmer architecture.

◁ **The ruins of Prasat Hin Muang Tam reflected in one of its four surrounding lotus-filled ponds**

Nong Khai (see pp282–3) is a rapidly developing commercial town that has retained a peaceful riverside atmosphere.

MEKHONG RIVER VALLEY
(see pp272–293)

Wat Phra That Phanom

Wat Phra That Phanom (see p287) *was, according to legend, built shortly after the death of the Buddha. It is the Northeast's most sacred shrine.*

Prasat Khao Phra Wihan

Prasat Khao Phra Wihan (see p292) *enjoys a stunning location on a mountain spur on the Thai-Cambodian border. Unfortunately, cross-border tensions mean it is not always open.*

0 kilometres   50

0 miles   25

The Lost Khmer Temples

Lintel at Phnom Rung

WHEN EUROPEANS first saw mysterious ruins in the forests far east of Ayutthaya they thought they had found an ancient Chinese, or even Greek, civilization. It was not until the 19th century that the history of the Khmers, who ruled an area covering much of modern Cambodia and Northeast Thailand from the 9th–14th centuries, began to be uncovered. The Khmers are now acknowledged to have been among the world's greatest architects. Many sites can be visited in Thailand today; in Cambodia, war has slowed the restoration of Angkor, the old capital.

THE KHMER EMPIRE

• *Major Khmer sites*

At the centre of Angkor Thom stands the Bayon, with its distinctive, colossal heads.

Bas-reliefs of battles *adorning the walls of many Khmer sites not only display the creative and technical abilities of the Khmer craftsmen but have also helped scholars to write Khmer history. The Khmers' main adversaries were the Thais: in 1444 Ayutthaya finally took Angkor and the Khmer Empire was vanquished.*

Restoration *of the most important of Thailand's 300-odd Khmer monuments was begun in 1925. The Thai Fine Arts Department has overseen work at temple complexes such as Phimai (see pp266–7) in the late 20th century.*

ROMANCE OF THE GREAT TEMPLES
Khmer temple complexes were built to symbolize kingship and the universe and are awesome in their scale and beauty. The Thais borrowed elements of Khmer temple design *(see p30)*, and a scale model, made in 1922, of Angkor Wat, the largest complex, stands at Bangkok's Wat Phra Kaeo *(see pp76–9)*. European views of romantic ruins abound, as exemplified by engravings such as this made in 1866–8. A reconstruction of Angkor Wat was also the centrepiece of the 1931 Colonial Exposition in Paris.

A shivalinga was the main object of worship at the centre of many Khmer temples. It is a phallus representing the creative force of the Hindu god Shiva.

THE REDISCOVERY OF ANGKOR

In about 1550 a Cambodian king is said to have come upon the ruins of Angkor while hunting for elephants. He cleared part of the site where his ancestors had once held court. Before long, news filtered to Europe from Portuguese and Spanish missionaries of a vast hidden city. But few ventured into the jungle, and the artistic feats of the Khmers were to remain largely unknown for another 300 years. Interest in the ruins increased when France colonized Indochina. Henri Mouhot (1826–61) earned the dubious posthumous status of "discoverer" of Angkor on publication of his engravings and drawings of the site that he made in 1860. From his work France decided to finance proper exploration. Louis Delaporte, George Coedès, Jean Boisselier and Henri Parmentier were among others who spent much of their lives piecing together Khmer history.

The French scholar Parmentier in 1923

Scenes from the Ramayana, *an ancient Indian epic, are found at many Khmer temples, and probably directly inspired the Thai version, the Ramakien (see pp36–7).*

The 19th-century artists were particularly inspired by imagery of the jungle encroaching upon the ruins.

The scale of the humans shown in the engraving is fairly accurate. The larger statues in the foreground are imaginary.

Marc Riboud, *a photographer for the renowned Magnum agency, visited Angkor in the 1960s and 1980s. He took some of the most evocative and widely published pictures of Angkor before and after the war in Cambodia.*

The gently smiling faces of the Buddha at the Bayon of Angkor Thom have found their way onto posters, book covers and, here, the score of a 1921 foxtrot.

Silk Production

Leaves from the mulberry bush

Finds at the prehistoric site of Ban Chiang *(see pp50–51)* indicate that silk production in Northeast Thailand may predate even that of China, where sericulture probably originated in about 2700 BC. In Thailand, silk production was beginning to die out until an American, Jim Thompson *(see pp116–17)*, revived it in the 1940s. Today, all manner of silk products are available, with silk shirts and sarongs popular with visitors. The silk industry is centred mostly in the Northeast, due to the suitability of soil in these areas for growing mulberry bushes, the main diet of the silkworm. Silk production in these areas is still based on traditional methods and comprises the stages outlined here.

2 *In three to four weeks the eggs grow into silkworms. These are placed on large, woven bamboo trays and, protected from mice, ants, flies and bright light, feed on mulberry leaves. In the larval stage, while they are still growing, each silkworm sheds its skin four times and increases its weight 10,000-fold.*

**Silkworm moth
(Bombyx mori)**

1 *Female silkworm moths spend their short life of about four days mating and laying eggs.*

SILKWORMS

REELING

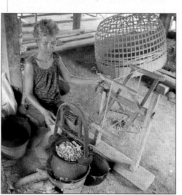

5 *The individual silk threads are lifted out of the pot using a special forked bamboo pole. They are twisted together to form a single, larger thread, which is then reeled onto a spool.*

6 *Silk skeins are inspected and graded. The outer layer of cocoon gives the coarsest yarn and is used for furnishings. The best silk, from the middle and inner layers, is used for weaving.*

DYEING

7 *The raw silk is soaked in soapy water to remove the sericin, a gum-like coating, leaving it softer and lighter.*

8 *The yarn is then dyed. The strength of the dye depends on the number of times the yarn is dipped in the solution. Tie-dyed yarn (ikat) is achieved by wrapping segments of yarn with dye-resistant strings, according to the design required. The thread is then dried and the strings removed, revealing the pattern.*

3 *At the end of the 30-day growth cycle, the fully developed silkworms are ready to spin a cocoon. They are moved to a large, circular, bamboo tray with a frame that leaves them just enough space to attach their cocoons. Silkworms build their cocoons from a single white or yellow fibre secreted from the mouth at a rate of 12 cm (4.5 in) per minute.*

Cocoons, which are spun in about 36 hours

4 *Cocoons have to be reeled within ten days or the moths will begin to hatch and damage the silk. The cocoons are placed in a pot of water just below boiling point. This kills them and releases the silk threads.*

COCOONS

PLYING	WEAVING

9 *Up to six threads can be plyed together to form a single thread, the weft.*

10 *The silk is woven on upright looms with foot treadles. The coarse weft is woven into fine, even warps, which even in traditional workshops are often pre-fabricated and imported from Japan, Korea and Europe – the production of the warp is a time-consuming business by any method. The combination of fine and coarse threads gives the fabric its unique lustre.*

TOOLS FOR SILK WEAVING

During the silk-weaving process, the fibres must be kept clean and free from obstructions that could tangle and damage them. Each implement has a unique and vital function: delicate brushes with ornamental wooden handles help to keep the silk free from particles of dust. Carved wooden pulleys, which are attached to traditional looms, ensure that the fibres run smoothly while they are being woven.

Traditional pulley

Decorative silk brushes

11 *The distinctive, brightly coloured silk is then made into umbrellas, scarves, ties, shirts and sarongs, and sold around Thailand (see p439).*

KHORAT PLATEAU

THOUGH ONE OF THE MOST *infertile areas of Thailand, and home to the nation's poorest people, the Khorat Plateau is rich in culture and historic sites from the days when the Khmer Empire held sway over the region. The people are welcoming, the cuisine fiery hot, often served with glutinous rice and raw vegetables, and the silk and cotton handicrafts are exquisite.*

The vast, sandstone Khorat Plateau dominates the Northeast, a region that the Thais call Isan. The plateau, which is about 200 m (660 ft) above sea level, takes up almost a third of Thailand's land mass and is home to about a third of the population. The uneven rainfall of the region causes both floods and droughts, and permits the cultivation of only one rice crop per year. As a result there is much rural poverty.

Although few tourists visit the region, there is much of historical interest to be discovered. To the north, at Ban Chiang, lies a site that has revolutionized archaeologists' views of prehistoric Southeast Asia. The Northeast is now thought to be one of the first areas in the world where rice growing, bronze making and silk weaving were pioneered. Silk production has flourished again since the mid-20th century, and visitors are drawn to modern-day weaving villages where a wide range of silk and cotton goods are sold.

In the 9th century AD, the Khorat Plateau came under Cambodian suzerainty, which was to endure until the end of the 13th century. It was during this period that the region's splendid Khmer temples were built. The magnificent stone temples at Phnom Rung and Phimai, which once stood on a road linking the plateau with the Khmer capital of Angkor, have been evocatively restored in recent years.

Bung Phlan Chai, a scenic lake in the centre of Roi Et town

◁ **Balustraded stone windows at Prasat Hin Muang Tam**

Exploring the Khorat Plateau

THE KHORAT PLATEAU occupies most of Northeast Thailand. It is a broad stretch of barren, arid hills some 300 m (985 ft) above sea level, separated from the Central Plains to the west by the Phetchabun mountain range. Much of the region is characterized by red earth and scrub forest. Khorat city, regarded as the gateway to the Northeast, is the centre of the region's transport network. Other towns and sights of interest in the region can be reached by road from here, though distances are considerable. North of Khorat lie the towns of Khon Kaen and Roi Et; further north still, the prehistoric site of Ban Chiang. East of Khorat the main attractions are the Khmer temples of Phimai and Phnom Rung. Nearby are Ta Klang and Surin, which are linked historically with the elephant trade.

SIGHTS AT A GLANCE

Phitsanulok

Huay Lan Reservoir

P H U K ... N A T I O ... P A R

Ubon Reser

PHETCHABUN

CHAIYAPHUM

Lam Chi

Lam Chi

Pa Sak

Lam Nam Pa Sak

Bangkok

PRASAT HIN PHIMAI

KHORAT **7**

DAN KWIAN **8**

Lam Thakong Reservoir

Bangkok

Lam Phra Phleong Reservoir

Mun

0 kilometres   50

0 miles   25

Prachin Buri

Chachoengsao

ARANYAPRATHE

Sisoph

The exquisitely restored Prasat Hin Phimai

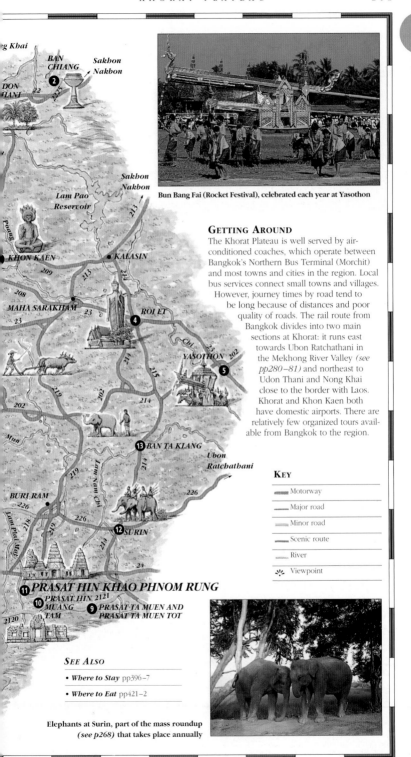

g Khai

BAN CHIANG

Sakhon Nakbon

DON HANI

22

Sakhon Nakbon

Lam Pao Reservoir

213

KHON KAEN

209

KALASIN

213

214

208

MAHA SARAKHAM

23

23

ROI ET

202

214

202

YASOTHON

23

202

214

219

202

214

Mun

219

Lam Nam Chi

BAN TA KLANG

214

Ubon Ratchathani

BURI RAM

226

226

226

219

Lam Plai Mat

216

219

226

214

SURIN

24

PRASAT HIN KHAO PHNOM RUNG

PRASAT HIN MUANG TAM

21

2120

PRASAT TA MUEN AND PRASAT TA MUEN TOT

Bun Bang Fai (Rocket Festival), celebrated each year at Yasothon

GETTING AROUND

The Khorat Plateau is well served by air-conditioned coaches, which operate between Bangkok's Northern Bus Terminal (Morchit) and most towns and cities in the region. Local bus services connect small towns and villages. However, journey times by road tend to be long because of distances and poor quality of roads. The rail route from Bangkok divides into two main sections at Khorat: it runs east towards Ubon Ratchathani in the Mekhong River Valley *(see pp280–81)* and northeast to Udon Thani and Nong Khai close to the border with Laos. Khorat and Khon Kaen both have domestic airports. There are relatively few organized tours available from Bangkok to the region.

KEY

- ▬ Motorway
- ▬ Major road
- ▬ Minor road
- ▬ Scenic route
- ▬ River
- ☼ Viewpoint

SEE ALSO

• *Where to Stay* pp396–7

• *Where to Eat* pp421–2

Elephants at Surin, part of the mass roundup
(see p268) that takes place annually

Nong Prachak Park, one of the more peaceful parts of Udon Thani

Udon Thani ❶
อุดรธานี

Udon Thani province. 150,000.
✈ ☒ ☐ ☐ ℹ *TAT, Mukmontri Rd,
Udon Thani (042) 325406.* 🛒 *daily.*

DURING the Vietnam War Udon Thani changed from a sleepy provincial capital into a booming support centre for a nearby American airbase. Since the withdrawal of the GIs in 1976, Udon has retained a little of that past vibrancy, together with some rather nondescript streets, lined with Western-style coffee shops, nightclubs and massage parlours. It has continued to grow as an industrial and commercial centre within the region. The most attractive part of town is **Nong Prachak Park**, where there are some open-air restaurants. The town makes a good base for travellers wanting to visit nearby Ban Chiang.

**Ban Chiang pot,
c.2000 BC**

The finds provided archaeological evidence that Northeast Thailand may have been one of the world's earliest centres of bronze production. Spearheads from the site are thought to date from around 3600 BC, while ceramics, dating from between 3000 BC and 500 AD, testify to a high degree of technical and artistic skill.

Today a collection of these artifacts is on display, together with ornaments such as bangles and rings, at the **Ban Chiang National Museum**.

A short walk from the museum, 2 km (1 mile) through dusty streets lined with quaint wooden shophouses, two covered excavation sites lie in the grounds of **Wat Pho Si Nai**. Here the main exhibits are graves containing skeletal remains and ceramics used for symbolic purposes in burial. Bodies were wrapped

in perishable material and laid on their backs. Pots were then arranged along the edge of the grave and over the bodies themselves. Other grave goods found at the burial site include pig skulls and mandibles, jewellery, tools, weapons and river pebbles.

Research associated with the discoveries at Wat Pho Si Nai indicates that the inhabitants of Ban Chiang were a strong, long-legged people with wide foreheads and prominent cheekbones with an average life expectancy of 31 years. The main causes of death were diseases such as malaria. As with other early peoples of Southeast Asia, the exact ethnic origins of the population of Ban Chiang remain a mystery.

🏛 **Ban Chiang
National Museum**
On edge of Ban Chiang village.
◷ *8:30am–4pm daily.* 🖼

Khon Kaen ❸
ขอนแก่น

Khon Kaen province. 165,000. ✈
☐ ☐ ☐ ℹ *TAT, 15/5 Prachasamoson
Rd, Khon Kaen (043) 244498.* 🛒 *daily.*
🎎 *Silk Festival (10 days Nov/Dec).*

ONCE THE QUIET capital of one of the poorest provinces in the Northeast of Thailand, this place has changed into a prosperous, bustling town. Located at the heart of the region, it has consequently been a focus of regional development projects – the town now boasts the

Ban Chiang ❷
บ้านเชียง

Udon Thani province. 80,000.
🚌 *from Udon Thani.* ℹ *TAT, Udon
Thani (042) 325406.* 🛒 *daily.*

THE PRINCIPAL attraction for visitors to Ban Chiang is its archaeological site *(see pp50–1)*. It was discovered by accident in 1966 by an American sociologist, who tripped over some remains.

Khon Kaen National Museum, home to Ban Chiang and Dvaravati relics

largest university in the Northeast, in addition to its own television studios. There are a number of modern hotels and shopping complexes, all of which nestle rather incongruously among the town's more traditional streets and market places.

Places of interest to tourists include **Khaen Nakhon lake**, an artificial lake beside which are some restaurants. **Khon Kaen National Museum** has a collection of Ban Chiang artifacts, and a number of Dvaravati *(see pp52–3)* stelae carved with excerpts from the life of the Buddha, as well as examples of local folk art.

⌂ Khon Kaen National Museum
At intersection of Kasikhon Thungsang Rd and Lungsun Rachakhan Rd.
◻ Wed–Sun. ◓ public hols. 🖼

Roi Et ❹
ร้อยเอ็ด

Roi Et province. 🏃 36,000. 🚌 🚉
TAT, Khon Kaen (043) 244498. 🚌 daily.

Founded in 1782, Roi Et literally means "one hundred and one", a name which is thought to be an exaggeration of 11, the number of vassal states over which the town once ruled. Today it is a steadily growing provincial capital. The modern skyline is dominated by an immense brown and ochre image of the Lord Buddha, the Phraphuttharattana-mongkol-maha-mani, which is situated within the grounds of **Wat Buraphaphiram**. Measuring 68 m (225 ft) from its base to the tip of its flame finial, this giant standing Buddha is reputed to be one of the tallest in the world. The

The Phraphuttha-rattana-mongkol-maha-mani image at Roi Et

climb up the stairs by the side of the statue offers an impressive view over the town and surrounding area. Silk and cotton are both good buys in Roi Et and can be found along Phadung Phanit Road.

THE KHAEN

Originating in Laos, and played widely in Northeast Thailand, the *khaen* is a large, free-reed pan-pipe, and is constructed primarily of bamboo. Although the length and pitch of the *khaen* are not standardized, the number of pipes and the tuning are. Each *khaen* is pitched according either to the personal preference of the player, or to the range of the singer which it accompanies, and has a range of two octaves – this gives a total of 15 pitches. Whereas most arts in Thailand are formally taught, *khaen* players tend to learn their skills by listening to relatives and neighbours in the village. There is no written music for the *khaen* its repertoire having been passed down through oral transmission. It was traditionally played by young men on their way to woo their sweethearts or by blind beggars in the hope of receiving a few coins for their performances. Women never play the *khaen*.

Craftsmen *assemble the* khaen *from bamboo reeds dried in the sun. Wax from the* khisut, *an insect, is used to glue the reeds together and attach them to the carved windchest.*

Phin (a type of guitar)   *Ranat* (a type of xylophone)

Khaen

The *khaen* comprises varying lengths of bamboo, each producing a different pitch.

Holes in the reeds are fingered to create different levels of pitch.

Notes are made by blowing into this carved windchest.

Orchestra with *khaen*, *phin* and *ranat* players

Bun Bang Fai or "Rocket" Festival held each year at Yasothon

Yasothon **5**
ยโสธร

Yasothon province. 🏯 *22,000.* 🚌
🛈 *TAT, Ubon Ratchathani (045)
243770.* 🚌 *daily.* 🎆 *Bun Bang Fai
(Rocket) Festival (May).*

LIKE MANY provincial towns
across Thailand, Yasothon
has only a few tourist sights.
There are one or two temples
that are worth visiting, in particular **Wat Thung Sawang**
and **Wat Mahathat Yasothon**.
Situated in the centre of the
town, the latter is home to the
Phra That Phra Anon *chedi*,
thought to have been built in
the 7th century to house
the relics of Phra Anon, the
closest disciple of the Buddha.
   Yasothon is best known,
however, as the principal
venue for the Bun Bang Fai or
"Rocket" Festival *(see pp43–4)*.
As a result of harsh weather
in Northeast Thailand, this
festival, the principal function
of which is to appease a Hindu
rain god, is one of great symbolic importance. Local people invest enormous sums of
money in the construction of
huge bamboo rockets. The
gunpowder that goes into the
rockets is pounded by young
girls in the temple grounds,
and, perhaps surprisingly, it is
Buddhist monks who possess
the expertise of building and
firing the rockets. The rockets
are paraded on floats through
the streets, surrounded by
revellers, then shot into the
clouds to "fertilize" them. The
festival's sexual overtones
come out in bawdy humour
and flirtation, not encouraged
at other times. The owners of
those rockets that fail to go
off are ritually coated in mud.

Prasat Hin Phimai **6**
ปราสาทหินพิมาย

See pp266–7.

Khorat **7**
โคราช

Khorat province. 🏯 *230,000.* ✈ 🚌
🚌 🛈 *TAT, 2102–4 Mittraphap Rd,
Khorat (044) 213666.* 🚌 *daily.*
🎆 *Thao Suranari Festival (late Mar/
early Apr).*

IN FORMER TIMES, Khorat, or
Nakhon Ratchasima, was
two separate towns, Khorakh-
apura and Sema; they were
joined during the reign of

KHORAT CITY CENTRE

National Museum ②
Night Market ④
Thao Suranari
   Monument ③

Wat Phra Narai Maharat ⑤
Wat Sala Loi ⑥
Wat Suthachinda ①

KEY

🚉 Train station

🚌 Coach station

🏯 Wat

0 metres   200
0 yards   200

Ornate pediment and façade of the *bot* at Wat Phra Narai Maharat

King Narai (1656–88). Today Khorat is a rapidly expanding business centre. Its recent development stems from playing host to a nearby US airbase during the Vietnam War. At first sight Khorat appears to the visitor as a sprawl of confusing roads and heavy traffic. The city centre has little of interest save for the **Night Market** which sells value-for-money street foods and local handicrafts.

At the city's western gate, Pratu Chumphon, is the **Thao Suranari Monument**, built in memory of Khunying Mo, a woman who successfully defended Khorat against an attack by an invading Lao army in 1826. While her husband, the deputy governor of Khorat, was away on business in Bangkok, Prince Anuwong of Vientiane (*see pp284–5*) seized the city. Khunying Mo and her fellow captives allegedly served the Lao army with liquor and were then able to kill them in their drunken stupor with whatever weapons were at hand. The Lao invasion was therefore held at bay until help arrived. Khunying Mo was given the title of Thao Suranari or "brave lady" from which the monument, built in 1934, derives its name. It shows Khunying Mo standing, hand on hip, on a tall pedestal. The

base of the statue is adorned with garlands and ornamental offerings made by local people in their respect for her; a week-long festival, including folk performances of dancing, theatre and song is also held in her honour each year.

Located in the grounds of **Wat Suthachinda** is Khorat's **Maha Weerawong National Museum**. The artifacts on display here range from skeletal remains of human corpses, Dvaravati and Ayutthaya Buddha images, ceramics and wood carvings, and were donated to Prince Maha Weerawong, from whom the museum derives its name.

Though quite a modern city, Khorat has a number of other Buddhist temples. In the *wihan* of **Wat Phra Narai Maharat** is a sandstone image of the Hindu god Vishnu, originally found at Khmer ruins near to the city.

One of the most strikingly innovative, modern Buddhist temples in Northeast Thailand is **Wat Sala Loi**, or the "temple of the floating pavilion", on the banks of the Lam Takhong River. Designed in the form of a Chinese junk, the main *wihan* of this *wat* has won architectural awards. It was constructed entirely from local materials, including distinctive earthenware tiles made only at the nearby village of Dan Kwian. The original site on which

Thao Suranari Monument

Wat Sala Loi now stands dates back to the time of Khunying Mo, and her ashes are still buried here, a fitting resting place for the heroine, without whom present-day Khorat would possibly not exist.

Just outside Khorat, **Wat Khao Chan Ngam**, is the site of prehistoric finds, while at **Wat Thep Phitak Punnaram**, a large white Buddha overlooks the road.

🏛 **Maha Weerawong National Museum**
Ratchadamnoen Rd. ⭕ Wed–Sun.
⬤ public hols. ♿

Dan Kwian ⑧
ด่านเกวียน

Khorat province. 🚍 600.
ℹ TAT, Khorat (044) 213666.

SOUTHEAST OF KHORAT is Dan Kwian, first inhabited in the mid-18th century by the Mon people travelling east from the Burmese border. Since then it has become renowned for its rust-coloured pottery, derived from the high iron content of the local clay.

Today Dan Kwian is essentially a collection of small ceramics factories with smoke billowing from their kilns. Shops selling the local pottery line the highway at the entrance point to the village. Items for sale include jewellery, elaborately decorated vases, often in the form of upstanding fish, chicken-shaped plant pots, leaf-shaped wind chimes and traditional water jars.

LUCKY KHORAT CATS

Silver-coloured Khorat cats are named after the Khorat Plateau. They are one of the most prized breeds in Thailand. A pair of Khorat cats is sometimes given as a wedding present in the Northeast, as they are believed to bring good fortune to their owners. They are mentioned in a book of cat poems, written during the Ayutthaya period. Khorat cats were first introduced to the West in 1896, but did not gain the same popularity as their cream-coloured relatives, who are still known as the original Siamese cats.

Thai stamp bearing a picture of a Khorat cat

Prasat Hin Phimai ⑥

ปราสาทหินพิมาย

Balustraded window

I N THE SMALL TOWN of Phimai, on the banks of the Mun River, lies one of Thailand's most extensively restored Khmer temple complexes. There is no definitive date for the construction of this temple, though the central sanctuary is likely to have been completed during the reign of Suryavarman I (1001–49). Prasat Hin Phimai lies on what was once a direct route to the Khmer capital at Angkor, and, unusually, is oriented in a southeasterly direction to face that city. Originally a Brahmanic shrine dedicated to Shiva, Prasat Hin Phimai was rededicated as a Mahayana Buddhist temple at the end of the 12th century. Its famous lintels and pediments depict scenes from the Ramayana *(see p36)*, and, unique among Khmer temples, Buddhist themes. Restoration of the site was carried out by the Fine Arts Department in 1964–9.

Front View of Central Sanctuary
The white sandstone edifice is topped with a rounded prang, the style of which may have influenced the builders of Angkor Wat (see pp254–5).

Naga Bridge
This symbolic bridge leads to the main entrance of the temple complex. The line of nagas that flank either side of the bridge are mythical guardian spirits.

CENTRAL SANCTUARY

The word *prasat*, which is used to refer to the central sanctuary, also describes the temple complex as a whole.

Southern Pediment
The southern pediment of the mandapa *shows a dancing Shiva, a classic Khmer theme. His mount, Nandin the bull, is to the right.*

Rama and Lakshman appear on the lintel over the western entrance to the *mandapa*. They have been tied up with a *naga*. The monkeys below despair, while above them a *garuda* (a mythical creature, half bird, half human) and more monkeys come to the rescue.

Mandapa (hallw of main entranc

Pilaster with Vajarasattva
On the southern face of the mandapa, *this pilaster shows a Vajarasattva (guardian spirit), holding a thunderbolt and a bell, protecting the door.*

STAR FEATURES

★ **Northern Porch**

★ **Northern Pediment**

★ **Buddha under Naga**

Rama and his monkeys,
building the causeway to Lanka
– a scene from the Ramayana
(see p36) – can
be seen on the
western pedi-
ment of the
prang.

Prang
(tower)

VISITORS' CHECKLIST

Centre of Phimai town, Khorat
province. ☐ TAT, Khorat (044)
213666. ☒ ☐ ☐ Khorat,
then songthaew. ☐ 6am–6pm
daily. ☒ ☒ Phimai Temple
Festival (Nov).

★ **Northern Porch**
*The centrepiece of the
northern porch is this
lintel depicting a three-
headed, six-armed
Vajarasattva. Below
him crouch a group
of dancing girls.*

★ **Northern Pediment**
*This scene from the
Ramayana includes Vishnu
holding a conch, a lotus,
a discus and a staff.*

★ **Buddha under Naga**
*Seated atop a coiled
naga and protected by an
umbrella formed by the
beast's head, this repro-
duction of a 13th-
century Buddha is in the
Bayon (see p254) style.*

The God of Justice, on the pediment of the
eastern porch, judges a feud between Rama
and Tosakan *(see p37)*, good and evil.

Trilokayavijaya, the most important Mahayana Bodhisattva (Enlightened being), can be
seen on the interior lintel of the eastern porch.

PLAN OF COMPLEX

1 Central sanctuary
2 Inner compound
3 Outer compound
4 Royal pavilions
5 *Gopuras* (entrance pavilions)
6 *Naga* (serpent) bridge

Novice Monks
*Though Prasat
Hin Phimai does
not function as a
working wat, it is
sometimes the set-
ting for Buddhist
gatherings and
celebrations.*

Prasat Ta Muen and Prasat Ta Muen Tot **9**

ปราสาทตาเมือนและตาเมือนโต๊ด

Off Hwy 2121, Surin province.
i *TAT, Khorat (044) 213666.* 🚉
🚌 *Surin, then preferably by organized tour.* ⬜ *daily.* 📷

I**N THE DISTRICT** of Ta Muen, in Surin province, the remains of two Khmer *prasats* stand 100 m (330 ft) apart. One, Prasat Ta Muen, is a laterite chapel marking what would once have been a resting place on the long, arduous road between Angkor *(see pp254–5)* and Prasat Hin Phimai *(see pp266–7)*. The other, Prasat Ta Muen Tot, is more decayed, and was originally a hospital to care for travellers along this route. Both were built by King Jayavarman VII (1181–1220).

Although both *prasats* are today largely in ruins, with their brickwork gripped and overrun by the roots of towering fig trees, they are potent reminders of the powerful Khmer Empire which once

held sway in this region. Because of their location along the rather dangerous Cambodian border, Ta Muen and Ta Muen Tot are best seen as part of a tour organized by one of the guesthouses in Surin, and may require a military escort. They are not easily accessible to lone tourists and cannot be visited at times of disputes and skirmishes between the various rival factions in the area.

Border police who act as armed escorts for visitors, Prasat Ta Muen

Prasat Hin Muang Tam **10**

ปราสาทหินเมืองต่ำ

Off Hwy 24, Buri Ram province.
i *TAT, Khorat (044) 213666.*
🚌 *from Surin to Prakhon Chai, then songthaew.* ⬜ *daily.* 📷

M**UANG TAM**, or "the lower city", stands at the foot of Khao Phnom Rung, an extinct volcano on top of which lies the Khmer site of Prasat Hin Khao Phnom Rung *(see pp270–1)*. Muang Tam post-dates the earliest stages of construction of the more elaborate and well-preserved temple above, and was built in brick, sandstone and laterite between the 10th and 12th centuries as a residence for the local governor. Today little remains, and at first sight Muang Tam appears to be nothing more than an exotic heap of decaying brickwork.

The remains of four brick sanctuaries surround what would once have been a central temple containing religious icons. The reliefs on the Muang Tam lintels indicate that these icons are most likely to have been Hindu. The lintel over the northern sanctuary shows Shiva and his consort Parvati riding on Nandin the bull, while another depicts the four-headed Hindu god of creation, Brahma.

All the sanctuaries in the complex face east and are encircled by galleries (now collapsed). On each side there are

THE SURIN ELEPHANT ROUNDUP

In the third weekend of November, Surin is transformed by the annual Elephant Roundup. The first roundup was held here in 1960, though nowadays the elephants are used less as working animals than as performers. Some 150 to 200 elephants from local farms are led into Surin by their *mahouts* (riders). Shows include demonstrations of how elephants are captured and raised, and war parades celebrating King Naresuan (1590–1605), who fought the Burmese on elephant back. During these, soldiers, dressed in Ayutthayan costume, march towards an imagined enemy, with spears and shields poised. There are demonstrations also of the elephants' strength and intelligence, as well as a chance for spectators to take rides.

Elephants and *mahouts* in traditional costume, Surin

also four *gopuras* or entrance pavilions. Beyond these lie four L-shaped ponds, decorated at each corner with majestic, multi-headed *nagas*. The ponds themselves are filled with colourful lotus blooms.

An immense reservoir or *baray*, 1,200 m (3,950 ft) wide and 500 m (1,650 ft) long, is situated to the north of Muang Tam, pointing to the fact that this site probably once supported a sizeable population.

Prasat Hin Khao Phnom Rung ⑪
ปราสาทหินเขาพนมรุ้ง

See pp270–1.

Boiling silkworm cocoons to release the silk threads, Surin

Surin ⑫
สุรินทร์

Surin province. 🏯 *38,000.* 🚉 🚌
🛈 *TAT, Khorat (044) 213666.* 🏪
daily. 🐘 *Elephant Roundup (Nov.)*

Surin is famous for its silk, its elephants, and its first ruler, Phraya Surin Phakdi Si Narong Wang, from whom it derives its name. A modern statue in the town depicts the leader dressed to go into battle. A member of the Suay tribe, Phraya Surin became ruler of Surin in 1760 when, according to legend, he was instrumental in recapturing an escaped royal white elephant *(see p102)*.

The process of silk production *(see pp256–7)* can be seen in the surrounding villages.

There are over 700 patterns used by silk-weavers in Surin province. Rhomboid designs are especially popular.

During the 1970s, when the Khmer Rouge seized control of, and terrorized, neighbouring Cambodia, thousands of Cambodian refugees crossed the Banthat mountains into Surin province and took up residence there, alongside already established Lao refugees, Thais, and Suay tribespeople. Although most immigrants have been repatriated, some remain.

Surin's main attraction is undoubtedly the annual Elephant Roundup, at the **Surin Sports Park**. At other times of the year, artifacts associated with elephant capture and training can be seen at the **Surin Museum**, including buffalo-hide ropes used by Suay tribesmen to catch wild elephants. There are also exhibits of the protective clothing and amulets, inscribed with magical incantations, worn during elephant hunts. The capture and training of elephants in Surin is traditionally a male preserve. In fact, women are strictly forbidden to touch the paraphernalia of the hunt, in case they destroy the magic needed to catch the elephants.

🏛 **Surin Museum**
Chitramboong Rd. ☐ *Wed–Sun.*

Road sign, advertising Ban Ta Klang, the Elephant Village

Ban Ta Klang ⑬
บ้านตากลาง

Surin province. 🏯 *1,600.* 🛈 *TAT, Khorat (044) 213666.* 🏪 *daily.* 🐘 *Elephant Roundup (Nov.)*

The Suay tribespeople make up the population of Ban Ta Klang, which is also known as the Elephant Village, a name which reflects the Suay people's skill in capturing and training wild elephants. The Suay are thought to have migrated to Thailand from Central Asia in the early 9th century and to have been the first people to make use of elephants for building, in particular for the construction of Khmer temples. Nowadays, Ban Ta Klang is the primary training ground for the Surin Elephant Roundup. Every October, approximately one month before the roundup in Surin itself, Suay tribesmen begin to practise their skills. In the days leading up to the roundup, the training becomes intense. To participate in the roundup, the *mahouts* must walk their elephants the 50 km (32 miles) or so south to the outskirts of Surin.

Statue of Phraya Surin

An elephant feeding, while the *mahout* takes a break, Surin

Prasat Hin Khao Phnom Rung ⓫

ปราสาทหินเขาพนมรุ้ง

Carved stone elephants

CROWNING THE EXTINCT VOLCANO of Khao Phnom Rung is the splendid Khmer temple complex Prasat Hin Khao Phnom Rung. A Hindu temple, it was built here to symbolize Shiva's abode on Mount Krailasa; hence the processional way leading to the central sanctuary, its stairways and *naga* bridges extending in total for 200 m (655 ft). The temple's construction began early in the 10th century, and, like other Khmer sites, it lies on a route to Angkor Wat in Cambodia *(see pp254–5)*. Its buildings are aligned so that at Songkran *(see p44)*, the rising sun can be seen through all 15 doors of the western *gopura*.

Western Porch Pediment
This carving shows monkeys rescuing Sita in a chariot which is itself a model of the temple.

★ **Central Sanctuary**
The corncob-shaped prang of the central sanctuary is the cosmological summit of the processional way.

Brick Sanctuary
Located just southeast of the central sanctuary, this 13th-century Bayon-style, laterite structure was a late addition to the compound. It was built as a library.

★ **Naga Bridge**
This naga bridge, which is located inside the main temple compound, links the east-facing entrance gopura to the central sanctuary. The body of the naga forms the bridge's balustrade.

STAR FEATURES

★ **Central Sanctuary**

★ **Naga Bridge**

★ **Ornamental Ponds**

★ **Processional Way**

Pediment over Porch of Mandapa
The carving on this pediment represents Shiva Nataraja, the dancing Shiva, his ten arms splayed out in a dance of death and destruction.

VISITORS' CHECKLIST

64 km (40 miles) S of Buriram, off Hwy 24, Buriram province.
🛈 TAT, Khorat (044) 213666.
🚌 from Khorat or Surin to Ban Ta Ko, then songthaew.
🕙 daily. 🎫 🚻 📷 Phnom Rung Festival (Apr).

Nandin the Bull
This image of Nandin the bull, the mythical mount of the Hindu deity Shiva, is located in the first, eastern chamber of the central sanctuary.

Main temple compound

Gopura

★ **Ornamental Ponds**
Located at the front of the entrance to the main temple compound are four ponds. They supposedly represent the four sacred rivers of the Indian subcontinent. In the background, a naga bridge leads into the complex.

Main entrance

Naga **bridge**

The stairway forms part of the processional way to the principal temple compound.

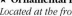

★ **Processional Way**
This processional walkway was built to symbolize the spiritual journey from earth to Hindu heaven.

MEKHONG RIVER VALLEY

S OME 2,000 KM (1,250 MILES) *from its source in the Tibetan Himalayas, having passed through China, Burma, the tip of Northern Thailand, then Laos, the Mekhong River reaches Chiang Khan in Northeast Thailand. From here the river forms the border with Laos until it flows into Cambodia. Although relatively few tourists visit this border country, it has many natural and cultural attractions.*

The agricultural basin of the Mekhong River Valley stands in contrast to the dusty, parched Khorat Plateau to the south and west and the rugged mountains on the Lao side of the river. The Mekhong River Valley's relatively fertile land means fruit and vegetables can be produced on a marketable scale. Furthermore, due to its distance from Bangkok, the area has escaped widespread development and remains one of the most beautiful, unspoilt regions in the country.

Lively Nong Khai is the most important border town in the region and the access point to the Lao capital, Vientiane. The stretch of river to the west of here is dotted with numerous picturesque towns and villages with traditional teak houses. At Phu Phrabat Historical Park (near Ban Phu), a variety of mesmerizing sandstone rock formations can be seen. Nearby are the extraordinary, huge Buddhist and Hindu statues of Wat Khaek.

As the river winds its way east and then south, past Nakhon Phanom, it passes one of the most important Buddhist pilgrimage sites in Thailand, Wat Phra That Phanom. The temple supposedly dates from the death of the Lord Buddha in 543 BC.

Further downriver is Pha Taem, a cliff face painted with huge prehistoric figures and unusual geometrical patterns. Not far away, at Khong Chiam, the Mun River flows into the Mekhong, creating the phenomenon of the "two-coloured river". From here the Mekhong flows into Laos and then Cambodia. The Cambodian border with Thailand has been the scene of skirmishes between rival factions and, as a result, it is not always possible to reach one of the most magnificent of all Khmer monuments, Prasat Khao Phra Wihan.

View from Nakhon Phanom, looking over the Mekhong River and into Laos

◁ Distinctive rock formations – a feature of the Northeast – near Phu Kradung

Exploring the Mekhong River Valley

THE MIGHTY MEKHONG RIVER forms a 750-km (465-mile) border between Northeast Thailand and Laos. The valley along which it flows is a relatively fertile area in an otherwise arid region of Thailand. It is possible to follow the length of the Mekhong from Chiang Khan to Pha Taem by road. Some of the most attractive areas are west of Nong Khai, where visitors pass through sleepy towns and villages of pretty wooden houses. South of the northern stretch of the Mekhong lie the Phu Rua, Phu Kradung and Phu Hin Rong Kla national parks. Further south is Ubon Rachathani, by far the largest city in the region.

VIENTIANE

PAK CHOM   SANGKHOM

CHIANG KHAN   SI CHIANGMAI

MEKHONG VILLAGES TOUR

NONG KHAI

PHU PHRABAT HISTORICAL PARK

Udon Thani

LOEI

PHU RUA NATIONAL PARK

Phitsanulok

PHU HIN RONG KLA NATIONAL PARK

PHU KRADUNG NATIONAL PARK

Bangkok

Khon Kaen

The colourful Phi Ta Khon Festival, held in Loei

KEY

- ▬▬ Motorway
- ▬▬ Major road
- ▬▬ Minor road
- ▬▬ Scenic route
- ≈≈ River
- ⚜ Viewpoint

SIGHTS AT A GLANCE

GETTING AROUND

Nong Khai, Loei, Nakhon Phanom and Ubon Rat-chathani are the best bases from which to tour the area. Two train lines run through the region: a direct line, which divides at Khorat, connects Bangkok to Ubon Ratchathani and to Udon Thani. Travellers can pick up a connection from Udon Thani to Nong Khai. The best way to get about is by bus, hired car or *songthaew*. Long-tail boats run on some sections of the Mekhong River.

Lao-style *chedi*, Sakhon Nakhon

SEE ALSO

- *Where to Stay* pp397–9
- *Where to Eat* pp422–3

Phu Kradung National Park ❶

อุทยานแห่งชาติภูกระดึง

Thai flower

THERE ARE TWO LEGENDS connected to Phu Kradung, or "bell mountain": the first is that the sound of a bell, said to be that of the god Indra, once rang out from its peak; the second is that the mountain rings like a bell when struck with a staff. This steep-sided, flat-topped mountain is now a national park covering 348 sq km (135 sq miles), its 60-km (37-mile) plateau 1,350 m (4,450 ft) above sea level. This plateau has a climate cool enough for plants that cannot survive in other parts of Thailand; many animals also live in its thin pine forests and grasslands.

Asiatic Black Bear
This bear lives in forests all over Southeast Asia; it feeds on ants, insect larvae, nuts and fruit.

Khun Phong waterfall

Pha Nam Pha wa

Waterfalls
Waterfalls are dotted all over Phu Kradung. They are most impressive in October (the end of the rainy season).

Asian Jackal
Thailand has two wild dogs. The handsome Asian jackal, which lives on Phu Kradung, has a bushy tail. The other common species is the red dog.

Pha Daeng

Pha Lom Sak
This unusually shaped sandstone ledge is situated on the southern edge of the plateau. It provides beautiful vistas over the rolling hills and valleys. A popular attraction, in summer there are queues of people lining up to photograph it.

Pha Nok An

"Swallow cliff", situated at the eastern edge of the plateau, offers breathtaking sunrise views. Its name refers to the many families of swallows who build their nests under the cliff's overhang.

VISITORS' CHECKLIST

Loei province. Park HQ about 70 km (43 miles) off Hwy 201, W of Khon Kaen. 🛈 *TAT, Khon Kaen (043) 244498; Forestry Dept (02) 579 0529 (inc bungalow bookings).* 🚌 *Loei, then songthaew to park entrance. Access to plateau on foot only.* ● *mid Jul–early Sep (rainy season).* 🗺 🚻 🍴

Pitcher Plants

Common in Phu Kradung, carnivorous pitcher plants gather nutrients lacking in the local acidic soil by "eating" insects.

Phen Pop Mai waterfall

• Tharn Yai waterfall

• Tharn Sawan waterfall

Sa Anodat pond

Phone Phop waterfall is named after the first World Champion Thai boxer, Phone Kingphet, who stumbled upon it when he was training. Phone chose the plateau as a training ground because its cool climate prepared him for fights abroad.

LOEI

Park entrance

0 kilometres   10

0 miles   10

Key

═══	Road
─ ·	Trail
🛈	National park office
Ⓐ	Camping and bungalows
〰	Viewpoint

THE BALLAD OF PHU KRADUNG

Phu Kradung was the inspiration for a long poem in 1969, by the award-winning Thai poet and artist Angkhan Kalyanaphong, who eulogized its unspoilt, natural beauties. *Lam Nam Phu Kradung* ("the ballad of Phu Kradung") reflects Angkhan's interest in nature and Buddhism. This excerpt translates poorly into English:

"Each time the sun went down I would sit at the Makduk cliff
And watch the beams of coloured light
Pierce the clouds and set alight the sky."

Sa Anodat pond, one of many inspiring sights

Rapids in Phu Hin Rong Kla National Park

Phu Hin Rong Kla National Park ❷

อุทยานแห่งชาติภูหินร่องกล้า

Phitsanulok province. Park HQ off Hwy 2331, 31 km (19 miles) SE of Nakhon Thai. 🛈 TAT, Phitsanulok (055) 252743; Forestry Dept (02) 579 0529 (inc bungalow bookings). 🚌 from Loei or Phitsanulok to Nakhon Thai, then songthaew. 🚗

COVERING AN AREA of 307 sq km (120 sq miles), Phu Hin Rong Kla National Park has a wide variety of flora and fauna, and an unusual open-air museum with exhibits of the Communist camp based here in the 1960s and '70s.

The spread of Communism in Southeast Asia from the 1950s increasingly alarmed the Thai goverment, and hostilities between the Communist Party of Thailand (CPT) and the military commenced in 1964. Soon after, the open forests of the Phu Hin Rong Kla mountain range became a CPT stronghold. An average elevation of 1,000 m (3,300 ft), proximity to Laos – run by the Communist Pathet Lao from 1975 (see p285) – and the access this facilitated to headquarters, at Kunming in China, all made it an ideal site. The CPT became especially active after 1976, when thousands of students fled here after a military coup in Bangkok. By 1979, disillusioned with Communism, many began to take advantage of an amnesty from the Thai government. Dwindling support and government attacks on Phu Hin Rong Kla in the early 1980s led the site to fall to the authorities in 1982.

Two years later it opened as a national park. Its highest peak, Phu Man Khao, rises to a height of 1,620 m (5,300 ft).

Phu Rua National Park ❸

อุทยานแห่งชาติภูเรือ

Loei province. Park HQ off Hwy 203, 50 km (30 miles) W of Loei. 🛈 TAT, Udon Thani (042) 325406; Forestry Dept (02) 579 0529 (inc bungalow bookings). 🚌 from Loei to Phu Rua village, then songthaew. 🚗

PHU RUA or "boat mountain" derives its name from its highest peak, which is shaped like a Chinese junk. It stands some 1,365 m (4,500 ft) above sea level and offers spectacular views over the town of Loei to the south and towards Laos. A modern Buddha image sits looking out over the plains in contemplation of their immense beauty.

It is possible to drive to the summit of Phu Rua, passing several bizarre rock formations on the way. The most remarkable is Hin Ta or "tortoise rock", with two huge sandstone boulders stacked, one on top of the other, surmounted by a third, giving the structure the appearance of a giant mushroom.

For the traveller with time to explore the 121 sq km (47 sq miles) of this national park, a number of marked trails lead

Unusual rock formation at Phu Rua National Park

through a beautiful landscape of meadows, rock gardens and pine and evergreen forests. Views across the surrounding lowlands can be seen from Phu Kut and the cliffs of Pha Lon Noi, Pha Dong Tham San, Pha Yat and Pha Sap Thong. There are also several waterfalls located around the park, namely Huai Phai, Huai Ta Wat and Lan Hin Taek.

Animals at Phu Rua National Park include barking deer, wild pigs, a wide variety of birds, including pheasant, and the rare *tao puru*, or Siamese big-headed turtle. Phu Rua is also famed for being one of the coolest areas of Thailand, with a record low temperature of -4° C (25° F) having been recorded here in 1981.

Relics of the war between the military and the CPT, Phu Hin Rong Kla

Rolling hills near Loei, typical of this part of the Northeast

Loei ❹

เลย

Loei province. 🏛 24,000. ✈ 🚌 🛈
TAT, Udon Thani (042) 325406. 🚌 daily.
🎎 Cotton Blossom Festival (Feb), Phi Ta
Khon Festival (Jul), Rocket Festival (May).

IN THAI, the word *loei* means "beyond" or "to the furthest extreme", a fitting name for a town and province that lie in the northernmost part of Northeast Thailand, straddling the edge of the Khorat Plateau. Though the province is administrated as part of Isan (the Northeast), its climate and landscape are more similar to those of Northern Thailand. In winter it is cold and foggy, in summer searingly hot. In the past, bureaucrats who had fallen out of favour with the Siamese government, based in Bangkok, were posted to the remote town of Loei as punishment for their inefficiency. One fortunate aspect of Loei's isolation is that it firmly retains its traditional flavour.

Lying along the west bank of the Loei River, Loei has a few sights of interest to visitors. There is a lively market by the bridge across the river and next to the bridge is the **Lak Muang** or "city pillar". The town also has an old Chinese shrine, **Chao Pho Kut Pong**, a popular place of worship for the local people. The surrounding valley is rich in minerals, and also produces some of the finest cotton in Thailand. Examples of this can be bought in Loei, in shops along Charoenraj Road and Ruamchai Road.

Loei also has a reasonable amount of cheap accommodation, making it a good base from which to visit Phu Rua and Phu Kradung *(see pp276–7)* national parks.

PHI TA KHON FESTIVAL

Although a less lively version of this festival is held in the provincial capital of Loei in July, its real home is in the town of Dan Sai, 80 km (50 miles) to the west. Here Phi Ta Khon takes place in June at the beginning of the rainy season *(see pp43–5)*. Its purpose is to make Buddhist merit and call for rain. The festival's origins are in the Buddhist tale of Prince Vessandorn, the Lord Buddha's final incarnation before he attained *nirvana*. Apparently, when Vessandorn returned to his city, the welcoming procession was so enchanting that the spirits emerged to celebrate. Today, the young men of Dan Sai dress up as spirits *(phi ta khon)*, draped in robes of patchwork rags and sporting painted masks made out of coconut tree trunks with huge, gaping mouths, beak-like noses and wicker-basket crowns. During the three-day festival, they make playful jibes at onlookers as they parade a sacred Buddha image around the town. Monks also recite the story of Vessandorn to the crowd. On the third day, the "spirits" bring the festival to a close by circumambulating the main building of the local *wat* three times, before finally casting their colourful masks into a nearby river.

Phi Ta Khon costume

Young men, dressed as spirits, preparing to parade a sacred Buddha around Loei town

Phi Ta Khon "spirits" making fun of onlookers

Ornate, Lao-style façade of Wat Tha Kok, Chiang Khan

Chiang Khan ❻

เชียงคาน

Loei province. 🏠 *61,000.* 🚌 *from Loei or Nong Khai.* ℹ️ *TAT, Udon Thani (042) 241968.*

CHIANG KHAN COMPRISES two parallel streets running close to the south bank of the Mekhong River, along which lie run-down teakwood shop-houses and restaurants, interspersed with temples. Those temples most worth a visit are Wat Santi, Wat Pa Klang, built over 100 years ago by Lao immigrants, Wat Si Khun Muang, Wat Tha Kok and Wat Mahathat. The latter is the oldest temple in Chiang Khan, its *bot* having been built in 1654. Like Wat Tha Kok, it shows French colonial influence in its colonnades and shutters.

Wat Tha Khok has a beautiful, painted ceiling. Its exterior walls are stained red, like the river, from dust. This possibly stems from deforestation in nearby Laos, which exposes the local red topsoil.

ENVIRONS: Located 2 km (1 mile) further east from Wat Tha Kok along the Mekhong River is Wat Tha Khaek. Neglected for years, this temple is now undergoing major reconstruction, albeit in a mixture of traditional and modern styles. A further 2 km (1 mile) down river are the scenic Kaeng Kut Khu rapids.

Pak Chom ❼

ปากชม

Loei province. 🏠 *10,000.* 🚌 *from Loei or Nong Khai.* ℹ️ *TAT, Udon Thani (042) 241968.* 🏠 *daily.*

PAK CHOM IS LITTLE MORE than a picturesque settlement of ramshackle, wooden buildings clustered by the bank of the Mekhong River, 40 km (25 miles) northeast of Chiang Khan. It's a good place to stop for refreshments and to enjoy the scenery. In the 1970s and 1980s the town had a somewhat higher profile thanks to Ban Winai, a Lao-Hmong *(see p196)* refugee camp of some 15,000 inhabitants. It was established when these tribespeople fled Laos in the wake of the Pathet Lao *(see p285)*, who overthrew the Lao monarchy and took control of the country in 1975. In 1992 the camp was disbanded and the Hmong moved to Chiang Kham in the Chiang Rai province of Northern Thailand.

Mekhong Villages Tour ❺

AS WELL AS VILLAGES, this tour takes in temples, lush forest and great river views. No river in the world is quite like the 4,025-km (2,500-mile) Mekhong, with its distinctive red waters. Its source is in the Himalayas, and it separates Laos and Thailand for 750 km (470 miles) before flowing through Cambodia and Vietnam out into the South China Sea. Rich in agriculture, its floodplain has been a source of wealth in an otherwise infertile region.

TIPS FOR TRAVELLERS

Length: 120 km (75 miles).
Stopping-off points: Chiang Khan has a couple of restaurants, and four or five good guesthouses which serve food. Pak Chom, Sangkhom and Si Chiangmai all have good guesthouses offering food. Some guesthouses hire out bicycles. Food vendors can also be found in most villages and towns.
Public transport: Local buses run between the main towns along the route. It is also possible to travel from Chiang Khan to Pak Chom by long-tail boat.

Ban Muang ④
Fishermen casting their nets are a common sight at this point in the Mekhong River.

Pha Baen ②
This small village is one of many with picturesque wooden buildings and river views.

Pak Chom ③
The journey along the stretch of river between Chiang Khan and Pak Chom can be made by road or by long-tail boat.

Chiang Khan ①
Many of the temples and shop-houses in Chiang Khan show Lao influences.

KEY

▬▬▬	Tour route
═══	Other roads
≈≈≈	Rivers

Sangkhom ⑧

สังคม

Nong Khai province. 🚶 *22,000.*
🚌 *from Loei or Nong Khai.* ℹ️ *TAT,
Udon Thani (042) 241968.*

THE MAIN ATTRACTIONS of this town are its peace and quiet and its location in a particularly lush part of the Mekhong River Valley. Ranged along the bank of the river are some quaint, wooden buildings. Sangkhom also makes a good base for excursions to the surrounding countryside.

ENVIRONS: The **Than Thip falls** are a major highlight of this area. Just outside Sangkhom, 3 km (2 miles) off the main highway, they are hidden in the midst of jungle and banana groves. The two main, and most accessible, levels of this waterfall have pools at their bases, making them ideal for a refreshing swim. More intrepid travellers can explore a further three levels higher up the falls.

Topiary in the gardens of the Fisheries Department, near Si Chiangmai

Si Chiangmai ⑨

ศรีเชียงใหม่

Nong Khai province. 🚶 *50,000.*
🚌 *from Loei or Nong Khai.* ℹ️ *TAT,
Udon Thani (042) 241968.* 🏪 *daily.*

THIS TOWN overlooks the Lao capital of Vientiane *(see pp284–5)* on the other side of the Mekhong River and has a large population of Lao and Vietnamese refugees. Its main claim to fame is as the world's largest producer of spring roll wrappers. When the weather is fine, they can be seen along the roadsides, spread out on bamboo racks to dry in the sun.

ENVIRONS: Located 5 km (3 miles) outside Si Chiangmai are the gardens of the **Fisheries Department**, featuring unusual elephant-shaped topiary.

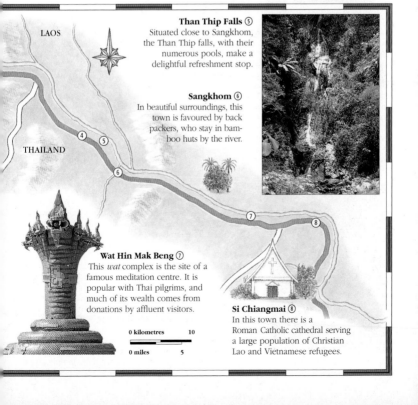

Than Thip Falls ⑤
Situated close to Sangkhom, the Than Thip falls, with their numerous pools, make a delightful refreshment stop.

Sangkhom ⑥
In beautiful surroundings, this town is favoured by backpackers, who stay in bamboo huts by the river.

LAOS

THAILAND

Wat Hin Mak Beng ⑦
This *wat* complex is the site of a famous meditation centre. It is popular with Thai pilgrims, and much of its wealth comes from donations by affluent visitors.

| 0 kilometres | 10 |
| 0 miles | 5 |

Si Chiangmai ⑧
In this town there is a Roman Catholic cathedral serving a large population of Christian Lao and Vietnamese refugees.

Nong Khai ⑩

หนองคาย

Village Weaver shop sign

ONCE A SLEEPY BORDER TOWN, Nong Khai has recently been transformed into one of the busiest commercial centres in the Northeast, partly because of the opening of the Friendship Bridge. The first bridge to span the Mekhong River between Thailand and Laos, its construction in 1994 was a factor in an increase in trade between the two countries. Nevertheless, the town centre retains much of its original charm, and Nong Khai's main attraction for travellers is still its peaceful riverside character.

Relative peace and quiet on Nong Khai's Meechai Street

Exploring Nong Khai

Nong Khai's streets and *sois* are lined with traditional wooden shop-houses. Its most vibrant neighbourhood is around the Sadet riverboat pier, with its market and adjacent restaurants overlooking the Mekhong River. A recent influx of prosperity in the town is made obvious by the burgeoning number of restaurants as well as modern shopping centres and banking facilities.

Intricate carving on the rear of the Lao-style Wat Si Muang

🖼 Indochina Market

ตลาดอินโดจีน

Off Rimkhong Rd. ◻ *daily.*

This market remains the focus of lively, local trade carried out between Thailand and Laos. Reciprocal visa arrangements allow merchants from either country to visit Vientiane *(see pp284–5)* or Nong Khai for up to three days. Merchandise that can be bought at the market includes clothing, pots and pans, foodstuffs, pestles and mortars, fishing nets and tables woven from bamboo.

Prap Ho Monument

อนุสาวรีย์ปราบฮ่อ

Off Chaiporn Rd.

The Prap Ho Monument, a symbol of municipal pride, was built to honour those who held off Ho Chinese invasions in 1855 and 1877. Built in 1886, and bearing Thai, Lao, Chinese and English inscriptions, it is the site of annual celebrations on 5 March.

🚩 Prajak Road

ถนนประจักษ์

Along Prajak Road, visitors can pay a call at the Village Weaver shop, where traditional silk-weaving is carried out. The factory-cum-shop specializes in *mut mee,* the name given to a method of tie-dying used in the Northeast. It was established as part of a scheme to encourage local girls to stay and work in Nong Khai, rather than moving to larger urban centres such as Bangkok. There is also a market on Prajak Road, to the rear of the bus station.

🛕 Wat Si Muang

วัดศรีเมือง

Off Meechai Rd. ◻ *daily.*

The temple buildings and *chedi* of Wat Si Muang are Lao in style. The *wat* has an ornate shrine at the main entrance, cluttered with Buddhist merit offerings. Wat Si Muang is one of many such temples that line the main Meechai Road leading west towards Wat Pho Chai.

🛕 Wat Pho Chai

วัดโพธิ์ชัย

Prasai Rd. ◻ *daily.*

The newly restored and somewhat gaudy Wat Pho Chai lies in the southwest of the city, adjacent to a street market of the same name. Its main chapel sports imposing *naga* balustrades and a pair of roaring lions at the top of the entrance stairs, protecting the highly revered Luang Pho Phra Sai Buddha image

Guardian lion, Wat Pho Chai

housed within. This solid gold Buddha with a ruby-studded, flame finial was originally moulded in the ancient Lao kingdom of Lan Xang. It later resided in Vientiane *(see pp274–5).* In 1778 it was taken by Prince Chakri, later Rama I (1782–1809), following the first Thai invasion of Laos. As he attempted to ferry it across the Mekhong, it fell into the river and, according to legend, miraculously resurfaced. After it had been rescued it was placed in Wat Pho Chai. Murals in the temple give a pictorial account of this story.

Luang Pho Phra Sai Buddha image, housed in Wat Pho Chai

🄰 Other Wats

Apart from its major sights, Nong Khai has a number of minor *wats* worth a visit. All of them have Lao-influenced architecture and include **Wat Haisoke**, **Wat Lamduan** and **Wat Si Sumang** which all offer views over the Mekhong River, and **Wat Si Khun Muang**.

ENVIRONS: Though always a major crossing point for tourists and traders bound for the Lao capital of Vientiane, Nong Khai gained significance as a commercial border post with the opening of the **Friendship Bridge** in 1994. Built with Thai, Lao and Australian cooperation, it

links Ban Chommani on the western outskirts of Nong Khai, to Tha Na Laeng on the opposite bank, some 20 km (12 miles) from Vientiane. By the foot of the bridge, on the Thai side, is a stretch of sand known as Chommani beach, a popular spot for picnicking Thais during the dry season, when the waters of the Mekhong River are low.

Closer to the town centre is the Lao *chedi* of **Phra That Nong Khai**, which collapsed into the Mekhong River in 1847. Over the years it has slowly drifted further and further into the middle of the river to the point where it can now be seen only when the water is low.

By far the most unusual site of interest at Nong Khai lies some 5 km (3 miles) to the east of the town. **Wat Khaek**, also known as Sala Kaew Ku, was founded in 1978 by the charismatic Luang Pu Bunleua Surirat. This Thai-Brahmin shaman allegedly trained under a Hindu guru in Vietnam, moved on to Laos and was then forced to Thailand by the hostile attentions of the Pathet Lao *(see p285)*. Wat Khaek is essentially an

Seven-headed *naga*, Wat Khaek

open-air theme park of enormous, concrete, Hindu and Buddhist sculptures.

Among the giant gods, saints and demons which are depicted here are Rahu, the god of eclipses and, tallest of all, a 25-m (82-ft) high seven-headed *naga* with a tiny Buddha seated on its coils. The atmosphere of a walk through this eccentric collection of images is intensified by the incense smoke and the piped music. The shrine building is an exhibition hall on two floors which contains, among other things, numerous photographs of the Luang Pu or "Venerable Grandfather".

He is said to have such charisma that anyone drinking holy water offered by him will immediately donate all their belongings to the temple.

VISITORS' CHECKLIST

Nong Khai province. 🄰 46,000. 🚊 3 km (2 miles) W of town on Kaeo Worawut Rd. 🚌 Praserm Rd. 🄸 TAT, Udon Thani (042) 325406. 🛒 daily. 🎊 Nong Khai Festival (Mar), Bun Bang Fai (Rocket) Festival (May).

NONG KHAI TOWN CENTRE

Indochina Market ③
Prajak Road ⑧
Prap Ho Monument ①
Wat Haisoke ②
Wat Lamduan ⑥
Wat Pho Chai ⑨
Wat Si Khun Muang ⑤
Wat Si Muang ④
Wat Si Sumang ⑦

KEY

🚍 Coach station
🛥 Riverboat pier
🄰 Wat

0 metres   500
0 yards   500

Vientiane ⑪

เวียงจันทน์

Temple door

IN ITS 1,000-YEAR HISTORY, Vientiane has come under Khmer, Vietnamese, Thai and French colonial influence. It was capital of the Lan Xang Kingdom in the 16th century and later a vassal of Ayutthaya. The Thais sacked Vientiane in 1828. In 1893 the French annexed Laos and made Vientiane its capital. Laos gained independence in 1953; in 1975 it became a Socialist Republic. A day trip from Nong Khai *(see pp282–3)*, today Vientiane shows a side of Southeast Asia that is fast disappearing.

Exploring Vientiane

Vientiane has been isolated from change for generations. However, trade with Thailand, encouraged by the Friendship Bridge *(see p283)*, means that the city is likely to start changing as fast as some Thai towns across the Mekhong River.

Vientiane was one of three important French Indochinese cities; the others were Ho Chi Minh City (or Saigon) and Phnom Penh. French colonial influence can still be felt in the city with its shuttered villas and broad, tree-lined boulevards, that sit somewhat incongruously next to traditional Lao- and Thai-influenced structures. Some drab apartment blocks, built with Russian aid, have also sprung up.

Shop-house in Vientiane

🏯 Haw Pha Kaew

Setthathirat Rd. ⬜ *Tue–Sun.* ⬤ *public hols.* 🔖

This temple was once home to the Phra Kaeo or Emerald Buddha *(see p79)*, which was taken by the Thais in 1778 and placed in Wat Phra Kaeo in Bangkok. (Phra Kaeo is the preferred transliteration in Thai; Pha Kaew in Lao.) A replica, a symbol of renewed friendship, was given to Laos by Thailand in 1994. The sack of 1828 left the temple in ruins. Restored in the 20th century, it is now a museum. The beautifully carved main door is all that remains of the original *wat*.

🏯 Wat Sisaket

Lane Xang Rd. ⬜ *Tue–Sun.* ⬤ *public hols.* 🔖

This *wat*, built in 1818, was one of the few buildings to survive the sack of 1828. It is now the oldest *wat* in Vientiane and one of the most interesting to visit. Its most memorable feature is the 2,052 tiny Buddha images made of terracotta, bronze and wood, which fill niches in the walls of the cloister. Over 300 Buddha images also rest on a long shelf below the niches.

🏯 Lao Revolutionary Museum

Samsenthai Rd. ⬜ *daily.* ⬤ *public hols.* 🔖

Artifacts and photographs here detail the period of French colonialism, independence in the 1940s and '50s and the rise of the Pathet Lao.

VIENTIANE CITY CENTRE

Haw Pha Kaew ⑥
Lao Revolutionary Museum ④
Wat Hai Sok ①
Wat Mixai ③
Wat Ong Teu ②
Wat Sisaket ⑤

KEY

🚌 Coach station
ℹ️ Tourist information
🏯 Wat
🕌 Mosque
⛪ Church

0 metres   250
0 yards   250

⬛ Wat Mixai

Setthathirat Rd. ⬤ *daily.*

Its gates flanked by two *nyaks* or guardian giants, parts of this *wat* complex were built in 19th-century Rattanakosin style.

⬛ Wat Ong Theu

Setthathirat Rd. ⬤ *daily.*

One of the most important *wat* complexes in all Laos, Wat Ong Theu was originally founded in the early 16th century. Destroyed in 1828, it was rebuilt in the 19th and 20th centuries. The *wat* houses a large, 16th-century bronze Buddha image, with two standing Buddhas either side of it. The *wat* also houses a school for monks.

⬛ Wat Hai Sok

Setthathirat Rd. ⬤ *daily.*

Like other *wats* in Vientiane, Wat Hai Sok recently underwent restoration. Its most distinctive feature is an impressive five-tiered roof.

ENVIRONS: The **Pha That Luang**, which perches, somewhat out of the way, halfway up a hill, on the northeastern outskirts of the city, is the most important national and Buddhist monument in Laos. According to legend a *chedi* was built here in the 3rd century BC to house a breastbone of the Lord Buddha. More tangible evidence suggests this was the site of a Khmer *prasat*. The present structure was built in 1566, when Vientiane became the capital of the Lan Xang Kingdom. It was damaged in the 18th and 19th centuries and restored, albeit badly, by the French in 1900. A better restoration of the site was undertaken in the 1930s.

Wat Si Muang, to the southeast of the city centre, is the most popular place of worship in Vientiane. According to legend, the site was chosen by Lao sages in 1563.

Wat Sok Pa Luang is known for its instruction in *vipassana*, a type of Buddhist meditation.

Ho Nang Ussa, a rock formation in Phu Phrabat Historical Park

Phu Phrabat Historical Park ⓬

อุทยานประวัติศาสตร์ภูพระบาท

Off Hwy 2020, 12 km (7.5 miles) S of Ban Phu, Nong Khai province. 🛈 TAT, Udon Thani (042) 325406. 🚌 from Nong Khai to Ban Phu, then songthaew. ⬤ daily. 🎫

THE DISTINCTIVE sandstone formations that are the central attraction of this historical park cannot fail to leave their imprint on the imagination. The local population has shrouded the site in many fantastic myths and legends. According to one of these, Princess Ussa was sent to Phu Phrabat by her father to study. However, she fell in love with Prince Barot. Outraged, her father challenged the prince to a temple-building duel, but lost. A huge sandstone slab in the park, known as Kok Ma Thao Barot, is supposedly Prince Barot's stable. The mushroom-shaped Ho Nang Ussa apparently represents Princess Ussa's residence, where she pined away many long years in exile.

The 6,000-year-old human history of this site is testified to by cave paintings found on the underside of two natural rock shelters, known locally as Tham Wua and Tham Khon or "ox cave" and "people cave".

At the entrance to the historical park stands a crude replica of Wat Phra That Phanom (*see p287*); the **Wat Phraphutthabat Bua Bok** houses the Bua Bok Buddha Footprint, and is an important pilgrimage site for local Thais.

THE PATHET LAO

The Lao Patriotic Front was formed after World War II and, with ties to Ho Chi Minh's Communist Party in Vietnam, opposed French rule. In 1953 Laos was declared a constitutional monarchy, backed by France and the USA. The LPF's armed wing, the Pathet Lao, mounted an armed struggle against the government in the 1960s. During the Vietnam War the USA repeatedly bombed Laos in order to stamp out Pathet Lao support for the North Vietnamese. With the withdrawal of American forces from the region in 1975, the Pathet Lao staged a bloodless coup and declared Laos the Lao People's Democratic Republic.

Poster supporting the Lao People's Democratic Party

Wat Phra That Choeng Chum, the main *wat* in the old, once Khmer, town of Sakhon Nakhon

Sakhon Nakhon ⓭

สกลนคร

Sakhon Nakhon province. 🏠 *50,000.*
✈ 🚌 🛈 *TAT, Nakhon Phanom
(042) 513490.* 🛒 *daily.* 🎎 *Wax
Castle Ceremony (Oct).*

THERE ARE TWO SIGHTS of
interest in the friendly town
of Sakhon Nakhon. **Wat Phra
That Choeng Chum** is a
beautiful temple complex
with a large *bot* and *wihan*, a
10th-century Khmer *prang*
and a whitewashed, 24-m (80-
ft) Lao-style *chedi* built during
the Ayutthaya period.

The old *prang* is reached
through a door in the *wihan*.
Etched into the *prang's* base
is an ancient Khmer inscription, and around it are Lao and
Khmer images of the Buddha.
Also in the compound is an
interesting display of *luk nimit*,
which are Brahmin foundation
markers that somewhat re-
semble giant cannon balls.

The five-layered, 11th-
century, Khmer *prang* of **Wat
Phra That Narai Cheng
Weng** was built as a Hindu
monument. The name Cheng
Weng is taken from the
princess responsible for its
construction; Narai is a Thai
and Khmer name for Vishnu.
The most important lintel –
over the only entrance, to the
east – shows Shiva dancing to
the destruction of the universe,
as he tramples the head of a
lion. On the northern portico
is a splendid depiction of Vishnu, with a lotus and baton in
two of his four hands.

Nakhon Phanom ⓮

นครพนม

Nakhon Phanom province.
🏠 *31,000.* ✈ 🚌 🛈 *TAT, 2/16
Salaklang Rd, Nakhon Phanom
(042) 513490.* 🛒 *daily.* 🎎 *Illuminated Boats Procession (Oct).*

NAKHON PHANOM – "city of
hills" – is a good town in
which to spend a few relaxing
days by the Mekhong. In the
dry season a beach by the
river, **Hat Sai Tai Muang**,
becomes exposed, and it is
possible to walk out almost
as far as Laos. The view of
Laos is splendid. However,
this town cannot be used as a
place to procure a visa for, or
as an entry point into, Laos.

To celebrate the end of the
rains, during the night of the
full moon in the 11th lunar
month, there is a resplendent
procession of illuminated boats
on the river here. Measuring
some 10 m (33 ft) in length,
the boats are traditionally
crafted from bamboo or banana trees. They are filled with
lighted candles, incense, paraf-
fin lamps and offerings of fragrant flowers and sweetmeats.

Renu Nakhon ⓯

เรณูนคร

Nakhon Phanom province.
🏠 *42,000.* 🚌 *from Nakhon
Phanom.* 🛈 *TAT, Nakhon Phanom
(042) 513490.* 🛒 *Wed.*

RENU NAKHON is a village
known primarily for its
weaving and fine embroidery.
At the popular Wednesday
market, colourful cottons and
silks are sold by the *phun*, a
measure 75 cm (2 ft) long.
Ready-made garments and
furnishings from all over the
Northeast and Laos are also
sold. There is a more permanent gathering of textile stalls
around **Phra That Renu**.
This was built in 1918 and
modelled loosely on the nearby *chedi* at That Phanom.

**Shop selling a range of locally
made textiles, Renu Nakhon**

Wat Phra That Phanom ⑯

วัดพระธาตุพนม

THIS WAT, in the remote town of That Phanom, is the most revered shrine in Northeast Thailand, famous for its central, Lao-style brick and plaster *chedi*. The *chedi* was constructed some 1,500 years ago, although according to legend it was built eight years after the death of the Buddha in 535 BC, when local dignitaries erected it as a burial place for his breastbone. The monument has been restored many times, most recently after devastating rains in 1975. Each year at the full moon of the third lunar month, during a farming holiday, a week-long temple festival attracts thousands of pilgrims from Thailand and Laos.

VISITORS' CHECKLIST

Centre of That Phanom, Nakhon Phanom province. 🛈 *TAT, Nakhon Phanom (042) 513490.* 🚌 *from Nakhon Phanom, Sakhon Nakhon or Mukdahan.* ⬜ *6am–7pm daily.* 🎫 🎏 *Ngan Phra That Phanom Festival (Feb/Mar).*

Stone Lion
One of two on either side of the outer compound's central path, this fierce, mythical beast is a temple guardian who wards off evil forces.

Pilgrims at Wat Phra That Phanom
Thousands come to pay homage at festival time and throughout the year. Many devotees are from Laos – the monument is the second most sacred site to them, the first being That Luang in Vientiane.

Gold decoration in the shape of a multi-leaved lotus flower represents the path to Enlightenment.

The *chedi* is studded with gemstones and gold rings.

Golden Buddha Image
In abhaya mudra posture (see p163) and shaded by an umbrella, this image sits near the entrance to the inner compound.

CENTRAL CHEDI

The famous, 57-m (185-ft) high *chedi* at the centre of the temple is in the shape of a stylized, elongated lotus bud. The present structure, rebuilt in 1977, is modelled on That Luang in Vientiane, Laos.

A *chat*, or ceremonial umbrella

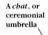

Numerous Buddha images line the inner compound wall of the *chedi*. Pilgrims paste squares of gold leaf onto them as a way of making merit.

Stone panels carved in the 10th century tell the legends of the five men who supposedly built the *chedi* in the 6th century BC.

The market along the river at Mukdahan, where Lao and Vietnamese merchandise is sold

Mukdahan ⑰

มุกดาหาร

Mukdahan province. 🚶 34,000.
🚌 🚹 TAT, Nakhon Phanom
(042) 513490. 🚪 daily. 🎎 Ruam
Pao Thai Ma Kham Wan Chai
Khong Fair (Jan).

MUKDAHAN IS THE CAPITAL of one of Thailand's newest provinces, created in 1980 from areas that were formerly part of Nakhon Phanom and Ubon Ratchathani provinces.

By far the most interesting street is Samran Chai Khong Road, which runs along the Mekhong River front. It faces the second largest city in Laos, Suwannakhet, on the

Seated Buddha at Wat Yot Kaew
Siwichai, Mukdahan

opposite bank. As a result of its proximity to this city, Mukdahan has grown up as a busy trading centre, and both Lao and Thai boats can be seen at the pier, loading and unloading their goods. Tourists with a visa (see p451) can cross into Laos at this point.

A market also runs most of the length of the riverside, between **Wat Si Mongkol Thai** and **Wat Yot Kaew Siwichai**. Goods on sale may be disappointing because there are few examples of traditional Lao and Vietnamese merchandise. Expect an excess of plastic ephemera, though the market is worth a visit for the local sweetmeats and its colourful atmosphere.

Wat Si Mongkhol Thai was built in 1956 by Vietnamese immigrants in the town and is distinguished by statues of mythical creatures at the entrance to its main chapel.

The gaudier Wat Yot Kaew Siwichai houses an enormous, seated, golden Buddha image. The figure sits in an open-fronted *wihan* with panelled glass on two of its sides. Near Wat Yot Kaew Siwichai, on Song Nang Sathit Road, is the Chinese **Chao Fa Mung Muang shrine**, home to Mukdahan's guardian spirit. Also here is the **Lak Muang**, or City Pillar, which is usually draped in colourful, plastic garlands.

ENVIRONS: Excellent views of the entire provincial capital can be captured from the 500-m (1,650-ft) peak of **Phu Manorom**. There is a pavilion at the top of the hill sheltering a replica of the Buddha's Footprint.

🏞 Phu Manorom
Off Hwy 2034, 5 km (3 miles) S of
Mukdahan. 🚪 daily. 🎫

Pha Taem ⑱

ผาแต้ม

18 km (11 miles) N of Khong Chiam,
Ubon Ratchathani province. 🚹 TAT,
Ubon Ratchathani (045) 243770.
🚌 from Ubon Ratchathani to Khong
Chiam, then tuk-tuk. 🚪 daily. 🎫

THE ROUTE, 18 km (11 miles) from Khong Chiam up to Pha Taem or "painted cliff", is a circuitous one, really accessible only by hire car or *tuk-tuk*. Along the way, a few kilometres before you arrive at the cliff top, an unusual, sandstone rock formation can be seen at the roadside. Known as Sao Chaliang, it is curiously reminiscent of the Ho Nang Ussa at Phu Phrabat Historical Park (see p285) in Udon Thani province.

At the end of the journey to Pha Taem, an unmarked trail leads from the car park to the cliff face. This is decorated with huge figures and geo-metrical designs. Painted in an indelible red pigment derived from soil, tree-gum and fat, the paintings are thought to date back some 4,000 years. Covering a 170-m (560-ft) length of the cliff face, they include depictions of fish traps, wild animals, giant, cock-roach-like fish, angular human beings and a 30-m (98-ft) stretch of handprints. The artists who created these unusual decorations are thought to have been related to the early inhabitants of Ban Chiang (see p262), and were rice cultivators rather than cave dwellers.

Pha Taem is particularly beautiful at sunset, when it affords tremendous views across the Mekong and of the wild Lao jungle beyond.

Prehistoric cliff-painting, Pha Taem

Khong Chiam ⓳

โขงเจียม

Ubon Ratchathani province.
🏛 28,000. 🚌 🛈 TAT, Ubon Ratchathani (045) 243770. 🎪 daily.

K HONG CHIAM IS NEAR the confluence of the muddy red Mekong and the indigo-blue Mun rivers, which creates the phenomenon of the maenam song si or "two-coloured river". The differing hues of the rivers derive from the amounts of sand and clay suspended in their waters.

Scenic views are offered from the bank at **Wat Khong Chiam**, while boat trips out to the confluence point itself allow a full appreciation of the blend of coloured waters, clearest in April. It is also possible to cross from Khong Chiam to the Lao town on the oppo-site side of the river, though this cannot be used by travellers as an official entry point into Laos. Visitors to Khong Chiam can also watch traditional, conical fish traps being made.

Chong Mek ⓴

ช่องเม็ก

Ubon Ratchathani province.
🏛 650. 🚌 from Ubon Ratchathani.
🛈 TAT, Ubon Ratchathani (045) 243770. 🎪 daily.

O N THE BORDER between Thailand and Laos, Chong Mek is one of the few places at which tourists can cross into Laos. Other Lao entry points include Nong Khai, (see pp282–3), and Chiang Khong (see p239). Visitors need a valid visa (see p451), which can be ob-tained in advance from Bangkok. For those who do not have a visa, it is possible, even with-out a passport, to walk some 200 m (660 ft) over the border to browse around the open-air market and duty-free shops that are set up there.

Chong Mek has all the feel of a re-mote, frontier post, and its Lao market, although small, is interesting and friendly. Young women vendors and children sell fruit, French bread

sticks, textiles and round wicker tables called tok, around which the Lao, Nor-thern and Northeastern Thais traditionally squat to eat.

In the market there may also be groups of old ladies selling rare plants and flowers. However, many of the plants are, sadly, taken from a fast-disappearing Lao jungle. Visitors to the market are advised not to buy these.

Boat on the Sirindhorn Dam

Sirindhorn Dam ㉑

เขื่อนสิรินธร

Ubon Ratchathani province. 🛈 TAT, Ubon Ratchathani (045) 243770.
🚌 from Ubon Ratchathani to Chong Mek, then songthaew.

N AMED AFTER the second daughter of King Bhumibol, the Sirindhorn Dam was built in 1971. The reservoir it created measures 43 km (27 miles) from north to south and the dam's tur-bines produce 24,000 kilo-watts of electricity.

There is a park at the dam headquarters, and a restaurant and bungalows for visitors. It is possible to walk out over the dam itself and to take a boat out onto the reservoir.

Dams in Thailand have been funded by the World Bank since the 1950s to meet Thai-land's ever-increasing need for electricity. They are given support mainly by politicians and the business community. Recently, residents and envir-onmental groups have begun to campaign against the con-struction of new dams.

Making wicker fish traps, Khong Chiam

Huge, intricately carved candles paraded through the streets of Ubon Ratchathani during the Candle Festival ▷

Prasat Khao Phra Wihan ②

ปราสาทเขาพระวิหาร

Off Hwy 221, 30 km (19 miles) S of
Kantharalak, just inside Cambodia.
🛈 TAT, Ubon Ratchathani (045)
243770. 🚌 from Ubon to Kantharalak,
then songthaew. ◯ daily. 🎫

Three ruined *prangs*, all on a single base, at Prasat Prang Ku

THE EXTRAORDINARY SITE of
this early Khmer temple,
laid out along a spur of the
Dongrek Mountains, makes it
one of the most distinctive
Khmer structures outside of
Angkor *(see pp254–5)*. Possibly older than Angkor, sadly,
it was long the victim of
disputes between Thailand
and Cambodia. After much
disagreement between the
two countries, in 1962 a
decision was taken by the
World Court: while the
easiest access to the temple
is through Thailand, the
temple stands firmly
in Cambodia.

During the
mid-1970s,
the years of
the Khmer
Rouge regime
in Cambodia,
the temple
became a
strictly no-go
area. After
the Vietnamese invaded
Cambodia in 1978, conflicts
between rival factions continued in the area until the
late 1980s. The site was finally
cleared of land mines and
opened to the public in the
early 1990s, but as civil unrest

**Stone relief on the Cambodian
sight of Prasat Khao Phra Wihan**

continues in Cambodia, this
magnificent temple is forced
to close down periodically.

When Khao Phra Wihan is
open, tourists can walk
through army checkpoints
to ascend a series of grand
staircases, pass through
stone *gopuras*, and then
walk along an 850-m
(2,800-ft) *naga*-
lined causeway
to arrive at the
central sanctuary, or *prasat*.
Dedicated to
the Hindu god
Shiva, it is now
largely in ruins.
The *prang* in
particular is in
need of restoration. Views from
the sheer cliffs here, over the
Cambodian plateau, are exhilarating. If the temple is closed,
elegant Khmer reliefs carved
in the cliff can be viewed from
the Thai side of the border.

Prasat Prang Ku ②

ปราสาทปรางค์กู่

Off Hwy 2234, 35 km (22 miles) W of
Si Sa Ket, Si Sa Ket province. 🛈 TAT,
Ubon Ratchathani (045) 243770.
🚌 from Ubon to Prang Ku, then
songthaew. ◯ daily. 🎫

LOCATED IN THE DISTRICT of
Prang Ku in Si Sa Ket
province, this 11th-century
Khmer monument comprises
three brick *prangs* on a single
platform. The most remarkable
feature is a well-preserved
lintel, divided horizontally
into two sections by the tails
of two long *nagas*. In the

centre stands Vishnu on his
mount, a *garuda*. On either
side of the *garuda* are two
lions with garlands of flowers
in their open mouths. The top
half of the lintel is decorated
with dancing deities. In front
of Prasat Prang Ku is a 1-km
(1,100-yd) long Khmer *baray*
(reservoir), a welcome feeding
ground for birds.

Ubon Ratchathani ②

อุบลราชธานี

Ubon Ratchathani province. 👥
154,000. ✈ 🚉 🚌 🛈 TAT, 164
Khuan Thani Rd, Ubon Ratchathani
(045) 243770. 🔄 daily. 🎫 Ubon
Candle Festival (late Jul).

FROM THE 10TH CENTURY, Ubon
Ratchathani province, often
simply known as Ubon, was
part of the Khmer Empire. It
later fell under the suzerainty
of the Ayutthaya Kingdom
(see pp56–7). The provincial
capital, the city of Ubon Ratchathani was founded by Lao
immigrants on the northern
bank of the Mun River at the
end of the 18th century, and
Lao influence can still be seen
in the architectural features of
some of the city's religious
buildings. Following the rapid
growth of Ubon during the
Vietnam War, when it played
host to a nearby American air
base, the city is, today, one of
the largest in Thailand.

At first sight, Ubon appears a
concrete sprawl, but the **Ubon
National Museum** is one of
the best in the Northeast, and
some fascinating temples are

**A beautifully preserved stone
gopura, Prasat Khao Phra Wihan**

dotted around the city. The museum is housed in the former country residence of King Vajiravudh (1910–25) and contains displays of Khmer, Hindu and Lao Buddhist iconography, as well as traditional tools, utensils and handicrafts. One of the rarest and most impressive exhibits is a giant, bronze drum, dating back as far as the 4th century AD, which was used originally for ceremonial purposes.

The most interesting of Ubon's temples is **Wat Thung Si Muang** on account of its teakwood library. Founded by King Rama III (1824–51) the *wat* houses 150-year-old murals showing some of the *jatakas* (*see p26*). The complex also includes a *mondop* with a Buddha Footprint.

Figure atop Wat Supattanaram

In 1853 King Mongkut (1851–68) gave his support to the construction of **Wat Supattanaram Worawihan** as the first temple in the Northeast dedicated to the Thammayut sect – a strict branch of Theravada Buddhism – of which the king was also a member. It comprises a highly eclectic blend of architectural styles, having been built by Vietnamese craftsmen who were under instruction to incorporate an unusual mixture of Khmer, Thai and European influences.

The more modern **Wat Phra That Nong Bua** was built in 1957 to commemorate the 2,500th anniversary of the death of the Lord Buddha. Its two, four-sided, whitewashed towers are decorated with standing Buddha images in niches and reliefs of tales of the Buddha in his previous lives. Ubon also has a small number of other interesting temples: **Wat Cheng**, with its elegant Lao-style wooden carvings; **Wat Si Ubon Rattanaram**, built in 1855 and housing a topaz Buddha image, originating from

Carved Buddha images in niches at Wat Phra That Nong Bua

Chiang Saen; and the main temple, **Wat Maha Wanaram**, in which local people worship.

Ubon becomes a place of pilgrimage at the beginning of Buddhist Lent, when, during the Ubon Candle Festival (*see p45*), large, sculpted candles are carried through the streets.

🏛 **Ubon National Museum**
Khuan Thani Rd. 📞 (045) 255071.
🕐 Wed–Sun. ⬤ public hols. 📷

UBON RATCHATHANI CITY CENTRE

Ubon National Museum ②
Wat Cheng ④
Wat Maha Wanaram ⑤
Wat Si Ubon Rattanaram ③
Wat Supattanaram Worawihan ①
Wat Thung Si Muang ⑥

0 metres   50
0 yards   50

KEY

🚌 Coach station
⛴ Riverboat pier
ℹ Tourist information
🛕 *Wat*
⛪ Church

THE GULF OF
THAILAND

Introducing the Gulf of Thailand

THAIS AND FOREIGNERS flock to the Gulf's resorts to unwind, relax on the many superb beaches and eat delicious seafood. Bangkok weekenders have long favoured Cha-am and Hua Hin, while built-up Pattaya draws lovers of sports and hectic nightlife. The towns of Chaiya and Phetchaburi contain architectural and artistic treasures and have the lively ethnic and cultural mix typical of the Western Seaboard and further south. Inland, breathtaking flora and fauna abound in beautiful, crowd-free national parks. Several islands burgeoned in popularity in the 1990s: sun-worshippers frequent Ko Samui's long, sandy beaches on the Western Seaboard, while other visitors favour Ko Samet and the sand, simplicity and solitude of Ko Chang, both on the east coast. The Gulf's sunniest days are from December to August.

Phetchaburi

WESTERN SEABOARD
(see pp314–331)

Phetchaburi (see pp318–20) *is an important cultural centre with more than 30 wats, including the splendid Wat Mahathat, founded in the 14th century. Despite a history dating back to the 11th century and an attractive old quarter, the town receives few visitors.*

Angthong National Marine Park
(see pp330–31), *easily accessible from Ko Samui, is a stunning group of tiny islands teeming with wildlife.*

Ko Samui
(see pp326–8) *is the premier beach destination of the Western Gulf. This large island caters for tourists on all budgets.*

Angthong National Marine Park

Ko Samui

◁ **Holiday-makers enjoying the sun, sand and sea on a section of Jomtien beach, Pattaya**

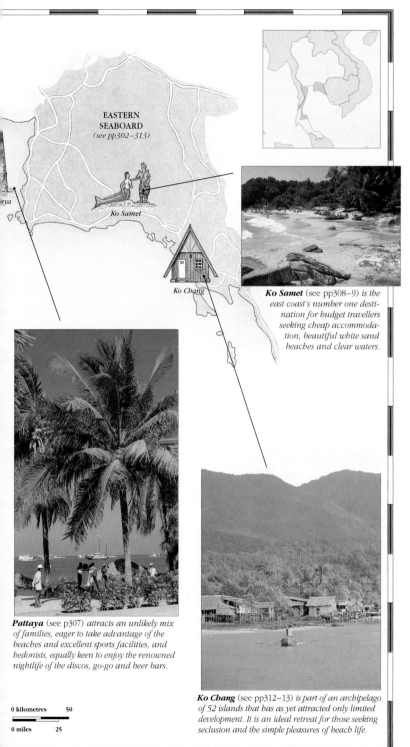

EASTERN SEABOARD
(see pp302–313)

Ko Samet

Ko Chang

Ko Samet (see pp308–9) *is the east coast's number one destination for budget travellers seeking cheap accommodation, beautiful white sand beaches and clear waters.*

Pattaya (see p307) *attracts an unlikely mix of families, eager to take advantage of the beaches and excellent sports facilities, and hedonists, equally keen to enjoy the renowned nightlife of the discos, go-go and beer bars.*

Ko Chang (see pp312–13) *is part of an archipelago of 52 islands that has as yet attracted only limited development. It is an ideal retreat for those seeking seclusion and the simple pleasures of beach life.*

0 kilometres   50

0 miles   25

Beach Life and Leisure in the Gulf

THAI BEACH CULTURE dates from the 1920s with the opening of both the railway from Bangkok to Hua Hin and the first golf club, the Royal Hua Hin, designed by Scottish railway engineer AO Robins. Hua Hin and its modern neighbour, Cha-am, continue to attract Thai weekenders from Bangkok, whose leisure pursuits centre more around sea-

Windsurfing, one of many sports available at Jomtien

food dining than swimming and sunbathing. Foreigners, meanwhile, are attracted to the Gulf's clear waters and fine sands, and exceptionally good water sports. The development of resort hotels and golf courses in the Gulf continues to boom, to the alarm of many environmentalists. However, it is still possible to find seclusion and simplicity, such as on Ko Chang.

***Bangpra Golf Course**, Pattaya, is one of many courses within the forested hills of Chon Buri province (see p445).*

***Cha-am** (see p320), a one-time fishing village, is now a stylish resort with a number of fine beach-side seafood restaurants.*

Hotel Sofitel Central at Hua Hin (see p321), *formerly famed as the Railway Hotel, has in recent years been restored to its original 1920s colonial-style elegance.*

BANGKOK

Kiarti T Golf Co
Royal Lakeside Golf Cours

Samut Songkhram

Chon Buri

Bangpra Golf Course

Sawang Resort Golf Course
Phetchaburi

Pattaya ③

② Cha-am
Springfield Golf Course
Royal Hua Hin Golf Course

① Hua Hin

BEST BEACHES OF THE NORTHERN GULF

Hua Hin Beach ①
Thailand's first beach resort. Good for the charm of the town and seafood restaurants.
Cha-am Beach ②
Popular with Thai weekenders but quiet during the week. Outstanding seafood restaurants.

Jomtien Beach, Pattaya ③
A 14-km (9-mile) long beach. Suitable for families and has excellent water sports facilities.
Glass Sand Beach (Hat Sai Kaeo), Ko Samet ④
Longest and liveliest beach on the island with

sand so clean it squeaks when walked on. Beautifully clear water, and good for water sports.
White Sand Beach (Hat Sai Khao), Ko Chang ⑤
The best and busiest beach on an unspoilt island. Fishing, snorkelling and boat trips.

PATTAYA

Thailand's biggest, brashest resort attracts single males and family package tourists in equal numbers. The former are drawn by the neon-lit go-go bars and reputation acquired when Pattaya was used for R&R by US servicemen during the Vietnam War. Families, meanwhile, are attracted by the restaurants, golf courses and beaches, particularly Jomtien beach (south of Pattaya beach) which has the best water sports facilities in the country.

Si Racha

Ko Sichang

Laem Chabang
Golf Course

Pattaya

Phoenix
Golf Course

Eastern Star
Golf Course

Sattahip   Rayong

0 kilometres   20

0 miles   10

Water sports – a major attraction of Pattaya

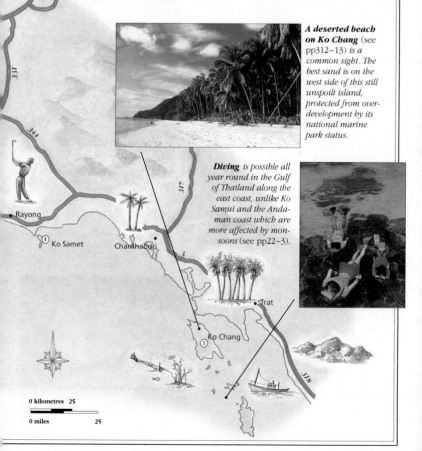

A deserted beach on Ko Chang (see pp312–13) *is a common sight. The best sand is on the west side of this still unspoilt island, protected from over-development by its national marine park status.*

Diving *is possible all year round in the Gulf of Thailand along the east coast, unlike Ko Samui and the Andaman coast which are more affected by monsoons (see pp22–3).*

Rayong

Ko Samet   Chanthaburi

Trat

Ko Chang

0 kilometres   25

0 miles   25

Thai Gemstones

SINCE THE 15TH CENTURY, Chanthaburi ("city of the moon") has been known to Western travellers for its abundance of gemstones. As a trading city its history dates back to the Khmer Empire in the 9th century *(see pp52–3)*. Along with Bangkok, Chanthaburi is world-renowned as a gem centre, and for its skilled gem cutters. The gemstones – mainly rubies and sapphires, with associated deposits of zircon, spinel and garnet – are found in alluvial deposits either on the surface or up to 6 m (20 ft) underground. Although rubies and sapphires are now over-mined around Chanthaburi, farmers have previously found gemstones while ploughing. Over 70 per cent of the world's rubies have come from Thailand.

Star ruby ring

GEM-MINING AREAS

■ *Ruby and sapphire mines*

Examining gemstones in the host rock helps formulate the correct cutting plan. This ensures the best yield and stone shapes are obtained.

This machine is pumping gravel and water that may contain gemstones such as rubies.

Simple grinding wheels are often used in small businesses, which are commonly run from the owner's home. More sophisticated operations use modern equipment such as diamond saws.

MINING FOR GEMSTONES

In Chanthaburi, gem stores can arrange visits to mines. Due to over-mining locally, many of the stones cut in Chanthaburi come from mines in Cambodia or Vietnam.

FACETTING GEMSTONES

Thai workers have a worldwide reputation for their skill and dexterity in facetting (precisely cutting) gemstones, often using simple equipment and judging angles by eye. A modern facetting machine may use a diamond blade or laser to improve speed and accuracy. After cutting, the stones are sorted and graded by size and quality, with quality being determined by sparkle, colour, brilliance and the presence or absence of imperfections.

Modern facetting equipment used to cut gemstones

Most gem buyers *prefer to buy gems "in the rough", using their expertise to judge the potential of the uncut material. Later the buyers arrange the cutting of the stones, often in their own workshops. Untrained buyers should beware potential scams (see p456).*

Bargaining *in gem-mining towns such as Bo Rai (see p311) is common practice. Since opinions differ as to the potential of rough material and the quality of cut stones, bargaining is hard but good natured.*

Designing and making jewellery *from gems demands a delicate touch and a keen eye, qualities renowned in Thai craftsmen and women. Most jewellery is made to highlight the beauty of the gems.*

Whole families can often be seen searching for gemstones. Children may begin helping from a very young age.

Pans are often used to scoop up gravel that may contain gemstones. The gemstones sink to the bottom of the pan.

Of all the Thai gemstones, deep blue sapphires and blood-red rubies are highly prized, as are unusually coloured (such as yellow) sapphires. Sometimes the colour is enhanced permanently by heating the stones to almost 2,000° C (3,650° F).

Star sapphire

Star ruby

Green sapphire

Zircon

Ruby

Peridot

Yellow sapphire

EASTERN SEABOARD

THE EASTERN SEABOARD *of the Gulf of Thailand, stretching from Bangkok to the Cambodian border, is a region of contrasts. Remarkably picturesque and unspoilt islands lie within easy reach of brash, over-developed resorts; oil refineries and industrial complexes are scattered along much of the coast, but not far inland are little-visited and spectacular national parks.*

The Eastern Seaboard was a frontier between the Khmer and Sukhothai empires in the early 15th century. As Khmer power waned, large numbers of ethnic Tais settled here and discovered gem-rich deposits in the lush countryside. Chanthaburi became a centre for gem trading and in the 18th and 19th centuries had to expel first Burmese then French occupying forces. Numerous Vietnamese refugees have since settled in the town.

Though still a forested region with orchards, gem-mining and fishing communities, the Eastern Seaboard has seen dramatic changes in the late 20th century as the oil and tourist industries have grown dramatically. However, some seaside towns have retained their charm, and in Si Racha excellent seafood can be sampled in open-air restaurants overlooking the bay. In contrast to this are the neon lights of Pattaya, an infamous destination for US marines on R&R during the Vietnam War.

Despite a seedy image, it is an excellent centre for water sports. South and east of Rayong there are beautiful mountainous islands and dense rainforest sheltering a wealth of fauna and flora. Trails, waterfalls and eerie limestone caves characterize Khao Chamao, Khao Kitchakut and Khao Sabap national parks.

The relaxed island of Ko Samet is a popular holiday destination, with its squeaky-sand beaches. Further south, Ko Chang has many idyllic deserted beaches and coves. It can be accessed from the market town of Trat, which is also the starting point for day trips to the gem market at Bo Rai.

Temple boys in a shrine cave within the Khao Chamao-Khao Wong National Park

◁ **Enjoying the good life on the blissfully quiet Ko Chang**

Exploring the Eastern Seaboard

Bᴸᴇꜱꜱᴇᴅ ᴡɪᴛʜ miles of idyllic beaches and soaring temperatures, the Eastern Seaboard is a sun-lover's paradise. Whether you want to unwind and sample the local seafood, or try out water sports, there is much to choose from. Beach resorts range from the chaotic Pattaya, with its lively nightlife, to lesser-known – and relatively undeveloped – islands such as Ko Chang, which is part of a stunning national marine park. The three other national parks in this region, characterized by tropical forests, mountains and waterfalls, are home to a wealth of wildlife. The main town in the area is Chanthaburi, centre of the thriving gem-mining industry.

KEY

▬▬	Motorway
▬▬	Major road
▬▬	Minor road
▬▬	Scenic route
▭▭	River
⁕	Viewpoint

Relaxing on Ko Samet's beautiful white beaches

Sɪɢʜᴛꜱ ᴀᴛ ᴀ Gʟᴀɴᴄᴇ

Bo Rai ⑫

Chanthaburi ⑩

Khao Chamao-Khao Wong
   National Park ⑦

Khao Khieo Zoo ①

Khao Kitchakut National Park ⑨

Khao Sabap National Park ⑪

Khlong Yai ⑮

Ko Chang ⑬

Ko Samet ⑥

Ko Sichang ③

Pattaya ④

Rayong ⑤

Si Racha ②

Trat ⑭

Wat Khao Sukim ⑧

GETTING AROUND

The Eastern Seaboard's transport system is comprehensive on the mainland and connects to the main islands. A twice daily train service runs from Hua Lamphong Station in Bangkok to Si Racha and Pattaya. Chon Buri and Sattahip are served by domestic airports. Coaches are the easiest way to get around the Eastern Seaboard: there is a regular service from Bangkok's Eastern Bus Terminal to the main towns. To visit places not on coach or bus routes, charter a *songthaew* from a local bus station. Transport in the mainland towns is provided by *songthaews*, rickshaws and *tuk-tuks*.

Several ferries leave Ban Phe each day for Ko Samet. On the island, *songthaews* service the main beaches, and fishing boats can be hired to surrounding islands. Ko Chang and Ko Mak are reached by ferry from Laem Ngop. Infrastructure on these islands is poor, though motorcycles and *songthaews* can be hired to get around the rough roads.

ARANYAPRATHET

KHAO KITCHAKUT

9

8 *WAT KHAO SUKIM*

10 *CHANTHABURI*

KHAO SABAP NATIONAL PARK **11**

12 *BO RAI*

14 *TRAT*

13 *KO CHANG*

KHLONG YAI **15**

BAN HAT LAK

The opulent interior of the main hall of Wat Khao Sukim

SEE ALSO

• *Where to Stay* pp399–401

• *Where to Eat* pp423–5

0 kilometres	25
0 miles	15

Bungalows on palm-fringed Ko Chang

Khao Khieo Zoo ❶

สวนสัตว์เขาเขียว

Off Route 3144, 10 km (6 miles) SE of Chon Buri, Chon Buri province. **(** (038) 338390. 🚌 🚗 *Chon Buri, then samlor.* 🕐 *8am–6pm daily.* 🏷

THIS "OPEN ZOO" has over 50 species of birds and animals, including deer, zebras and tigers – many of them indigenous to Southeast Asia. The animals inhabit spacious, semi-free enclosures, while the birds are kept in a large aviary. The zoo is in a peaceful, hilly setting amid woodland scenery, and is best reached by car.

For bird enthusiasts, 20 km (12 miles) south of Khao Khieo is the beautiful wild marshland of **Bang Phra Reservoir**, where, among other species, the brown-spotted wimbrel can be seen in winter.

Si Racha ❷

ศรีราชา

Chon Buri province. 🏠 *100,000.* 🚌 🚗 ⛴ 🛈 *TAT, Pattaya (038) 427667.* 🗓 *daily.*

FAMED FOR ITS SEAFOOD and its spicy Si Racha sauce *(nam phrik si racha)* – Thailand's answer to Tabasco – this small seaside town is the launching point for trips to Ko Sichang. Running off busy Jermjompol Road, Si Racha's main seafront street, are several tentacle-like piers. At the end of the piers are breezy, open-air restaurants ideal for sampling the local delicacies: oysters *(hoi nang rom)* or mussels *(hoi thot)* dipped in Si Racha sauce.

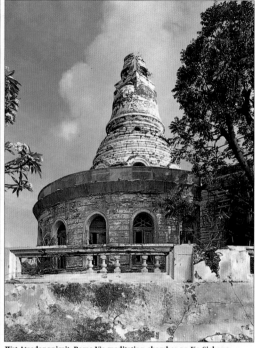

Wat Atsadangnimit, Rama V's meditation chamber on Ko Sichang

On a rocky promontory, which is also an occasional ferry pier, is **Ko Loi**, a Thai-Chinese Buddhist temple. Of interest are a Buddha Footprint, an image of Kuan Yin (the Chinese goddess of mercy) and a pond full of turtles. Buddhists feed the turtles as an act of merit-making *(see p125)*.

The streets of Si Racha (and Ko Sichang) resonate to the sound of spluttering motorcycle rickshaws. They are unique to the area – their sidecars are positioned at the rear.

Ko Sichang ❸

เกาะสีชัง

Chon Buri province. 🏠 *4,300.* ⛴ *from Si Racha.* 🛈 *TAT, Pattaya (038) 427667.*

A FORMER HAUNT of King Chulalongkorn (Rama V), this small island, with a rugged coastline, once functioned as the customs checkpoint for Bangkok-bound ships. Now it is a relatively quiet place with some architectural ruins and a handful of guesthouses catering for visitors who want to avoid the bustle and commercialism of the resorts.

There is only one ramshackle fishing village, **Tha Bon**, on the eastern side of the island. Just north of it is the **Chinese Temple**, with colourfully decorated shrine caves.

On the west coast of the island are the quiet beaches of **Hat Sai Khao** and **Hat Tham**. On the southern side, sprawling over a hillside, are the overgrown ruins of **Rama V's Summer Palace**. The palace was built in the 1890s but abandoned after a fleeting

Motorcycle rickshaws provide the transport on Si Racha and Ko Sichang

occupation by the French in 1893. In 1901 it was moved and reconstructed as Vimanmek Palace at Dusit Park in Bangkok *(see pp98–101)*.

Restoration work on the remains of the palace complex is being carried out – two elegant, pistachio-green villas, just behind the beach at **Hat Tha Wang**, are now finished.

For the most part, though, only foundations remain – a riddle of staircases, rock pools and tattered mosaic floors and fragrant frangipani trees. The only structure to remain intact is the circular **Wat Atsadangnimit**, at the top of the hill and crowned by a crumbling *chedi*. This was once a meditation chamber used by King Chulalongkorn.

The deserted rocky hilltop offers pleasant walks and fine views. It is home to nesting seabirds and the yellow squirrel, which is endemic here.

Pattaya ❹

พัทยา

Chon Buri province. 🛉 71,000. 🚍 🚌 🛳 🚏 TAT, 382/1 Mu 10 Chaihat Rd, Pattaya (038) 427667. 🏛 daily. 🎉 Pattaya Festival (Apr).

PATTAYA'S faded beauty is now difficult to discern. The once-idyllic beaches attracted visitors as early as the 1950s and later became a destination for American troops on R&R during the Vietnam War. Now dubbed "Patpong by the Sea" *(see p112)*, the

A jet ski sitting ready for use on one of Pattaya's beaches

Picnicking Thais relaxing at Suan Son, a beach park near Rayong

town has become one of Thailand's infamous red light districts, with a menagerie of neon lights, go-go bars and glitzy transvestite shows.

Despite its seedy image, families come in their thousands to Pattaya on fortnight package tours. They come for the good, cheap accommodation, extensive beaches (though the sea is often polluted), excellent restaurants and the best sports facilities in Thailand.

Pattaya consists of three bays. At its centre is the 3-km (2-mile) long **Pattaya beach**. Central Pattaya Road is packed with condominiums, fast-food restaurants and souvenir shops.

South Pattaya Road or "the strip", as the locals call it, is where the sex industry plies its trade. North Pattaya Road, on the other hand, is more sedate, with open-air drinking spots, called "bar beers".

Many tourists prefer the more family-oriented 14-km (9-mile) long **Jomtien beach**, around the southern headland of Pattaya. This is also the best place for water sports, as the sea here is cleaner. Scores of companies offer water-skiing and jet-skiing, windsurfing, sailing, parasailing, game-fishing and scuba diving. Land-based activities include golf (there are numerous golf courses), target shooting, horseback riding and tennis.

Quieter **Naklua bay**, to the north of Pattaya beach, has a fishing village which, despite tourism, has kept its charm.

Parrot fish, a common sight for divers in Pattaya's waters

Rayong ❺

ระยอง

Rayong province. 🛉 97,000. 🚍 🚌 🚏 TAT, 153/4 Sukhumvit Rd, Rayong (038) 655420. 🏛 daily. 🎉 Fruit Fair (May).

RAYONG is a busy and prosperous fishing town best known locally for its statue of Thailand's most famous poet, Sunthorn Phu *(see p309)*.

The main attractions lie outside the town. For good beaches, head 25 km (16 miles) southeast to **Ban Phe**. A 20-km (12-mile) coast road winds along from here to Laem Mae Phim.

From Ban Phe there are boats to Ko Samet *(see pp308–9)*. Ferries also run to nearby **Ko Saket**, **Ko Man Nok** and **Ko Man Klang** – the latter two islands are part of the Laem Ya-Mu Ko Samet National Park. The park authorities have managed to limit excessive development here, though jet-skiing is gradually eroding the coral reef.

Five km (3 miles) past Ban Phe is the beach park of **Suan Son** ("pine park"). This has crystal-white sand beaches and is a popular picnic area for Thais. It offers seafood snacks and home-grown water sports such as wave-riding on inner tubes.

Rayong province is known for its succulent fruit, particularly the pineapple and durian *(see p309)*, and its *nam pla* (fish sauce) and *nam phrik kapi* (shrimp paste).

Ko Samet ⑥

เกาะเสม็ด

Rayong province. 👥 *1,700*. ⛴ *from Ban Phe (Rayong) to Na Dan pier.* ℹ *TAT, Rayong (038) 655420.* 🚪 *daily.*

KO SAMET, blessed as it is with clear blue waters and crystalline sand, is popular with foreigners and Thai weekenders. Because it is only 6 km (4 miles) long and 3 km (2 miles) wide, most of the island is accessible on foot. The interior's dense jungle, home to the usual geckos and hornbills, is riddled with trails.

Although the island now has some tourist accommodation, when it attained national park status in 1981 all but the most rustic development was halted. In 1990 the park authorities closed Ko Samet to overnight visitors but met angry opposition from local residents and businessmen. The island was reopened after four days.

The small fishing town of **Na Dan**, which links Ko Samet to Ban Phe on the mainland, was an ancient checkpoint for Chinese junks. Legend has it that its calm, sheltered waters were once the hunting ground of pirates. Several beaches on Ko Samet offer one-way boat trips back to Ban Phe.

The kite-shaped island's prettiest beaches are on the east coast. With its clear shallow waters, **Hat Sai Kaeo** ("glass sand beach") is the longest and liveliest beach. Water sports on the beach include windsurfing. Boat trips around Ko Samet

KEY

🏖	Beach
🏄	Water sports
🚌	Bus station
⛴	Ferry service
= = =	Dirt track
- - -	Footpath
🌿	Viewpoint

Sunset walk along the coast of picturesque Ko Samet

and snorkelling day-trips to nearby islands leave from here.

Heading southwards along the east coast are the equally popular **Ao Hin Khok**, **Ao Phai** and **Ao Nuan**. Near the first is a wind-battered statue of the prince and the mermaid in *Phra Aphaimani*, a poem by Sunthorn Phu, Thailand's most famous poet.

Further south, the bays are less crowded, with the exception of the wide beach at **Ao Wong Duan** ("moon bay"), which is packed with bungalows and can get quite busy. At the narrow isthmus of **Ao Kui**, solitude and beauty are guaranteed. It is merely a short stroll between sunrise and sunset viewing points of Ao Kui Na Nok and Ao Kui Na Nai. The island's best coral is found just off the southern tip.

The only area to have undergone development on the largely inaccessible west coast is **Ao Phrao** ("paradise bay"). Due to its isolation, the beach here doesn't receive as many overnight visitors as those on the east coast.

There have been reports of malaria on Ko Samet in the past, so precautions are necessary. A health clinic, located near Na Dan, can deal with any urgent problems.

Wat Khao Sukim's cable car, which transports visitors up to the temple

Up-market bungalows on peaceful Ao Phrao, Ko Samet

Khao Chamao-Khao Wong National Park ❼

อุทยานแห่งชาติเขาชะเมา–เขาวง

Rayong province. Park HQ 17 km (11 miles) N of Hwy 3 at Klaeng.
i *TAT, Rayong (038) 655420; Forestry Dept, Bangkok (02) 579 0529 (inc bungalow bookings).* 🚌 *Rayong or Chanthaburi, then songthaew.* 🏕

THE TWO MOUNTAINS in this national park, Khao Wong and Khao Chamao, loom above the farming lowlands of the Eastern Seaboard.

Mammals such as tigers, elephants and Asiatic black bears find refuge in the park's tropical, broadleaved, evergreen forests, away from farmers and hunters. Also resident is the *tor soro* carp. Village folklore claims that the name of Chamao mountain, which means

"to get drunk", derives from the curious light-headedness induced by eating the carp.

Park highlights include the pools of the **Khao Chamao waterfall** and the 80 or so **Khao Wong caves**. Tham Pet ("diamond cave") and Tham Lakhon ("theatre cave"), situated 4 km (2 miles) southeast of the park headquarters, are the most spectacular of these limestone caverns. When the waters are low it is possible to proceed to **Hok Sai waterfall** and camp on the summit.

There are few developed trails in the park. The best route climbs alongside the cascading Khao Chamao waterfall and ends near the top of the falls at Chong Kaep.

From the park's northwest station, former elephant trails lead through the fertile and wildlife-rich forest of the stunning Khlong Phlu valley.

Wat Khao Sukim ❽

วัดเขาสุกิม

Khao Bay Si, Tha-Mai district, 20 km (12 miles) N of Chanthaburi.
i *TAT, Rayong (038) 655420.*
🚌 *Chanthaburi, then songthaew.*

THIS HUGE, pale orange *wat* is perched on the side of Sukim mountain. The temple, the home of Luang Pho Somchai, one of Thailand's most popular meditation masters, is reached via a cable car or the *naga*-lined staircase. Inside are a number of tables inlaid with mother-of-pearl, while exhibits housed in a museum include an ostentatious display of jewellery and a collection of Bencharong, Khmer and Ban Chiang pottery. They show the surprising wealth that a revered monk can accumulate from donations by merit-makers.

THE POETRY OF SUNTHORN PHU

Sunthorn Phu (1786–1855) is Thailand's most respected poet. His long, lyrical travel verses, often with a moral lesson, made him the favourite poet of kings Rama II and Rama III. The epic *Phra Aphaimani*, Sunthorn's first poem, was inspired by the surroundings of Ko Samet (then called Ko Kaew Pisadan), where he settled. The poem tells the story of a prince, Phra Aphaimani, exiled to an underwater kingdom ruled by a giantess, who is in love with him. Helped by a mermaid, the prince escapes by fleeing to Ko Samet. The giantess follows, but is defeated when the prince plays his magic flute, sending her to sleep. The prince is subsequently betrothed to a beautiful princess.

Statue on Ko Samet depicting characters in *Phra Aphaimani*

Khao Kitchakut National Park ❾

อุทยานแห่งชาติเขาคิชฌกูฏ

Chanthaburi province. Park HQ off Hwy 20, 28 km (17 miles) N of Chanthaburi. **ℹ** *Park HQ (039) 431983.* 🚌 *Chanthaburi, then songthaew.* 🌐

COVERING AN AREA of just 59 sq km (23 sq miles), this is one of Thailand's smallest national parks. It encompasses Khao Kitchakut, a granite mountain just over 1,000 m (3,300 ft) high. The park's best known site, the 13-tier **Krathin waterfall**, is located near park headquarters. From here a relatively easy trail can be taken to the top.

More ambitious hikers and large numbers of pilgrims make the arduous four-hour climb to the summit of the impressive Phrabat mountain. They come to see two sights: an image of the Buddha's Footprint, which is etched here in granite, and a strange collec-

Logo of the Thai national parks

tion of natural rock formations shaped like an elephant, a large turtle, a pagoda and a monk's bowl.

Khao Kitchakut is near the much larger, but less visited, **Khao Soi Dao Wildlife Sanctuary** (745 sq km, 290 sq miles). Both protected areas enclose some of the last surviving tracts of a once-great lowland forest. They are vital to the economy of the region as their slopes collect water for orchards. They also provide protection for many endangered species, including sun bears, spot-bellied eagle owls, silver pheasants, spinybreasted giant frogs, binturongs (bear cats) and elephants. The upland forests of Khao Soi Dao provide a habitat for the treedwelling pileated gibbon.

✦ Khao Soi Dao Wildlife Sanctuary

Off Hwy 317, 25 km (16 miles) NW of Chanthaburi. **ℹ** *TAT, Rayong (038) 655420.* 🚌 *Chanthaburi, then songthaew.* 🌐

A refreshing shower at the base of Krathin waterfall, Khao Kitchakut

Shrine inside the Church of the Immaculate Conception, Chanthaburi

Chanthaburi ❿

จันทบุรี

Chanthaburi province. 🏠 *69,000.* 🚌 **ℹ** *TAT, Rayong (038) 655420.* 🏪 *daily.* 🎉 *Fruit Festival (May/Jun).*

SURROUNDED BY verdant chilli and rubber plantations, this prosperous and friendly town is arguably Thailand's most charming settlement. Known as a centre for gem trading *(see pp300–1)* since the 15th century, Chanthaburi has attracted a wide ethnic mix. Vietnamese refugees form the largest group. They came in three waves: in the 19th century, fleeing the anti-Catholic persecutions of Cochin China; in the early 20th century, escaping French colonial rule; and after the 1975 victory in South Vietnam by North Vietnamese Communists. The Vietnamese quarter, running parallel to the river on Rim Nam Road, is lined with latticework wooden shop-houses.

The monarch most revered in the town today is King Taksin. In the 18th century he expelled the Burmese from the town, their last Thai stronghold, thus reuniting Thailand. Two monuments celebrate Taksin and his famous victory: **San Sadej Prachao Taksin** on Tha Luang Road is a huge statue in the shape of Taksin's hat. **Taksin Park** sports a dynamic bronze statue of the king in battle as seen on the 20-*baht* note.

On the bank of the Chanthaburi River is the **Church of the Immaculate Conception**, a French-style Catholic cathedral built on the site of

MAYTIME FRUIT FESTIVALS

Held in three neighbouring provinces – Rayong, Chanthaburi and Trat – this annual fruit festival, lasting for a few days in either May or June (whenever the harvest is ripe), is a colourful, celebratory affair. These provinces are known for their flavoursome rambutan, durian and mangosteen, which all come into season during May. Stalls selling the produce of local orchards are set up on the main streets of each town. Parades of floral-and-fruit floats are held along with gaudy beauty pageants, which are a ubiquitous element of every provincial Thai festival. Contests for the ripest durian or most beautifully shaped fruit, among other titles, are a highlight of the year for local farmers and a great spectacle for tourists. Visitors can also see cultural shows and excellent displays of local handicrafts. In Chanthaburi there are many stalls selling one of the specialities of the province, intricately woven straw mats.

Fruit festival float, Chanthaburi

an 18th-century missionary chapel. It is the largest cathedral in the country and a legacy of French occupation. The French held Chanthaburi hostage from 1893 to 1904 as a guarantee that Thailand would relinquish her hold on Lao and Cambodian land. To keep the country intact, King Chulalongkorn reluctantly agreed to surrender the territories.

The **Gem Quarter** *(talat phloi)*, at the intersection of Si Chan and Thetsaban 4 roads, attracts gem traders from all over the world. At weekends, a rainbow array of gemstones from Burma, Cambodia and the rich mines of Chanthaburi province are traded at street stalls. However, most of the best quality stones are dispatched directly to Bangkok.

Statue of King Taksin, Chanthaburi

Khao Sabap National Park ⓫
อุทยานแห่งชาติน้ำตกพลิ้ว

Chanthaburi province. Park HQ off Hwy 3, 14 km (9 miles) SE of Chanthaburi. 🛈 *TAT, Rayong (038) 655420; Forestry Dept (02) 579 4842 (inc bungalow bookings).* 🚌 *Chanthaburi, then songthaew.* 🐾

IMMENSELY POPULAR with Thais, this 135-sq km (52-sq mile) park contains some of Thailand's richest rainforest. It is also a haven for wildlife, with over 156 species of birds and 32 of mammals, including the Asiatic black bear, tiger, leopard, barking deer and macaque. The park's other attractions are its spectacular waterfalls – the most impressive being **Phliu waterfall**. Facing this are two *chedis*: the Alongkon *chedi* and a 3-m (10-ft) high pyramid-shaped *chedi*, built by King Chulalongkorn in honour of one of his queens, Sunantha, who drowned at Bang Pa-in *(see p171)* in 1876. The region was much loved by Chulalongkorn.

Less popular with visitors, due to the harder hike required, are the 20-m (66-ft) roaring Trok Nong falls and the forest-encircled Klang waterfall. The entrance road to the park is lined with souvenir shops.

Bo Rai ⓬
บ่อไร่

Trat province. 🏠 *41,000.* 🚌 🛈 *TAT, 100 Mu 1 Trat–Laem Ngop Rd, Laem Ngop, Trat province (039) 597255.* 🛍 *daily.*

THIS SMALL TOWN used to be the thriving centre of the Eastern Seaboard's gem trade. The surrounding mines, once renowned for the quality of their rubies *(tab tim)*, have almost dried up, so nowadays the Bo Rai gem trade is small. Only one morning market of any significance, the **Khlong Yaw market**, remains. The market has a reverse system of buying and selling – buyers sit at makeshift tables and vendors stroll around displaying their wares.

Sadly, gem mining has destroyed large areas of Trat province, exposing the topsoil, and leaving acres of despoiled land in rusty-orange mud.

Customer carefully inspecting a vendor's gems in Bo Rai market

Bungalows amid coconut trees along Khlong Phrao, Ko Chang

Ko Chang ⑬

เกาะช้าง

Trat province. 🏠 4,000. 🛥 from Laem Ngop. ℹ TAT, 100 Mu 1 Trat–Laem Ngop Rd, Laem Ngop, Trat province 📞 (039) 597255.

MOUNTAINOUS KO CHANG is the largest of the 50 or so islands that form the Ko Chang National Marine Park, which covers an area of 650 sq km (250 sq miles), two-thirds of which is sea. Despite their gin-clear waters and postcard-perfect beaches, the islands' tourist industry is, surprisingly, still in its infancy. One drawback is that several of the islands consist solely of expensive, privately owned resorts.

Since Thai-Chinese agricultural families first settled on Ko Chang in the mid-19th century, most of the island's wildlife has been destroyed, although some small mammals, including the barking deer, stumptailed macaque and small

KEY

🏖	Beach
🔱	Water sports
ℹ	Tourist information
⛴	Ferry service
══	Dirt track
🌿	Viewpoint

Indian civet, remain. Also resident are some 75 bird species, and reptiles and amphibians such as monitor lizards, pythons, king cobras and the endemic Ko Chang frog.

Inland exploration is difficult due to the rugged terrain. The coast road, which was begun in the early 1990s, is the first construction to improve accessibility on the island. Ko Chang's best beaches are

on the west coast, especially along Ao Sai Khao, where the shell-sprinkled, bungalow-lined **Hat Sai Khao** ("white sand beach"), the island's longest and busiest beach, is located. An information centre on the beach arranges boat trips, fishing and snorkelling. Most guesthouses also offer fishing, snorkelling and motorbike hire. **Hat Khlong Phrao**, south of here, is prettier and quieter. Nearby is a fishing village, Ban Khlong Phrao. Because tourism is growing only gradually on the island, fishing is, for now, still the main industry.

The beaches in the south are still relatively isolated. Of these, the beach at the sheltered bay of **Ao Bang Bao**, in the southwest corner, is particularly beautiful. East of here is a long beach encircling a bay, Ao Sa Lak Phet, where there are a few fishing villages and bungalows. The wrecks of two Thai Navy ships can be visited off the coast here.

Of the island's many waterfalls, two are worth the hike. On the east coast, near the park headquarters, is the three-tiered **Than Mayom waterfall**, which has good views of the

View of Hat Khlong Phrao, one of the best beaches on Ko Chang

island. The other is **Khlong Phlu waterfall**, along Khlong Phrao on the west coast. The uppermost level, accessible via a gentle 3-km (2-mile) hike, has a freshwater pool.

For snorkellers, divers and day-trippers there are stunning smaller islands off the coast of Ko Chang, with a good variety of hard and soft corals and a proliferation of giant clams.

Ko Kut, the second largest island within the group, falls outside the park boundaries. It has excellent beaches and breathtaking waterfalls.

The rocky, coral-lined coast of **Ko Wai**, south of Ko Chang, is popular for fishing. Around **Ko Rang**, further south, is a cluster of coral-rich rocky islets.

Ko Mak, a predominantly flat island, is covered mainly in coconut plantations. Its attractions include a secluded beach on the northwest bay, a fishing village and good coral reefs.

Barrel sponge, seen off Ko Chang

Northeast of Ko Mak is the coconut-fringed **Ko Kradat**, a tiny island with some of the prettiest beaches in the island cluster. Although the entire island is a privately owned resort with expensive hotels, bungalows can also be hired.

Sandflies and mosquitoes are a problem on the islands, so precautions are necessary.

Trat ⑭

ตราด

Trat province. 🚶 15,000. ✈ ⚓ 🛈 TAT, 100 Mu 1 Trat–Laem Ngop Rd, Laem Ngop, Trat province (039) 597255. 🏪 daily. 🎏 Rakham Fruit Fair (Jan).

THIS PROVINCIAL CAPITAL is a small but busy commercial town. Currently, most tourists pass through Trat only en route to Ko Chang. However, the town's popularity is likely to increase in line with that of the archipelago. Trat has several attractions, including its markets, most of which are centred around Tait Mai and Sukhumvit roads. The covered market on Sukhumvit Road has a good selection of food and drink stalls. Also of interest are the gem-mining villages around Trat, such as Bo Rai, where rubies are mined *(see pp300–1)*. Trips can be arranged at local guesthouses.

Located about 2 km (1 mile) southwest of Trat is **Wat Bupharam** ("flower temple"), set in pleasant grounds with large, shady trees. Some of the original buildings within the temple complex, including the *wihan*, the bell tower and the monks' residences, or *kutis*, date from the late Ayutthaya period *(see pp56–7)*.

Durian vendor at one of Trat's bustling markets

Khlong Yai ⑮

คลองใหญ่

Trat province. 🚶 18,000. 🛈 TAT, 100 Mu 1 Trat–Laem Ngop Rd, Laem Ngop, Trat province (039) 597255. 🏪 daily.

SITUATED near the Cambodian border, this picturesque seaside town sports a handful of bustling Thai-Cambodian markets and stalls selling delicious noodles with seafood.

The road from Khlong Yai to the border checkpoint of **Hat Lek** passes through spectacular scenery: Cambodia's Cardamom Mountains are on one side, fish farms and sea on the other. Hat Lek is Thailand's narrowest point and marks the end of Sukhumvit Road, which starts in Bangkok *(see p132)*. Currently, visitors may not cross into Cambodia.

Fishing trawlers, harboured on Ko Chang, which provide the main source of income on the island

WESTERN SEABOARD

THE ROLLING LANDSCAPE *of the Western Seaboard extends some 600 km (370 miles) from Bangkok to Surat Thani. Its major attraction is, without doubt, the islands that make up the beautiful Ko Samui archipelago, such as Ko Pha Ngan, Ko Tao and the Ang Thong National Marine Park. Yet visitors should not ignore the many charms of the mainland – lively towns, fine beaches and national parks.*

Miles of remote sandy beaches dominate long stretches of the Western Seaboard, which unites the Buddhist heartland of the nation with the maritime, Muslim-influenced South. Temples reflecting pre-Thai influences, simple fishing villages, verdant fruit orchards, and sand-rimmed resorts characterize this region.

The Tenasserim Mountains, rising to 1,329 m (4,350 ft), form a spine down the peninsula. They absorb much of the rain that falls during the southwest monsoon, keeping the coastal strip relatively dry. However, this coastal region is still a fertile growing area, famed for its pineapples, sweetcorn, sugar cane, "lady-finger" bananas, asparagus and mangosteens.

Beaches easily reached from the capital cater primarily to weekenders from Bangkok. Particularly popular are the casuarina-lined waterfronts of Cha-am and Hua Hin. The latter was Thailand's first beach resort. The many golf courses within easy reach of these two tourist centres make this area arguably the country's premier golf destination. Further south, the stunning islands of the Ko Samui archipelago offer excellent diving and sunbathing, and a well-developed tourist infrastructure.

Trekkers and bird-watchers will be drawn to Khao Sam Roi Yot and Kaeng Krachan national parks where migratory birds rest and feed in the salt marshes from August to April.

Among the most interesting of the towns along the Western Seaboard is Phetchaburi, with its crumbling architectural remnants of Khmer, Mon, Ayutthaya and Rattanakosin epochs. Further to the south, Chaiya still contains archaeological remains that reveal its important role in the Srivijaya Empire *(see pp336–7)*.

Fishing boats in the bay of the peaceful town of Prachuap Khiri Khan

◁ **Devotees making offerings inside Phetchaburi's Wat Mahathat**

Exploring the Western Seaboard

T HIS LONG, NARROW COASTAL STRIP, backed by mountains along the
Burmese border, stretches from the cultural centre of Phetchaburi to the commercial town of Surat Thani. In the north is one
of Thailand's oldest beach resorts, Hua Hin, while further north still
is the modern resort of Cha-am. The area also offers natural beauty
inland in the huge, hilly Kaeng Krachan National Park and the
limestone outcrops of the coastal Khao Sam Roi Yot National Park.
The more recently developed islands of the stunning Ko Samui
archipelago are the major attractions further south. Ko Samui itself
is the main resort island while Ko Tao and Ko Pha Ngan are popular with backpackers. For spectacular, unspoilt island scenery, it
is hard to beat the beautiful Angthong National Marine Park.

SIGHTS AT A GLANCE

**Towering stacks of TV aerials on the houses along the
Phet River in the centre of Phetchaburi**

GETTING THERE

Most of the attractions of the Western Seaboard
are easily accessible from the main highways 4
and 41. The major towns are linked to each
other and Bangkok by several air-conditioned
bus services and trains daily (Bangkok to Hua
Hin is 3–4 hours by bus or train; Bangkok to
Surat Thani is 11 hours by bus, 11–13 hours by
train). Ko Samui, Surat Thani, Prachuap Khiri
Khan and Hua Hin have domestic airports.
Songthaews and bicycle rickshaws can be hired
for trips to local sights. Cha-am, Hua Hin and
Ko Samui have car hire facilities. Surat Thani
and Don Sak are the main gateways to the Ko
Samui archipelago. Ko Tao is also accessible
via Chumphon. The train/bus/ferry journey
from Bangkok to Ko Samui takes 16 hours.

Lapping up the sun on Ko Samui's Chaweng beach

SEE ALSO

• *Where to Stay* pp401–3

• *Where to Eat* pp425–7

Bangkok

1 *PHETCHABURI*

KAENG KRACHAN NATIONAL PARK

2   **3** *CHA-AM*

4 *MAREUKATHAYAWAN PALACE*

5 *HUA HIN*

6 *KHAO SAM ROI YOT NATIONAL PARK*

7 *PRACHUAP KHIRI KHAN*

KEY

- ▦ Motorway
- ▬ Major road
- ▬ Minor road
- ▬ Scenic route
- ═ River
- ☀ Viewpoint

8 *CHUMPHON*

Ranong
Phuket

KO TAO **14**

KO PHA NGAN

12

ANGTHONG NATIONAL MARINE PARK

13

11 *KO SAMUI*

9 *CHAIYA*

● *DON SAK*

10 *SURAT THANI*

Khlong Yan

Khlong Phum Duong

401

4009

4188   *4186*

4224

4189

4140

Ta Pi

Trang

Nakhon Si Thammarat

Limestone outcrops at Khao Sam Roi Yot National Park

0 kilometres   50

0 miles   25

Street-by-Street: Phetchaburi ●

เพชรบุรี

Detail, Phra
Nakhon Khiri

SETTLED SINCE AT LEAST the 11th century,
Phetchaburi (often spelt Phetburi) is one of
Thailand's oldest towns. It has long been an
important trading and cultural centre, and
Mon, Khmer and Ayutthayan influences can
be seen in its 30 temples. During the 19th
century it became a favourite royal retreat, and
King Mongkut built a summer house here on a
hill, Khao Wang, west of the centre.
This is now part of the Phra Nakhon
Khiri Historical Park *(see p320)*.
Other major sights are the 17th-century Wat Yai
Suwannaram, the five Khmer *prangs* of Wat Kamphaeng Laeng and an old quarter that has retained
much of its original charm. Despite such attractions, accommodation is scant. Most visitors come
on day trips from Bangkok, 123 km (76 miles) away.

Phra Song Road
Several wats *are located on this busy road.*

To Phra Nakhon
Khiri Historical
Park

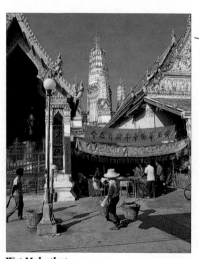

Wat Mahathat
*The five white Khmer-style
prangs of this much restored
14th-century temple domi-
nate the town's central skyline. The figures of angels
and gods decorate the roofs
of the main* wihan *and* bot.

STAR SIGHTS

★ **Phra Nakhon Khiri
Historical Park**

★ **Wat Kamphaeng
Laeng**

★ **Wat Yai Suwannaram**

To Wat Tho

**Wooden
Shop-Houses**
*Concrete may have re-
placed wood in many
Thai towns but attrac-
tive wooden buildings,
many lining the river
bank, are still a feature
of Phetchaburi.*

★ Phra Nakhon Khiri Historical Park

As a keen astronomer, King Mongkut had this observatory conveniently sited next to his hilltop summer palace; this is now a museum (see p320). The magnificently landscaped and forested surrounding park offers extensive views over Phetchaburi.

VISITORS' CHECKLIST

Phetchaburi province. 60,000.
Rot Fai Rd, 1.5 km (1 mile) NW of town. Chisa-in Rd, near Chomrut Bridge.
TAT, Cha-am (032) 471005.
daily. Phra Nakhon Khiri Fair (8 days in early Feb).

To Wat Chisa-in

★ Wat Yai Suwannaram

Built during the Ayutthaya period (see pp56–7), the temple is notable for the splendid original murals of Hindu gods in the bot. A scripture library stands on stilts in the middle of a large pond in the grounds.

To Wat Yai Suwannaram

| 0 metres | 75 |
| 0 yards | 75 |

KEY

– – – Suggested route

Market

To Wat Kamphaeng Laeng

★ Wat Kamphaeng Laeng

This is one of the few surviving Khmer shrines in Thailand outside the Northeast. The five laterite prangs of the temple, in varying states of disrepair, are typically Khmer in design and may date from the 12th century. Originally a Hindu temple, it was later adapted for Buddhist use.

Phra Nakhon Khiri, Rama IV's ambitious 19th-century palace complex

Exploring Phetchaburi's Outer Sights

Phetchaburi is divided by the Phet River which weaves its way past this provincial capital's 30 historic temples. Many, especially the Ayutthayan *wats*, are excellently preserved, their pinnacles dominating the skyline. In the distance, to the west, three large hills loom imperiously over the city.

Phra Nakhon Khiri, locally referred to as Khao Wang, translates as the "celestial city of the mountain". This palace complex, perched on top of 92-m (302-ft) Maha Samana hill, was commissioned by King Mongkut (Rama IV) as a summer house in the 1850s. Extravagant use of European, Chinese and Japanese architectural styles make this a bold study in Thai and foreign architecture. Set among natural woods, rocks and caverns, it also offers fine vistas of Phetchaburi town and panoramic views of the province.

The complex extends over three peaks. The Royal Palace and the Ho Chatchawan Wiangchai, an observatory tower (Rama IV was an accomplished amateur astronomer), are both perched on the west rise; the Phra That Chomphet, a white *chedi* erected by Rama V, stands on the central rise; and Wat Maha Samanaram, containing some fine murals, takes up the east rise. In 1988 the complex was made a Historical Park. A cable car takes visitors up the steep ascent to the palace buildings.

A short distance north of town is **Tham Khao Luang**, a cave containing stalactites,

chedis and Buddha images. To the right of the cave's mouth lies **Wat Bun Thawi**, notable for its intricately carved wooden door panels.

🏛 **Phra Nakhon Khiri**
Khao Wang, Phetchaburi. ☎ (032) 425600. ○ daily. 🎫

🦇 **Tham Khao Luang**
Hwy 3173, 3 km (2 miles) N of Phetchaburi. ○ daily. 🎫 donation.

Kaeng Krachan National Park ➋
อุทยานแห่งชาติแก่งกระจาน

Phetchaburi province. Park HQ off Hwy 3175, 47 km (29 miles) S of Phetchaburi. 🚩 TAT (032) 471005; Forestry Dept (02) 579 0529 (inc bungalow bookings). 🚌 🚏 Phetchaburi then songthaew. 🎫

THAILAND'S LARGEST national park is home to at least 40 species of large mammal, such as tiger, leopard, elephant, gibbon, two types of Asiatic bear and two types of leaf-monkey (langur). Established in 1981, this 2,920-sq km (1,150-sq mile)

Tiger, one of many species at Kaeng Krachan National Park

reserve covers nearly half of Phetchaburi province and contains some of the most pristine tracts of tropical evergreen forest in the country.

The park is relatively unknown to tourists yet offers some excellent trailwalking.

Its western flank is marked out by the dramatic Tenasserim mountain range and the Thai-Burmese border. Streams and rivers are the water source for the 45-sq km (17-sq mile) **Kaeng Krachan reservoir** which can be explored by boat. Thousands of migratory birds coming from as far afield as China and Siberia rest, feed and breed in the salt marshes.

Horse for hire at Cha-am beach

Cha-am ➌
ชะอำ

Phetchaburi province. 🏠 36,000. 🚌 🚏 🚩 TAT, 500/51 Phetkasem Rd, Cha-am (032) 471005. 🛒 daily.

SINCE THE MID-1980s, Cha-am has experienced a dramatic surge in popularity. It has been developed from a quiet fishing and market village into a lively playground for Bangkok weekenders. Tall condominiums and huge resort hotels have sprung up alongside the long, sandy beach. During the week, however, it can be remarkably quiet.

The resort caters primarily for Thais, who focus their attentions on eating and drinking rather than swimming. At umbrella-shaded tables, strung along the beach like a high tide mark, holidaymakers feast on delicious grilled fish, squid, prawns and mussels. Spicy dips and cold beer complete the culinary adventure.

Those who prefer more formal eating will find restaurants serving the same range of succulent fare at the northern end of the beach.

Mareukathayawan Palace ❹

พระราชนิเวศน์มฤคทายวัน

Off Hwy 4, 32 km (20 miles) S of Cha-am. 🚩 *TAT, Cha-am (032) 471005.* 🚌 *from Cha-am.* ⏰ *8am–5pm daily.* 🎫 *donation.* 🚫 *in bedroom.*

MAREUKATHAYAWAN PALACE ("the palace of love and hope") was the summer residence of Rama VI. Built midway between Cha-am and Hua Hin, this grand golden teak building was designed by an Italian architect and constructed in just 16 days in 1923. However, it was abandoned when Rama VI died two years later and stood neglected for decades. The palace has undergone restoration since the 1970s and is now close to its original appearance.

The building is cool and airy; its wooden halls, verandas and royal chambers are decorated simply and painted in pastel shades. Although the palace is easily accessible, it is rarely visited by tourists.

Hua Hin ❺

หัวหิน

Prachuap Khiri Khan province. 🏛 *40,000.* ✈ 🚆 🚌 🚌 *Municipality Tourist Office, 114 Phetkasem Rd, Hua Hin (032) 512120.* 🍴 *daily.*

HUA HIN WAS Thailand's first beach resort. Its rail connection to Bangkok, completed in 1911, was central to its success, making the 190-km (118-mile) journey from Bangkok a manageable seaside excursion.

A nine-hole golf course, commissioned by King Rama VI, and the splendid colonial-style Railway Hotel were built in 1922 and 1923.

Hua Hin Station, vital to the resort's early success

Following the international trend for recuperative spa resorts at the time, Hua Hin became a popular retreat for minor Thai royalty, Bangkok's high society and affluent foreigners. Prince Chulachakra-bongse built a summer palace in the town which he called **Klai Klangwon** (meaning "far from worries") in 1926. It is still used by the Royal Family and is not open to the public. Although Hua Hin's fortunes declined after World War II,

its historical connections have helped it become popular again with a new generation of Bangkokians. Activities such as pony riding, seafood dining, golf and shopping for polished seashell curios in the town's market give Hua Hin a relaxed, family feel.

For an insight into the Hua Hin of the 1920s, visit the Railway Hotel, now called the **Hotel Sofitel Central**. By the 1960s it had fallen into disrepair, but a sensitive restoration of the elegant 1920s' decor, museum tea room and intricate topiaries won it an Outstanding Conservation Award from the Architects' Association of Thailand in 1993. Before its refurbishment the hotel and its environs were used extensively in the making of the film *The Killing Fields*, where it stood in for the Phnom Penh Hotel.

South of Hua Hin's main beach lies Khao Takiap (or "chopstick hill"), which is covered with miniature *chedis* and shrines. Nearby stands **Wat Khao Lad**, fronted by an impressive 20-m (66-ft) standing Buddha, which faces the sea.

The majestic, open hall and first-floor gallery in the north wing of Mareukathayawan Palace

Khao Sam Roi Yot National Park ❻

อุทยานแห่งชาติเขาสามร้อยยอด

Prachuap Khiri Khan province. Visitors' Centre off Hwy 4, 35 km (22 miles) S of Pranburi. **🛈** TAT, Cha-am (032) 471005; Forestry Dept (02) 5790529 (inc bungalow bookings). 🚌 Pranburi, then songthaew. 📷 🚗

THIS SMALL COASTAL PARK sits in the narrowest part of the Thai peninsula, overlooking the Gulf of Thailand. Covering 98 sq km (38 sq miles), it is a region of contrasts: sea, sand and marsh backed by mountains and caves. The park is best known for its distinctive limestone pinnacles (Khao Sam Roi Yot means "mountain of 300 peaks"), which rise vertically from the marshland to a height of 650 m (2,150 ft).

The park's wetlands provide a sanctuary for water birds. Millions of migratory birds flying from Siberia to Sumatra and Australia rest, feed and breed here between August and April. It is home to many other animals such as the rare dusky langur, the nocturnal slow loris and the crab-eating macaque. Other attractions include extensive forest walks and large caves. **Tham Phraya Nakon** houses a grand pavilion, built for King Rama V in 1896 and **Tham Sai** contains fossilized falls.

Beware monkeys sign, Khao Sam Roi Yot

Wat Chong Kra Chok, overlooking sedate Prachuap Khiri Khan

Prachuap Khiri Khan ❼

ประจวบคีรีขันธ์

Prachuap Khiri Khan province. 🏠 58,000. 🚌 🚗 ⛴ **🛈** TAT, Cha-am (032) 471005. 🏨 daily.

PRACHUAP KHIRI KHAN means "town among the mountain chain". And it is certainly true that its coastal sugar-loaf limestone outcrops at either end of a sandy bay give it a "little Rio" appearance. The local economy primarily relies on fishing; freshly caught seafood can be purchased from a number of good restaurants and stalls along the promenade. This peaceful administrative town has pleasant swimming beaches to the north and south of its main bay. The top of the delightful **Wat Chong Kra Chok** – perched on one of the surrounding hills – offers the best view of the area. Around 200 macaques live on the hill and every evening they climb to the top to feed from the pretty frangipani trees.

Chumphon ❽

ชุมพร

Chumphon province. 🏠 44,000. 🚌 🚗 ⛴ **🛈** TAT, Surat Thani (077) 288818. 🏨 daily. 🎉 Luan Suan Buddha Image Parade and Boat Race (5 days in Oct).

CHUMPHON IS REGARDED by some as the point of cultural transition between the heartland of the Buddhist Tai peoples, and the peninsular south of the country, where Muslim culture is strong. The town was the home of Prince Chumphon, the Father of the Royal Thai Navy, who died in 1923. Nearby, the 68-m (225-ft) long **HMS Chumphon** torpedo boat, decommissioned in 1975, has been preserved. It forms a distinctive landmark.

The reefs around the 47 tiny islands off Chumphon's 222-km long (140-mile) coast are becoming increasingly popular with divers. Tour companies in town will arrange diving day trips to such islands as **Samet**, **Mattra**, **Ngam Yai** and **Ngam Noi**. Chumphon is also the most convenient place from which to get a ferry to Ko Tao (see p331).

CHAIYA'S ROLE IN THE SRIVIJAYA EMPIRE

The Mahayana Buddhist Empire of Srivijaya (see pp52–3) dominated the whole Malaysian peninsula and parts of Indonesia between the 7th and 13th centuries AD. Although the majority of scholars now believe that Palembang in Sumatra was the Srivijayan capital, discoveries of temple remains and some exquisite stone and bronze statues (many now in the National Museum in Bangkok) in Chaiya provide evidence of Chaiya's importance. Its strategic geographical position, as a then coastal port, meant the town played an important role in the east–west trade between India, the peninsula and China. In fact, Chaiya was mentioned in the writings of the Chinese monk I Chinga, who, while visiting the area in the late 7th century, testified to its religious and cultural sophistication. It is known that some of Chaiya's rulers were connected by marriage to those of central Java. Furthermore, it is possible that the name "Chaiya" originated as a contraction of "Siwichaiya" (a different transliteration of Srivijaya), which follows the local tendency to emphasize the final syllable of a word.

Srivijayan votive tablet

8th-century bronze found at Chaiya

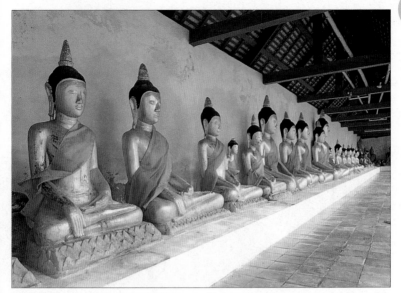

A line of Buddha images at Phra Boromathat Chaiya, one of the few remaining temples from the Srivijaya period

Chaiya ❾

ไชยา

Surat Thani province. 🏠 *42,000.*
🚌 🚉 ℹ️ *TAT, Surat Thani (077)
288818.* 🛒 *daily.* 🎊 *Chak Phra
Festival (Oct–Nov).*

DESPITE THE SOMEWHAT dreary
look of the small railway
town of Chaiya, the settlement
is actually one of the oldest
and most historically significant in Southern Thailand. A
number of superb examples
of sculpture dating from the
Srivijaya period (7th–13th centuries) have been found here.

Many of the sculptures show
clear Mon and Indian influences, depicting figures such
as Bengali-style Buddha images and multi-armed Hindu
deities. These, and a variety
of votive tablets, can be seen
at the **Chaiya National Museum**. It also holds examples
of Ayutthayan art. The museum is 2 km (1 mile) west of
Chaiya and a ten-minute walk
from the train station.

Right beside the museum is
Phra Boromathat Chaiya
(see pp336–7), an important
Srivijayan temple. Within the
main compound is the central
chedi, which has been pain-
stakingly restored. Square in
plan, it has four porches which
ascend in tiers and are topped

with mini towers. The 8th-
century *chedi* is built of brick
and vegetable mortar. Though
the site is old, it is the memory
of Phra Chaiya Wiwat, a locally venerated monk who
died in 1949, which attracts the
majority of worshippers today.

🏛️ Chaiya National Museum

Phra Boromathat Chaiya. 📞 *(077)
431066.* 🕐 *Mon–Sat.* ⭕ *public
hols.* 🏷️

ENVIRONS: The International
Dhamma Hermitage *(see
p446)*, based at **Wat Suan
Mok**, southwest of Chaiya, is
a popular and famous retreat
for Buddhists from all over
the world. Its attraction is its
back-to-basics religious philosophy established by the
wat's founder, Buddhadhasa
Bhikkhu, who died in 1993.
Within the temple a regimen of

**Murals relating the story of the
Buddha at Wat Suan Mok**

physical labour underpins a
simple monastic life devoid of
elaborate religious ceremony.
Ten-day residential meditation
retreats are held here, starting
on the first day of each month.

🏯 Wat Suan Mok

5 km (3 miles) SW of Chaiya off Hwy
41. 📞 *(077) 431552.* 🕐 *daily.*

Surat Thani ❿

สุราษฎร์ธานี

Surat Thani province. 🏠 *135,000.*
✈️ 🚉 *Phun Phin, 14 km (9 miles) W
of Surat Thani, then bus.* 🚌 🚢 *Ban
Don (in town); Thong, 6 km (4 miles)
E of town.* ℹ️ *TAT, 5 Talat Mai Rd,
Surat Thani (077) 288818.* 🎊
*Rambutan Fair (Aug), Chak Phra
Festival (Oct–Nov).*

SURAT THANI, a business centre
and port dealing in rubber
and coconuts, first grew to
prominence in the Srivijaya
period as it was strategically
located at the mouth of the
Tapi and Phum Duang rivers.
The riverside is still intriguing
today with its numerous small
boats ferrying people to the
city's busy waterfront markets,
which sell fresh products and
flowers. But Surat Thani is best
known as a transport gateway
to the beach havens of Ko
Samui and Ko Pha Ngan.

Lofty palm trees and clear blue waters of a near-deserted beach on Ko Samui ▷

Ko Samui ⑪

เกาะสมุย

Coconuts, a key crop on Samui

Aᴛ 247 ꜱꞯ ᴋᴍ (95 ꜱꞯ ᴍɪʟᴇꜱ), Samui is Thailand's third largest island, after Ko Phuket and Ko Chang. Dubbed the biggest coconut plantation in the world until the first backpackers arrived in the 1970s, this island has now seen tourism become its main income earner. Samui's beaches are world famous – its long, perfect strands attract around 500,000 visitors each year. Chaweng beach, in particular, has a reputation as something of a hang-out for an international party crowd. It is likely, however, that as more and more luxury accommodation is built for package tourists, the character of Ko Samui will change somewhat.

Naton

Naton is Samui's capital and main ferry port. The island was first settled in the 1850s by Chinese merchants who had come in search of trade in cotton and coconuts. Naton was founded around 1905 when the site was chosen as the island's administrative centre.

Few visitors stay here, except in order to take an early morning boat to Surat Thani on the mainland. The town has a supermarket, post office, and exchange facilities.

The main transport route on the island is the 50-km (31-mile) circular road, which passes through Naton. *Songthaews* departing from Naton ferry port travel either northwards (clockwise) towards Chaweng beach and the airport, or southwards (anticlockwise) towards Lamai.

The 12-m (38-ft) "Big Buddha" on Ko Faan, just off the Samui coast

Maenam

This 4-km (2-mile) long beach is the most westerly stretch of sand on the north coast. It has extensive views of Ko Pha Ngan *(see p329)*. Visitors flock here for the excellent windsurfing opportunities, which are aided by the strong directional breezes that blow on

KEY

🏖	Beach
🏄	Water sports
🛈	Tourist information
🛕	*Wat*
✈	Airport
🚌	Bus station
⛴	Ferry service
▬▬	Main road
▬▬	Minor road
🌼	Viewpoint

Maenam, on the north coast, one of the quietest beaches on Ko Samui

Thong Son •
Ao Choeng Mon
Ko Faan
(Big Buddha) •
Bangrak
Maenam •
Bophut •
Hin Lat waterfall •
• Chaweng
• Khao Pom
• Namuang waterfall
• Lamai
Hin Ta & Hin Yai
Hua Thanon •

Ko Pha Ngan

0 kilometres   2
0 miles   1

VISITORS' CHECKLIST

Surat Thani province. 🚶 33,000.
✈ 23 km (14 miles) from Naton.
⛴ from Surat Thani, Tha Thong
and Don Sak. ℹ TAT, Naton
(077) 420504 or TAT, Surat Thani
(077) 288818; Songserm Travel,
64/1–2 Naton Pier, Chonvithi Rd,
Naton (077) 421316 (for ferry
bookings). 🚌 3 km (2 miles) S of
Naton (077) 421281. 🎪 daily.

**Parascending over Chaweng beach,
one of many activities on offer**

Asian tourists, who come here
to make merit *(see p125)*. A
gaudy bazaar of souvenir stalls
and cafés has sprung up at
the foot of the *naga* staircase
leading to the Buddha image.

Thong Son and Choeng Mon
Further along the coast, on
Samui's northeastern cape,
are a series of secluded rocky
coves. Hat Thong Son is a
peaceful inlet with marvellous
views across to Ko Pha Ngan.
Most of the accommodation
on the headland is concentrated at Ao Choeng Mon, an
attractive bay with a pleasant
beach and good swimming.

shore during the northeasterly
monsoon from December to
February. However, the beach
is very narrow and not as
pretty as others on the island.

Bophut
Bophut has better facilities
than Maenam. Its village, at
the eastern end of the next
bay to the east, includes bungalows, a bank, bars, restaurants and a range of water
sports. The tranquil 2-km
(1-mile) long beach is popular
with families and backpackers.
From Bophut there is a daily
boat service to Hat Rin, a
beach on Ko Pha Ngan.

Bangrak
Adjacent to Bophut is Bangrak,
also known as "Big Buddha"
beach. The sea is not as clear
here as it is off Chaweng and

Lamai beaches *(see p328)*, but
it does offer plenty of budget
accommodation. A causeway
links the eastern end of
Bangrak beach to the tiny
island of Faan, home to
the large, gold-covered Big
Buddha. The imposing statue
is popular with islanders and

Palm trees shading typical beachside huts on Ko Samui

Exploring Ko Samui: the East Coast and Minor Sights

T HE BEAUTIFUL BEACHES and buzzing nightlife of Chaweng and Lamai on Samui's east coast draw tourists from all over the world. Many visitors never stray from these resorts, leaving the quieter beaches on the south and west coasts, the island's *wats* and Samui's spectacular mountainous and forested interior relatively untouched.

Muslim fishermen landing their boats on Samui's east coast

Chaweng
Chaweng is the longest, busiest and prettiest beach on the island, stretching 5 km (3 miles) down the east coast. Its warm waters, white sands and back-to-nature beach bungalows have attracted budget travellers for many years. Today, though, more and more up-market developments are being built to accommodate package tourists.

At the northern end of Chaweng is a tranquil 1-m (3-ft) deep lagoon, ideal for children and novice windsurfers. The long, inviting sweep of the middle and southern end of the beach is bordered by

coconut palms. Chaweng is at its most scenic along its southern section where large boulders alternate with discreet sandy coves.

For the active, the beach has a wide range of sports including windsurfing, canoeing, parascending, scuba diving, tennis and volleyball.

Chaweng has the most developed tourist infrastructure on Samui with travel agencies, banks, supermarkets and car and bike hire among the facilities available. Although it does attract a few families, Chaweng is still predominantly visited by young travellers. Many come to enjoy the ever-increasing numbers of bars, restaurants and clubs.

Lamai
Samui's second largest beach caters primarily for the European budget tourist. The main focus is at the centre of the 4-km (2-mile) long beach. Set back from the beach are a huddle of riotous bars and nightclubs and restaurants serving Western food.

Lamai village is at the quieter, northern end of the beach, away from the crowds. It still has many old teak houses with thatched roofs. The village's main sight is Wat

Lamai Cultural Hall, built in 1826, which has a small folk museum dedicated to arts and crafts found on Samui.

On the southern promontory of Lamai beach are the Hin Ta and Hin Yai rock formations which are famous for their similarity in shape to male and female sexual organs.

South and West Coasts
There are many quiet beaches with simple huts along the south and west coasts, such as around Thong Krut. Another is Thong Yang which – although only 1.5 km (1 mile) south of the pier where the vehicle ferries from Don Sak dock – is perfect for those seeking peaceful seclusion.

Swimming in Namuang waterfall, in the centre of Samui

The Interior
For visitors tiring of the beach, the interior of Samui offers an adventurous alternative. The mix of dense tropical forest and large coconut plantations seems impenetrable, but there are rough trails – which can be negotiated by four-wheel-drive jeep or by motorcycle – and two roads leading to Samui's picturesque waterfalls.

Namuang, an impressive 30-m (98-ft) high waterfall, is a popular destination for picnics and swimming. It is situated 10 km (6 miles) from Naton and 5 km (3 miles) from the circular coast road. Hin Lat, 3 km (2 miles) from Naton, is smaller than Namuang and less interesting. Both falls are at their most spectacular in December or January at the end of the rainy season, when they swell with rainwater.

Chaweng, the longest and most attractive beach on Ko Samui

Ko Pha Ngan 12

เกาะพะงัน

Surat Thani province. 🏠 9,000.
🚢 from Naton on Ko Samui to
Tong Sala. 🛈 TAT, Surat Thani
(077) 288818. 🗓 daily.

K O PHA NGAN is 7 km (4
miles) north of Ko Samui,
and is two-thirds its size. The
island has the same tropical
combination of powdery
beaches, accessible coral reefs
and rugged, forested interior.
Budget travellers come to enjoy a bohemian life, staying
in rattan huts beside idyllic
bays. The island is much less
developed for tourism than
Samui, due mainly to its bad
road system. Much of it is accessible only by sea or along
rutted tracks by pick-up truck.

Tong Sala

This town is the entrance port
to Ko Pha Ngan, and, like
Naton on Ko Samui, acts as a
service town with a bank, post
restante, supermarket, travel
agent and photo processing
shop. Next to the pier, an
armada of *songthaews* waits to
take visitors around the island.

Hat Rin

The greatest number of bungalows on the island is at Hat
Rin, located at the southeastern
tip, 10 km (6 miles) from Tong
Sala. It has become a popular
destination with backpackers,
many of whom now consider
Samui's resorts to be too
commercialized. Hat Rin has
two wide beaches flanking
the headland. Its accommodation is often fully booked
for a week either side of the

**The white sands of Hat Rin beach
on Ko Pha Ngan**

monthly full moon beach
party which starts after dark
and goes on beyond sunrise.

Chaloklam

A strong smell of dried, salted
fish emanates from Chalo-
klam's shop-fronts. Asian visitors often stop here to
buy fish after visiting
the revered Chao Mae
Koan Im shrine in the
centre of the island.
In Chaloklam, fishing-
related activities, such
as mending nets and
gutting fish, co-exist
with shop-houses
selling pizzas and
other tourist snacks.
The beaches near the
town tend to be rath-
er dirty but improve further
to the east, especially as far
out of town as Khom beach.

Tong Nai Pan

Although the majority of the
beaches are on the east side
of the island, most are accessible only from a rough track
running along the coast. The
twin bays of Tong Nai Pan
Noi and Tong Nai Pan Yai in

**Dried fish at
Chaloklam village**

KEY

🏖	Beach
🏄	Water sports
🛕	*Wat*
🚌	Bus station
⚓	Ferry service
▬	Main road
▬	Minor road
▬ ▬	Dirt track
☀	Viewpoint

the northeast offer arguably
the prettiest scenery. They
can be reached by pick-up
truck from Tong Sala
or, between January
and September, by
long-tail boats, which
sail from Maenam
beach on Ko Samui.
Tansadet, 3 km (2
miles) to the south,
is the island's biggest
stream and waterfall.
It owes its name,
"royal stream", to
the ten visits King
Chulalongkorn made
between 1888 and 1909. Since
then most Thai monarchs have
left large stone inscriptions on
rocks alongside the stream –
finding the signatures requires
scrambling among the rocks.
The stream has two falls, Sam-
pan and Daeng. Both are suitable for bathing, but heavy
rainfall from September to December makes the stream bed
too dangerous to walk along.

Angthong National Marine Park ⑬

อุทยานแห่งชาติทางทะเลอ่างทอง

Surat Thani province. Park HQ on Ko Wua Talab. 🚤 *from Ko Samui.* 🛈 *TAT, Surat Thani (077) 288818; Park HQ (077) 286025 (inc bungalow bookings).*

T HE 40 VIRTUALLY uninhabited islands of the Angthong National Marine Park display a rugged beauty distinct from palm-fringed Ko Samui 31 km (19 miles) away to the south-east. The Angthong ("golden basin") islands, covering an area of 102 sq km (39 sq miles), are the submerged peaks of a flooded range of limestone mountains which, further south in Nakhon Si Thammarat province, rise to 1,835 m (6,000 ft).

Angthong's pristine beauty owes much to it being the preserve of the Royal Thai Navy, and therefore off limits until 1980 when it was declared a National Marine Park. Now naval boats have been replaced by tourist ferries. Most visitors come on day-trips from Ko Samui to relax on the mica-white sands, explore the lush forests and limestone caves, sea canoe around the islands' jagged coastlines and snorkel among the colourful fan corals.

Another attraction is the abundant wildlife, both on land and in the sea. Leopard cats, squirrels, long-tailed macaques, sea otters and pythons may be glimpsed,

KEY

🏖	Beach
🏄	Water sports
🛈	Tourist information
🚤	Ferry service
--	Footpath
⛰	Viewpoint

and a lack of natural predators has made the endearingly friendly dusky langur easy to spot. Among the 40 bird species found in the archipelago are the black baza, the edible-nest swiftlet, the brahminy kite and the Eurasian woodcock.

Divers taking advantage of the excellent coral off **Ko Sam Sao** will probably see short-bodied mackerel *(pla thu).* A staple of the Thai diet, the sea around the Angthong islands is favoured by the fish as a breeding ground. It is also sometimes possible to spot dolphins although they are wary of humans because fisherman in the area catch them for their meat.

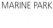

Ferry to Angthong National Marine Park

Ko Naayphud

Ko Hindab

Ko Wuakantang

Ko Sam Sao

Ko Mae Ko

Ko Phi
National Park Headquarters

Ko Wua Talab

Ko Samui

ANGTHONG NATIONAL MARINE PARK

Ko Tao-Pun

Ko Phaluai

0 kilometres 2

0 miles 1

View from a trail on Ko Wua Talab, Angthong National Marine Park

Boat for carrying visitors from the ferry to the beach on Ko Mae Ko

The park headquarters, and the islands' only tourist accommodation and facilities, are located on the largest island, **Ko Wua Talab** ("sleeping cow island"). A steep 400-m (1300-ft) climb from here leads to a viewpoint offering wonderful panoramas of the whole archipelago and beyond to Ko Pha Ngan, Ko Samui and the mainland. The view is at its best at sunrise and sunset. Another fairly tough climb leads to Tham Buabok ("waving lotus cave"), so named because of the shape of some of its stalactites and stalagmites.

On **Ko Mae Ko** there is a swimming beach as well as the stunning Thale Noi, a wide turquoise lake bordered by sheer cliffs. This is the "golden basin" that gives the islands their name.

Cowrie shell, Ko Tao

Ko Tao ⑭
เกาะเต่า

Surat Thani province. 🏠 750. 🚢 from Chumphon, Surat Thani and Ko Pha Ngan. 🛈 TAT, Ko Samui (077) 281828.

LOCATED 40 KM (25 miles) northwest of Ko Pha Ngan, "turtle island" is the smallest and prettiest of the islands in the Samui archipelago that offer visitors accommodation.

Ko Tao's major attraction is its superb offshore diving. Excellent visibility, a wide range of diving sites and a rich variety of coral and marine life make for some of the most rewarding diving in the country. The main dive sites are Green Rock, Chumphon Pinnacle and Southwest Pinnacle. Many sites are suitable for beginners thanks to the shallow inshore bays and clear waters. In May water visibility can approach 40 m (130 ft), which is often claimed to be the maximum possible. The island has ten or so dive companies which operate all year round, although the main season is from December to April.

The island itself is rugged, with dense forest inland, quiet coves along the east coast and a fine sweep of sandy beach on the west side. Plenty of simple bungalow accommodation is available, although it can be difficult to find a room in high season.

Just to the northwest of Ko Tao lie three immensely scenic islands known collectively as **Ko Nang Yuan**. Linked by sandbars and surrounded by coral, these are a delightful place to linger for a few days.

Diving among the rich marine life and fine coral off Ko Tao

BIRD'S-NEST SOUP

Unlike such misleadingly named delicacies as Bombay duck, the main ingredient of bird's-nest soup is, indeed, birds' nests. Not just any nest will do, however. Only the homes of birds such as the brown-rumped swift, the edible-nest swiftlet and the sea swallow are acceptable. When these delicate, saliva-thread constructions are cooked they are transformed into smooth, noodle-like strands which are considered to have aphrodisiac properties by peoples throughout Southeast and East Asia. Such is the perceived potency of the soup that the nests change hands for huge sums of money. A government licence is required to collect the nests, and many of the most important sites, such as those in caves on Ko Phi Phi Ley (see p363) are protected by armed guards. The dangerous job of nest harvesting is allowed only between February and April and in September when agile collectors must scale the cave walls on flimsy bamboo scaffolds.

Birds' nests: a regional delicacy

SOUTHERN
THAILAND

Introducing Southern Thailand

THE NARROW PENINSULA of Southern Thailand, stretching from Ranong, on the Burmese border, to Malaysia, is a unique region with a rich, multi-cultural heritage. Forest-cloaked mountains run along much of the interior, while the hinterland and islands of Phangnga Bay in the Andaman Sea form Thailand's most spectacular natural landscape. Here the shallow waters are dotted with limestone stacks and craggy islands up to 300 m (985 feet) high. Some of the country's best sandy beaches and dive sites are also found along the southern coasts and around the Andaman islands. Though the beach resorts of Phuket and Krabi draw most visitors to the area, the South also offers historic cultural sites, such as the towns of Songkhla and Nakhon Si Thammarat, and areas of unspoilt wilderness. The South is hot and humid year-round, with the monsoons bringing most rain to the Andaman coast from May to October and the Gulf coast from November to April.

UPPER ANDAMAN COAST
(see pp342–363)

Phangnga Bay

Phuket

Phangnga Bay (see pp354–7), *with its weird and wonderful towering limestone stacks, is one of Southern Thailand's most famous natural beauty spots. The most memorable way to explore the mangrove-lined bay and its hidden caves is by sea canoe (see p445).*

Phuket (see pp348–53) *is Thailand's largest island and richest province. Prosperous even during the 19th century, when Chinese merchants used the island as a base for sea trade, today it is one of the most popular tourist resorts in Thailand. Phuket is now a largely up-market destination with luxury hotels, restaurants and shops lining many of the island's stunning beaches. A wide range of water sports is available, including superb diving facilities.*

◁ **A row of golden, seated Buddha images in the interior courtyard of Wat Wang, near Phatthalung town**

Nakhon Si Thammarat (see pp368–9), *once the regional capital of the Srivijaya Empire (see pp 336–7), is today the South's cultural centre. Despite some fine sights, including Southern Thailand's holiest shrine, Wat Mahathat, and one of the few remaining* nang talung *shadow puppet theatres, the city is still not visited by many tourists.*

Songkhla National Museum (see pp374–5), *contains an eclectic collection of ceramics, art and furniture. It occupies the one-time deputy governor's residence, a splendid 19th-century, Chinese-style mansion.*

Nakhon Si Thammarat

Korlae *fishing boats (see p378), with painted hulls, are a colourful feature of the Muslim South. Some of the best ones can be seen at Pattani, once an independent Muslim state.*

Songkhla

| 0 kilometres | 50 |
| 0 miles | 25 |

Tarutao National Marine Park

Pattani

DEEP SOUTH
(see pp364–379)

Tarutao National Marine Park (see p376) *has a wide diversity of wildlife, and offers some of the most stunning, unspoilt beaches and island scenery in Thailand.*

The Peninsula as a Cultural Crossroads

For over 2,000 years, the peninsula that is now divided between Malaysia, Thailand and Burma has been a major cultural crossroads. Finds from the Isthmus of Kra (especially the historic entrepôts of Nakhon Si Thammarat, Chaiya, Sathing Phra and Takua Pa) testify to strong links with China, India, the Middle East and even the Roman Empire before the first millennium AD. In the 7th–13th centuries the Hindu-Buddhist Srivijaya Empire held sway over much of the region. After Srivijaya's decline, Burma and Siam, both Buddhist, pushed south, while Islam, brought by Arab traders, made a lasting impact in the southernmost part of the peninsula. There was even greater cultural diversity from the 16th century, when the British, Dutch, Portuguese, and other colonial powers developed trade routes through the Straits of Malacca.

***Islam**, the main religion in Malaysia, is widely practised in Southern Thailand today – minarets compete with Buddhist shrines in many towns.*

TO ARABIA

INDIA

BURMA (MYANMAR)

INDIAN OCEAN

TO AFRICA, EUROPE

***Prehistoric paintings** can be found in Phangnga Bay (see pp354–7) and other parts of the peninsula. Humans have lived here at least since the last Ice Age, when the peninsula did not exist as such – the area from Borneo to Sumatra was then dry land.*

TRADE ROUTES

The Straits of Malacca have always been a natural channel for sea routes. Chinese, Indian and Arab vessels were trading, gathering provisions and "wintering" at entrepôts along the peninsula at least 2,000 years ago. European ships joined them from the 16th century. As seafaring technology developed ships became less dependent on some ports, which subsequently declined.

***Ceremonial drums** found at the ancient cities of Chaiya and Nakhon Si Thammarat, and in Sumatra, were made in Dong Son in North Vietnam c.500 BC, testifying to early trade.*

***The Srivijaya Empire** ruled the peninsula as far north as Chaiya in the 7th–13th centuries. As first a Hindu and then a Mahayana Buddhist state, it produced many statues of Bodhisattvas – Enlightened beings who delay nirvana in order to save mankind.*

0 kilometres		1,000

0 miles		500

KEY

———	Local routes (c. 5th century BC onwards)
———	Major routes during the Srivijaya period (7th–13th centuries AD)
———	Major European routes (16th century onwards)

This Dutch East India Company cannon *is in Nakhon Si Thammarat, an ancient town in Southern Thailand (see pp368–9). The company traded all over Southeast Asia and was drawn to the peninsula by access to Chinese and Japanese goods.*

SRIVIJAYAN ARCHITECTURE

The Srivijaya Empire controlled trade at ports such as Chaiya *(see pp322–3)* and Takua Pa, in the Isthmus of Kra. Numerous Srivijayan artifacts have been found in the Gulf and South of Thailand, but most *chedis*, which were built of stucco and brick, have been built over. The main example to survive is an outstanding, complete *chedi* at Wat Phra Boromathat in Chaiya. Cruciform in shape, it has four tiers,

Chedi of the Javan-influenced **Wat Phra Boromathat, Chaiya**

decreasing in size as they ascend. On each corner is a smaller *chedi*. Built in the 9th–10th centuries, it has been restored many times, most recently in 1930.

TO CHINA

VIETNAM

THAILAND

CAMBODIA

ISTHMUS OF KRA

MALAYSIA

SOUTH CHINA SEA

BORNEO

SUMATRA

JAVA

TO AFRICA, EUROPE

TO THE SPICE ISLANDS (MOLUCCAS)

This European engraving shows a march in Pattani (see p378), one of several Muslim states in the peninsula that lost autonomy to Bangkok in the early part of the 20th century.

The Thais and Burmese *battled over the northern peninsula after Srivijaya waned. A fight for Phuket, or Junkceylon (see pp348–53), took place in 1785.*

European trade *led to extensive mapping of Southeast Asia. This 17th-century French map shows the local trade route up the east coast of the peninsula, from Batavia (Jakarta) in Java to the city of Ayutthaya in Siam.*

Coral Reefs

Red saddleback anemonefish

THAILAND'S BEST CORAL REEFS are found in the Andaman Sea. These reefs, which are composed of countless tiny marine animals, grow extremely slowly: 1 m (3 ft) of coral reef can take 1,000 years to form. As a coral reef is an excellent source of food and shelter, it provides the base for a unique and diverse marine ecosystem. The reef comprises reef builders (mainly hard corals, whose limestone skeletons form the basis of the reef) and reef dwellers, such as sea urchins, whose remains may also help build the reef when they die. Thousands of plants and animals – from large sharks to tiny algae – live around a coral reef. About 30 per cent of the world's fish species are found near coral reefs.

Snorkelling *is a cheap and easy way to explore a coral reef. Many reefs can be found in relatively shallow, clear water, which is excellent for snorkelling.*

Gobies – *small, spiny-finned fish with large heads – live mainly in tropical waters. They often share sand burrows with shrimps.*

Coconut grove

West-facing wall

The clown triggerfish *has an upright spine in its dorsal fin. The spine is raised to wedge the fish under rocks and ledges; this stops predators from pulling the fish out.*

Moray eels *are voracious predators, hiding in crevices and lunging out at unsuspecting prey swimming by. Food left between a moray's teeth may be picked clean by hungry cleaner shrimps.*

A TYPICAL REEF

On the island's east side, the reef flat slopes away from the beach, rises to a crest, then slopes steeply to the sea bed. Mostly hard corals are found on the east side. The reef's west walls tend to be much steeper and rockier than the east side. Its boulders provide protection for soft corals, and nooks in which creatures such as eels live.

Leopard sharks, *also known as zebra sharks, pose no threat to people. At Shark Point, near Ko Phi Phi, divers often see these timid creatures resting or cruising along the outskirts of the coral reef.*

Many species of sea bird *gather around islands with coral reefs to feed on the abundant fish life. This is a great egret, a large wading bird that feeds by stabbing small fish with its razor-sharp bill.*

Scuba diving *is an excellent way to experience diverse reef ecosystems (see p444). In the South, Phuket has the most diving operators offering instruction, equipment rental and trips to offshore islands such as Ko Phi Phi. When exploring a coral reef, you should not touch the delicate corals, as this causes permanent damage to the reef.*

Rays *are often seen around coral reefs. Manta rays have impressive wingspans of up to 6 m (20 ft), while blue-spotted rays have a poisonous spine in their tail.*

Sandy beach

Reef flat

Reef crest

Snapper *often follow schools of feeding goatfish, devouring any small fish that escape the latter.*

Reef slope

Giant hermit crabs *are soft-bodied crustaceans. They protect their bodies by living and moving around the sea bed in the empty shells of molluscs such as whelks.*

CORAL: THE REEF'S BUILDING BLOCK

Coral is made of the skeletons of polyps, small animals related to sea anemones and jellyfish. Polyps are unusual in that they build their skeletons outside their bodies. As the polyps divide, the coral colony slowly builds up. There may be as many as 200 different species of coral in a reef, divided into hard corals such as brain coral, and colourful soft corals, which have no stony outer skeleton.

Hard, rock-like coral

Soft, plant-like coral

Mangrove Forests

White-throated kingfisher

MANGROVE FORESTS develop only in the tropics, in brackish and saltwater areas of estuaries. In Thailand they are found in pockets of the South, particularly at Phangnga Bay *(see pp354–7)*. Mangrove species are the only trees to have adapted to the inhospitable conditions of these muddy, intertidal zones. The forests typically cover networks of channels and levees created from the build-up of silt that becomes trapped in the cage-like root systems of the trees. Though often dismissed as wasteland, in its natural state a mangrove forest is a vital ecosystem – a fertile spawning, nursing, feeding and sheltering ground for crustaceans, fish, birds, snakes and even mammals. "Primary" mangrove grows to over 25 m (80 ft) high. However, most mangrove in Thailand is "secondary", meaning it has been cut by humans and reaches only 5–10 m (16–33 ft).

The characteristic stilt-like roots of most mangrove trees support the tree against the constant movement of tidal waters. As well as holding the trunk of the tree above the high tide level, the roots trap nutrient-rich sediments.

The upward-growing roots (pneumatophores) of some trees have special "breathing" pores used during low tide.

The mud skipper, so called for its skipping gait across mud flats at low tide, is the ubiquitous mangrove dweller. It can survive for short periods out of water.

Sonneratia are sturdy trees, tolerant of high salinity.

Avicennia are sustained by large cable root systems below the mud.

Rhizophora species are associated with soft mud under strong tidal influence.

Breathing roots, or pneumatophores, can excrete excess salt.

CROSS SECTION OF A MANGROVE LEVEE

This cross section shows a typical gradation of trees in a Thai mangrove forest. The waters are at high tide, a time when small fish and invertebrates feed in the sheltered, nutrient-rich waters around the roots of the trees. At low tide, when the roots of the trees are exposed, crabs and wading birds scour the mud flats for trapped fish and decaying matter.

The estuarine crocodile was once king of the mangroves. Nowadays it is bred in farms and is very rarely seen in the wild.

Small-clawed otters are often spotted in mangrove regions. They eat the smaller inhabitants such as molluscs and crabs.

Male fiddler crabs sift the silt with their one enlarged claw, selecting tiny organic particles to eat. As with most other types of crab, their colourful claws are also used in courtship displays.

Rhizophora trees, *such as these at Phangnga Bay, are common in Thai mangrove forests. Their colonizing ability is largely due to the unusual shape of their seed pods. With dagger-shaped stalks, these penetrate the ooze rather than floating away with the tide.*

Yellow-ringed cat snakes, *like other mangrove snakes, are adept swimmers and tree climbers. They rest by day and hunt fish and frogs by night.*

Nipa palms thrive in soft mud away from wave action. Nipa is used by Thais to wrap tobacco and as an ingredient in sweetmeats and alcohol.

Bruguiera trees grow in compacted mud which is inundated with water only during high spring tides.

Crab-eating macaques *inhabit Thai mangrove forests; they are capable swimmers and forage for crabs at low tide. Seeds also form part of the macaques' diet.*

THE DESTRUCTION OF THAILAND'S MANGROVE FORESTS

Despite the provision of a national mangrove management scheme (set up in 1946), some 60 per cent of Thailand's mangrove has been cleared since the 1960s – just 121,400 ha (300,000 acres) were thought to remain by 1996. Not only has this loss of habitat decimated marine life but coastal erosion has also started to become a problem in parts of the South. Without the roots of mangrove trees to trap it, estuarine silt is deposited over a progressively larger area, and sea water seeps over more and more of the land. The rate of loss peaked in the late 1980s with the boom in tiger prawn farming in former mangrove areas.

Prawn farm in a former area of mangrove forest

After clearing mangrove trees to make way for prawn farms, farmers use the tide-flushed mangrove channels to discharge nutrient-rich excreta from the prawn pools. This reduces oxygen levels in the adjacent natural breeding grounds of prawns, fish and crabs. Charcoal production is also to blame: tall mangrove species have been select-cut for decades in order to be incinerated and turned into charcoal. The fuel is sold cheaply in Thailand or shipped to Singapore for distribution within Asia. Road and harbour construction are other factors responsible for the loss of mangrove forests in Thailand.

UPPER ANDAMAN COAST

THE ABIDING IMAGE *of Thailand's Andaman coast is of long sandy beaches backed by swaying palms and a verdant hinterland of rainforest. Centred on Ko Phuket, the upper half of this coast has many attractions for visitors, whether they want to dive amid spectacular reefs, party in hectic resorts, canoe around the tall limestone stacks of Phangnga Bay, or find solitude on deserted islands.*

The Andaman coast around Phuket has long been a magnet for Thais and foreigners. Merchants were drawn by its strategic position on the spice routes between East and West *(see pp336–7)*; prospectors came for the rich tin deposits. This is a lush, fertile region. Much of the interior is cloaked in rainforest, and rubber, coffee, cashew, banana and durian plantations are common.

The outstanding natural beauty of the Andaman coast is known the world over. The biggest draw in the region is Phuket, now a resort island, which has superb beaches, excellent diving facilities and the most developed tourist infrastructure in Southern Thailand. Over the last 20 years, many traditional sea gypsy and Muslim fishing villages on Phuket and around Krabi have been transformed into holiday resorts. Long-tail boats take visitors to sights like the extraordinary limestone stacks of Phangnga Bay. In remote mangrove channels – accessible only by canoe – otters, monkeys and sea eagles still live undisturbed.

There is outstanding scenery and diving around Ko Phi Phi, though it is now firmly on the tourist trail. Visitors wanting sand and sun without the crowds head for relatively undeveloped islands such as Ko Lanta. Unspoilt beach resorts can be found along the stretch of coast from Ranong to Phuket, and the virgin rainforest of Khao Sok National Park is located inland. West of here, the Ko Surin and Ko Similan archipelagos offer some of the world's best dive sites.

The southwest monsoon, which lasts from about June to October, makes some of the outer islands inaccessible.

A typical beach scene in this part of Thailand: sun, sand and water sports

◁ **Not just a holiday island – the productive rice paddies of Phuket**

Exploring the Upper Andaman Coast

THIS PART OF THAILAND's Andaman Sea coast contains some of the most inviting beach scenery in Southeast Asia. Using the international resort of Phuket as a base, visitors have 12 long sandy beaches on their doorstep and a full range of shopping, dining, entertainment, land and water sport services. The towering limestone stacks of Phangnga Bay can readily be explored in a daytrip. An alternative base is quieter Krabi, which combines fine beaches with spectacular cliff landscapes. Accessible from Krabi, and from Phuket, is the idyllic island scenery of Ko Phi Phi. The monsoon forests of the Tenasserim mountain range provide a backdrop to the little frequented beaches of Khao Lak. Avid divers and snorkellers can visit the remote Similan and Surin archipelagos acclaimed for their superlative corals and aquatic life.

RANONG

❹ *KO SURIN*

Yachting off the coast of the un-spoilt Similan archipelago

*KHAO SOK ❷
NATIONAL PARK*

TAKUA PA ●

KO SIMILAN

KHAO LAK COAST ❸

0 kilometres   25

0 miles   15

*PHANGNGA
TOWN* ●

❻

PHANGNGA BAY

THALANG ●

❺ *PHUKET*

● *PHUKET
TOWN*

A deserted beach on Ko Phi Phi – still possible to find despite its ever-increasing popularity

SIGHTS AT A GLANCE

SEE ALSO

**The thickly forested hillside and limestone
cliffs near Khao Sok National Park**

GETTING THERE

Most visitors make use of Phuket's modern airport, and Phuket or Krabi make the best bases
to explore the Upper Andaman Coast. Reliable
air-conditioned bus services link Phuket, Krabi,
Phangnga and Ranong, although car hire in Phuket
or Krabi is much more convenient. There is no
railway in the region. Ko Similan is accessible from
Phuket, Ko Surin from Ranong and also by air from
Phuket. Thailand's water taxi, the long-tail boat,
is the best way to explore smaller bays once in
the Phi Phi, Phangnga Bay or Ko Lanta areas.

KEY

▬▬	Major road
▭▭	Minor road
▭▭	Scenic route
⌁	River
☀	Viewpoint

Long-tail boats on a beach on Ko Poda, near Krabi

Collecting water from one of Ranong's geothermal springs

Ranong ❶

ระนอง

Ranong province. 🏛 17,000. 🚌 🚢 🛳 daily. 🛈 TAT, Surat Thani (077) 288818.

RANONG WAS originally settled in the late 18th century by Hokkien Chinese, who were hired to work as labourers in the region's tin mines. The area grew rich, and Ranong is now a major border town. From here Thai nationals may travel to **Victoria Point** in Burma on a half- or full-day boat trip. Referred to as Kaw Thaung by the Burmese, the town is well known for bargain duty-free goods and handicrafts. Officially, foreigners may not go to Victoria Point without a visa, but this is not always enforced.

In Ranong, the natural hot springs are the main attraction. They rise beside the Khlong Hat Sompen River at **Wat Tapotaram**, 1 km (1,100 yds) east of the town centre, and

are channelled into three concrete tubs called Mother, Father and Child. At an average temperature of 65° C (150° F), the water is too hot for bathing. A short walk down the river, the Jansom Thara Spa Resort Hotel has tapped and cooled the water to a more bearable 42° C (110° F). Those not staying at the hotel can take a spa bath for a nominal fee.

Khao Sok National Park ❷

อุทยานแห่งชาติเขาสก

Surat Thani province. Park HQ off Hwy 401, 40 km (25 miles) E of Takua Pa. 🛈 TAT, Surat Thani (077) 288818 or Forestry Dept (02) 579 0529 (inc bungalow bookings). 🚌 from Surat Thani or Takua Pa. 🗺

TOGETHER WITH nearby reserves, Khao Sok National Park forms the largest and most dramatic tract of virgin forest in South Thailand. The 738-sq km (285-sq mile) park rises to a height of 960 m (3,150 ft) and includes 100 spectacular islands, formed when the Racha-brapha Dam was built in 1982.

Elephants, tigers, bears, boars and monkeys live in the park, along with at least 188 species of birds, including hornbills and the argus pheasant. Sightings of the larger mammals are quite rare since they are usually active only at night. Animal tracks, however, are regularly seen

Barking deer at Khao Lak

along the park's many marked trails. Sadly, poaching of tigers and elephants persists despite the efforts of national park officers. The area is increasingly popular with tourists keen to trek, canoe, watch birds and spot animals. The park also contains interesting flora, such as the rare, giant Rafflesia flower. Many of the hiking trails are suitable for all ability levels, with more demanding hikes for the experienced. Khao Sok receives the brunt of both summer and winter monsoons, causing a long wet season from May to November. The best time to visit the park is between January and April, when the skies are clear.

Khao Lak Coast ❸

เขาลัก

Ranong province. 🛈 TAT, Surat Thani (077) 288818. 🚌 from Takua Pa or Phuket.

MUCH OF THE coastline south of Takua Pa, which was once a major trading port, consists of long stretches of virtually deserted beach with few signs of commercial development. Khao Lak, a small coastal village halfway between Takua Pa and Thai Muang, is a good base from which to explore the area. It has a few simple bungalows and a fine beach. The nearby **Khao Lak National Park** is famous for its spectacular scenery. Steep ridges of monsoon forest extend to the winding coast, giving views of rocky capes and sandy coves. Barking deer and small bears are among the wildlife still living in the forest, but the park, like most others in Thailand, is plagued by encroachment and poaching.

Between November and April, Tap Lamu fishing port and Hat Khao Lak operate as ferry points for Ko Similan.

🦌 **Khao Lak National Park**
Park HQ 33 km (20 miles) S of Takua Pa. 🛈 Forestry Dept (02) 579 0529. 🗺

Khao Sok, a wilderness of virgin forest, limestone cliffs and waterfalls

Similan's boulders, beneath which are massive underwater grottoes

Ko Surin and Ko Similan ❹

เกาะสุรินทร์และสิมิลัน

Phangnga province. 🅸 *TAT, Phuket (076) 212046 or Forestry Dept (02) 579 0529 (inc bungalow bookings for Similan).* **Surin** 🚌 *from Ban Hin Lat, off Hwy 4, 50 km (31 miles) N of Takua Pa.* 🚤 **Similan** 🚌 *from Hat Khao Lak or Tap Lamu, off Hwy 4, 30 km (19 miles) or 40 km (25 miles) S of Takua Pa; or by diving trips from Ko Phuket.* 🚤

KO SURIN and Ko Similan, 60 km (37 miles) off the west coast and 100 km (62 miles) apart, are the most remote islands in Thailand. Owing to the southwesterly monsoon, from May to October they are virtually inaccessible. In season, however, the two archipelagos offer some of the best diving sites in the world and some of the most spectacular wildlife and scenery in Thailand.

The five **Surin** islands are virtually uninhabited, home only to a few sea gypsies and national park officials. There is a park dormitory on Ko Surin Nua, but most people camp on the islands.

The two largest islands, Ko Surin Nua and Ko Surin Tai, are heavily forested with tall hardwood trees. Sea eagles, monitor lizards and crab-eating macaques are common sights. The surrounding sea offers an outstanding array of soft corals and frequent sightings of shovel-nose rays, bow-mouthed guitar fish and whale sharks. However, overfishing has led to the depletion of the marine life of Ko Surin, and many divers maintain that the best sightings of sealife are around the Similans instead.

The nine **Similan** islands became a national marine park in the mid-1980s. The name Similan is thought to derive from the Malaysian word *sembilan*, meaning nine, and the islands are numbered Ko 1 through to Ko 9. Ko 4 (Ko Miang) has the park HQ, a restaurant, bungalows and camp site (with a stock of two-man tents). Also important is Ko 9, where the ranger sub-station can be found. The interiors of these islands consist of crystal-white sand and lush rainforest, while the headlands are made up of distinctive, giant granite boulders the size of houses. Beneath these rocks are underwater grottoes and swim-through tunnels, which enhance the islands' appeal to divers and snorkellers.

The stunning sea bed is decorated with staghorn, star and branching corals and a breathtaking range of fish, including lithe manta rays, and giant sea turtles. Other, more threatening, fish include giant groupers, and poisonous stone-fish and lionfish. Sharks seen around the islands include black and white tips, leopard sharks, hammerheads, bull sharks and whale sharks.

Diver exploring the colourful coral around Ko Similan

THE WORLD'S LARGEST FLOWER

Khao Sok is one of the few places in the world where the giant *Rafflesia kerri* grows. This foul-smelling tropical plant has no roots or leaves and is wholly parasitic. For most of the year it lies dormant in the form of microscopic threads inside the roots of a host tree. Once a year, however, a small flower breaks the surface of the host's bark. Over a period of months the bud swells to the size of a watermelon and eventually opens to become the largest flower on earth, with a diameter up to 80 cm (31 inches). The flower's fetid smell attracts insects which assist in the pollination process. After a few days the orange-red flower shrivels to an unsightly, putrescent mass. Occasionally a Rafflesia in flower may be found at the end of a sign-posted path at Khao Sok.

Rafflesia flower in full bloom, Khao Sok National Park

Phuket ⑤

ภูเก็ต

Patong beach on Phuket

Phuket is Thailand's largest island and one of the most popular holiday destinations in Southeast Asia, attracting up to one million visitors each year. At 48 km (30 miles) long and covering 550 sq km (210 sq miles), it is a province in itself – and the wealthiest in the country. Originally this prosperity was based on tin production but tourism is now the major earner. The northern tip of the island is separated from the mainland only by a narrow channel of sea, over which runs the 700-m (765-yd) long Sarasin Bridge.

Game fishing
Tuna, barracuda and other fish are hunted from boats in the waters off Phuket.

Half-Buried Buddha
Wat Phra Tong is built around a curious, gold-leafed Buddha image, half buried in the ground. Legend says that whoever tries to remove it will die.

★ **West Coast Beaches**
The clearest waters, best sand and most luxurious hotels are on the west coast. Patong is the most densely developed resort; Karon and Kata are quieter.

KEY

🏖	Beach
⬛	Water sports
ℹ	Tourist information
🚶	*Wat*
✈	Airport
🚌	Coach station
⛴	Ferry service
▬▬▬	Main road
▬▬	Minor road
☀	Viewpoint

STAR SIGHTS

★ **West Coast Beaches**

★ **Thai Village**

★ **Marine Research Centre**

Cape Promthep is the southernmost point on Ko Phuket. The views from this rugged headland are some of the most stunning on the island, particularly at sunset.

Sarasin Bridge ●

Hat Mai Khao ●

Hat Nai Yang ●

Hat Nai Thon ●

Wat Phra To

Thalang

Hat Bang Tao

Hat Pansea ●

Hat Surin ●

Hat Kamala

Kathu waterfall ●

Hat Patong ●

● Hat Karon Noi

Wat Chalong

Hat Karon ●

Hat Kata Yai ●

Hat Kata Noi ●

Ao Nai Harn ●

Hat Rav

Cape Promthep   Ko Bon

The Gibbon Rehabilitation Centre in the Khao Phra Taew Forest Reserve encourages once-domesticated gibbons to fend for themselves in the wild.

VISITORS' CHECKLIST

Phuket province. 210,000.
29 km (18 miles) NW of
Phuket town. Phangnga Rd,
Phuket town. from Ko Phi
Phi to Phuket Deep Sea Port.
TAT, 73–75 Phuket Rd (076)
212213. Phuket Rd (076)
212046. Vegetarian Festival
(late Sep/early Oct, for nine days).

Thalang
Thalang is famous for its wooden houses and surrounding rubber plantations.

Ko Ngam

Cape Khut

Gibbon
Rehabilitation
Centre

Ko Raet

Ko Naga Yai

• Bang Pae waterfall

Ko Naga Noi

• Khao Phra
Ton Sai Taew Forest
waterfall Park

Naga Pearl Farm

Heroines' Monument
Two brave sisters rallied the women of Phuket to successfully defend the island against Burmese invaders during the Battle of Thalang in 1785.

Thalang Museum

Heroines'
monument

Ko Rang

Phuket Butterfly Garden and Aquarium
Numerous species of butterflies are cultivated in a large, covered garden. There are also 50 fish tanks with examples of local sealife.

Ko Maphrao

Butterfly Garden
and Aquarium

Thai Village

PHUKET TOWN

• Ko Sire Gypsy Village

Phuket town is notable for its 19th-century Sino-Portuguese-style residences. It acts as a transport and service centre.

Chalong

• Phuket Deep Sea Port

→ Ko Phi Phi

Marine Research
Centre

Lone

★ Thai Village
Orchids are sold at this village and there is a show on Thai culture with elephants, Thai boxing and classical dancing.

★ Marine Research Centre
A well-designed aquarium at the centre includes salt- and freshwater fish, lobsters, turtles and molluscs.

0 kilometres   5

0 miles   5

Phuket Town

PHUKET TOWN grew to prominence around the beginning of the 19th century, when the island's tin resources attracted thousands of Chinese migrants. Many merchants made fortunes from tin, built splendid residences and sent their children to British Penang to be educated. Hokkien-speaking tin-mining families soon intermarried with the indigenous Thai population. Today, the bustling downtown area retains some of its earlier charm though, unlike most of the island, it is geared towards residents rather than tourists. The Chinese heritage is preserved in the Sino-Portuguese shop-houses, temples, the local cuisine and the Vegetarian Festival.

Dragon detail at a temple

One of the grand old Chinese mansions in Phuket town

🏠 Chinese Mansions
Thalang, Yaowarat, Ranong and Damrong roads.

The heart of Phuket town is the old Sino-Portuguese quarter with its spacious, if now rather run-down, colonial-style residences set in large grounds. Most date from the reigns of Rama IV and Rama V (1851–1910). Among the best examples are those used today as offices by the Standard Chartered Bank and Thai Airways on Ranong Road. Unfortunately, no-one has yet seen fit to convert any of the old mansions into a museum and none can be visited. Many of the commercial Chinese shop-houses are also dilapidated.

🏠 Thavorn Hotel Lobby Exhibition
ห้องแสดงของเก่าโรงแรมถาวร
74 Rasada Rd. **[** (076) 211334.
◯ daily.

The owner of this hotel in the centre of town has assembled a collection of Phuket artifacts

and pictures which he now displays in the lobby and adjacent function rooms. Among the exhibits are models of tin mines, pictures of the town

centre in the 19th century, Chinese treasure chests and weavers' tables, all of which are imaginatively displayed.

🏠 Fresh Produce Market
ตลาดสด
Ranong Rd. ◯ daily.

The 24-hour wet market is a treat which assaults the senses. The market and adjacent lanes are full of colourful characters hawking condiments, dried herbs and spices, pungent pickled *kapi* fish, squirming eels and succulent durians.

♣ Rang Hill
เขารัง

On the top of this hill overlooking the town stands a statue of Khaw Sim Bee Na-Ranong (1857–1913), governor of Phuket for 12 years from 1901. He enjoyed considerable autonomy from Bangkok but is credited with bringing the island firmly under central rule, and also with importing the first rubber tree into Thailand.

🏠 Bang Niew Temple
ศาลเจ้าบางเหนียว
Phuket Rd. ◯ daily.

This temple is where *naga* devotees climb knife-ladders during the Vegetarian Festival. The inner compound is devoted to a number of Chinese mythological gods, the most prominent being Siew, Hok and Lok who represent longevity, power and happiness.

PHUKET TOWN'S VEGETARIAN FESTIVAL

At the start of the ninth Chinese lunar month, Phuket town hosts a nine-day Vegetarian Festival accompanied by gruesome rites. The tradition began over 150 years ago when a troupe of Chinese entertainers in Phuket recovered from the plague by adhering to austere rituals practised in China. Today believers use the festival to purge the body and soul of impure thoughts and deeds. Devotees dress in white, follow a vegetarian diet and refrain from alcohol and sex. The highlight is the parade of *nagas* (spirit mediums) with their flesh pierced by metal rods. Other *nagas* climb ladders of knives, plunge their hands into hot oil or walk on burning coals. The worse the suffering, the greater reward for the *naga* and his temple.

***Nagas* parading through the town**

Wat Mongkol Nimit, a typical example of Rattanakosin architecture

VISITORS' CHECKLIST

Phuket province. 🚶 69,000.
🚌 Southern Bus Terminal, near
Phang Nga Rd. ℹ️ TAT, 73–75
Phuket Rd (076) 212213.
🚓 Phuket Rd (076) 219878.
📅 daily. 🎭 Vegetarian Festival
(late Sep/early Oct, for nine days).

🏛 Wat Mongkol Nimit

วัดมงคลนิมิต

Yaowarat Rd. ⬡ daily.
This large, Rattanakosin-style temple has finely carved doors. Its compound acts as a community centre where monks play *takraw* with the laity.

🏛 Chui Tui Temple

ศาลเจ้าจุ้ยตุ่ย

Ranong Rd. ⬡ daily.
A steady flow of people visit this Chinese temple to shake numbered sticks from a canister dedicated to vegetarian god Kiu Wong In. Each number corresponds to a pre-printed fate which, according to belief, the person will inherit.

ENVIRONS: Three km (2 miles) to the north of Phuket town is the **Phuket Butterfly Garden and Aquarium**. The garden's warm and humid atmosphere provides ideal conditions for hundreds of tropical butterflies as well as scorpions, stag beetles, other assorted insects and a playful otter. Among the highlights of the aquarium are the strange dog-face pufferfish and the black-tip sharks.

The **Thai Village**, located 4 km (2.5 miles) north of Phuket town, puts on cultural performances and animal shows from the different regions of Thailand.

There are demonstrations of *muay thai* boxing *(see pp40–41)*, traditional dancing, cock fighting, sword fighting, and a re-enactment of a Thai wedding. The fisherman's, tin miner's, and rubber-tapping dances were invented here. There is also an elephant show with log-towing and a tug-of-war with tourists.

The village is a good place to buy *yan lipao (see p101)* reed grass bags and ornaments, made by a weaving method unique to Southern Thailand. You can watch the artisans at work. There is also an **Orchid Garden**, with orchids for sale – 40,000 are grown here each year.

♣ Phuket Butterfly Garden and Aquarium

Yaowarat Rd. ⬡ daily. 🎫

♣ Thai Village and Orchid Garden

Thepkasattri Rd. ☎ (076) 214860.
⬡ daily. 🎫

PHUKET TOWN CENTRE

Bang Niew Temple ⑦
Chinese Mansions ②
Chui Tui Temple ④
Fresh Produce Market ⑤
Rang Hill ①
Thavorn Hotel Lobby
  Exhibition ⑥
Wat Mongkol Nimit ③

KEY

🚌 Coach station

🚓 Tourist police

ℹ️ Tourist information

🏛 Wat

⛪ Church

0 metres   500
0 yards   500

Exploring Phuket

PHUKET WAS CALLED Junkceylon by early European traders, but its modern name may derive from the Malay word *bukit*, meaning hill. On arrival, many visitors head straight for a beach resort and do not leave it for the duration of their holi-day – the best of the island's beaches are strung out along the west coast. However, there are several historical and cultural sights to complement the beachside attractions, and the lush, hilly interior is also worth exploring.

Hibiscus flower, typical of Phuket

High-rise hotel overlooking the popular, tree-lined beach at Patong

Hat Patong
Phuket's most developed strand is the 3-km (2-mile) long Hat Patong. Once a quiet banana plantation, it is now almost a city by the sea. This cosmopolitan area has a vibrant mix of hotels, restaurants, discos and raucous beer bars, resulting in a lively nightlife. During the day there are many water activities, such as parasailing, waterskiing, diving and deep-sea fishing on offer.

Although Patong continues to expand brazenly along its connecting roads, relative serenity still prevails for the moment at the beaches along the southern headland of Patong bay. It is possible to ride to the cape on elephant back, passing almond, cashew and tamarind trees on the way.

Hat Karon and Hat Kata
South of Patong, and almost as popular, are the beaches of Karon and Kata. Karon has one long stretch of sand lined with accommodation, and a second beach at tiny Karon Noi. Kata's beaches, along the bays of Kata Yai and Kata Noi, are smaller and prettier, sheltered by rocky promontories. There are a number of good restaurants on the headland between Karon and Kata.

Other Western Beaches
North of Patong lie the smaller beaches of Kamala, Surin and Pansea, fringed by palm-covered headlands. Perfectly curved Hat Kamala is relatively undeveloped, with Muslim fishermen's houses interspersed with a few restaurants.

Further north, Hat Bang Tao offers a quiet, enchanting retreat, popular with families. This long stretch is fronted by a few exclusive hotels. The beach is good for water sports.

Round the next few headlands are three beaches: Hat Nai Thon, a gorgeous, undeveloped strand; Hat Nai Yang, which is visited by Thais at weekends; and Hat Mai Khao, a deserted 12-km (7.5-mile) stretch of sand.

Southeastern Capes and Bays
Ao Nai Harn, a bay near the southern tip of Phuket, is home to the exclusive Phuket Yacht

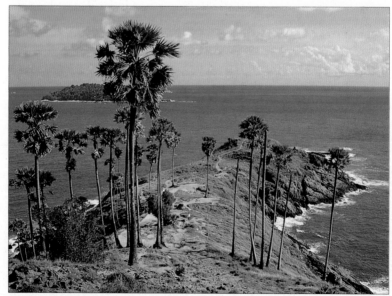

Cape Promthep, one of the best viewpoints on Phuket – a good place for spectacular sunsets

SEA GYPSIES OF THE ANDAMAN SEA

Sea gypsies, known as *chao ley* in Thai, may originate from the Andaman or Nicobar islands, across the Andaman Sea from Thailand. Phuket's sea gypsy population settled the area around 200 years ago, following routes from the Mergui archipelago, west of the Burmese mainland. Today, they can be found in Phuket at Rawai, Ko Sire, near Sapam village, and in northern Phuket's villages of Laem La and Nua.

Ethnically, they comprise three groups: Moklen, Moken and Urak Lawoi. Sea gypsies live throughout the Andaman Sea at Ko Surin, Ko Phra Tong in Phangnga and further south at the islands of Phi Phi, Lanta, Talibong, Tarutao and Langkawi. They speak their own language and have animistic beliefs. Once a year they hold a spiritual cleansing ceremony, placing human mementoes on a small boat before pushing it out to sea to get rid of bad spirits.

Cleaning fish, an everyday part of life for Andaman sea gypsies

Club. The beach (open to all) is considered to be one of the most beautiful on the island. Cape Promthep, 2 km (1 mile) away on the southernmost point of Phuket, offers wonderful views, especially at sunset.

North of Promthep, on the east side of the island, is the unexceptional Hat Rawai, and further along the coast is Ao Chalong. The sands around this bay are not as white as those on the west coast but there are many excellent seafood shacks here favoured by locals.

Ghost crab at Marine Centre

Ao Chalong acts as an anchorage for international yachts taking advantage of its sheltered location. It is also a departure point for boat excursions to the charming islands of Lone, Hai and Bon, where there is good snorkelling.

Further up the coast at Cape Phanwa is the much-visited Phuket Aquarium, which forms part of the **Marine Research Centre**. Numerous species of fish, corals, crabs and turtles are displayed here in tanks filled with sea water.

🏊 Marine Research Centre
Tip of Cape Phanwa. ☎ *(076) 391128.* ⭕ *daily.* 📷

Northeast Coast

Ko Naga Noi, an island off Phuket's northeast coast, has a tranquil, sandy beach that makes a fine halt for swimming and relaxing. The island is home to the **Naga Pearl Farm**, whose owners give demonstrations of the process of culturing South Sea pearls.

At Phuket's northeasternmost point, on the Cape Khut headland, there are sweeping views of the monoliths of Phangnga Bay *(see pp354–7)*. The placid waters of the narrow channel between Phuket and Phangnga province are exploited by Muslim fishermen who farm sea bass here.

🏊 Naga Pearl Farm
Ko Naga Noi. ☎ *(076) 219870.* ⭕ *daily.* 📷

Thalang

This town in central Phuket was the site of a famous battle in 1785 against the Burmese, which is commemorated by the Heroines' Monument 8 km (5 miles) to the south. A short walk east of the monument is the Thalang Museum which outlines the rich heritage of Phuket. Among the exhibits are

5th-century religious icons, Chinese porcelain, life-size figures recreated from the Burmese battle and information on the sea gypsies.

In Thalang itself there is a good market and, nearby, Wat Phra Tong. In the centre of the *wat* lies a gold-covered Buddha image, half buried in the ground. Legend has it that disaster will come to anyone who tries to move the image.

🏛 Thalang Museum
Off Hwy 4027, opposite Heroines' Monument. ⭕ *Wed–Sun.* ⬤ *public hols.* 📷

Khao Phra Taew Forest Park

Four km (2.5 miles) east of Thalang is the spectacular Khao Phra Taew Forest Park. The reserve is important as it preserves the last of Phuket's primary rainforest.

Within the park are two fine waterfalls. Ton Sai waterfall is the prettiest and is at its best from June to December. On the eastern fringe of the reserve is the Bang Pae waterfall, which offers cooling plunge pools all year.

Near the latter is the **Gibbon Rehabilitation Centre**. This volunteer-run scheme aims to reintroduce domesticated gibbons into the forest by encouraging them to fend for themselves. Visitors' donations buy food for the gibbons.

🌲 Khao Phra Taew Forest Park
Thalang district. ⭕ *daily.* 📷
🌲 Gibbon Rehabilitation Centre
Off Hwy 4027. ⭕ *daily.*

A barrel of limes for sale at Thalang market in central Phuket

Phangnga Bay ❻

อ่าวพังงา

No ONE AREA EPITOMIZES the splendour of the South's landscape as succinctly as 400-sq km (155-sq mile) Phangnga Bay. Its scenic grandeur derives from towering limestone stacks rising sheer from calm, shallow waters up to 350 m (1,150 ft) high. Inside many of the 40-odd stacks are narrow tunnels and sea chambers. Inland, too, this coastal area boasts majestic, scrub-clad pinnacles.

Sea eagle, Phangnga Bay

Phangnga is, in fact, the most spectacular remnant of the once mighty Tenasserim Mountains, which still form a spine through Thailand to China.

Protected Mangroves
The heavily silted, northern end of Phangnga Bay, where several rivers meet the sea, is Thailand's largest and best preserved area of mangrove (see pp340–41).

Undercut Cliffs
The action of waves erodes the base of the stacks at a rate of about 1 m (3 ft) every 5,000 years.

Caves form quickly at sea level. Some are exposed only at low tide.

Fissures allow water to penetrate and erode the limestone.

Calcite Deposits in Caves
Within most caves are stalagmites, stalactites and other structures formed from dripping calcite.

CROSS SECTION OF TYPICAL STACKS IN PHANGNGA BAY

The limestone landscape at Phangnga Bay is known by geologists as drowned karstland. Karst is characterized by its internal drainage system, whereby water finds its way into the interior of the limestone through fissures, then erodes the rock from within. A riddle of tunnels is typical; chasms and vast sea chambers *(hongs)* are also common at Phangnga.

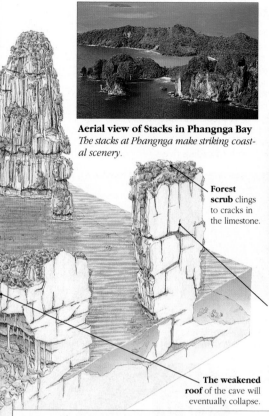

Aerial view of Stacks in Phangnga Bay
The stacks at Phangnga make striking coast-al scenery.

VISITORS' CHECKLIST

Phangnga province. ℹ *TAT, Phuket (076) 212213.* 🚌 *from Phuket or Krabi to Phangnga town, then hire a long-tail; or join ferry tour from Phuket or Phangnga.*

Forest scrub clings to cracks in the limestone.

Isolated Stacks
There are a number of sheer, thin stacks in the bay. These columns of rock are splinters of limestone that have been heavily eroded by the sea.

The weakened roof of the cave will eventually collapse.

HOW PHANGNGA BAY WAS FORMED

Hard and soft corals

Deposits of calcite from dead coral build up.

130 million years ago *the area was under-water and part of a vast coral reef. Calcite deposits from dead coral built up in thick layers.*

Calcite turns into limestone over millions of years.

Fissures form from rain action.

Gaps occur where calcite de-posits are uneven.

75 million years ago *plate movements pushed these deposits, which had turned to limestone, out of the sea. The inelastic rock ruptured.*

Meltwater from ice caps begins to flood Phangnga.

The gap erodes into a cave.

20,000 years ago, *at the end of the last Ice Age, the sea level rose, flooding Phangnga. Wave and tide action accelerated the process of erosion.*

Wave action sculpts the stacks.

The cave is much larger.

8,000 years ago *the sea reached its highest level, about 4 m (13 ft) above its present height, sculpting a shelf, visible on most of the stacks.*

Exploring Phangnga Bay

MOST BOAT TOURS of the best known sights, such as the unique fishing village built over water in the shadow of Ko Panyi, and "James Bond Island", as well as a number of

Seashell, Phangnga

fascinating caves. Some of the eerie caverns contain prehistoric paintings and Buddhist shrines; others are home to bats. Canoes and small boats allow access to narrow mangrove channels and tunnels through the rock leading to open sea chambers *(hongs)*. The karst scenery continues inland to the east, where cliffs soar above hidden valleys with cascading rivers.

Tham Lot is a 50-m (165-ft) long sea tunnel through limestone with stalactites hanging from its roof.

• Phangnga town

★ Panyi Fishing Village
About 120 Muslim families live in this village, which is built on stilts above the water. Islanders sell fish sauce, dried prawns and shrimp paste.

Suwan Kuha Cave (Wat Tham)
A reclining Buddha, tiny shrines and chedis *are found among stalactites and stalagmites in this cave temple.*

Ko Phanak contains a number of sea *hongs* with vegetation-clad walls and marooned snakes and monkeys.

★ James Bond Island
This island (Ko Khao Phing Kan) and nearby Ko Tapu ("nail island") were made famous in a James Bond film. The two islands are the highlight of numerous boat tours.

Ko Hong
This network of lagoons, chasms and tunnels is best explored in a small boat such as a sea canoe (see p445). Parts of the island are accessible only at low tide.

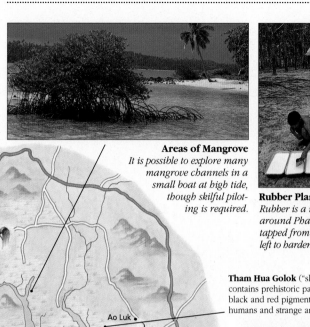

Areas of Mangrove
It is possible to explore many mangrove channels in a small boat at high tide, though skilful piloting is required.

Rubber Plantations
Rubber is a major industry around Phangnga. Latex, tapped from rubber trees, is left to harden in shallow trays.

Tham Hua Golok ("skull cave") contains prehistoric paintings, in black and red pigment, of humans and strange animals.

Ao Luk

Tanboke Koranee National Park
In Ao Luk district, this national park is known for its series of miniature waterfalls amid beautiful limestone scenery.

0 kilometres 10

0 miles 5

STAR SIGHTS

★ **Panyi Fishing Village**

★ **James Bond Island**

JAMES BOND AND THE ISLAND HIDEOUT

In the film *The Man With the Golden Gun* (1974), James Bond (Roger Moore) comes to the Orient in search of the villain Scaramanga (Christopher Lee). Bond is eventually taken to Scaramanga's hideout, an island just off China. In fact, the island seen is Ko Khao Phing Kan in Phangnga Bay; the sheer rock nearby, containing the secret weapon, is Ko Tapu.

Scaramanga and Bond

The extraordinary Ko Tapu ("nail island") in Phangnga Bay ▷

Khao Phanom Bencha National Park ❼

อุทยานแห่งชาติเขาพนมเบญจา

Krabi province. Park HQ off Hwy 4, 20 km (12.5 miles) N of Krabi. **TAT, Phuket (076) 211036; Forestry Dept (02) 579 0529.** *Krabi, then local bus.*

THIS 500-SQ KM (193-sq mile) national park of mostly tropical monsoon forest is named for the five-shouldered peak of Khao Phanom Bencha, which rises to a height of 1,350 m (4,400 ft).

Despite illegal logging and poaching, the park's rainforest still holds at least 156 species of bird, including the white-crowned hornbill and the striped wren-babbler. Among the 32 mammal species catalogued are the Asiatic black bear, Malaysian sun bear, clouded leopard, wild boar, binturong and serow.

The thundering **Huay To waterfall** and **Huay Sadeh waterfall** are located less than 3 km (2 miles) from the park headquarters. Park attendants can arrange treks to the summit. The climb is difficult but rewarding – from the top there are spectacular views over the surrounding forest.

Clouded leopard in Khao Phanom Bencha

Ao Nang ❽

อ่าวนาง

18 km (11 miles) W of Krabi town, Krabi province. **TAT, Krabi (075) 612740.** *Krabi, then songthaew.*

FROM NOVEMBER TO APRIL, this scenic bay becomes a popular holiday base for tourists who are seeking a less hectic atmosphere than Phuket.

Until the early 1980s, fishing and coconut and rubber plantations were the mainstay for the Muslim villagers at Ao Nang. Today the 2-km (1-mile) sandy beach sports a growing number of hotels, seafood restaurants, scuba diving outlets and canoe tour companies. Visitors can hire a sea canoe to paddle in the turquoise waters in the shadow of the 100-m (330-ft) rocky eastern end of the bay. Nearby is uncrowded Pai Plong beach.

In season, Ao Nang is a pleasant base for day trips by long-tail boat to the striking **Railae-Phra Nang headland**, located 3 km (2 miles) to the southeast. Its sheer limestone cliffs, pure white sand and emerald sea attract many visitors.

Hat Tham Phra Nang, west of the Phra Nang headland, is the most attractive beach in the area. Rising above it is a high

Strolling along a beach on Ko Poda, a small island near Ao Nang

limestone cliff into which **Tham Phra Nang Nok** ("outer princess cave") is carved. Inside is a shrine to the lost spirit of a princess, Phra Nang, whose ship allegedly sank near the beach in the 4th century BC. Today, local fishermen place offerings of incense, fruit and water at the shrine to bring them a plentiful catch. Inside the cliff is **Sa Phra Nang**, a lagoon reached by a steep path.

Flanking Phra Nang are the white sand beaches of East and West Railae, the latter being much finer. There are boats from West Railae and Phra Nang beaches to **Ko Poda**, southwest of Phra Nang, where striped tiger fish can be fed by hand from the shallow shore, and **Ko Hua Khwan**, or Chicken Island, located further south. Both islands offer excellent diving and snorkelling.

On **Ko Hong**, 25 km (16 miles) northwest of Ao Nang, the prized nests of the edible-nest swiftlet (*see p331*) are collected from the island's intricate network of caves.

The headquarters of the **Phi Phi-Hat Nopparat Thara National Marine Park**, to the west of Ao Nang, overlook stunning beaches. The park covers an area of 390 sq km (150 sq miles), which includes Ko Phi Phi (*see pp362–3*), Ko Mai Phai and Ko Yung (also known as Ko Mosquito).

❌ Phi Phi-Hat Nopparat Thara National Marine Park Park HQ 3 km (2 miles) W of Ao Nang. **Forestry Dept (02) 579 0529 (inc bungalow bookings).** *Krabi, then songthaew.*

Idyllic bay within the Phi Phi-Hat Nopparat Thara National Marine Park

Krabi ❾
กระบี่

Krabi province. 🏛 21,000. ⬛ ⬛
ℹ TAT, Uttarakit Rd, Krabi (075)
612740. ⬛ daily.

THIS SMALL FISHING TOWN, the capital of beautiful Krabi province, has an important role as the ferry embarkation point for islands such as Ko Lanta to the south, Ko Phi Phi to the southwest, and the beaches around Ao Nang to the west. Set on the banks of the Krabi Estuary, the town takes its name from a sword, or *krabi*, allegedly discovered nearby. It is surrounded by towering limestone outcrops, similar to those in Phangnga Bay *(see pp354–7)*, which have become the symbol of Krabi province. Among the most notable are **Kanap Nam twin limestone peaks**, which stand like sentinels at each side of the river. To the east, the town is flanked by mangrove-lined shorelines. These outcrops and mangroves can be toured by renting a long-tail boat from the Chao Fa pier in the centre of town.

ENVIRONS: Located 8 km (5 miles) north of town is **Wat Tham Sua** ("tiger cave temple"), named after a rock formation that resembles a tiger paw. It is one of the most renowned forest *wats* in Southern Thailand, with the main hall built inside a cave. Here, meditation is practised in peaceful surroundings.

Bathers enjoying a hot spring spa in the forest near Khlong Thom

A circular path in the nearby forest dell offers a pleasant walk among towering, buttressed trees and *kutis*, simple huts inhabited by monks and nuns. A 300-m (985-ft) high staircase leads to a large Buddha image and Buddha Footprint on top of the cliff. From here there are panoramic views of the province.

Buddha image on the cliff top by Wat Tham Sua, Krabi province

Khlong Thom ❿
คลองท่อม

Krabi province. 🏛 55,000. ⬛ ℹ
TAT, Phuket (076) 211036. ⬛ daily.

SOME 40 KM (25 MILES) south of Krabi town, Khlong Thom is known locally for the small museum within **Wat Khlong Thom**. The temple's abbot has assembled an array of archaeological icons and weapons from the area. One of the most interesting exhibits is a collection of distinctive beads called *lukbat*.

A maritime port, Kuan Lukbat, was once located on the site of Khlong Thom. From the 5th century AD onwards, the port was used by foreign merchants and emissaries crossing the peninsula to Nakhon Si Thammarat and Surat Thani *(see pp336–7)*. Few traders wanted to sail through the treacherous, pirate-infested Straits of Malacca, so they travelled overland instead.

ENVIRONS: A bumpy 12-km (7.5-mile) ride inland from Khlong Thom leads to a natural hot spring in the forest, which is ideal for bathing.

About 8 km (5 miles) further on is the rewarding **Tung Tieo forest trail** in Khao No Chuchi lowland forest. The signposted paths lead through this protected area, skirting emerald pools along the way. The surrounding woodland is the only known area in the world where the colourful ground-dwelling Gurney's pitta survives. Previously, this bird was thought to be extinct.

CLIMBING KRABI'S STACKS

Krabi and Ko Phi Phi are the only places in Thailand where organized rock-climbing takes place. The honeycombed limestone stacks around the Phra Nang headland, near Krabi, and Ko Phi Phi offer challenging conditions and attract rock climbers from around the world. Only the south of France is said to offer such arduous climbs. They vary in difficulty from an easy "4" according to the French system, to a very difficult "8b". Climbers can cool off with a swim between climbs.

Climber on 'Thaiwand Wall', Tham Phra Nang near Ao Nang

Ko Phi Phi ⑪

เกาะเสม็ด

Krabi province. 1,200. from Phuket or Krabi. TAT, Phuket (076) 212213.

SPECTACULAR Ko Phi Phi, pronounced "PP", 40 km (25 miles) south of Krabi town, is in fact two separate islands: Phi Phi Don and Phi Phi Ley. Both islands belong to the **Phi Phi-Hat Nopparat Thara National Park**, which also takes in part of the mainland near Ao Nang *(see p360)*.

The islands are famed for their spectacular landscapes. Rock climbers are attracted by the breathtaking cliffs *(see p361)*, with tall sheer walls of limestone rising to 314 m (1,030 ft) on Phi Phi Don, and 374 m (1,230 ft) on Phi Phi Ley. Nature lovers, meanwhile, find a haven in the islands' transparent seas and coral beds, which are home to a wide range of sea life.

Phi Phi Don

The two sections of Phi Phi Don, the larger of the two islands, are linked by a 1-km (1,100-yd) isthmus of sand. Here stands the island's original Muslim fishing village, Ban Ton Sai, now enveloped by an ever-expanding belt of bungalows, cafés, exchange booths and hotels. Since development began on Phi Phi Don following the arrival of the first visitors in the 1970s, the island has unashamedly given itself up to

Ban Laem Tong

Laem Tong

PHI PHI DON

Ban Ton Sai

Hat Yao

Krabi

Phuket

0 kilometres 2

0 miles 1

KEY

🏖 Beach

🏄 Water sports

⛴ Ferry service

--- Footpath

☀ Viewpoint

Viking Cave

PHI PHI LEY

Ao Maya

tourism. However, there is still plenty of natural beauty to enjoy here. A pleasant one-hour coastal walk from Ban Ton Sai leads to Hat Yao ("long

beach"), with tantalizing white sands, vibrant offshore marine life and unhindered views to the soaring flanks of Phi Phi Ley, 4 km (2.5 miles) away.

It is also worth climbing the steep trails on Phi Phi Don's two massifs, which afford wonderful vistas over the island. The eastern route is well signposted and the least strenuous.

Superb coral beds at Hin Pae off Hat Yao, and at Ko Phai ("bamboo island"), to the northeast of Phi Phi Don, provide some of the best diving and snorkelling in Thailand.

To the north is Ban Laem Tong. This village's sea gypsy population still survives on fish caught in the isolated coves of nearby Laem Tong.

A typical view of Ko Phi Phi's stunning scenery, now enjoyed by large numbers of holidaymakers

One of Ko Phi Phi's enticing, dazzling, white-sand beaches

Phi Phi Ley

In contrast to Phi Phi Don, Phi Phi Ley remains uninhabited and unspoilt. Boats from Phi Phi Don bring visitors on day trips to see the paintings in Viking Cave. Another feature of the cave are the nests of the edible-nest swiftlet *(see p331)*, which are used in bird's nest soup. Agile collectors climb rickety bamboo scaffolding to reach the nests, which are so valuable that the caves are protected by armed guards. In a bid to halt the illegal trade of the nests, staying overnight on the island is prohibited. There is excellent snorkelling at the coral reefs of Ao Maya, a bay in the southwest corner of the island.

ENVIRONS: Many of the islands in the area shelter endangered bird species such as the white-bellied sea eagle and the *mukimaki* flycatcher.

Ko Lanta ⑫

เกาะเสม็ด

Krabi province. 👥 *23,000.* ⛴ *from Krabi or Bo Muang.* ℹ *TAT, Phuket (076) 212213.*

Close to the mainland in the southeast corner of Krabi province, Ko Lanta is a group of 52 islands, 15 of which belong to the Ko Lanta National Marine Park. The park is home to many animals, including lemurs, langurs, civets,

CAVE PAINTINGS OF THE ANDAMAN ISLANDS

There are many prehistoric paintings in Phangnga *(see pp354–9)* and Krabi *(see p361)* provinces, especially in caves on the Andaman Islands. Most are stylized red and black outlines depicting human forms, hands, fish, and, in some cases, broken line patterns which are thought to have had symbolic value. Some of the unidentifiable images are of monstrous beings – half-human, half sea-creatures – which still mystify archaeologists. Such paintings may have been drawn as part of magical-religious rituals to bring good fortune for hunting, fishing, food gathering and tribal battles.

Many paintings can be reliably dated to Neolithic times, but the drawings of junk-like boats at Phangnga Bay and in the misleadingly named Viking Cave on Phi Phi Ley may be only a few hundred years old.

Paintings of boats in a cave at Phangnga Bay

mouse deer and over 100 types of bird. Most of the wildlife is on the smaller, remoter islands.

The ramshackle wooden port of Ban Sala Dan is the gateway to **Ko Lanta Yai**, a predominantly Muslim fishing island. Some 25 km (15 miles) long, this is the main island in the archipelago. It is covered with undulating forested hills sweeping down to numerous west-facing sandy bays, and, although it cannot match Ko Phi Phi for scenery, it is a good alternative for those seeking solitude.

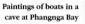

A rare white-bellied sea eagle

Monkey and lizard footprints are still more common on its beaches than human prints.

The Laem Kaw Kwang headland in the northwest of the island gives views across to Ko Phi Phi. At the southern tip, a 3-km (2-mile) coastal footpath leads to a solar-powered lighthouse on a steep promontory beside the park headquarters.

Sea gypsies inhabit the nearby village, Ban Sangka-u. They are renowned for their colourful rituals, such as the *loi rua* ceremony. As part of the festivities, a 2-m (6-ft) replica boat is sent out to sea to banish the ill fate built up throughout the past year.

Bungalow accommodation on the unspoilt island of Ko Lanta

DEEP SOUTH

THE DEEP SOUTH OF THAILAND *has more in common with Malaysia than with the distant Thai heartland to the north. Many visitors come here to experience the region's distinct culture, dialect and food, and to learn about the local history and religion. The scenery, with spectacular mountains in the interior of the peninsula and unspoilt beaches and islands on the west coast, is equally alluring.*

In many ways Thailand's Deep South doesn't feel like Thailand at all. The influence of Indian, Chinese and Malaysian culture can be seen in the region's architecture and ethnic make-up. Skin tones are noticeably darker than the rest of the country. The population speaks an unusually intonated dialect of Thai, and Yawi, a language related to Malay and Indonesian. Also, the food is spicier, characterized by often bitter curries laced with turmeric.

South of Songkhla, especially near the coasts, most people are Muslim, and the minarets of mosques replace the gilded peaks of Buddhist temples. Indeed, Pattani, an important Malay kingdom in the 17th century, is still a centre of Islamic scholarship. Nevertheless, Wat Mahathat in Nakhon Si Thammarat, the South's cultural capi-

tal, is one of the most revered Buddhist temples in Thailand. Also, numerous Hindu shrines and customs, not least the Hindu-inspired *manohra* dance, are evidence of Nakhon's role as a major religious centre on the ocean trade routes between India and China. Modern Songkhla has become the educational capital of the South. Nearby Hat Yai has grown from an agricultural service and railway town into an important shopping and entertainment centre. However, tourism is still low-key around the west coast's superb beaches and on the stunning islands of the Tarutao National Marine Park. The wild interior is even less developed. A few tigers, elephants and Negrito tribes still roam the South's forested mountains which, until the mid-1970s, sheltered bands of Communist guerrillas.

Two Muslim girls – the Islamic religion is strong in the Deep South

◁ **Detail from the staircase to Wat Pha Kho, Sathing Phra**

Exploring the Deep South

THE EASTERN LOWLANDS of the Deep South are among the most fertile in the country. Year-round heat and high humidity are ideal conditions for fast-growing coffee beans, pineapples, cashews, rambutans, and oil and rubber palms. The South's commercial capital, Hat Yai, is in this region, but Nakhon Si Thammarat and Songkhla are the cultural centres. In the west, the Trang coast and Tarutao archipelago both have fine sand beaches, spectacular corals and few visitors by virtue of undeveloped tourist facilities. The east coast offers fewer natural attractions, but charming towns such as Songkhla are well worth visiting. The three provinces south of Hat Yai – Yala, Pattani and Narathiwat – are strongly influenced by Muslim Malaysia. The differences in language, cuisine and religion are obvious even to casual visitors. Densely forested mountains near the Malaysian border shelter tigers, elephants and other wildlife.

Minaret of Friday Mosque, Nakhon Si Thammarat

SIGHTS AT A GLANCE

Typically deserted beach in the Tarutao archipelago

GETTING AROUND

Hat Yai is the main transport hub of the Deep South. The 930-km (580-mile) journey to Hat Yai from Bangkok takes about 14 hours by coach and 17 hours by train. Most of the other big towns have coach and rail connections. Highways 4 and 41 are the major north-south roads. Most roads are paved, and local buses run to many sights. There are six small regional airports. Many Singaporeans and Malaysians visit the area on organized tours; most other visitors are independent travellers. A hire car is the easiest way to get around. The east coast islands can be reached from Pak Meng, Pak Bara and Kantang.

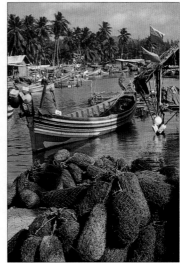

Fishing village in Narathiwat province

● SATHING PHRA

8 SONGKHLA

9 HAT YAI

KEY

▭▭	Motorway
▭▭	Major road
▭▭	Minor road
▭▭	Scenic route
▭▭	River
☆	Viewpoint

PATTANI **12**

13 YALA

BACHO NATIONAL PARK

15 NARATHIWAT

Alor Setar (Malaysia)

TAK BAI

SUNGAI KO-LOK

0 kilometres   50

0 miles   25

PIYA MIT COMMUNIST CAMP

14 BETONG

SEE ALSO

• *Where to Stay* p405

• *Where to Eat* p429

Nakhon Si Thammarat ❶

นครศรีธรรมราช

Silver figure

ALTHOUGH NAKHON SI THAMMARAT features on few tourist itineraries, the most historic town in the South is a lively centre with several attractions. Under the name of Ligor, it is thought to have been the capital of Tambralinga, a peninsular kingdom prior to the 7th century. From the 7th–13th centuries it was an important city of the Srivijaya Empire *(see pp336–7)*. During this time, it became a religious centre with the Sanskrit name Nagara Sri Dhammaraja, meaning "city of the sacred dharma king". Many Indian traders settled in Nakhon – as the town is popularly known – and Hindu shrines are a feature here, together with *nang talung* shadow puppet plays *(see p373)* and intricately etched nielloware *(see p433)*.

The relaxing way to take in Nakhon's sights

🗿 Wat Mahathat

วัดมหาธาตุ
Rachadamnoen Rd, 2 km (1 mile) S of railway station. ⬜ *daily.*

Wat Mahathat is one of Thailand's most sacred temples. Although its age is disputed, the *wat* is thought to be at least 1,000 years old. The present *chedi* dates from the 13th century and was supposedly built to house relics of the Buddha which were brought

here from Sri Lanka. It is 77 m (255 ft) high and topped with gold variously estimated to weigh between 600 and 1,000 kg (1,350 to 2,200 lbs).

The Wihan Luang chapel has an intricately painted 18th-century ceiling, although the Wihan Phra Ma hall is perhaps more impressive. It features an elaborate, emerald-inlay door from the Sukhothai period, carved with the figures of

Phrom and Vishnu. A small museum displays an evocative but unlabelled selection of archaeological finds, jewellery and religious sculptures including Dvaravati pieces from the 6th to 13th centuries.

🏛 Nakhon Si Thammarat National Museum

พิพิธภัณฑสถานแห่งชาตินครศรีธรรมราช
Rachadamnoen Rd, 2.5 km (1.5 miles) S of railway station. ☎ *(075) 324480.* ⬜ *Wed–Sun.* ⬛ *public hols.* ✍

The centrepiece of this branch of the National Museum is the 9th-century statue of Vishnu in the Pala style of South India. It was found in the base of a tree in Kapong district near Takua Pha in Phangnga, then a major entrepôt for Indian migrants colonizing the South.

Two rare bronze drums made by the Dong Son people of northern Vietnam are another highlight. The Thai gallery displays religious art from Dvaravati and Srivijayan periods to the Rattanakosin era. Look out for Buddha images in the distinctive local Sing style, characterized by stumpy features and animated faces.

🎭 Shadow Puppet Theatre (Suchart House)

บ้านหนังตะลุงสุชาติ
110/18 Si Thammasok Soi 3. ⬜ *daily.*

The *nang talung* workshop of Suchart Subsin keeps alive a uniquely Southeast Asian form of entertainment that is in danger of dying out in Thailand. Visitors can watch the puppets being cut from leather and buy the finished product. Sometimes Suchart puts on an impromptu show.

The gold-topped *chedi* of Nakhon's splendid Wat Mahathat

⚑ Ho Phra I-suan (Shiva)
หอพระอิศวร

Rachadamnoen Rd. ◯ daily.

In the hall of this shrine is a 1-m (3-ft) *shivalinga*, a phallic image of the Hindu god Shiva, which may date back to the 6th century AD. The worship of Shiva was a potent force in the early peninsular city states of the first millennium AD.

⚑ Ho Phra Buddha Sing
หอพระพุทธสิหิงค์

Rachadamnoen Rd. ◯ Wed–Sun.

The Phra Buddha Sing is one of Thailand's most revered images. The replica kept in this shrine is of an original cast in Sri Lanka in AD 157 and brought to Nakhon at the end of the 13th century. Local

Ho Phra Buddha Sing, home of the sacred Phra Buddha Sing image

artisans put their characteristic stamp on the Buddha by giving it a half smile, a rounder face and a full chest. It is similar to Buddha images in Wat Phra Sing in Chiang Mai and the National Museum in Bangkok.

⚑ Ho Vishnu Phra Narai
หอพระนารายณ์

Rachadamnoen Rd. ◯ daily.

Five *lingas* (phallic sculptures) discovered on the site of this shrine may date from before AD 1000. They are now in the Wat Mahathat Museum.

🏮 Tha Chang Road
ถนนท่าช้าง

The tradition of gold and silver shops along this road dates from 1804, when migrants from Saiburi district moved to Nakhon. Only skilled gold- and silversmiths were allowed to settle in this area, to the west of Sanam Na Muang parade ground.

Typical nielloware pot

⛩ North Gate
กำแพงเมืองเก่า

Just E of Rachadamnoen Rd.

The ancient city wall originally contained an area 400 m by 2,320 m (440 yds by 2,550 yds). The red brick North Gate is a reconstruction of the original.

⚑ Wat Sao Thong
วัดเสาทอง

Rachadamnoen Rd. ◯ daily.

Adjoining the compound of Wang Tawan Tok temple, this *wat's* main attraction is the Southern Thai wooden house, started in 1888 and finished in 1901. It is actually three houses joined together and features delicately carved wooden door panels, gables and window surrounds.

The Architects' Association of Thailand gave a conservation award to the building in 1993.

🏪 Bovorn Bazaar
ตลาดบวร

Rachadamnoen Rd. ◯ daily.

The city centre bazaar is a peaceful courtyard and popular meeting place with cafés, bars and two good restaurants.

NAKHON SI THAMMARAT TOWN CENTRE

Bovorn Bazaar ①
Ho Phra Buddha Sing ⑦
Ho Phra I-suan (Shiva) ⑤
Ho Vishnu Phra Narai ⑥
North Gate ④
Shadow Puppet Theatre ⑧
Tha Chang Road ③
Wat Mahathat ⑨
Wat Sao Thong ②

KEY

🚉 Railway station

🚌 Coach station

🛈 Tourist information

⚑ Wat

0 metres 500
0 yards 500

Lush lowland scenery at Hat Chao Mai National Park

Trang's Andaman Islands ❷

หมู่เกาะอันดามันจังหวัดตรัง

Trang province. 🛥 *long-tail from Kantang to Ko Muk, Ko Kradan and Ko Libong, and from Pak Meng to Ko Hai and Ko Muk.* 🛈 *TAT, Hat Yai (074) 243747; Forestry Dept (02) 579 0529.*

Tourist development has barely touched the 50 or so small islands off the coast of Trang province. For the moment at least, their stunning sands, pristine corals and rich bird and marine life remain the preserve of a handful of solitude seekers.

Forested **Ko Hai** is the island most easily reached from Pak Meng on the mainland and offers the widest choice of accommodation. There are wonderful beaches, particularly on the east coast, and magnificent coral offshore.

Ko Muk, 8 km (5 miles) southeast of Ko Hai, is best known for Tham Morakhot ("emerald cave") on its west coast. A long limestone tunnel leads from the sea to an inland beach surrounded by vegetation-clad cliffs. It can be entered only by boat at low tide.

Arguably the most beautiful of Trang's Andaman islands, **Ko Kradan** is also one of the most remote. White sand beaches and good snorkelling are the major attractions.

Further south and close to the mainland, **Ko Libong** is the largest of the islands. It is famed for its spectacular birdlife, which is at its best during March and April.

Hat Chao Mai National Park ❸

อุทยานแห่งชาติหาดเจ้าไหม

Trang province. 🛈 *TAT, Hat Yai (074) 243747; Forestry Dept (02) 579 0529 (inc bungalow bookings).* 🚌 *from Trang to Kantang, then songthaew.*

Around 50 km (31 miles) west of Trang town, Hat Chao Mai National Park has a varied coastal geography. Mangrove creeks are interspersed with coastal karsts, and hidden beaches accessed through caves around Yao and Yongling beaches. Seafood dining under casuarina trees lining Pak Meng beach in the north of the park is popular.

***Tuk-tuk* in Trang town**

This is also the main departure point for boat tours around Trang's islands, nine of which are also under park control. Dugongs can sometimes be spotted between the mainland and the islands.

Trang ❹

ตรัง

Trang province. 👫 *80,000.* ✈ 🚉 🏣
🛈 *TAT, Hat Yai (074) 243747.*
🏪 *daily.* 🎉 *Vegetarian Festival (Oct).*

Trang has been a trading centre since at least the 1st century AD. It grew to prosperity between the 7th and 13th centuries during the Srivijaya period and remains an important commercial town today. Rubber, palm oil and fishing are the mainstays of its economy. Tourism has not yet made much impact, although this may change if Trang's Andaman islands start to be more intensively developed.

The town has a strong Chinese character (and good Chinese restaurants) as a result of an influx of immigrant labour in the latter half of the 19th century. Trang's Vegetarian Festival, mirroring its better-known counterpart on Phuket (*see p350*), is renowned for the intensity of its ascetic rites which include body piercing.

The **Rubber Museum** displays tools used in making the pressed rubber sheets which can be seen hanging to dry outside plantation houses all over Southern Thailand. It also explains the right and wrong ways to tap rubber.

A monument to Khaw Sim Bee Na-Ranong, the first governor of Trang from 1890 to 1901, stands in the Fitness Park at the eastern end of Phatthalung Road. The statue attracts many merit-makers, especially on

Tranquil landing pier on the estuary of the Trang River

10 April, the day dedicated to the former governor. A few minutes' walk away, the Clarion MP Hotel is notable for being partially built in the shape of an ocean liner.

Rubber Museum
Trang Non-Formal Education Centre, Phatthalung Rd. *(075) 218440.* ○ Mon–Fri.

ENVIRONS: Trang province was dependent on tin mining until the first rubber tree seedlings were brought into Thailand from Indonesia and British Malaya around 1901. The first rubber tree in the country can still be seen in Kantang, 22 km (14 miles) southwest of Trang, near a small museum dedicated to Khaw Sim Bee Na-Ranong. Boats run from Kantang to many of the nearby islands.

Dense rainforest on the steep slopes of the Banthat Mountains

Slender rubber trees in one of Trang province's many plantations

Banthat Mountains ❺
เขาบรรทัด

Trang province. ▮ TAT, Hat Yai (074) 243747; Forestry Dept (02) 579 0529.

THE VERDANT Banthat Mountains, which run down the peninsula as far as the Malaysian border, mark the eastern boundary of Trang province.

The forested higher elevations of the mountains, which rise to 1,350 m (4,430 ft) at Khao Ron, are one of the few places in South Thailand where the Sakai tribe still maintain their hunter-gatherer existence. These ethnically unique Negrito people speak a language related to Mon-Khmer. Traditionally they live in groups of 10 to 30 in simple lean-to leaf and grass shelters near running water, and hunt with poison blow darts. Forest clearance and exposure to lowland culture has led to some Sakai becoming agricultural labourers.

The mountains are also home to many amphibian and reptile species, such as dwarf geckos, wrinkled frogs and slender toads, and rare bird species, including hornbills, spiderhunters, hawk cuckoos and the narcissus flycatcher. A worthwhile excursion is to the **Khao Chong Nature and Wildlife Study Centre**, 20 km (12 miles) east of Trang off Highway 4. It contains an impressive open zoo and two waterfalls. Just to the south, a bird sanctuary at **Khlong Lam-chan** has a reservoir which attracts many species of duck.

The minor road heading south along the western flanks of the Banthat Mountains gives access to a series of spectacular waterfalls, caves and shady picnic places. Highlights include the huge **Ton Tay falls**, the spray rainbow that often forms by mid-afternoon over the **Sairung falls**, and the stalactites and stalagmites of **Tham Chang Hai** ("lost elephant cave") near Muansari village in Nayong district.

Much further south, and easily accessible from Satun, is the spectacular Thale Ban National Park (see p376).

DUGONGS
The once common dugong, or sea cow, was brought to the brink of extinction in Thai waters by hunting and by accidental drowning in commercial fishing nets. Today numbers are slowly increasing. The area around the Trang islands of the Andaman Sea is one of the few places they can be spotted. These herbivores feed on the seagrass beds around Ko Libong and the Trang Estuary. They grow up to 3 m (10 ft) long and can weigh 400 kg (880 lbs). In local folklore, the tears of a dugong act as a love potion.

The dugong – a rare, gentle giant now protected by law

Phatthalung ⑥

พัทลุง

Phatthalung province. 🏛 *38,000.*
🚉 🚌 ⛴ ℹ *TAT, Nakhon Si*
Thammarat (075) 346515. 🛍 *daily.*
🎭 *Phon Lak Phra Competition*
(3 days in Oct or Nov).

O NE OF THE FEW rice-growing areas in Southern
Thailand, Phatthalung province has earned a steady income from the crop throughout its history. It is better
known, though, as the place
where *nang talung* (shadow
puppetry) was first performed
in Thailand – the name *nang
talung* may even derive from
Phatthalung. This theatre, related to Indonesian shadow
puppetry, is performed mainly in Phatthalung and Nakhon
Si Thammarat provinces.

Phatthalung town was established in the 19th century
during the reign of Rama III
(see pp60–1). Today's modern
town is set out in a grid and is
surrounded by limestone hills
to the north and the fertile
Thale Luang lake to the east.

Phatthalung lies between
two attractive peaks: **Khao
Ok Talu** ("punctured chest
mountain"), and **Khao Hua
Taek** ("broken head mountain") to the north-
west. According to local
legend, these two mountains,
"the mistress" and "the wife",
fought over Khao Muang (the
male mountain), located to
the north. It is said that they
still nurse their battle scars
from this confrontation. In
fact, Khao Ok Talu has a
naturally occurring tunnel in
its peak (the punctured chest),

Khao Ok Talu ("punctured chest mountain") overlooking Phatthalung

while Khao Hua Taek has a
dent in its peak (the broken
head). In the latter are the
Buddhist grottoes of **Wat Kuha
Sawan**. Inside the lower cave
are statues of monks and the
Buddha, while the upper cave
has views of Khao Ok Talu
and most of Phatthalung and
the surrounding area.

ENVIRONS: Lush rice fields surround Phatthalung. At **Lam
Pam**, a small fishing village
6 km (4 miles) east of Phat-

thalung, slow-flowing canals
empty into the large Thale
Luang inland sea. The breezy
but peaceful area at Sansuk
beach has a few restaurants
serving good seafood. Boats
can be hired to the nearby
islands, Ko Si and Ko Ha.

Two km (1 mile) before
Lam Pam is **Wat Wang**, Phatthalung's oldest temple,
thought to have been founded
at the same time as the town.
Next to the *chedi* is a *bot*
whose walls are decorated
with faded murals depicting
Buddhist and Ramakien *(see
pp36–7)* themes.

The restored **Governor's
Palace** occupies a peaceful
site nearby. Built in 1889, the
palace comprises two individual buildings. The outer teak
structure, nearer the road,
functioned as living quarters
for the governor's family. The
main building, beside the river,
is built around a courtyard
with a large tree.

🏠 **Governor's Palace**
Hwy 4047, 4 km (2 miles) E of
Phatthalung. ◯ *8:30–4pm daily.*

The elevated structures of the Governor's Palace in Lam Pam

Thale Noi Waterfowl Park 7

ทะเลน้อย

32 km (20 miles) NE of Phatthalung, Phatthalung province. ▮ TAT, Nakhon Si Thammarat (075) 346515; Forestry Dept, Bangkok (02) 579 0529. ▭ from Phatthalung, then hire a long-tail. ◯ 8:30–4pm daily.

Long-tail boat at Thale Noi Waterfowl Park

THE LARGEST wetland bird reserve in Thailand, this park serves as a resting and feeding ground for thousands of exotic migratory birds flying to Sumatra and Australia to escape winter in Siberia and China. The best way to explore the watery reserve, covering 30 sq km (12 sq miles), is by long-tail boat, which can be hired from Phatthalung for a two-hour round trip.

With its reeds and water vines, Thale Noi has the appearance of a swamp, but it is predominantly a freshwater lake, with a depth of up to 1.5 m (5 ft). Only in periods of high southerly winds does the lake become brackish, when saltier water from Thale Luang and Songkhla

White-throated kingfisher

Lake to the south is pushed northwards. Dawn is the best time for bird-watching, especially between the months of January and April. Many of the 150 or so species of birds who visit the park arrive during this time, swelling its population to as much as 100,000. In May the population begins to shrink, and from October to December there are only small numbers of native species left. A viewing platform in the middle of the lake is the ideal place for bird-watching.

Among the birds to be seen at the park are the purple swamp hen, bronze-winged jaçana, whistling teal, white-throated kingfisher, the long-legged *nok i-kong*, and the rarer white ibis and grey heron.

One of the major forms of vegetation in the park is *don kok*, a reed which the *nok i-kong* use to build "platforms" over the water for nesting.

Around 100 families live along the shores of Thale Noi, mostly in raised wooden houses. They make a living from fishing and by weaving bulrush reeds into mats.

SHADOW PUPPETS – NANG TALUNG

Nang talung is the popular Thai version of shadow puppetry, an art form that originated as early as 400 BC in Asia. *Nang talung* performances, which begin late at night and last several hours, are still an essential part of village life in the Deep South. It is the task of a single person, the *nai nag* (puppet master), to create the whole show. Sitting behind an illuminated screen, he manoeuvres up to six puppets per scene. The puppets, about 50 cm (20 in) high, are made from leather, or *nang*, which is carved, coloured and rendered movable by joints. The changing tone of the puppeteer's voice differentiates between the characters, while a band of musicians adds tension to the plot. While the more formal *nang yai* is based on the Ramakien (*see pp36–7*), *nang talung* takes its inspiration from everyday life, with themes such as family problems. Each story is created by the *nai nag* and includes easily recognizable characters, such as comic figures with exaggerated features. Once a year the apprentices commemorate the puppet master in a *wai kru* ("paying respect to the teacher") ceremony.

Shadow puppet of a Ramakien character

A puppeteer, sitting behind a screen, using his skills to perform *nang talung*

The audience's view of *nang talung*

Songkhla ❽

สงขลา

Songkhla province. 👥 80,000.
✈ 🚌 at Hat Yai, 36 km (22 miles)
SW of Songkhla. 🚌 ⛴ ℹ TAT,
Hat Yai (074) 243747. 🛒 daily.
🎋 Chinese Lunar Festival (Sep/Oct).

ONCE KNOWN as Singora
("lion city"), Songkhla
grew to prominence
as a coastal port dur-
ing the Srivijaya peri-
od (see pp336–7). It
once had a reputa-
tion as a pirate base
but gradually grew
in respectability, at-
tracting Arab, Indian,
Khmer and Chinese
traders. The cuisine
and language of
Songkhla reflect its
multi-cultural heritage, while a
subtle Portuguese influence is
evident in the architecture of
the houses along Nakhon
Nok and Nakhon Nai roads.

Today the city, built on the
headland between the Gulf of
Thailand and Thale Sap – the
country's largest lake – is a
fishing port and an administrative and educational centre.

Songkhla's main beach, **Hat
Samila**, which is presided over
by a bronze **mermaid statue**,
has several good seafood restaurants. Further south, at

**Wat Chai Mongkhon,
Songkhla**

Khao Seng, is a Muslim fishing village, where colourful
korlae fishing boats *(see p378)*
can be seen. A local myth
says that if you can move the
Nai Bang's Head boulder on
the headland beside the
village, you will inherit the
gold buried underneath.

The beautiful, evocative
building housing the **Songkhla
National Museum** is
an attraction in itself.
It was built in 1878
in the Southern Thai-
Chinese style as the
residence of deputy
Songkhla governor
Phraya Suntharanur-
aksa. A hidden grass
courtyard flanks two
spiralling staircases
leading to the wood-
en panelled second
storey where most exhibits
are kept. Highlights include
Bencharong pottery, earthenware jars recovered from the
sea around Songkhla, 7th- to
9th-century Dvaravati plinths
and Buddha images, and Ban
Chiang pottery said to date
from 3000 BC.

The **Patrsee Museum** in
Wat Matchimawat (sometimes
called Wat Klang), south of the
National Museum, is no less
important. Its 35-cm (14-in)
stone image of Ganesh, the elephant god, is thought to date

from the late 6th century, making it the earliest such image
found in the peninsula. Chinese painted enamelware from
the Qwing Ching dynasty,
15th-century U Thong wares
and 18th-century European
plates all indicate the importance of Songkhla's former
maritime trade links.

The city's other main temple, **Wat Chai Mongkhon**,
has a Buddha relic from Sri
Lanka buried beneath it.

Songkhla is an attractive
city to walk around, taking in
the topiary garden at **Khao
Noi**, and the view of Thale
Sap from the peak of **Khao
Tung Kuan**. Restaurants and
live music bars can be found
around Chaiya Road.

**Elaborately decorated door at the
Songkhla National Museum**

SONGKHLA TOWN CENTRE

Khao Noi ②
Khao Tung Kuan ③
Mermaid Statue ①
Old Portuguese Houses ⑦
Patrsee Museum ⑥
Songkhla National
　Museum ④
Wat Chai Mongkhon ⑤

KEY

🚌 Coach station

⛴ Ferry pier

🛕 *Wat*

━━ Major road

0 metres　　500
0 yards　　　500

🏛 **Songkhla National Museum**
Rong Muang Rd. ◯ *Wed – Sun.*
● *public hols.* 🖼

🏛 **Patrsee Museum**
Wat Matchimawat, Saiburi Rd.
◯ *Wed – Sun.* ● *public hols.* 🖼

ENVIRONS: The Prem Tinsula-nond bridge connects Songkhla with the narrow coastal strip to the north. The longest bridge in Thailand, it traverses Thale Sap via the island of **Ko Yo** on the western side of the lake. The link has boosted the island's active cotton-weaving industry and fish farms.

Ko Yo is home to the excellent **Folklore Museum**, on a hill top overlooking the lake. The museum, which aims to preserve the rich folk traditions of the South, houses displays on history, ethnology and religion. Exhibits include fabrics, pottery and metalware, and traditional arts from the South. Examples of these Southern crafts are rattan and brassware from Ranong, Muslim *kris* knives from Pattani, *krajude* grass mats from Chumphon, and dove cages from Songkhla.

Wat Pha Kho, in **Sathing Phra** district, to the north of Songkhla, is believed to be the oldest temple in Songkhla province. Archaeological finds around the *wat* suggest Sathing Phra was once an important port selling ceramics, produced at nearby Pa-o, to Khmer, Cham and Chinese traders.

🏛 **Folklore Museum**
Institute of Southern Thai Studies, Ko Yo, 14 km (8 miles) SW of Songkhla.
◯ *daily.* 🖼

Three young devotees venerating a Buddhist shrine in Hat Yai

Hat Yai ❾
หาดใหญ่

Songkhla province. 🏠 *150,000.* ✈ 12 km (7 miles) W of Hat Yai. 🚌 🚐 ℹ *TAT, 1/1 Soi 2, Niphat U-thit Rd, Hat Yai (074) 243747.* 🚉 *same address as TAT (074) 246733.* 🛍 *daily.* 🎊 *Chinese Lunar Festival (Sep/Oct).*

ALTHOUGH IT IS the commercial and transport capital of Southern Thailand, Hat Yai wins no prizes for beauty. It has grown affluent on the strength of its strategic railway junction, its cut-price market products and a constant flow of Malaysian tourists who converge on the city at weekends to enjoy its dining, shopping and nightlife. Malay, English, Yawi, Hokkien, Mandarin and the clipped syllables of Southern Thai dialect can be heard around the

A woman displaying her produce at Hat Yai market

cosmopolitan downtown area. Be aware that some parlours here advertising "ancient massage" will probably offer more than a quick rub down.

As Hat Yai's cultural attractions are few, most visitors spend daylight hours shopping in Thailand's third largest city. Electrical goods at the Kim Yong market, durians and apples from street vendors, and Bangkok-made leather goods and fashions in the department stores are a few of Hat Yai's popular buys. Bullfighting takes place in the city on the first Saturday of every month at different locations. Bulls are pitted against each other, and the winner is the animal that forces its opponent to retreat. The furious betting is often as much of a spectacle as the fight itself.

Wat Hat Yai Nai, 2 km (1 mile) west of the city centre, has the third largest reclining Buddha image in the world, measuring 35 m (115 ft) long and 15 m (49 ft) high. You can walk inside the image, entering via a small shrine room. Herbal saunas and massages are offered in the temple grounds.

ENVIRONS: Ton Nga Chang ("elephant tusk") waterfall, 24 km (15 miles) west of Hat Yai, takes its name from the two streams of water that tumble over the seven tiers of falls. They are best seen in the cool season, starting in November.

Extensive fish farms beside Ko Yo on Thale Sap lake, near Songkhla

Taking the ferry from Pak Bara to Tarutao National Marine Park

Thale Ban National Park ⓾

อุทยานแห่งชาติทะเลบัน

Satun province. Off Hwy 4184, 37 km (23 miles) from Satun. TAT (074) 231055; Forestry Dept (02) 579 0529 (inc bungalow bookings). Satun, then songthaew.

THALE BAN is a lush expanse of dense tropical rainforest scattered with waterfalls, which extends over the Banthat Mountains (*see p371*) close to the Malaysian border. It covers only 102 sq km (40 sq miles) but contains a staggering variety of wildlife including sun bears, tigers and rare birds such as bat hawks. The park has some marked trails, the Yaroy waterfall, 5 km (3 miles) north of the park headquarters, and several bathing pools.

Satun is the nearest town and gateway to the park. It is within easy reach of Pak Bara, from where ferries depart for Tarutao and the west coast.

Tarutao National Marine Park ⓫

อุทยานแห่งชาติตะรุเตา

Satun province. 22 km (14 miles) from Pak Bara. TAT (074) 231055 or Park HQ (074) 711383. from Pak Bara; regular crossings mid-Nov to mid-May only.

THE 51 ISLANDS of the Tarutao National Marine Park are the most southwesterly in Thailand, located only 8 km (5 miles) from the Malaysian island of Langkawi. Tarutao is renowned for its superb diving sites, considered to be among the best in the world.

Offshore sightings of sperm and minke whales, dugongs and dolphins are common. There is also a rich concentration of fish life with 92 species of coral fish and around 25 per cent of all the world's fish species in the surrounding seas.

For centuries the islands had a more sinister reputation as a lair for pirates. It wasn't until the 1960s that the British Royal Navy finally curtailed the pirate raids. The archipelago, extending over 1,490 sq km (580 sq miles), became Thailand's first national marine park in 1974.

Hawksbill turtle, a resident of Tarutao

The park includes spectacular, unspoilt scenery, a wide variety of wildlife and good coral. However, these attractions are accessible to visitors only from mid-November to mid-May as monsoon storms make the ferry trip from Pak Bara too risky at other times.

The largest island in the group, 26-km (16-mile) long **Ko Tarutao**, offers the greatest scenic variety. Semi-evergreen rainforest covers most of its surface, which reaches a height of 708 m (2,300 ft). Most accommodation and the best facilities for visitors are found near the wonderful, pristine beaches of the west coast.

Ferries from Pak Bara dock at Ao Phante Malaka, which is where the park headquarters, bungalows, two restaurants and the island's only shop are located. Worthwhile excursions from here include the half-hour climb to To-bo cliff with its fine views, particularly at sunset, and the 2-km (1-mile) boat trip to stalagmite-filled Crocodile cave. No crocodiles have been seen for many years, but the island does support a wide variety of fauna including deer, wild pigs, macaques, otters and soft-shelled turtles.

Ko Adang and **Ko Lipey** are the only other islands in the park to offer (rudimentary) accommodation and food for visitors. Rugged Ko Adang, 62 km (39 miles) west of the mainland, rises to 703 m (2,300 ft). It is thickly forested and has many year-round waterfalls, such as the Rattana falls on the southwest coast. Here, you can take a freshwater rock pool bath while overlooking the sea.

The smaller island of Ko Lipey, 2 km (1 mile) south of Ko Adang, has pleasant footpaths through coconut plantations and the immaculate sands of Pattaya beach. It is also home to a community of sea gypsies, displaced from Ko Rawi and Ko Adang when the park was created. Relations between the gypsies and the park authorities are strained.

Ko Kra, off Lipey's east coast, has excellent corals, as has Ko Yang, midway between Rawi and Adang islands.

Tiny Ko Khai ("egg island"), west of Tarutao, has a dramatic rock arch and is surrounded by fine sands. These area a major breeding ground for sea turtles, hence the island's name.

Colourful corals, part of a reef in the Tarutao National Marine Park

Seafood of the South

ONE OF THE GREATEST culinary treats Thailand provides is the abundant fresh seafood of the South. Throughout the year, a wide range of fish, crabs, lobsters, mussels, prawns, molluscs and squid are available along both the Gulf of Thailand and Andaman Sea coasts. Although flash-frozen and container-freighted seafood is avail-

Ho mok, **a seafood mousse with fresh mint**

able all over the country today, it is hard to beat the flavour of a freshly caught fish, simply cooked and served up whole on a plate by the shore. Nor does it have to be expensive: for every five-star restaurant offering lobster bisque there are half a dozen street cafés serving an enormous range of seafood cooked in an amazing variety of styles.

Hoi nang lom sot, *a simple Thai hors d'oeuvre of fresh oysters, is served out of the shell with slices of zesty lime.*

Green mussels from the Gulf of Thailand　　**Whelks from the Andaman Sea**

Andaman Sea cockles

Fresh crab from Phuket | **Saltwater tiger prawns**

Charamet fish, *prized for its succulent, soft flesh, is cooked here in sweet plum sauce* (neung buay), *accompanied by ginger, lemon grass and chilli peppers.*

BARBECUED SEAFOOD

Barbecued seafood, known as *thale phao*, is popular with both Thais and foreign visitors. Diners make their selection of freshly caught fish and shellfish displayed on banks of crushed ice. Pricing is usually by weight.

Thot man kung (deep fried prawn cakes) *are served with a sweet sauce dip. This is a favourite dish with those who don't like very spicy food.*

Pla meuk op sos noei (squid baked in butter sauce) *is decorated with exquisitely carved vegetable "flowers" and "leaves". Garnishes of this type accompany many Thai dishes and are generally not eaten.*

Phanaeng kung makheuathet *is a creamy, fragrant dish of tomatoes stuffed with a prawn and coconut milk curry. It is a speciality of Hat Yai and Phuket.*

Kung mangkon phat phrik phao (barbecued lobster with chilli sauce) *is particularly popular around Phuket, where lobsters abound.*

Pattani ⑫

ปัตตานี

Pattani province. 👥 55,000. ✈ 🚌
🚂 ℹ Sungai Kolok, Narathiwat
(073) 612126. 🔔 daily. 🎭 Lim Ko
Niaw Festival (Mar).

F OUNDED IN THE EARLY 15th
century, Pattani was once
a semi-autonomous Malay-
speaking sultanate. Today, it
is the heart of Muslim South
Thailand (75 per cent of the
province's population are
followers of Islam). There is
also a sizeable Chinese presence, and the cultural mix
between these two commu-
nities is the most interesting
feature of modern Pattani.

Wat Khuha Phimuk, with its adjacent cave containing a reclining Buddha

Apart from the **Matsayit
Klang** mosque, there
are few notable sights
but the town is lively,
particularly around
the harbour with its
brightly-coloured boats.

ENVIRONS: The mosque
of **Kru Se**, 7 km (4 miles)
east of town, is unre-
markable in design but
has an interesting story
behind it. In the 1570s,
Lim To Khieng, a Chinese merchant, married a local woman

**Muslim women
in Pattani**

and converted to Islam. To
show his devotion to his new
faith he started the construction
of a mosque. His sister,
Lim Ko Niaw, sailed from
China to protest about
his conversion, and she
swore he would return
to China as soon as the
mosque was finished.
However, he ensured
that it never was, and
his sister, on her death-
bed, cursed the build-
ing and anyone who
attempted to complete
it. Her shrine and the
still unfinished mosque attract
huge numbers of devotees.

KORLAE FISHING BOATS

Along mainly the east coast of the peninsula, from Ko Samui
southwards, colourful, painted fishing boats called *korlae*
have been built and decorated by Muslim fishermen for
hundreds of years. The finest examples of this now declining industry originate in the boat yards of Saiburi district,
Pattani. Originally sail boats, they are now run with engines
by fishermen. Among the characters commonly depicted on
the superbly detailed hull designs are the *singha* lion, the
gagasura horned bird, *payanak* sea serpent and the *garuda*
bird from Asian mythologies. Artists, however, don't feel
anything is amiss if they add a Swiss Alpine background.

Battling mythical beasts, intricately painted on a *korlae* boat

Yala ⑬

ยะลา

Yala province. 👥 96,000. ✈ 🚂 🚌
ℹ Sungai Kolok, Narathiwat (073)
612126. 🎭 ASEAN Barred Ground
Dove Festival (1st weekend Mar); Yala
City Pillar Celebrations (May/Jun).

Y ALA, OFTEN HERALDED as the
cleanest town in Thailand,
is laid out in an orderly fashion
with a grid-pattern of streets
and tree-lined boulevards. It's
a prosperous and rather staid
place, at its most lively during
the annual cooing competition
of the ASEAN Barred Ground
Dove Festival which attracts
entrants from all over Southeast
Asia. Yala's mosque is the
largest in Thailand.

ENVIRONS: For many people,
the main reason to visit Yala is
to see **Wat Khuha Phimuk**,
called Wat Na Tham locally,
located 8 km (5 miles) outside
the town. It is one of the most
sacred and important archaeological sites in South Thailand.
A cave next to the temple
contains a 25-m (82-ft) long
reclining Buddha. The statue,
which allegedly once had
the head of the Hindu god
Vishnu, dates from the 8th
century, the beginning of
the Srivijaya period.

Among the priceless icons
from that era found here are
votive *stupas* from Northeast
India and 9th-century bronze
standing Buddha images in
the style of South India.

The small museum hall, at
the foot of the *naga* staircase
leading up to the temple cave,
displays a range of Srivijayan
artifacts found in the area.

Betong ❶
เบตง

Yala province. 🏛 27,000. 🚌
ℹ Sungai Kolok, Narathiwat (073)
612126. 🕑 daily.

BETONG IS THE southernmost town in Thailand. It sits high in the hills, 5 km (3 miles) from the Malaysian border and 140 km (87 miles) from Yala.

The surrounding countryside is of more interest than the town itself, which has few sights other than the 40-m (130-ft) high *stupa* in **Wat Phuttha Tiwat**. This was built in the late 1980s in a modified Srivijayan style.

ENVIRONS: The winding road from Yala to Betong climbs through remote mountain forests where bands of the Sakai tribe still hunt.

From the 1940s until the 1980s this dense forest was home to an active unit of the Communist Party of Malaya, taking refuge in Thailand. A surfaced road leads to their former underground guerrilla camp, **Piya Mit**, which has now been converted into a museum. Around 180 Communists lived here undetected in 1 km (1,100 yds) of tunnels, 10 m (33 ft) below the surface.

The end came peacefully in 1989 when "an honourable settlement" was reached with the Malaysian and Thai governments. Most of the former revolutionaries settled in the area and some now guide visitors through the network of dank tunnels and explain the camp's facilities. The cleverly constructed kitchen area has a flue which would disperse smoke on the other side of the hill, thus concealing the camp's location. It was so successful that the stronghold remained undetected until the end. Other items on display include old shoes, uniforms, knives and torches used by the fugitive comrades. Simple accommodation is available in modern bungalows.

🏛 **Piya Mit**
Betong province. Off Hwy 410, 19 km (12 miles) N of Betong. ☐ daily.

Narathiwat ❶
นราธิวาส

Narathiwat province. 🏛 77,000.
✈ 🚌 🚌 ℹ Sungai Kolok Tourist Information Centre, Asia 18 Rd, Narathiwat (073) 612126.
🎎 Narathiwat Fair (3rd week Sep).

THE PLEASANT, SEDATE town of Narathiwat is visited by few tourists, but it makes a useful base for exploring the surrounding region. It has a few decent hotels and restaurants and an easygoing atmosphere befitting one of Thailand's smallest provincial capitals. The Muslim fishing village, five minutes' walk from the centre, is a good place to see the traditional painted *korlae* boats. There are a number of good beaches near the town – the best is Ao Manao, 6 km (4 miles) to the south.

Immense golden-tiled Buddha on Khao Kong, Narathiwat

ENVIRONS: Taksin Palace, south of town, is the summer residence of the King and Queen. It is open to the public when the royal family is not in residence. The gardens afford views of the adjacent beach and contain an aviary with peacocks and cockatoos.

On the road to Rangae is the hill **Khao Kong**, perched upon which is the tallest seated Buddha image in Thailand. The 24-m (79-ft) statue is covered in golden tiles.

Close to the Malaysian border, 34 km (21 miles) south of Narathiwat, is the village of **Tak Bai**. Its main attraction is Wat Chonthara Sing He: an outpost of Thai Buddhism in an almost exclusively Malay-speaking, Muslim area. The *wat* was erected in 1873 by King Chulalongkorn to stake his claim to a region that the British wanted to incorporate into Malaya (Malaysia).

The architecture of the temple mixes Southern Thai with Chinese influences, the latter being particularly evident in the tiered roof. One of the buildings in the large grounds contains a reclining Buddha decorated with Chinese ceramics from the Song dynasty. Another is adorned with fine murals depicting many aspects of local life painted during the reign of King Mongkut.

🏛 **Taksin Palace**
Off Hwy 4048, 8 km (5 miles) S of Narathiwat. ☐ daily.
🌑 usually Aug & Sep.

A lively scene of daily life from a mural at Wat Chonthara Sing He

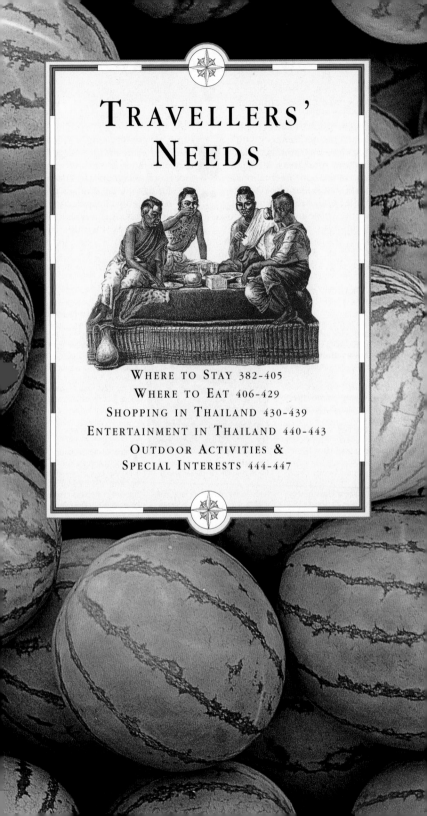

TRAVELLERS' NEEDS

WHERE TO STAY

Accommodation in Thailand comes in all price ranges, although the distribution of hotels is very uneven: massive development in the beach resorts contrasts with basic guesthouses (or no facilities at all) in many rural areas. All major cities have at least one international-class hotel, while Bangkok boasts some of the best hotels anywhere in the world. These are equipped with swimming pools, gyms, restaurants, business services and other luxury facilities. Middle-range accommodation is available in most towns

Bell boy at the Oriental Hotel

and, although much lacks character, it is uniformly clean, efficient and friendly. Western-style bathrooms are the rule rather than the exception, air-conditioning is widespread (though some middle-range hotels may offer fan rooms as well), and services such as laundry and safe deposit are standard. Guesthouses provide remarkably cheap accommodation for budget travellers. Other alternatives include, for the hardy, camping or staying in bungalows in the national parks, and, for the ascetic, bedding down in a monastery.

HOTEL GRADING AND FACILITIES

Hotels are not officially graded, although some are registered with the **Thai Hotels Association**. Price is therefore the only indication of what to expect *(see p384)*. Accommodation ranges from basic to luxury. At the cheap end of the market cleanliness is not always a priority.

Often the best value is to be found in the once-luxury establishments which have been downgraded since the arrival of international luxury chains. These hotels offer the facilities available in first-class hotels at a fraction of the cost.

LUXURY HOTELS

Thailand's luxury hotels are probably the equal of any in the world – and their number and standards are rising year after year. Expect to be treated like a visiting dignitary in the air-conditioned oases of Bangkok and the other major cities. Rooms are sure to have every conceivable luxury, from a king-size bed and massive television to a well-stocked mini-bar and perhaps even a marble Jacuzzi. In such world-famous hotels as the Oriental and the Shangri-La in Bangkok, the magnificent views over the Chao Phraya River are an added privilege.

These first-class hotels offer their guests a huge range of facilities, including business centres, banqueting halls, con-

The Melia Hotel, Hua Hin, noted for its fine sea views (see p401)

ference rooms, shopping malls, coffee shops, fitness centres and swimming pools, as well as numerous food outlets.

All luxury hotels in Thailand provide an extensive range of cuisines, some having as many as ten restaurants; Thai is, of course, standard, and Chinese – often with a regional

variant such as Cantonese or Szechuan – is common. Italian and French restaurants are very popular, usually complete with imported European chef. Less popular, but increasingly available, are German, English, Japanese and Mexican cuisines. Compared with similar establishments in the West, these hotels offer extraordinarily good value for money.

RESORT HOTELS

Like the urban luxury hotels, the resort hotels of Thailand are unsurpassed in style, comfort and elegance by the majority of their counterparts elsewhere in the world. They also usually offer stunning views. Such resorts as the Regent in Chiang Mai, Maiton Island in Phuket, and the Dusit Resort in Cha-am are luxury designer-built oases of tranquillity and opulence. You should expect – and will usually get

The Conrad Room at the Oriental Hotel, Bangkok (see p390)

◁ **Fresh watermelons on display at the Damnoen Saduak Floating Market, near Bangkok**

Felix River Kwai Resort, on the Khwae Yai River, Kanchanaburi *(see p391)*

– the very best of everything. Charming service is provided by traditionally dressed waiting staff, and you should not be surprised if waitresses approach your table on their knees. (Height etiquette dictates that you, as an honoured guest, should be physically higher than servants.) The food available is varied and generally of an excellent standard.

Most resorts offer their guests a wide range of entertainments and distractions, such as swimming – for which there might be several pools – outdoor Jacuzzis, saunas, tennis courts, water sports facilities, even horse-riding or polo. In Chiang Mai resorts may be able to organize elephant trekking.

GUESTHOUSES

GUESTHOUSES are a relatively new phenomenon in Thailand, dating from the backpacker explosion of the 1970s. Still frequented primarily by Western travellers, they offer superb value for money and often a great deal of charm.

In Bangkok, Khao San Road is the primary haunt of budget travellers. Offering low-cost accommodation in an otherwise expensive capital city seems to have taken priority over comfort, and, with few exceptions, Bangkok guesthouses are at best unremarkable.

Outside the capital, however, and especially in Chiang Mai, guesthouses are usually clean, friendly, and astoundingly cheap. Most have rooms with air-conditioning or fans, as well as bathrooms. Some establishments offer swimming pools, restaurants and good service for around 400 *baht* a

night, just a fraction of the cost of a top resort hotel. Cheap guesthouses may cost as little as 100 *baht*, but for this expect basic facilities, with communal Asian toilets and showers, although the quality of service should still be good.

THAI AND CHINESE HOTELS

THAI AND CHINESE hotels can be found just about everywhere in Thailand, though relatively few foreign visitors choose to stay in them. They generally offer basic facilities, often without Western-style toilets (they are clean, but you must squat rather than sit), and are cheap, functional and unexceptional.

Thai hotels are architecturally unexciting, generally being multi-storey concrete blocks containing numerous identical rooms. As ever in Thailand, however, they are usually clean and the service is

friendly. Most will offer you a choice between air-conditioned rooms *(hong air)* and fan-cooled rooms *(hong patlom)*.

Chinese hotels, by contrast, are readily identifiable by a number of distinctly "Middle Kingdom" features – and not just the serious-looking concierge who usually guards the keys. Wall partitions generally stop a foot short of the ground, and several feet below the ceiling, making privacy distinctly elusive. Mirrors are strategically placed to repel evil spirits, and Chinese decorative features, such as dragons and red-and-gold Chinese characters (for good luck), are much in evidence.

Only a few Thai and Chinese hotels are equipped with restaurants. However, in some remote areas, particularly little-visited areas of the Central Plains and Northeast Thailand, these hotels may well provide the only option for travellers.

STAYING IN MONASTERIES

MONASTERIES are traditionally places of refuge and contemplation. Whether you are a Buddhist, or want to learn more about Buddhism, it is often possible to stay overnight in a *wat* for a small donation.

Facilities are basic, and early rising is the norm. Mixed-sex accommodation is not available. Clean, tidy dress and an appropriate demeanour are also important. For temple etiquette see page 455.

Nong Sam Guest House, Chiang Khan, Northeast Thailand *(see p397)*

SELF-CATERING

SELF-CATERING accommodation is widely available throughout Thailand at very reasonable rates. However, self-catering is an option rarely taken up by short-term visitors. This is for a number of reasons: dining out is inexpensive in Thailand; landlords rarely speak other languages; and advertisements of apartments for rent are generally aimed solely at Thais. However, it may make sense for visitors staying in one place for more than a few weeks to rent a room or a small apartment. Thai friends will normally be happy to act as intermediaries in arranging a short-term let.

STAYING IN NATIONAL PARKS

THE MAJORITY of national parks allow camping (for a minimal fee), although the facilities provided are invariably extremely basic when compared to those available in Europe and North America. Camping has never taken off in Thailand, as Thais do not understand why anyone would choose to sleep under canvas when there is a cheap hotel

A traditional-style bedroom with mattresses on the floor

nearby. Additionally, campers have to face the perils of the outdoors. Mosquito nets and coils, and copious amounts of insect repellent are essential.

In many national parks visitors can also stay in clean, if usually charmless, concrete bungalows. As there are only limited numbers of these, it is advisable to book ahead by phoning the **Forestry Department** in Bangkok.

PRICES

THAILAND'S EXTRAORDINARY range of accommodation includes something to suit every visitor's budget. At the top end of the market, which

includes such hotels as Bangkok's Oriental and Chiang Mai's Regent, the sky is the limit. Celebrities and heads of state may take suites at 40,000 *baht* a night, although for more everyday luxury expect to pay between 10,000 and 15,000 *baht* a night.

Tourist accommodation costs from 1,000 to 4,000 *baht* a night in Bangkok, Chiang Mai, Pattaya, Phuket or Ko Samui. A comfortable air-conditioned room in a standard provincial hotel goes for between 700 and 1,500 *baht*, depending on the season. Prices everywhere are at their highest in the cool season. In the hot season (March to May) and the rainy season (May to October) rates often fall, except in the capital, which is open for business all year round. A clean but spartan room in a Thai or Chinese hotel in Bangkok will cost around 500 *baht*, falling to 150 to 250 *baht* in the regions.

Local factors should also be taken into consideration. For example, in Surin the hotel prices soar during the Elephant Roundup in November, when rooms in this otherwise moderately priced city are booked out months in advance.

The best deals available are probably the guesthouses of Chiang Mai and other tourism-oriented towns. It is possible to stay in traditional Thai houses, with teak walls and stilts, for between 100 and 500 *baht* a night. This is difficult to beat, and visitors often stay for weeks longer than planned. Beach bungalow accommodation is similarly priced, but less comfortable, and more prone to invasion by insects.

An idyllic setting: tent and bungalows at Ao Phrao on Ko Samet

BOOKING

ADVANCE BOOKING is advisable for luxury hotels and mid-range establishments, especially during national and local festivals. Thai and Chinese hotels and guesthouses are unlikely to take bookings. In popular tourist areas, and at luxury hotels, staff speak English. Elsewhere, making a booking may be difficult unless you speak some Thai. TAT offices are able to make bookings on behalf of tourists.

TAX

THE TAX SITUATION in Thailand is rather confusing and apparently anomalous. All hotels should charge 11 per cent government tax, and some luxury hotels will also add a 10 per cent service charge on top of their basic rates. Some of the top hotels – such as the Oriental, Shangri-La and others in this category – include tax in the room rates quoted. Less expensive hotels, catering for tourists, may simply add on tax when the final bill is presented. Thus, it is important to ask whether it is included in the price when booking or before checking in.

At small hotels outside the main resorts, tax is rarely (if ever) charged, and service is paid for (if at all) by tipping.

BARGAINING

IT IS ALWAYS a good idea to ask about "special rates" or the possibility of a reduction in price. The worst that can happen is a polite refusal, and very often, especially outside Bangkok and out of season, such an enquiry can lead to substantial savings. It is not considered impolite to ask, but it is bad manners to press the point. Many hotels give discounts if bookings are low, and if special rates are available, most Thai proprietors will certainly let you know.

TIPPING

OUTSIDE THE CAPITAL and the major destinations of Ko Samui, Phuket, Pattaya and Chiang Mai, tipping is unusual. Porters will expect a tip, and staff are rewarded for good service. Use your discretion: if you have received particularly good service, then leave a tip if you wish. Thanks, and a smile, are also much appreciated.

There are no hard and fast rules, and the standard British 10 per cent – let alone the American 15 per cent – would be far too much on a large bill. Between 10 and 50 *baht* is adequate in almost every circumstance. Expensive hotels will automatically include a service charge on the bill.

FACILITIES FOR CHILDREN

THAIS LOVE CHILDREN, and are incredibly tolerant of them, especially if they are blond-haired and blue-eyed. Such kids seem as exotic and doll-like to Thais as their own offspring do to the average Westerner. However, few mid-range hotels have facilities for children or nursing mothers (breast-feeding in public is considered improper), and supervised play areas are rare.

By contrast, the majority of seaside resorts and luxury hotels offer some kind of babysitting services, and children can often stay in their parents' room for free. Paddling pools may be provided, but you must look after your own children.

Khon Kaen Hotel, Northeast Thailand *(see p397)*

DISABLED TRAVELLERS

EVEN LUXURY HOTELS have few special facilities for disabled visitors. Ramps for wheelchairs are beginning to make an appearance in newly commissioned luxury hotels, and nearly every luxury or tourist-class establishment has a lift. However, that is the limit of facilities in nearly all hotels.

Thailand has a fast developing economy and a booming tourist trade, but it is likely to be many years before a serious awareness of the needs of the disabled develops. Hotels should be carefully chosen, with the help of the Thai Hotels Association, and bookings made well in advance.

DIRECTORY

THAI HOTELS ASSOCIATION

Bangkok Airport.
 (02) 535 2558.

FORESTRY DEPARTMENT

Phahon Yothin Rd, Bangkok.
 (02) 579 0529.

MAIN TAT OFFICES

Bangkok
 (02) 226 0060.

Chiang Mai
 (053) 248604.

Ko Samui
 (077) 281828.

Pattaya
 (038) 428750.

Phuket
 (076) 212213.

Bungalows and coconut palms on Ko Chang

Thailand's Best Luxury Hotels

THAILAND BOASTS A remarkable number of superb, inter-national-class hotels. These tend to be clustered in major cities like Bangkok and Chiang Mai, and around the big resorts such as Pattaya and on Phuket. However, as tourism increases still further in Thailand, fine new hotels are appearing in smaller towns and resorts, and few countries in Southeast Asia can boast a similar range and quantity of first-rate accommodation. Many hotels also represent excellent value for money when compared with similar standard hotels in Europe and the USA. Some Thai hotels, such as the renowned Oriental in Bangkok and Amanpuri Resort on Phuket have been acclaimed the best in the world. Listed here are the top luxury hotels in each region.

Westin Hotel

NORTHWEST HEARTLAND

F NOR

NORTH CENTRAL PLAINS

Westin Hotel, Chiang Mai (see p394), attracts the rich and famous, providing luxury at high prices.

Dusit Island Resort, Chiang Rai (see p395), is located on an island in the Kok River. Its attractions include spacious grounds, pool, tennis courts and excellent restaurants.

SOUTH CENTRAL PLAINS

Pailyn Hotel, Phitsanulok (see p392), offers stylishly furnished rooms with river views, a sauna and two good restaurants.

BANGKOK

Melia Hotel

Felix River Kwai Resort, Kanchanaburi (see p391), is artfully set in landscaped grounds next to the Khwae River. Extensive amenities include two swimming pools, 24-hour room service and rooms for non-smokers and disabled people.

WESTERN SEABOARD

Melia Hotel, Hua Hin (see p401), stands on the beachfront of this popular, long-established resort. In addition to international-standard facilities, all rooms have balconies with sea views.

UPPER ANDAMAN COAST

Amanpuri Resort

Amanpuri Resort, Phuket (see p404), is architecturally stunning and offers facilities of unparalled luxury. Guests stay in spacious individual pavilions within a shady coconut grove.

Sima Thani Hotel, Khorat *(see p397)*, situated out of the centre of town, is spacious and attractively decorated. Amenities are first rate and include swimming pool, fitness centre, sauna, two restaurants and two bars. The five-storey atrium lounge is particularly striking.

MEKHONG RIVER VALLEY

Pathumrat Hotel, Ubon Ratchathani (see p399), is a modern seven-storey hotel near the town centre. Rooms are comfortably furnished and come equipped with air-conditioning, mini-bar and TV. Facilities include a coffee shop and a swimming pool.

KHORAT PLATEAU

Pathumrat Hotel

Grand Hyatt Erawan

EASTERN SEABOARD

Oriental Hotel, Bangkok (see p390), has long been recognized as one of the world's great hotels. Its standards of luxury and superlative service make a stay here a memorable experience.

Grand Hyatt Erawan, Bangkok (see p389), is one of the finest luxury hotels in the capital.

Royal Cliff Beach Resort, Pattaya (see p400), located near Jomtien beach, is the best family resort in the area. It offers high quality accommodation, excellent service and a wide range of sports and leisure facilities. Most rooms have sea views.

DEEP SOUTH

Royal Crown Hotel, Songkhla *(see p405)*, is a popular hotel, notable for its central location, friendly service and restaurant.

| 0 kilometres | | 200 |
| 0 miles | | 100 |

Choosing a Hotel

THE HOTELS in this guide have been selected across a wide price range for their locations and value for money. Many have excellent facilities, and some are splendidly designed. The chart lists the hotels by region, starting with Bangkok; colour-coded thumb tabs show the regions covered on each page. For restaurant listings see pages 412–29.

BANGKOK

	CREDIT CARDS	SWIMMING POOL	WESTERN BATHROOMS	COFFEE SHOP	GARDEN/TERRACE

OLD CITY: *BK Guest House.* **Map** 2 D3.
11/1 Soi Surao, Chakrabongse Rd. ☎ *(02) 281 3048.* FAX *(02) 281 3048.*
Clean, very low-priced rooms with shared bathrooms. Well placed for the Chao Phraya River and the Old City. *Rooms: 25.* 📋 *5.*

Credit Cards: Ⓑ — Western Bathrooms: ■

OLD CITY: *Peachy Guest House.* **Map** 1 C4.
10 Phra Athit Rd. ☎ *(02) 281 6471.*
A pleasant garden makes this place stand out among the many cheap guesthouses in and around Banglamphu. *Rooms: 30.* 📋 *5.*

Credit Cards: Ⓑ — Garden/Terrace: ■

OLD CITY: *Khao San Palace.* **Map** 2 D4.
139 Khao San Rd. ☎ *(02) 282 0578.*
In recent years Khao San Road has replaced Soi Ngam Duphli to the south of Lumphini Park as the backpackers' haunt in Bangkok. This place is among the best – though rates are high for the area. *Rooms: 32.* 📋 *32.*

Credit Cards: ⒷⒷ

OLD CITY: *Miramar.* **Map** 6 D1.
777 Maha Chai Rd. *(02) 222 4191.* FAX *(02) 225 4994.*
Tourist-class hotel close to Phahurat Market, Bangkok's "Little India". Nearby, too, are Wat Saket and the Golden Mount. 🍴 📺 *Rooms: 160.* 📋 *60.*

Credit Cards: ⒷⒷ / MC V — Western Bathrooms: ■ — Garden/Terrace: ■

OLD CITY: *Phra Athit Mansion.* **Map** 1 C4.
22 Phra Athit Rd. ☎ *(02) 280 0744.* FAX *(02) 280 0742.*
Basic, clean, airy accommodation very close to the Phra Athit ferry pier. Suitable for young travellers watching their funds. *Rooms: 35.* 📋 *35.*

Credit Cards: ⒷⒷ / MC V — Western Bathrooms: ■

OLD CITY: *Royal.* **Map** 2 D4.
2 Ratchadamnoen Klang Ave. ☎ *(02) 222 9111.* FAX *(02) 224 2083.*
One of Bangkok's oldest hotels. Majestic accommodation, despite its recent history: in 1992 there was much bloodshed in the foyer during a pro-democracy demonstration. 🍴 24 📺 *Rooms: 297.* 📋 *297.*

Credit Cards: ⒷⒷⒷ / AE MC V — Swimming Pool: ● — Western Bathrooms: ■ — Coffee Shop: ●

CHINATOWN: *River View Guest House.* **Map** 6 F3.
768 Soi Phanu Rang Si, Songwat Rd. ☎ *(02) 234 5429.* FAX *(02) 237 5428.*
A real bargain, right by the river. The view from the 8th-floor restaurant is wonderful, even if the food is only mediocre. A clean and friendly establishment, though the service is a little slow. 🍴 📺 *Rooms: 45.* 📋 *12.*

Credit Cards: ⒷⒷ / AE MC V — Western Bathrooms: ■

CHINATOWN: *Grand China Hotel.* **Map** 6 F2.
295 Yaowarat Rd. ☎ *02) 226 1267.* FAX *(02) 224 7999.*
Mid-range, plain hotel situated right in the heart of Bangkok's busy Chinatown. Good access to diverse restaurants in the area serving Thai, Indian and Chinese cuisine. 🍴 📺 🔸 *Rooms: 150.* 📋 *150.*

Credit Cards: ⒷⒷⒷ / AE DC MC V — Western Bathrooms: ■ — Coffee Shop: ●

CHINATOWN: *White Orchid.* **Map** 6 E2.
409–21 Yaowarat Rd. ☎ *(02) 226 0026.* FAX *(02) 225 6403.*
Plain but respectably turned out establishment, well located for the many gold and herbalist shops in the main shopping area of Chinatown, Sampeng Lane. 🍴 📺 *Rooms: 300.* 📋 *300.*

Credit Cards: ⒷⒷⒷ / AE DC MC V — Western Bathrooms: ■ — Coffee Shop: ●

DUSIT: *Bangkok International Youth Hostel.* **Map** 2 F2.
25/2 Phitsanulok Rd. ☎ *(02) 282 0950.* FAX *(02) 628 7416.*
Clean, with reasonable rates and a downstairs restaurant serving good food. Usual youth hostel rules apply. Situated close to Vimanmek Palace in the relatively peaceful Dusit quarter. 🍴 *Rooms: 20 (40 beds).* 📋 *16.*

Credit Cards: Ⓑ — Garden/Terrace: ■

DUSIT: *Villa Guest House.* **Map** 2 D3.
Samsen Soi 1. ☎ No telephone.
A small, basic and plain but unusual establishment for Bangkok – so quiet and friendly that it's more like a private home than a hotel. Extremely cheap rates mean that it is often full with budget travellers. 🍴 *Rooms: 10.* 📋 *0.*

Credit Cards: Ⓑ — Western Bathrooms: ■

<table>
<tr><td>

Price categories for a standard double room per night, including tax for luxury hotels.

ⓑ under B350
ⓑⓑ B350–800
ⓑⓑⓑ B800–1,600
ⓑⓑⓑⓑ B1,600–3,200
ⓑⓑⓑⓑⓑ over B3,200

</td><td>

CREDIT CARDS
AE American Express; DC Diners Club; MC MasterCard; V VISA; JCB Japanese Credit Bureau.

WESTERN BATHROOMS
Indicates sit-down, flush toilets; showers and/or baths. Others have squat toilets and trough-and-dipper baths.

COFFEE SHOP
Hotel with coffee shop.

GARDEN/TERRACE
Hotel with garden, courtyard or terrace.

</td></tr>
</table>

	CREDIT CARDS	SWIMMING POOL	WESTERN BATHROOMS	COFFEE SHOP	GARDEN/TERRACE
DUSIT: *Trang*. **Map** 2 D2. 99/8 Wisut Kasat Rd. (02) 281 2083. FAX (02) 280 3610. A mid-range hotel near the river north of the Old City. Particularly well placed for the key sights of Dusit. 🍽 📶 📺 **Rooms:** *150.* 🛏 *150.* — ⓑⓑⓑ	AE DC MC V	●	■	●	
DUSIT: *Royal Princess*. **Map** 3 A4. 269 Lan Luang Rd. (02) 281 3088. FAX (02) 280 1314. A luxurious establishment conveniently located for the sights of Dusit and the Old City. Excellent Chinese restaurant, as well as Italian and meticulously prepared Japanese fare. 🍽 📶 24 📺 🛁 **Rooms:** *170.* 🛏 *170.* — ⓑⓑⓑⓑ	AE DC MC V JCB	●	■	●	■
DOWNTOWN: *Niagara*. **Map** 7 B5. 26 Soi Suksa Witthaya. (02) 233 5783. FAX (02) 233 6563. The best low-cost accommodation in the Silom area. Just far enough from Patpong to escape the late-night bar and traffic noise. 🍽 **Rooms:** *60.* 🛏 *60.* — ⓑⓑ			■	●	
DOWNTOWN: *White Lodge*. **Map** 7 C1. 36/8 Soi Kasem San 1. (02) 216 8867. FAX (02) 216 8228. Clean, friendly and good value for money. Located in the centre of Siam Square business district. Jim Thompson's House can be found nearby. 🍽 **Rooms:** *26.* 🛏 *26.* — ⓑⓑ			■		■
DOWNTOWN: *Asia*. **Map** 3 C5. 296 Phaya Thai Rd. (02) 215 0808. FAX (02) 215 4360. Established in 1970, the Asia has five good restaurants serving Chinese, Vietnamese and Thai food. Convenient for the Siam Center, Siam Square and the World Trade Center. 🍽 📶 24 📺 🛁 **Rooms:** *650.* 🛏 *650.* — ⓑⓑⓑⓑ	AE DC MC V JCB	●	■	●	
DOWNTOWN: *Mandarin Bangkok*. **Map** 7 B3. 662 Rama IV Rd. (02) 238 0230. FAX (02) 234 3363. Fresh, pleasingly airy rooms in a reasonably priced high-class hotel. Every luxury imaginable, right down to sumptuous Italian marble bathrooms. 🍽 📶 24 📺 🛁 **Rooms:** *400.* 🛏 *400.* — ⓑⓑⓑⓑ	AE DC MC V JCB	●	■	●	
DOWNTOWN: *Mercure*. **Map** 4 F5. City Square, 35 New Petchaburi Rd. (02) 253 0510. FAX (02) 253 0556. Huge complex with special facilities for business travellers, 11 function rooms and a ballroom. 🍽 📶 24 📺 🛁 **Rooms:** *668.* 🛏 *668.* — ⓑⓑⓑⓑ	AE DC MC V JCB	●	■	●	
DOWNTOWN: *Amari Watergate*. **Map** 4 E5. 847 Petchaburi Rd. (02) 653 9000. FAX (02) 653 9045. Attractive luxury accommodation in the core of the Pratunam business district. This establishment has several in-house restaurants – the Italian regularly attracts high praise. 🍽 📶 24 📺 🛁 **Rooms:** *575.* 🛏 *575.* — ⓑⓑⓑⓑⓑ	AE DC MC V JCB	●	■	●	■
DOWNTOWN: *Dusit Thani*. **Map** 8 D4. 946 Rama IV Rd. (02) 236 0450. FAX (02) 236 6400. One of the best views of Bangkok can be seen from the top-floor restaurant. This 23-storey hotel has pyramid-style architecture, a relaxing, tree-lined pool area and eight restaurants. 🍽 📶 24 📺 🛁 **Rooms:** *530.* 🛏 *530.* — ⓑⓑⓑⓑⓑ	AE DC MC V JCB	●	■	●	■
DOWNTOWN: *Grand Hyatt Erawan*. **Map** 8 D1. 494 Ratchadamri Rd. (02) 254 1234. FAX (02) 253 5856. Spacious rooms and luxurious decoration are features of this smart hotel, which has a four-storey atrium and an extensive art collection. Centrally located by downtown Ploenchit. 🍽 📶 24 📺 🛁 **Rooms:** *389.* 🛏 *389.* — ⓑⓑⓑⓑⓑ	AE DC MC V JCB	●	■	●	■
DOWNTOWN: *Hilton International Bangkok*. **Map** 8 E1. 2 Witthayu (Wireless) Rd. (02) 253 0123. FAX (02) 253 6509. Absolutely everything you would expect in a Hilton International: luxury, comfort, taste – there is even a Thai Brahmin fertility shrine in the hotel grounds. 🍽 📶 24 📺 🛁 **Rooms:** *343.* 🛏 *343.* — ⓑⓑⓑⓑⓑ	AE DC MC V JCB	●	■	●	■

	CREDIT CARDS	SWIMMING POOL	WESTERN BATHROOMS	COFFEE SHOP	GARDEN/TERRACE
DOWNTOWN: *Holiday Inn Crowne Plaza.* **Map** 7 A5. ⒷⒷⒷⒷ 981 Silom Rd. (02) 238 4300. FAX (02) 238 5289. Immaculate, marble-clad establishment offering every comfort. Positioned towards the western end of Silom Road near Bangkok's financial, shopping and sightseeing areas. 🍴 📶 24 TV 🛁 *Rooms: 724.* 🛏 724.	AE DC MC V JCB	●	■	●	
DOWNTOWN: *Indra Regent.* **Map** 4 E5. ⒷⒷⒷⒷ 120/126 Ratchaprarop Rd. (02) 208 0022. FAX (02) 208 0388. Located in the busy Pratunam area, this 1970s hotel has business facilities and luxurious rooms. Most long-distance, air-conditioned, luxury coaches to Bangkok stop in this area. 🍴 📶 24 TV 🛁 *Rooms: 500.* 🛏 500.	AE DC MC V JCB	●	■	●	■
DOWNTOWN: *Montien.* **Map** 7 C3. ⒷⒷⒷⒷ 54 Surawong Rd. (02) 233 7060. FAX (02) 236 5218. Rooms are a little plain for this price range, but the location for business and pleasure is perfect: close to Silom financial district and just a stone's throw from the nightlife in Patpong. 🍴 📶 24 TV 🛁 *Rooms: 475.* 🛏 475.	AE DC MC V JCB	●	■	●	■
DOWNTOWN: *Oriental.* **Map** 6 F4. ⒷⒷⒷⒷ 48 Oriental Ave. (02) 236 0400. FAX (02) 236 1937. Excelling in comfort, elegant decor and service, this legendary establishment, founded in 1876 *(see p110)*, still ranks as one of world's top hotels. Notable, too, are its gardens and river view. 🍴 📶 24 TV 🛁 *Rooms: 396.* 🛏 396.	AE DC MC V JCB	●	■	●	■
DOWNTOWN: *Regent.* **Map** 8 D2. ⒷⒷⒷⒷ 155 Ratchadamri Rd. (02) 251 6127. FAX (02) 253 9195. A world-class, centrally located, luxury hotel offering every facility including yoga and ballroom dancing. 🍴 📶 24 TV 🛁 *Rooms: 363.* 🛏 363.	AE DC MC V JCB	●	■	●	■
DOWNTOWN: *Royal Orchid Sheraton.* **Map** 6 F3. ⒷⒷⒷⒷ 2 Captain Bush Lane, Si Praya Rd. (02) 266 0123. FAX (02) 236 8320. This smart, spacious, business hotel shares a helicopter service to the airport with the Oriental. There are startlingly good views over the Chao Phraya River from its 28 floors. 🍴 📶 24 TV 🛁 *Rooms: 773.* 🛏 773.	AE DC MC V JCB	●	■	●	■
DOWNTOWN: *Siam Inter Continental.* **Map** 8 D1. ⒷⒷⒷⒷ 967 Rama I Rd. (02) 253 0355. FAX (02) 253 2275. A magnificent, top-class hotel set in 26 acres of landscaped parkland. A good place to stay if downtown shopping or Jim Thompson's House are on your itinerary. 🍴 📶 24 TV 🛁 *Rooms: 400.* 🛏 400.	AE DC MC V JCB	●	■	●	■
THON BURI: *Royal River.* **Map** 1 A2. ⒷⒷⒷ 670/805 Charan Sanit Wong Rd. (02) 433 0300. FAX (02) 433 5880. Generally considered to be the best, well-facilitated, luxury hotel on the west bank of the Chao Phraya River. 🍴 📶 24 TV 🛁 *Rooms: 454.* 🛏 454.	AE DC MC V JCB	●	■	●	■
THON BURI: *Marriott Royal Garden Riverside.* **Map** 6 E4. ⒷⒷⒷⒷ 257/1–3 Charoen Nakhon Rd. (02) 476 0021. FAX (02) 460 1805. Set on the west bank of the Chao Phraya River, this spacious, luxury hotel has five restaurants (one international), 11 acres of landscaped gardens and a hot spa that can take up to ten people. 🍴 📶 24 TV 🛁 *Rooms: 430.* 🛏 430.	AE DC MC V JCB	●	■	●	■
THON BURI: *Royal City* ⒷⒷⒷⒷ 212/14 Borom Ratchonni Rd. (02) 435 8888. FAX (02) 434 3636. This Thon Buri hotel near the Chao Phraya River offers first-class accommodation, rather off the beaten track. A garden café and smart French restaurant add to its appeal. 🍴 📶 24 TV 🛁 *Rooms: 401.* 🛏 401.	AE DC MC V JCB	●	■	●	■
FURTHER AFIELD: *Ambassador* ⒷⒷⒷ Soi 11, Sukhumvit Rd. (02) 254 0444. FAX (02) 253 4123. Yet another huge luxury hotel, with every service, located in the busy heart of Sukhumvit. This one, though, has a selection of "ethnic" restaurants on the ground-floor terrace. 🍴 📶 24 TV 🛁 *Rooms: 1,050.* 🛏 1,050.	AE DC MC V JCB	●	■	●	■

FURTHER AFIELD: *Golden Plaza*   ⒷⒷⒷ | AE MC V
76/1 Mu 5, Khok Mo Rd, Ratchaburi. **(** *(032) 322026.*
Ratchaburi's newest hotel and the only up-market establishment in
town. Offers clean and comfortable accommodation, delicious food and
friendly, efficient service. **Ⅱ 24 TV** ⚡ *Rooms: 215.* 🔲 *215.*

FURTHER AFIELD: *Park Hotel*   ⒷⒷⒷ | AE DC MC V JCB
6 Sukhumvit, Soi 7. **(** *(02) 255 4300.* **FAX** *(02) 255 4309.*
Very comfortable indeed – with pool, gym and sauna facilities – yet
reasonably priced for western Sukhumvit. Close proximity to the expressway allows easy access to the airport. **Ⅱ ▼ 24 TV** ⚡ *Rooms: 139.* 🔲 *139.*

FURTHER AFIELD: *Fortune Blue Wave*   ⒷⒷⒷⒷ | AE DC MC V JCB
Fortune Town Building, 1 Ratchadaphisek Rd. **(** *(02) 641 1500.* **FAX** *(02) 641 1551.*
A large and comfortable establishment with a good business centre. Has
three Asian-based restaurants, a coffee shop and a bar. Well located for the
Thailand Cultural Center. **Ⅱ ▼ 24 TV** ⚡ *Rooms: 428.* 🔲 *428.*

FURTHER AFIELD: *Amari Airport*   ⒷⒷⒷⒷ | AE DC MC V JCB
333 Chert Wudthakas Rd, Don Muang. **(** *(02) 566 1020.* **FAX** *(02) 566 1941.*
A plush hotel connected by walkway to the International and Domestic
terminals of Bangkok Airport and Don Muang train station. Ideal for
passengers in transit, but overpriced. **Ⅱ ▼ 24 TV** ⚡ *Rooms: 305.* 🔲 *305.*

FURTHER AFIELD: *Landmark Plaza.* **Map 8 F2.**   ⒷⒷⒷⒷ | AE DC MC V JCB
138 Sukhumvit Rd. **(** *02) 254 0404.* **FAX** *(02) 253 4259.*
Near to the National Convention Centre and ideal for downtown
Sukhumvit, this extensive complex has a four-floor shopping plaza and
ten quality restaurants. **Ⅱ ▼ 24 TV** ⚡ *Rooms: 415.* 🔲 *415.*

FURTHER AFIELD: *Sukhothai Bangkok.* **Map 8 D4.**   ⒷⒷⒷⒷ | AE DC MC V JCB
13/3 Sathorn Tai Rd. **(** *(02) 287 0222.* **FAX** *(02) 287 4980.*
A series of courtyards, pagodas and small ponds peacefully set in six
acres of landscaped gardens make this hotel very attractive. Near the top
of the price range for Bangkok. **Ⅱ ▼ 24 TV** ⚡ *Rooms: 226.* 🔲 *226.*

SOUTH CENTRAL PLAINS

AYUTTHAYA: *BJ Guest House*   Ⓑ
16/7 Naresuan Rd. **(** *(035) 251526.*
Centrally located and clean – the best place for budget travellers visiting
Ayutthaya. Bicycle rentals and good food are on offer. **Ⅱ** *Rooms: 10.* 🔲 *0.*

AYUTTHAYA: *U Thong Inn*   ⒷⒷⒷ | AE DC MC V
210 Rodjana Rd. **(** *(035) 242236.* **FAX** *(035) 242235.*
The best-appointed hotel in Ayutthaya, within easy striking distance of all
the most important historical sights. **Ⅱ ▼ 24 TV** ⚡ *Rooms: 87.* 🔲 *87.*

BANG PA-IN: *Phra Intaracha*   ⒷⒷ
136 Mu 7, Tambon Chiangraknoi. **(** *(035) 361081.*
Few people stay in Bang Pa-in – it's too convenient a day trip from Bangkok.
But if you do stop here, then this hotel is better than most. *Rooms: 50.* 🔲 *18.*

KANCHANABURI: *Jolly Frog Back-Packers*   Ⓑ
Just off Rong Hip Awee Rd. **(** *(034) 514579.*
Original name, original concept: a unique bamboo "motel" situated right
on the river bank, with a very popular restaurant. **Ⅱ** *Rooms: 50.* 🔲 *0.*

KANCHANABURI: *Felix River Kwai Resort*   ⒷⒷⒷⒷ | AE DC MC V
9/1 Mu 3, Thamakhan. **(** *(034) 515061.* **FAX** *(034) 515095.*
Luxurious hotel with landscaped gardens, next to the Khwae River.
Facilities include tennis courts, two good-sized swimming pools and a
private safe in every room. **Ⅱ ▼ 24 TV** ⚡ *Rooms: 255.* 🔲 *255.*

LOP BURI: *Asia Lopburi Hotel*   ⒷⒷ
1/7–8 Sorasak Rd. **(** *(036) 411892.* **FAX** *(036) 411892.*
Could not be more central, overlooking King Narai's Palace. Good value,
though fairly basic, accommodation. *Rooms: 110.* 🔲 *20.*

LOP BURI: *Lopburi Inn*   ⒷⒷ | AE MC V
28/9 Narai Maharat Rd. **(** *(036) 412300.* **FAX** *(036) 411917.*
One of the best hotels in the Central Plains, with pleasant, air-conditioned
rooms. However, it is more than 3 km (2 miles) from Lop Buri's historic
sites. **Ⅱ 24 TV** ⚡ *Rooms: 134.* 🔲 *134.*

Price categories for a standard double room per night, including tax for luxury hotels.

- (B) under B350
- (B)(B) B350–800
- (B)(B)(B) B800–1,600
- (B)(B)(B)(B) B1,600–3,200
- (B)(B)(B)(B)(B) over B3,200

CREDIT CARDS
AE American Express; DC Diners Club; MC MasterCard; V VISA; JCB Japanese Credit Bureau.

WESTERN BATHROOMS
Indicates sit-down, flush toilets; showers and/or baths. Others have squat toilets and trough-and-dipper baths.

COFFEE SHOP
Hotel with coffee shop.

GARDEN/TERRACE
Hotel with garden, courtyard or terrace.

	Credit Cards	Swimming Pool	Western Bathrooms	Coffee Shop	Garden/Terrace
NAKHON PATHOM: *Nakhon Inn* (B)(B) 55 Ratwithi Rd. (034) 254998. FAX (034) 532600. A pleasant, clean place offering all the usual facilities. Without much character, but smart compared with other options. 11 TV Rooms: 70. 70.			■	●	■
SANGKHLA BURI: *Three Pagodas Resort* (B)(B)(B) Three Pagodas Pass, Amphoe Sangkhla Buri. (034) 124159. Probably the best place to stay at the Three Pagodas Pass near the Burmese frontier point. Attractive, well-appointed bungalows in a rustic setting. Booking in advance is advisable. 11 TV Rooms: 32. 0.	MC V		■	●	

NORTH CENTRAL PLAINS

	Credit Cards	Swimming Pool	Western Bathrooms	Coffee Shop	Garden/Terrace
KAMPHAENG PHET: *Phet* (B)(B) 99 Wichit Rd. (055) 712810. FAX (055) 512816. Near the market in the south of Khampaeng Phet, this clean hotel with a small pool offers good value for money. 11 24 TV Rooms: 234. 234.	MC V	●	■	●	■
KAMPHAENG PHET: *Cha Kang Rao* (B)(B)(B) 123/1 Thesa Rd. (055) 711315. FAX (055) 711326. In the newer part of Khampaeng Phet, yet within easy distance of the old historic city. There are also tennis courts. 11 24 TV Rooms: 100. 100.	MC V		■	●	
MAE SOT: *Central Mae Sot Hill Resort* (B)(B)(B) 100 Asia Highway. (055) 532601. FAX (055) 532600. Features include tennis courts, disco, cocktail lounge, ballroom, supper club and an excellent restaurant. Children are particularly well catered for, with a water spa and children's pool. 11 24 TV Rooms: 120. 120.	AE DC MC V	●	■	●	■
PHITSANULOK: *Phitsanulok Youth Hostel* (B) 38 Sanam Bin Rd. (055) 242060. This friendly youth hostel occupies an old, jasmine-covered wooden house with a large teak veranda. Rooms: 30. 0.			■		■
PHITSANULOK: *Pailyn* (B)(B)(B)(B) 38 Baromatrailokanart Rd. (055) 252412. FAX (055) 252411. The best hotel in Phitsanulok, offering luxurious, tastefully furnished rooms, river views and two restaurants. 11 24 TV Rooms: 200. 200.	AE MC V		■	●	
SAWANKHALOK: *Muang Inn* (B)(B) 21 Kasem Rat Rd. (055) 641662. The only place worth staying in Sawankhalok. Pleasant atmosphere, with good Central Thai cooking available in the restaurant. 11 Rooms: 30. 20.			■	●	
SUKHOTHAI: *Hana Sukho* (B) 234/6 Chodwithithong Rd. (055) 611315. Large and comfortable, this place was formerly one of three "No. 4 Guest Houses" dotted around New Sukhothai. 11 Rooms: 12. 0.					■
SUKHOTHAI: *Sawasdiphong* (B)(B) 56/2–5 Singhawat Rd. (055) 611567. FAX (055) 612268. Clean, comfortable and unremarkable accommodation in New Sukhothai, though the restaurant is highly rated. 11 Rooms: 41. 15.	AE MC V		■		
SUKHOTHAI: *Thai Village House* (B)(B) 241 Chodwithithong Rd. (055) 612275. FAX (055) 612583. Attractive teak bungalows owned by the Sukhothai Cultural Centre. The only place to stay in Old Sukhothai itself – book ahead. 11 Rooms: 13. 13.			■		■
TAK: *Wiang Tak* (B)(B) 25/3 Mahathai Bamrung Rd. (055) 511910. FAX (055) 512169. Tak has only a small number of plain hotels, which line the town's main street. This is the largest and best establishment. 11 Rooms: 100. 100.	AE MC V JCB		■	●	

UMPHANG: *Umphang Country Huts* ⒷⒷⒷ
141 Mu, 1 Tambon Umphang. 【 *(055) 561079.*
These basic huts on the outskirts of Umphang are the most comfortable
"jungle" accommodation in the province. 🍴 *Rooms: 20.* 📋 *0.*

NORTHWEST HEARTLAND

CHIANG DAO: *Chiang Dao Hills* ⒷⒷⒷ
28 Mu 6, Ping Kong, Chiang Dao. 【 *(053) 232434.* FAX *(053) 251372.*
An isolated and tranquil bungalow resort set in rolling hill country. The
hotel restaurant is highly recommended. 🍴 *Rooms: 38.* 📋 *0.*

CHIANG MAI: *Daret's Guest House* Ⓑ
4/5 Chaiyaphum Rd. 【 *(053) 235440.*
Long-established and popular backpacker hang-out in the central Tha
Phae Gate area. Good information on activities is provided, and Daret's
restaurant is well known for cheap, non-spicy, tasty fare. 🍴 *Rooms: 20.* 📋 *0.*

CHIANG MAI: *La Maloon* Ⓑ
1 Chaban Rd. 【 *(053) 271001.*
Very attractive wooden guesthouse with a garden bar under French
management. The food is good and reasonably priced. 🍴 *Rooms: 15.* 📋 *0.*

CHIANG MAI: *Al Farooq* ⒷⒷ
341 Charoen Prathet Rd. 【 *(053) 821107.* FAX *(053) 821106.*
A mid-range hotel located in Chiang Mai's Muslim neighbourhood in the
south of the city. Notable mainly for its restaurant, where vegetarian fare
and excellent halal dishes are prepared. 🍴 24 TV *Rooms: 100.* 📋 *100.*

CHIANG MAI: *Anodard* ⒷⒷ — MC V
57/9 Ratchamankha Rd. 【 *(053) 270755.* FAX *(053) 270759.*
An old-fashioned hotel in the heart of the walled city. Clean and
unpretentious. 🍴 24 TV *Rooms: 135.* 📋 *42.*

CHIANG MAI: *Baan Jong Come* ⒷⒷ
47 Tha Phae Rd, Soi 4. 【 *(053) 274823.*
Central but quiet location in one of Chiang Mai's many back lanes. Has a
pleasant garden atmosphere and friendly staff who are well informed on
trekking and other activities in the area. 🍴 *Rooms: 74.* 📋 *5.*

CHIANG MAI: *Chatree Guest House* ⒷⒷ — MC V
11/10 Suriyawong Rd. 【 *(053) 279221.* FAX *(053) 279085.*
This place offers an approachable, relaxed atmosphere rather removed
from its location in the Night Bazaar area. 🍴 🍴 24 TV *Rooms: 60.* 📋 *60.*

CHIANG MAI: *Lai Thai Guest House* ⒷⒷ — AE MC V
111/4–5 Khotchasan Rd. 【 *(053) 271725.* FAX *(053) 272724.*
A guesthouse with good facilities next to the moat surrounding Chiang Mai's
walled city. This is an ideal place to stay during the Songkran Festival in
April, when you can see revellers hurling water. 🍴 24 TV *Rooms: 120.* 📋 *40.*

CHIANG MAI: *Top North Guest House* ⒷⒷ — MC V
15 Mun Muang Rd, Soi 2. 【 *(053) 278900.* FAX *(053) 278485.*
This modern building, with Northern Thai style motifs, is in the old
walled city close to the small five star strip on Mun Muang Road. Provides
motorbike rental as well as trekking services. 🍴 24 🏊 *Rooms: 90.* 📋 *50.*

CHIANG MAI: *Diamond Riverside* ⒷⒷⒷ — AE DC MC V JCB
33/10 Charoen Prathet Rd. 【 *(053) 270080.* FAX *(053) 271482.*
A luxury hotel by the Ping River right in the city centre, within easy walking
distance of the Night Bazaar. A fine, 150-year-old teak house functions as
a restaurant in the grounds. 🍴 🍴 24 TV 🏊 *Rooms: 423.* 📋 *423.*

CHIANG MAI: *River View Lodge* ⒷⒷⒷ — MC V
25 Charoen Prathet Rd, Soi 2. 【 *(053) 271110.* FAX *(053) 279019.*
Looks like a large Swiss chalet from the outside, while all the rooms have
touches of traditional Lanna style. The lodge has fine views of the river,
and you can bathe in its riverside pool. 🍴 *Rooms: 36.* 📋 *36.*

CHIANG MAI: *Tapae Place* ⒷⒷⒷ — AE DC MC V JCB
2 Tha Phae Rd, Soi 3. 【 *(053) 281842.* FAX *(053) 271982.*
This hotel has a lot of charm and character and is situated on one of
Chiang Mai's quiet and attractive back lanes. Within easy striking distance
of Tha Phae Gate and the Night Bazaar. 🍴 24 TV *Rooms: 90.* 📋 *90.*

For key to symbols see back flap

Price categories for a standard double room per night, including tax for luxury hotels.

Ⓑ under B350
ⒷⒷ B350–800
ⒷⒷⒷ B800–1,600
ⒷⒷⒷⒷ B1,600–3,200
ⒷⒷⒷⒷⒷ over B3,200

CREDIT CARDS
AE American Express; DC Diners Club; MC MasterCard; V VISA; JCB Japanese Credit Bureau.

WESTERN BATHROOMS
Indicates sit-down, flush toilets; showers and/or baths. Others have squat toilets and trough-and-dipper baths.

COFFEE SHOP
Hotel with coffee shop.

GARDEN/TERRACE
Hotel with garden, courtyard or terrace.

	CREDIT CARDS	SWIMMING POOL	WESTERN BATHROOMS	COFFEE SHOP	GARDEN/TERRACE
CHIANG MAI: Chiang Mai Orchid ⒷⒷⒷⒷ 22 Huai Kaeo Rd. 📞 (053) 222099. FAX (053) 221625. Popular with high society, this long-established, grand hotel has a reputation for fine wine and extensive cellars. Facilities include a health club. Located in the northwest part of town. 🍴 🍴 24 TV 🏊 *Rooms: 266.* 266.	AE DC MC V JCB	●	■	●	■
CHIANG MAI: Lotus ⒷⒷⒷⒷ 99/4 Huai Kaeo Rd, Mu 2. 📞 (053) 224333. FAX (053) 224493. Linked to one of the biggest shopping complexes in Chiang Mai, this hotel attracts visitors who like shopping and nightlife. The adjacent Kad Theatre is the largest in Southeast Asia. 🍴 🍴 24 TV 🏊 *Rooms: 750.* 750.	AE DC MC V JCB	●	■	●	
CHIANG MAI: Novotel Chiang Mai ⒷⒷⒷⒷ 183 Chang Puek Rd. 📞 (053) 225500. FAX (053) 225505. A modern, airy hotel in northern Chiang Mai. The adjacent theme park, run by the hotel, features Mexican food and has fountains, pools and a wave-making machine. 🍴 24 TV 🏊 *Rooms: 159.* 159.	AE DC MC V JCB	●	■	●	
CHIANG MAI: Chiang Mai Sports Club ⒷⒷⒷⒷⒷ 284 Mu 3, Tambon Don Kaew, Mae Rim. 📞 (053) 298330. FAX (053) 297897. Fabulous sporting facilities with everything available from horse riding to swimming in the Olympic-size pool. Even if you aren't athletic, its beautiful location is a great draw. 🍴 🍴 24 TV 🏊 *Rooms: 48.* 48.	AE DC MC V JCB	●	■	●	■
CHIANG MAI: Regent Chiang Mai ⒷⒷⒷⒷⒷ Mae Rim–Samoeng Old Rd. 📞 (053) 298181. FAX (053) 298189. In the Mae Sai valley with 20 acres of landscaped gardens featuring lakes, lily ponds and terraced rice fields, the Regent has the most spectacular setting of the Chiang Mai luxury hotels. 🍴 🍴 24 TV 🏊 *Rooms: 69.* 69.	AE DC MC V JCB	●	■	●	
CHIANG MAI: Westin Chiang Mai ⒷⒷⒷⒷⒷ 318/1 Chiang Mai–Lamphun Rd. 📞 (053) 275300. FAX (053) 275299. The Westin has some of the most expensive rooms in Chiang Mai, which gives it an exclusivity that attracts the rich and famous. Notable guests have included Elizabeth Taylor. 🍴 🍴 24 TV 🏊 *Rooms: 525.* 525.	AE DC MC V JCB	●	■	●	■
LAMPHUN: Suan Kaew Bungalow Ⓑ 209 Lamphun–Lampang Highway, Mu 4. 📞 No telephone. Good value, basic hotel just outside a town with little accommodation. A far nicer place to stay than the run-down Si Lamphun Hotel. *Rooms: 8.* 0.			■		
LAMPANG: Asia Lampang ⒷⒷ 229 Boonyawat Rd. 📞 (054) 227844. FAX (054) 224436. An old hotel that has been refurbished to compete with other local establishments like the Wiengthong. Now with an air of plushness, this hotel still offers good value for money. 🍴 24 TV *Rooms: 73.* 73.	MC V		■	●	
LAMPANG: Lampang Wiengthong ⒷⒷⒷ 138/109 Paholyothin Rd. 📞 (054) 225801. FAX (054) 225803. A luxurious hotel in downtown Lampang, in stark contrast to the town's average, dirty hotels. Very comfortable, with all modern conveniences, including business facilities. 🍴 🍴 24 TV 🏊 *Rooms: 235.* 235.	AE DC MC V JCB	●	■	●	■
MAE HONG SON: Piya Guest House Ⓑ 1 Khunlum Phrapat Rd. 📞 (053) 611260. FAX (053) 612308. Perfectly located on the shores of Chong Kham Lake, this is the best place for budget travellers wanting to check out Mae Hong Son's famous early morning mists. For this reason it is often full. 🍴 TV *Rooms: 10.* 10.			■		■
MAE HONG SON: Holiday Inn ⒷⒷⒷ 114/5–7 Khunlum Phrapat Rd. 📞 (053) 612324. FAX (053) 611524. Nestling at the foot of Doi Kong Mu, this 1990s hotel offers picture-postcard sunsets and misty dawn views. 🍴 24 TV 🏊 *Rooms: 114.* 114.	AE DC MC V	●	■	●	■

MAE HONG SON: *Imperial Tara* ⒷⒷⒷ
149 Mu 8, Tambon Pang Mu. 【 (053) 611021. FAX (053) 611252.
In the heart of trekking country, a short distance out of town, is this
beautifully appointed resort with grand Northern architecture set in
landscaped, tropical gardens. 🍴 🍴 TV 🛁 *Rooms: 104.* 🗐 *104.*

| | AE DC MC V JCB | ● | ■ | ● | |

MAE HONG SON: *Rooks Resort* ⒷⒷⒷ
114/5–7 Khunlum Phrapat Rd. 【 053) 612108. FAX (053) 611524.
Billed as "mountain view detached bungalows", these luxurious chalet-
type accommodations share some of the facilities of the neighbouring
Holiday Inn, but offer more privacy. 🍴 24 TV 🛁 *Rooms: 70.* 🗐 *70.*

| | AE DC MC V | ● | ■ | ● | |

PAI: *Rim Pai Cottages* ⒷⒷ
17, Mu 3, Viang Tai Rd. 【 (053) 699133. FAX (053) 699234.
The best place to stay in the small town of Pai, by the river. Thai houses
are available. The price includes breakfast. 🍴 *Rooms: 22.* 🗐 *0.*

| | | | ■ | | |

FAR NORTH

CHIANG KHONG: *Wiangkaeo Guest House* Ⓑ
8/1–8/4 Sai Klang Rd. 【 No telephone.
A handful of clean and attractive rooms in a teak house. Its terrace, right
on the bank of the Mekhong, allows good views of Laos. 🍴 *Rooms: 5.* 🗐 *0.*

| | | | ■ | | ■ |

CHIANG RAI: *Boonbundan Guest House* Ⓑ
1005/13 Chet Yot Rd. 【 (053) 717040.
In a quiet, shaded area not far from the town centre, and with an
attractive outdoor restaurant. Fans cool down the bungalows; air-
conditioning is in the newer, main building. 🍴 *Rooms: 53.* 🗐 *12.*

| | | | ■ | | |

CHIANG RAI: *Chiang Rai Inn* ⒷⒷ
661 Uttarakit Rd. 【 (053) 712673. FAX (053) 711483.
Modern Northern Thai architecture distinguishes this smart hotel from
many of its nondescript competitors. The rooms are spotlessly clean and
comfortable; the staff attentive and friendly. 🍴 24 TV *Rooms: 77.* 🗐 *77.*

| | AE MC V | | ■ | ● | ■ |

CHIANG RAI: *Golden Triangle Inn* ⒷⒷ
590 Paholyothin Rd. 【 (053) 711339. FAX (053) 713963.
A mid-range hotel with a Japanese garden and rooms in traditional Thai
decor. The price includes American breakfast. 🍴 *Rooms: 34.* 🗐 *34.*

| | MC V | | ■ | ● | ■ |

CHIANG RAI: *Dusit Island Resort* ⒷⒷⒷ
1129 Kraisorn Sit Rd. 【 (053) 715777. FAX (053) 715801.
Set on an island in the middle of the Kok River, and so a great place from
which to view the river activity, this attractive hotel has a relaxed atmosphere
and lovely outdoor restaurant. 🍴 🍴 24 TV 🛁 *Rooms: 271.* 🗐 *271.*

| | AE DC MC V JCB | | ■ | ● | ■ |

CHIANG RAI: *Little Duck* ⒷⒷⒷ
199 Paholyothin Rd. 【 (053) 715620. FAX (053) 715639.
Despite its name, this is not a little place at all, rather, a massive hotel complex wedded to a shopping mall with many facilities, including a snooker
hall and convention rooms. 🍴 24 TV 🛁 *Rooms: 330.* 🗐 *330.*

| | AE DC MC V JCB | ● | ■ | ● | ■ |

CHIANG RAI: *Wiang Inn* ⒷⒷⒷ
893 Paholyothin Rd. 【 (053) 711533. FAX (053) 711877.
A fairly typical, large, provincial hotel with every sort of facility including
disco and masseurs. 🍴 24 TV 🛁 *Rooms: 258.* 🗐 *258.*

| | AE DC MC V JCB | ● | ■ | ● | |

CHIANG SAEN: *Gin Guest House* Ⓑ
71 Chiang Saen–Sop Ruak Rd Mu 8. 【 No telephone.
Set in a lychee orchard, this guesthouse offers secluded, pretty bungalows
and bicycles for visiting the Golden Triangle. 🍴 *Rooms: 13.* 🗐 *0.*

| | | | ■ | | ■ |

DOI MAE SALONG (SANTIKHIREE): *Mae Salong Resort* ⒷⒷⒷ
Chiang Rai–Mae Chan Rd. 【 (053) 765014. FAX (053) 765135.
The best hotel with the finest views, over the mountains on the Thai-
Burmese border, in a beautiful, remote town. The restaurant has a
considerable reputation for Yunnanese food. 🍴 24 TV *Rooms: 59.* 🗐 *0.*

| | MC V | | ■ | | |

GOLDEN TRIANGLE: *Delta Golden Triangle* ⒷⒷⒷ
222 Golden Triangle, Sop Ruak. 【 (053) 784001. FAX (053) 784006.
All rooms face the river and offer a fine view of the Golden Triangle –
the confluence of the Ruak and Mekhong rivers. The excellent restaurant
serves Thai and Western fare. 🍴 24 TV 🛁 *Rooms: 70.* 🗐 *70.*

| | AE DC MC V | ● | ■ | ● | ■ |

Price categories for a standard double room per night, including tax for luxury hotels.

(B) under B350
(B)(B) B350–800
(B)(B)(B) B800–1,600
(B)(B)(B)(B) B1,600–3,200
(B)(B)(B)(B)(B) over B3,200

CREDIT CARDS
AE American Express; DC Diners Club; MC MasterCard; V VISA; JCB Japanese Credit Bureau.

WESTERN BATHROOMS
Indicates sit-down, flush toilets; showers and/or baths. Others have squat toilets and trough-and-dipper baths.

COFFEE SHOP
Hotel with coffee shop.

GARDEN/TERRACE
Hotel with garden, courtyard or terrace.

		CREDIT CARDS	SWIMMING POOL	WESTERN BATHROOMS	COFFEE SHOP	GARDEN/TERRACE
GOLDEN TRIANGLE: *Meridien Baan Boran* (B)(B)(B)(B) 229 Mu 1, Golden Triangle, Sop Ruak. (053) 784084. FAX (053) 784090. Probably one of Northern Thailand's most luxurious hotels, designed in traditional style. A lively resort specializing in mountain biking, elephant rides, boat trips and assorted tours. ⚫ Rooms: 110. 110.		AE DC MC V JCB	●	■	●	■
MAE SAI: *Mae Sai Guest House* (B) Rim Sai Rd. (053) 732021. Attractive, relaxing bungalow accommodation by the fascinating Sai River. So close to Burma that you can watch the women washing clothes on the opposite bank each morning. Rooms: 25. 0.				■		■
MAE SAI: *Mae Sai Plaza* (B) 383/6 Sailomchoi Rd. (053) 732230. Having the appearance of a medieval fortress, this extraordinary collection of rooms and huts is built into the side of a cliff. Views over the river towards Burma are captivating. Rooms: 60. 0.				■		■
NAN: *Sukkasem* (B) 119–121 Ananta Worarittidet Rd. (054) 710141. A basic, ferro-concrete hotel in history-steeped Nan, with little to recommend it but low price and relatively clean rooms. Rooms: 43. 4.				■		
NAN: *Dheveraj* (B)(B)(B) 466 Sumon Dheveraj Rd. (054) 710094. FAX (054) 4171365. The best hotel in Nan, albeit somewhat in need of modernization. Built around a courtyard featuring a fountain. Large, clean rooms and friendly staff. Rooms: 154. 115.		MC V		■	●	■
PHRAE: *Nakhon Phrae Tower* (B)(B) 3 Muang Hit Rd. (054) 521321. FAX (054) 523503. This hotel tower block has comfortable rooms with all modern facilities. Tours can be organized to visit hill-tribe villages and nearby craft centres. Rooms: 139. 139.		AE DC MC V JCB		■	●	■
PHRAE: *Mae Yom Palace* (B)(B)(B) 181/6 Yantrakit Koson Rd. (054) 521028. FAX (054) 522904. Definitely the best hotel in town, offering tours to hill-tribe villages. Well run, amiable, and with spotless rooms. Rooms: 104. 104.		AE MC V	●	■	●	■
THA TON: *Mae Kok River Lodge* (B)(B)(B) 3 Chiang Mai–Tha Ton Rd. (053) 459328. FAX (053) 459329. A small hotel in a beautiful, remote location, by the Burmese frontier. Specializes in "Track of the Tiger" trekking. Rooms: 22. 0.		MC V		■		■

KHORAT PLATEAU

		CREDIT CARDS	SWIMMING POOL	WESTERN BATHROOMS	COFFEE SHOP	GARDEN/TERRACE
BURIRAM: *Sang Rung Interpark* (B)(B)(B)(B) 38 Mu 1, Tambon Isaan, Amphur Muang. (044) 621203. FAX (044) 612392. Though in the nondescript town of Buriram, this is the nearest quality hotel to the Khmer ruins at Phnom Rung. Rooms: 250. 250.		AE MC V		■	●	■
CHAIYAPHUM: *Lertnimitra* (B)(B) 447/1 Nivesrat Rd. (044) 811522. FAX (044) 822335. Chaiyaphum is the most convenient base for visiting the nearby silk villages. This hotel offers some air-conditioned bungalows as well as fan and air-conditioned rooms in the main building. Rooms: 79. 59.		AE DC MC V JCB		■	●	
KHON KAEN: *Suksawat* (B) 2/2 Klang Muang Rd. (043) 236472. An old wooden building located on the quiet back streets of this busy Northeastern city. No special facilities, but with more personality and character than many of the larger establishments. Rooms: 33. 0.				■		■

KHON KAEN: *Khon Kaen* ⓑⓑ
43/2 Pimpasute Rd. 📞 (043) 244883. FAX (043) 242458.
Large, modern hotel with nightclub and karaoke. The restaurant serves
good Thai, Western and Japanese fare. 🍽 24 TV 🛗 *Rooms: 124.* 📇 *124.*

AE DC MC V		■	●

KHORAT: *Doctor's House* ⓑ
78 Sueb Siri Rd, Soi 4. 📞 (044) 255846.
Fine, very reasonably priced rooms, and a relaxing garden seating area.
Helpful staff are always glad to give you information on local area. Guests
keep coming back because of the family atmosphere. 🍽 *Rooms: 6.* 📇 *0.*

		■	■

KHORAT: *Siri* ⓑⓑ
688–90 Pho Klang Rd. 📞 (044) 242831.
Quiet and friendly accommodation, popular with budget travellers. On
the ground floor is the Veterans of Foreign Wars Café – Khorat was a US air
base during the Vietnam War. Serves US-style fast food. 🍽 *Rooms: 40.* 📇 *10.*

	■

KHORAT: *Royal Princess* ⓑⓑⓑⓑ
1137 Sura Narai Rd. 📞 (044) 256629. FAX (044) 256601.
Luxurious hotel decorated tastefully in Northeastern Thai style. The
Empress Chinese restaurant is excellent; it has a reputation for serving
good local food, too. 🍽 24 TV 🛗 *Rooms: 188.* 📇 *188.*

AE DC MC V JCB	●	■	●

KHORAT: *Sima Thani* ⓑⓑⓑⓑ
Mittraphap Rd. 📞 (044) 213100. FAX (044) 213122.
The top hotel in Khorat, but quite far from the centre of town. All
modern facilities, very spacious, and with a pleasant garden atrium dotted
with Khmer-style sculptures. 🍽 🍴 24 TV 🛗 *Rooms: 265.* 📇 *265.*

AE DC MC V JCB	●	■	●

PHIMAI: *Old Phimai Guest House* ⓑ
Off Chonsudasadet Drive. 📞 (044) 471918.
Under friendly management, and with a tranquil atmosphere, this
enchanting wooden guesthouse has attractive bedrooms and a pleasant roof
garden. Very close to the temple at Phimai. 🍽 *Rooms: 8.* 📇 *0.*

	■

ROI ET: *Petcharat* ⓑⓑ
66–80 Haisok Rd. 📞 (043) 511741. FAX (043) 514078.
A typical Thai provincial hotel: clean, but plain. Ask for rooms away from the
road, which can be noisy at night. 🍽 24 TV *Rooms: 150.* 📇 *150.*

MC V	■	●

SURIN: *Petchkasem* ⓑⓑⓑ
104 Chitbumrung Rd. 📞 (044) 511274. FAX (044) 514041.
Medium-sized luxurious hotel with large, air-conditioned rooms, good
business facilities and attentive staff. 🍽 24 TV 🛗 *Rooms: 162.* 📇 *162.*

MC V	■	●

SURIN: *Tarin* ⓑⓑⓑⓑ
60 Sirirat Rd. 📞 (044) 514281. FAX (044) 511580.
Surin's top hotel, located slightly out of town. It has a cool, airy feel with
a marble atrium and all the usual trappings and facilities of a luxury
hotel. 🍽 🍴 24 TV 🛗 *Rooms: 240.* 📇 *240.*

MC V	●	■	●

UDON THANI: *Charoen* ⓑⓑⓑ
549 Phosri Rd. 📞 (042) 248155. FAX (042) 241093.
The Charoen is a large, well-appointed business hotel with air-conditioned rooms and glitzy bar and disco. 🍽 24 TV 🛗 *Rooms: 242.* 📇 *242.*

AE DC MC V		■	●

UDON THANI: *Charoensri Grand* ⓑⓑⓑ
277/1 Prajak Rd. 📞 (042) 343555. FAX (042) 343550.
Luxury tower hotel providing the best accommodation for miles around.
Lacks character, but its clean, spacious bedrooms with good views from
the upper floors more than make up. 🍽 🍴 24 TV 🛗 *Rooms: 255.* 📇 *255.*

MC V JCB	●	■	●

MEKHONG RIVER VALLEY

CHIANG KHAN: *Nong Sam Guest House* ⓑ
Rim Kong Rd. 📞 No telephone.
Very friendly establishment run by an Englishman and his Thai wife,
consisting of large, comfortable, screened rooms in brick and wood
bungalows. Try the delicious, home-cooked Thai food. 🍽 *Rooms: 6.* 📇 *0.*

	■

LOEI: *Phuluang* ⓑⓑⓑ
55 Charoen Rat Rd. 📞 (042) 811532. FAX (042) 812558.
A typical upcountry Thai hotel – clean, spartan rooms complemented by
adequate facilities and a small nightclub. 🍽 TV *Rooms: 86.* 📇 *86.*

■	●

Price categories for a standard double room per night, including tax for luxury hotels.

B under B350
BB B350–800
BBB B800–1,600
BBBB B1,600–3,200
BBBBB over B3,200

CREDIT CARDS
AE American Express; DC Diners Club; MC MasterCard; V VISA; JCB Japanese Credit Bureau.

WESTERN BATHROOMS
Indicates sit-down, flush toilets; showers and/or baths. Others have squat toilets and trough-and-dipper baths.

COFFEE SHOP
Hotel with coffee shop.

GARDEN/TERRACE
Hotel with garden, courtyard or terrace.

	CREDIT CARDS	SWIMMING POOL	WESTERN BATHROOMS	COFFEE SHOP	GARDEN/TERRACE

MUKDAHAN: *Hua Nam*   B
20 Samut Sakdarak Rd. 📞 (042) 611137.
No facilities whatsoever, but clean and reasonably priced, with large rooms. Close to the pier for Suwannakhet in Laos. **Rooms:** 32. ▤ 10.

MUKDAHAN: *Mukdahan*   BB
8/8 Samut Sakdarat Rd. 📞 (042) 611619.
This is a no-frills hotel, just out of town near the river, but it is clean and friendly, and Northeastern food is available. 🍴 **Rooms:** 55. ▤ 30.
Western Bathrooms · Coffee Shop · Garden/Terrace

MUKDAHAN: *Mukdahan Grand*   BBB
78 Songnang Sathit Rd. 📞 (042) 612020. FAX (042) 612021.
With good views across the Mekhong to Suwannakhet in Laos and high standards unmatched in Mukdahan. 🍴 24 📺 🛏 **Rooms:** 200. ▤ 200.
AE MC V · Western Bathrooms · Coffee Shop · Garden/Terrace

NAKHON PHANOM: *River Inn*   B
137 Sunthorn Wichit Rd. 📞 (042) 511305.
A rather shabby and run-down hotel in one of Thailand's oldest towns, but well located beside the Mekhong River. 🍴 **Rooms:** 16. ▤ 8.
Western Bathrooms · Coffee Shop · Garden/Terrace

NAKHON PHANOM: *Maenam Khong Grand View*   BBB
527 Sunthorn Wichit Rd. 📞 (042) 513564. FAX (042) 511037.
Nakhon Phanom's most luxurious accommodation, with every modern convenience. Spectacular views over the Mekhong River to Laos make staying here a memorable experience. 🍴 24 📺 🛏 **Rooms:** 150. ▤ 150.
AE DC MC V JCB · Swimming Pool · Western Bathrooms · Coffee Shop · Garden/Terrace

NONG KHAI: *Mut Mee Guest House*   B
1111/4 Kaew Worawut Rd. 📞 No telephone.
In a beautiful mango orchard overlooking the Mekhong, this welcoming establishment, run by an Englishman and his Thai wife, consists of rooms or bamboo huts. Bicycles can be hired. **Rooms:** 10. ▤ 0.
Garden/Terrace

NONG KHAI: *Nong Khai Grand Thani*   BBB
589 Nong Khai–Ponephisai Rd. 📞 (042) 420033. FAX (042) 412026.
A mid-range hotel to the south of the main city on the route to Wat Khaek. Facilities include a disco. 🍴 24 📺 🛏 **Rooms:** 130. ▤ 130.
AE DC MC V JCB · Swimming Pool · Western Bathrooms · Coffee Shop

NONG KHAI: *Mekong Royal Nong Khai*   BBBB
222 Had Jommani Rd. 📞 (042) 420024. FAX (042) 421280.
A luxurious, riverside establishment near the Friendship Bridge, which opened in 1993 in anticipation of the increased number of visitors crossing to and from Laos. 🍴 24 📺 🛏 **Rooms:** 198. ▤ 198.
AE DC MC V JCB · Swimming Pool · Western Bathrooms · Coffee Shop · Garden/Terrace

THAT PHANOM: *Niyana Guest House*   B
73 Rimkhong Rd, Soi Withi Sawrachon. 📞 (042) 298181.
This friendly guesthouse by the Mekhong, with small roof-top garden, is notable for its baguettes and Lao coffee. 🍴 **Rooms:** 10. ▤ 0.
Garden/Terrace

PHU KRADUNG: *Phu Kradung National Park Bungalows*   BB
Phu Kradung National Park. 📞 (02) 579 0529.
Attractive, well-appointed bungalows arranged in the lee of a hill in the middle of the national park. Book well in advance. 🍴 **Rooms:** 6. ▤ 0.
Western Bathrooms · Garden/Terrace

UBON RATCHATHANI: *Tokyo*   B
360 Upparat Rd. 📞 (045) 241739.
The Tokyo is a friendly, reasonably priced hotel with clean rooms. Popular, despite lacking distinguishing features. **Rooms:** 48. ▤ 10.
Western Bathrooms

UBON RATCHATHANI: *Regent Palace*   BB
265–271 Kulyangkun Rd. 📞 (045) 255529. FAX (045) 245597.
Facilities include a snooker club and a cocktail lounge. The hotel is clean, comfortable and quiet, but not particularly inspiring.
🍴 24 📺 🛏 **Rooms:** 159. ▤ 159.
AE DC MC V · Western Bathrooms · Coffee Shop

UBON RATCHATHANI: *Pathumrat*   ⓑⓑⓑ
337 Chayangkun Rd. 📞 *(045) 241501.* 𝐅𝐀𝐗 *(045) 242313.*
A luxury hotel, close to the town centre. Favoured by tour companies,
facilities include a disco and nightclub. 🍽 24 TV 🛗 *Rooms: 168.* 🗄 *168.*

AE MC V

EASTERN SEABOARD

BANG SAEN: *Bang Saen Villa*   ⓑⓑⓑ
190 Mu 13 Beach Rd. 📞 *(038) 282088.* 𝐅𝐀𝐗 *(038) 383333.*
One of several resort hotels north of Si Racha, with the best view over
the bay and a reputation for delicious seafood. Good range of facilities.
🍽 24 TV 🛗 *Rooms: 70.* 🗄 *70.*

MC V

CHANTHABURI: *Chanthaburi Riverside*   ⓑⓑⓑ
63 Mu 9, Chantanimit V Rd. 📞 *(039) 311726.* 𝐅𝐀𝐗 *(039) 311726.*
A very plush resort hotel near the river, with courteous, efficient staff and
good attention to detail. With regard to facilities, it has just about everything, including its own botanical garden. 🍽 24 TV 🛗 *Rooms: 72.* 🗄 *72.*

MC V

CHANTHABURI: *KP Grand*   ⓑⓑⓑ
35/200–201 Trirat Rd. 📞 *(039) 323201.* 𝐅𝐀𝐗 *(039) 323214.*
Luxurious and spacious hotel offering perhaps the best accommodation
in town. Try the sticky rice and durian at the restaurant when this fruit
is in season (Mar–May). 🍽 🍹 24 TV 🛗 *Rooms: 202.* 🗄 *202.*

AE DC MC V JCB

KO CHANG: *White Sand Beach Resort*   ⓑⓑ
Hat Sai Khao. 📞 *No telephone.*
Paradise – sturdy huts roofed with nipa palm; hammocks strung between
palm trees; and white, coral sands. 🍽 *Rooms: 12.* 🗄 *0.*

KO CHANG: *Ko Chang Resort*   ⓑⓑⓑ
39 Mu 4. 📞 *(039) 597212.* 𝐅𝐀𝐗 *(039) 597028.*
Lovely bungalows set amid leaning palms overlooking the South China
Sea – a Robinson Crusoe-style getaway. 🍽 TV 🛗 *Rooms: 60.* 🗄 *60.*

AE DC MC V

KO SAMET: *Naga*   ⓑ
Ao Hin Kok. 📞 *(01) 3210732.* 𝐅𝐀𝐗 *(01) 3210732.*
Simple bungalows set on a low hill overlooking Hin Kok bay. The attached
restaurant sells delicious home-made bread and cakes. 🍽 *Rooms: 21.* 🗄 *0.*

KO SAMET: *Sea Breeze*   ⓑⓑ
Ao Phai. 📞 *(01) 3294780.*
Convivial staff and a good restaurant serving – inevitably – fresh seafood of
all descriptions. The management organizes interesting boat, snorkelling
and fishing trips around the enchanting island. 🍽 *Rooms: 60.* 🗄 *0.*

KO SAMET: *Wongduan Resort*   ⓑⓑ
Ao Wong Duan. 📞 *(038) 651777.* 𝐅𝐀𝐗 *(038) 651819.*
Comfortable bungalow resort next to the calm, azure waters of Wong
Duan bay. Unfortunately, the peace is often broken by jet-skiers. It is out of
the price range of most backpackers. 🍽 *Rooms: 54.* 🗄 *54.*

MC V

KO SAMET: *Diamond Beach and Sea View*   ⓑⓑⓑ
Hat Sai Kaeo. 📞 *(01) 239 0208.*
Well-located and generously spaced cluster of simple bungalows beside
a pristine beach. The on-site restaurant serves delicious and very fresh
seafood for the fun-loving, lively clientele. 🍽 *Rooms: 15.* 🗄 *0.*

MC V

KO SAMET: *Samet Ville Resort*   ⓑⓑⓑ
299 Mu 4. 📞 *(01) 321 1284.* 𝐅𝐀𝐗 *(02) 246 3196.*
Secluded, well away from the sprawl of bungalows on the more
developed beaches, this relaxing resort, rather up-market for Samet,
offers luxurious accommodation in an idyllic setting. 🍽 *Rooms: 64.* 🗄 *12.*

PATTAYA: *Diamond Beach*   ⓑⓑ
373/8 South Pattaya Beach Rd. 📞 *(038) 429885.* 𝐅𝐀𝐗 *(038) 424888.*
If you want to stay in the vibrant heart of South Pattaya's "strip", then this
is the place for you. A beauty salon, videotheque and massage parlour
are among the facilities. 🍽 🍹 24 TV 🛗 *Rooms: 152.* 🗄 *152.*

AE DC MC V JCB

PATTAYA: *Diana Inn*   ⓑⓑ
216/6–9 Pattaya 2nd Rd. 📞 *(038) 429870.* 𝐅𝐀𝐗 *(038) 424566.*
Friendly, clean and very good value. The restaurant has a wide range of
reasonably priced Thai and Western fare. 🍽 24 TV 🛗 *Rooms: 114.* 🗄 *114.*

AE MC V

<table>
<tr><td colspan="2">

Price categories for a standard double room per night, including tax for luxury hotels.

Ⓑ under B350
ⒷⒷ B350–800
ⒷⒷⒷ B800–1,600
ⒷⒷⒷⒷ B1,600–3,200
ⒷⒷⒷⒷⒷ over B3,200

</td><td colspan="2">

CREDIT CARDS
AE American Express; DC Diners Club; MC MasterCard; V VISA; JCB Japanese Credit Bureau.

WESTERN BATHROOMS
Indicates sit-down, flush toilets; showers and/or baths. Others have squat toilets and trough-and-dipper baths.

COFFEE SHOP
Hotel with coffee shop.

GARDEN/TERRACE
Hotel with garden, courtyard or terrace.

</td></tr>
</table>

	CREDIT CARDS	SWIMMING POOL	WESTERN BATHROOMS	COFFEE SHOP	GARDEN/TERRACE
PATTAYA: *Peace Resort* ⒷⒷ 179/40 Mu 5, Pattaya–Naklua Rd. 📞 *(038) 426605.* 📠 *(038) 426607.* As the name suggests, this is a refuge from the noisy, southern part of town. The landscaped gardens are attractive. 🍴 24 📺 🛁 *Rooms: 130.* 🗐 *130.*	MC V	●	▣	●	▣
PATTAYA: *Grand Jomtien Palace* ⒷⒷⒷ 356 Jomtien Beach Rd. 📞 *(038) 231405.* 📠 *(038) 231404.* Situated far down Jomtien Road to the south of Pattaya's bustling night life, with fine views across Jomtien bay. 🍽 24 📺 🛁 *Rooms: 250.* 🗐 *250.*	AE MC V	●	▣	●	▣
PATTAYA: *Little Duck Pattaya Resort* ⒷⒷⒷ 336/22 Pattaya Klang Rd. 📞 *(038) 428065.* 📠 *(038) 426043.* This hi-tech, medium-sized hotel is located in the centre of Pattaya's entertainment area. Hosts a popular disco. 🍴 24 📺 🛁 *Rooms: 160.* 🗐 *160.*	AE DC MC V	●	▣	●	▣
PATTAYA: *Mermaid's Beach Resort* ⒷⒷⒷ 75/1 Mu 12, Nong Pru Jomtien Beach Rd. 📞 *(038) 231907.* 📠 *(038) 231908.* One of the best run and most attractive hotels on family-oriented Jomtien beach, with a good reputation for fresh seafood. 🍴 📺 *Rooms: 112.* 🗐 *112.*	AE DC MC V	●	▣	●	▣
PATTAYA: *Palm Garden* ⒷⒷⒷ 240/1 Mu 5, Pattaya 2nd Rd. 📞 *(038) 429188.* 📠 *(038) 429188.* Located in the quiet, northern part of town, this hotel is clean, reasonably priced, and has attractive gardens. 🍴 24 📺 *Rooms: 115.* 🗐 *115.*	AE DC MC V	●	▣	●	▣
PATTAYA: *A-One Royal Cruise* ⒷⒷⒷⒷ 499 Beach Rd North. 📞 *(038) 424875.* 📠 *(038) 424242.* Designed to resemble a cruise liner, with spectacular views over Pattaya bay. Facilities include a disco, barber's salon, beauty shop and shopping arcade. 🍴 🍽 24 📺 🛁 *Rooms: 200.* 🗐 *200.*	AE DC MC V JCB	●	▣	●	
PATTAYA: *Amari Orchid Resort* ⒷⒷⒷⒷ 240 Mu 5, Pattaya Beach Rd. 📞 *(038) 428161.* 📠 *(038) 428165.* Situated in extensive grounds at the quiet, north end of Pattaya's crescent-shaped bay, hidden from noisy discos and beer bars. The resort has Asian and Western restaurants. 🍴 24 📺 🛁 *Rooms: 236.* 🗐 *236.*	AE DC MC V	●	▣	●	▣
PATTAYA: *Asia Pattaya* ⒷⒷⒷ Pratumnak Rd. 📞 *(038) 250602.* 📠 *(038) 250491.* On a low cliff overlooking Ao Noi or "little bay" is this very private, very exclusive, hotel with good views. Facilities include tennis courts, a golf course and water sports equipment. 🍴 🍽 24 📺 🛁 *Rooms: 314.* 🗐 *314.*	AE DC MC V JCB	●	▣	●	▣
PATTAYA: *Wong Amat* ⒷⒷⒷ Pattaya–Naklua Rd. 📞 *(038) 426990.* 📠 *(038) 428599.* Well-appointed establishment with everything on the premises from videotheque to tennis courts. 🍴 24 📺 🛁 *Rooms: 178.* 🗐 *178.*	AE DC MC V JCB	●	▣	●	▣
PATTAYA: *Woodland Resort* ⒷⒷⒷⒷ 164/1 Mu 5, Pattaya–Naklua Rd. 📞 *(038) 425661.* 📠 *(038) 425663.* Attractive colonial-lodge style resort set in well-maintained gardens far away from the traffic fumes of central Pattaya. 🍴 24 📺 🛁 *Rooms: 81.* 🗐 *81.*	AE DC MC V	●	▣	●	▣
PATTAYA: *Royal Cliff Beach Resort* ⒷⒷⒷⒷⒷ 378 Pratumnak Rd. 📞 *(038) 428513.* 📠 *(038) 250511.* Quite simply an institution. Every conceivable facility, including four swimming pools and eight restaurants, and set on top of a cliff overlooking Jomtien bay. 🍴 🍽 24 📺 🛁 *Rooms: 650.* 🗐 *650.*	AE DC MC V JCB	●	▣	●	▣
RAYONG: *Rayong* Ⓑ 65/1–3 Sukhumvit Rd. 📞 *(038) 611073.* A reasonably priced Thai hotel with friendly staff and clean rooms. Restaurant and food stalls nearby. *Rooms: 51.* 🗐 *10.*			▣		▣

RAYONG: *Hin Suay Nam Sai* ⒷⒷⒷⒷ — AE DC MC
250 Mu 2, Sakpon District, Klang. 【 *(038) 638260*. FAX *(038) 638034*.
Luxury resort set in landscaped grounds with a private beach. A haven
for racket sports enthusiasts. 🍽 🛒 24 TV 🏊 *Rooms: 174.* 🗖 *174*.

RAYONG: *Novotel Rimpae Rayong* ⒷⒷⒷⒷⒷ — AE DC MC V JCB
4/5 Mu 3, Pae Klang Kam Rd. 【 *(038) 648008*. FAX *(038) 648002*.
A spectacularly well-appointed resort hotel, which is not at all unusual
along this part of Thailand's Gulf coast, but in this case there are no less
than four swimming pools. 🍽 🛒 24 TV 🏊 *Rooms: 189.* 🗖 *189*.

TRAT: *Laem Ngop Inn* ⒷⒷ
19/14 Tambon Laem Ngop. 【 *(039) 597044*. FAX *(039) 597144*.
For most people Laem Ngop will be no more than a brief halt on the
way to or from Ko Chang. This basic hotel is actually the best in Trat
province, and it has lovely views of Ko Chang. TV *Rooms: 31.* 🗖 *26*.

TRAT: *Muang Trat* ⒷⒷ — MC V
40 Withiyoanya Rd. 【 *(039) 511091*.
An unremarkable hotel located in downtown Trat, but it is clean and
comfortable and has courteous staff. 🍽 TV *Rooms: 140.* 🗖 *140*.

WESTERN SEABOARD

CHA-AM: *Santisuk Bungalows and Beach Resort* ⒷⒷ — MC V
263/3 Ruamchit Rd. 【 *(032) 471212*.
Tastefully decorated, popular and reasonably priced establishment
offering both rooms and bungalow accommodation. 🍽 *Rooms: 12.* 🗖 *3*.

CHA-AM: *Beach Garden* ⒷⒷⒷⒷ — AE DC MC V JCB
949/21 Cha-am Beach. 【 *(032) 471334*. FAX *(032) 471334*.
South of central Cha-am on a clean, wide beach, this hotel offers water
sports, four swimming pools, tennis, fishing and even a mini golf course.
It is favoured by European tour groups. 🛒 24 TV 🏊 *Rooms: 230.* 🗖 *230*.

CHA-AM: *Cha-am Methavali* ⒷⒷⒷⒷ — AE DC MC V
220 Ruamchit Rd. 【 *(032) 471028*. FAX *(032) 471590*.
Well suited to families, with several multi-roomed bungalows. Clean,
quiet and attractive. 🍽 24 TV 🏊 *Rooms: 115.* 🗖 *115*.

CHA-AM: *Regent Cha-am* ⒷⒷⒷⒷ — AE DC MC V JCB
849/21 Phetkasem Rd. 【 *(032) 471482*. FAX *(032) 471492*.
Luxurious hotel and cottage accommodation on an enormous site – about
300 acres altogether – almost a village in its own right. Facilities include
squash and tennis courts. 🍽 🛒 24 TV 🏊 *Rooms: 600.* 🗖 *600*.

CHA-AM: *Dusit Resort and Polo Club* ⒷⒷⒷⒷⒷ — AE DC MC V JCB
1349 Phetkasem Rd. 【 *(032) 520009*. FAX *(032) 520296*.
A stylish resort with an English country and polo club theme. Rooms are
big and luxurious with oversized marble bathrooms. Facilities include
horse-riding, polo and water sports. 🍽 🛒 24 TV 🏊 *Rooms: 308.* 🗖 *308*.

CHUMPHON: *Pornsawan Home and Beach Resort* ⒷⒷⒷ — V
110 Mu 4, Paknam Rd. 【 *(077) 521521*. FAX *(077) 521529*.
The best establishment in town, with all modern conveniences. Tennis
courts and lovely sea views add to the attraction. 🍽 *Rooms: 60.* 🗖 *60*.

HUA HIN: *Ban Boosarin* ⒷⒷⒷ
8/8 Poonsuk Rd. 【 *(032) 512076*. FAX *(077) 521529*.
Hua Hin was Thailand's first beach resort when it became popular back
in the 1920s. This is good, cheaper accommodation in a town of expensive, luxurious resorts and it's close to the beach. TV *Rooms: 10.* 🗖 *10*.

HUA HIN: *Sofitel Central* ⒷⒷⒷⒷⒷ — AE DC MC V JCB
1 Damnoen Kasem Rd. 【 *(032) 512021*. FAX *(032) 512089*.
A luxurious and architecturally impressive colonial-style hotel *(see p321)*.
It has park-like grounds, which include a topiary garden, wide lawns, and
an orchid and butterfly farm. 🍽 🛒 24 TV 🏊 *Rooms: 216.* 🗖 *216*.

HUA HIN: *Melia Hua Hin* ⒷⒷⒷⒷⒷ — AE DC MC V JCB
33 Naresdamri Rd. 【 *(032) 511612*. FAX *(032) 511135*.
This luxurious, high-rise hotel stands right on Hua Hin's beach and offers
every facility. A big bonus is that all rooms have balconies that provide
excellent sea views. 🍽 🛒 24 TV 🏊 *Rooms: 297.* 🗖 *297*.

Price categories for a standard double room per night, including tax for luxury hotels.

Ⓑ under B350
ⒷⒷ B350–800
ⒷⒷⒷ B800–1,600
ⒷⒷⒷⒷ B1,600–3,200
ⒷⒷⒷⒷⒷ over B3,200

CREDIT CARDS
AE American Express; DC Diners Club; MC MasterCard; V VISA; JCB Japanese Credit Bureau.

WESTERN BATHROOMS
Indicates sit-down, flush toilets; showers and/or baths. Others have squat toilets and trough-and-dipper baths.

COFFEE SHOP
Hotel with coffee shop.

GARDEN/TERRACE
Hotel with garden, courtyard or terrace.

	CREDIT CARDS	SWIMMING POOL	WESTERN BATHROOMS	COFFEE SHOP	GARDEN/TERRACE
HUA HIN: *Mercure Hua Hin Resort* ⒷⒷⒷⒷⒷ 1 Damnoen Kasem Rd. ℂ (032) 512035. FAX (032) 511014. This Thai-style village in a garden setting complete with fountains, rock pools and ponds is a luxury resort for the well-heeled Bangkok weekender or wealthy foreign tourist. ⑪ 🍴 24 TV 🛁 *Rooms: 41.* ▤ *41.*	AE DC MC V JCB	●	▦	●	▦
HUA HIN: *Royal Garden Resort* ⒷⒷⒷⒷⒷ 107/1 Phetkasem Rd. ℂ (032) 511881. FAX (032) 512422. A large and luxurious resort for those in search of good sports facilities, which include golf, tennis and water sports. Also boasts a shopping arcade and a children's playground. ⑪ 🍴 24 TV 🛁 *Rooms: 220.* ▤ *220.*	AE DC MC V JCB	●	▦	●	▦
HUA HIN: *Royal Garden Village* ⒷⒷⒷⒷⒷ 43/1 Phetkasem Rd. ℂ (032) 520250. FAX (032) 520259. Traditional Thai housing set amid large, lush, tropical gardens. Rooms are Thai-style with teak and rattan furniture. Sports on offer include golf, sailing, surfing and sea kayaking. ⑪ TV 🛁 *Rooms: 162.* ▤ *162.*	AE DC MC V JCB	●	▦	●	▦
KO PHA NGAN: *Island View Cabana* Ⓑ 106 Mu 7, Mae Hat Beach. ℂ *No telephone.* Clean, friendly, basic accommodation on the island's northwestern coast. Its restaurant serves fresh seafood. Ko Mae, a small island just offshore, makes a beautiful backdrop to this beach paradise. ⑪ *Rooms: 25.* ▤ *0.*					▦
KO PHA NGAN: *Pha Ngan Bayshore Resort* ⒷⒷ Thong Nai Pan Beach. ℂ (01) 7250430. A relaxed and appealing resort in perfect surroundings. Coral sands, azure waters and plentiful coconut palms. ⑪ *Rooms: 50.* ▤ *50.*	MC V		▦		▦
KO SAMUI: *Golden Sand Resort* ⒷⒷⒷ 124/2 Lamai Beach. ℂ (077) 424031. FAX (077) 424430. This lively beach resort includes a snooker club, tennis court and videotheque. There's no swimming pool, but access to the appealing, shimmering ocean is easy. ⑪ TV *Rooms: 75.* ▤ *10.*	AE MC V		▦		
KO SAMUI: *Blue Lagoon* ⒷⒷⒷⒷ 99 Mu 2, Chaweng Beach. ℂ (077) 422037. FAX (077) 422401. Beautiful Thai buildings flanking Chaweng beach are complemented by a large swimming pool, children's pool and playground. Extensive water sports facilities include sea kayaking. ⑪ 🍴 TV 🛁 *Rooms: 71.* ▤ *71.*	AE DC MC V JCB	●	▦	●	▦
KO SAMUI: *Chaweng Regent Beach Resort* ⒷⒷⒷⒷ 155/4, Mu 2 Chaweng Beach. ℂ (077) 422008. FAX (077) 422222. Yet another beautifully appointed luxury resort with fine views over Chaweng beach. The restaurant specializes in delicious crayfish, lobster, crab and giant sizzling prawns. ⑪ 🍴 24 TV 🛁 *Rooms: 137.* ▤ *137.*	AE DC MC V JCB	●	▦	●	▦
KO SAMUI: *Coral Bay Resort* ⒷⒷⒷⒷ 9 Mu 2, Tambon Bophut. ℂ (077) 422223. FAX (077) 422392. Located at the northern end of Chaweng beach, this all-bungalow resort offers every comfort and a wide range of water sports. The bungalows are furnished with coconut wood furniture. ⑪ TV *Rooms: 42.* ▤ *42.*	AE MC V JCB	●	▦	●	▦
KO SAMUI: *Coral Cove Chalet* ⒷⒷⒷⒷ 210 Coral Cove Beach, Lamai. ℂ (077) 422260. FAX (077) 422496. At the top end of Lamai beach accommodation, very comfortable and with great views. The bright, chalets, grouped around a pool, are set in a cove framed by thousands of coconut palms. ⑪ TV *Rooms: 65.* ▤ *65.*	AE MC V	●	▦	▦	▦
KO SAMUI: *Imperial Boat House* ⒷⒷⒷⒷ 83 Mu 5, Tambon Bophut. ℂ (077) 425041. FAX (077) 425460. Extraordinary luxury resort featuring a boat-shaped swimming pool and teak rice barges for accommodation. ⑪ 24 TV 🛁 *Rooms: 216.* ▤ *216.*	AE DC MC V JCB	●	▦	●	▦

KO SAMUI: *Samui Euphoria* ⓑⓑⓑ
Bophut Beach. 【 *(077) 425100.* FAX *(077) 425107.*
Quiet, peaceful resort with an attractive, U-shaped tropical garden.
Leisure facilities include tennis courts, a games room and a huge pool.
Excellent sea views and a private beach. ⓘⓘ ⓘⓘ TV ⓘ *Rooms: 124.* 目 *124.*
AE DC MC V

KO SAMUI: *Central Samui Beach Resort* ⓑⓑⓑⓑ
38/2 Mu 3, Borpud, Chaweng Beach. 【 *(077) 230500.* FAX *(077) 422385.*
Immaculately maintained gardens and marvellous beach views from the
most beautiful, central stretch of Chaweng beach. Facilities include a
beauty salon and boutique. ⓘⓘ ⓘⓘ 24 TV ⓘ *Rooms: 208.* 目 *208.*
AE DC MC V JCB

KO SAMUI: *Poppies Samui* ⓑⓑⓑⓑ
PO Box 1, Chaweng. 【 *(077) 422419.* FAX *(077) 422420.*
A village of tastefully furnished, comfortable cottages, each secluded from
its neighbours by lush tropical gardens. ⓘⓘ TV *Rooms: 24.* 目 *24.*
AE DC MC V JCB

KO TAO: *Ko Nang Yuan Dive Resort* ⓑⓑ
Ko Nang Yuan, nr Ko Tao, Surat Thani. 【 *(01) 726 0085.* FAX *(01) 7260212.*
This bungalow and cottage resort is located on an island in a small,
three-island archipelago, encircled by a turquoise ring of coral. Excellent
diving around the island. ⓘⓘ *Rooms: 70.* 目 *70.*
MC V

PHETCHABURI: *Khao Wang Hotel* ⓑⓑ
123 Ratwithi Rd. 【 *(032) 425167.* FAX *(032) 410750.*
This basic hotel, in one of the country's oldest towns, is well positioned
for the attractions of the extravagant architecture of Khao Wang Palace and
the surrounding temples on Phra Nakhon Khiri hill. TV *Rooms: 58.* 目 *12.*
MC V

PRACHUAP KHIRI KHAN: *Hadthong* ⓑⓑ
7 Susuk Rd. 【 *(032) 611960.* FAX *(032) 601057.*
Comfortable modern hotel offering the best lodgings in town. Views both
over the bay and of nearby "mirror mountain". ⓘⓘ TV *Rooms: 140.* 目 *140.*
AE DC MC V

SURAT THANI: *Wang Tai* ⓑⓑⓑ
1 Talat Mai Rd. 【 *(077) 283020.* FAX *(077) 281007.*
The coffee shop of this modern hotel tower, just out of town, has wide
ranging views of the Tapi Estuary. The hotel also has a restaurant, a bar, a
discotheque and a golf course. ⓘⓘ 24 TV ⓘ *Rooms: 230.* 目 *230.*
AE DC MC V JCB

UPPER ANDAMAN COAST

KO PHI PHI: *Charlies* ⓑⓑ
Ao Lo Dalam. 【 *(075) 620615.*
Beachfront bungalows in a beautiful setting but somewhat over-priced for
the facilities offered. ⓘⓘ 24 TV ⓘ ⓘ *Rooms: 79.* 目 *0.*

KO PHI PHI: *Phi Phi Palm Beach* ⓑⓑⓑ
Laem Tong, Ko Phi Phi Don. 【 *(01) 7230922.* FAX *(01) 7230052.*
The most exclusive resort on the island. The design of its luxury cottages and
larger, family-style suites, has won a design award. Facilities include tennis
courts, a freshwater pool and a Jacuzzi. ⓘⓘ ⓘⓘ TV *Rooms: 80.* 目 *80.*
AE DC MC V

KO PHI PHI: *Pee Pee Island Cabana* ⓑⓑⓑⓑ
Ton Sai Bay, Ko Phi Phi Don. 【 *(076) 214941.* FAX *(076) 612196.*
Phi Phi comprises two islands: Phi Phi Don is the busier, Ton Sai bay its
main accommodation centre. These well-appointed bungalows are in a
jungle setting with superb sea views. ⓘⓘ TV *Rooms: 209.* 目 *150.*
AE MC V

KO LANTA: *Lanta Royal Resort* ⓑⓑ
Ko Lanta Yai. 【 *(075) 612524.*
Cottages and a restaurant set on the western side of the island in almost
completely unspoilt coconut groves. ⓘⓘ *Rooms: 73.* 目 *73.*

KRABI: *Phra Nang Place* ⓑⓑ
Ao Phra Nang. 【 *(075) 512172.* FAX *(075) 612251.*
Set in a private plantation, well off the beaten track. Part of the attraction
is catching the boat from Krabi or Ao Nang to get there. ⓘⓘ *Rooms: 26.* 目 *0.*

KRABI: *Phra Nang Inn* ⓑⓑⓑ
119 Mu 2, Ao Nang Beach. 【 *(075) 612174.* FAX *(075) 612174.*
This hotel has a rustic feel and is constructed out of pine and palms. It
has good views over Ao Nang beach. Facilities include a restaurant and a
small pool. ⓘⓘ TV *Rooms: 51.* 目 *30.*
AE MC V

Price categories for a standard double room per night, including tax for luxury hotels. (B) under B350 (B)(B) B350–800 (B)(B)(B) B800–1,600 (B)(B)(B)(B) B1,600–3,200 (B)(B)(B)(B)(B) over B3,200	**CREDIT CARDS** AE American Express; DC Diners Club; MC MasterCard; V VISA; JCB Japanese Credit Bureau. **WESTERN BATHROOMS** Indicates sit-down, flush toilets; showers and/or baths. Others have squat toilets and trough-and-dipper baths. **COFFEE SHOP** Hotel with coffee shop. **GARDEN/TERRACE** Hotel with garden, courtyard or terrace.			

	CREDIT CARDS	SWIMMING POOL	WESTERN BATHROOMS	COFFEE SHOP	GARDEN/TERRACE
KRABI: *Krabi Maritime* (B)(B)(B)(B) 1 Thungfah Rd. (075) 620028. FAX (075) 612992. Expensive, recently built establishment offering every facility including a beauty salon. This hotel is close to Krabi town, but some distance away from the main beach attractions. Rooms: 221. 221.	AE MC V	●	■	●	■
KRABI: *Krabi Resort* (B)(B)(B)(B) 232 Ao Nang Beach. (075) 637031. FAX (075) 637052. The most luxurious accommodation available at Ao Nang. Stay in the modern hotel buildings or try the beach-facing, thatched-roof bungalows. The gardens are well-tended and colourful. Rooms: 95. 95.	AE DC MC V JCB	●	■	●	■
PHANGNGA: *Phangnga Bay Resort* (B)(B)(B) 20 Thadan Rd, Panyi. (076) 412067. FAX (076) 412057. A mid-range, modern resort on the edge of Phangnga Bay. Views are disappointing, but facilities include a swimming pool and a recommended restaurant. Rooms: 80. 80.	AE MC V	●	■	●	■
PHUKET: *Thara Patong Beach Resort* (B)(B)(B) 81 Thaweewongse Rd. (076) 340135. FAX (076) 340446. An attractive seaside resort with just about everything from an outdoor Jacuzzi to tennis courts and a sauna room. There is a pool for children, and an excellent seafood restaurant. Rooms: 128. 128.	AE DC MC V	●	■	●	■
PHUKET: *Felix Karon* (B)(B)(B)(B) 4/8 Patak Rd, Karon Beach. (076) 396666. FAX (076) 396853. This hotel has good facilities for families with children and is well located for popular Karon Beach. Rooms: 126. 126.	AE DC MC V	●	■	●	■
PHUKET: *Amanpuri* (B)(B)(B)(B)(B) Sri Santhorn Rd. (076) 324333. FAX (076) 324100. *Amanpuri* is a Sanskrit word meaning place of peace, and is aptly applied to this elegant pavilion complex. In the evening there is a cultural performance including dancing and sword fights. Rooms: 40. 40.	AE DC MC V JCB	●	■	●	■
PHUKET: *Diamond Cliff Resort* (B)(B)(B)(B)(B) 61/9 Kalim Beach, Patong. (076) 340501. FAX (076) 340507. This resort nestles on the hillside above the clear waters of Patong bay, yet is only a short walk from Patong's vibrant nightlife. Has a fine choice of Asian and European restaurants. Rooms: 222. 222.	AE DC MC V JCB	●	■	●	■
PHUKET: *Dusit Laguna Resort* (B)(B)(B)(B)(B) 390 Sri Sunthorn Rd, Cherngtalay. (076) 324320. FAX (076) 324174. An astonishing resort hotel surrounded by a clear lagoon. All modern facilities including excellent restaurants. Rooms: 226. 226.	AE DC MC V JCB	●	■	●	■
PHUKET: *Laguna Beach Club* (B)(B)(B)(B)(B) 323 Sri Sunthorn Rd, Cherngtalay. (076) 324352. FAX (076) 324353. Another resort with just about everything in the way of amenities. Of special interest to parents, there is a supervized "Kids Club" where children can be safely left to play. Rooms: 252. 252.	AE DC MC V JCB	●	■	●	■
PHUKET: *Maiton Island Resort* (B)(B)(B)(B)(B) 100 Mu 7, Tambon Wichit, Phuket. (076) 214954. FAX (076) 214959. Maiton is an isolated, offshore island about 2 km (1 mile) long and just 400 m (1,300 ft) wide. There is no town or village – the resort offers peace and quiet in extraordinary comfort. Rooms: 75. 75.	AE DC MC V JCB	●	■		■
PHUKET: *Pearl Village* (B)(B)(B)(B)(B) Nai Yang Beach and National Park. (076) 327006. FAX (076) 327338. This resort lies on the fringes of a national park, north of Phuket town. Facilities include two pools, one with a waterfall. Famous guests have included Prince Philip and Michael Jackson. Rooms: 215. 215.	AE DC MC V JCB	●	■	●	■

DEEP SOUTH

HAT YAI: *Garden Home* ⓑⓑ MC V
51/2 Hoi Muk Rd. 【 (074) 234444. FAX (074) 234444.
Attractive modern hotel built around a waterfall and garden. Well located
for the tasty food stalls at the junction of Kimpradit and Phadung Phakdi
roads and good value for money. 🍴 24 TV **Rooms:** *103.* 🛏 *103.*

HAT YAI: *Diamond Plaza* ⓑⓑ AE MC V
62 Niphat Uthit 3 Rd. 【 (074) 230130. FAX (074) 239824.
This hotel is friendly and reasonably priced. It is located near the centre of
Hat Yai's nightlife. 🍴 24 TV **Rooms:** *272.* 🛏 *272.*

HAT YAI: *J B Hotel* ⓑⓑⓑ AE DC MC V JCB
99 Jootee Anusorn Rd. 【 (074) 234300. FAX (074) 234328.
The classiest hotel in Hat Yai, but rather away from the city centre on the
north side of town. 🍴 📺 24 TV 🏊 **Rooms:** *432.* 🛏 *432.*

KO TARUTAO: *National Park Bungalows* ⓑⓑ
Tarutao and Adang National Marine Park. 【 (02) 579 0529. FAX (02) 579 1154.
Rather short on facilities, but in incredibly beautiful natural surroundings.
The national park authority has an effective monopoly. 🍴 **Rooms:** *16.* 🛏 *0.*

NAKHON SI THAMMARAT: *Taksin* ⓑⓑ
1584/23 Sriprad Rd. 【 (075) 342790. FAX (075) 342794.
Most of Nakhon Si Thammarat's hotels are undistinguished, and this is no
exception. However, rooms are clean, the staff friendly and the tariff
remarkably good value. Large rooms. 🍴 TV **Rooms:** *155.* 🛏 *155.*

NAKHON SI THAMMARAT: *Thai* ⓑⓑ MC V
1375 Rachadamnoen Rd. 【 (075) 341512. FAX (075) 344858.
Conveniently located two blocks from the railway station, this clean but
unremarkable hotel boasts a videotheque, a discotheque and a shopping
mall. 🍴 TV **Rooms:** *210.* 🛏 *120.*

NARATHIWAT: *Tanyong* ⓑⓑ MC V
16/1 Sopha Phisai Rd. 【 (073) 511477. FAX (073) 511834.
Chinese-style hotel with good Malay cuisine. Try the mangoes and sticky
rice speciality during the hot season. 🍴 TV **Rooms:** *84.* 🛏 *84.*

PATTANI: *My Garden* ⓑⓑ MC V
8/28 Charoen Pradit Rd. 【 (073) 331055. FAX (073) 348200.
Located about 1 km (1,100 yds) out of town. The best accommodation in
Pattani, with a very popular disco. Try the Diana Restaurant directly
opposite, which specializes in seafood. 🍴 TV **Rooms:** *150.* 🛏 *150.*

PHATTHALUNG: *Lam Pam Resort* ⓑⓑ V
88 Mu 6, Tambon Lam Pam. 【 (074) 611486. FAX (074) 610213.
This resort has clean, simple chalets, a good restaurant and is situated 15
minutes' drive out of town on the banks of the Thale Sap lake. Many
think it is the best option available in Phatthalung. TV **Rooms:** *50.* 🛏 *0.*

SONGKHLA: *Lake Inn* ⓑⓑ AE DC MC V
301–3 Nakhon Nok Rd. 【 (074) 321441. FAX (074) 321441.
A mid-range establishment located on the western side of Songkhla,
overlooking the main fishing wharf for the Thale Sap lake. As might be
expected, the Lake Inn serves good seafood. 🍴 TV **Rooms:** *80.* 🛏 *80.*

SONGKHLA: *Royal Crown Songkhla* ⓑⓑ AE MC V
8 Sai Ngam Rd. 【 (074) 312174. FAX (074) 321027.
A clean, pleasant and centrally located establishment, popular with Songkhla's expatriate oil workers and their families. 🍴 24 TV **Rooms:** *52.* 🛏 *52.*

TRANG: *Clarion MP Resort Hotel* ⓑⓑ MC V
184 Trang–Phatthalung Rd. 【 (075) 214230. FAX (075) 211177.
Shaped like a luxury liner, this opulent establishment offers every sort of
facility including a lovely garden restaurant, extensive swimming pools,
karaoke and lobby bar. 🍴 📺 24 TV 🏊 **Rooms:** *191.* 🛏 *191.*

TRANG: *Thumrin* ⓑⓑ AE MC V
99 Thumrin Square. 【 (075) 211011. FAX (075) 218057.
An up-market, high-rise hotel located in central Trang near the railway
station. It is starting to look a little shabby, nevertheless, it still ranks as
one of the better hotels in Trang. 🍴 TV **Rooms:** *117.* 🛏 *117.*

For key to symbols see back flap

WHERE TO EAT

THAILAND IS FORTUNATE in being a land of plenty. As much of the land is fertile and the population has always been small relative to the size of the country, famine is all but unknown. In the 13th century King Ramkamhaeng of Sukhothai, the first Thai kingdom, recorded: "This land is thriving... in the water are fish, in the fields there is rice." He might also have mentioned the wide range of tropical fruits, vegetables and spices – to which have been added, since his day, a wealth of imports from

The usual eating implements

tropical America, thriving in their new Old World setting. The range of dishes, as well as the variety and freshness of the ingredients, make for one of the world's great cuisines. Thais love to eat: six or seven times a day is not uncommon. Wherever there are people there are restaurants and food stalls. As well as flavour and freshness, Thais also appreciate the harmonious presentation of food. The dishes of even a modest meal will often be garnished with flowers and rosettes carved out of colourful vegetables and fruit.

The Grand Ballroom of the Holiday Inn on Silom Road, Bangkok

RESTAURANTS

THERE IS A GREAT RANGE and diversity of eating establishments, from "hole in the wall" cafés, through the leafy *aban suan* "garden restaurants" to air-conditioned oases of luxury. Unlike the ubiquitous roadside stalls, all these are fairly restricted in their opening times. Most urban restaurants, especially those serving Western food, open at about 11am and close between 10pm and midnight. This is not really a problem, as opening times – together with details of credit cards accepted – are usually posted on the door. But it can mean that finding an early Western-style breakfast is difficult away from the tourist scene, in which case a Thai omelette may have to serve as a substitute.

Virtually every major city and resort in Thailand has at least one free monthly tourist advi-

sory magazine. They can be picked up in hotel reception lobbies, at banks and money changers, as well as in many restaurants. These list restaurants by cuisine and speciality, often giving details of how to get there, along with telephone numbers for booking tables. Away from the major tourist destinations, you can be sure that the main hotels in every

Restaurant in the Sadet Market at Nong Khai, by the Mekhong River

town will have air-conditioned restaurants offering a mixture of Thai and Chinese cuisine.

Thais have taken to Western cuisine, and especially to the Western fast food culture, with enthusiasm. McDonalds and Kentucky Fried Chicken are increasingly visible, but the most popular imports appear to be pizza and pasta, which can be found in just about any provincial capital. However, quality does vary from place to place.

COFFEE SHOPS

IN TOURIST RESORTS and international hotels, coffee shops are just that – places to sit and drink cappuccino or espresso, eat snacks, refresh oneself or kill time. In this they differ little from their counterparts in New York or London. It is not so in the smaller provincial towns or Thai hotels, however. Here, "coffee bars" are more like nightclubs, with live music, darkened windows and a plethora of "hostesses" whose job is to entertain the customer and encourage the spending of money. It is generally easy to tell the difference between the two types of establishment, even from the outside.

ROADSIDE AND MARKET FOOD STALLS

SOME OF THE BEST and most reasonably priced food in Thailand can be found at any of the numerous roadside food stalls. Generally speaking, such establishments are clean and

Street vendor's cart selling fruit and drinks, Phuket

unpretentious. These stalls are often mobile, allowing the proprietors to push them home and clean them every night. The ingredients are openly displayed behind glass panels. Fast cooking processes, such as flash-frying, grilling over charcoal, or boiling are used. This means that the fare, invariably fresh, will also be well cooked, piping hot and safe to eat.

A sure way of measuring a stall's popularity, as anywhere in the world, is by its patrons. If there are plenty of locals sitting at the simple tables most stalls provide, then the chances are the food is good. Don't be surprised to find a businessman with a Mercedes parked nearby sitting at the same stall as a *tuk-tuk* driver. Thais from all sectors of society know how to appreciate good, cheap food.

Menus are rarely given in English, so it is a good idea to memorize the names of your favourite dishes from the food glossary (see pp410–11). Alternatively, you can point and ask to taste – few Thais expect foreign visitors to speak their language, and they are always willing to help and advise.

KHANTOKE DINING

A TRADITIONAL STYLE of dining in Northern Thailand, *khantoke* dinners are often arranged for guests by hotels in Chiang Mai and other Northern cities. Diners sit on raised platforms around a circular table. The meal includes a variety of Northern dishes such as *nam phrik naw* (a very spicy dip), *kap mu* (pork skin) and *kaeng kai* (a chicken-and-vegetable curry), all of which are served with *khao niaw* (sticky rice) and washed down with local beer. A *khantoke* dinner is often accompanied by displays of traditional Thai dancing.

PRICES

B UYING MEALS is one of the cheapest aspects of a visit to Thailand. The cost of alcohol, however, can often be more than the meal itself. It is common practice for prices to be displayed. Menus invariably list them next to each dish. The prices for shellfish are often given by weight. In larger establishments

Neon sign for a restaurant

and international-class hotels a service charge and VAT will usually be levied. These extra costs will be clearly detailed on the bill.

Even at very small establishments prices are nearly always fixed and marked (in Arabic numerals) on a board. Bargaining for foodstuffs is rare – surprising in a country where shoppers delight in haggling.

TIPPING

T IPPING WAS once unknown, but its popularity is increasing as Thais grow accustomed to tips from tourists. Do not apply a percentage: ten per cent of 50 *baht* may well be appropriate, but ten per cent of an expensive meal would be far too much.

EATING HABITS IN THAILAND

T HE THAI PHILOSOPHY of nutrition is simple – if you are hungry, eat. Nothing should stand in the way. Most Thais, moreover, eat little but often, sometimes "snacking" six or seven times a day. The concept of three meals simply does not apply in Thailand. Even though people do indeed eat breakfast, lunch and dinner, they may also stop for a bowl of noodles, or a fried snack or a sweet at any time of day.

Eating is a simple pleasure, and does not involve complex rituals of etiquette, although visitors should note a few rules. Thais eat with a fork held in the left hand and a spoon held in the right hand. The fork is used solely to push food onto the spoon; eating straight from a fork is considered crude. Since food – especially meat – is cut into pieces before it is cooked, knives are not needed.

Thai noodle dishes are often strongly influenced by Chinese culinary traditions and they are eaten using chopsticks and a spoon. Another exception to the general rule is sticky rice (*khao niaw*), which is eaten – delicately – with the fingers.

Food in Thailand is generally served communally in a series of large bowls. Only small rice bowls are reserved for individual use. Rice is traditionally served first, and then a spoon is used to ladle two or three spoonfuls from the communal bowls on top of the rice. You should feel free to come back later for more as necessary. Overloading your plate is regarded as uncouth – there is no hurry, and there is always plenty more in the kitchen.

Street vendor cooking satay for passers-by in a Bangkok park

What to Eat in Thailand

Thai food is famous for its spicy qualities. Chilli peppers were imported to Thailand, from the New World, in the 16th century by European traders *(see p153)*. The Thais took to them (especially the small, fiery ones) with great enthusiasm. In spite of this, mild dishes are also widely available in Thailand. Rice is, of course, the staple food, while rice noodles come second, appearing in dry, fried dishes and in soups. The cuisine is nutritious and flavoursome: meats are lightly fried, the vegetables boiled.

Three chilli varieties

Rice porridge (khao tom) *is a standard breakfast. Often an egg is added, which cooks as it is stirred in. The best condiment for this dish is chillies in rice vinegar.*

Condiment of chillies in fish sauce (*nam pla phrik*)

Condiments of fish sauce and chilli flakes

Noodle soup (kuaytiaw nam) *is the only Thai dish to be eaten with chopsticks. It includes vegetables and usually meat balls.*

Fried rice dishes (khao phat), *made with egg, slivers of meat and vegetables, are a delicious and filling all-in-one meal that can be enjoyed any time of day.*

Phat thai *is a mixture of flat rice noodles fried with bean curd, vegetables, egg, peanuts and dried shrimps. It is claimed to be Thailand's national dish.*

Wheat noodles served with slices of red pork (bami haeng mu daeng) *is a typical dish that can be bought from street vendors throughout the country.*

Tom yam*, typically made with prawns and tomatoes, is the most famous of all Thai soups. It is spiced with coriander, lemongrass and chillies, and is often cooked and served in a tureen.*

Mu sap bai kraphao *(fried pork flavoured with holy basil) is a delicious meat dish that may form part of a communal meal.*

Phanaeng curry (kaeng phanaeng) *is a "dry" chicken curry. Ingredients include shrimp, coriander seeds, red chillies and a small amount of basil.*

Green curry (kaeng khiaw wan), *like many Central Thai curries, is cooked in coconut milk, which gives it a quite mild, almost sweet flavour. Green chillies add spice.*

Steamed rice (khao suay), *the mainstay of communal meals in Thailand, is always served first. It is the best thing for cooling the mouth when eating very hot food.*

Sticky rice (khao niaw) *cooked and served in a lidded basket is common in the North and Northeast. This glutinous rice is eaten with the fingers; sometimes the rice is rolled into a ball and used to carry food to the mouth.*

Raw Thai aubergine

Carved raw carrot

Crispy pork crackling

Nam phrik ong, a pork and chilli dip

Carved yellow aubergine

Nam phrik *is a family of popular dishes where an elaborately prepared chilli paste is eaten as a dip with raw vegetables and deep-fried meat. Regional specialities include* nam phrik ong *from Northern Thailand, with pork crackling. On special occasions and at high-class restaurants, the vegetables are carved, often in the shape of flowers.*

Fried water lilies (phat pak bung) *are just one of many simple, mild dishes that may be served as part of a main meal. They take only a minute to cook.*

Papaya salad (som tam) *is very popular throughout Thailand. The papaya is sliced thinly and mixed with chillies. Chicken is a good accompaniment.*

Seafood salad (yam thalay) *is often served as a starter in the South. Like many other Thai salads, the warm, cooked seafood is placed on a bed of lettuce.*

Mango with sticky rice (khao niaw mamuang), *which is sweetened with coconut cream, is the country's best-known dessert. Only the sweetest mangoes are used.*

DRINKS

Thailand has a wealth of fruits *(see p129)*, many of which can be juiced. Coconut juice, drunk with a straw straight from the coconut, is also popular. Tea and coffee are usually served chilled. Beer is the preferred alcoholic accompaniment to meals – it complements spicy food better than wine. Plain water *(nam plao)* is served with main meals.

Coconut custard (sangkhaya) *is a dessert of coconut milk, eggs and sugar. It may be served either with sticky rice or baked in a hollowed-out pumpkin.*

Roselle juice

Iced tea

Singha beer

Chang beer

A Glossary of Typical Thai Dishes

Khanom khrok –
coconut puddings

THAI CUISINE IS FAMOUSLY creative and varied *(see pp34–5)*. Even street vendors delight in their culinary skills, and it is not uncommon to see food being encased in a banana leaf as delicately as if it were being gift wrapped. Such artful presentations and the sheer range of dishes can be bewildering to newcomers: it may not even be obvious what is savoury or sweet. This glossary covers typical dishes; phonetic guidance for food words is on page 503.

A street vendor cooking over charcoal on a road-side stall

CHOOSING DISHES

RESTAURANT MENUS in tourist areas may include descriptions in English, and sometimes other languages. The Thai names of dishes often derive simply from the main elements – for instance, the dish *khao mu daeng* translates literally as "rice, pork, red". Thus, the basic components of any dish can often be worked out with only a little knowledge of Thai. If there is no menu, the dishes of the day will be on display. If you don't recognize the dish, pointing and saying "*nee arai na?*" ("what's this?") should elicit a list of ingredients.

Vegetarians should find it easy to order food without meat (*mai ao nua*), but ought to be aware that fish sauce is used in many dishes. Dairy products feature only rarely in Thai cuisine, so vegans should not fare worse than vegetarians.

Thais are accustomed to foreigners asking if a dish is spicy (*phet mai?*), or requesting a non-spicy meal (*mai ao phet na*). To enliven any dish, diners can use the ubiquitous condiments of chillies in vinegar, chilli flakes, sugar (for savoury dishes) and fish sauce usually found on tables.

SNACKS

Thais love to snack. Almost every street corner has a selection of food stalls selling raw and freshly cooked snacks.

Chicken satay

Bami mu daeng
บะหมี่หมูแดง
Egg noodles with red pork.
Kai ping
ไก่ปิ้ง
Charcoal-roasted eggs.
Kai yang
ไก่ย่าง
Charcoal-grilled chicken.
Khanom beuang
ขนมเบื้อง
Filled, sweet, crispy pancakes.

Khanom khrok
ขนมครก
Coconut puddings.
Khao tom mat
ข้าวต้มมัด
Sticky rice served in banana leaves.
Kluay ping
กล้วยปิ้ง
Charcoal-grilled bananas.
Luk chin ping
ลูกชิ้นปิ้ง
Meatballs with a chilli sauce.
Po pia
ปอเปี๊ยะ
Deep-fried spring rolls.
Sai krok
ไส้กรอก
Thai beef or pork sausages.

Satay
สะเต๊ะ
Slivers of beef, pork or chicken grilled on a stick, served with peanut sauce and cucumber.
Tua thot
ถั่วทอด
Roasted cashews or peanuts.

NOODLES

Rice noodles come as *sen yai* (broad), *sen lek* (medium) and *sen mi* (vermicelli). *Bami* are egg noodles. *Wun sen* are thin, transparent soya noodles.
Bami nam
บะหมี่น้ำ
Egg noodles in a broth with vegetables and meat or fish.
Kuaytiaw haeng
ก๋วยเตี๋ยวแห้ง
Rice noodles served "dry" with vegetables and meat or fish.
Kuaytiaw nam
ก๋วยเตี๋ยวน้ำ
Rice noodles in a broth with vegetables and meat or fish.
Luk chin pla
ลูกชิ้นปลา
Grilled fish with noodles.
Phat thai
ผัดไทย
Rice noodles fried with beancurd, egg, dried shrimp, peanuts, beansprouts and chilli.

Street sellers and their customers in a Bangkok market

RICE DISHES

Rice is the staple food. A familiar Thai greeting, equivalent to "how are you?" is *kin khao mai?*, literally "have you eaten rice?"

Khao man kai
ข้าวมันไก่
Chinese-style chicken with rice cooked in chicken stock.

Khao mok kai
ข้าวหมกไก่
Thai-style chicken biriyani.

Khao mu daeng
ข้าวหมูแดง
Chinese-style red pork served on a bed of fragrant rice.

Khao na pet
ข้าวหน้าเป็ด
Roast duck served on a bed of fragrant rice.

Khao phat mu/kung
ข้าวผัดหมูหรือกุ้ง
Fried rice with pork or prawns.

SOUPS

Soups are diverse and inventive. Some, such as *jok*, are eaten for breakfast. The word *"sup"* is widely recognized.

Jok
โจ๊ก
Ground rice soup with minced pork and ginger.

Khao tom
ข้าวต้ม
Rice soup with a selection of meat and vegetable side dishes.

Tom jeut tao hu
ต้มจืดเต้าหู้
Mild broth with beancurd and minced pork.

Tom kha kai
ต้มข่าไก่
Chicken soup with galingale, coconut milk and lemon grass.

Tom yam kung
ต้มยำกุ้ง
Prawns, mushrooms, lemon grass, galingale and coriander.

CURRIES

Curries are served either *rat khao* (on a plate of rice) or in a bowl as an accompaniment to a central bowl of rice.

Kaeng kari kai
แกงกะหรี่ไก่
Indian-style chicken and potato.

Kaeng khiaw wan
แกงเขียวหวาน
Slightly sweet green curry.

Khao tom mat – sticky rice wrapped in banana leaves

Kaeng matsaman
แกงมัสมั่น
A mild curry from the Muslim South with beef, peanuts, potatoes and coconut milk.

Kaeng phanaeng
แกงแพนง
Southern-style "dry" curry with coconut and basil.

Kaeng phet
แกงเผ็ด
A hot curry with red chillies, lemon grass and coriander.

Kaeng som
แกงส้ม
Hot and sour curry, often with fish.

SEAFOOD

An amazing variety of seafood is available at reasonable prices, particularly in the South.

Hoi malaeng pu op
หอยแมลงภู่อบ
Steamed green mussels.

Hoi thot
หอยทอด
Oysters fried in batter with egg on a bed of beansprouts.

Hu chalam
หูฉลาม
Shark's fin soup.

Southern seafood, including crab

Kung mangkon phao
กุ้งมังกรเผา
Grilled lobster.

Pla meuk yang
ปลาหมึกย่าง
Roasted sliced squid.

Pla nung khing
ปลานึ่งขิง
Steamed fish with ginger, chilli and mushrooms.

Pla thot
ปลาทอด
Deep fried fish.

Pu neung
ปูนึ่ง
Steamed crab.

REGIONAL DISHES

Kaeng hang le
แกงฮังเล
Pork, peanut and ginger curry from Chiang Mai.

Khao soi
ข้าวซอย
Chicken or beef broth served with wheat noodles, fresh lime and pickled cabbage. A Northern speciality.

Larb pet
ลาบเป็ด
Northern spicy minced duck.

Som tam
ส้มตำ
Green papaya salad with peanuts, from the Northeast.

Yam thalay
ยำทะเล
Southern spicy seafood salad.

DESSERTS

Known as *khong wan* or "sweet things", these are mostly coconut or fruit based.

Foy thong
ฝอยทอง
Sweet, shredded egg yolks.

Khao niaw mamuang
ข้าวเหนียวมะม่วง
Fresh mango served with sticky rice and coconut milk.

Kluay buat chi
กล้วยบวดชี
Bananas in coconut milk.

Mo kaeng
หม้อแกง
Thai-style egg custard.

DRINKS

Bia
เบียร์
Beer. Usually served in bottles.

Cha ron
ชาร้อน
Tea with condensed milk.

Kafae
กาแฟ
Coffee, often instant.

Nam cha
น้ำชา
Chinese-style tea without milk.

Nam kuat
น้ำขวด
Bottled water.

Coconut seller on the Floating Market

Choosing a Restaurant

T<small>HE</small> <small>RESTAURANTS</small> in this guide have been selected for their good value, exceptional food and interesting location. This chart highlights some of the factors which may influence your choice. Use the colour-coded thumb tabs, which indicate the regions covered on each page, to guide you to the relevant sections of the chart.

	C<small>REDIT</small> C<small>ARDS</small>	T<small>HAI</small> S<small>PECIALITIES</small>	A<small>SIAN</small> (N<small>ON</small>-T<small>HAI</small>) D<small>ISHES</small>	W<small>ESTERN</small> D<small>ISHES</small>	O<small>UTDOOR</small> T<small>ABLES</small>
BANGKOK					
OLD CITY: *Vegetarian Restaurant.* **Map** 2 D4. ⓑ 85/2 Soi Wat Bowon, off Tanao Rd. 【 *No telephone.* A wide range of good-value vegetarian food, such as Indian-style potato curries, *khanom chin* (noodles) and coconut-milk desserts.	ⓑ	●	■		
OLD CITY: *Maharajah.* **Map** 2 D4. ⓑⓑ Khao San Rd. 【 *No telephone.* Tasty Indian food at reasonable prices is served at this restaurant, which caters chiefly to budget travellers on hectic Khao San Road. 🍽	ⓑⓑ		■		
OLD CITY: *Sorn Daeng.* **Map** 2 E4. ⓑⓑ Dinso Rd. 【 *(02) 224 3088.* Enjoy tasty Thai food and seafood at this eatery near the Democracy Monument. The dishes, which are excellent value for money, include Southern Thai specialities such as *kaeng matsaman* (beef curry). 🍽	ⓑⓑ	●		●	
CHINATOWN: *Royal India.* **Map** 6 D1. ⓑ 392/1 Chak Phet Rd. 【 *(02) 221 6565.* Good, solid, North Indian cooking at reasonable prices that should not be missed. Both vegetarian and non-vegetarian dishes are featured on the menu. Try the Indian breads, which are especially tasty. 🍽	ⓑ		■		
CHINATOWN: *Samrat.* **Map** 6 D1. ⓑ Chak Phet Rd. 【 *No telephone.* Set in a tiny alley to the side of the ATM Department Store, this friendly Sikh-run establishment dishes up wonderful dhals and curries. These can all be washed down with *chai* (hot, sweet Indian tea).	ⓑ		■		
CHINATOWN: *Likee.* **Map** 6 E1. ⓑⓑ Soi Bamrung Rat. 【 *No telephone.* A large Chinese restaurant with an extensive menu of Cantonese dishes. Dim sum specialities are served in the mornings.	ⓑⓑ		■		
DUSIT: *Empress.* **Map** 3 A4. ⓑⓑⓑⓑ Royal Princess Hotel, 269 Lan Luang Rd. 【 *(02) 281 3088.* A well-known Chinese restaurant, in the Royal Princess Hotel, with a considerable reputation for its Southern Chinese cuisine. Cantonese specialities such as dim sum are recommended. 🍽 🍷	ⓑⓑⓑⓑ AE DC MC V JCB		■		
DUSIT: *Piccolo.* **Map** 3 A5. ⓑⓑⓑⓑ Royal Princess Hotel, 269 Lan Luang Rd. 【 *(02) 281 3088.* A fine restaurant, specializing in North Italian food. Some delicious dishes feature veal – this is unusual, as it's a rarity in Bangkok. The various pasta dishes are also recommended. 🍽 🍷 🍷	ⓑⓑⓑⓑ AE DC MC V JCB			●	
DOWNTOWN: *Arirang.* **Map** 8 C4. ⓑⓑ 106–108 Silom Rd, Soi 4. 【 *(02) 234 1096.* The Korean barbecued beef here is so tender it virtually melts in the mouth. Try the *kimchi* (pickled garlic) dishes. Friendly staff. 🍽	ⓑⓑ AE		■		
DOWNTOWN: *Bobby's Arms.* **Map** 7 C3. ⓑⓑ 2nd Floor, Car park bldg, Patpong, Soi 2. 【 *(02) 233 6828.* This enduringly popular English pub is tucked away behind the second floor of Patpong car park. It serves the whole gamut of pub food, from steak and kidney pie to bangers and mash. 🍽 🍷	ⓑⓑ AE DC MC V			●	
DOWNTOWN: *El Gordo's Cantina.* **Map** 7 C4. ⓑⓑ 130/8 Soi 8, Silom Rd. 【 *(02) 237 1415.* Popular Mexican and Tex-Mex food. If you crave burritos, nachos, tortillas and other Mexican dishes, this is the place to come. The management are deservedly proud of their margaritas. 🍽 🍷	ⓑⓑ AE DC MC V			●	

		THAI SPECIALITIES	ASIAN (NON-THAI) DISHES	WESTERN DISHES	OUTDOOR TABLES

Price categories for an evening meal for one, including service, but not alcohol:

⑧ under B100
⑧⑧ B100–200
⑧⑧⑧ B200–500
⑧⑧⑧⑧ B500–1,000
⑧⑧⑧⑧⑧ over B1,000

THAI SPECIALITIES
The restaurant has Thai dishes.

ASIAN (NON-THAI) DISHES
Cuisine from other parts of Asia, such as China, Korea, Japan or India, is served.

WESTERN DISHES
French, Italian or other Western fare is on the menu.

OUTDOOR TABLES
Facilities for eating outdoors *(suan ahan)*, on a terrace, or in a garden or courtyard.

	CREDIT CARDS	THAI SPECIALITIES	ASIAN (NON-THAI) DISHES	WESTERN DISHES	OUTDOOR TABLES
DOWNTOWN: *Thai Room* ⑧⑧ 30/37 Patpong, Soi 2. 📞 *(02) 233 7920.* Set in the heart of Patpong, most regulars patronize this old favourite for its tasty Mexican specialities, such as tacos, nachos and fajitas. There are also over 100 Thai dishes and delicious club sandwiches. 🍽	AE DC MC V	●		●	
DOWNTOWN: *Bussaracum*. **Map 7 C4.** ⑧⑧⑧ Psethiwan Bldg, Silom Rd. 📞 *(02) 266 6312.* This renowned restaurant concentrates on Royal Thai cuisine *(see p34).* Specialist dishes, such as *foi thong,* or "golden threads" (an egg-yolk concoction), are enhanced by the elegant surroundings. 🍽 🍷 🍸	AE DC MC V JCB	●			
DOWNTOWN: *Himali Cha Cha* ⑧⑧⑧ 1229/11 Charoen Krung (New) Rd. 📞 *(02) 235 1569.* Mouthwatering Mogul-style cooking in one of Bangkok's oldest Indian restaurants. The fresh breads are delicious, the dhals superb. 🍽 🍷	AE MC V		▪		
DOWNTOWN: *Scala Shark's Fin*. **Map 7 C1.** ⑧⑧⑧ 218/1 Siam Square, Soi 1. 📞 *(02) 250 1633.* Some of the best shark's-fin soup in town, together with other Chinese specialities, such as bird's-nest soup. Don't be put off by the decor – which is slightly shabby – the emphasis is on the cuisine. 🍽	MC V		▪		
DOWNTOWN: *Sichuan Garden*. **Map 8 E1.** ⑧⑧⑧ World Trade Center, Ratchadamri Rd. 📞 *(02) 255 9840.* Sichuan cuisine is spicier, sharper and more pungent than other Chinese schools of cookery and is very popular in Bangkok. Here it is served in smart, agreeable surroundings. 🍽 🍷	AE DC MC V JCB		▪		
DOWNTOWN: *Spice Market*. **Map 8 D2.** ⑧⑧⑧ Regent Hotel, 155 Ratchadamri Rd. 📞 *(02) 251 6127.* One of the city's best Thai restaurants, offering a wide range of dishes in a setting decorated to resemble an old Thai spice shop. Enjoy delicious curries and old-fashioned Thai sweets. 🍽 🍷	AE DC MC V JCB	●			▪
DOWNTOWN: *Trattoria da Roberto*. **Map 7 C4.** ⑧⑧⑧ 37/9 Patpong, Soi 2. 📞 *(02) 233 6851.* Savour fine Italian food in an authentically Italian ambience, right in the heart of Bangkok's premier night entertainment area. The veal *parmigiani* is memorable, the seafood spaghetti sublime. 🍽 🍷	AE DC MC V			●	
DOWNTOWN: *Gaddi's Grill*. **Map 7 B3.** ⑧⑧⑧⑧ Mandarin Bangkok Hotel, 662 Rama IV Rd. 📞 *(02) 238 0230.* This prestigious grillroom offers a wide range of imported food. Choose from American steaks, New Zealand lamb, Scottish smoked salmon and local seafoods. Desserts include French cheesecake. 🍽 🍷	AE DC MC V JCB			●	
DOWNTOWN: *Le Bistrot*. **Map 8 F2.** ⑧⑧⑧⑧ 20/17–19 Soi Ruam Rudi. 📞 *(02) 251 2523.* Some of the best French cuisine in Bangkok, in suitably refined surroundings. The wine list is extensive for Thailand. 🍽 🍷 🍸	AE MC V			●	
DOWNTOWN: *Mayflower*. **Map 8 D4.** ⑧⑧⑧⑧ Dusit Thani Hotel, 946 Rama IV Rd. 📞 *(02) 236 0450.* An award-winning Chinese restaurant – one of the best in Bangkok – specializing in Cantonese cuisine. The sumptuous, intricately designed interior features authentic Chinese antiques. 🍽 🍷	AE DC MC V JCB		▪		
DOWNTOWN: *Noble House*. **Map 8 E1.** ⑧⑧⑧⑧ Hilton International Bangkok, 2 Witthayu (Wireless) Rd. 📞 *(02) 253 0123.* Superior Cantonese cuisine in surroundings designed to resemble an old Chinese trading house. The lunchtime dim sum, served by waitresses dressed in Chinese traditional dress, is exceptional. 🍽 🍷	AE DC MC V JCB		▪		

For key to symbols see back flap

<table>
<tr><td colspan="2"></td><td>CREDIT CARDS</td><td>THAI SPECIALITIES</td><td>ASIAN (NON-THAI) DISHES</td><td>WESTERN DISHES</td><td>OUTDOOR TABLES</td></tr>
</table>

Price categories for an evening meal for one, including service, but not alcohol:

ⓑ under B100
ⓑⓑ B100–200
ⓑⓑⓑ B200–500
ⓑⓑⓑⓑ B500–1,000
ⓑⓑⓑⓑⓑ over B1,000

THAI SPECIALITIES
The restaurant has Thai dishes.

ASIAN (NON-THAI) DISHES
Cuisine from other parts of Asia, such as China, Korea, Japan or India, is served.

WESTERN DISHES
French, Italian or other Western fare is on the menu.

OUTDOOR TABLES
Facilities for eating outdoors *(suan aban)*, on a terrace, or in a garden or courtyard.

Restaurant	Credit Cards	Thai Specialities	Asian (Non-Thai) Dishes	Western Dishes	Outdoor Tables
DOWNTOWN: *Captain Bush Grill*. **Map** 6 F3. ⓑⓑⓑⓑⓑ Royal Orchid Sheraton Hotel, 2 Captain Bush Lane. 【 *(02) 266 0123.* Top-notch Western cuisine is featured on the menu here. Diners can enjoy delicious imported steaks, lamb and fresh salmon in a classic English grillhouse ambience. 🍴 ▮ ● *lunch times.*	AE DC MC V JCB			●	
THON BURI: *Rim Nam*. **Map** 6 D2. ⓑⓑ 111 Somdet Phra Pin Klao Rd. 【 *(02) 424 1112.* Enjoy Thai- and Chinese-style seafood at reasonable prices on the bank of the Chao Phraya, next to Phra Pin Klao Bridge. 🍴 ▮	V	●	▪		▪
THON BURI: *Sala Rim Nam (or Djit Pochana)*. **Map** 6 F4. ⓑⓑⓑⓑ Opposite Oriental Hotel, 48 Oriental Ave. 【 *(02) 236 0420.* Good food in a romantic riverside setting. Cross-river from the Oriental pier (with regular ferry links to the hotel), the restaurant is renowned for its excellent seafood and classical Thai dancing. 🍴 ▮	AE DC M V JCB	●			▪
FURTHER AFIELD: *Mangsawirat* ⓑ Just off Ratwithi Rd, Nakhon Pathom, Nakhon Pathom province. 【 *No telephone.* A popular vegetarian restaurant offering a wide range of tasty dishes. Well worth trying is the *kaeng kari* (Indian-style potato curry).		●			
FURTHER AFIELD: *Cabbages and Condoms* ⓑⓑ 10 Sukhumvit, Soi 12. 【 *(02) 229 4610.* A distinctive restaurant serving organically grown Thai food. The unusual name derives from the work of Mechai Viravaidya, a promoter of family planning. Profits go towards his work. 🍴 ▮	AE DC MC V JCB	●			▪
FURTHER AFIELD: *Nakhon Inn* ⓑⓑ 55 Ratwithi Rd, Nakhon Pathom, Nakhon Pathom province. 【 *(034) 251152.* This restaurant and coffee shop prepares standard Central Thai fare like *tom yam kung* (spicy soup with prawns) and some basic Western cuisine. If you want steak and chips, this is the place. 🍴 ▮	AE	●		●	
FURTHER AFIELD: *Señor Pico* ⓑⓑ Rembrandt Hotel, Sukhumvit, Soi 18. 【 *(02) 261 7100.* Some of the best Mexican and Tex-Mex cuisine in town, including fajitas, nachos and combination platters, as well as good steaks. These are served in a bright and cheery atmosphere. 🍴 ▮	AE DC MC V JCB			●	
FURTHER AFIELD: *Bei Otto* ⓑⓑⓑ 1 Sukhumvit, Soi 20. 【 *(02) 260 0869.* A popular German establishment with its own *bierhaus*, delicatessen and bakery. The house specialities include a mixed sausage platter, leg of pork with sauerkraut, wiener schnitzel and *rösti*. 🍴 ▮	AE DC MC V JCB			●	
FURTHER AFIELD: *Bourbon Street* ⓑⓑⓑ Washington Square, Sukhumvit, Soi 22. 【 *(02) 259 0328.* Located quite unexpectedly in downtown Bangkok is this Cajun-Creole restaurant. Gumbo, jambalaya, red beans and rice, blackened redfish and Cajun boiled fish are among the dishes. 🍴 ▮	AE MC V				
FURTHER AFIELD: *Cedar* ⓑⓑⓑ 4/1 Sukhumvit, Soi 49/9. 【 *(02) 391 4482.* Lebanese, Levantine and Greek dishes are a feature of this restaurant decorated to resemble a (rather sophisticated) Arab tent. Try the wonderful tzatziki, moussaka, hummus, felafel and kebabs. 🍴 ▮	AE DC V		▪	●	
FURTHER AFIELD: *Celadon*. **Map** 8 D4 ⓑⓑⓑ Sukhothai Bangkok Hotel, 13/3 Sathorn Tai Rd. 【 *(02) 287 0222.* This superb Thai restaurant features delicious specialities such as *gai hor phai toey* (chicken grilled in screw pine leaves) and *tom kha kai* (chicken soup flavoured with coconut and galangal). 🍴 ▮ ▯	AE DC MC V JCB	●			▪

FURTHER AFIELD: *Le Dalat*   ⓑⓑⓑ   AE DC MC V
47/1 Sukhumvit, Soi 23. 【 (02) 258 4192.
One of three branches of the most celebrated Vietnamese restaurant in
Bangkok. Enjoy *cha glo* (spring rolls) or *naem meuang* (spicy grilled
meatballs wrapped in lettuce leaves) in elegant surroundings. 🍽 🍷

FURTHER AFIELD: *La Grenouille.* **Map** 8 F1.   ⓑⓑⓑ   AE DC MC V
220/4 Sukhumvit, Soi 1. 【 (02) 253 9080.
Good quality traditional French food. The excellent bistro-style cooking,
such as profiteroles, is accompanied by a long wine list. 🍽 🍷

FURTHER AFIELD: *Huntsman Pub.* **Map** 8 F2.   ⓑⓑⓑ   AE DC MC V JCB
Landmark Plaza Hotel, 138 Sukhumvit Rd. 【 (02) 254 0404.
An up-market, British-style pub serving typical dishes such as a mixed
grill and steak and kidney pie, as well as general Thai food. There is a
well-stocked bar and live entertainment every night. 🍽 🍷

FURTHER AFIELD: *Kisso*   ⓑⓑⓑ   AE DC MC V JCB
Delta Grand Pacific Hotel, 259 Sukhumvit Rd. 【 (02) 254 4998.
This exclusive Japanese restaurant excels in sushi, tempura, sashimi,
teppanyaki and other classic dishes. Choose from the fixed-price lunch
menu, the à la carte dinner and the Japanese buffet at weekends. 🍽

FURTHER AFIELD: *Lemongrass*   ⓑⓑⓑ   AE DC MC V
5/1 Soi 24, Sukhumvit Rd. 【 (02) 258 8637.
This popular establishment cooks up moderately spiced, Central Thai
food in an elegant old wooden house. The speciality is *kai yang phak
phanaeng* (sweet and spicy Southern-style grilled chicken). 🍽 🍷 🎵

FURTHER AFIELD: *Mrs Balbir's*   ⓑⓑⓑ   AE MC V
155/18 Sukhumvit, Soi 11. 【 (02) 253 2281.
Diners come here for the delicious North Indian specialities, using
imported Indian spices such as saffron (which is a rare ingredient in
Thai cooking). The chicken tandoori is one of the best dishes. 🍽

FURTHER AFIELD: *Nang Yuan Restaurant*   ⓑⓑⓑ   AE DC MC V
Fortune Town Bldg, 1 Ratchadaphisek Rd. 【 (02) 641 1500.
Chinese specialities, including steamed bird's nest with red dates and
ginseng. The dim sum lunch buffets are recommended. 🍽 🍷

FURTHER AFIELD: *Pan Pan 33*   ⓑⓑⓑ   AE DC MC V
Soi 33, Sukhumvit Rd. 【 (02) 258 5071.
Everything is delicious, from the salami and wood-fired calzone
pizzas, salads and pasta dishes to the rich, dark coffee. 🍽 🍷

FURTHER AFIELD: *Tum Nak Thai*   ⓑⓑⓑ   AE DC MC V JCB
131 Ratchadaphisek Rd. 【 (02) 274 6420.
This is said to be the largest restaurant in the world – so big that the
staff use roller skates to get around. It is a fun place to take the family
(especially children) and the Thai food is good. Seats 2,000 people! 🍽

FURTHER AFIELD: *Trader Vic's*   ⓑⓑⓑⓑⓑ   AE DC MC V JCB
Marriott Royal Garden Riverside, Charoen Nakhon Rd. 【 (02) 476 0021.
Polynesian cuisine – dishes such as suckling pig, and smoked or fried
breadfruit – in addition to some international food. Veal cutlets are a
speciality: try them pan fried. 🍽 🍷 🎵

SOUTH CENTRAL PLAINS

AYUTTHAYA: *Chainam*   ⓑⓑ
36/2 Uthong Rd. 【 (035) 252013.
Good Thai and Western dishes for reasonable prices are characteristic
of this restaurant. It is a good place to go for Western breakfasts.

AYUTTHAYA: *Phae Krung Kao*   ⓑⓑ   AE MC V
4 Mu 2, Uthong Rd. 【 (035) 241555.
This attractive, floating restaurant specializes in seafood, but the menu
also has a wide range of chicken and pork dishes. The cuisine is
mainly Thai, though some Chinese delicacies are also available. 🍽 🍷

KANCHANABURI: *Punnee Café and Bar*   ⓑ
Saengchuto Rd. 【 (034) 513503.
This café has a mix of Western-style Thai and Thai-style European
dishes on its menu. It also advertises "the coldest beer in town". 🍷

		CREDIT CARDS	THAI SPECIALITIES	ASIAN (NON-THAI) DISHES	WESTERN DISHES	OUTDOOR TABLES
Price categories for an evening meal for one, including service, but not alcohol: ⓑ under B100 ⓑⓑ B100–200 ⓑⓑⓑ B200–500 ⓑⓑⓑⓑ B500–1,000 ⓑⓑⓑⓑⓑ over B1,000	**THAI SPECIALITIES** The restaurant has Thai dishes. **ASIAN (NON-THAI) DISHES** Cuisine from other parts of Asia, such as China, Korea, Japan or India, is served. **WESTERN DISHES** French, Italian or other Western fare is on the menu. **OUTDOOR TABLES** Facilities for eating outdoors *(suan ahan)*, on a terrace, or in a garden or courtyard.					
KANCHANABURI: *Mae Nam* End of Lak Muang Rd. 【 *(034) 512811*. A large floating restaurant with a pleasant atmosphere. The specialities tend to be fish- and seafood-oriented. A band plays Thai pop or light Western music in the evenings.	ⓑⓑ		●	■		
KANCHANABURI: *New Isaan* 292/1–2 Saengchuto Rd. 【 *No telephone.* A simple, clean establishment serving typical Northeastern delicacies. Try the *kai yang* (grilled chicken) or the *som tam* (papaya salad).	ⓑⓑ		●			
LOP BURI: *Phikul Kaeo* Nah Phra Kan Rd. 【 *(036) 441318*. Cheap and reliable wok-fried Thai and Chinese food is the order of the day here. Enjoy the *hoi thot*, a delicious omelette of oysters on a bed of fresh bean sprouts, served with a sweet, piquant sauce. 🍽	ⓑ		●	■		
LOP BURI: *Anodard* Sa Kaeo Circle. 【 *(036) 411433*. Quality Chinese and Thai food at reasonable prices. This is an ideal place to try popular *priaw wan* (sweet and sour) dishes or *kai phat pet mamuang* (chicken fried with cashew nuts). 🍽	ⓑⓑ		●	■		
SUPHAN BURI: *Wang Kung* Nang Pim Rd. 【 *No telephone.* A pleasant restaurant with good value Chinese and Thai-Chinese food. It is easily identified by the Chinese lanterns hanging outside. 🍽	ⓑⓑ	MC V	●	■		
NORTH CENTRAL PLAINS						
KAMPHAENG PHET: *Malai* 77 Thesa Rd. 【 *(055) 711630*. A small eatery serving tasty Northeastern Thai food. There is no English signboard, so look out for the rice baskets hanging outside. Try the *nam phrik* pepper-based dips. 🍽 ● *evenings.*	ⓑ		●			■
KAMPHAENG PHET: *Phayao* 217–219 Thesa Rd. 【 *(055) 712174*. This bakery offers bread and sweet pastries, washed down with tea or coffee. It is a good place for breakfast in Kamphaeng Phet.	ⓑ				●	
KAMPHAENG PHET: *Ruan Phae Rim Ping* 120 Soi 1, Thesa 2 Rd. 【 *(055) 712767*. Located on the bank of the Ping River, this pleasant garden restaurant rustles up *miang sawoei* – a spicy Thai hors d'oeuvre with fresh ginger, peanuts and piquant sauces – among other specialities.	ⓑⓑ	MC V	●	■		■
MAE SOT: *Pim Hut* 415/11–12 Intharakiri, Tang Kim Chiang Rd. 【 *(055) 532818*. One of a number of clean, reasonably priced restaurants along this road, Pim Hut has a selection of Western, Thai and Chinese dishes. The moderately priced Western breakfasts are recommended.	ⓑ		●	■	●	
MAE SOT: *Kengtung* 2/1 Sri Phanich Rd. 【 *No telephone.* Excellent Cantonese cuisine in the best Chinese restaurant in town. Dim sum is a delicious option at lunch time on most days.	ⓑⓑ			■		
PHITSANULOK: *Rim Nam Food Market* Phuttha Bucha Rd. 【 *No telephone.* This large group of food stalls is a good place for *phak bung loy fa* (flash-fried morning-glory) – tossed spectacularly through the air from chef to server – for which Phitsanulok is renowned.	ⓑ		●	■		■

PHITSANULOK: *Fah Thai* (B)(B)
Reua Pier, Phuttha Bucha Rd. (055) 258078.
This boat-restaurant cruises the Nan River each evening. Its extensive
Thai menu includes *kluay tak* (sweet banana), a local speciality.

PHITSANULOK: *Ketnikaa* (B)(B) MC V
66 Phuttha Bucha Rd. (055) 241333.
Seafood specialities, such as local freshwater shrimps, are offered at
this rather plush establishment. There is a live band every night.

PHITSANULOK: *Laap Phet Nong Khai* (B)(B) MC V
27/36 Ekhatotsarot Rd. (055) 244804.
The speciality of the house here is a delicious *lap phet* (duck salad).
Many other Central and Northeast dishes are available.

SUKHOTHAI: *Rainbow Restaurant* (B)
Nikhon Kasem Rd. (055) 613461.
A range of Thai and Western food is served at this clean and very
reasonably priced restaurant. Western breakfasts and a selection of
sandwiches are offered. The ice cream is particularly good.

SUKHOTHAI: *Coca Sukhothai* (B)(B) MC V
Sawasdiphong Hotel, 56/2–5 Singhawat Rd. (055) 611567.
A Thai-style *suki* place: that is, where diners cook their own food at
the table. Meals are a delicious concoction of fresh fish, chicken, pork,
beef and assorted seafood with fresh vegetables in a tasty broth.

SUKHOTHAI: *Dream Café and Antique House* (B)(B)
86/1 Singhawat Rd. (055) 612081.
An extensive selection of Thai and Western food in this characterful
restaurant decorated with 19th-century Thai antiques. Choose from a
range of Thai herbal liquors, which are said to boost stamina.

TAK: *Jintana* (B)(B)
2/46 Paholyothin Rd. (055) 511638.
A large restaurant with a pleasant garden terrace. The house
specialities include fish dishes and spare ribs cooked with garlic.

NORTHWEST HEARTLAND

CHIANG MAI: *Galare Food Centre* (B)
89/2 Chang Khlan Rd. (053) 272067.
This good selection of food stalls close to the Night Bazaar includes a
wide range of Northern and Central Thai dishes, Indian food and seafood. On most nights traditional Thai dancers perform next to diners.

CHIANG MAI: *New Lamduan Faham Khao Soi* (B)
North of Rama IX Bridge, Charoen Rat Rd. No telephone.
This restaurant, which serves delicious food in unpretentious surroundings, enjoys the distinction of royal patronage. HM King Bhumibol is
said to favour the *khao soi* (chicken and noodles in a spicy broth).

CHIANG MAI: *Raan Khao Soi Islam* (B)
Charoen Prathet Rd, Soi 1. No telephone.
A halal establishment with the best *khao soi* (broth served with
noodles) in Thailand. Other dishes include samosas and *khao mok kai*
(chicken biryani). It is clean and the staff are friendly. after 3pm.

CHIANG MAI: *Sri Pen* (B)
103 Inthawarorot Rd. (053) 215328.
Top quality Northern Thai food. Local specialities are cooked to the
highest standards and come with a selection of fresh green vegetables
and sticky rice. Incredibly good value for money. after 3pm.

CHIANG MAI: *Brasserie Restaurant* (B)(B) MC V
37 Charoen Rat Rd. (053) 241665.
Pla meuk krathiam phrik tai (fried, stuffed squid with garlic and pep-
per) is just one of the good dishes at this riverside restaurant.

CHIANG MAI: *Chiang Mai Ban Yuan* (B)(B)
8 Phra Pok Klao Rd, Soi 11. (053) 416083.
Vietnamese specialities, all freshly prepared by a Vietnamese family.
The *nam nyang* (barbecued pork), which is cooked to a secret recipe,
is just one example of the delicious specialities available here.

For key to symbols see back flap

Price categories for an evening meal for one, including service, but not alcohol: ⓑ under B100 ⓑⓑ B100–200 ⓑⓑⓑ B200–500 ⓑⓑⓑⓑ B500–1,000 ⓑⓑⓑⓑⓑ over B1,000	**THAI SPECIALITIES** The restaurant has Thai dishes. **ASIAN (NON-THAI) DISHES** Cuisine from other parts of Asia, such as China, Korea, Japan or India, is served. **WESTERN DISHES** French, Italian or other Western fare is on the menu. **OUTDOOR TABLES** Facilities for eating outdoors *(suan aban)*, on a terrace, or in a garden or courtyard.	**CREDIT CARDS**	**THAI SPECIALITIES**	**ASIAN (NON-THAI) DISHES**	**WESTERN DISHES**	**OUTDOOR TABLES**

Restaurant		CREDIT CARDS	THAI SPECIALITIES	ASIAN (NON-THAI) DISHES	WESTERN DISHES	OUTDOOR TABLES
CHIANG MAI: *Crusty Loaf Bakery and Irish Pub* 24/1 Rachawithi Rd. [(053) 214554. Irish and English home cooking, with favourites such as sandwiches and ice cream dished up in a welcoming Irish-pub atmosphere. The fresh breads include baguettes and delicious soda bread. 🍴 ● Mon.	ⓑⓑ		●		●	▦
CHIANG MAI: *Gallery* 25–29 Charoen Rat Rd. [(053) 248601. Excellent food such as *nam phrik ong* (spicy tomato and minced pork curry) in a delightful garden by the river. Booking is essential. 🍴 🍴	ⓑⓑ	MC V	●		●	▦
CHIANG MAI: *JJ Bakery* 2–6 Ratchadamnoen Rd. [(053) 211070. This is an enduringly popular place with both travellers and locals. The menu features good Thai food, though most people come here for the salads, sandwiches and other snacks. 📋	ⓑⓑ	V	●		●	
CHIANG MAI: *Smiling Monkey* 40/1 Bamrung Buri Rd. [(053) 277538. A pretty garden restaurant under English management. Try one of the tasty dishes such as *kaeng khiaw wan* (green curry), or have a drink at the bar in the charming, old teak house. 📋 🍴	ⓑⓑ	MC V JCB	●			▦
CHIANG MAI: *Ta-Krite* 12 Huai Kaew Rd. [(053) 404371. Set between two old wooden buildings surrounded by small trees, this garden restaurant serves beautifully prepared Thai food. It is one of the few places open at night inside the old walled city. 📋 🍴	ⓑⓑ		●			▦
CHIANG MAI: *Whole Earth* 88 Si Don Chai Rd. [(053) 282463. A long-established vegetarian and South Asian restaurant set in attractive grounds, not far from the Night Bazaar. It is one of the few restaurants in Chiang Mai offering Indian cuisine. 📋 🍴	ⓑⓑ		●	▦		
CHIANG MAI: *Antique House* 71 Charoen Prathet Rd. [(053) 276810. Enjoy a delicious Northern or Central Thai meal in a late 19th-century restored wooden house, or dine in its small garden which is decorated with antique Lanna furniture and handicrafts. 🍴	ⓑⓑⓑ	MC V	●	▦		▦
CHIANG MAI: *Babylon* 100/63 Huai Kaew Rd. [(053) 212180. The atmosphere is that of a small, charming, Italian village café. Spaghetti with blue cheese is just one of the superb dishes.	ⓑⓑⓑ	MC V			●	
CHIANG MAI: *Kaeng Ron Ban Suan* 149/3 Soi Chom Doi Mu 2. [(053) 213762. Beautifully located at the foot of Doi Suthep, this restaurant specializes in Northern Thai food. Try the *sai wua* (Northern-style sausage) or the *pak kut* (a Thai vegetable harvested only in the wild). 🍴	ⓑⓑⓑ	AE DC MC V	●			▦
CHIANG MAI: *Old Chiang Mai Cultural Center* 185/3 Wualai Rd. [(053) 275097. This is a good place to enjoy a traditional Northern Thai *khantoke* dinner, with classical Thai dance and music. The restaurant is set in a series of old Lanna-style houses. 📋 🍴 ● after 9pm.	ⓑⓑⓑ	MC V	●			▦
CHIANG MAI: *Le Coq d'Or* 68/1 Ko Klang Rd. [(053) 282024. Chiang Mai's best French restaurant is part of an elegant house that once belonged to the first British consul in Chiang Mai. The wine list is unusually comprehensive for Thailand. 📋 🍴	ⓑⓑⓑ	AE DC MC V			●	

CHIANG MAI: *Piccola Roma*　　　　　　　　　　ⒷⒷⒷⒷⒷ
3/2–3 Charoen Prathet Rd. 【 *(053) 271256.*
A first-class restaurant whose fresh seafood is flown in daily. The
Italian owner, Angelo, has a wine list unsurpassed in Northern Thailand. Luxurious surroundings are matched by authentic food. 🍴 🍷

	AE			●	
MC				
V				

LAMPANG: *Mackenna Pub*　　　　　　　　　　　　Ⓑ
Tipchang Rd, next to Riverside Bar and Restaurant. 【 *No telephone.*
Popular for *kap klaem* (snacks), which can accompany iced beer or
Thai whisky. Dine on the excellent *mu sap bai kaprao* (minced pork
with holy basil) while enjoying views of the Yom River. 🍴

| MC | ● | | | ▦ |
| V | | | |

LAMPANG: *Khrua Tai Rim Nam*　　　　　　　　　ⒷⒷ
Pamai Rd, Amphur Wiang Neua. 【 *No telephone.*
Located on the bank of the Wang River in a large teak house, this is
the best restaurant in the old Wiang Neua part of the city. Try the *tot
man kung* – prawn cakes with sweet tamarind sauce. 🍴 🍷

| ● | | | ▦ |

LAMPANG: *Riverside Bar and Restaurant*　　　　ⒷⒷ
328 Tipchang Rd, next to Mackenna Pub. 【 *No telephone.*
A very popular place situated, as its name suggests, by the river. The
cuisine is excellent, including Thai dishes such as *phat kari pu* (crab
meat in yellow curry sauce). There is live folk music every night.

| MC | ● | | ● | ● |
| V | | | |

LAMPANG: *Suki Bhami Coca*　　　　　　　　　　ⒷⒷ
138/72–74 Paholyothin Rd. 【 *(054) 316440.*
Thai-style *suki* cuisine, where diners cook their own food at the table
on hot plates. Enduringly popular with the locals. 🍴

| MC | ● | | | |
| V | | | |

LAMPHUN: *Ba-Mii Kwangtung*　　　　　　　　　Ⓑ
On the corner of Rot Kaew and Inthayongyot roads. 【 *No telephone.*
An excellent selection of fresh noodles makes this just about the best
place to eat in Lamphun. There is no English sign, but as the cooking
is done by the entrance, it is easy to find. ● *by nightfall most evenings.*

| ● | | | |

MAE HONG SON: *Good Luck Restaurant*　　　　Ⓑ
Khunlum Phraphat Rd. 【 *No telephone.*
This little place juggles a remarkably international range of dishes – Thai,
Greek, Turkish, Jewish, Arab and vegetarian – all to a high standard.

| ● | ▦ | ● | |

MAE HONG SON: *Bai Fern*　　　　　　　　　　　ⒷⒷ
Khunlum Phraphat Rd. 【 *(053) 611374.*
An attractive restaurant in a large wooden house, offering a variety of
good, inexpensive Central Thai and Chinese food, as well as simple
Western dishes. A pleasant atmosphere adds to the experience.

| ● | | ● | ▦ |

MAE HONG SON: *Khai Muk*　　　　　　　　　　ⒷⒷ
Khunlum Phraphat Rd. 【 *No telephone.*
Chinese and Thai dishes in simple yet attractive surroundings make
this place a favourite with locals and visitors alike. The *kai phat met
mamuang* (chicken fried with cashew nuts) is recommended.

| ● | ▦ | | ▦ |

MAE HONG SON: *Holiday Food Centre*　　　　　ⒷⒷⒷ
114/5–7 Khunlum Phraphat Rd. 【 *(053) 677524.*
Top-quality food at reasonable prices for such a prestigious establishment. The best place for seafood in this landlocked town. 🍴 🍷 🍴

AE	●	▦	●	▦
DC			
MC			
V			

MAE SARIANG: *Inthira Restaurant*　　　　　　　Ⓑ
Wiang Mai Rd. 【 *(053) 681529.*
The best Thai and Chinese food in remote Mae Sariang. The restaurant
is well known for its breakfast *patthong ko* (deep-fried "Chinese
doughnuts"), and for its lunchtime *kop krob* (batter-fried frogs).

| ● | ▦ | | |

PAI: *Own Home Restaurant*　　　　　　　　　　Ⓑ
Ratchadamrong Rd. 【 *No telephone.*
Good-quality mixed cuisine in this out-of-the-way spot. Try the felafel
with hummus, tzatziki and other Middle Eastern fare. The menu also
includes Indian samosas, Mexican burritos and vegetarian Thai food.

| ● | ▦ | ● | ▦ |

PAI: *Tai Yai Restaurant*　　　　　　　　　　　　Ⓑ
Ratchadamnoen Rd. 【 *No telephone.*
Enjoy the best Western breakfast in Pai, featuring home-baked
wholemeal bread, muesli and locally grown coffee. The majority of
Pai's restaurants are closed by 10pm – this stays open later than most.

| ● | | ● | |

For key to symbols see back flap

<table>
<tr><td colspan="2">

Price categories for an evening meal for one, including service, but not alcohol:

B under B100
B B B100–200
B B B B200–500
B B B B B500–1,000
B B B B B over B1,000

</td><td colspan="6">

THAI SPECIALITIES
The restaurant has Thai dishes.

ASIAN (NON-THAI) DISHES
Cuisine from other parts of Asia, such as China, Korea, Japan or India, is served.

WESTERN DISHES
French, Italian or other Western fare is on the menu.

OUTDOOR TABLES
Facilities for eating outdoors *(suan aban)*, on a terrace, or in a garden or courtyard.

</td></tr>
</table>

		CREDIT CARDS	THAI SPECIALITIES	ASIAN (NON-THAI) DISHES	WESTERN DISHES	OUTDOOR TABLES

FAR NORTH

	Price	CREDIT CARDS	THAI SPECIALITIES	ASIAN (NON-THAI) DISHES	WESTERN DISHES	OUTDOOR TABLES
CHIANG KHONG: *Lawt Tin Lu* Sai Klang Rd, Soi 2. **(** No telephone. Simple but delicious Chinese and Thai food is served at this branch of a renowned Shan-Chinese restaurant in Kengtung, eastern Burma.	**B**			●	■	
CHIANG RAI: *Mae Oui Kiaw* 106/9 Ngam Muang Rd. **(** (053) 753172. An exceptional place for Northern Thai cuisine, with all the common dishes, including *nam phrik ong* (a spicy curry of tomato and minced pork) and *kaeng hang le* (pork and ginger curry). ● after 6pm.	**B**			●		
CHIANG RAI: *Raan Ahaan Islam* 142 Itsaraphap Rd. **(** No telephone. One of the top halal establishments in town. The house specialities include *khao mok kai* (chicken biryani) and *khao soi* (a wheat noodle and coconut milk curry with beef or chicken). ● after 3pm.	**B**			●		■
CHIANG RAI: *Golden Triangle International Café* 590 Paholyothin Rd. **(** (053) 711339. Central Thai food made to Western tastes – not too hot unless requested. Many Western dishes, too, including breakfasts. 目	**B B**	MC V	●		●	
CHIANG RAI: *Yunnan* 211/6 Khwae Wai Rd. **(** (053) 713263. Specializing in regional Chinese food including Sichuan, with dishes such as Yunnanese ham and Kunming-style fried milk. ▌	**B B**			■		
CHIANG RAI: *Chinatown* Dusit Island Resort, 1129 Kraisorn Sit Rd. **(** (053) 715777. An extremely extensive Chinese menu. Dim sum is a lunchtime speciality, while Peking duck is an excellent dish served in the evenings in a classy ambience. 目 ▌	**B B B**	AE DC MC V JCB		■		
CHIANG RAI: *La Cantina* 528/20 Banpha Prakan Rd. **(** (053) 716808. Chiang Rai's best Italian restaurant. The menu features a wide range of antipasto, pizza, pasta and meat dishes. The pleasant atmosphere is enhanced by piped opera music in the background. 目 ▌	**B B B**	MC V			●	
CHIANG SAEN: *Bierstübe* 897/6 Paholyothin Rd. **(** (053) 714195. If you're pining for rich, hearty German fare, then this is the place to come. All the usual German favourites – such as wiener schnitzel (veal in breadcrumbs) – come with draught beer or schnapps. 目 ▌	**B B B**	MC V			●	
DOI MAE SALONG (SANTIKHIREE): *Mae Salong Villa* 5 Mu 1, Doi Mae Salong. **(** (053) 765115. A popular restaurant, which has good views across the hills. Often at night, a barbecue is held around a warming log fire. The menu consists of Chinese – in particular, Yunnanese – specialities. ▌	**B B B**	AE DC MC V JCB	●	■	●	■
FANG: *Parichat Road* Rawp Wiang Rd. **(** No telephone. This small, clean Thai restaurant specializes in noodles. Try the excellent *khao soi* – a bowl of wheat noodles served in a chicken or beef curry broth, eaten with lime and chilli peppers.	**B**	'	●			
GOLDEN TRIANGLE: *Border View* Delta Golden Triangle Hotel, 222 Golden Triangle, Sop Ruak. **(** (053) 784001. Elegant dining on a terrace overlooking the Mekhong. Excellent Thai and Chinese food, as well as good, genuine Western cuisine. 目 ▌ ▌	**B B B**	AE DC MC V	●	■	●	

GOLDEN TRIANGLE: *Yuan Lue Lao* ⓑⓑⓑ | AE DC MC V JCB
Golden Triangle, Sop Ruak. 【 (053) 784084.
Despite its name, this up-market establishment does not offer Lao food, but Thai, Chinese and Western cuisine. The dishes are good, and the setting, at the heart of the Golden Triangle, is even better. 🍴 🍷

MAE SAI: *Mae Sai Plaza* ⓑ
383/6 Sailomchoi Rd. 【 (053) 732230.
Situated on a covered terrace on the hill, the Mae Sai Plaza has views across the river to the Burmese town of Tachilek. The Thai food is good; the Western food is standard budget travellers' fare.

MAE SAI: *Rabieng Kaew* ⓑⓑ | AE DC MC V
356/2 Mu 1, Paholyothin Rd. 【 (053) 640463.
Excellent Central and Northern Thai food, as well as some unexpected Asian specialities. Try the fresh, tender Korean barbecued beef. Northern Thai music is played in the evenings. 🍴

NAN: *No Name* ⓑ
38/1 Suriyapong Rd. 【 No telephone.
Noodle dishes at very reasonable prices. Try the *kuaytiaw reua* – literally "boat noodles" – a delicious, spicy broth.

PHRAE: *Night Market* ⓑ
Pratuchai intersection. 【 No telephone.
Not an individual restaurant, but a collection of food stalls with street-side tables and chairs. An excellent place to enjoy incredibly cheap and tasty Central Thai and Thai-Chinese food.

PHRAE: *Ban Fai* ⓑⓑⓑ | MC V
57/6 Mu 1, Yantrakit Koson Rd. 【 (054) 523114.
On the menu at this large restaurant is good Central Thai food, and perhaps the best seafood in town. 🍴 🍷

KHORAT PLATEAU

BURIRAM: *Phnom Rung Park* ⓑ
Phnom Rung Hill. 【 No telephone.
These stalls and small restaurants offer a delicious array of dishes including *som tam* (papaya salad), grilled chicken and sticky rice. This is the only refreshment stop at Prasat Hin Khao Phnom Rung.

CHAIYAPHUM: *Phaibun* ⓑ
Ratchathan Rd. 【 No telephone.
Good Central Thai and Chinese cuisine is offered at this large, comfortable, clean and dependable restaurant. Try the *mu prio wan* (sweet and sour pork) or the *kaeng khiaw wan* (green curry). 🍴 🍷

KHON KAEN: *Krua Weh* ⓑⓑ
1/1 Klang Muang Rd. 【 No telephone.
Authentic Vietnamese food, as well as Northeast Thai dishes, served in an attractive old teak house. The Thai *ka yaw sot* (spring rolls) are excellent, as is the *nam nyang* (Vietnamese barbecue). 🍴

KHON KAEN: *Nong Lek* ⓑⓑ
54/1–3 Klang Muang Rd. 【 (043) 261759.
Good Thai and Chinese food in a restaurant patronized by locals. The specialities are *khao na pet* (duck served with rice) and seafood.

KHORAT: *Veterans of Foreign Wars Café* ⓑ
167–168 Pho Klang Rd. 【 (044) 242831.
This café, founded by ex-US servicemen, specializes in American-style fast food and simple Thai dishes. It is a good place for breakfasts. 🍴

KHORAT: *Great Wall* ⓑⓑ | MC V JCB
Chomphon Rd. 【 No telephone.
Khorat has an extensive Sino-Thai population, and this Chinese establishment is one of the community's favourite eating places. Enjoy the excellent Cantonese cuisine in comfortable, relaxing surroundings. 🍴

PHIMAI: *Bai Toey* ⓑ
Phimai Main Street. 【 No telephone.
Simple Thai and Western fare in a garden setting. Try the vegetarian dishes and the sweets made from sticky rice and coconut milk.

For key to symbols see back flap

			CREDIT CARDS	THAI SPECIALITIES	ASIAN (NON-THAI) DISHES	WESTERN DISHES	OUTDOOR TABLES

Price categories for an evening meal for one, including service, but not alcohol:

B under B100
B **B** B100–200
B **B** **B** B200–500
B **B** **B** **B** B500–1,000
B **B** **B** **B** **B** over B1,000

THAI SPECIALITIES
The restaurant has Thai dishes.

ASIAN (NON-THAI) DISHES
Cuisine from other parts of Asia, such as China, Korea, Japan or India, is served.

WESTERN DISHES
French, Italian or other Western fare is on the menu.

OUTDOOR TABLES
Facilities for eating outdoors (suan ahan), on a terrace, or in a garden or courtyard.

	Credit Cards	Thai Specialities	Asian (Non-Thai) Dishes	Western Dishes	Outdoor Tables
ROI ET: *Neua Yang Kaolee* **B** **B** Rim Beung Plan Chai Rd. **C** No telephone. This excellent garden restaurant is located on the northeastern side of Beung Phlan Chai Lake, in the centre of town. It is named after the house speciality, Korean barbecued beef, which is cooked at the table.	MC V		■		■
SURIN: *Cocaa* **B** **B** 21/1 Soi Tessaban 2. **C** (044) 512390. Good Thai and Chinese cuisine, with seafood specialities. Don't be put off by the dull appearance – there isn't a better place in Surin. ▤		●	■		■
UDON THANI: *Rung Thong* **B** Hor Nalika Clock Tower. **C** (042) 223154. A simple establishment that excels at delicious, reasonably priced Central and Northeastern food, including Thai curries. Try the *tom kha kai* (chicken soup with coconut milk and lemon grass).		●			
UDON THANI: *Madame Kiu* **B** **B** Adunyadet Rd. **C** No telephone. A late-night place which stays open until 4am providing good Central Thai and Chinese food, as well as some basic Western fare. *Kung phat phrik phao* (prawns fried with chillies) is one of the specialities. ▤		●	■	●	
UDON THANI: *Mayfair* **B** **B** **B** Charoen Hotel, 549 Phosri Rd. **C** (042) 248155. This award-winning restaurant has the best reputation for good food in Udon Thani. There is an extensive menu that features Thai and Chinese cuisine in addition to good Western breakfasts. ▤ 🍴 🛏	AE DC MC V JCB	●	■	●	

MEKHONG RIVER VALLEY

	Credit Cards	Thai Specialities	Asian (Non-Thai) Dishes	Western Dishes	Outdoor Tables
CHIANG KHAN: *Suksomboon Hotel* **B** 243/3 Chai Khong Rd. **C** (042) 821064. Situated on the Mekhong River. If you have the stomach for it, sample the *gung ten* – live shrimps taken straight from the river, immersed in a bowl of lemon and chilli sauce and eaten while still alive.		●	■	●	
LOEI: *Savita* **B** **B** 139 Charoen Rat Rd. **C** No telephone. Savita is a restaurant-cum-coffee shop, serving Central Thai food and Thai-style Western fast food including burgers and sandwiches. ▤	MC V	●		●	
MUKDAHAN: *Night Market* **B** Songnang Sathit Rd. **C** No telephone. This extensive group of food stalls near the bus station sells Thai, Lao and Vietnamese specialities at excellent prices.		●	■		
MUKDAHAN: *Riverside* **B** **B** Samran Chai Khong Rd. **C** No telephone. A shady riverside terrace that has pleasant views of Suwannakhet in Laos across the water. The menu features Thai and Chinese cuisine and cold beer. One of the best dishes is *lap phet* (spicy duck salad).		●	■		■
NAKHON PHANOM: *Mekhong Golden Giant Catfish* **B** 257–261 Sunthon Wichit Rd. **C** (042) 511218. *Pla buk* – giant Mekhong catfish – is the speciality here. Try it stir-fried with holy basil *(phat kraphao)* or baked in a clay pot *(op mo din)*. 🍴	AE DC V	●			■
NAKHON PHANOM: *Nawt Laap Phet* **B** 494 Aphiban Bancha Rd. **C** No telephone. Northeastern specialities, as well as common dishes such as spicy grilled chicken and papaya salad. Especially recommended is the *yang seua rong hai* – literally "grilled crying tiger" – beef with chillies.		●			

NONG KHAI: *Udom Rot* Ⓑ
423 Rim Khong Rd. 【 *(042) 421084.*
Good views of the Mekhong and the river traffic to Laos. Enjoy the
excellent *phat tai*, which is thin rice noodles fried with bean sprouts,
egg, pork and dried prawns, served with a slice of fresh lime.

NONG KHAI: *Indochine* ⒷⒷ
189/1 Meechai Rd. 【 *No telephone.*
This is an excellent place to sample Vietnamese cooking. Among the
typical dishes are spring rolls accompanied by fresh green vegetables,
barbecued sausages and various egg-based concoctions.

THAT PHANOM: *That Phanom Pochana* Ⓑ
Phanom Phanarak Rd. 【 *(042) 541189.*
Situated near the triumphal arch in the centre of town, this restaurant
specializes in reasonably priced Thai and Chinese fish dishes.

UBON RATCHATHANI: *Jiaw Kii* Ⓑ
Khuan Thani Rd. 【 *No telephone.*
An excellent place for breakfast, whether you like Thai *khao tom* (rice
soup) or Western-style ham and eggs with warm baps. ▤

UBON RATCHATHANI: *Indochine* ⒷⒷ V
Wat Cheng, 168–170 Sapphasit Rd. 【 *(045) 245584.*
People travel from all over the country to enjoy the great Vietnamese
cooking – the omelettes in particular are praised – and the pleasant,
relaxed atmosphere of this old teak house. ▤

EASTERN SEABOARD

CHANTHABURI: *Chanthon Phochana* Ⓑ
98/1 Benchamarachutit Rd. 【 *(039) 312340.*
Tasty Thai and Chinese fare is served at this spotlessly clean
restaurant. Chanthaburi is known for its noodle dishes, and this is the
place to taste dishes such as *sen mi phat pu* (crab fried with noodles).

CHANTHABURI: *Mangsawirat* Ⓑ
Tha Chalab Rd, Soi 3. 【 *No telephone.*
A tiny vegetarian establishment by Taksin Park. As well as delicious
and reasonably priced food, there are many fresh fruit juices, including
guava, *roselle* (similar to blackcurrant), coconut and tamarind.

KO CHANG: *Sunset (Tawanplob)* ⒷⒷⒷ AE DC MC V
39 Mu 4, Ko Chang. 【 *(039) 5380549.*
An up-market place for this relatively undeveloped island, with
seafood specialities and a wide range of dishes. 🍴

PATTAYA: *Ali Baba* ⒷⒷ AE V MC
1/13–14 Central Pattaya Rd. 【 *(038) 429262.*
This restaurant has two menus: good North Indian cuisine inside, and
South Indian vegetarian food outside. Choose from a variety of curries,
dhals, Indian breads and cooling raitas. ▤ 🍴

PATTAYA: *Bahay Filipino* ⒷⒷ MC V
485/3 Pattaya 2nd Rd. 【 *(038) 426191.*
This establishment features Filipino specialities, accompanied by live
music. Try the suckling pig, *gambas al ajillio* (raw shrimps in garlic
and olive oil) or *gambas rebosado* (prawns baked in butter). ▤ 🍴

PATTAYA: *Poteen Still* ⒷⒷ
219/68 Soi Yamato. 【 *(038) 420644.*
Uniquely, this place serves a mixture of Irish pub fare, such as fish
and chips, and (canned) Guinness, plus various Thai dishes. ▤ 🍴

PATTAYA: *Russkii* ⒷⒷ
205/8–9 Pattaya 2nd Rd. 【 *(038) 429662.*
This is the best of several Russian places in the resort. On offer are
borsch (beetroot soup), *pelmeni* (small dumplings), chicken Kiev and
a host of other traditional dishes. ▤ 🍴

PATTAYA: *Vientiane* ⒷⒷ MC V
485/18 Pattaya 2nd Rd. 【 *(038) 411298.*
Pattaya's foremost Indochinese restaurant has a varied menu that features Lao, Vietnamese, Thai and Chinese dishes, as well as seafood. ▤

For key to symbols see back flap

		THAI SPECIALITIES	**ASIAN (NON-THAI) DISHES**	**WESTERN DISHES**	**OUTDOOR TABLES**
	CREDIT CARDS				

Price categories for an evening meal for one, including service, but not alcohol:

Ⓑ under B100
ⒷⒷ B100–200
ⒷⒷⒷ B200–500
ⒷⒷⒷⒷ B500–1,000
ⒷⒷⒷⒷⒷ over B1,000

THAI SPECIALITIES
The restaurant has Thai dishes.

ASIAN (NON-THAI) DISHES
Cuisine from other parts of Asia, such as China, Korea, Japan or India, is served.

WESTERN DISHES
French, Italian or other Western fare is on the menu.

OUTDOOR TABLES
Facilities for eating outdoors *(suan ahan)*, on a terrace, or in a garden or courtyard.

PATTAYA: *La Brassero*   ⒷⒷⒷ
Central Shopping Arcade, Pattaya 2nd Rd. 【 *No telephone.*
A pleasant French bistro. The fixed-price menu is especially good value for money, and typically features such dishes as smoked chicken salad, steak and chips and a choice of desserts. 📋 🍴 🍷

Credit Cards	Thai	Asian	Western	Outdoor
			●	■

PATTAYA: *Green Bottle*   ⒷⒷⒷ
Diana Inn, 216/6–9 Pattaya 2nd Rd. 【 *(038) 429675.*
Great food in this friendly English-style pub. The specialities include lobster thermidor, roast duck in a red wine sauce and fillet steak stuffed with goose liver paté and wrapped in bacon. 📋 🍴

AE DC MC V | ● | | ● |

PATTAYA: *La Gritta*   ⒷⒷⒷ
Amari Orchid Resort, 240 Mu 5, Pattaya Beach Rd. 【 *(038) 428161.*
Allegedly Pattaya's top Italian restaurant, specializing in seafood. Typical fare includes pizzas and pasta dishes, as well as monthly promotions featuring local produce cooked in Italian style. 📋 🍴 🍷

AE MC V | | | ● |

PATTAYA: *Lobster Pot*   ⒷⒷⒷ
288 Beach Rd, South Pattaya. 【 *(038) 426083.*
A fine seafood restaurant. The extensive menu is matched by a pleasant atmosphere. Renowned for its fresh seafood – this is the best place for lobster thermidor in Pattaya. 📋 🍴

AE MC V | ● | | ● |

PATTAYA: *Mai Kai Supper Club*   ⒷⒷⒷ
Hotel Tropicana, Pattaya Beach Rd. 【 *(038) 428645.*
Polynesian specialities and standard Western fare in air-conditioned comfort overlooking Pattaya bay. At Mai Kai Supper Club there is live music from a Haitian band every evening. 📋 🍴

AE DC MC V | | ■ | ● |

PATTAYA: *Pan Pan San Domenico*   ⒷⒷⒷ
Tappaya Rd. 【 *(038) 251874.*
An outstanding Italian restaurant. Everything about this place, from the food to the decor, is first class. The rather limited menu is rescued by a wide range of fresh desserts and pastries. 📋 🍴

AE MC V | | | ● |

PATTAYA: *Pattaya Park Tower*   ⒷⒷⒷ
345 Jomtien Beach Rd. 【 *(038) 251201.*
The food is good, and the views are superb, at this revolving seafood restaurant located on the 52nd floor of Pattaya's tallest building. The buffet includes Japanese, Thai, Chinese and European food. 📋

AE MC V | ● | ■ | ● |

PATTAYA: *PIC Kitchen*   ⒷⒷⒷ
Soi 5, Pattaya Beach Rd. 【 *(038) 428387.*
Top quality traditional Thai food at a restaurant composed of a series of teak houses. Classical Thai dancing is a feature every week. 📋

AE MC V | ● | | ● | ■ |

PATTAYA: *Red Baron*   ⒷⒷⒷ
Amari Orchid Resort, 240 Mu 5, Pattaya Beach Rd. 【 *(038) 428161.*
German and Swiss specialities are the order of the day at this stylish restaurant, in a peaceful location near the beach. 📋 🍴 🍷

AE DC MC V | | | ● |

PATTAYA: *Ruen Thai*   ⒷⒷⒷ
485/3 Pattaya 2nd Rd. 【 *(038) 425911.*
Thai food of great quality is served in a cluster of open-air wooden pavilions, accompanied by jazz music and classical Thai dancing every night. The children's facilities include a playground. 📋 🍴

AE DC MC V | ● | | | ■ |

PATTAYA: *Sugar Hut*   ⒷⒷⒷ
Tappaya Rd. 【 *(038) 251689.*
Sumptuous teak houses in a setting that is hard to fault. The menu focuses on Central Thai cuisine, with delicious and well presented dishes. It is excellent value for money. 📋 🍴

AE DC MC V | ● | ■ | ● | ■ |

PATTAYA: *Yamato*   ⒷⒷⒷ
Soi Yamato. 【 *(038) 429686.*
Classic Japanese cuisine served by waitresses dressed in kimonos. The
house specialities include sushi, tempura and sashimi. Though the
experience is not particularly cheap, the authenticity is worth it. ▤ ▯
AE MC V JCB

PATTAYA: *Angus Steak House*   ⒷⒷⒷⒷ
485/2 Pattaya 2nd Rd. 【 *(038) 426193.*
Imported beef, lamb and chargrilled salmon dished up in a traditional
steakhouse atmosphere. There is a menu for children. ▤ ▯
AE MC V

SI RACHA: *Chua Li*   ⒷⒷⒷ
Jermjonpol Rd, Soi 10. 【 *No telephone.*
An excellent seafood place, concentrating on Thai and Chinese dishes.
Si Racha gives its name to the local speciality: a delicious, spicy sauce
called *nam phrik si racha*. Try it with grilled lobster or crayfish. ▤
MC V

TRAT: *Sang Fah*   ⒷⒷ
156–157 Sukhumvit Rd. 【 *(039) 511222.*
An extensive menu featuring many seafood dishes; the *tom yam pla
chon* (spicy fish stew) is recommended. ▤

WESTERN SEABOARD

CHA-AM: *Family Shop*   ⒷⒷ
Ruamchit Rd. 【 *No telephone.*
This basic restaurant offers delicious, fresh seafood barbecues right on
the seashore. Enjoy the huge, succulent king prawns.

CHA-AM: *Sorndaeng*   ⒷⒷ
Cha-am Methavali Hotel, 220 Ruamchit Rd. 【 *(032) 471480.*
Cha-am is well known for its seafood, and this restaurant serves some
of the best, cooked to both Western and Thai recipes. ▤ ▯

HUA HIN: *Maria Ice Cream*   Ⓑ
54/2 Decha Nuchit Rd. 【 *No telephone.*
Wonderful home-made ice cream, ideal for cooling down in the heat.
Choose from a whole spectrum of flavours, including papaya, durian,
watermelon and coconut. Simple Thai snacks are also on the menu.

HUA HIN: *Museum*   ⒷⒷ
Hotel Sofitel Central, 1 Damnoen Kasem Rd. 【 *(032) 512031.*
In keeping with its surroundings in the Sofitel (formerly Railway)
Hotel *(see p321)*, the Museum is decorated in 1920s style. Traditional
high tea, with delicious pastries, can be taken here. ▤ ▯
AE DC MC V

HUA HIN: *Charlie's Seafood*   ⒷⒷⒷ
Naresdamri Rd. 【 *No telephone.*
A wide range of freshly caught seafood at reasonable prices. House
specialities worth sampling include *pla samli* (cotton fish), *pla kapong*
(perch) and *hoi malaeng pu* (mussels).

HUA HIN: *Goya*   ⒷⒷⒷ
Melia Hua Hin Hotel, 33 Naresdamri Rd. 【 *(032) 512888.*
One of Thailand's very few Spanish restaurants. The menu features
Iberian favourites such as paella, gazpacho and various tapas. The
seafood specialities are particularly good. ▤ ▯ ▮
AE DC MC V

HUA HIN: *Railway*   ⒷⒷⒷ
Hotel Sofitel Central, 1 Damnoen Kasem Rd. 【 *(032) 512031.*
This restaurant in the former Railway Hotel specializes in French and
Asian cuisine, and there is a daily buffet with either Italian or Thai
food. Eat against the backdrop of a 1920s railway station. ▤ ▯
AE DC MC V

HUA HIN: *Saeng Thai*   ⒷⒷⒷ
By the pier on Naresdamri Rd. 【 *(032) 512144.*
A large, open-air place right on the seafront, this is one of the oldest
seafood restaurants in town. The menu constantly proves very popular
with residents and visitors alike.
MC V

HUA HIN: *Suan Guang*   ⒷⒷⒷ
43/1 Phetkasem Rd. 【 *(032) 520250.*
Excellent Thai food is served here in a traditional antique Thai setting.
Live classical Thai music accompanies the meal. ▤ ▯

<table>
<tr><td colspan="2">

Price categories for an evening meal for one, including service, but not alcohol:

Ⓑ under B100
ⒷⒷ B100–200
ⒷⒷⒷ B200–500
ⒷⒷⒷⒷ B500–1,000
ⒷⒷⒷⒷⒷ over B1,000

</td></tr>
</table>

THAI SPECIALITIES
The restaurant has Thai dishes.

ASIAN (NON-THAI) DISHES
Cuisine from other parts of Asia, such as China, Korea, Japan or India, is served.

WESTERN DISHES
French, Italian or other Western fare is on the menu.

OUTDOOR TABLES
Facilities for eating outdoors *(suan aban)*, on a terrace, or in a garden or courtyard.

	CREDIT CARDS	THAI SPECIALITIES	ASIAN (NON-THAI) DISHES	WESTERN DISHES	OUTDOOR TABLES
HUA HIN: *Palm Pavilion* ⒷⒷⒷⒷ Hotel Sofitel Central, 1 Damnoen Kasem Rd. 【 *(032) 512031.* Another elegant, 1920s restaurant within this delightful hotel. Food includes a creative seafood menu and fine cuts of imported beef and lamb. It is very popular, so reservations are recommended. ▤ ▮ ▯	AE DC MC V	●		●	▦
KO PHA NGAN: *Island View Cabana* Ⓑ Mae Hat Beach. 【 *No telephone.* Travellers in search of reasonably priced, international fare should go to this quiet, outdoor restaurant. When it is available, the steak *pla chalam* (chargrilled fresh shark steak) is memorable.		●		●	▦
KO SAMUI: *Brasserie* ⒷⒷ Cumber Hotel, 3–5 Mu 2, Chaweng Beach. 【 *(077) 422041.* The usual excellent seafood for which Ko Samui is famed, but with a difference: at this restaurant the chefs specialize in Italian cooking. ▮	MC V	●		●	▦
KO SAMUI: *Happy Elephant* ⒷⒷ 19/1 Mu 1, Tambon Bophut. 【 *(077) 245347.* Both Thai and Western dishes, at reasonable prices. The seafood specialities are good, particularly the *kung pan oy*, prawn cakes grilled on fresh sugar cane sticks, then dipped in sweet tamarind sauce. ▮		●		●	
KO SAMUI: *Osteria* ⒷⒷ Chaweng Arcade, Chaweng Beach Rd. 【 *(077) 230057.* A pizza and pasta restaurant in a terrific location, near Ko Samui's longest and prettiest beach. The calzone (stuffed pizza) is particularly good, and the prices are extremely reasonable. ▮	AE MC V			●	▦
KO SAMUI: *Captain's Choice* ⒷⒷⒷ Boathouse Hotel, Choeng Mon Beach. 【 *(077) 425041.* One of Ko Samui's top restaurants, with a wide range of fresh sea-foods. All the usual maritime favourites, including prawns, squid, crab, lobster and crayfish, plus less common seafoods such as shark. ▤ ▮	AE DC MC V JCB	●	▦	●	▦
KO SAMUI: *Coral Cove Chalet Restaurant* ⒷⒷⒷ Lamai Beach. 【 *(077) 422260.* A beautiful location, matched by tasty and fresh food. The specialities include *tom kha kai* (chicken cooked in coconut milk) and *kung phao* (grilled prawns). Good Western breakfasts are also available. ▮	AE MC V	●		●	▦
KO SAMUI: *Island Restaurant* ⒷⒷⒷ North Chaweng Beach. 【 *No telephone.* Reputed to give the largest helpings on Ko Samui, this restaurant specializes in seafood and Italian dishes. Imported meat, including Australian beefsteaks and New Zealand lamb, is another feature. ▮	AE MC V	●		●	▦
KO SAMUI: *Kinaree* ⒷⒷⒷ 14/3 Mu 2, Tambon Bophut. 【 *(077) 422015.* This smart, fern-filled restaurant offers seafood dishes including lobster thermidor, stuffed crab and many other delicious specialities. ▤ ▮ ▯	AE DC MC V	●		●	
KO SAMUI: *Laguna Terrace* ⒷⒷⒷ Blue Lagoon Hotel, 99 Mu 2, Chaweng Beach. 【 *(077) 422037.* A combination of seafood, Thai and European cuisine. The lunchtime buffet, on Tuesdays, Thursdays and Saturdays, is huge and reasonably priced. There is Thai dancing in the evenings. ▮	AE MC V	●	▦	●	▦
KO TAO: *Ko Tao Cottage* ⒷⒷ Chalok Ban Khao Beach. 【 *(01) 7250751.* One of the best restaurants on this tiny island, pleasantly isolated from the main centre of activity at Ban Hat Sairee. Not surprisingly, the menu features seafood, as well as Thai and Western dishes.	AE MC V	●	▦	●	▦

PHETCHABURI: *Ban Khanom Thai* ⓑ
130 Petchkasem Rd. ((032) 425618.
Phetchaburi is famed for its Thai sweets, and the name of this establishment means "house of Thai desserts". Sample the *khanom mo kaeng*, a firm custard of mung beans, eggs, coconut and sugar.

PRACHUAP KHIRI KHAN: *Phloen Samut* ⓑⓑ V
44 Beach Rd. ((032) 601866.
A good place to try the local speciality, *pla samli taet diaw*, which is flash-fried, sun-dried cotton fish, served with mango salad. 🔋

SURAT THANI: *Suan Isaan* ⓑⓑ
Off Donnok Rd, 1 Damnoen Kasem Rd. (No telephone.
A traditional Thai house with delicious Northeastern food, such as *kai yang* (grilled chicken), *som tam* (papaya salad) and other delicacies.

UPPER ANDAMAN COAST

KO LANTA: *La Crêperie* ⓑⓑ
Ko Lanta Yai. (No telephone.
Seafood is the mainstay of Ko Lanta cooking, and at this restaurant it is given a French touch. The seafood pancakes are outstanding.

KO PHI PHI: *Pizza House* ⓑⓑ AE MC V
Ton Sai Village, Ko Phi Phi Don. (No telephone.
Just about the only place on Ko Phi Phi that doesn't specialize in seafood – though this, too, is on the menu. The pizzas are tasty and the spaghetti with seafood sauce is recommended.

KO PHI PHI: *Patcharee Seafood* ⓑⓑⓑ
Ton Sai Village, Ko Phi Phi Don. (No telephone.
Excellent fresh seafood at relatively steep prices. Indulge in the barbecued shark steak, just one of several great dishes available.

KRABI: *Panan Makanan Islam* ⓑ
At the corner of Ruen Rudi and Maharat roads. (No telephone.
Krabi is far enough south for Malay cuisine to be available. On offer are biryanis and satay, as well as the more unusual *kaeng matsaman*, or beef curry served with a peanut sauce.

KRABI: *Kotung* ⓑⓑ
36 Kongkha Rd. ((075) 611522.
A seafood restaurant serving Central and Southern Thai dishes. Clean, friendly and cheap, this place can be relied upon. The *tom yam kung* (a spicy broth with prawns and mushrooms) is recommended.

PHANGNGA: *Duang* ⓑ
122 Phetkasem Rd. ((076) 412216.
Chinese and Southern Thai cuisine features on this restaurant's menu. The seafood is particularly fresh, with tasty dishes such as *tom yam thalay* (spicy seafood stew) and *kung phao* (grilled prawns).

PHUKET: *Somjit Noodles* ⓑ
214/6 Phuket Rd. (No telephone.
A small, clean, unassuming place that makes really excellent Thai and Hokkien noodles. Try the island's best known dish – *khanom chin nam ya phuket* (Chinese noodles in a curried fish sauce).

PHUKET: *Pop & Jazz* ⓑⓑ AE MC V
43 Phuket Villa 1, Soi 1 Yaowarat Rd. (No telephone.
Unusually for Phuket, this establishment features Central Plains and Northern Thai specialities. Enjoy *khao soi* (a spicy, curried broth with chicken or beef) and *nam phrik ong* (a spicy pork curry). 🍽

PHUKET: *Sundown Café* ⓑⓑ MC V
Surin Beach. ((076) 270230.
A Tex-Mex place with an assortment of food including burritos, nachos, tacos, fajitas and superb home-made ice cream. 🍽 🔋 ● Mon.

PHUKET: *Bluefin Tavern* ⓑⓑⓑ
111/17 Taina Rd, Kata Beach. ((076) 330856.
This New England-style pub serves up a range of tasty dishes. Typical favourites include corned beef, pastrami, roast beef sandwiches, Cuban black bean soup, Texas chilli and fish chowder. 🍽

For key to symbols see back flap

		CREDIT CARDS	**THAI SPECIALITIES**	**ASIAN (NON-THAI) DISHES**	**WESTERN DISHES**	**OUTDOOR TABLES**

Price categories for an evening meal for one, including service, but not alcohol:

Ⓑ under B100
ⒷⒷ B100–200
ⒷⒷⒷ B200–500
ⒷⒷⒷⒷ B500–1,000
ⒷⒷⒷⒷⒷ over B1,000

THAI SPECIALITIES
The restaurant has Thai dishes.

ASIAN (NON-THAI) DISHES
Cuisine from other parts of Asia, such as China, Korea, Japan or India, is served.

WESTERN DISHES
French, Italian or other Western fare is on the menu.

OUTDOOR TABLES
Facilities for eating outdoors *(suan ahan)*, on a terrace, or in a garden or courtyard.

	Credit Cards	Thai	Asian	Western	Outdoor
PHUKET: *Giorgio's* ⒷⒷⒷ Beach Rd, Patong. 【 *No telephone.* Mainly Italian food in a lush tropical garden setting. Choose from pizzas, pasta and specialities such as seafood soup. The Swiss pastries are good, and the list of Italian wines is extensive. ☘	AE MC V			●	▦
PHUKET: *Kan Eang Seafood* ⒷⒷⒷ Chalong Bay. 【 *(076) 381323.* Diners can select their own seafood from the display at this restaurant. The Thai cuisine is delectable, with specialities such as *ho mok* (curried seafood mousse). ☘ 🍽	AE DC MC V	●			▦
PHUKET: *Kiko* ⒷⒷⒷ Diamond Cliff Resort, 61/9 Kalim Beach, Patong. 【 *(076) 340501.* A beach-side restaurant that creates fine Japanese food with ingredients imported fresh from Japan. The house specialities are traditional dishes such as *teppanyaki*, sushi and sashimi. ▤ ☘	AE DC MC V JCB		▦		
PHUKET: *Old Siam* ⒷⒷⒷ Beach Rd, Patong. 【 *(076) 341193.* Thai cuisine of royal standards is served in this traditional wooden *sala*. Classical Thai dancing can be enjoyed on Wednesdays and Saturdays. Good food in a lovely setting. 🍽	AE DC MC V	●			▦
PHUKET: *Pae Thip* ⒷⒷⒷ Pearl Village Hotel, Nai Yang Beach and National Park. 【 *(076) 327006.* Set in the middle of a lake and surrounded by landscaped gardens, this restaurant specializes in Japanese cuisine and Korean barbecues. Beautifully prepared Thai food is also available. ▤ ☘ ● *Wed.*	AE DC MC V JCB	●	▦		▦
PHUKET: *Saffron* ⒷⒷⒷ Banyan Tree Hotel, 393 Mu 2, Cherngtalay. 【 *(076) 324374.* An assortment of Middle Eastern and South Asian dishes. The *fukulmas peggadu badun* (stir-fried chicken livers with onions) and the Singapore chilli crab are both recommended. ☘ 🍽	AE DC MC V		▦		
PHUKET: *La Trattoria* ⒷⒷⒷⒷ Dusit Laguna Resort, 390 Sri Sunthorn Rd, Cherngtalay. 【 *(076) 324320.* Traditional Italian food of excellent quality is served in this open-air setting. The dishes are not cheap by Phuket standards, but this is the place to go if you want first-rate Italian food. ☘ 🍽	AE DC MC V JCB			●	▦
PHUKET: *Lighthouse* ⒷⒷⒷⒷ Cape Panwa Hotel, Ao Makham. 【 *(076) 391123.* The Lighthouse has an extensive and sophisticated seafood menu. Oysters, lobster thermidor and stuffed crab are all featured. ▤ ☘ 🍽	AE DC MC V			●	
PHUKET: *Regatta Bar and Grill* ⒷⒷⒷⒷⒷ Phuket Yacht Club, Nai Harn Beach. 【 *(076) 381156.* Top-of-the-range *nouvelle cuisine* is prepared by the Regatta's resident European chef. Enjoy stunning views of Nai Harn bay as you dine. The ambience is wonderful, with live music every night. ▤ ☘ 🍽	AE DC MC V JCB			●	
RANONG: *Raan Ahaan Islam* Ⓑ Ruangrat Rd. 【 *(077) 832534.* A small and inexpensive Muslim-run place where it is possible to try Burmese fare as well as traditional Thai food. It is also good for breakfasts if you like curry and roti, washed down with milky tea.		●	▦		
RANONG: *Palm Court* ⒷⒷⒷ Jansom Thara Hotel, 2/10 Phetkasem Rd. 【 *(077) 811510.* The best restaurant in Ranong has a wide selection of Thai and Chinese dishes. The house speciality is grilled suckling pig. ☘	AE MC V	●	▦	●	

DEEP SOUTH

HAT YAI: *Ruby*   Ⓑ
Niyomrat Rd. 📞 *No telephone.*
An extensive range of North Indian dhals, curries, biryanis and tandoori dishes in this Muslim establishment, where all the food is halal.

HAT YAI: *Sumatera*   Ⓑ
Cheevanusorn Rd. 📞 *No telephone.*
This restaurant specializes in Malay cuisine with a distinct Indonesian flavour. Try the *mee goreng* (noodles with eggs and shrimps), the *nasi goreng* (rice with eggs and shrimps) or the *rojak* (peanut sauce salad).

HAT YAI: *Hua Lee*   ⒷⒷⒷ   AE
Niphat Uthit 3 Rd. 📞 *No telephone.*   DC
Enjoy Chinese dishes such as *rang nok* (bird's-nest soup) and *hu*   MC
chalam (shark's-fin soup). This place is popular with Hat Yai's Chinese   V
community, and stays open late into the night.

NAKHON SI THAMMARAT: *Hao Coffee*   Ⓑ
Bovorn Bazaar, Ratchadamnoen Rd. 📞 *No telephone.*
A very pleasant coffee shop, attractively decorated with Thai antiques.
Tasty Thai snacks, good Western breakfasts and international coffees.

NAKHON SI THAMMARAT: *Tamnak Thai*   ⒷⒷ
378 Omkhai Rd. 📞 *No telephone.*
A delightful series of pavilions, ornamented in the Northern Thai style,
set in a lake with fountains and connected by walkways. The cuisine
(mainly Thai) and the atmosphere are good, with live bands. 🎴

NARATHIWAT: *Rim Nam*   ⒷⒷ
Jaturong Ratsami Rd. 📞 *No telephone.*
Well worth the 2-km (1-mile) trip out of town, this is Narathiwat's best
restaurant. Good Southern Thai and Malay seafood and curries, such
as *kaeng matsaman* (a curry of beef and peanut sauce).

PATTANI: *Chong Ah*   ⒷⒷ
190 Prida Rd. 📞 *No telephone.*
An extensive selection of Southern Thai, Central Thai and Chinese
dishes. This place is popular with the locals, which is a recommen-
dation, but means you may have to wait for a table.

PHATTHALUNG: *Khrua Cook*   Ⓑ
Prachabamrung Rd. 📞 *No telephone.*
Excellent seafood – try the *pla samli taet diaw* (fried cotton fish served
with fresh mango salad) or the deep-fried prawns served with a dip.

SONGKHLA: *Khunying*   Ⓑ
Srisuda Rd. 📞 *No telephone.*
Enjoy curries and noodle dishes here, including *khanom chin nam ya*
(noodles with fish curry) and *kaeng khiaw wan* (green curry).

SONGKHLA: *Bua Kaew*   ⒷⒷ   MC
13 Ratchadamnoen Rd. 📞 *(074) 314816.*   V
This restaurant conjures up first-class seafood at reasonable rates. Try
the *phat pla meuk* (spicy fried squid) or the *phat kari pu* (yellow
curried crab). Chinese dishes are also available. 🎴

SONGKHLA: *Ou-en*   ⒷⒷ
Srisuda Rd. 📞 *No telephone.*
Mandarin-style cuisine and various Southern Thai dishes at this very
popular Chinese restaurant. The house speciality is Peking duck.

TRANG: *Khao Tom Phui*   Ⓑ
111 Talat Rd. 📞 *(075) 210127.*
This establishment serves Thai and Chinese food, such as tasty
pumpui kha na fai daeng (stir-fried greens in a bean sauce) and *pla*
kaphong nam daeng (sea bass in a sweet, piquant sauce).

TRANG: *Sin Jiew*   Ⓑ
152–154 Kantang Rd. 📞 *(075) 218552.*
One of Trang's numerous *kopii* shops – which make real filtered
coffee. It is run by a Hokkien Chinese family, who dish up tasty
snacks such as *mu yang* (barbecued pork), a local speciality.

For key to symbols see back flap

SHOPPING IN THAILAND

THAILAND IS WELL known as a country that offers good shopping. The high quality, wide variety and keen prices of many Thai goods are a major attraction for tourists. Arts and crafts are probably the most tempting buys. These range from inexpensive wicker rice steamers to valuable antiques, and include many typically Thai items such as triangular cushions, colourful hilltribe artifacts and finely crafted silver jewellery. Many are available from specialist crafts centres. Thai silk has

Market stall selling herbs

an international reputation and comes in a huge variety of designs, both traditional and modern. Tailors, particularly in Bangkok, can make clothes in silk or any other fabric to high standards for low prices. The country is also known for its rich supply of gems, and the capital is a major gem trading centre. With the appearance of huge, luxurious shopping malls in Bangkok alongside vibrant, chaotic markets and street stalls, Thailand offers shoppers a mix of the contemporary and the traditional.

Asia Books – one of the best book chains in Thailand

OPENING HOURS

MOST SMALL SHOPS open from about 8am to 8pm or 9pm, while department stores, shopping malls and tourist shops typically open from 9:30am until 9pm or 10pm in busy areas. Trading days are normally Monday to Saturday, but most shops in Bangkok, tourist areas and resorts also open on Sundays and public holidays. During the Chinese and Thai new years (in February and April) many shops shut for several days. Market hours are usually dawn to mid-afternoon for fresh produce, or late afternoon to midnight or even later for tourist markets.

HOW TO PAY

THE THAI BAHT, linked to the US dollar, has been a stable currency since the mid-1980s. *Baht* will always be accepted throughout the country (and in Laos). Credit cards can be used in many shops in Bangkok and resorts, and

increasingly so in provincial towns. VISA and American Express are probably the most widely accepted, followed by MasterCard. Up-market places usually take all major cards. Be warned, though, that many shops will add on a surcharge of up to five per cent if you pay by credit card.

RIGHTS AND REFUNDS

WHEN BUYING expensive items, ask for a written receipt (*bai set*) bearing the shop's address and tax number. For goods on which you want to reclaim the seven per cent value added tax, shops should fill out a form for you to present to customs officers at the airport. However, the hassle and handling fees involved mean that this is rarely worth the trouble.

If you are arranging to have goods shipped home make sure you confirm all the costs involved with the supplier in advance, including insurance, tax and shipping charges.

Refunds are almost unheard of, but exchange of faulty or ill-fitting non-sale goods from reputable stores should be possible, if sometimes complicated. For small shops and markets you may succeed through charm.

BARGAINING

THE TREND IN CITIES, especially Bangkok, is towards chain stores with fixed prices and endless discount sales. However, the Thai love of bargaining means you can still often negotiate at small shops, specialist retailers and, of course, market stalls. There are a few tips for successful bargaining. Be aware of the going rate for items so as not to offer embarrassingly low sums. Talking in Thai numbers may restrain the vendor's initial bid. You can try faking disinterest if the seller's bids remain high. This is a better policy than enthusiastically bargaining, then deciding not to buy when the vendor agrees your price.

Jewellery stall on Khao San Road, Bangkok

Fashion Island: one of Bangkok's new hi-tech shopping malls

DEPARTMENT STORES AND MALLS

INTERNATIONAL-STYLE department stores are a mainstay of Bangkok shopping. However, Thai market habits die hard and many stores fill their aisles with bargain stalls.

The two main Thai chains are **Robinson's**, which has branches in Bang Rak district on Silom and Sukhumvit roads among others; and the more up-market **Central** at the Silom Complex, further down Silom Road, and Lad Phrao.

The scale of the change in Thai shopping habits is remarkable. Residents of Bangkok already have countless downtown malls, such as **Peninsula Plaza**, to choose from, as well as luxury shopping complexes like **Gay Sorn Plaza** and **World Trade Center** which specialize in designer brands. But the trend is for vast new malls out of the centre of the city – such as **Fashion Island** on Ramindra Road. These are the focus for growing suburbs and resemble self-contained, air-conditioned towns, selling not only fashion and domestic items, but even houses and cars. They incorporate huge food courts, water parks, cinemas, concert halls, skating rinks, bowling alleys and entertainment theme parks.

Two of the world's five biggest shopping malls are in outer Bangkok. **Seacon Square** on Srinakharin Road, southeast of the city, contains a fun fair and stretches for more than 1 km (1,100 yds).

The rest of Thailand has yet to experience such excesses, but a few modern malls are now appearing in the larger towns and resorts. Examples include **Kad Suan Kaew** in Chiang Mai and the **Mike Shopping Mall** in Pattaya.

ENGLISH-LANGUAGE BOOKSHOPS

THAILAND HAS THREE English-language book and magazine chains: **Asia Books**, **DK Book House** and **Bookazine**. All have several branches in Bangkok; there are two DK outlets in Chiang Mai, and a Bookazine in Pattaya. DK's Seacon Square branch is Southeast Asia's largest bookshop.

MARKETS AND STREET VENDORS

THERE IS A MARKET at the heart of every Thai town. Even the smallest will offer a good range of fresh produce, and the larger markets often sell everything from arts and crafts through to fruit and vegetables and household items. The most notable are Chatuchak Market *(see p131)*, north of Bangkok, the massive Chiang Mai Night Bazaar *(see p216)* and the smaller night market in Chiang Rai. For markets in central Bangkok, see pages 436–7.

Impromptu road-side stalls are also found all over the country. Some sell devotional items such as jasmine rings *(see p27)* while others are good for souvenirs (though many of the goods are of dubious legality). Chiang Mai, Pattaya, and Patong in Phuket have many such stalls. In Bangkok they are found on Silom and Sukhumvit roads, and in Banglampu and Patpong districts.

FACTORIES AND CRAFTS CENTRES

TOURS OF FACTORY outlets and crafts centres are popular, particularly in the North and Northeast. No bargaining is required as prices are fixed but be aware that guides and touts take commission.

FAKE GOODS

Thailand's trade in fakes is so notorious that many people seek out the most kitsch items as souvenirs. Most prized are goods with a deliberately fake quality, using famous logos on products they'd never normally grace, such as Louis Vuitton bum-bags or Chanel T-shirts. Conversely, identical copies with spoof labels like Live's Jeans are even becoming collectors' items. Original manufacturers are understandably outraged by the piracy. However, it could be argued that aping or deconstructing an original is a way for a developing country to gain a skills base on which to build innovative industries. In fact, an increasingly effective copyright clampdown has shrunk the trade in fakes and even led to some forgers becoming official import agents. Be warned that customs officers may confiscate fakes.

Street stall in Pattaya selling fake versions of expensive watches

Thai Silk

The ancient art of Thai silk-weaving *(see pp256–7)* was revived by American Jim Thompson *(see pp114–15)* after World War II and is now a booming export business. Silk can be plain, patterned or in the subtle *mut mee* style made from pre-tie-dyed *(ikat)* thread. Aside from Thai designs, this heavy, bright and slightly rough cloth is now imaginatively used for ties, dresses, shirts, skirts and other Western fashion items, plus cushions, hangings and sundry ornaments. Many shops will tailor clothes to your measurements, even to your own designs.

Most silk comes from the Northeast and the North, but some is woven in and around Bangkok. For range and quality, Surawong Road in Bangkok is reliable, particularly **Jim Thompson's** and **Khanitha**, as well as **Shinawatra** on Sukhumvit Road. Chiang Mai's San Kamphaeng Road is renowned for its silk, the most famous producer being **Shinawatra Thai Silk**.

The Thai Silk Fair is held annually in Khon Kaen in late November or early December, when the town is packed with vendors and their bolts of cloth. If you miss the fair, **Prathamakant** sells a superb selection of silk all year round.

A dazzling selection of swatches of colourful Thai silk

Clothes

Thai tailors can make suits and dresses to order for low prices. Resist the rip-off 24-hour package deals including a "free gift". You get better service by seriously assessing

Made-to-measure suits are a speciality of many Thai tailors

the designs, fabric and cut, and insisting on one or two intermediate fittings. In Bangkok, countless Chinese and Indian tailors advertise in tourist magazines and outside their shops along Sukhumvit, Charoen Krung and Khao San roads. Designs are usually copied, often with considerable skill, from magazines or catalogues of famous brands such as Armani and Hugo Boss. The quality of workmanship can vary considerably. Ask around for recommendations.

Other popular items of Thai clothing include baggy fishermen's pants; batik sarongs (especially in the South, such as at Ko Yo, Songkhla); waistcoats and trousers made from hill-tribe fabrics; Thai silk and other Northeastern fabrics.

Arts and Crafts

Most Thai handicrafts are produced in the North and Northeast, and Chiang Mai is undoubtedly where visitors will find the widest choice of goods. The vibrant, diverse Night Bazaar sells everything from lacquerware to teak furniture, and you will need several hours if you want to peruse the often overpriced shops on San Kamphaeng Road (Highway 1006).

Prathamakant in Khon Kaen stocks a fine selection of Northeastern items such as the colourful triangular pillows.

Ayutthaya is a good source of crafts and antiques, particularly around Wat Phra Si Sanphet and on Si Sanphet Road,

where you can find unique stone carvings at **Arun-casem Antique**. Nearby **Bang Sai Folk Arts and Crafts Centre** is the focus of Queen Sirikit's SUPPORT Foundation, which enables villagers to make a living from preserving their traditions *(see p101)*. The fine pieces they produce are also sold at the dozen **Chitrlada** shops around Thailand.

High-quality ethnic crafts at fixed prices are available from boutiques in most of the top hotels, **Silom Village**, **River City** and the less expensive **Narayanaphand** department store in Bangkok. In the South, **Thai Village** in Phuket town is a good bet for crafts.

Hill-Tribe Artifacts

The costumes and artifacts of the hill tribes make fascinating anthropological souvenirs. Items might include Akha coin headdresses, Lahu geometric blankets and cushion covers, Hmong red-ruffled black jackets, brightly coloured Lisu tunics, wooden cattle bells, almond-shaped bamboo boxes, wooden boxes with carvings and woven rattan.

Some of the best outlets in Chiang Mai are the **Hill Tribe Products Foundation**, **Thai Tribal Crafts** and the **Old Chiang Mai Cultural Center**. The **Chiang Rai Handicraft Center** also has a large range. In Bangkok, the best selection is found at Chatuchak Market *(see p131)*. Buying from the shop at **Cabbages and Condoms** will ensure that your money goes to the tribes.

Lisu tribeswoman, selling tribal goods at a Chiang Rai bazaar

Road-side basket seller in Northern Thailand

WOOD, BAMBOO AND RATTAN

BAMBOO, RATTAN and wooden items are very cheap and can be shipped home. Carved wooden friezes, screens, bedheads, doors and lintels are readily available. Chiang Mai is the best source – **Beau Siam** is excellent for wooden furniture; **Raeng Jai** is good for rattan/bamboo. Woodcarving is a speciality of Mae Tha and Ban Luk near Lampang, as well as the Bo Hang district of Chiang Mai. Hang Dong and Saraphi to the south of Chiang Mai are known for their intricate basketware.

Be aware that if you buy wooden items, you may be contributing to Thailand's already disastrous deforestation.

Attractive celadon and blue and white ceramics in Bangkok

CERAMICS

DELICATE BENCHARONG pottery was historically made in China and sent to Thailand to be decorated with intricate floral patterns using five colours. Today the entire process occurs in Thailand. You can buy complete dinner services in Bencharong, and myriad designs, including the more typical spherical pots. In Bangkok,

Chatuchak Market is cheaper and offers a wider choice than the downtown shops. The heavy celadon pottery style is distinguished by its etched designs under a thick, translucent green, blue or brown glaze with a cracked patina. It's best bought direct from the potteries in Chiang Mai, where the top producer is **Mengrai Kilns**, but is also available in Bangkok from **Thai Celadon House** and many crafts shops, including those on Silom and Charoen Krung roads.

Lampang is notable for its fine blue and white ceramics, produced by companies such as **Indra Ceramics**.

LACQUERWARE

LACQUERWARE is a Northern Thai speciality. It usually has floral, flame or portrait designs in black and gold on bamboo and wood. More common is the Burmese style of red ochre on bamboo and rattan with pictorial scenes or floral designs. Traditional items include boxes for food and jewellery. Lacquerware is plentiful in the craft shops of Chiang Mai and Bangkok.

NIELLOWARE AND PEWTERWARE

NIELLOWARE, the intricate process of silver (or, more rarely, gold) inlay in a black metal amalgam in floral and flame patterns, makes for beautiful items like cufflinks, pill pots and jewellery. Some of the finest is from Nakhon Si Thammarat.

Southern Thailand has significant tin deposits, so pewterware has become a major craft. Typical items include tankards, plates, vases and boxes. Department stores in Bangkok and shops in Phuket town stock good selections.

KALAGA TAPESTRIES

THE WEAVING of *kalaga* tapestries involves metallic and multicoloured threads, beads, patches and sequins sewn on to a padded black background. It is a 200-year-old Burmese art but has only recently been revived, so antique examples are rare and very expensive. The ubiquitous modern embroideries are often gaudy and sloppily made, but the more carefully constructed (and more expensive) simple traditional designs can make attractive cushions, hangings, bags and even caps. Towns near to the Burmese border such as Mae Sot and Mae Sai are usually the best sources.

MUSICAL INSTRUMENTS, MASKS AND PUPPETS

MUSICAL INSTRUMENTS including *khaens* (Northeastern "pan pipes"), *phiphat* ensemble gongs and drums make impressive souvenirs. They are available at Chiang Mai's Night Bazaar and at Silom Village, Narayanaphand and Chatuchak and Nakorn Kasem markets in Bangkok. These places are also good sources of *khon* masks and theatrical items such as intricate *hun krabok* puppets, and *nang talung* and *nang yai* shadow puppets.

In the South, Nakhon Si Thammarat is the place for shadow puppets. They can be bought from the **Shadow Puppet Theatre** and, if you phone in advance, the master puppet-maker will show you how the puppets are made.

Narayanaphand department store in Bangkok

ANTIQUES

THE DELICACY and charm of Thai antiques are so appealing to shoppers that the few antiques remaining in the country are very expensive, fakes or illegally obtained. Thailand is, in fact, one of the principal outlets for antiques from all over Southeast Asia. Some shops resemble museums, jumbled with tapestries, statues, cabinets, bells, puppets, ceramics, baskets, lacquerware and temple artifacts. They're enchanting even if you're not buying.

Bargains are rare, although prices are lower than in Hong Kong or Singapore. Chiang Mai's Tha Phae and Loi Khro roads are a bit cheaper than the main sources in Bangkok: Charoen Krung Road, River City, Chatuchak Market and in Chinatown at Wang Burapha and Nakorn Kasem Market. There are antique auctions at River City on the first Saturday of each month. The excellent copies available are a cheaper, more culturally responsible alternative.

Recommended shops include **Amaravadee Antiques** and **Borisoothi Antiques** in Chiang Mai, and Bangkok's **Elephant House** and **NeOld**.

Export permits are required for antiques and all Buddha images from the Fine Arts Department via the **National Museum** and take at least a week to obtain *(see p451)*. Not surprisingly, given that so much of their cultural heritage has left the country, Thai customs officers are vigilant in enforcing this regulation.

Antiques in one of Bangkok's more exclusive shops

Shoppers admiring gold jewellery in Bangkok's Chinatown

JEWELLERY

THAI JEWELLERY tends to be large and expressive, often with superb detailing. The country has a long history of silverwork, particularly in the North, Northeast and among the hill tribes. The Wualai Road shops in Chiang Mai offer a good selection.

Necklaces, bracelets, earrings and Lao-style belts are typical in employing silver thread and filigree detail, often incorporating silver beads and large, plate-like pendants. Contemporary and international styles are increasingly preferred in cities and resorts. Affordable modern costume jewellery sells well in Siam Square and Chatuchak Market in Bangkok, where you can buy cheap ethnic wares and jewellery imaginatively created out of such materials as nuts, seeds, shells and beans.

Intricate bejewelled silver pendant

Some of Thailand's best jewellery is found in Bangkok's **Peninsula Plaza** and hotels such as the Dusit Thani. Some shops will work to your own specifications, notably **Uthai's Gems** and **Siam Royal Orchid**, which specializes in yellow and white gold-dipped flowers. Richard Brown designs personalized Vedic astrological jewellery at **Astral Gemstone Talismans**.

Gold is a popular, age-old form of portable wealth, and the most common type is the very yellow, Chinese-style gold. There are Chinese-owned gold shops in most sizeable towns.

Be warned that amulets are not classed as jewellery and the trade in these sacred items is widely disapproved of, not least by the Buddhist authorities who believe it exploits and encourages superstition. You need a licence to export them.

GEMS

BANGKOK IS POSSIBLY the world's biggest gem trading centre. The local stones are rubies, red and blue spinels, orange and white zircons, and yellow and blue sapphires *(see pp300–301)*. Markets operate around Chanthaburi, Kanchanaburi, Mae Sai and in Mae Sot on the Burmese border, where gems are cheaper than in Bangkok. However, you'll need an expert eye to pick out the bargains and should be wary of illegally smuggled gems. Phuket is Thailand's only good source of high quality pearls (try **Pearl Center** in Phuket town).

Gem scams are notorious in Bangkok and Chiang Mai, so run a mile if someone friendly says it's a public holiday so there's a government suspension of tax. Countless people have fallen for this ruse before being coaxed into parting with large sums of money by clever salesmanship and even, sometimes, drugged drinks.

It is possible to learn gemology and have stones authenticated and graded (but not valued) at the **Asian Institute of Gemological Sciences** in Bangkok.

DIRECTORY

DEPARTMENT STORES AND MALLS

Central Department Store
Silom Complex, 191 Silom Rd, Bangkok. **Map** 7 A4.
((02) 235 5105.

Fashion Island
505 Ramindra Rd, Bangkok.
((02) 947 5000.

Gay Sorn Plaza
Corner of Ploen Chit and Ratchadamri rds, Bangkok.
Map 8 D1.
((02) 656 1149.

Kad Suan Kaew
99/4 Mu 2, Huai Kaew Rd, Chiang Mai.
((053) 224444.

Mike Shopping Mall
262 Mu 10, Pattaya Beach Rd, Pattaya.
((038) 412000.

Peninsula Plaza
153 Ratchadamri Rd, Bangkok. **Map** 8 D1.
((02) 253 9762.

Robinson's
2 Silom Rd, Bang Rak, Bangkok. **Map** 8 D3.
((02) 255 3340.

Seacon Square
904 Srinakharin Rd, Bangkok.
((02) 721 8888.

World Trade Center
Ratchadamri Rd, Bangkok.
Map 8 D1.
((02) 255 9500.

ENGLISH-LANGUAGE BOOKSHOPS

Asia Books
221 Sukhumvit Rd, Bangkok.
((02) 252 7277.

Bookazine
Floor 1, CP Tower, 313 Silom Rd, Bangkok.
Map 7 C4.
((02) 252 7277.

DK Book House
224–6 Soi 2, Rama I Rd, Siam Square, Bangkok.
Map 7 C1.
((02) 251 1467.

THAI SILK

Jim Thompson's
9 Surawong Rd, Bangkok.
Map 7 C3.
((02) 234 4900.

Khanitha
113 Surawong Rd, Bangkok. **Map** 7 C3.
((02) 235 0464.

Prathamakant
81–85 Ruenrom Rd, Khon Kaen.
((043) 224080.

Shinawatra
94 Sukhumvit Rd, Soi 23, Bangkok.
((02) 258 0515.

Shinawatra Thai Silk
145/1–2 San Kamphaeng Rd, Chiang Mai.
((053) 338053.

ARTS AND CRAFTS

Arun-casem Antique
79/3 Sri Sam Phet Rd, Ayutthaya.
((035) 251193.

Bang Sai Folk Arts and Crafts Centre
Tambon Chang Yai, Bang Sai, Lop Buri province.
((035) 366092.

Chitrlada Shop
Chitrlada Palace, Bangkok. **Map** 3 B2.
((02) 281 1111.

Narayanaphand Department Store
127 Ratchadamri Rd, Bangkok.
Map 8 D1.
((02) 252 4670.

River City
23 Trok Rongnamkaeng, Yotha Rd, Bangkok.
Map 6 F3.
((02) 237 0077.

Silom Village
286 Silom Rd, Bangkok.
Map 7 A4.
((02) 233 9447.

Thai Village
52/11 Thepkasattri Rd, Muang Phuket.
((076) 214860.

HILL-TRIBE ARTIFACTS

Cabbages and Condoms
10 Sukhumvit, Soi 12, Bangkok. **Map** 8 F1.
((02) 229 4611.

Chiang Rai Handicrafts Center
3 km (2 miles) N of Chiang Rai on Phahon Yothin Rd.
((053) 713355.

Hill Tribe Products Foundation
21/17 Suthep Rd, Chiang Mai.
((053) 277743.

Old Chiang Mai Cultural Center
185/3 Wualai Rd, Chiang Mai.
((053) 275097.

Thai Tribal Crafts
208 Bamrung Rad Rd, Chiang Mai.
((053) 241043.

WOOD, BAMBOO AND RATTAN

Beau Siam
41 Loi Khro Rd, Chiang Mai.
((053) 209111.

Raeng Jai
46/2 Chiang Mai–San Kamphaeng Rd, Chiang Mai.
((053) 331213.

CERAMICS

Indra Ceramics
Lampang–Denchai Rd, Lampang.
((054) 221189.

Mengrai Kilns
79/2 Arak Rd, Chiang Mai.
((053) 272063.

Thai Celadon House
Soi Asoke, opposite Sukhumvit Soi 16, Bangkok.
((02) 229 4383.

PUPPETS

Shadow Puppet Theatre
110/18 Si Thammasok Soi 3, Nakhon Si Thammarat.
((075) 346394.

ANTIQUES

Amaravadee Antiques
141 Chiang Mai–Hot Rd, Chiang Mai.
((053) 441628.

Borisoothi Antiques
15/2 San Kamphaeng Rd, Chiang Mai.
((053) 338462.

Elephant House
67/12 Soi Phra Phinit, Soi Suanphlu, Sathorn Tai Rd, Bangkok. **Map** 8 D5.
((02) 286 5280.

National Museum
Fine Arts Department, 1 Na Phra That Rd, Bangkok.
Map 1 C4.
((02) 224 1370.

NeOld
149/2–3 Surawong Rd, Bangkok. **Map** 7 B4.
((02) 235 8352.

JEWELLERY

Astral Gemstone Talismans
3rd Floor, Lang Suan Balcony, 99/22 Soi Lang Suan, Bangkok.
Map 8 E2.
((02) 251 0577.

Siam Royal Orchid
94–120 Charoen Muang Rd, Chiang Mai.
((053) 242282.

Thai Lapidary
1009–11 Silom Rd, Bangkok. **Map** 7 C4.
((02) 236 2134.

Uthai's Gems
28/7 Soi Ruam Rudi, Phloen Chit Rd, Bangkok.
Map 8 F2.
((02) 253 8582.

GEMS

Asian Institute of Gemological Sciences
6th Floor, Jewellery Trade Center, 919 Silom Rd, Bangkok. **Map** 7 B4.
((02) 267 4325.

Pearl Center
83 Ranong Rd, Soi Phutorn, Phuket town.
((076) 211707.

Bangkok's Markets

MARKETS ARE A FUNDAMENTAL part of Bangkok life. Both specialist and general markets provide great browsing, whether you are interested in flowers or fabrics, sarongs or stamps. Do not try to take in too many markets in one outing – focus on one area and explore that in depth. Nancy Chandler's *Market Map and Much More*, readily available in Bangkok, can be a great help in planning a market sortie.

Market vendor selling Thai flowers

Khao San Road Market *may take up only one tiny road but it has become a legend among backpackers as a source of almost anything imaginable. In addition to rucksacks, hiking boots and other travellers' equipment, it is good for second-hand books, jewellery, clothes, bags and cheap cassette tapes.*

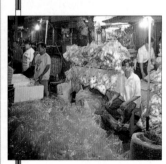

Thewet Flower Market *(see p100), located in a sedate backwater of the city, offers a riotously colourful spectacle of flowers and plants from all over Thailand.*

Banglamphu Market *is a typical neighbourhood market with general stalls displaying food, shoes, clothes and assorted bric-a-brac.*

Bo Be Market, on the corner of Ratchadamnoen Klang and Tanao roads, is one of the city's main cloth markets and a good source of Chinese silk.

Pak Khlong Market (see p94) *is the most lively and atmospheric wholesale fresh produce market in the capital. Open 24 hours a day, it is best viewed – and cheapest – between 10pm and 5am when exotic blooms line the pavements along with fruit and vegetables.*

KEY TO MARKET LOCATIONS IN BANGKOK

Banglamphu Market ②
Bangrak Market ⑬
Bo Be Market ④
Kao Market ⑩
Khao San Road Market ③
Nakorn Kasem (Thieves' Market) ⑤
Pak Khlong Market ⑧
Patpong/Silom Market ⑫
Phahurat Market ⑦
Pratunam Market ⑪
Sampeng Lane Market ⑨
Stamp Market ⑥
Thewet Flower Market ①

Phahurat Market (see p94) *is the commercial hub of Bangkok's Indian community. Fabric sellers and tailors predominate, and the air is filled with the aroma of Indian food and spices.*

Nakorn Kasem (see p94), otherwise known as the Thieves' Market, in Chinatown was once a focus for stolen goods. Today, it is a good place to pick up pots and pans, antiques, ceramics and furniture. Hard bargaining and a keen eye for spotting fakes is recommended.

0 metres 500

0 yards 500

The Stamp Market is held every Sunday outside the General Post Office on Charoen Krung Road. Thailand has long been issuing fine stamp designs, collected by philatelists around the world.

Pratunam Market *(see pp114–15)* occupies a maze of covered stalls. It is particularly good for cheap Indian fabrics and sewing accessories, and also has general domestic items.

Kao Market, *(see pp92–3)* between Yaowarat Road and Sampeng Lane, has been supplying the Chinese community with traditional ceremonial and decorative items – from lanterns to paper models for cremations – for more than 200 years.

Sampeng Lane Market occupies a former red light district. Bargain-priced high quality fabrics as well as toys, Chinese items and household goods are sold here.

Patpong/Silom Market (see pp111–12) is a neon-lit jumble of stalls displaying cheap souvenirs and fake goods. Stalls on Silom Road have fashionable clothes.

Bangrak Market (see p111) is a small but thriving local bazaar. Many of the top hotels buy their fruit, vegetables, meat and seafood from here. The market also has fabric and clothes stalls.

What to Buy in Thailand

Toy
tuk-tuk

Thai market stalls, crafts centres and specialist shops offer a wide and tempting range of souvenirs and gifts. Handicrafts are particularly good buys, and there are few regions of the country without their own speciality. In the South you can find delicately worked nielloware, pewter and shadow puppets; colourful hill-tribe artifacts, lacquerware and silver jewellery are made in the North; the Northeast is famed for its silk and cushions. The widest selection is available in major cities such as Bangkok and Chiang Mai.

Nang talung puppet

TRADITIONAL MASKS AND PUPPETS

Thailand has a rich tradition of masked dance and puppetry, and although performances are becoming increasingly rare, masks and puppets make evocative souvenirs. Most depict characters from the Ramakien *(see pp36–7)* and include huge leather *nang yai* figures, smaller *nang talung* shadow puppets, *hun krabok* marionettes and the smaller *hun lek (see pp38–9)*. Puppets can be bought in the South as well as at markets such as Chatuchak in Bangkok.

Figure of a Thai musician

Khon mask of a demon

Rattan and wickerwork come in many guises, from simple rice steamers to attractive and durable suites of rattan furniture. Trays, boxes and bags are popular and can be found for sale in many Thai markets, particularly in Bangkok and Chiang Mai. Reputable shops can arrange for large items to be shipped overseas.

Nielloware is an ancient craft which has been practised in the South of Thailand for several centuries. Nakhon Si Thammarat province is the centre of Thai nielloware production today. The process involves the decorative etching of silver and gold items which are then rubbed with a black metal alloy. Jewellery and small boxes are the most afford-able items.

Wood-carving is a highly skilled profession and visitors can buy everything from tiny carved bowls and pill boxes to huge screens, cabinets and beds. However, be aware that some hardwood items may be made from illegally felled trees.

Lacquerware items include jewellery boxes, bangles, bowls and trays. The process of coating split bamboo or wood with lacquer and then adding delicate hand-paintings is a speciality of the North. The two most common styles of decoration are gold on black lacquer and the Burmese style of yellow and green on red. Chiang Mai is the best source.

Hill-tribe artifacts are sold in towns and villages all over Northern Thailand, although Chiang Mai undoubtedly has the widest range of handicrafts. Among the most attractive items are patchwork bags, brightly coloured blankets, delicately wrought silver jewellery and hand-embroidered jackets and hats. If you go on a trek it is likely that you will visit at least one hill-tribe village, enabling you to buy the local handicrafts direct from the producers and, sometimes, see them being made.

Ceramics have been produced in Thailand for hundreds of years. Although many styles show a pronounced Chinese influence there are also several types of ceramics that are given a distinctive Thai stamp. One is the colourfully enamelled Bencharong pottery which is most commonly found as small pots and vases. Celadon is another example. It is recognizable by its characteristic cracked patina over a typically light green glaze.

Blue and white dinner service

Bencharong pot

Celadon vase

Silverware is another traditional Northern Thai craft. Beaten silver bowls, vases and boxes, often with expertly worked relief patterns, are popular buys, particularly in Chiang Mai. Delicate silver jewellery in traditional and modern designs is also widely available throughout the North and in Bangkok.

Silver bird

Orchid jewellery

Yellow and blue sapphire ring

A selection of sapphires

Silver bowl

Hanuman on silver box lid

Jewellery and gems are particularly tempting purchases in Thailand. Not only is the country one of the world's major sources of rubies and sapphires but it is also well known for skilfully crafted jewellery. Jewellers who display their work in the shops within the top hotels usually offer good quality at fair prices. But it is unwise to buy gems with the intention of reselling at a profit unless you are an expert.

THAI FABRICS

Silk is without doubt the best known Thai fabric and probably the number one buy for visitors *(see p432)*. It comes in an enormous range of styles, weights and designs, both ancient and modern, including tie-dyed *mut mee*. Thai cotton goods are also excellent – *pha sin* skirts and triangular *mawn sam liam* cushions often feature complex patterns. The hill tribes are known for their bold, geometric fabric designs. In the South, batik sarongs and baggy fishermen's trousers are widely available.

Colourful silk hanging

Mawn sam liam cushion

Patterned silk tie

Scarf of raw Thai silk

Traditional cotton fishermen's trousers

Cotton *pha sin* skirt

ENTERTAINMENT IN THAILAND

MODERN THAILAND MAY have adopted many foreign pursuits, from Hollywood movies to karaoke, but traditional entertainments still flourish. Although the graceful movements of classical *khon* dance-dramas survive mainly as tourist shows, the grass roots following of such typically Thai obsessions as *muay thai* boxing remains as strong

Thai dancers at the Rose Garden, Bangkok

as ever. High-spirited *sanuk* (fun) is an all-embracing activity, even on the most serious of occasions such as religious festivals. Indulging in the local passions is essential to understanding life in Thailand, whether it be a song-filled night out at a bar or folk music club, a colourful temple fair, a classical concert, a *takraw* game or watching the latest Thai film.

The Thailand Cultural Center, the country's premier concert venue

INFORMATION SOURCES

DETAILS OF THE major events and festivals throughout Thailand are provided in a booklet available from TAT offices. For more detailed entertainment listings, *Metro* is not only the best source for what's going on in the capital but also provides useful information on events in the rest of the country. It is also worthwhile consulting the English-language newspapers, the *Bangkok Post* and the *Nation*, and the many free tourist magazines. Good hotels should also be able to provide information.

Bangkok's listings magazine

BOOKING TICKETS

MAJOR HOTELS and travel agencies can book tickets for cultural shows and sporting events. Alternatively, you can buy tickets direct from venues or, for major events, from **DK Book House** in Siam Square, **Asia Books** on Sukhumvit Road and at the ticket counters in all branches of **Robinson's** department stores (*see p435*).

TRADITIONAL THEATRE AND DANCE

WATCHING THE STYLIZED royal all-male masked dance *khon* is like seeing the murals of Wat Phra Kaeo come to life. Sadly, popular interest in the mostly Ramakien-based dance-dramas is waning and performances of *khon*, and of the equally elaborate but less formal *lakhon*, are becoming increasingly rare. In even greater danger of extinction are the *hun lek* marionette shows (*see pp38–9*).

The most atmospheric place to watch traditional dance is at Sanam Luang on the evening of royal ceremonies such as the king's birthday or a funeral. At such times dozens of stages provide entertainment long into the night. Complete performances can last days, so abridged scenes are chosen for shows at the **National Theatre** (indoors on the last Saturday and Sunday of the month; outdoors every Saturday and Sunday from December to May) and the hi-tech **Royal Chalermkrung Theatre** in Bangkok and at the **Old Chiang Mai Cultural Center**.

Countless tourist dinner shows in the major cities and resorts offer bills of dances from all over the country. Chiang Mai's famous *khantoke* dinners (*see p34*), including dancing, can be experienced at the

Khantoke Palace, **Khun Kaew Khantoke Palace** and **Lanna Khantoke**. Reliable venues in Bangkok include the **Rose Garden**, **Silom Village** and **Tum Nak Thai**, while the Oriental's **Sala Rim Nam** restaurant presents authentic *khon*. *Lakhon* can also be witnessed at Bangkok's Lak Muang near Sanam Luang, and the Erawan Shrine, where devotees make merit by paying the dancers to perform (*see p116*).

The most widespread dance-drama is *likay*, a regular feature of temple fairs, festivals and TV. Its bawdy, slapstick and satirical elements have enabled it to retain a popular contemporary following. The ancient equivalent from the South of Thailand is *manora*.

Still widespread in Malaysia and Indonesia, *nang talung* shadow puppet shows only survive in the Deep South at Phatthalung and particularly Nakhon Si Thammarat (*see p373*). Performances at local festivals can run all night, but an hour or two is enough for most tourists. Even rarer is *nang yai*, in which enormous, flat, leather puppets are manipulated by a team of puppeteers.

A traditional *khon* performance

CONCERTS, EXHIBITIONS AND MODERN THEATRE

THAILAND'S MAJOR concert and exhibition venues are located in Bangkok. The state-of-the-art **Thailand Cultural Center** has the country's best performance facilities and attracts international names. **Saeng Arun Arts Centre** holds interesting occasional events, but mostly in Thai. The German **Goethe-Institut** and the **Alliance Française** host first rate exhibitions, concerts and art movies. Top stars frequently perform in the ballrooms of hotels such as the **Dusit Thani** and **Siam Inter-Continental** (see pp389–90).

Bangkok Playhouse frequently stages plays in English and also houses **Art Corner** gallery, though **Tadu** is the best place to see contemporary Thai art. The **Patravadi The-atre** puts on superb, highly visual musicals based on classical stories, which are easily understandable to non-Thais.

Hand-painted movie poster – a common sight in Thai cities

cinemas in Bangkok (such as **The Lido** and **Siam Cinema**), Chiang Mai, Pattaya, Phuket and Hat Yai show films with their original soundtracks.

DISCOS, BARS, COMEDY, MUSIC AND FOLK CLUBS

CHALLENGED BY international rock and sugary Thai pop, folk music has retained its popularity. It can be heard on the radio and TV, in bars, at festivals and impromptu gatherings, particularly outside the capital, although concerts are rarely publicized in English. It is also played in the unsalubrious cafés staging *talok* (comedy), which don't welcome tourists.

The main styles include the exuberant, rhythmic *lam wong*, which is often accompanied by a jocular dance; *luk thung* ("country music"), combining big band music, costumed dance troupes and singing; and the schmaltzy, ballad-based *luk krung*. Favoured by bus and taxi drivers, the faster Northeastern *mo'lam* sound is distinguished by *khaen* pipes and rap-like vocals. The Khmer-style *kantrum* music of the southern region of the Northeast can be heard in Surin's **Petchkasem Hotel** at weekends. The plain-

tive, radical *phleng phua chiwit* ("songs for life") emerged during the student protests of the 1970s and has dedicated venues such as **Raintree**.

Emerging rock bands are often showcased at the **Front Page**, while classier music venues are often in the hotels: **Riva's** (Sheraton Grande), **Spasso** (Grand Hyatt Erawan), **Angelini** (Shangri-La) and the Oriental's **Lord Jim's** and jazzy **Bamboo Bar**.

Friends sharing food and whisky while listening to live music is the nightlife formula throughout Thailand, although karaoke, discos and themed bars are gaining ground. In Bangkok, fashionable districts come and go at great speed. Sarasin is an enduring strip, where arty types frequent **Blue's Bar**. The original trendy hangout, Silom Soi 4, is still packed with bright young things, while the gay scene is centred on Silom Soi 2 and the multi-purpose centre, **Utopia**. The most impressive internet café is **Cyberia**. In Chiang Mai, **The Riverside** leads a string of venues beside the Ping River.

Discos can be found in all the major resorts. Large Bangkok clubs include the space-age **Phoebus**, flashy **Discovery**, up-market **Taurus** and kitsch **Narcissus**.

The flesh-trade districts such as Patpong (see p112), Nana Entertainment Plaza (Sukhumvit Soi 3) and Soi Cowboy (off Soi Asoke) in Bangkok, plus Pattaya, and Patong in Phuket, are notorious for their bizarre gynaecological "entertainments". Rip-offs are common, although the King's Group's bars are among the most "reputable".

One of Thailand's most infamous and popular attractions on stage and TV is its cross-dressing *katoeys*, or "lady-boys". Tourists flock to their sanitized transvestite shows at **Calypso Cabaret** in Bangkok, **Blue Moon Cabaret** in Chiang Mai, **Simon Cabaret** in Patong, and **Alcazar** in Pattaya, which boasts the best performers.

Glitzy modern cabaret show, popular in the brash beach resorts and Bangkok

CINEMA

THAIS ARE KEEN cinema-goers. Bangkok now has huge multiplexes but there are still 2,000 mobile units in the country which offer impromptu open-air screenings in villages.

The Thai film industry has a long, erratic history and, despite socially aware classics like *Luk Isan* (1978), tends to produce formulaic melodramas, comedies and violent action films. Hong Kong action movies have long been popular but, since the early 1990s, Hollywood movies have dominated the Thai market. Some

"Adult" entertainment from the King's Group

TEMPLE FAIRS AND FESTIVALS

THE THAI CALENDAR is packed with national holidays and local festivals (see pp42–7). These festivals may be religious or in honour of a local hero, to promote seasonal produce or dedicated to other activities like boat racing and kite flying.

As well as often hosting other events, most *wats* stage temple fairs. But apart from scheduled major fairs such as the Golden Mount Temple Fair in Bangkok at Loy Krathong (see p46), it's usually a matter of chance whether you encounter one. The sideshows are often as entertaining as the ceremonies with vendors selling food and trinkets, colourful characters like the cross-dressing *katoeys*, folk music such as *likay* and *lam wong*, beauty contests and who-can-eat-the-hottest-*som-tam* competitions. Other activities might include cock fighting or Siamese fighting fish contests.

Staged spectaculars aimed at tourists include the *son et lumières*, fireworks and other festivities at the Sukhothai ruins during Loy Krathong in November and during the Khwae River Bridge Week at Kanchanaburi (see p46).

Parade during the Loy Krathong festival in Lampang

MUAY THAI AND KRABI-KRABONG

THAI KICK BOXING, *muay thai*, is a national passion (see pp40–41). Most provinces have a boxing arena, although the nation's top two venues are in the capital. **Lumphini Stadium** has bouts on Tuesdays, Fridays and Saturdays, while boxing can be seen at

Muay thai boxing – passionately followed all over Thailand

Ratchadamnoen Boxing Stadium on Mondays, Wednesdays, Thursdays and Sundays. If you are interested in learning, rather than simply watching, the skills involved in *muay thai*, then contact the **International Amateur Muay Thai Federation** who should be able to recommend suitable gyms and instructors.

Another revered, long-established Thai martial art is *krabi-krabong*, named "sword-staff" after some of the hand weaponry used. The techniques are taught to ancient standards, although skill and stamina rather than injuries inflicted are now the measures of an accomplished fighter. Demonstrations are often included in tourist cultural shows, and you can learn the intricacies of *krabi-krabong* at the **Buddhai Sawan Fencing School of Thailand**.

TAKRAW

THE ACROBATIC Southeast Asian sport of *takraw* is played by young males at seemingly any clear patch of ground in Thailand. The idea is to keep a woven rattan ball in the air using any part of your body except your hands. The players' extraordinary agility, balletic leaps and speed of reactions are a revelation to visitors reared on more ponderous sports.

There are elaborate versions emphasizing individual skill but the classic original style has a team trying to get the ball into a basketball-like net more times in a set period than their rivals. Despite the

competitive version, *sepak takraw*, which resembles volleyball, now being incorporated into the Olympics and Asian Games, professional games are played surprisingly rarely.

The remarkably acrobatic *takraw*

FOOTBALL, RUGBY AND SNOOKER

IN RECENT YEARS Thais have developed a feverish enthusiasm for football. In 1996 a professional football league was introduced. Rugby has also sparked remarkable interest, with established clubs competing in a league and the Hong Kong Sevens. Games are mostly held in Bangkok at the **Pathumwan Stadium**, **Hua Mark Stadiums**, **Army Stadium** and **Royal Bangkok Sports Club**.

Thailand is the most successful non-Anglophone country to adopt snooker, which has become hugely popular. Its dangerous association with underground gambling makes it hard for players to emulate champions like James Wattana, though there are safe clubs like **Max Break**. Thailand hosts world ranking tournaments in March and September.

DIRECTORY

TRADITIONAL THEATRE AND DANCE

Khantoke Palace
174/7 Chang Khlan Rd,
Chiang Mai.
(053) 272757.

Khun Kaew Khantoke Palace
252/19–23 Phra Pok Klao Rd, Chiang Mai.
(053) 214315.

Lanna Khantoke
33/10 Charoen Prathet Rd,
Chiang Mai.
(053) 270080.

National Theatre
1 Na Phra That Rd,
Bangkok. **Map** 1 C4.
(02) 224 1342.

Old Chiang Mai Cultural Center
185/3 Wualai Rd,
Chiang Mai.
(053) 275097.

Rose Garden
Off Hwy 4, 32 km (20 miles) W of Bangkok.
(02) 295 3261.

Royal Chalermkrung Theatre
66 Charoen Krung Rd,
Bangkok. **Map** 6 D1.
(02) 222 0434.

Sala Rim Nam
Oriental Hotel, 48 Oriental Ave, Bangkok.
Map 6 F4.
(02) 236 0400.

Silom Village
286 Silom Rd, Bangkok.
Map 7 A4.
(02) 234 4581.

Tum Nak Thai
131 Ratchadaphisek Rd,
Bangkok.
(02) 274 6422.

CONCERTS, EXHIBITIONS AND MODERN THEATRE

Alliance Française
29 Sathorn Tai Rd,
Yannawa, Bangkok.
Map 8 D4.
(02) 213 2122.

Bangkok Playhouse/Art Corner
2884/2 New Phetchaburi Rd, Bangkok.
(02) 319 7641.

Goethe-Institut
18/1 Soi Atthakan Prasit, Sathorn Tai Rd, Bangkok.
Map 8 E4.
(02) 287 0942.

Patravadi Theatre
69/1 Soi Wat Rakhang,
Arun Amarin Rd, Thon Buri, Bangkok. **Map** 1 B5.
(02) 412 7287.

Saeng Arun Arts Centre
5th floor, Plan Bldg, 4 Soi Suksa Witthaya, Bangkok.
Map 7 B5.
(02) 237 0080
(extension 801–7).

Tadu
Pavilion Y Bldg, Royal City Avenue, between Rama IX and New Petchaburi rds, Bangkok. **Map** 8 D1.
(02) 203 0216.

Thailand Cultural Center
Ratchadaphisek Rd,
Bangkok.
(02) 247 0028.

CINEMA

The Lido
256 Rama I Rd, Siam Square, Bangkok.
Map 7 C1.
(02) 252 6498.

Siam Cinema
Siam Square, Rama I Rd,
Bangkok. **Map** 7 C1.
(02) 251 1735.

DISCOS, BARS, COMEDY, MUSIC AND FOLK CLUBS

Alcazar
Pattaya Second Rd, Pattaya.
(038) 428746.

Angelini
Shangri-La Hotel, 89 Soi Wat Suan Phu, Bangkok.
Map 6 F5.
(02) 237 3766.

Blue Moon Cabaret
5/3 Mun Muang Rd,
Chiang Mai.
(053) 206048.

Blue's Bar
231/16 Soi Sarasin,
Ratchadamri Rd, Bangkok.
Map 8 E3.
(02) 252 7335.

Calypso Cabaret
Ambassador Hotel, Sukhumvit Soi 11, Bangkok.
(02) 261 6355.

Cyberia
Sukhumvit Soi 24,
Bangkok.
(02) 259 3356.

Discovery
4 Sukhumvit Soi 12,
Bangkok.
(02) 653 0246.

Front Page
14/10 Soi Sala Daeng 1, off Rama IV Rd, Bangkok.
Map 8 D4.
(02) 233 6315.

Lord Jim's/ Bamboo Bar
Oriental Hotel, 48 Oriental Ave, Bangkok. **Map** 6 F4.
(02) 236 0400.

Narcissus
112 Sukhumvit Soi 23,
Bangkok.
(02) 258 4805.

Petchkasem Hotel
104 Chitbumrung Rd, Surin.
(044) 511274.

Phoebus
Ratchadaphisek Rd,
Bangkok.
(02) 245 5545.

Raintree
116/64 Soi Rang Nam, off Phaya Thai Rd, Bangkok.
(02) 245 7230.

Riva's
Sheraton Grande Hotel,
250 Sukhumvit Rd,
Bangkok.
(02) 653 0334.

The Riverside
9–11 Charoenrat Rd,
Chiang Mai.
(053) 243239.

Simon Cabaret
100/6–8 Mu 4, Patong-Karon Rd, Patong, Phuket.
(076) 342011.

Spasso
Grand Hyatt Erawan Hotel, 494 Ratchadamri Rd, Bangkok. **Map** 8 D1.
(02) 254 1234.

Taurus
Sukhumvit Soi 26,
Bangkok.
(02) 261 3991.

Utopia
116/1 Sukhumvit Soi 23,
Bangkok.
(02) 259 9619.

MUAY THAI AND KRABI-KRABONG

Buddhai Sawan Fencing School
5/1 Phet Kasem Rd, Thon Buri, Bangkok. **Map** 5 A4.
(02) 421 1906.

International Amateur Muay Thai Federation
Pathumwan Stadium,
54 Rama I Rd, Bangkok.
Map 7 B1.
(02) 215 4631.

Lumphini Stadium
Rama IV Rd, Bangkok.
Map 8 E4.
(02) 280 4550.

Ratchadamnoen Boxing Stadium
1 Ratchadamnoen Nok Rd,
Bangkok. **Map** 2 F4.
(02) 281 4205.

FOOTBALL, RUGBY AND SNOOKER

Army Stadium
Wiphawadirangsit Rd,
Bangkok.
(02) 278 5095.

Hua Mark Indoor and Outdoor Stadiums
2088 Ramkhamhaeng Rd,
Bangkok.
(02) 214 0120.

Max Break
251/2 Thonglor Soi 13, Sukhumvit Soi 55, Bangkok.
(02) 392 3291.

Pathumwan Stadium
54 Rama I Rd, Bangkok.
Map 7 B1.
(02) 214 0120.

Royal Bangkok Sports Club
1 Henri Dunant Rd,
Pathumwan, Bangkok.
Map 8 D2.
(02) 255 1420.

OUTDOOR ACTIVITIES & SPECIAL INTERESTS

I N THAILAND an impressive range of special interest activities is on offer. The South's spectacular coastline is ideal for aquatic fun, from sailing, water skiing and wind-surfing to big game fishing and diving to see some of the most spectacular coral reefs in the world. Northern Thailand's moun-tainous forests are famous for their waterfalls, caves and wildlife, including rare birds, gibbons, ele-phants and tigers. Trekking in this beautiful region to see hill tribes has become controversial in recent years and care should be taken

Windsurfing off the coast

in choosing a responsible trekking company with knowledgeable guides. Thailand has an extensive network of beautiful national parks. Exciting ways to explore Thailand's natural wilderness include sea canoeing, leisurely bamboo rafting, thrilling whitewater rafting, elephant riding and rock climbing. Some visitors take advantage of the country's growing number of excellent golf courses. Others come to learn cultural skills such as Buddhist meditation, traditional massage and Thai cookery techniques which include vegetable carving.

Spectacular diving around the reefs off Thailand's coasts and islands

DIVING AND SNORKELLING

A BUNDANT CORAL REEFS throng-ing with aquatic life – serviced by countless diving operations – make Thailand one of the most accessible and rewarding destinations for underwater exploration in the world. The Andaman coast and islands *(see pp338–63)* in particular have some stunning fringing reefs, ocean drop-offs and submerged pinnacles – plus visibility often exceeding 30 m (100 ft). A rich variety of marine life can be spotted, such as whale sharks off the famous Burma Banks.

Much of the best diving is to be found in the national ma-rine parks containing the Surin, Similan and Tarutao archipela-gos in the Andaman Sea, Ang-thong in the western Gulf of Thailand and Ko Chang in the eastern Gulf. The once magni-ficent Ko Phi Phi has not been protected by this reserve status, though, and has been heart-breakingly damaged by care-less anchoring and snorkellers breaking the coral. Reckless fishing with dragnets, harpoons and explosives has also killed some reefs, while siltation and pollution pose growing threats.

Due to the rough weather brought on by the monsoons *(see pp22–3)*, the Andaman dive sites are accessible only from November to April, while the shallower waters of the western Gulf coast are best visited between January and October. The Eastern Seaboard is accessible all year round.

Trips vary in length from one to several days. Many sightsee-ing tours include snorkelling. Access to many untouched reefs around Burma's Andaman islands is slowly becoming es-tablished via Phuket. In Bang-kok, **Divelink Thailand** runs special trips. Selected dive companies are listed in the directory *(see p447)* while fuller listings and details of sites appear in the books *Asian Diver Scuba Guide: Thailand* (Asian Diver) and *Diving in Thailand* (Asia Books).

PADI- and NAUI-approved diving courses are widely avail-able. In order of importance the main centres are Phuket, Pattaya, Ko Tao, Ko Samui, Ko Phi Phi and Krabi.

Basic diving rules include: inspect your equipment and get the right fit; don't dive un-less you are confident in your instructor and have been well trained; ensure there's a buddy system in operation; check that your group is small enough for the divemasters to monitor; and never touch the coral.

SAILING

T HAILAND'S DRAMATIC coast-line is popular with the yachting fraternity, who come to Phuket every December for the King's Cup Regatta. Chartering a yacht or joining a crew is possible from Hua

Hin and with **Ocean Marina** from Pattaya. However, the best facilities and scenery, and the widest choice of sailing companies, are found on Phuket, where **Yacht Haven**, **Southeast Asia Live-aboards**, **Thai Marine Leisure** and **Sunsail** operate.

Sea canoeing – the best, and often only, way to explore the coast

WATER SPORTS

RECENT YEARS HAVE witnessed a mushrooming in the popularity of water sports, although the disturbance they cause is of concern. In places such as Krabi water sports are banned. However, in most resorts windsurfing boards can be rented, while jet skis and "inflatable banana rides" are becoming commonplace even in national marine parks such as Ko Samet.

For the best range of water sports, including parascending, waterskiing and motorboat hire, head for Jomtien beach at Pattaya, Hua Hin and Cha-am, and Patong and Karon beaches on Phuket.

Anglers make for the excellent facilities for big game fishing at Pattaya and Phuket.

Sea canoeing is not just the most peaceful way to enjoy the strange karst islets of Phangnga Bay and the Angthong archipelago but also the only way to explore their collapsed sea caves. Ringed by forest and often containing tiny beaches, many of these spectacular *bongs* were first discovered by **Sea Canoe Thailand**, who run the most responsible tours to these fragile "lost worlds".

WHITEWATER RAFTING

SEDATE BAMBOO RAFTING is a popular tourist pastime, particularly on the rivers in the North. More exciting, though, is whitewater rafting on hardy inflatables. The upper reaches of the Pai and Moei rivers are ideal for this fast-growing sport, and Umphang's Mae Klong district near Mai Sat is particularly notable for world class rafting. **Thai Adventure Rafting** and **The Wild Planet** are two of the best trip organizers.

GOLF

GOLF IS REACHING near fanatical popularity levels in Thailand, which has hosted international competitions at its fast-growing number of courses. The many around Bangkok are mostly flat and uninteresting, but there are some staggeringly scenic backdrops at golfing resorts in Phuket, Khao Yai, Chiang Mai and Kanchanaburi.

Exclusivity is a feature of many clubs, but golfing holiday packages are particularly popular at places such as Pattaya, Phuket and Hua Hin. The best guides to courses are the *Thailand Golf Map* and *Thailand Golf Guide*, while TAT publishes a free directory of the country's top 75 courses. For improving your handicap, there's a David Leadbetter Academy of Golf at the excellent **Thana City Golf and Country Club**.

Enjoying the unique sensation of elephant riding through the forest

ELEPHANT RIDING

AFTER THE MECHANIZATION of logging, and then its supposed ban in 1989, working elephants suddenly found themselves unemployed. Offering rides is a relatively positive means of ensuring the survival of this national symbol since their lowland forest habitat has been largely destroyed. However, some unscrupulous *mahouts* ply their mounts with drugs to lengthen their working day.

An hour's ride is frankly all the time you need to appreciate the pachyderm's vehicular novelty, take photos, lurch through forest and be sprayed by its trunk. Most treks include a ride which are also available from elephant camps. Most of these are clustered around Chiang Mai and include the **Elephant Training Centre Chiang Dao**, **Mae Sa Elephant Camp** and **Young Elephant Training Centre**. You can also ride elephants in Bangkok's **Dusit Zoo** and **Safari World**.

Natural Park Golf Club, Pattaya: superb golf and a spectacular backdrop

TREKKING

THAILAND HAS SOME ideal terrain for hiking, from the precipitous karst forests of Krabi and Khao Sok to the undulating mountains surrounding Mae Hong Son and Loei.

Aside from the country's natural beauty, it is the opportunity to visit hill tribes that has undoubtedly caused the trekking business to boom. The novelty of encountering hill tribespeople in elaborate costumes undeniably adds cultural frisson to a trek. However, over time traditional tribal values cannot but be eroded by continued exposure to tourists. Additionally, there is the problem of trekkers feeling like voyeurs, particularly at cynical freak shows such as the long-necked Padaung *(see p206)*. Try to establish a rapport with tribespeople and ask their permission before taking photos.

Villages close to Chiang Mai and Chiang Rai (and, increasingly, Pai and Mae Hong Son) are all depressingly exploited. Be wary of Burmese border areas, especially in Tak, where there is the chance of encountering fighting. Malaria is also a risk here, as it is in Kanchanaburi. In general, the health risks increase the further you travel away from the towns.

For exclusively nature-based treks, head for Khao Yai *(see pp174–5)* and the South. Most treks also include an elephant ride and, if the rivers are high enough, punting on a bamboo raft. Treks can last a week, but most are over two to three

Trekkers resting on a trail in the popular Khao Yai National Park

nights and include a visit to at least one village. Scams are commonplace and TAT keeps lists of companies recognized by the professional **Guide Association of Chiang Mai** or the **Jungle Tour Club of Northern Thailand**, but word of mouth is often best.

All treks should be led by at least two competent guides (who should speak the necessary tribal languages and be aware of local customs). Check that the group doesn't exceed about eight trekkers, that the trek is registered with the police and that transportation is not by public buses. Tips for trekkers include lining backpacks with plastic bags to keep wet clothes in and damp out; always sleep in dry clothes – even if it means putting on wet clothes by day; wear a sun hat and cream, long trousers to protect against leeches, insect repellent (Jaico is the best)

Delicately carved vegetables

and worn-in hiking boots – or at least supportive trainers. Nights are cold in the mountains, so take warm layers – thermal tops and leggings, and silk sleeping bags. The best times to trek are November to February and early in the wet season in June and July.

Eco-tourism is an abused term, but **Siam Safari**, **The Trekking Collective** and **Phuket Trekking Club** have a good reputation and **Friends of Nature** organize genuinely ecological treks. **The Wild Planet** is equally well respected and, like **Bike and Travel**, also runs professional mountain bike trips into the wild.

CULTURAL STUDY

COURSES IN MEDITATION and Buddhism can give a great insight into Thai culture and a skill for life. For meditation sessions in English and longer, disciplined retreats, contact the **World Fellowship of Buddhists**. Non-Thais are most welcome at the **Northern Insight Meditation Centre's** month-long retreats; at the strict **Wat Pa Nanachat Beung Rai**; at **Wat Phra Dhammakaya**'s retreats and Sunday sessions; and at the modern-minded **International Dhamma Hermitage** over the first ten days of each month. The latter two are most accepting of women; many *wats* are male-only.

Visitors also come to Thailand to study traditional Thai massage, a vigorous combination of yoga, reflexology and acupressure. Popular training in English is conducted at **Wat Pho** *(see pp88–9)* and in Chiang Mai's subtler style at centres including the **Old Medicine Hospital** and **Institute of Thai Massage**.

The techniques of Thai cuisine – including fruit and vegetable carving – can be learned at the cookery schools in the **Dusit Thani** and **Oriental** hotels *(see pp389–90)* and **UFM Baking and Cooking School** and **Community Services of Bangkok**.

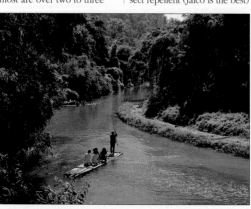
Leisurely rafting down the Ping River near Chiang Mai

DIRECTORY

DIVING AND SNORKELLING

Dive Asia
PO Box 70, Kata Beach, Phuket.
[(076) 330598.

Divelink Thailand
PO Box 53, Suntisuk Post Office, Bangkok.
[(02) 392 2267.

Fantasea Divers
219 Rat U-thit Rd, Patong, Phuket.
[(076) 295511.

H2O Sports
Palm Beach Resort, Ko Phi Phi.
[(01) 723 0052.

Marina Divers
120/2 Patak Rd, Kata Beach, Phuket.
[(076) 330272.

Mermaid's Dive School
75/124 Mu 12, Jomtien Beach Rd, Pattaya.
[(03) 232220.

Planet Scuba
Holiday Mansion Hotel, 53 Witthayu (Wireless) Rd, Bangkok.
Map 8 E1.
[(02) 253 8043.

Samui International Diving School
Angthong Rd, Naton, Ko Samui.
[(077) 421465.

Samui International Diving School
Ko Tao.
[(077) 421316.

SAILING

Ocean Marina
274 Sukhumvit Rd, Jomtien, Pattaya.
[(038) 237310.

Southeast Asia Live-aboards
113/12 Song Roi Pi Patong, Patong Beach, Phuket.
[(076) 340406.

Sunsail
Boat Lagoon, Thepkas-attri Rd, Ko Kaew, Phuket.
[(076) 239057.

Thai Marine Leisure
70/176 Paradise Complex, Rat U-thit Rd, Patong, Phuket.
[(076) 344261.

Yacht Haven
Laem Phrao, Ko Aien, Phuket.
[(076) 327109.

WATER SPORTS

Deutsches Haus
(deep-sea fishing)
Soi 4 Beach Rd, Pattaya.
[(038) 428725.

Phuket Sport Fishing Center
PO Box 214, Phuket town.
[(076) 214713.

Santana Canoeing
92/18 Sawatdirak Rd, Patong, Phuket.
[(076) 340360.

Sea Canoe Thailand
367/14 Yaowarat Rd, Muang Phuket.
[(076) 212172.

Sun & Sand Tour
Pearl Hotel, Montri Rd, Phuket town.
[(076) 211044.

WHITEWATER RAFTING

Thai Adventure Rafting
Rungsiyanon Rd, Pai.
[(053) 699111.

The Wild Planet
42 Sukhumvit Soi 22, Bangkok.
[(02) 258 2249.

GOLF

Natural Park Golf Club
Off Hwy 3, km 83, near Pattaya.
[(038) 349370.

Thana City Golf and Country Club
Bang Na Trat Rd, off Hwy 34, km 14, near Bangkok.
[(02) 336 1968.

ELEPHANT RIDING

Elephant Training Centre Chiang Dao
Off Hwy 107, 56 km (35 miles) N of Chiang Mai.
[(053) 298553.

Mae Sa Elephant Camp
Mae Rim, 20 km (12 miles) N of Chiang Mai.
[(053) 297060.

Young Elephant Training Centre
Thung Kwian, 25 km (16 miles) NW of Lampang.
[(054) 229042.

TREKKING

Bike and Travel
801/45 Wang Thong Trade Center, Phahon Yothin Rd, Mu 8, Lam Lukka, Pathum Thani.
[(02) 992 5925.

Friends of Nature
133/21 Ratchaprarop Rd, Bangkok.
Map 4 E4–5.
[(02) 642 4426.

Guide Association of Chiang Mai
Sarika Tour Co, 1/1 Nimmanhamin Soi 4, Chiang Mai.
[(053) 212942.

Jungle Tour Club of Northern Thailand
Gem Travel Company, Charoen Prathet Rd, Chiang Mai
[(053) 271680.

Phuket Trekking Club
94/23 Soi Patong Resort, Bangla Rd, Patong, Phuket.
[(076) 341453.

Siam Safari
PO Box 296, Phuket 3000.
[(076) 280116.

The Trekking Collective
22 Ratchadamnoen Rd, Chiang Mai.
[(053) 419080.

CULTURAL STUDY

Community Services of Bangkok
15/1 Sukhumvit Rd, Soi 33, Bangkok.
[(02) 258 5652.

Institute of Thai Massage
17/7 Morakot Rd, Chiang Mai.
[(053) 218632.

International Dhamma Hermitage
Wat Suan Mok, Chaiya, Surat Thani.
[(077) 431552.

Northern Insight Meditation Centre
Wat Ram Poeng, Canal Rd, Chiang Mai.
[(053) 278620.

Old Medicine Hospital
78/1 Soi Moh Shivagah Komarapaj, Wualai Road, Chiang Mai.
[(053) 275085.

UFM Baking and Cooking School
593/29–39 Sukhumvit Soi 33/1, Bangkok.
[(02) 259 0620 (extension 286).

Wat Pa Nanachat Beung Rai
Baan Bung Wai, Amphoe Warinchamrab, Ubon Ratchathani.

Wat Phra Dhammakaya
23/2 Mu 7 Khlong Sam, Khlong Luang, Pathum Thani.
[(02) 524 0257.

World Fellowship of Buddhists
33 Sukhumvit Rd, Bangkok.
[(02) 251 1188.

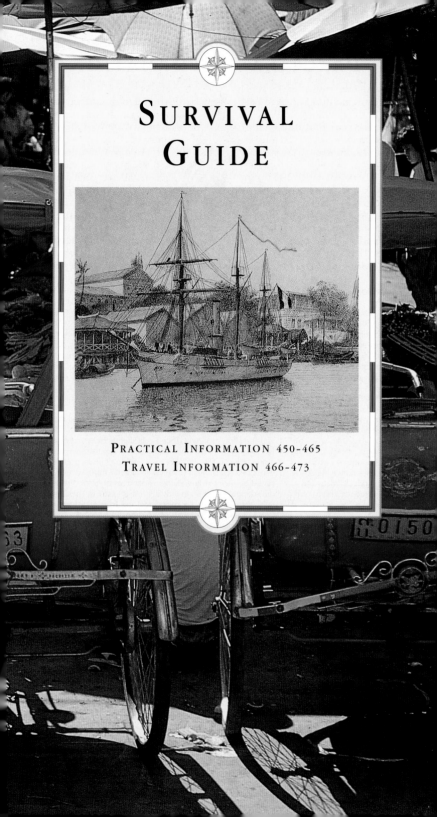

SURVIVAL
GUIDE

PRACTICAL INFORMATION

THAILAND CATERS WELL for its growing number of tourists. The six million people who visit each year find one of the biggest and best-organized tourist industries in Asia. The headquarters of the helpful Tourism Authority of Thailand (TAT) is in Bangkok, and there are offices across the country and several overseas branches. The relevant address and telephone number is given for each town and sight throughout this guide. The tourist industry is developing rapidly, and the

Changing of the Royal Guard, Bangkok

adventurous traveller no longer need be restricted to organized tours or major tourist destinations such as Bangkok and Phuket, as the country becomes more accessible to independent travellers. There are many reputable travel agencies all over Thailand. They offer advice, book flights and accommodation, and organize sightseeing tours. Some pre-travel planning is necessary to avoid the worst of the rainy season and holiday periods such as the Chinese New Year (*see pp44–7*).

WHEN TO GO

THAILAND'S WEATHER can be tempestuous, with year-round humidity, rocketing temperatures and rains of biblical proportions. However, the optimum time to visit is during the cooler, drier months from November to February. It is no coincidence that this is the peak tourist season, when sights may get crowded. The hot season, from March to July, can be unbearable, while the rainy season, which generally lasts from June to October, is the least predictable of the three periods. Climate and rainfall charts can be found on pages 44–7.

WHAT TO TAKE

AS THE CLIMATE in Thailand is generally hot and humid, it is advisable to dress in cool, non-restricting clothes made from natural fibres. A jumper may be needed in Northern and Northeastern regions during the cool season. Throughout Thailand, the rainy season brings sudden downpours; a light raincoat is handy. If visiting temples, appropriate dress is required (*see p455*), as is easily removable footwear. A first-aid kit is also useful (*see p458*).

ADVANCE BOOKING

BANGKOK IS a popular launching point for other Southeast Asian destinations, so it is necessary to book airline tickets well in advance. This is

especially so during Thailand's peak tourist season, November to February, when flights and hotels are heavily booked. If you plan to travel during this period, it is wise to make arrangements at least three to six months prior to departure.

VISAS AND PASSPORTS

MANY NATIONALITIES, including the citizens of most European countries, Australia and the USA, can enter Thailand for up to 30 days without a pre-arranged visa. Proof of a confirmed return flight or other on-going travel arrangements must be presented upon arrival in Thailand. This 30-day period is not extendible. Nationals of several smaller European countries, such as Andorra, must obtain a visa before travelling. For those wishing to stay longer, a 60-day tourist visa

can be arranged from a Thai embassy or consulate prior to arrival in Thailand. This usually takes two to three working days to process, but may take longer during busy periods.

A 90-day non-immigrant visa must be applied for in your home country and requires a letter of verification from a Thai source giving a valid reason, such as business or study, for spending three months in Thailand. This visa is slightly more expensive than the 60-day tourist visa.

With all visas, entry into Thailand must occur within 90 days of issue. Visa extensions are at the discretion of the **Immigration Department** in Bangkok or any other immigration office in Thailand. Over-staying a visa carries a fine of 100 *baht* per day and can result in serious penalties. Re-entry visas, allowing the

Tourists relaxing in the sun at Patong beach, Phuket

◁ **A row of *samlors* at the market in Lop Buri**

visitor to leave the country and return within 60 days, can be applied for at the Bangkok Immigration Department. Proof of funds sufficient to support the traveller while in Thailand may be required in some cases. Strictly speaking, travellers entering Thailand should have at least six months left on their passport. It is best to confirm all such details with a Thai embassy or consulate in your home country before travelling.

Crossing the border into neighbouring countries generally depends on the current political situation *(see p456)*. A four-week tourist visa for Burma, which costs 250 *baht*, can be obtained from the Burmese Embassy in Bangkok. A 15-day tourist visa for Laos can be issued by the Lao Embassy, though it is often quicker to apply for it at a travel agency in major cities such as Bangkok or Chiang Mai. A four-week tourist visa for Cambodia can be issued upon arrival at Phnom Penh airport.

IMMUNIZATION

THERE ARE no legal immunization requirements unless you are travelling from a country known to be infected with yellow fever. It is recommended that everyone be immunized against polio, tetanus, typhoid and hepatitis A. In addition – for those travellers going to remote or rural areas, or who are staying more than two to three weeks – BCG, hepatitis B, rabies, diphtheria, and Japanese encephalitis are advised *(see pp458–9)*. For the latest advice, contact a travel clinic or your GP, who will also be able to advise on the current guidelines for malaria prevention, as the drug recommendations change fairly often.

Some vaccines need to be given separately or in stages. Malaria tablets, meanwhile, are started a week before leaving and continued for several weeks after returning. For these reasons it is advisable to contact your doctor at least six weeks before departure.

CUSTOMS INFORMATION

CUSTOMS REGULATIONS when entering Thailand are standard. During an inbound flight you will be given a white customs form which must be filled in and handed over at the customs desk after claiming your baggage. Thai customs restrictions for goods carried into the country are the following: 200 cigarettes, one litre of wine or spirits, one video camera, five rolls of still film, three rolls of video film and one item of electrical goods per person.

A car or motorbike can be brought into the country for touring purposes for up to six months but this requires prior arrangement through the Thai embassy in your home country. The carrying of drugs *(see p456)*, firearms or pornography is strictly prohibited.

Although there are no restrictions on the maximum amount of money an individual may bring into the country, there is a minimum requirement, which varies according to the type of visa on which you are travelling. Check with your local Thai embassy for current requirements.

Antiques and Buddha images are not allowed out of Thailand without authorization. If you wish to export such items, you must first contact the **Fine Arts Department** of the National Museum in Bangkok. Authorization involves some minor red tape: a couple of forms accompanied by two frontal photographs of the object being purchased. Some of the more up-market antique shops can organize this for you. Contemporary "works of art", such as paintings bought in markets, can be taken out of the country without permission. It is illegal to leave Thailand with more than 50,000 *baht* without the correct authorization.

TAT Duty Free logo

DIRECTORY

Immigration Department
Soi Suanphlu, Sathorn Tai Rd, Bangkok.
((02) 287 3101.

Fine Arts Department
National Museum, 1 Na Phra That Rd, Phra Nakhon, Bangkok.
((02) 224 1370.

EMBASSIES

Australia
37 Sathorn Tai Rd, Bangkok.
((02) 287 2680, (02) 287 4843.

Burma
116 Sathorn Nua Rd, Bangkok.
((02) 234 2258.

Laos
520 and 502/1–3 Soi 39, Ruam Klamhaeng Rd, Bangkok.
((02) 539 6679.

Malaysia
35 Sathorn Tai Rd, Bangkok.
((02) 286 1390.

United Kingdom
1031 Wireless Rd, Bangkok.
((02) 253 0191.

DEPARTURE TAX

FOR INTERNATIONAL FLIGHTS out of Thailand *(see pp466–7)* there is a departure tax of 250 *baht* per person. For domestic flights the departure tax is 20 *baht*. These taxes should be paid at the check-in counters at the relevant airport.

Buddha images wrapped and ready for sale

TOURIST INFORMATION

THE MANY BRANCHES of the Tourism Authority of Thailand (TAT) are very helpful, offering plenty of practical and background information on sights and festivals, as well as maps, brochures, mini-guides and posters. They also have a useful list of reputable travel agents and hotels. There is a small information kiosk in Don Muang airport. Many of the provincial capitals in Thailand have a TAT office (listed throughout this guide), as do some overseas countries.

Logo of TAT

ADMISSION CHARGES

ADMISSION CHARGES to sights in Thailand are usually nominal, ranging from 10–50 *baht* for government-run establishments (including most national parks), to 100 *baht* or more for private museums. Occasionally, foreigners may (legitimately) be charged a higher admission price than locals, on the assumption that they earn more than most Thais. Major tourist *wats* charge a set fee; in others there is usually a box for donations.

Typical entrance tickets to major historical sites

OPENING HOURS

THIS GUIDE INDICATES the days of the week when sights are open. Almost all destinations and sights in Thailand can be visited throughout the year, though accommodation on, and ferries to, some of the southern islands may be limited during the rainy season. In general, major tourist attractions open at 8am or 9am and close any time between 3:30pm and 6pm. A few also shut for lunch between noon and 1pm. Most major sights are open daily, but some national museums close for public holidays and on Mondays and Tuesdays.

Large department stores are usually open daily 10am–9pm, while smaller shops are open 8am–9pm. In small towns markets are generally held on a daily basis. Commercial offices are invariably open 8am–noon and 1pm–5pm Monday to Friday. Government offices are open 8:30am–noon and 1pm–4:30pm Monday to Friday. During the Chinese New Year, many businesses may close, especially in the South. Details of banking hours are given on page 460.

FACILITIES FOR THE DISABLED

THERE ARE few facilities for disabled travellers in Thailand. Pavements can be uneven and pedestrian bridges are often accessed only by steep staircases. Wheelchair access is limited to the top-class hotels in major cities. The easiest way to travel is to book an organized tour *(see p471)* or to contact the **Association of Physically Handicapped People** for further information.

Colourful tourist brochures about Thailand, available from TAT

FACILITIES FOR CHILDREN

THAIS ADORE CHILDREN and will go out of their way to help you make them happy. The larger hotels have child-minding services, and TAT offers advice on attractions that have special appeal to kids, such as zoos. Hats and sunblock are a must for children (and adults) out in the sun. There are plenty of fast-food outlets and adaptable chefs who will willingly provide a choice of suitable alternatives to spicy meals.

CENTRES OF WORSHIP FOR VISITORS

THERE ARE MANY FACILITIES for visitors to undertake Buddhist studies *(see p446)*. The **International Buddhist Meditation Centre** has details of English-language courses at *wats* in and around Bangkok.

Most other religious denominations are represented in Thailand – listed below are religious centres in Bangkok offering services in English. **Christ Church** holds Anglican and Episcopalian services. The **Holy Redeemer Catholic Church** holds services every Sunday. The Jewish Association of Thailand has occasional services at the **Jewish Community Centre**. The **Haroon Mosque** has services for Muslims. Places of worship are listed in the telephone directories available in hotels and guesthouses in Bangkok and provincial capitals.

Phra Si Rattana Chedi, Wat Phra Kaeo, Bangkok

A sign at Hat Phrao, Ko Samet, asking visitors to keep the beach clean

LANGUAGE

IT IS USEFUL to learn a few Thai phrases *(see pp500–504)*, and Thais will be delighted that you have made the effort. Many local people in popular tourist towns speak some English, as do most hotel receptionists. Sight and road names in these areas are transliterated, and menus are often in English as well as Thai. Prices and road numbers are in Arabic numerals. Transliterated spellings vary wildly in different maps and guides, and on signposts. Note that "j" and "ch" are interchangeable, as are "d" and "t". The letters "ph" (e.g. as in Phuket) are pronounced "p", never "f". Likewise, the "h" in "th" is always silent (e.g. Thailand).

THAI TIME SYSTEM AND CALENDAR

BANGKOK TIME is seven hours ahead of Greenwich Mean Time (GMT) and six hours ahead of British Summer Time (BST). It is 12 hours ahead of Eastern Standard Time and 15 hours ahead of Pacific Standard Time. Although the standard clock and 24-hour clock are used and widely understood, Thailand also has its own system which can be confusing to foreigners. Thais divide the day into four segments of six hours each. For example, "7am" is one in the morning and "7pm" is one in the evening.

Two calendars are used in Thailand: the Gregorian (Western) and the Buddhist calendars. The Buddhist Era (BE) starts 543 years before the Gregorian era. To convert from the Gregorian calendar to the Buddhist calendar, add 543 years. For example, AD 1957 is the equivalent of 2500 BE.

MEASUREMENTS

THE METRIC SYSTEM is generally used in Thailand, although traditional weight and measurement systems are sometimes used in markets and outside Bangkok. As well as being a unit of currency, the *baht* is also a unit of weight which is used when pricing gold.

CONVERSION CHART

Imperial to Metric
1 inch = 2.5 centimetres
1 foot = 30 centimetres
1 mile = 1.6 kilometres
1 ounce = 28 grams
1 pound = 454 grams
1 pint = 0.6 litre
1 gallon = 4.5 litres

Metric to Imperial
1 centimetre = 0.4 inch
1 metre = 3 feet 3 inches
1 kilometre = 0.6 mile
1 gram = 0.04 ounce
1 kilogram = 2.2 pounds
1 litre = 1.8 pints

ELECTRICITY

THE ELECTRIC CURRENT for the whole of Thailand is 220 volts AC, 50 cycles. Dual-prong rounded plugs as well as flat-pin plugs can be used in sockets. Major hotels in Bangkok also have 110-volt outlets for electric razors. Adaptors can be bought in any department store or electrical store. These outlets also sell power-surge cables, which are vital if you are travelling with a laptop computer.

Power failures are increasingly rare but not unheard of in smaller towns, especially during the rainy season. In some rural areas it is a good idea to keep a torch handy.

PHOTOGRAPHY

CAMERA FILM in Thailand should be stored in relatively cool conditions as heat and humidity lead to rapid deterioration. As in any country, it is polite to ask first before photographing people, especially monks or tribespeople, whose spiritual beliefs may not welcome such intrusions.

A range of plugs and adaptors that can be used in Thailand

Etiquette

IT IS NOT BY ACCIDENT that Thailand is often referred to as "the land of smiles". The Thais are exceptionally friendly and helpful people and getting along with them is easy – simply smile wide and laugh a lot. Being Buddhists, they are an amazingly tolerant people. Avoiding offensive behaviour can generally be achieved through simple courtesy and common sense. A few taboos do exist, though, mostly with regard to the monarchy and Buddhism. Visitors should be particularly careful to behave respectfully at *wats* and in front of any Buddha image. Confrontation is also considered extremely rude, and Thais will bend over backwards to avoid arguments of any sort. Losing your temper or shouting, whatever the situation, is seen as an embarrassing loss of face.

King Bhumibol taking part in a ceremony, Wat Benchamabophit

Two Thais addressing each other with a *wai*, the traditional greeting

GREETING PEOPLE

THE THAI GREETING is known as the *wai* and consists of the palms being pressed together and lifted towards the chin. The *wai* evolved from an ancient greeting used to show that neither party was carrying weapons. The *wai* is layered with intricacies of class, gender and age: each of these dictates a certain height at which the two hands must be held. The inferior party initiates the *wai* and holds it higher and for longer than the superior, who returns it according to his or her social standing. Non-Thais are not expected to be familiar with these complexities, and the easiest method is simply to mirror whatever greeting you receive. As a general rule of thumb, however, you should not *wai* children or workers such as waiters, waitresses and street vendors.

Thais use first names to address people, even in formal situations. The polite form of address is the androgynous title Khun, followed by the first name or nickname. Every Thai person has a nickname, usually a one- or two-syllable name with a simple meaning, such as Mu ("pig") or Kung ("prawn").

BODY LANGUAGE

THE HEAD IS CONSIDERED a sacred part of the body by Thais. Never touch someone's head, not even that of a child. The feet are seen as the lowliest part of the body and to point your feet towards someone or rest them on a table is considered rude. When sitting on the floor, especially inside a temple, tuck your legs away behind you or to the side and try not to step over people sitting around you; allow them time to move out of your way.

ROYALTY

THE ROYAL FAMILY is the most revered institution in Thailand. Criticizing or defaming it in any way can be considered lese-majesty. Not only could this mean a jail sentence, but Thai people will nearly always be deeply offended. Coins, banknotes and stamps bear the images of kings and therefore should not be treated lightly. Similarly, you cannot photograph certain sacred sights connected to royalty, such as the *bot* of Wat Phra Kaeo, which houses the highly revered Emerald Buddha image.

THE NATIONAL ANTHEM

THE NATIONAL ANTHEM is played twice a day, at 8am and 6pm, on the radio and through tannoys in small towns and some public parks and buildings, such as Lumphini

Devotees kneeling before a Buddha, their feet facing away from the image

A man offering food to a queue of monks on the daily alms round

Park and Hua Lamphong Station in Bangkok. At these times it is polite to stop whatever you are doing and stand still. In cinemas the national anthem is played before all performances. When it is playing the audience stands in silent respect to a portrait of the king on the screen.

MONKS

THE MONKHOOD *(sangha)* is a respected institution that comes just below royalty in the social hierarchy. Most taboos in dealing with monks concern women: it is prohibited for a monk to touch a woman or for him to receive anything directly from her. Therefore, when travelling by public transport, women should avoid sitting near or next to a monk. If she has to offer anything to a monk she should either use a middleman or place the item nearby for him to pick up. These rules are confined to monks and do not apply to nuns.

It is not forbidden for people to talk to monks – many are eager to try out their basic English on visitors. However, monks never return *wais*.

ETIQUETTE AT WATS

AS IN CHURCHES and other houses of worship, a certain decorum should be observed when entering the grounds of any *wat*. Temples are calm, quiet places, so try

to avoid disturbing the peace. Dress should be clean, respectable, and unrevealing (strictly speaking, the upper arms and legs down to mid-calf should be covered). Shoes should be removed when entering any temple building. Step over, not on, the thresholds of *wat* buildings as Thais believe that one of the nine spirits that inhabit buildings lives in the threshold.

All Buddha images are sacred no matter how small, ruined or neglected, and you must never sit with your feet pointing towards them.

Some areas of a temple may be off limits for women – there is usually a sign indicating so.

SUITABLE DRESS

BECAUSE THE THAIS are a modest people, clothing should be kept respectable whether you are in the city or in the country. Women especially should take care not to wear revealing skirts, shorts or skimpy tops. In formal settings and restaurants you will rarely see Thai women with bare shoulders; sleeveless dresses or tops are considered too revealing for such situations. Topless sunbathing is frowned upon greatly – regardless of whether others are doing it – even in resorts dominated by Western tourists. Most Thais find the practice embarrassing and many of them find it offensive.

"No shoes" sign outside Wat Phra Kaeo, Bangkok

COMMUNICATING

BARGAINING is common throughout Thailand *(see p430)*. Though everyone develops a personal technique – whether it involves smiling or remaining poker-faced – it is important not to get too tough or too mean. Likewise, be patient with receptionists, waitresses and others whom you may deal with. In general, you should avoid raising your voice or becoming obviously irritable – Thais learn in childhood always to speak softly and avoid direct conflict. Foreigners who may be used to getting results if they show impatience are likely to find Thais ignoring them rather than attempting to continue communicating with them.

Tourists bargaining with vendors on the platform of Hua Hin station

TIPPING

TRADITIONALLY, tipping is not common practice in Thailand, though in Westernized establishments it is becoming so. Taxi drivers expect tips – you should round up the fare to the nearest ten *baht* if you have not already bargained the fare. Porters, hairdressers and barbers also often expect tips. A service charge of ten per cent is common on upmarket restaurant and hotel bills, even if they also charge government tax *(see p391)*.

SMOKING

MOST RESTAURANTS in Thailand provide smoking areas. The exception is Western fast-food chains, where smoking is generally banned. It is also prohibited in cinemas, department stores and on public transport in Bangkok. Provincial bus services and trains often allow smoking.

Personal Security and Health

THAILAND IS A FAIRLY SAFE COUNTRY, and simple health and safety precautions keep the vast majority of travellers out of trouble. For instance, ignore touts, keep away from troubled border areas, take care of valuables and avoid staying or eating in unsanitary conditions. The infrastructure of emergency services for both health and crime are efficient throughout Bangkok and provincial capitals. As a rule of thumb, the more remote the area, the higher the health risk and less support available in the event of any mishap. The main hospitals in Bangkok, Chiang Mai, the main resorts and other large cities have modern equipment and well trained doctors, many of whom speak some English.

Tourist policeman wearing a beret, and an ordinary officer

IN AN EMERGENCY

THERE ARE NO national emergency telephone lines, and operators do not speak English. For English-speaking help, call the Tourist Assistance Centre which will contact the appropriate service for you. Lines are open from 8am to midnight, after which you will have to rely on English-speaking hotel staff. During office hours, TAT *(see p452)* may also be able to help. The Metropolitan Mobile Police cover general emergencies in Bangkok. All Bangkok's hospitals have 24-hour accident and emergency departments.

Fire engine

Ambulance

GENERAL PRECAUTIONS

DESPITE ITS SIZE, Bangkok is relatively safe. Crime and violence do exist in the city, but the vast majority of travellers remain untouched by it. Usually discretion and sobriety are the best means of avoiding problems. Be on your guard at tourist sights, and at bus and railway stations which are rife with touts and pickpockets. Do not flash large amounts of cash around, or leave your luggage unattended. If you are leaving valuables in a hotel safe, make sure that you get a receipt, and do not let credit cards out of your sight when paying for shopping.

The drugging, then robbing, of tourists on long-distance trains and buses has occurred, so politely decline food or drink from strangers. Thailand is an excellent place to buy gems *(see p434)*, but do not be tempted into buying large quantities to sell back at home unless you are familiar with the market and its pitfalls. Extra care is necessary in remote areas of the country, or in poorer parts of cities at night, or if travelling alone.

DRUGS

THAI LAW PROHIBITS the sale or purchase of opium, heroin or marijuana. Charges for possession, smuggling or dealing can lead to a 2–15 year jail sentence or, in extreme cases, the death sentence. Border areas in the North attract drug runners. Be wary of strangers in these areas, and do not leave baggage unattended, or offer to check-in a "friendly" stranger's suitcase at airports.

DANGER SPOTS

BORDER AREAS are sometimes precarious places. Changing political conditions, tribal skirmishes and the haziness of border lines have made some areas of Thailand dangerous. Khmer Rouge insurgents are sometimes a threat along the Cambodian border, as are land mines and booby-traps.

There are frequent clashes on the Burmese border, and it is best to avoid travelling alone along remote roads in the region. In some parts of the Deep South, the militant Malay-Muslim group, PULO (Pattani United Liberation Organization) can present danger. Again, common sense should prevail and it is wise to stay away from the most remote border areas.

WOMEN TRAVELLERS

FEMALE TRAVELLERS are unlikely to be harassed in Thailand. Bangkok itself is not dangerous for women; hotels are safe and taxis are readily avai-

Patrol car used by the tourist police, seen mainly in cities lable. If travelling alone it is a good idea to keep in touch with someone in Bangkok and let them know where you are going and for how long. Note that Thais perceive lone travellers as people to be pitied, and may offer to accompany you without any ulterior motive.

TOURIST POLICE

THERE ARE tourist police stations in the main tourist cities. Tourist police officers all speak some English and are attached to TAT offices. Set up in 1982 to deal with tourist-related crime, they are happy to help with anything from credit card scams to ludicrous bar surcharges. They are also helpful in emergencies, and can act as an English-speaking liaison. The Bangkok branch of the tourist police is located in front of the southwest entrance to Lumphini Park. The Tourist Assistance Centre is also helpful in emergencies, and is experienced in dealing with complaints such as fraudulent business charges.

Badge identifying the tourist police

LEGAL ASSISTANCE

SOME INSURANCE POLICIES cover legal costs, for instance after an accident. Contrary to advice given in other countries, if involved in an accident when in a hire car, it may be wiser to drive to the nearest telephone and call the tourist police or Tourist Assistance Centre rather than remain at the scene. There are no legal bodies specifically representing foreigners.

In a severe emergency, contact your embassy (see p451). At night there is an answering service, giving the number of the duty officer. If you are not insured for legal proceedings, then you should contact your nearest consulate for advice.

Pharmacy sign found throughout Thailand

Logo of the Thai Red Cross Society, part of Chulalongkorn University

MEDICAL FACILITIES

MEDICAL INSURANCE is advisable when travelling in Thailand. Some policies pay bills direct, while others refund you later. Hospitals in Bangkok, both public and private, are modern, clean and efficient, although waiting times are longer at public ones. Some doctors are Western-trained and speak good English.

Outside the capital the best facilities are in the large towns: Khon Kaen in the Northeast, Chiang Mai in the North, or Phuket in the South. Emergency care is available from military hospitals, which treat tourists in urgent cases. For dental or eye care, it is best to seek treatment in Bangkok. The Thai Red Cross on Rama IV Road does not offer medical treatment, but is able to deal with vaccinations and snake bites.

PHARMACIES

THERE IS NO SHORTAGE of well-stocked pharmacies in Bangkok – there will be several in every main street and shopping mall, and supermarkets will have drug store kiosks. They are all supplied with up-to-date medications and can dispense antibiotics over the counter without a prescription.

Most pharmacies are open from 8am to 9pm. In the central areas of Bangkok, around Silom and Sukhumvit roads, a few stay open until 10pm or 11pm. Pharmacy signs are the same all over the country. In small towns pharmacies are less prolific and have fewer supplies. For instance, disposable nappies and tampons can be hard to find in remote areas.

PUBLIC TOILETS

ALL HOTELS AND MANY guesthouses have Western-style flush toilets. In general, paper is erratically supplied. Some toilets have a water spray which is used instead of toilet paper. In some restaurants and at many major sights, you will encounter the Asian squat toilet. Nearby will be a ladle and a bucket of water, which are used to wash the body and to sluice out the toilet after use. Paper is disposed of in a bin.

COPING WITH THE HEAT

ACCLIMATIZATION TO THE sometimes oppressive humidity and heat of Thailand can often take longer than expected. In the first few days it is not advisable to exert yourself. Make sure you drink lots of fluids, take plenty of rest in the shade and avoid being out and about in the midday sun. Once you are acclimatized, dehydration and salt deficiency can still be a problem – always keep up a high intake of fluids, especially bottled water, and perhaps add extra salt to food.

A fan to beat the heat

Minor fungal infections can occur due to the heat, especially if tight clothing or shoes are worn. Perspiration trapped beneath the skin can cause the itchy rash called prickly heat. The local remedy and prophylactic for this is a talcum powder which contains a tingling cooling agent. Clothing should be loose and light – 100 per cent cotton is best.

The sun, especially at midday and on the islands, is very powerful; sunscreen and a wide-brimmed hat are indispensable.

Treatment for prickly heat

FIRST-AID KIT

ALTHOUGH MOST first-aid items can be obtained from any pharmacy in main towns, when travelling to rural areas or quiet islands it is advisable to carry a basic first-aid kit. This should include the following: any personal medication; aspirin or pain killers for fevers and minor aches and pains; an antiseptic for minor

Tiger Balm – provides relief from aches, pains, bites and strains

cuts and bites; a digestive preparation to soothe upset stomachs; insect repellent; plasters; scissors, tweezers and a thermometer. Tiger Balm, available at any pharmacist, is Asia's miracle cure-all, relieving headaches, muscle pains and insect bites.

MINOR STOMACH UPSETS

DIARRHOEA, a common complaint for travellers the world over, is caused by bacteria in food and water.

Should diarrhoea occur, eat plain foods for a few days and drink plenty of fluids. It is never wise to drink tap water – bottled water is readily available over most of the country. Ice should be fine in main hotels and restaurants, but avoid crushed iced drinks from street vendors. Eating in hotels and good restaurants is generally safe. It is when you venture into the street vendors' moveable feasts that the danger of "Bangkok belly" can arise. Choose food stalls that are popular with locals, and watch how the dishes are prepared. It can take time for visitors' stomachs to adjust to new foods. If your constitution is delicate, stick to unpeeled fruits and well-cooked foods, and eat dishes while they are still hot. Avoid eating spicy dishes on an empty stomach. Fried noodle or rice dishes and noodle soups are usually easy to digest.

Drugs such as Lomotil and Imodium can bring relief to diarrhoea, but rehydrating solutions, available at pharmacies, are usually the best remedy. For immediate relief, a single 500 mg dose of the prescription antibiotic called Ciproxin is effective and safe.

CUTS AND BITES

ALWAYS TAKE PRECAUTIONS in rural areas: wear boots and long trousers when walking through grassland or forested areas to protect against snake bites and discourage leeches (in the rainy season).

Few snake bites are dangerous. If you are bitten, apply a crepe bandage firmly to the bite, keep the limb immobile and seek immediate medical help.

Jellyfish stings are painful – vinegar will soothe the wound. Coral cuts are slow to heal as coral contains a mild poison. Cuts should be treated with an antiseptic to prevent infection. Bandages and plasters keep wounds wet so should be used only sparingly.

INSECT-BORNE DISEASES

SEVEN OF THAILAND'S 410 mosquito species carry malaria. Symptoms of the disease include headache, fever and violent chills. If you experience such symptoms, seek medical advice immediately. Pollution in the main towns and resorts keeps them largely free of malarial mosquitoes. The areas of greatest risk are the Burmese and Cambodian border regions and, to a lesser degree, some rural areas north of Chiang Mai. However, malarial zones are continually changing. For up-to-date information and advice on the most suitable prophylactic drug, call a travel clinic or, in the UK, **MASTA** (Medical Advisory Service for Travellers Abroad) for a free, comprehensive health report *(see p457)*.

Mosquitoes have become resistant to certain malaria tablets. Prevention is by far the best defence against the disease. Malarial mosquitoes are active from sun-down till sunrise, during which time you should spray on plenty of repellent, wear long-sleeved clothing in light colours (dark attracts mosquitoes) and use mosquito nets and coils. Another mosquito-borne dis-

Essentials for the outdoor life – mosquito coil and insect repellent

Spicy curries from food stalls – best avoided if your stomach is delicate

ease – dengue fever – is a risk during the day-time. However, few mosquitoes are infected with the virus and the symptoms, though intense and unpleasant, are rarely fatal. These include fever, headache, severe joint and muscle pains, and a rash. No preventative treatment or vaccination is available.

In Northern Thailand and some rural areas there is a risk of contracting Japanese encephalitis. Spread by night-biting mosquitoes and ticks, the symptoms are headache, fever, chills and vomiting. Vaccination is advisable if your plans include travelling to rural areas (particularly during the rainy season), or trekking. Should any of the above symptoms occur seek immediate medical help.

As with malaria, the best way to counter the risk of dengue fever and Japanese encephalitis is to try to avoid being bitten in the first place.

PEOPLE- AND ANIMAL-BORNE DISEASES

ACQUIRED IMMUNE deficiency syndrome (AIDS) is passed through bodily fluids. Blood transfusion methods in Thailand are not always reliable – it is safest to seek treatment in the main hospitals. The same goes for inoculations – make sure needles are new or bring your own supply. Be wary of any procedure involving needles, including tattooing, ear-piercing and dentistry.

The high turnover of clients in Thailand's infamous and pervasive sex industry means that unprotected sex carries a serious risk *(see p112)*. Not only AIDS, but other sexually transmitted diseases are commonplace. Some strains have become so virulent that they are penicillin-resistant.

Hepatitis B is also transmitted through bodily fluids. Symptoms include fever, nausea, fatigue and jaundice, and it can lead to severe liver damage. A prophylactic vaccine is available.

Rabies is carried in the saliva of infected animals and can be passed on by a bite or lick to a wound or scratch. Any bite from a dog, cat or monkey should be cleaned immediately and checked by a doctor. If rabies is detected, treatment involves a long series of inoculations. A prophylactic vaccine is now available.

Tetanus is a potentially lethal disease transmitted through infected cuts and animal bites. The first symptoms are difficulty in swallowing (tetanus is also known as lockjaw) and muscle stiffness in the neck area, which can lead to convulsions. As with rabies, all wounds should be speedily cleaned and examined by a doctor. Effective vaccinations are available and a booster is necessary every ten years.

Tuberculosis is prevalent throughout Asia but the visitor is not at serious risk. Vaccines are available and unpasteurized dairy products should be avoided, particularly by children.

Bilharzia is contracted from tiny worms which infect some types of freshwater snail. They burrow into the skin and cause a general feeling of sickness followed by abdominal pain. Avoid swimming in untested rivers and lakes.

FOOD- AND WATER-BORNE DISEASES

DYSENTERY IS A severe form of food or water poisoning. Bacillary dysentery – characterized by stomach pains, vomiting and fever – is highly contagious but rarely lasts longer than a week. Amoebic dysentery has similar symptoms but takes longer to develop. It can recur and cause chronic health problems. Medical help should be sought without delay if you suspect you have either type.

Hepatitis A is passed on in conditions of poor sanitation – contaminated water or food – and can now be prevented with a vaccine. Symptoms include extreme fatigue, aching, fever, chills and jaundice. Little can be done to treat the disease beyond rest.

Cholera is a water-borne disease and symptoms include severe diarrhoea, weakness and cramps. A vaccination is available but is generally considered to be unreliable. Fluid replacement is the most important treatment, while the best prevention is to avoid unsanitary conditions and areas where cholera is present.

Typhoid is transmitted through contaminated water or food, so the same precautions apply. Symptoms are similar to those of flu but quickly accelerate to high fever, weight loss and severe dehydration. Medical attention is essential as complications, such as pneumonia, can easily occur. Although a vaccination is available, it is not always reliable.

Bottled water

Banking and Local Currency

Siam Commercial Bank logo

Throughout Bangkok and the main provincial towns, banking facilities and exchange services are plentiful, well-run and easy to access. In the major centres, tellers often speak some English. Exchange booths are usually located in the central parts of towns, and mobile exchange units are stationed near larger tourist attractions. Automatic Teller Machines (ATMs) can be found in all cities. Smaller towns are less likely to have exchange facilities, but most have banks or ATMs. Rural villages, unless they are tourist destinations, probably will not have banking or currency exchange services.

Hongkong and Shanghai Bank head office, Silom Road, Bangkok

BANKS AND BANKING HOURS

The three main banks are the Bangkok Bank, the Thai Farmers Bank and the Siam Commercial Bank. The Bank of Ayudhya and Thai Danu Bank also have branches throughout the country. Foreign-owned banks offering full commercial banking services include the Bank of America, Banque Indosuez, Citibank, Chase Manhattan Bank, Deutsche Bank, Hongkong and Shanghai Bank and Standard Chartered Bank.

Banking hours are generally 8:30am–3:30pm, Monday to Friday. Some Bangkok banks have shorter hours in an effort to lessen the rush-hour traffic problems. Exchange booths are often open daily, early until late. As well as providing day-to-day banking services, the major banks can also organize international money transfers. Most banks, especially in cities, will have an associated ATM.

ATM SERVICES

Most atm services provide instructions in both Thai and English. Any ATM displaying the VISA or MasterCard

Automatic Teller Machine: found in Bangkok and many Thai towns

sign will accept these cards, and dispense cash in *baht* using your regular PIN. There are surcharges for such

transactions. If you are staying in Thailand for several months or more, it might be a good idea to open an account at a Thai bank. This allows access to any ATM or main bank without having to worry about exchange rates or charges. Although not all banks have application forms in English, one of the tellers should be able to help. The account should take about a week to set up.

CHANGING MONEY

Banks almost always offer the best exchange rates, and rates differ little between banks. Hotels usually offer the worst rates, while those at exchange booths can vary considerably. US dollars are the mostly widely accepted foreign currency when buying *baht*, although sterling is also generally taken. In Bangkok, hole-in-the-wall exchange booths can be found in most major department stores and shopping malls and on major roads. Mobile exchange units

---

DIRECTORY

THAI BANKS

Bangkok Bank
333 Silom Rd, Bangkok.
((02) 231 4333.

Bank of Ayudhya
550 Phloen Chit, Bangkok.
((02) 253 8601.

Siam Commercial Bank
1060 Petchaburi Rd, Bangkok.
((02) 256 1234.

Thai Danu Bank
393 Silom Rd, Bangkok.
((02) 230 5000.

Thai Farmers Bank
1 Thai Farmers Lane, Ratburana Rd, Bangkok.
((02) 470 1122.

FOREIGN BANKS

Bank of America
2/2 Wireless Rd, Bangkok.
((02) 251 6333.

Banque Indosuez
152 Wireless Rd, Bangkok.
((02) 651 4590.

Citibank
127 South Sathorn Rd, Bangkok.
((02) 232 2972.

Deutsche Bank
208 Wireless Rd, Bangkok.
((02) 651 5000.

Hongkong and Shanghai Bank
Silom Rd, Bangkok.
((02) 233 1904–17.

Standard Chartered Bank
990 Rama IV Rd, Abdul Rahim Building, Bangkok.
((02) 636 1000.

CARDS

American Express
((02) 273 0033;
(02) 273 0044 (hotline).

MasterCard
((02) 271 0234;

VISA
((02) 256 7326.

can often be found near tourist attractions and around tourist market areas. These are generally open daily between 7am and 9pm. Exchange rates are published daily in the *Bangkok Post* and the *Nation*.

CREDIT AND DEBIT CARDS

CREDIT CARDS are accepted in major hotels, department stores and up-market shops and restaurants. They can also be used at major banks (and some exchange kiosks) for cash advances. A surcharge will be applied. VISA and MasterCard are the most widely accepted cards; the use of Diners Club and American Express is more limited.

MasterCard debit cards can be used to withdraw cash at most foreign exchange booths, and at Bangkok Bank and Siam Commercial Bank. VISA debit cards can do the same at the Thai Farmers Bank. Debit cards can also be used at local ATMs, but a surcharge will be levied.

As the popularity of plastic money increases, so too does the incidence of credit-card fraud. Visitors should always carefully check what they sign.

CURRENCY

THE THAI UNIT of currency is the *baht*, usually seen abbreviated to "B". There are 100 *satang* in a *baht*, but the *satang* represents such a small sum today that it is scarcely used. You may hear 25 *satang* referred to as a *saleng*. However, inflation is rendering this colloquial term redundant. Bank notes come in the following denominations: 10 *baht* (slowly being phased out), 20 *baht*, 50 *baht*, 100 *baht*, 500 *baht* and 1,000 *baht*.

Logos for two of Thailand's long-established banks

Changing large denomination notes in rural areas may prove difficult. The coin denominations are 25 *satang* (1 *saleng*), 50 *satang*, 1 *baht*, 5 *baht*, 10 *baht*. Possible confusion over different sized coins of the same denomination is becoming less likely as older, larger 1 and 5 *baht* coins are gradually phased out in favour of smaller versions. Old coins feature Thai numerals only, while newer coins have both Thai and Arabic numerals.

TRAVELLERS' CHEQUES

BANKS, MAIN HOTELS and most exchange booths cash travellers' cheques, but banks provide the best value as their surcharge is minimal. Travellers' cheques are the safest method of carrying money and are exchanged at better rates than cash. Banks charge a fee per cheque changed, so using large-domination cheques works out cheapest.

VAT

THAILAND IMPOSES a 7 per cent Value Added Tax (VAT) on goods and services, generally levied only in up-market hotels, restaurants and shops. It is not possible to claim VAT back.

20 baht

50 baht

100 baht

500 baht

1,000 baht

Coins shown at actual size

25 satang   **50 satang**   **1 baht**   **5 baht**   **10 baht**

Communications

THAILAND'S COMMUNICATION NETWORK is becoming increasingly sophisticated. The telephone system is run by the Telephone Organization of Thailand (TOT) under the umbrella of the Communications Authority of Thailand (CAT). It is possible to make international calls and send faxes from all business centres and main hotels. Public phones can be found on all main roads and many minor ones. The postal system, however, can be erratic; if you are sending valuables it is advisable to use courier services. Many major international newspapers and magazines can be easily obtained. Locally published English-language newspapers and magazines can be bought in almost every hotel and bookshop, and at many kerb-side news kiosks.

A domestic telephone box

A green card-phone for local and long distance domestic calls

INTERNATIONAL CALLS

ALL MAJOR HOTELS and most guesthouses offer international dialling services, but will add a surcharge of 30–40 per cent. Business centres in small towns offer fax and phone services which are accompanied by high surcharges.

Bangkok's Central Post Office on Charoen Krung (New) Road and some major post offices around the country have a CAT centre which can arrange reverse-charge and credit card calls. In Bangkok these are open from 7am to midnight, with reduced hours in the provinces.

To dial directly from a hotel room, either contact reception, or dial 001 (for an international line) followed by the country code and telephone number. Alternatively, dial the international operator on 100. Full rates are charged from 7am to 9pm, with a 30 per cent discount between midnight and 5am, and a 20 per cent discount at other times.

Blue and yellow international payphones can be found on the street, in shopping malls and in airports. These take some credit cards, and Lenso phonecards, which are sold in the post office and by agents displaying the Lenso logo.

LOCAL CALLS

LOCAL PHONE CALLS can be made from any public payphone other than the blue and yellow Lenso phones, which can be used for international calls only.

Domestic calls can be made from blue and silver coin phones or green card-phones. All coin-operated phones accept one *baht* and five *baht* coins; and some of them will also accept ten *baht* coins. Hotel phones may accept only five *baht* coins. Local calls (within the same area code) cost one *baht* a minute. There are also some red coin phones, from which it is possible to make only local calls, but these are being phased out.

The long-distance domestic service covers Malaysia and Laos as well as regional Thai calls. These countries can be dialled directly using the appropriate area code.

Green card-phones can be found in department stores and airports throughout the country. Cards for these can be bought at most post offices, bookshops and hotels, and come in several denominations: 25 *baht*, 50 *baht*, 100 *baht* and 240 *baht*.

Comprehensive telephone directories are published by Shinawatra. An English edition can be found in major hotels and most restaurants in Bangkok. Such directories are to be found in most provincial capitals, but outside these there is unlikely to be an English edition available.

USING AN INTERNATIONAL PHONE

5 Listen for the dialling tone and dial 001 and then the number.

4 The display will show you how much credit is left.

3 To make a follow-on call press the "Next Call" button.

2 Select your language using the "Language Select" button.

1 Lift receiver, then insert phonecard here. Press the button when the call ends.

Phonecard for international calls

TELEVISION AND RADIO

THAILAND HAS FIVE television channels; programmes are mostly in Thai, though in Bangkok some are broadcast with an English soundtrack on FM radio. Some towns may receive only one national channel and a local station. Satellite and cable networks are fast expanding all over Asia, and most international English-language networks such as the BBC and CNN are readily available. Many hotels provide satellite and cable television as well as an in-house video channel. Check the *Bangkok Post* and the *Nation* for details.

There are over 400 radio stations nationwide. In Bangkok, there are 41 FM and 35 AM stations. The vast majority of these are in Thai, but English-language stations manned by local DJs are listed in the *Outlook* section of the *Bangkok Post*. The national public radio station, Radio Thailand, broadcasts English-language programmes on 97 FM from 6am to 11pm, while listings for short-wave frequencies receiving the BBC, VOA, Radio Australia, Radio Canada, RFI (French) and Deutsche Welle are found in the *Focus* section of the *Nation*.

NEWSPAPERS AND MAGAZINES

THE TWO MAIN English-language newspapers, arguably the best in Asia, are the *Bangkok Post* and the *Nation*. These provide reliable local, regional and international

Three popular English-language newspapers in Thailand

coverage. Their daily broadsheet inserts *Outlook (Post)* and *Focus (Nation)*, include features on lifestyle, travel and human interest as well as listings for food, films, concerts and exhibitions in Bangkok. Both are sold in news kiosks and shops.

Smaller, less comprehensive papers, which rely heavily on the wire service are *Business Day* and *Thailand Times*. The *Asia Times*, launched in 1996, is a Thailand-based regional business paper. The Singapore

DIRECTORY

DIRECTORY ASSISTANCE

Greater Bangkok Metropolitan Area
(13.

Provincial Areas
(183.

OPERATOR

Long Distance Service for Thailand, Malaysia and Laos
(101.

International Service
(100.

Road-side newspaper kiosk selling a variety of publications

edition of the *International Herald Tribune* and the *Asian Wall Street Journal* are sold in hotels and English-language bookshops such as Asia Books and DK Books which also stock a good selection of international magazines such as *Esquire, Cosmopolitan* and *Vanity Fair*. News weeklies, *The Economist, Time* and *Newsweek* are widely available, as are their Hong Kong-based Asian counterparts, *Far Eastern Economic Review* (FEER) and *AsiaWeek*.

Among the local English-language monthly publications are the useful listings guide *Metro*, the business and lifestyle magazine *Manager*, and society rag *Thailand Tatler*. Free guides available in restaurants, bars and bookshops include *This Week Thailand, Bangkok Guide* and the pocket-sized *Bangkok Dining and Entertainment*.

USEFUL DIALLING CODES

- To make a call within a province dial the last six digits of the number, or seven digits if in Bangkok.
- To call another province, first dial the area code, (beginning with 0). The code for Bangkok is 02, all other provinces have three-figure codes.
- To make an international call, dial 001, then the country code.
- Country codes are: UK 44; Ireland 353; France 33; USA & Canada 1; Australia 61; New Zealand 64. It may be necessary to omit the first digit of the destination area code.

- For directory assistance dial 13 in Bangkok, or 183 outside the capital.
- To put a call through the international operator, or to report technical faults, dial 100.
- To speak to the domestic operator, dial 101.
- To make a reverse charge (collect) call dial the international operator on 100.
- Note that the speaking clock and similar telephone services such as directory enquiries are all in Thai.
- For an alarm-call, contact your hotel switchboard or reception.

Phra Sing Post Office, in the centre of Chiang Mai

POST

L ETTERS AND POSTCARDS generally take at least one week to reach Europe and North America from Thailand. Stamps are available at all post offices, and can also be bought at many hotels. The major hotels will also post letters and packages for you.

Be wary of sending valuable items through the post as parcels have been known to go astray. Greater reliability can usually be assured by sending letters and packages by registered post or via International Express Mail (EMS).

Parcels must be wrapped in officially approved packaging. This will be done for you at a special counter at most post offices. Having queued to have your parcel packed, you might find that you must then queue again for the parcel to be weighed, and once again to buy the stamps.

Poste restante facilities are available at all main post offices in the country. Letters will normally be held for up to three months. To claim mail from a poste restante it is necessary to show your passport and sometimes pay a

small fee. Letters should be addressed to you (with your last name written in capitals and underlined), poste restante, GPO, address, town, Thailand. Thus for Bangkok's main GPO, correspondents should send mail care of GPO, Charoen Krung Road, Bangkok.

Larger post offices are usually open from Monday to Friday between 8am and 8pm and at weekends between 8am and 1pm. Smaller post offices in cities, and those in most provincial towns, are generally open Monday to Friday between 8:30am and 4:30pm and between 9am and 12 noon on Saturdays.

FAX, TELEX AND TELEGRAPH SERVICES

M AJOR HOTELS often provide fax and telex facilities for guests. However, you should be aware that, as with phone calls, hotels add a heavy mark-up for the use of such services.

It can be cheaper to take advantage of the fax, telex and telegraph services available at the Overseas Telegraph and Telephone offices. These can be found in many towns and, usefully, are often open 24 hours a day. Additionally, some of the TAT offices and independent agencies may offer fax facilities.

COURIER SERVICES

T HE MAJOR INTERNATIONAL courier companies, such as **DHL** and **FedEx**, operate in Thailand so it is easy to have goods air freighted home. However, for very heavy or large items, such as furniture, the cost is prohibitive, and shipping will be the only viable option. Many shops will arrange this for you and provide the necessary paperwork.

Thai postbox

ADDRESSES

T HAI ADDRESSES are complicated. What may look like a street number may in fact be a block number. For instance, 349/2–3 Sukhumvit Road, indicates block number 349 with the premises occupying numbers 2–3 of that block. Most main roads have numerous numbered *sois* (lanes) leading off them. Sometimes these are written before the road name, sometimes after. Thus, 123 Sukhumvit Soi 14, Khlong Toey, Bangkok indicates house number 123 on Soi 14 off Sukhumvit Road in Bangkok's Khlong Toey district. Some major *sois* have a name as well as a number.

An added complication is *mu* numbers. These refer to a specific, small geographical area, which is often a village. However, *mu* numbers may still be encountered in cities, reflecting the expansion of the cities as they encompassed outlying settlements within their boundaries.

Addresses outside large cities are usually the number and street name, village, village group, district and province.

The familiar figure of King Bhumibol on all the standard issue Thai stamps

Provinces of Thailand
Thailand's 76 provinces, known as *changwats*, are grouped into four main administrative areas.

Provinces Around Bangkok

THE PROVINCES OF THAILAND

PAK NUA

1 Mae Hong Son
2 Chiang Mai
3 Chiang Rai
4 Phayao
5 Nan
6 Lamphun
7 Lampang
8 Phrae
9 Tak
10 Sukhothai
11 Uttaradit
12 Kamphaeng Phet
13 Phitsanulok
14 Phichit
15 Phetchabun
16 Uthai Thani
17 Nakhon Sawan

ISAN

18 Loei
19 Nong Khai
20 Nong Bua Lum Phu
21 Udon Thani
22 Sakhon Nakhon
23 Nakhon Phanom
24 Chaiyaphum
25 Khon Kaen
26 Kalasin
27 Mukdahan
28 Maha Sarakham
29 Roi Et
30 Yasothon
31 Amnat Charoen
32 Khorat (Nakhon Ratchasima)
33 Buri Ram
34 Surin
35 Si Sa Ket
36 Ubon Ratchathani

PAK KLANG

37 Chai Nat
38 Lop Buri
39 Kanchanaburi
40 Suphan Buri
41 Sing Buri
42 Ang Thong
43 Nakhon Pathom
44 Phra Nakhon Si Ayutthaya
45 Saraburi
46 Nonthaburi
47 Pathum Thani
48 Nakhon Nayok
49 Samut Sakhon
50 Krung Thep Maha Nakhon (Bangkok)
51 Samut Prakan
52 Samut Songkhram
53 Prachin Buri
54 Sa Kaeo
55 Chachoengsao
56 Chon Buri
57 Rayong
58 Chanthaburi
59 Trat
60 Ratchaburi
61 Phetchaburi
62 Prachuap Khiri Khan

PAK THAI

63 Chumphon
64 Ranong
65 Phangnga
66 Surat Thani
67 Phuket
68 Krabi
69 Nakhon Si Thammarat
70 Trang
71 Phatthalung
72 Satun
73 Songkhla
74 Pattani
75 Yala
76 Narathiwat

ADMINISTRATIVE REGIONS

THAILAND'S 500,000 sq km (193,000 sq miles) is home to 60 million people. The country is split into four main regions: Pak Nua (the North), Isan (the Northeast), Pak Klang (Bangkok, the Central Plains and the Gulf of Thailand) and Pak Tai (the South).

The regions are subdivided into 76 provinces (*changwats*), each administered by a governor. Provincial capitals are known as *amphoe muangs*. Each province consists of a number of *amphoes*, or districts (722 in total), which are headed by a district officer. These are, in turn, divided into sub-districts (*king amphoes*), and then into village groups (*tambons*). There are a total of 7,109 of these village groups in the country, each of which is administered by a *kamnan*. At the most basic level are the 64,450 individual villages (*mu bans*). Every village is represented by its own elected headman or *phuyaiban*.

These administrative boundaries are useful to understand when working out addresses or travelling to locations that are off the beaten track.

TRAVEL INFORMATION

FOR MOST VISITORS, flying is the most convenient way of getting to Thailand – the only other routes at present are by ferry, road and rail via Malaysia, or by limited but rapidly improving road links via Laos. Domestic flights within Thailand are easy and cut journey times considerably, with provincial airports dotted generously around the country. Flights to surrounding countries are cheaper if booked

Thai Airways logo

within Thailand. Regular rail services run between Bangkok and Singapore, via Kuala Lumpur, Butterworth (for Penang) and some Southern Thai towns. Rail travel is efficient, clean and comfortable, though there is a limited number of lines. Long-distance coaches and provincial buses of varying quality run to all towns and most villages. At a local level there is a variety of taxis, *songthaews, tuk-tuks* and rickshaws.

A Boeing 747 in the traditional livery of Thai Airways

ARRIVING BY AIR

THAILAND IS SERVED BY numerous airlines from all over the world. Direct flights are available from North America, Europe, Australasia and Asia. A direct flight from London will take approximately 12 hours. The national airline, **Thai Airways**, operates out of London's Heathrow airport, as does **British Airways**. Some other carriers fly from Gatwick. Most flights arrive in Bangkok, but charters and flights from Asian countries may land at Phuket, Chiang Mai or Hat Yai.

AIR FARES

THE COST OF FLYING to and from Thailand varies according to the destination, the airline and the time of year. In the northern hemisphere the cheap fares are available from September to April, and in the southern hemisphere from March to November. Bangkok is one of the cheapest cities in the world to fly out of due to loose government restrictions on air fares, and fierce competition between the airlines and Bangkok's travel agencies.

DON MUANG AIRPORT

BANGKOK'S INTERNATIONAL airport, called Don Muang, is the entry point for the vast majority of visitors to Thailand. The airport is well-equipped and signposted, and is one of the most modern and efficient in Asia. Immigration lines can admittedly be a bit slow, but the baggage claim is reliable, and the green customs channel (nothing to declare) nearly always runs smoothly.

There are two international terminals, 1 and 2, as well as a domestic terminal. The international terminals are within easy walking distance of each other, while an elevated walkway connects them to the domestic terminal. There is also a free shuttle-bus service that runs every 15 minutes along the short distance between the terminals. The arrivals hall of Terminal 1 has by far the best facilities, including currency exchange booths, automatic teller machines (ATM), a 24-hour post office with international telephone facilities, an airport

clinic, a tourist information kiosk, and a hotel reservation desk. At the latter you can book rooms in any of the hotels that belong to the Thai Hotels Association (*see p382*) for a small commission. The departure hall of Terminal 1 has restaurants and bars, as well as a left-luggage facility of up to four months. There are fewer facilities at Terminal 2.

The airport is within 100 m (100 yards) of a busy metropolitan area with a market, shops, restaurants, food stalls, and even a *wat*, all of which may provide a welcome distraction for travellers. Nearby hotels offer daytime "ministays" of three hours as well as overnight accommodation.

GETTING TO AND FROM DON MUANG AIRPORT

TRAVEL TIME BY ROAD between the airport and central Bangkok depends on the traffic conditions. The Expressway (for which a toll must be paid) can take as little as 20 minutes in optimum conditions. However, it may take over three hours if there is heavy congestion, so try to avoid rush hours. There are a variety of ways to travel the 25 km (16 miles) into

Planes on the tarmac at Bangkok airport

An airport limousine, identified by its green registration plates

A licensed airport taxi, with yellow registration plates

An ordinary city taxi, characterized by white registration plates

Bangkok from Don Muang. If you are already booked into a hotel, you should check to see if it offers a complimentary limousine or mini-bus service from the airport. The Thai Hotels Association desk should have this information. One or two luxury hotels operate a helicopter service to and from

the airport for their guests. Thai Airways offers limousines, taxis, and a minibus service to major hotels. The taxi ranks are now controlled by the airport. This rule applies even to meter taxis. Ignore any touts offering cheap rates (they may not be all they seem) and seek out the taxi desk in the arrivals hall of each terminal, where a price will be set for your journey (typically 300 *baht*). Licensed airport limousines and airport taxis can be identified by their respective green or yellow licence plates. An experimental airport bus service to town began in 1996.

The train station, directly opposite the airport, is reached via a covered walkway from the arrivals hall. Trains depart from here every 15–30 minutes for Hua Lamphong Station in the centre of Bangkok. Normal meter taxis operate in the city.

Adventurous travellers without much baggage can try the public buses which stop on the highway outside the airport (a bus map can be found in any airport kiosk). Women travelling alone are advised to take either an airport-licensed taxi, or the minibus service that is provided by Thai Airways.

DIRECTORY

AIRLINES

Bangkok Airways
(02) 229 3456.

British Airways
(02) 636 1747.

Cathay Pacific Airways
(02) 263 0606.

Malaysia Airlines
(02) 263 0565.

Orient Airlines
(02) 267 3211.

Qantas Airways
(02) 636 1747.

Singapore Airlines
(02) 236 0440.

Thai Airways
(02) 628 2000.

United Airlines
(02) 253 0558.

DOMESTIC FLIGHTS

LOCAL CARRIERS **Thai Airways** and **Bangkok Airways** fly to all major provincial capitals such as Chiang Mai, Hat Yai and Phuket. They also serve towns such as Ranong, Mae Sot and Phrae. Some destinations, such as Ko Samui and Sukhothai, are serviced only by Bangkok Airways. **Orient Airlines** began operating in late 1996 serving popular destinations from Bangkok such as Pattaya, Phuket and Chiang Mai. Tickets can be bought through travel agents and hotels, or booked directly through the airlines and picked up at the airport an hour before flying.

On the many public holidays and at weekends it can be difficult to get a flight, so try to book tickets well in advance or to travel during the week.

Bus from Don Muang airport to the centre of Bangkok

AIRPORT	INFORMATION	DISTANCE TO TOWN OR RESORT	AVERAGE TAXI FARE	AVERAGE JOURNEY TIME
Bangkok domestic:	(02) 535 1111 (02) 535 1253	City centre 25 km (16 miles)	300 *baht*	Rail: 50 minutes Road: 1–2 hours
Chiang Mai	(053) 270222	City centre 7 km (4.5 miles)	250 *baht*	Road: 30 minutes
Phuket	(076) 3272307	Patong 50 km (31 miles)	400 *baht*	Road: 45 minutes
Ko Samui	(077) 245601	Chaweng 26 km (16 miles)	150 *baht*	Road: 30 minutes

Travelling Around by Train, Coach and Boat

THAILAND HAS AN efficient railway system known as the SRT (State Railway of Thailand), with four major lines connecting Bangkok with the North, Northeast, East and South. Though trains are comfortable and safe, journey times are similar, sometimes even longer, than by coach, and the number of towns on the network is limited. Phuket and Chiang Rai, for instance, do not have train stations. By contrast, well-maintained, long-distance coaches connect all major cities to Bangkok, and provincial buses serve all smaller towns and many villages. The main islands are accessible via scheduled ferry services.

Queuing for train tickets at Hua Lamphong Station in Bangkok

THE RAILWAY NETWORK

THE MAIN STATION in Bangkok is Hua Lamphong, which serves all four major lines. The first line runs to Chiang Mai via the Central Plains. A second, which later divides in two, runs to Nong Khai and Ubon Ratchathani in Northeast Thailand. A third connects Bangkok to the Eastern Seaboard and Cambodia and a fourth runs down the peninsula to Malaysia. However, Thon Buri Station in Bangkok Noi is the principal departure point for trains to the South. It also has lines to Kanchanaburi and Suphan Buri.

Window of a first-class train carriage

TRAINS

TRAIN SERVICES are labelled Special Express (the fastest), Express, Rapid (slower than Express) and Ordinary. Journey times, even on

Express trains, can be longer than by road. Bangkok to Chiang Mai, for instance, takes 11 to 13 hours.

First-class carriages (available on Express and Special Express trains) consist of individual cabins with air-conditioning. Second-class carriages have reclining seats and a choice of fans or air-conditioning. Sleepers in this class have individual seats which are converted into curtained-off beds at night. Toilets (there should be at least one Western toilet) and washing facilities are at the end of carriages. Most tourists find that second class is comfortable enough for long distances, and far more relaxing than a coach journey.

Third-class carriages have wooden benches each seating two or three passengers: they are cheap but not recommended for long distances.

Most trains are clean and well maintained. Uniformed vendors stroll up and down the aisles with refreshments, and buffet cars are attached to trains on long-distance routes.

TRAIN TICKETS AND FARES

A TRAIN TIMETABLE in English is available from Hua Lamphong Station in Bangkok. Trains at peak periods (weekends and holidays) can be sold out days in advance. Hua Lamphong has an advance booking office with English-speaking staff. Some travel agents will also book train tickets.

Fares depend on the speed of the train and the class of the carriage. A second-class journey between Bangkok and Chiang Mai is about 250 *baht*, with supplements of around 20–50 *baht* for Rapid and Express services. Shorter journeys, such as from Bangkok to Ayutthaya, cost anything between 15–90 *baht*.

Tourists can also buy 20-day rail passes. These cost 1,000–2,000 *baht*. Information about these is available from Hua Lamphong Station.

LONG-DISTANCE COACHES

LONG-DISTANCE coaches run from the Eastern (Ekamai), Northern (Morchit) and Southern (Pin Klao) coach terminals in Bangkok. Most provincial capitals can be reached direct

Fountain in front of Hua Lamphong Station, Bangkok

THE EASTERN & ORIENTAL EXPRESS

The world-renowned Eastern & Oriental Express operates between Bangkok and Singapore. The journey takes three days and two nights, including stops at Butterworth (Penang) and Kuala Lumpur in Malaysia. The 22 carriages are bedecked with fabrics and fittings evocative of 1930s rail travel. Double and single cabins come in private and presidential classes, and there are two restaurants, a saloon car, a bar and an observation deck. Such luxuries are, of course, reflected in the price.

Dining car on the Eastern & Oriental Express

from Bangkok. Large cities such as Chiang Mai, Phitsanulok, Khorat and Surat Thani also act as transport hubs, with both long-distance and local connections. Coaches can be faster than trains: Bangkok to Chiang Mai takes about ten hours. Vehicles are air-conditioned, with a toilet, reclining seats and plenty of leg room. "VIP" coaches have the best facilities, including free refreshments served by a stewardess. Overnight services are popular, though they can get rather chilly – blankets should be provided.

Typical bus tickets

COACH TICKETS AND FARES

Fares for long-distance coach trips are similar in price to second-class train tickets. "VIP" coaches are at the top of the price range. Book a day or two in advance through a travel agent or at the coach station if travelling at the weekend or during a public holiday. Otherwise, just turn up at the coach station at least half an hour before departure. Tickets are always bought as singles.

PROVINCIAL BUSES

The government bus company is called *Bor Kor Sor* (BKS). Its buses are frequent, relatively reliable and they are the cheapest form of transport in Thailand. Booking is rarely necessary. On many buses simply pay the driver or conductor. Almost every town will have a BKS terminal. The non air-conditioned *(rot thamadaa)* buses are the cheapest and slowest, and they stop almost everywhere along the way. Air-conditioned *(rot aer)* local buses do not necessarily provide blankets, so take a jacket or jumper, especially at night-time.

Travelling on provincial buses is a good way to meet local people and reach many villages and sights. Beware, though, that refreshment and toilet stops may be infrequent, the buses may be in a poor state of repair, and the road skills of drivers will vary. Local services are nearly always slow and crowded. Back seats are reserved for monks, so be prepared to move or stand. Women should avoid sitting next to monks *(see p455)*.

(see p455)

A blue and white air-conditioned *(rot aer)* coach

DIRECTORY

TRAIN INFORMATION

Hua Lamphong Station
Krung Kasem Rd, Bangkok.
((02) 223 0341.
Advance booking office open
7am–4pm daily.

Thon Buri/Bangkok Noi Station
Arun Amarin Rd, Bangkok Noi.
((02) 411 3102.

Chiang Mai Station
Charoen Muang Rd, Chiang Mai.
((053) 242094.

Eastern & Oriental Express
((0171) 928 6000 (UK).
((02) 216 8661 (Bangkok).
((65) 227 2068 (Singapore).

COACH TERMINALS

Bangkok
Eastern/Ekamai Bus Terminal
Sukhumvit Rd, Bangkok.
((02) 391 2504.

Northern/Morchit Bus Terminal
Kampheng Phet Rd, Morchit, Bangkok.
((02) 272 5299.

Southern/Pin Klao Bus Terminal
Nakhon Chai Si Rd, Phra Pin Klao, Bangkok.
((02) 435 1199.

Chiang Mai
Chiang Mai Arcade, Kaew Nawarat Rd, Chiang Mai.
((053) 242664.

BOATS TO THE ISLANDS

Scheduled ferries are always erratic as their service is dependent on the weather conditions. Regular services are available to Ko Samui, Ko Pha Ngan and Ko Tao from Surat Thani. Ko Phi Phi is served by ferries from Phuket and Krabi. Smaller islands have less regular services – sometimes just a make-shift ferry run by local fishermen. Travel agents will be able to give you rough timetables, but these may be dependent on filling enough seats in the boat. Many services stop in the rainy season.

Local Transport

**Bangkok
tuk-tuk**

BANGKOK IS POSSIBLY the world's most congested city. The traffic jams and pollution are notorious, so take the riverboats of the Chao Phraya Express service wherever possible. Local transport in the provinces is far less frenetic, where bicycle rickshaws *(samlors)* and colourful *tuk-tuks* run alongside services such as *songthaews*. Visitors will find that they cannot walk far without being offered some mode of transport. Bargaining for the fare on *samlors* is part of the experience. Do not climb on before agreeing a price, and beware being taken for a ride in more ways than one.

A *songthaew* – uncomfortable, but cheaper and safer than a *tuk-tuk*

GETTING AROUND BANGKOK

TRANSPORT in the capital comes in the form of riverboats and public buses, as well as limousines and tour buses run by hotels, and the usual assortment of taxis and *tuk-tuks* seen in the rest of Thailand. The Skytrain, which was begun in the mid-1990s, is an elevated railway, unique in Thailand: you should check with your hotel to find out how much of the network is open.

Express riverboats with conductors serve popular piers on the Chao Phraya River, running every 10–20 minutes. Ferries also link east and west banks, and it is possible to hire a long-tail boat *(see pp70–71)* at some piers to explore the *khlongs*. The routes of the Skytrain and the Chao Phraya Express are plotted on the Bangkok Street Finder *(see pp138–45)*.

In Bangkok, one-way bus lanes can make buses the fastest form of road transport. The *Tourist Map Bangkok City* and *Tour 'n' Guide Map Bangkok* show the bus routes. Blue air-conditioned buses ("AC" in the transport details for each Bangkok sight), and pink and grey microbuses (indicated by "M") are comfortable and cover the popular routes. Ordinary (non air-conditioned) buses are cheap, cover all of Bangkok and run into the night.

Few tourists use city buses outside Bangkok: routes are ever-changing, non-Thai

speakers are at a disadvantage and taxis, *tuk-tuks* and *songthaews* are more readily available and convenient.

TAXIS

METER TAXIS operate in Bangkok, Chiang Mai and Hat Yai, distinguishable by a prominent "Taxi-Meter" sign on the roof. Drivers tend to know only the names and locations of the major hotels and sights. In non-meter taxis (in Bangkok these are now quite rare and not recommended), you need to bargain for the fare before getting in.

Motorcycle taxis operate in some towns. Drivers tend to congregate near markets and long *sois* and can be identified by their colourful numbered vests. Prices are negotiated.

TAXI-METER

Sign on the roof of a metered taxi in Bangkok

SONGTHAEWS, SAMLORS AND TUK-TUKS

SONGTHAEWS (literally translated as "two rows") are vans with two rows of seats in the back. They are more common than city buses outside Bangkok and run popular routes for set fares, typically between 20 and 40 *baht*. Drivers may wait until they are at least half full before setting off. Routes are sometimes written in English on the sides of the vans. *Songthaews* can be hired like taxis, but are less comfortable.

Samlors are three-wheeled vehicles that can transport one or two people up to a few kilometres. Motorized *samlors* are known as *tuk-tuks* – their two-stroke engines, introduced by the Japanese during World War II, are notoriously noisy. In heavy traffic or during the rainy season, *tuk-tuks* can be uncomfortable and unstable, but are always popular with tourists. Non-motorized *samlors* are often in the form of bicycle rickshaws. You need to negotiate a price before climbing into either type: 30–60 *baht* is reasonable for short hops.

Three-wheeled bicycle rickshaw, or *samlor*, in a seaside resort

Organized Tours

H UNDREDS OF TOUR COMPANIES are based in Bangkok, Chiang Mai and major resorts such as Phuket, and most hotels throughout the country offer tours of one sort or another. Typical excursions on offer range from one-day city tours covering the main sights, to more comprehensive itineraries taking in several towns and locations over several days. Costs are naturally higher than taking public transport, but in some cases – for instance many sights in the Greater Bangkok region – much time and effort simply in getting to the destination may be saved. The drawback of most organized tours is, of course, that there is rarely time to linger.

BOOKING A TOUR

I T SHOULD BE POSSIBLE to book a tour of Thailand from your home country, which will include all travel and accommodation. Such all-inclusive tours typically last between one and two weeks and include a few nights in Bangkok followed by excursions to Chiang Mai and other Northern locations, or to a beach resort. Other packages are more specialized, concentrating, say, on trekking in the North *(see p446)*, and may vary from a few days to several weeks in duration. Based in Bangkok, **Thai Overland Travel & Tour** and **NS Travel & Tours** are major operators.

Most regional hotels and many guesthouses offer tours of the surrounding area, or are in close contact with local tour companies. The local TAT office will also be able to recommend reputable tour companies. Day trips to the most popular sights can usually be booked just one day in advance. Tours to more distant sights should include arrange-

ments for accommodation, and usually have at least one departure day each week. In most cases, the tour company will pick you up direct from your hotel or guesthouse.

TOUR BUSES AND BOATS

M ANY TOUR COMPANIES use luxury, or "VIP," coaches, with reclining seats, on-board refreshments, air-conditioning and a toilet. Air-conditioned minibuses are also common,

as are jeeps for gaining access to remote areas. Most vehicles are well maintained and safe.

Boat tours are popular in many resorts, though the majority of operators follow the same routes. Day trips to islands, including opportunities for water sports, are common. Transfers to and from hotels are often part of the deal. Trips to remote islands, often with diving facilities on board *(see p446)* can span several days, and accommodation may be provided on the boat itself.

GUIDED TOURS

B ILINGUAL GUIDES accompany many tours, especially to cultural sights, such as Ayutthaya. In Northern Thailand a knowledgeable guide is essential for safety reasons when trekking through the jungle and visiting hill-tribe villages. The quality of guides varies considerably: a listing of reputable ones is published by the Professional Guide Association, available from TAT.

Elephant trekking, a popular tour option in Northern Thailand

---

DIRECTORY	Inthanon Tour	Silver Queen	Thai-Indochina
MAJOR TOUR COMPANIES	95 Huay Kaew Rd, Chiang Mai. [(053) 212373.	291 Chaofa Rd, Phuket. [(076) 222623.	**Tour Co** 753 Silom Rd, Bangkok. [(02) 635 0500.
Chiang Mai Green Tour & Trekking 29/31 Chiang Mai–Lamphun Rd, Chiang Mai. [(053) 247374.	**NS Travel & Tours** 133/19–20 Ratchaprarop Rd, Bangkok. [(02) 246 5659.	**Songserm Travel** 51 Satun Rd, Phuket. [(076) 222570.	**Thai Overland Travel & Tour** 407 Sukhumvit Rd, Bangkok. [(02) 258 4778.
Diethelm Travel Kian Gwan Building II, 140/1 Witthayu Rd, Bangkok. [(02) 255 9150.	**Perfect Tour** 103/34 Soi Saphankhu, Rama IV Rd, Bangkok. [(02) 679 8501.	**STA Travel** 14th Floor, Wall Street Tower Building, Suriwong Rd, Bangkok. [(02) 233 2582.	**Traveller's World** 4/33–34 Sukhumvit, Soi 21 (Soi Asoke), Bangkok. [(02) 258 3743.

Hiring a Car, Moped or Bicycle

Kilometre marker

DRIVING IN THAILAND is not for the faint-hearted. Hazards come in the form of pot-holed roads, confusing junctions, poorly maintained vehicles and dangerous driving. For many visitors wanting to explore away from the usual tour routes, hiring a car with a driver who is used to the roads is by far the best option. International car hire firms operate in Bangkok and provincial capitals. The standard of local rental companies varies enormously. In the resorts, mopeds and jeeps are popular with tourists.

Sign for a local car hire company: check if insurance is included

HIRING A CAR

A VALID INTERNATIONAL driving licence is a necessity for most visitors, while those from ASEAN countries (Association of Southeast Asian Nations) need only have a permit from their home countries. International rental agencies offer safe cars and the most extensive insurance and back-up services. **Avis** and **Hertz** have desks at some airports and in major cities. Charges range from about 1,000 *baht* for a day to 20,000 *baht* for a month.

With other car rental companies, you should check the small print on the contract for liabilities. Insurance may not be included. Obtain a copy of the vehicle registration and carry it around with you.

HIRING A CHAUFFEUR-DRIVEN CAR

HIRING AN experienced driver with a car is gaining popularity in Thailand. The cost can be surprisingly low – often less than 50 per cent extra on top of the normal price of car hire. Some drivers are knowledgeable about sights and will suggest interesting itineraries. Most car rental firms can arrange drivers. **Siam Express** offers packages including a chauffeur, car and accommodation in a wide range of hotels.

HIRING A MOPED

MOPEDS AND MOTORBIKES are widely available for hire in the resorts, provincial capitals and other large towns. In areas with a lot of guesthouses you can hire anything from a moped to a heavy-duty dirt-bike. Driving licences are rarely requested, and few firms bother with insurance. Costs are low: 200–300 *baht* is average for a day's hire.

Safety precautions are essential. Check tyres, oil and brakes before you set out. Wear a helmet (compulsory in many towns) and proper shoes. Long sleeves and trousers will minimize cuts and grazes in a minor accident. Take great care on dirt roads and avoid driving alone in rural areas. Bear in mind that medical help is not always easily available.

PETROL AND SERVICING

P ETROL STATIONS in Thailand are well manned and are located on main roads in towns and along highways. They are modern and most provide unleaded petrol. Attendants will fill your tank, wash your windows and pump up your tyres. Some garages have a resident mechanic for bigger jobs, or will at least be able to recommend one. Most of them have a small general shop, and all have Asian toilet facilities. Many garages are open 24 hours, while others close at about 8pm. Petrol itself is often cheaper than in the West.

Logo of PTT, a petrol company with stations throughout Thailand

PARKING

M ULTI-STOREY car parks in Bangkok are generally attached to major hotels and department stores. Parking is usually free for hotel guests, and for visitors for up to two or three hours. A ticket is issued on entry, which should be stamped by a cashier; pay on the way out. Besides these arrangements, parking can be difficult in Bangkok.

Throughout Thailand, pavements painted with red and white stripes indicate a no-parking zone. In provincial cities, many hotels and large guesthouses provide free parking facilities for guests. In quieter towns you can generally park anywhere that is not obviously going to be in the way of passing traffic.

Mopeds for hire in Naton town, Ko Samui

Traffic policeman waving vehicles through at a Bangkok intersection

ROADWAYS AND ROAD SIGNS

MULTI-LANE NATIONAL highways exist mostly in and around Bangkok. A toll is charged to travel on the expressways, including the one to Bangkok airport. The fee is indicated above the booth – the exact change is required at manually operated booths. The expressways are less congested than other Bangkok roads, but they are still prone to traffic jams. Many roads in Bangkok are one-way, though a lane may be reserved for buses travelling in the opposite direction.

National highways (in some places also known as routes), such as Highway 1 through the Central Plains, are fast and furious, and can be congested in places. Provincial highways are paved and vary in quality. Smaller roads linking villages are sometimes no more than dirt tracks. Main roads in towns are called *thanons*; numbered lanes leading off these are called *sois* and *troks*. In the rainy season, all roads can become flooded.

Destinations are often given in Roman as well as Thai script. Arabic numerals are always used for distances, and kilometre markers are placed along all main roads. Road markings and traffic symbols are easy to understand.

Auto Guide Company map

RULES OF THE ROAD

DRIVING is on the left. The speed limit is 60 kph (35 mph) within city limits, unless signed otherwise, and 80 kph (50 mph) on open roads. The standard international road rules apply, but are of little interest to Thai drivers. Indeed, the only consistent rule of thumb is that "size wins".

The eccentric use of indicators and headlights can be unnerving. A left signal can indicate to another driver that it is alright to overtake, while a right signal can indicate hazardous on-coming traffic, and a flash of the headlights means: "I'm coming through."

Horns are used constantly, often as a warning of presence rather than obvious danger. Drivers think nothing of straddling lanes and overtaking on bends and up hill. Give way to larger vehicles at unmarked junctions. It is legal to turn left at red traffic lights if there is a blue sign with a white left arrow, or occasionally if you are in the left lane. On minor roads, beware of buffalo herds and roaming dogs.

Traffic fines are most commonly imposed for illegal turns. If you get a ticket and your licence is retained, go to the local police station, the address of which will be on the ticket, and pay the fine. Drive slowly through army checkpoints in border areas and be prepared to stop if necessary.

Typical road scene in Thailand's notoriously busy capital city

ROAD MAPS

MOST THAIS RELY ON mental maps and see no need for the level of cartography favoured in the West. Tourist maps are widely available but cover major roads only. Some provincial, fold-out maps produced by the Prannok Witthaya Map Center are excellent, showing all roads and reliefs, but are sold in few outlets. The *Thailand Highways Map* by the Auto Guide Company and the *Thailand Highway Map* by the Roads Association are the best atlases, and are written in Thai and Roman scripts.

HIRING A BICYCLE

IN THE COOL SEASON, cycling in quiet areas is a pleasant way to get around. Guesthouses and small agencies often have bicycles for hire for 20–100 *baht* a day, though the bikes may be rickety. New mountain bikes may be on offer, though, perhaps surprisingly, costs may exceed those of mopeds. Taking plenty of water is essential and, of course, great care is always necessary on the roads.

General Index

Acknowledgments

DORLING KINDERSLEY would like to thank the following people whose contributions and assistance have made the preparation of this book possible.

MAIN CONTRIBUTORS

PHILIP CORNWEL-SMITH is a journalist focusing on entertainment, lifestyle and topical issues. After working on guides to London, in 1994 he moved to Thailand and was founding editor of the Bangkok listings magazine *Metro*.

ANDREW FORBES has studied Thai history and culture for more than 20 years and has lived in the country on and off since 1984. He writes for the *Asian Wall Street Journal* and *Far Eastern Economic Review* among other publications.

TIM FORSYTH is a writer and lecturer at the London School of Economics. He has travelled extensively throughout Northern Thailand and other parts of Southeast Asia.

RACHEL HARRISON has lectured at the School of Oriental and African Studies in London and contributed to Thai phrase books. She has a special interest in Northeast Thailand.

DAVID HENLEY is director of Crescent Press Agency's Thailand Bureau and has lived in Thailand for more than a decade. An authority on Thai cuisine, he contributes regularly to the *Bangkok Post* and *The Australian*.

JOHN HOSKIN has been based in Bangkok since 1980. He is the author of several books on travel, art and culture in Thailand and Indochina, including *The Mekong: A River and Its People*.

GAVIN PATTISON is a London-based writer who has contributed to the *Blue Guide to Thailand* among other titles. He has travelled extensively in Thailand, Indonesia and other parts of Southeast Asia.

JONATHAN RIGG is a reader in human geography at Durham University, with a special interest in Southeast Asia. He has lived in Thailand, speaks Thai and Lao and continues to travel widely throughout the region.

SARAH ROONEY is a Bangkok-based journalist who contributes to Asian publications such as *Art and Asia Pacific*, *Metro*, *Thailand Tatler* and the renowned English-language Thai newspaper *The Nation*.

KEN SCOTT, a journalist, lives in Krabi, Southern Thailand. He specializes in the culture and history of the Southern Thai-Malay Peninsula. His features appear regularly in the *Bangkok Post* and other publications.

ADDITIONAL CONTRIBUTORS

Paul Dennison, Paul Lees, James Mahon, Tim Redford, Francis Silkstone, Tym Srisawat.

TRANSLITERATION ADVISER

David Smyth (London School of Oriental and African Studies).

TRANSLATION ASSISTANCE

AThaiS (Bristol), Vantana Cornwell, Dutjapun Williams.

ADDITIONAL ILLUSTRATIONS

Robert Ashby, Graham Bell, Peter Bull, Joanna Cameron, Chris Forsey, Paul Guest, Stephen Gyapay, Ruth Lindsay, Maltings Partnership, Mel Pickering, Robbie Polley, Sally Anne Reisen, Mike Taylor, Pat Thorne, Paul Weston.

ADDITIONAL PHOTOGRAPHY

Alberto Cassio, Peter Chadwick, Crescent Press Agency, Philip Dowell, Neil Fletcher, Dave King, Alan Newnham, Harry Taylor.

ADDITIONAL CARTOGRAPHY

Christine Purcell and Gary Bowes (ERA-Maptec Ltd).

DESIGN AND EDITORIAL ASSISTANCE

Alexander Allan, Vicky Barber, Tessa Bindloss, Louise Boulton, Catherine Day, Jonathan Fiber, Silvia Gaillard, Leanne Hogbin, Lee Redmond, Julian Sheather, Veronica Wood.

ADDITIONAL RESEARCH

Parita Boonyoo, Debbie Guthrie Haer, Elizabeth Lu, Sathorn Leelakachornjit, Pharadee Narkkarphunchiwan, Wanee Tipchindachaikul, Somchai Worasart.

PROOFREADER

Denise Heywood.

INDEX

Hilary Bird.

SPECIAL ASSISTANCE

Dorling Kindersley would like to thank all the regional branches of the Tourism Authority of Thailand (TAT). Particular thanks also to: the Ayutthaya Historical Studies Centre (Thailand), Dr Peter Barrett (Medical Advisory Service for Travellers Abroad, London), William Booth (Jim Thompson's House, Bangkok), Alberto Cassio (Photobank, Bangkok), Crescent Press Agency (Chiang Mai), Gerald Cubitt, John Dransfield (Kew Gardens Herbarium, London), Michael Freeman, Helen Goldie (Durham University), Philip Harris (Bahn Thai Restaurant, London), Kietisak Itchayanan (National Culture Commission, Bangkok), Elizabeth Moore (London School of Oriental and African Studies), Tony Moore (British Thai Boxing Council), Phra Maha Pradit Panyatulo (Wat Buddhapadipa, London), Paisarn Piammattawat, Rattika Rhienpanish (Mai Thai Restaurant, London), Vidhisha Nayanthara Samarasekara, Philip Stott (London School of Oriental and African Studies), Dusadee Swangviboonpong (London School of Oriental and African Studies), Thai Airways (London), William Warren (Bangkok), Terri S Yamaka (TAT, London).

PHOTOGRAPHY PERMISSIONS

Dorling Kindersely would like to thank the following for their assistance and kind permission to photograph at their establishments: Ancient City, Ayutthaya Historical Park, Ban Chiang National Museum, Ban Phin (House of Opium), Chakra Bongse House, Chan Kasem National Museum, Chao Sam Phraya National Museum, Chiang Mai National Museum, In Buri National Museum, Jim Thompson's Thai Silk Shop, Kamphaeng Phet Historical Park, Khon Kaen National Museum, Khorat (Nakhon Ratchasima) National Museum, Lampang National Museum, Lamphun National Museum, Lop Buri National Museum, Muang Tam Historical Park, Nakhon Pathom National Museum, Nakhon Si Thammarat National Museum, Nan National Museum, Narai Ratchaniwet Palace, National Gallery, National Museum (Bangkok), Oriental Hotel, Pha Taem, Phimai National Museum, Phnom Rung Historical Park, Prasart Museum, Ramkamhaeng National Museum, Ratchaburi National Museum, Royal Barge Museum, Sawankha Woranayok National Museum, Siriraj Hospital, Si Satchanalai-Chalieng Historical Park, Songkhla National Museum, Sukhothai Historical Park, Surin National Museum, Ubon Ratchathani National Museum, U Thong National Museum. Also all the other temples, museums, hotels, restaurants, shops, galleries and sights too numerous to thank individually.

PICTURE CREDITS

t = top; tl = top left; tlc = top left centre; tc = top centre; trc = top right centre; tr = top right; cla = centre left above; ca = centre above; cra - centre right above; cl = centre left; c = centre; cr = centre right; clb = centre left below;

cb = centre below; crb = centre right below; bl = bottom left; bc = bottom centre; bcl - bottom centre left; br = bottom right; (d) = detail.

The publisher would like to thank the following individuals, companies and picture libraries for kind permission to reproduce their photographs.

THE NATIONAL MUSEUM (BANGKOK): 50tl, 51cl, tc, 58tl, 58–59cs, 84tl, tr, cl, 85tcb, cr, crb, 75cr.

ARDEA LONDON: Francois Gohier 201tl; Wardene Weisser 201clb; ASIA ACCESS: Jeffrey Alford 370tr; Naomi Duguid 18bl, 228, 370b; ASIA IMAGES: © 1988 38–39c, 42b; © 1993 Matthew Burns 43cr, 257br, 342, 471crb; © 1995 Matthew Burns 34br; © 1990 Allen W Hopkins 273b, 298tr; © 1991 Allen W Hopkins 445b; © 1995 Allen W Hopkins 83br, 431t; AUSCAPES INTERNATIONAL/ Kevin Deacon 339c; AXIOM: © 1995 Jim Holmes 292cl, bl.

BAN PHIN (HOUSE OF OPIUM): 223clb, 238b; CHACRIT BOONSOM: 446t; BFI STILLS POSTERS & DESIGNS: © 1974 Danjaq, LLC and United Artists Corporation Inc. All Rights Reserved 357br; THE BOWERS MUSEUM OF CULTURAL ART: 50cl, clb; ASHLEY J BOYD: 307crb, 313cl, 331cl, cr, 335bl, 338tl, cla, clb, bla, br, 339cr, br, bc, bl, 347cr, 349cbc, 376c, bl; BY PERMISSION OF THE BRITISH LIBRARY Manuscript Or. 14025: 26–27c.

DEMETRIO CARRASCO: 21br, 28cla, 42tl, 43bl, 274cb, 290–291; JEAN-LOUP CHARMET 223cra, 254–255c, 255br; BRUCE COLEMAN LTD: © Werner Layer 201cra; © J Zwaenepoel 201tr; CRESCENT PRESS AGENCY: 383tl; Joe Cummings 285bl; Ron Emmons 299cb; David Henley 21c, 22tr, 26tr, 34tl, 35crb, 36bl, bra, 37bra, br, 40clb, 47cra, 49b, 57br, 59ca, 60tl, br, 61tl, ca, b, 62tl, ca, 63tc, 64b, 65b, 77cra, 87b, 95t, bca, 116tl, clb, 117cra, br, 121tl, 129t, cra, cr, clb, cb, cbr, rb, bl, bc, br, 130b, 152tl, 153tl, br, bl, 165tl, 196tl, tr, clb, br, 197tl, br, 198tr, 214tl, 215br, 216tl, b, 243t, 244tr, 265br, 272, 337tl, br, bl, 366cl, 367tr, 381c, 382c, 386cl, 387bla, 442cr, 432br, 454tr, 464br; John Hobday 24bla, 209crb; Daniel Kestenholz 98ca; Rainer Krack 26tl, 345br, 355cra, 386bl, 407tl, 450br; GERALD CUBITT: 18tc, 24tl, tr, cl, cr, clb, crb, blb, bcb, brb, 25cla, tc, trc, cra, cl, cr, clb, bc, bca, br, 51tl, 77tl, 79tl, 101br, 127t, 129cla, 149tc, crb, 174tl, tr, bl, 175t, ca, crb, br, 181t, 195br, 197bl, 200cla, c, clb, 204bl, 209clb, bl, 211tl, 213bl, 220tl, clb, bl, 221tl, cra, crb, 223bl, 239bl, 244cb, 245tr, 246bc, 270cla, 276bca, 279tl, 287cla, 296c, clb, 297br, 300–301cla, 302, 305br, 313b, 316c, 317crb, 336tr, 339tl, 340tl, cl, clb, bl, bc, 341tlb, tr, cr, 344bl, 345tr, 346crb, 360ca, bl, 363clb, 371tr, cl, 375crb, 385bl, 433tl, 434bl, 446bl, 459tl; MICHAEL CUTHBERT: 360tr, 361clb, 366br.

JAMES DAVIS TRAVEL PHOTOGRAPHY: 149br, 298clb, 334cl; JEAN-LEO DUGAST: 116cr, 26cl, 441tc.

JOHN EVERINGHAM: 4cra, cr, 5tl, 22bl, 23tl, 26br, 34cl, 35tc, 36–37b, 37cra, cr, crb, bl, 41cra, 44bl, 47br, 75bl, 128tl, 210bl, 211cra, 230bl, 257clb, 299bra, 326b, 327cra, br, 328bl, 338tr, 341bc, 344cl, 348cl, 352tr, 353ca, 354cl, 356cla, 442tr, 444tc, 445cla.

FEATURE MAGAZINE: 311tr, 371br; MICHAEL FREEMAN: 21tl, 22tl, 34tr, 38cla, ca, 45cla, 52–53c, 53tl, 54clb, bla, 57tl, ca, crb, 59tl, bla, 60cb, 65tc, cla, 79br, 80bl, 81br, 101tr, 103br, 116bc, 150cla, cb, br, brb, 151cb, bl, 168tlb, 169trb, 170tl, 177b, 181b, 190clb, 194tr, 196ca, 197tr, cra, 198bl, 199tca, bla, br, 202, 203b, 215cra, 250–251, 253br, 254cla, 255tl, 260bl, 300cla, 301cr, 320tl, 321b, 132bla, 347tl, 407cr, 434crb, 439cl.

GRAMMY ENTERTAINMENT PUBLIC COMPANY LTD: 441cl.

ROBERT HARDING PICTURE LIBRARY: 44tc, 68bla, 70cla, 78cl, 226br, 256cr, 257tl, 279bl, br, 339tr, 442clb; © Alain Evrard 16, 22cb, 43t, 45crb, 112bl; © Robert McCleod

45br; © Luca Tettoni 261tr, 268bl; © Ken Wilson 171b; CHRISTINE HEMMET: 27bl, 373bra; THE HUTCHISON LIBRARY: 3c, © Robert Francis 470tl.

THE IMAGE BANK: 11tr; © Peter Hendrie 76tr; © Andrea Pistolesi 126.

JEWELRY REALTY LTD, BANGKOK: 300tl, 301tr. DR OY KANCHAVANIT: 387bc; SUTHEP KRITSANAVARIN: 125cl.

FRANK LANE PICTURE AGENCY: © D Fleetham/Silvestris 25bra; © T & P Garner 340bra; © David Hosking 158b; © E & D Hosking 174cb, 200bl, 353clb; © L Lee Rue 25bl; © T Whittaker 276tr; © De Zylva 331bl.

MAGNUM: © Marc Riboud 255bc; STUART MILLER: 361bl; TONY MOORE British Thai Boxing Council: 40tl.

THE ORIENTAL BANGKOK: 108br.

PHOTOBANK (BANGKOK): 1c, 8–9, 18c, 19tl, 22–23c, 23tr, cra, 27tl, cra, 34–35c, 35bl, 36tr, cla, 37t, 38tl, tr, clb, br, 39tl, tr, ca, br, bc, bl, 42c, 49t, 50ca, cr, 51cra, bra, 52tl, ca, cl, 53ca, crb, 54cla, 55crb, 56clb, 58cb, clb, 60cla, 62–63c, 63crb, 64–65c, 65cra, 68tr, 71tc, 76bla, 84bl, 85tl, 95crb, bl, br, 125cr, cb, bl, 146–147, 148cla, bl, 149cra, 150–151c, 151ca, 152cl, 153cr, 155b, 160b, 166tl, 172–173, 174cl, 185br, 194cl, 206bc, 220cl, 223br, 239bra, 245br, 253cra, 254bl, 284ca, 294–295, 297clb, 298tl, 299cla, 300br, 307bl, 314, 315b, 318cl, 320b, 322bl, br, 336bla, bc, 340tr, 349c, 350b, 355tc, 357tl, tr, 362b, 363tl, cra, br, 374cr, 406c, 407b, 410tr, bl, 436cla, 437cb, 439cra, 440t, cla, br, 444cl, 466br, 472b; PHOTO EFEO: 255tr; PHOTOBANK (SINGAPORE): 20t, 26bla, 35cr, 38bl, 39cra, bra, 40cla, 40–41c, 41tc, 48, 50–51c, 51c, 52bca, 54tl, 55tc, ca, 56cla, cra, 59bca, 60ca, cr, 60–61c, 61br, 62bla, bc, 64cra, 69cra, bl, 81t, 82bl, 88cra, 91tc, 102b, 116tr, cl, 117tc, cr, 120bl, 121bc, 151tl, 152b, 152–153c, 154, 168br, 169tl, 170cl, 176, 196bl, 196–197c, 198cl, 198–199c, 199tr, cr, cb, bra, 214cla, 215tc, 216cl, 231tr, 243cla, crb, clb, bl, br, 246tr, 247tl, cra, bra, bl, 252clb, bc, 255cr, 257bl, bc, 258, 337cr, 373br, 434tr; PICTOR INTERNATIONAL: 2–3, 4br, 47bl, 66–67, 194br, 334b, 343b, 356bla, 358–359; PICTURES COLOUR LIBRARY: 65cr, 237tr, 296bl; POPPERFOTO: 111b.

RIVER BOOKS (BANGKOK): 27cr, 64cl, 98clb, 151tr.

SEACO PICTURE LIBRARY: 455cr, 469ca; CNE, 1988 Distribution Spot Image/SCIENCE PHOTO LIBRARY 10bl; TONY STONE IMAGES: Glen Allison 44c, 324–325; Marcus Brooke 387bra; David Hanson 20b; Hideo Kurihara 104–105; Ed Pritchard 473b; SUPERSTOCK LTD: 122cl, 328cla.

THAI AIRWAYS INTERNATIONAL PUBLIC COMPANY LTD: 466t, cl; JIM THOMPSON'S THAI SILK COMPANY: 256cl, c, b; TOURISM AUTHORITY OF THAILAND: 19cr, 46b, 263cr, bl; TRAVEL INK: Alan Hartley 68cl, 121tc, 297cra, 298cl, 304bl, 316bl, 386cb; Pauline Thornton 17ca, 122bla.

WELLCOME INSTITUTE LIBRARY (LONDON): 223cla.

Cover: All special photography except GERALD CUBITT: Front ca, bra; IMAGE BANK: © Andrea Pistolesi cra; PHOTOBANK (BANGKOK) cb.

Front endpaper: All special photography except Asia Access/ Naomi Duguid tlc; Asia Images © 1993 Matthew Burns bl; CRESCENT PRESS AGENCY: Photo David Henley tc; GERALD CUBITT cr; JAMES DAVIS TRAVEL PHOTOGRAPHY bc; MICHAEL FREEMAN tl; PHOTOBANK BANGKOK r; PHOTOBANK (SINGAPORE) l, cl, trc.

Back endpaper: All special photography.

Phrase Book

THAI IS A TONAL LANGUAGE, and regarded by most linguists as head of a distinct language group, though it incorporates many Sanskrit words from ancient India, and some modern English ones, too. There are five tones: mid, high, low, rising and falling. The particular tone, or pitch, at which each syllable is pronounced determines its meaning. For instance "mâi" (falling tone) means "not", but "mǎi"

(rising tone) is "silk". The Thai script, meanwhile, is one of the most elaborate in the world, running left to right and using over 80 letters. In the third column of this phrase book is a phonetic transliteration for English speakers, including guidance for tones in the form of accents. This differs from the system used elsewhere in the guide, which follows the Thai Royal Institute's recommended romanization of common names.

GUIDELINES FOR PRONUNCIATION

When reading the phonetics, pronounce syllables as if they form English words. For instance:

a	as in "**a**go"
e	as in "h**e**n"
i	as in "th**i**n"
o	as in "**o**n"
u	as in "g**u**n"
ah	as in "r**a**ther"
ai	as in "Th**ai**"
air	as in "p**air**"
ao	as in "M**ao** Tse-Tung"
ay	as in "d**ay**"
er	as in "**e**nter"
ew	as in "f**ew**"
oh	as in "g**o**"
oo	as in "b**oo**t"
OO	as in "b**oo**k"
oy	as in "t**oy**"
g	as in "**g**ive"
ng	as in "si**ng**"

These sounds have no close equivalents in English:

eu	can be likened to a sound of disgust – the sound could be written as "**errgh**"
bp	a single sound between a "b" and a "p"
dt	a single sound between a "d" and a "t"

Note that when "p", "t" and "k" occur at the end of Thai words, the sound is "swallowed". Also note that many Thais use an "l" instead of an "r" sound.

THE FIVE TONES

Accents indicate the tone of each syllable.

no mark	The **mid tone** is voiced at the speaker's normal, even pitch.
á é í ó ú	The **high tone** is pitched slightly higher than the mid tone.
à è ì ò ù	The **low tone** is pitched slightly lower than the mid tone.
ǎ ě ǐ ǒ ǔ	The **rising tone** sounds like a questioning pitch, starting low and rising.
â ê î ô û	The **falling tone** sounds similar to an English speaker stressing a one-syllable word for emphasis.

MALE AND FEMALE POLITE FORMS

In polite speech, Thai men add the particle "**krúp**" at the end of each sentence; women add "**ká**" at the end of questions and "**kâ**" at the end of statements. These particles have been omitted from all but the most essential polite terms in this phrase book, but should be used as much as possible. The polite forms of the word "I" are, for men, "**pǒm**" and, for women, "**dee-chún**".

IN AN EMERGENCY

Help!	ช่วยด้วย	chôo-ay dôo-ay!
Fire!	ไฟไหม้	fai mâi!
Where is the nearest hospital?	แถวนี้มีโรงพยาบาล อยู่ที่ไหน	tǎir-o née mee rohng pa-yah-bahn yòo têe-nǎi?
Call an ambulance!	เรียกรถพยาบาล ให้หน่อย	rêe-uk rót pa-yah-bahn hâi nòy!
Call the police!	เรียกตำรวจให้หน่อย	rêe-uk dtum ròo-ut hâi nòy!
Call a doctor!	เรียกหมอให้หน่อย	rêe-uk mǒr hâi nòy!

COMMUNICATION ESSENTIALS

Yes.	ใช่ or ครับ/ค่ะ	châi or krúp/kâ
No.	ไม่ใช่ or ไม่ครับ/ไม่ค่ะ	mâi châi or mâi krúp/ mâi kâ
May I have ...?	ขอ ...	kǒr ...
Please can you ...?	ช่วย ...	chôo-ay ...
Thank you.	ขอบคุณ	kòrp-kOOn
No, thank you.	ไม่เอา ขอบคุณ	mâi ao kòrp-kOOn
Excuse me/sorry.	ขอโทษ (ครับ/ค่ะ)	kǒr-tôht (krúp/kâ)
Never mind.	ไม่เป็นไร	mâi bpen rai
Hello.	สวัสดี (ครับ/ค่ะ)	sa-wùt dee (krúp/kâ)
Goodbye.	ลาก่อนนะ	lah gòrn ná
Here.	ที่นี่	têe-nêe
There.	ที่โน่น	têe-nûn
What?	อะไร	a-rai?
Why?	ทำไม	tum-mai?
Where?	ที่ไหน	têe nǎi?
How?	ยังไง	yung ngai?

USEFUL PHRASES

How are you?	คุณสบายดีหรือ (ครับ/คะ)	kOOn sa-bai dee reu (krúp/kâ)?
Very well, thank you – and you?	สบายดี (ครับ/ค่ะ) แล้วคุณล่ะ	sa-bai dee (krúp/kâ) – láir-o kOOn lâ?
What is your name?	คุณชื่ออะไร (ครับ/คะ)	kOOn chêu a-rai (krúp/kâ)?
My name is ...	(ผม/ดิฉัน) ชื่อ ...	(pǒm/dee-chún) chêu ....
Where is/are ...?	... อยู่ที่ไหน	.... yòo têe-nǎi?
How do I get to ...?	... ไปยังไง	... bpai yung- ngai?
Do you speak English?	คุณพูดภาษาอังกฤษ เป็นไหม	kOOn pôot pah-sǎh ung-grìt bpen mái?
I understand.	เข้าใจ	kâo-jai
I don't understand.	ไม่เข้าใจ	mâi kâo-jai
Could you speak slowly?	ช่วยพูดช้าๆหน่อย ได้ไหม	chôo-ay pôot cháh cháh nòy dâi mái?
I can't speak Thai.	พูดภาษาไทย ไม่เป็น	pôot pah-sǎh tai mâi bpen
I don't know.	ไม่ทราบ or ไม่รู้	mâi sâhp or mâi ròo

USEFUL WORDS

wife	ภรรยา	pun-ra-yah
husband	สามี	săh-mee
daughter(s)	ลูกสาว	lôok săo
son(s)	ลูกชาย	lôok chai
woman/women	ผู้หญิง	pôo-yĭng
man/men	ผู้ชาย	pôo-chai
child/children	เด็ก	dèk
big	ใหญ่	yài
small	เล็ก	lék
hot	ร้อน	rórn
cold	เย็น or หนาว	yen or năo
good	ดี	dee
bad	ไม่ดี	mâi dee
enough	พอ	por
well	สบายดี	sa-bai dee
open	เปิด	bpèrt
closed	ปิด	bpìt
left	ซ้าย	sái
right	ขวา	kwăh
straight on	อยู่ตรงหน้า	yòo dtrong nâh
between	ระหว่าง	ra-wàhng
on the corner of	ตรงหัวมุม	dtrong hŏo-a mOOm
near	ใกล้	glâi
far	ไกล	glai
up	ขึ้น	kêun
down	ลง	long
early	เช้า	cháo
late	ช้า or สาย	cháh or săi
entrance	ทางเข้า	tahng kâo
exit	ทางออก	tahng òrk
toilet	ห้องน้ำ	hôrng náhm
free/no charge	ฟรี	free

TELEPHONING

Where is the nearest public telephone?	แถวนี้มีโทรศัพท์ อยู่ที่ไหน	tăir-o née mee toh-ra-sùp yòo têe-nǎi?
Can I call abroad from here?	จะโทรศัพท์ไปต่าง ประเทศจาก ที่นี่ได้ไหม	ja toh bpai dtàhng bpra-tâyt jàhk têe née dâi mái?
I'd like to reverse the charges.	ขอให้เก็บเงิน ปลายทาง	kŏr hâi gèp ngern bplai tahng
Hello, this is ... speaking.	ฮันโล (ผม/ดิฉัน) ... พูด (ครับ/ค่ะ)	hello (pŏm/dee-chún) ... pôot (krúp/kâ)
I would like to speak to ...	ขอพูดกับคุณ ... หน่อย (ครับ/ค่ะ)	kŏr pôot gùp khun ... nòy (krúp/kâ)
May I leave a message?	ขอฝากสั่งอะไร หน่อยได้ไหม	kŏr fàhk sùng a-rai nòy dâi mái?
Could you speak up a little, please?	ช่วยพูดดังๆหน่อย ได้ไหม	chôo-ay pôot dung dung nòy dâi mái?
Hold on.	รอสักครู่	ror sùk krôo
I'll ring back later.	เดี๋ยวจะโทรมาใหม่	dĕe-o ja toh mah mài
local call	โทรศัพท์ภายใน ท้องถิ่น	toh-ra-sùp pai nai tórng tìn
phone box/kiosk	ตู้โทรศัพท์	dtôo toh-ra-sùp
phone card	บัตรโทรศัพท์	but toh-ra-sùp

SHOPPING

How much does this cost?	นี่ราคาเท่าไร	nêe rah-kah tâo-rài?
I would like ...	ต้องการ ...	dtôrng-gahn ...
Do you have ...?	มี ... ไหม	mee ... mái?
I am just looking.	ชมดูเท่านั้น	chom doo tâo-nún
Do you take credit cards/travellers' cheques?	รับบัตรเครดิต/เช็คเดิน ทางไหม	rub but cray-dit/ chék dern tang mái?
What time do you open/close?	เปิด/ปิดกี่โมง	bpèrt/bpìt gèe mohng?
Can you ship this overseas?	ส่งของนี้ไปต่าง ประเทศได้ไหม	sòng kŏng nee bpai dtàhng bpra-tâyt dâi mái?
Does it come in other colours?	มีสีอื่นอีกไหม	mee sĕe èun èek mái?
black	สีดำ	sĕe dum
blue	สีน้ำเงิน	sĕe núm ngern
green	สีเขียว	sĕe kĕe-o
red	สีแดง	sĕe dairng
white	สีขาว	sĕe kăo
yellow	สีเหลือง	sĕe lĕu-ung
cheap	ถูก	tòok
expensive	แพง	pairng
gold	ทอง	torng
hill-tribe handicrafts	หัตถกรรมชาวเขา	hùt-ta-gum chao kăo
ladies' wear	เสื้อผ้าสตรี	sêu-pâh sa-dtree
silver	เงิน	ngern
Thai silk	ผ้าไหมไทย	pâh-măi tai
bookshop	ร้านขายหนังสือ	ráhn kăi núng-sĕu
chemist	ร้านขายยา	ráhn kăi yah
department store	ห้าง	hâhng
market	ตลาด	dta-làht
newsagent	ร้านขายหนังสือพิมพ์	ráhn kăi núng-sĕu pim
shoe shop	ร้านขายรองเท้า	ráhn kăi rorng táo
supermarket	ซุปเปอร์มาเก็ต	sÓOp-bpêr-mah-gèt
tailor	ร้านตัดเสื้อ	ráhn dtùt sêu-a

SIGHTSEEING

travel agent	บริษัทนำเที่ยว	bor-ri-sùt num têe-o
tourist office	สำนักงานการ ท่องเที่ยว	sŭm-núk ngahn gahn tôrng têe-o
tourist police	ตำรวจท่องเที่ยว	dtum-ròo-ut tôrng têe-o
closed on public holidays	ปิดวันหยุดราชการ	bpìt wun yÒOt râht-cha-gahn
beach	หาด or ชายหาด	hàht or chai-hàht
cave	ถ้ำ	thûm
cliff	หน้าผา	nâh păh
coral	หินปะการัง	hĭn bpa-gah-rung
elephant camp	ค่ายช้าง	kâi cháhng
festival	งานออกร้าน	ngahn òrk ráhn
hill/mountain	เขา	kăo
hill-tribe village	หมู่บ้านชาวเขา	mòo bâhn chao kăo
historical park	อุทยานประวัติศาสตร์	ÒO-ta-yahn bpra wùt sàht
island (ko)	เกาะ	gòr

lake	ทะเลสาบ	ta-lay sàhp
temple (wat)	วัด	wút
museum	พิพิธภัณฑ์	pí-pít-ta-pun
national park	อุทยานแห่งชาติ	ÒO-ta yahn hàirng châht
old town	เมืองเก่า	meu-ung gòw
palace	วัง	wang
park/garden	สวน	sŏo-un
river	แม่น้ำ	mâir náhm
ruins	โบราณสถาน	boh-rahn sa-tăhn
Thai boxing	มวยไทย	moo-ay tai
Thai massage	นวด	nôo-ut
trekking	การเดินทางเท้า	gahn dern tahng táo
waterfall	น้ำตก	náhm dtòk
zoo	สวนสัตว์	sŏo-un sàt

TRANSPORT

When does the train for ... leave?	รถไฟไป ... ออกเมื่อไร	rót fai bpai ... òrk meu-rài?
How long does it take to get to ...?	ใช้เวลานาน เท่าไวไปถึงที่ ...	chái way-lah nahn tâo-rài bpai tĕung têe ...?
A ticket to ... please.	ขอตั๋วไป ... หน่อย (ครับ/ค่ะ)	kŏr dtŏo-a bpai ... nòy (krúp/kâ)
Do I have to change?	ต้องเปลี่ยนรถ หรือเปล่า	dtôrng bplèe-un rót réu bplào?
I'd like to reserve a seat, please.	ขอจองที่นั่ง	kŏr jorng têe nûng
Which platform for the ... train?	รถไฟไป ... อยู่ ชานชาลาไหน	rót fai bpai ... yòo chahn cha-lah năi?
What station is this?	ที่นี่สถานีอะไร	têe nêe sa-tăhn-nee a-rai?
Where is the bus stop?	ป้ายรถเมล์อยู่ที่ไหน	bpai rót may yòo têe-năi?
Where is the bus station?	สถานีรถเมล์อยู่ที่ไหน	sa-tăhn-nee rót may yòo têe-năi?
Which buses go to ...?	รถเมล์สายไหนไป ...	rót may săi năi bpai ...?
What time does the bus for ... leave?	รถเมล์ไป ... ออกกี่โมง	rót may bpai ... òrk gèe mohng?
Would you tell me when we get to ...?	ถึง ... แล้ว ช่วยบอกด้วย	tĕung ... láir-o chôo-ay bòrk dôo-ay?
Do you know... Road?	รู้จักถนน ... ไหม	róo-jùk ta-nŏn ... mái?
Is it far?	ไกลไหม	glai mái?
Turn left.	เลี้ยวซ้าย	lée-o sái
Turn right.	เลี้ยวขวา	lée-o kwăh
Go straight on.	เลยไปอีก	ler-ee bpai èek
Park over there.	จอดที่โน่น	jòrt têe-nôhn
Park right here.	จอดตรงนี้	jòrt dtrong née
air-conditioned bus	รถปรับอากาศ	rót bprùp ah-gàht
arrivals	ถึง	tĕung
booking office	ที่จองตั๋ว	têe jorng dtŏo-a
bus station	สถานีรถเมล์	sa-tăhn-nee rót may
departures	ออก	òrk
left luggage	ที่ฝากของ	têe fàhk kŏrng
ordinary bus	รถธรรมดา	rót tum-ma-dah
tour bus	รถทัวร์	rót too-a

ticket	ตั๋ว	dtŏo-a
ferry	เรือข้ามฟาก	reu-a kâhm fâhk
train	รถไฟ	rót fai
railway station	สถานีรถไฟ	sa-tăhn-nee rót fai
moped	รถมอเตอร์ไซค์	rót mor-dter-sai
bicycle	รถจักรยานต์	rót jùk-gra-yahn
taxi	แท็กซี่	táirk-sêe
airport	สนามบิน	sa-năhm bin

BARGAINING

How much is this?	นี่ราคาเท่าไร	nêe rah-kah tâo-rai?
How much to go to ...?	ไป ... เท่าไร	bpai ... tâo-rài?
That's a little expensive.	แพงไปหน่อย	pairng bpai nòy
Could you lower the price a bit?	ลดราคาหน่อยได้ไหม	lót rah-kah nòy dâi mái?
How about ... baht?	... บาทได้ไหม	... bàht dâi mái?
Will you go for ... baht?	... บาทไปไหม	... bàht bpai mái?
I'll settle for ... baht.	... บาทก็แล้วกัน	... bàht gôr láir-o gun

STAYING IN A HOTEL

Do you have a vacant room?	มีห้องว่างไหม	mee hôrng wâhng mái?
double/twin room	ห้องคู่	hôrng kôo
single room	ห้องเดี่ยว	hôrng dèe-o
air-conditioned room	ห้องแอร์	hôrng air
I have a reservation.	จองห้องไว้แล้ว	jorng hôrng wái láir-o
I'd like a room for one night/three nights.	(ผม/ดิฉัน) จะพักอยู่ คืนหนึ่ง/สามคืน	(pŏm/dee-chún) ja púk yòo keun nèung / săhm keun
What is the charge per night?	ค่าห้องวันละเท่าไร	kâh hôrng wun la tâo-rài?
I don't know yet how long I'll stay.	ไม่ทราบว่าจะอยู่นาน เท่าไร	mâi sâhp wâh ja yòo nahn tâo-rài
Can I see the room first please?	ขอดูห้องก่อนได้ไหม	kŏr doo hôrng gòrn dâi mái?
Can I leave some things in the safe?	ขอฝากของไว้ในตู้เซฟ ได้ไหม	kŏr fàhk kŏrng wái nai dtôo sáyf dâi mái?
Can you spray some mosquito repellent, please?	ช่วยฉีดยากันยุงให้ หน่อยได้ไหม	chôo-ay chèet yah gun yOOng hâi nòy dâi mái?
air conditioner	เครื่องปรับอากาศ	krêu-ung bprùp ah-gàht
bedroom	ห้องนอน	hôrng norn
bill	บิล	bin
fan	พัดลม	pùt lom
hotel	โรงแรม	rohng-rairm
key	กุญแจ	gOOn-jair
manager	ผู้จัดการ	pôo-jùt-gahn
mosquito screen	มุ้งลวด	mÓOng lôo-ut
shower	ฝักบัว	fùk boo-a
swimming pool	สระว่ายน้ำ	sà wâi náhm
toilet/bathroom	ห้องน้ำ	hôrng náhm

EATING OUT

A table for two please.	ขอโต๊ะสำหรับ สองคน	kŏr dtó sŭm-rùp sŏrng kon
May I see the menu?	ขอดูเมนูหน่อย	kŏr doo may-noo nòy
Do you have ...?	มี ... ไหม	mee ... mái?
I'd like ...	ขอ	kŏr ...
Not too spicy, ok?	ไม่เอาเผ็ดมากนะ	mâi ao pèt mâhk na
Is it spicy?	เผ็ดไหม	pèt mái?
I can eat Thai food.	ทานอาหารไทยเป็น	tahn ah-hăhn tai bpen
May I have a glass of water, please.	ขอน้ำแข็งเปล่า แก้วหนึ่ง	kŏr núm kăirng bplào gâir-o nèung
I didn't order this.	นี่ไม่ได้สั่ง (ครับ/ค่ะ)	nêe mâi dâi sùng (krúp/kâ)
Waiter/waitress!	คุณ (ครับ/คะ)	kOOn (krúp/kâ)
That was an excellent meal.	อร่อยมาก (ครับ/ค่ะ)	a-ròy mâhk (krúp/kâ)
The bill, please.	ขอบิลหน่อย (ครับ/ค่ะ)	kŏr bin nòy (krúp/kâ)
ashtray	ที่เขี่ยบุหรี่	têe-kèe-a bOO-rèe
bamboo shoots	หน่อไม้	nòr mái
banana	กล้วย	glôo-ay
beef	เนื้อวัว	néu-a woo-a
beer	เบียร์	bee-a
boiled	ต้ม	dtôm
bottle	ขวด	kòo-ut
bowl	ชาม	chahm
char-grilled	ย่าง	yâhng
chicken	ไก่	gài
chilli	พริก	prík
chilli paste	น้ำพริก	núm prík
chopsticks	ตะเกียบ	dta-gèe-up
coconut	มะพร้าว	ma-práo
coffee	กาแฟ	gah-fair
crab	ปู	bpoo
crispy noodles	หมี่กรอบ	mèe gròrp
custard apple	น้อยหน่า	nóy-nàh
deep fried	ทอด	tôrt
drink(s)	เครื่องดื่ม	krêu-ung dèum
dry noodles	ก๋วยเตี๋ยวแห้ง	gŏo-ay dtĕe-o hâirng
duck	เป็ด	bpèt
durian	ทุเรียน	tÓO-ree-un
egg	ไข่	kài
egg noodles	บะหมี่	ba-mèe
fish	ปลา	bplah
fish sauce	น้ำปลา	núm bplah
fork	ส้อม	sôrm
fruit	ผลไม้	pŏn-la-mái
fruit juice	น้ำผลไม้	núm pŏn-la-mái
ginger	ขิง	kĭng
glass	แก้ว	gâir-o
iced coffee	กาแฟเย็น	ga-fair yen
iced water	น้ำแข็งเปล่า	núm kăirng bplào
jackfruit	ขนุน	ka-nŎOn
mango	มะม่วง	ma-môo-ung
Mekong whisky	แม่โขง	mâir-kŏhng
menu	เมนู	may-noo
morning glory	ผักบุ้ง	pùk bÔOng

mushroom	เห็ด	hèt
noodle soup	ก๋วยเตี๋ยวน้ำ	gŏo-ay dtĕe-o náhm
oven-cooked	อบ	òp
papaya	มะละกอ	ma-la-gor
pineapple	สับปะรด	sùp-bpa-rót
plate	จาน	jahn
pomelo	ส้มโอ	sôm oh
pork	เนื้อหมู	néu-a mŏo
prawns	กุ้ง	gÔOng
rambutan	เงาะ	ngór
restaurant	ร้านอาหาร	ráhn ah-hăhn
rice	ข้าว	kâo
rice noodles	ก๋วยเตี๋ยว	gŏo-ay dtĕe-o
snack	อาหารว่าง	ah-hăhn wâhng
soy sauce	น้ำซีอิ๊ว	núm see éw
spoon	ช้อน	chórn
spring greens	ผักคะน้า	pùk ka-náh
squid	ปลาหมึก	bplah-mèuk
sticky rice	ข้าวเหนียว	kâo-nĕe-o
stir fried	ผัด	pùt
sweet corn	ข้าวโพด	kâo pôht
tea	น้ำชา	núm chah
vegetables	ผัก	pùk
vinegar	น้ำส้ม	núm sôm
waiter	คนเสริฟ	kon sèrp
waitress	คนเสริฟหญิง	kon sèrp yíng
water	น้ำ	náhm

HEALTH

I do not feel well.	รู้สึกไม่สบาย	róo-sèuk mâi sa-bai
I have a pain in ...	เจ็บที่ ...	jèp têe ...
It hurts here.	เจ็บตรงนี้	jèp dtrong née
It hurts all the time.	เจ็บตลอดเวลา	jèp dta-lòrt way-lah
It hurts only now and then.	เจ็บเป็นบางครั้ง บางคราว	jèp bpen bahng krúng bahng krao
I have a temperature.	ตัวร้อนเป็นไข้	dtoo-a rórn bpen kâi
I'm allergic to ...	(ผม/ดิฉัน) แพ้ ...	(pŏm/dee-chún) páir ...
How many tablets do I take?	ต้องกินยากี่เม็ด ต่อครั้ง	dtôrng gin yah gèe mét dtòr krúng
accident	อุบัติเหตุ	OO-bùt-dti-hàyt
acupuncture	ฝังเข็ม	fŭng kĕm
ambulance	รถพยาบาล	rót pa-yah-bahn
aspirin	แอสพริน or ยาแก้ไข้	air-sa-bprin or yah-gâir-kâi
asthma	โรคหืด	rôhk hèut
bite (by dog)	หมากัด	măh gùt
bite (by insect)	แมลงกัด	ma-lairng gùt
blood	เลือด	lêu-ut
burn	ไหม้	mâi
cholera	อหิวาต์	a-hì-wah
cough	ไอ	ai
dentist	ทันตแพทย์ or หมอฟัน	tun-dta-pâirt or mŏr fun
diabetes	โรคเบาหวาน	rôhk bao wăhn
diarrhoea	ท้องเสีย	tórng sĕe-a
dizzy	เวียนหัว	wee-un hŏo-a
doctor	หมอ	mŏr
dysentery	โรคบิด	rôhk bìt

earache	ปวดหู	bpòo-ut hŏo
fever	ไข้	kâi
filling	อุดฟัน	ÒOt fun
hayfever	ไข้จาม	kâi jahm
headache	ปวดหัว	bpòo-ut hŏo-a
heart attack	หัวใจวาย	hŏo-a jai wai
hepatitis	ตับอักเสบ	dtùp ùk-sàyp
hospital	โรงพยาบาล	rohng pa-yah-bahn
injection	ฉีดยา	chèet yah
malaria	มาเลเรีย	mah-lay-ree-a
medicine	ยา	yah
penicillin	ยาเพนนิซิลลิน	yah pen-ní-seen-lin
prescription	ใบสั่งยา	bai sùng yah
prickly heat	ผด	pòt
rabies	โรคสุนัขบ้า	rôhk sŎO-nùk bâh
sore throat	เจ็บคอ	jèp kor
stomach ache	ปวดท้อง	bpòo-ut tórng
temperature	ตัวร้อน	dtoo-ah rórn
toothache	ปวดฟัน	boo-ut fun
traditional medicine	ยาแผนโบราณ	yah pǎirn boh-rahn
vomit	อาเจียน	ah-jee-un

NUMBERS

0	๐ or ศูนย์	sŏon
1	๑ or หนึ่ง	nèung
2	๒ or สอง	sŏrng
3	๓ or สาม	sǎhm
4	๔ or สี่	sèe
5	๕ or ห้า	hâh
6	๖ or หก	hòk
7	๗ or เจ็ด	jèt
8	๘ or แปด	bpàirt
9	๙ or เก้า	gâo
10	๑๐ or สิบ	sìp
11	๑๑ or สิบเอ็ด	sìp-èt
12	๑๒ or สิบสอง	sìp-sŏrng
13	๑๓ or สิบสาม	sìp-sǎhm
14	๑๔ or สิบสี่	sìp-sèe
15	๑๕ or สิบห้า	sìp-hâh
16	๑๖ or สิบหก	sìp-hòk
17	๑๗ or สิบเจ็ด	sìp-jèt
18	๑๘ or สิบแปด	sìp-bpàirt
19	๑๙ or สิบเก้า	sìp-gâo
20	๒๐ or ยี่สิบ	yêe-sìp
21	๒๑ or ยี่สิบเอ็ด	yêe-sìp-èt
22	๒๒ or ยี่สิบสอง	yêe-sìp-sŏrng
30	๓๐ or สามสิบ	sǎhm-sìp
40	๔๐ or สี่สิบ	sèe-sìp
50	๕๐ or ห้าสิบ	hâh-sìp
60	๖๐ or หกสิบ	hòk-sìp
70	๗๐ or เจ็ดสิบ	jèt-sìp
80	๘๐ or แปดสิบ	bpàirt-sìp
90	๙๐ or เก้าสิบ	gâo-sìp
100	๑๐๐ or หนึ่งร้อย	nèung róy
101	๑๐๑ or ร้อยเอ็ด	róy-èt
200	๒๐๐ or สองร้อย	sŏrng róy
1,000	๑๐๐๐ or หนึ่งพัน	nèung pun
1,001	๑๐๐๑ or หนึ่งพันหนึ่ง	nèung pun nèung
10,000	๑๐,๐๐๐ or หนึ่งหมื่น	nèung mèun
100,000	๑๐๐,๐๐๐ or หนึ่งแสน	nèung sǎirn

TIME AND SEASONS

one minute	หนึ่งนาที	nèung nah-tee
one hour	หนึ่งชั่วโมง	nèung chôo-a mohng
half an hour	ครึ่งชั่วโมง	krêung chôo-a mohng
quarter of an hour	สิบห้านาที	sìp-hâh nah-tee
midnight	เที่ยงคืน	têe-ung keun
1am	ตีหนึ่ง	dtee nèung
2am	ตีสอง	dtee sŏrng
3am	ตีสาม	dtee sǎhm
4am	ตีสี่	dtee sèe
5am	ตีห้า	dtee hâh
6am	หกโมงเช้า	hòk mohng cháo
7am	เจ็ดโมงเช้า or โมงเช้า	jèt mohng cháo or mohng cháo
8am	สองโมงเช้า	sŏrng mohng cháo
9am	สามโมงเช้า	sǎhm mohng cháo
10am	สี่โมงเช้า	sèe mohng cháo
11am	ห้าโมงเช้า	hâh mohng cháo
noon	เที่ยงวัน	têe-ung wun
1pm	บ่ายโมง	bài mohng
2pm	บ่ายสองโมง	bài sŏrng mohng
3pm	บ่ายสามโมง	bài sǎhm mohng
4pm	บ่ายสี่โมง	bài sèe mohng
5pm	ห้าโมงเย็น	hâh mohng yen
6pm	หกโมงเย็น	hòk mohng yen
7pm	ทุ่มหนึ่ง	tÔOm nèung
8pm	สองทุ่ม	sŏrng tÔOm
9pm	สามทุ่ม	sǎhm tÔOm
10pm	สี่ทุ่ม	sèe tÔOm
11pm	ห้าทุ่ม	hâh tÔOm
half past one (pm)	บ่ายโมงครึ่ง	bài mohng krêung
quarter past one (pm)	บ่ายโมงสิบห้านาที	bài mohng sìp-hâh nah-tee
quarter to two (pm)	อีกสิบห้านาทีบ่ายสองโมง	èek sìp-hâh nah-tee bài sŏrng mohng
a day	หนึ่งวัน	neung wun
a weekend	สุดสัปดาห์	sÒOt sùp-pah-dah
a week	หนึ่งอาทิตย์	nèung ah-tít
a month	หนึ่งเดือน	nèung deu-un
a year	หนึ่งปี	nèung bpee
Monday	วันจันทร์	wun jun
Tuesday	วันอังคาร	wun ung-kahn
Wednesday	วันพุธ	wun pÓOt
Thursday	วันพฤหัส	wun pa-réu-hùt
Friday	วันศุกร์	wun sÒOk
Saturday	วันเสาร์	wun sǎo
Sunday	วันอาทิตย์	wun ah-tít
cool season	หน้าหนาว	nâh nǎo
hot season	หน้าร้อน	nâh rórn
rainy season	หน้าฝน	nâh fŏn
holiday	วันหยุด	wun yÒOt
public holiday	วันหยุดประจำปี	wun yÒOt bpra-jum-bpee
Christmas	คริสต์มาส	krít-sa-maht
New Year	ปีใหม่	bpee mài
Thai New Year	สงกรานต์	sŏng-grahn
Chinese New Year	ตรุษจีน	dtrÒOt jeen

Bangkok City Centre

THON BURI
Pages 118–125
Street Finder maps 1, 5, 6

CHAO PHRAYA EXPRESS

This service operates daily from 6am to 6pm. Boats serve the piers shown here about every 10 minutes at peak times and about every 20 minutes otherwise.

- Nonthaburi (Phibun 3)
- Phibun 2
- Wat Khian
- Wat Salari
- Wat Khema
- Phibun 1
- *Rama VI Bridge*
- Rama VI
- Bang Pho
- Kiek Kai
- Wat Chan Samoson
- Wat Thep Nari
- Cholapatan
- Sang Hee
- Phayap
- *Krung Thon Bridge*
- Phra Pin Klao (Wat Dao Dung)
- Thewet
- Wisut Kasat
- Wat Sam Phraya
- Bangkok Noi/ Thon Buri Railway Station
- Phra Athit
- *Phra Pin Klao Bridge*
- Phrannok
- Maharaj
- Chang
- Tien
- Rachinee
- Saphan Phut
- Ratchawong
- *Memorial Bridge*
- *Phra Pok Klao Bridge*
- Krom Chaotha (Harbour Dept)
- Si Phraya
- Wat Muang Khae
- Oriental
- *Taksin Bridge*
- Wat Sawetchat
- Sathorn
- Wat Worachanyawat
- Wat Ratcha Singkhon

Map labels: CHARAN SANIT WONG, SOMDET PHRA PIN KLAO, Khlong Bangkok Noi, AMARIN, ITSARAPHAP, Chao Phraya, SAMSEN, Phra Pin Klao Bridge, Bangkok Noi/Thon Buri Railway Station, BANGLAMPHU, National Museum, SANAM LUANG, RATCHADAMNOEN KL, PHRA NAKHON, ATSADANG, BANGKOK NOI, PHRANNOK, ARUN, Wat Phra Kaeo, SANAM, Grand Palace, SUAN SARANROM, RATTANA KOSIN, SUAN ROMMA NART, BAMRUN, TI THONG, Khlong Mon, CHAI, Wat Pho, PHAHURAT, CHARON, TRI PHET, CHAK PHET, CHA, Wat Arun, Chao Phraya, Khlong Bangkok Yai, ITSARAPHAP, Memorial Bridge, Phra Pok Klao Bridge, BANGKOK YAI, SOMDET CHA, PRACHATHIPOK, ITSARAPHAP, THA DIN DAENG, LAD, Wongwian Yai Railway Station

OLD CITY
Pages 72–89
Street Finder maps 1, 2, 5